Crimes against the State

Sedition, Rebellion, and Treason since America's Founding

JAMES A. BECKMAN AND ERIC MERRIAM

BLOOMSBURY ACADEMIC
NEW YORK • LONDON • OXFORD • NEW DELHI • SYDNEY

BLOOMSBURY ACADEMIC
Bloomsbury Publishing Inc
1385 Broadway, New York, NY 10018, USA
50 Bedford Square, London, WC1B 3DP, UK
29 Earlsfort Terrace, Dublin 2, Ireland

BLOOMSBURY, BLOOMSBURY ACADEMIC and the Diana logo are trademarks of Bloomsbury Publishing Plc

First published in the United States of America 2024

Cover images: (Top) Waco, Texas, March 1993. A protester denouncing what he calls heavy-handed police tactics against the Branch Davidians. (Bottom) Protestors storm the Capitol building during a joint session of Congress in Washington, DC on Wednesday, January 6, 2021. © Bob Daemmrich/Alamy Stock Photo; Sipa USA/Alamy Stock Photo

Library of Congress Cataloging-in-Publication Data
Names: Beckman, James A., author. | Merriam, Eric, author.
Title: Crimes against the state : sedition, rebellion, and treason since America's founding / James A. Beckman, Eric Merriam.
Description: New York : Bloomsbury Academic, 2024. |
Cases – Crimes/crime prevention – Events – Individuals – Laws – Movements/organizations.
Identifiers: LCCN 2024006299 (print) | LCCN 2024006300 (ebook) | ISBN 9781440879074 (hardback) | ISBN 9798765124123 (paperback) | ISBN 9798216171188 (epub) | ISBN 9781440879081 (ebook)
Subjects: LCSH: Political crimes and offenses–Law and legislation–United States–History. | Sedition–Law and legislation–United States–History. | Treason–Law and legislation–United States–History. | Terrorism–Law and legislation–United States–History. | Civil disobedience–Law and legislation–United States.
Classification: LCC KF9390 .B43 2024 (print) | LCC KF9390 (ebook) | DDC 345.73/0231–dc23/eng/20240411
LC record available at https://lccn.loc.gov/2024006299
LC ebook record available at https://lccn.loc.gov/2024006300

ISBN: HB: 978-1-4408-7907-4
ePDF: 978-1-4408-7908-1
eBook: 979-8-2161-7118-8

Typeset by Integra Software Services Pvt. Ltd.
Printed and bound in Great Britain

To find out more about our authors and books visit www.bloomsbury.com and sign up for our newsletters.

Contents

Alphabetical List of Entries vi
Topical List of Entries ix
Acknowledgments xvi

Introduction 1

Timeline of Major Events Involving Crimes against the State 6

A–Z Entries 17–442

Index 445

Alphabetical List of Entries

Abel, Rudolf Ivanovich

Abrams v. United States (1919)

Aid and Comfort (Aid to Enemies of the State)

Al-Arian, United States v. (2005)

Alien Act (1798)

Alien and Sedition Acts (1798)

Alien Enemies Act (1798)

American Civil War—Amnesty and Pardons

American Civil War and Treason

American Revolution and Treason

Ames, Aldrich Hazen "Rich"

Anarchy, Criminal

Anthrax Attacks (2001)

Anti-Terrorism and Effective Death Penalty Act (1996)

Arnold, Benedict

Assassination

Axis Sally (Mildred Gillars)

Bacon's Rebellion (1676–7)

Battle of Athens, Tennessee (1946)

Battle of Liberty Place (1874)

Booth, John Wilkes

Boston Marathon Bombing (2013)

Brandenburg v. Ohio (1969)

Brown, John

Bundy Standoffs (2014–16)

Burr, Aaron

Burr, United States v. (1807)

Capitol Insurrection on January 6, 2021

Chin, Larry Wu-Tai

Christiana Revolt (1851)

Civil Disobedience and Crimes against the State

Civil Rights Movement and Crimes against the State

Clear and Present Danger Test

Colfax Massacre (1873)

Communist Control Act (1954)

Conspiracy, Criminal

Cook, John E.

Copeland, John Anthony, Jr.

Coppoc, Edwin

Corruption of Blood

Cramer v. United States (1945)

Crimes Act of 1790

Criminal Syndicalism

Cruikshank, United States v. (1876)

Cybersecurity

Davis, Jefferson

Debs v. United States (1919)

DeJonge v. Oregon (1937)

Dennis v. United States (1951)

Disqualification Clause

Dorr's Rebellion (1841–42)

Enforcement Acts (including the Ku Klux Klan Act) (1870–71)

English Treason Statute of 1351

Espionage

Espionage Act of 1917 and Sedition Act of 1918

Eufaula Election Massacre and Spring Hill Riot (1874)

Ex Parte Bollman (1807)

Ex Parte Milligan (1866)

Ex Parte Quirin (1942)

Ex Parte Vallandigham (1864)

First Red Scare and the Palmer Raids (1919–20)

Flag Disrespect as Crime against the State

Fries's Rebellion (1799)

Fuchs, Klaus

Fuerzas Armadas de Liberacion Nacional (FALN)

Gabriel's Rebellion (1800)

Gadahn, Adam Yahiye

Gitlow v. New York (1925)

Greathouse, United States v. (1863)

Green Corn Rebellion

Green, Shields

Greenwood, New York, Insurrection (1882)

Hamdi v. Rumsfeld (2004)

Hanssen, Robert Philip

Hanway, United States v. (1851)

Hasan, Nidal

Haupt v. United States (1947)

Haymarket Affair (1886)

Hazlett, Albert

Hess v. Indiana (1973)

Hirabayashi v. United States (1943)

Hiss, Alger

Homeland Security Act (2002)

Hoxie, United States v. (1808)

Insurrection

Insurrection Act

Intelligence Identities Protection Act

Internal Security Act of 1950

Jefferson, Thomas

John Brown's Raid (1859)

Kaczynski, Theodore ("Unabomber")

Kawakita v. United States (1952)

Keyishian v. Board of Regents (1967)

Korematsu v. United States (1944)

Leaks of National Defense Information

Levying War

Lincoln Assassination (1865)

Lindh, John Walker

Luther v. Borden (1849)

Martial Law

Material Support Crimes

McKinley Assassination (1901)

Militia Movement (Modern)

Mitchell, United States v. (1795)

Monti, United States v. (1949)

Mumford, William Bruce

Mutiny

Near v. Minnesota (1931)

New York Times v. United States (1971)

New York v. Lynch (1814)

O'Brien, United States v. (1968)

Oklahoma City Bombing (1995)

Padilla, United States v. (including *Rumsfeld v. Padilla* and *Padilla v. Hanft*) (2004–2014)

Pelton, Ronald William

Pennsylvania v. Nelson (1956)

Pentagon Papers and Trials of Daniel Ellsberg and Anthony Russo

Perjury, False Statements, and Obstruction of Justice

Pollard, Jonathan Jay

Pottawatomie Massacre (1856)

Prize Cases (1862)

Puerto Rican Nationalist Party Revolt

Radio Traitors and Anti-State Propaganda during the Second World War

Rebellion

Riot and Incitement to Riot

Rosenberg, Julius and Ethel

Ruby Ridge (1992)

Rudolph, Eric Roberts

Sabotage

Sacco–Vanzetti Case (1921)

Salazar, Hipolito

Schenck v. United States (1919)

Second Red Scare (McCarthyism)

Sedition

Sedition Act of 1798

Seditious Conspiracy

September 11, 2001

Shay's Rebellion (1786–7)

Smith Act

Sovereign Citizen Movement

Speech as Crime against the State

Stevens, Aaron

Surratt, Mary E.

Terrorism

Texas v. White (1869)

Threats against Government Officials

Tokyo Rose (Iva Toguri D'Aquino)

Treason

Turner, Nat

United States v. U.S. District Court (1972)

USA PATRIOT Act

Vesey's Rebellion (1822)

Virginia v. Brown (1859)

Waco (1993)

Walker, John Anthony, Jr.

War of 1812 and Treason

Weapons of Mass Destruction

Weather Underground

West Virginia Coal Wars

Whiskey Rebellion

Whitney v. California (1927)

Wilmington Insurrection of 1898

Wolverine Watchmen

World Trade Center Bombing of 1993

Yates v. United States (1957)

Year of the Spy (1985)

Zenger, John Peter

Topical List of Entries

Cases

Abrams v. United States (1919)

Al-Arian, United States v. (2005)

Brandenburg v. Ohio (1969)

Burr, United States v. (1807)

Carlisle v. United States (1872)

Cramer v. United States (1945)

Cruikshank, United States v. (1876)

Debs v. United States (1919)

DeJonge v. Oregon (1937)

Dennis v. United States (1951)

Ex Parte Bollman (1807)

Ex Parte Milligan (1866)

Ex Parte Quirin (1942)

Ex Parte Vallandigham (1864)

Gitlow v. New York (1925)

Greathouse, United States v. (1863)

Hamdi v. Rumsfeld (2004)

Hanway, United States v. (1851)

Haupt v. United States (1947)

Hess v. Indiana (1973)

Hirabayashi v. United States (1943)

Hoxie, United States v. (1808)

Kawakita v. United States (1952)

Keyishian v. Board of Regents (1967)

Korematsu v. United States (1944)

Luther v. Borden (1849)

Mitchell, United States v. (1795)

Monti, United States v. (1949)

Near v. Minnesota (1931)

New York Times v. United States (1971)

New York v. Lynch (1814)

O'Brien, United States v. (1968)

Padilla, United States v. (including *Rumsfeld v. Padilla* and *Padilla v. Hanft*) (2004–14)

Pennsylvania v. Nelson (1956)

Prize Cases (1862)

Sacco–Vanzetti Case (1921)

Schenck v. United States (1919)

Texas v. White (1869)

United States v. U.S. District Court (1972)

Virginia v. Brown (1859)

Whitney v. California (1927)

Yates v. United States (1957)

Crimes/Crime Prevention

Aid and Comfort (Aid to Enemies of the State)

Anarchy, Criminal

Assassination

Civil Disobedience and Crimes against the State

Conspiracy, Criminal

Criminal Syndicalism

Cybersecurity

Espionage

Flag Disrespect as Crime against the State

Insurrection

Leaks of National Defense Information

Levying War

Material Support Crimes

Mutiny

Perjury, False Statements, and Obstruction of Justice

Rebellion

Riot and Incitement to Riot

Sabotage

Sedition

Seditious Conspiracy

Speech as Crime against the State

Terrorism

Threats against Government Officials

Treason

Weapons of Mass Destruction

Events

American Civil War—Amnesty and Pardons

American Civil War and Treason

American Revolution and Treason

Anthrax Attacks (2001)

Bacon's Rebellion (1676–7)

Battle of Athens, Tennessee (1946)

Battle of Liberty Place (1874)

Boston Marathon Bombing (2013)

Bundy Standoffs (2014–16)

Capitol Insurrection on January 6, 2021

Christiana Revolt (1851)

Colfax Massacre (1873)

Dorr's Rebellion (1841–2)

Eufaula Election Massacre and Spring Hill Riot (1874)

First Red Scare and the Palmer Raids (1919–20)

Fries's Rebellion (1799)

Gabriel's Rebellion (1800)

Green Corn Rebellion (1917)

Greenwood, New York, Insurrection (1882)

Haymarket Affair (1886)

John Brown's Raid (1859)

Lincoln Assassination (1865)

McKinley Assassination (1901)

Oklahoma City Bombing (1995)

Pentagon Papers and Trials of Daniel Ellsberg and Anthony Russo

Pottawatomie Massacre (1856)

Puerto Rican Nationalist Party Revolt

Radio Traitors and Anti-State Propaganda during the Second World War

Ruby Ridge (1992)

Second Red Scare (McCarthyism)

September 11, 2001

Shay's Rebellion (1786–7)

Vesey's Rebellion (1822)

Waco (1993)

War of 1812 and Treason

West Virginia Coal Wars

Whiskey Rebellion

Wilmington Insurrection of 1898

World Trade Center Bombing of 1993

Year of the Spy (1985)

Individuals

Abel, Rudolf Ivanovich

Ames, Aldrich Hazen "Rich"

Arnold, Benedict

Axis Sally (Mildred Gillars)

Booth, John Wilkes

Brown, John

Burr, Aaron

Chin, Larry Wu-Tai

Cook, John E.

Copeland, John Anthony, Jr.

Coppoc, Edwin

Davis, Jefferson

Fuchs, Klaus

Gadahn, Adam Yahiye

Green, Shields

Hanssen, Robert Philip

Hasan, Nidal

Hazlett, Albert

Hiss, Alger

Jefferson, Thomas

Kaczynski, Theodore ("Unabomber")

Lindh, John Walker

Mumford, William Bruce

Pelton, Ronald William

Pollard, Jonathan Jay

Rosenberg, Julius and Ethel

Rudolph, Eric Roberts

Salazar, Hipolito

Stevens, Aaron

Surratt, Mary E.

Tokyo Rose (Iva Toguri D'Aquino)

Turner, Nat

Walker, John Anthony, Jr.

Zenger, John Peter

Laws

Alien Act (1798)

Alien and Sedition Acts (1798)

Alien Enemies Act (1798)

Anti-Terrorism and Effective Death Penalty Act (1996)

Clear and Present Danger Test

Communist Control Act (1954)

Corruption of Blood

Crimes Act of 1790

Disqualification Clause

Enforcement Acts (including the Ku Klux Klan Act) (1870–71)

English Treason Statute of 1351

Espionage Act of 1917 and Sedition Act of 1918

Homeland Security Act (2002)

Insurrection Act

Intelligence Identities Protection Act (1982)

Internal Security Act of 1950

Martial Law

Sedition Act of 1798

Smith Act

USA PATRIOT Act

Movements/Organizations

Civil Rights Movement and Crimes against the State

Fuerzas Armadas de Liberacion Nacional (FALN)

Militia Movement (Modern)

Sovereign Citizen Movement

Weather Underground

Wolverine Watchmen

Acknowledgments

This book would not have been possible without the guidance and support of several key individuals and institutions. First, the authors are incredibly grateful and appreciative of the support of ABC-CLIO/Bloomsbury Publishing in recognizing the potential of a book of this nature and seeing this book through to publication. Without ABC-CLIO/Bloomsbury, and regardless of the independent importance of the topic and arguable merits of the work, this book simply would not have been possible. Likewise, from the very earliest point in the process more than two years ago, Senior Acquisitions Editor Kevin Hillstrom recognized the value of this project, offered essential guidance and support in getting this project off the ground, and provided inspiration and patience in keeping us on track to complete this manuscript. For his invaluable assistance, we are appreciative. We are also grateful to Development Editor Nicole Azze for all the recommended revisions and improvements to the draft manuscript, which undoubtedly resulted in a much-improved final version.

The authors also extend thanks and gratitude to the University of Central Florida (UCF) in allowing its professors the leeway to pursue scholarly projects of merit and in providing resources to complete a book project of this magnitude. The authors were aided by several UCF students who enthusiastically offered assistance and helped us formulate our thoughts on several entries. Those students included Noah Galper, Sebastian Delgado, and Jan Soto.

Finally, the authors are deeply grateful for the enduring and essential support of their spouses, Maria Beckman and Dr. Erica Merriam.

All views expressed in this book are those of the authors alone, and not those of UCF, the State of Florida, or the United States government. Every effort was taken to ensure this book was free from errors. But to err is human, and any remaining mistakes are the authors' sole responsibility.

Introduction

In the days after the Capitol Insurrection on January 6, 2021, countless questions were raised regarding the legality and legal consequences of the day's events. These questions have been debated repeatedly on social media, news programs, talk radio, print media, in Congressional hearing rooms, in courts, and at dinner table conversations around the country. Did those who stormed the Capitol threatening to "hang Mike Pence," "stop the steal," or enact "regime change" commit treason? Sedition? Insurrection? How do these differ? What about those who attended the rally and called for actions to keep Donald Trump in the White House but did not engage in any such speech? Does the Constitution not protect citizens and permit them to participate in such activities? Where does the Right of Assembly or Free Speech under the First Amendment end and the right of the government to protect itself begin? Does the First Amendment protect the conduct of President Donald Trump in imploring his supporters to march on the Capitol?

Long before January 6, 2021, historian Bill Coate (2007) wrote, "a fear exists that America may be losing its memory—that our shared collective consciousness may be fading" and that it is as if Americans "have been afflicted with a kind of historical amnesia" (IX). To understand and make sense of an event like January 6 requires knowledge and understanding of similar events in the nation's past. As Coate urged, "a common understanding based upon some common knowledge of our nation's past is imperative. It draws people together. It gives us a common, civic identity. Indeed, the promise of America is premised on the need for an educated citizenry" (IX). This is perhaps what Thomas Jefferson meant when he wrote that "if a nation expects to be ignorant and free, it expects what never was and never will be" (Coate 2007, IX). A collective understanding and knowledge of our past undoubtedly helps us make sense of the present and provides a roadmap to navigate problems in the future. As ancient religious texts remind us, "The thing that hath been, it is that which shall be; and that which is done is that which shall be done: and there is no new thing under the sun" (Ecclesiastes 1:9). As the reader of our modest book will realize, "there is nothing new under the sun" when it comes to crimes against the state.

Indeed, the history of the United States is replete with examples of insurrection, rebellion, treason, espionage, sabotage, mutiny, and other crimes committed against the government. The American Revolution was itself a treasonous rebellion against Great Britain, and its leaders were traitors. Benedict Arnold was one of the first traitors against the United States, before the nation even came into existence. The nation's third vice president, Aaron Burr, was the subject of one of America's earliest treason prosecutions after he attempted to split the country. The United States was faced with other early acts of rebellion, collective disobedience, and treason prosecutions in events such as the Whiskey Rebellion and Fries's Rebellion. State governments dealt with numerous rebellions and insurrections and treason in the antebellum era, from Nat Turner's Slavery Insurrection in 1831 to Dorr's Rebellion in 1842 to John Brown's Raid in 1859. Over 150 years ago, the American Civil War constituted the largest single act of treason and rebellion in the history of the United States. During the First and Second World Wars, the country witnessed hundreds of prosecutions ranging from seditious speech to espionage and treason. Though the events involving the Capitol Insurrection on January 6, 2021, may appear to be a new low in American history, reviewing entries in this book on topics ranging from the American Civil War to the Colfax Massacre, the Eufaula Election Massacre and Spring Hill Insurrection, and the Wilmington Insurrection of 1898 will sadly illustrate otherwise.

"Crimes against the state" traditionally include criminal offenses like treason, sedition, seditious conspiracy, sabotage, espionage, mutiny, assassination, and conspiracies to harm the government, among other things. Indeed, the primary factor that distinguishes crimes against the state from other crimes is that the intended "victim" of a crime against the state is the sovereign. That is, such crimes are intended to injure the government in some way. In announcing the decision to impose the death sentence in the Second World War treason prosecution of Tomoya Kawakita (*Kawakita v. United States,* 1952), the presiding trial judge made an observation that is helpful in understanding how crimes against the state differ from other crimes. The judge stated:

> As I view this matter, it is not a question of whether the defendant kicked some American prisoner of war or a dozen of them. His crime might be briefly put in two sentences. [The defendant] said that from 1943 on he did everything he could to help the Japanese Government win the war [and t]he jury found that he owed a duty of loyalty at that time to the United States. So, his crime cannot be considered … in terms of beating up someone, no matter how brutal. His crime is a crime against the country of his birth. His crime is not against a few American prisoners of war. His crime is against the whole people of this country where he was born and where he was fed and where he was educated. Throughout history treason has always been the crime most abhorred by English-speaking peoples. The traitor has always been considered even worse than a murderer. And the distinction is based upon reason: for the murderer violates at most only a few, while the traitor violates all the members of his society, all the members of the group to which he owes his allegiance.

Stating it somewhat more succinctly, in commenting on why he would not commute the death sentences of Julius and Ethel Rosenberg for committing espionage by providing nuclear secrets to the Soviet Union, President Dwight D. Eisenhower said that the "nature of the crime for which they have been found guilty and sentenced far exceeds that of the taking of the life of another citizen; it involves the deliberate betrayal of the entire nation and could very well result in the death of many, many thousands of innocent citizens" (Eisenhower 1953). Crimes against the state are those offenses that target the sovereign and in so doing aim to impact the entire society.

This book is a study of crimes against the state in the United States. In most nation states under a unitary system of government, the "state" is the national government as all the power resides in a central government. So too, in the United States, crimes against the state are primarily considered to be crimes against the national government, where continued existence of the nation itself, or at least its existence under the current form of government, may be jeopardized. Indeed, when one considers crimes like treason, sedition, insurrection, or espionage, one naturally thinks of a national government as the target. By contrast, one does not typically think of spying against Massachusetts or sedition against Florida. Yet, unlike in a unitary system, some offenses directed toward state or local governments (as opposed to the national government) may also constitute crimes against the state. And state governments may protect themselves with laws to the extent those laws are intended to protect the state government (and not the federal government).

In *Pennsylvania v. Nelson* (1956), the United States Supreme Court held that states could not criminalize sedition against the United States because the federal government already had outlawed such speech and activities. But the Court took care to observe that it was not declaring state sedition laws to be unconstitutional when the state government is the target of seditious activity or speech. The Court explicitly explained that states could protect themselves. So, under the United States' federalist system of dual sovereigns where the federal government and each individual state are sovereign, "crimes against the state" include offenses where either the federal government or the state government is the intended victim. For example, state criminal anarchy, criminal syndicalism, and sedition laws can be constitutional to the extent the state government is endeavoring to protect itself rather than the national government (and consistent with the Supreme Court's jurisprudence regarding speech as crime against the state).

Given state sovereignty and police powers over citizens, attacks against state governments take on a character quite like crimes against a national government. Indeed, as detailed in this book, several of the most significant crimes against the state in United States history were crimes against a state or subsidiary local government, rather than against the federal government. An early example of this was Dorr's Rebellion, an attempt to overthrow the government of Rhode Island by force and install a shadow government. In the subsequent prosecution of Thomas Wilson Dorr, the court decided that prosecution for treason against Rhode Island was appropriate because Rhode Island had a right to protect itself as a sovereign. Another example includes *Virginia v. Brown* (1859), where John Brown was charged with treason against the Commonwealth of Virginia, even though Brown's crimes targeted both the federal government's arsenal and armory and the state government's slavery policy. Often, crimes against both the state and federal government are intermingled. For instance, other early examples include the West Virginia Coal Wars, where local government was the victim of the mine workers' insurrection, but the insurrection was quelled in part by federal military forces, and *United States v. Cruikshank* (1876), where the federal government attempted to prosecute individuals under federal law for the Colfax Massacre, a violent insurrection that overthrew local government officials.

As the book title suggests, and the Timeline of Major Events indicates, the book covers the period from America's founding through the present. Thus, the book covers a lot of ground. The reader will find notable laws, concepts, cases, people, and events in American history. Included in this book are discussions ranging from treason and rebellion in the American Revolution and the Civil War, to how antebellum rebellions like Dorr's Rebellion in 1842 and John Brown's Raid in 1859 were handled, to twentieth-century events like Ruby Ridge, Waco, and the Oklahoma City bombing. The book attempts to address the root causes of these events, and the legal and constitutional constraints on the government's reaction to such events. As William Faulkner once argued, the reading and study of historical events is not the study of "was," but rather the study of "is." Thus, this book is the study of crimes against the United States in 2024, even if the entry at issue in the book originally occurred with an event, person, or law in the 1800s or 1900s. Analyzing these events is important to understanding events happening in the United States in 2024.

A few comments about topic inclusion and exclusion are appropriate. Some malevolent individuals like Eric Rudolph, Timothy McVeigh (Oklahoma City Bombing), and Ted Kaczynski (the "Unabomber") are profiled in this book, while other notorious mass murderers, bombers, or shooters are not. For instance, the heinous and deplorable criminal behavior of individuals like serial killers Ted Bundy and Jeffrey Dahmer is not covered. Bundy and Dahmer were not motivated to attack the government, but rather by the perverse gratification they got from killing their victims. As heinous and repugnant as their actions were, they were not crimes against the state. On the other hand, the violent actions of individuals like Rudolph, McVeigh, and Kaczynski were directed at the government as the intended victim. For example, Eric Rudolph's views about the government, coupled with his violent actions directed toward the sovereign state, transformed his "ordinary" criminal law offenses of abortion clinic bombings and the 1996 Olympic Bombing into what we classify as a crime against the state. A bombing or killing to stop a government policy or law (in this instance, government policy in support of early-stage abortions) is ultimately directed at injuring the state itself, not merely effecting policy change. On the point of prompting changes in government policy alone, readers may wish to consider the entry on Civil Disobedience and Crimes against the State, which includes our conclusion that traditional civil disobedience is not a crime against the state because government policy (only) is the target, not the government itself.

Another example illustrating this methodology of topic inclusion/exclusion can be seen with presidential assassinations. The crime of assassination is a classic crime against the state and has its own entry in this book. Additionally, there are entries in this book on the specific assassinations of Abraham Lincoln in 1865 and William McKinley in 1901. Yet, for purposes of this book, assassinations or attempted assassination plots are not considered a crime against the state if the perpetrator attempted the assassination for personal reasons independent of a desire to harm the government or the nation (i.e., the sovereign). For example, John Hinckley, Jr., attempted to assassinate Ronald Reagan not to harm the government, but rather in a misguided attempt to impress actress Jodie Foster, with whom Hinckley had become infatuated. Similarly, Lynette “Squeaky” Fromme, who was associated with the Manson Family cult, attempted to assassinate President Gerald Ford in 1975. Fromme’s crime was clearly a violation of federal law and subject to prosecution and conviction, but Fromme was not apparently motivated by the goal to attack the government. Rather, Fromme’s actions were driven by her devotion to Manson and the Manson Family’s ideologies. Conversely, the Lincoln assassination is a textbook example of a “crime against the state.” The perpetrators of the assassination plot contemplated decapitating the entire upper echelon of the federal government, including killing the president, vice president, Secretary of State, and the commanding General of the Union Army, with the goal of changing government policy toward the South. Similarly, the McKinley Assassination was committed by an avowed anarchist, who sought eradication of the government. As such, the Lincoln and McKinley Assassinations are included in this book, while the assassinations of President John F. Kennedy and James Garfield are not.

The concept for this book is to provide the reader with a reference to explore crimes against the state throughout US history. While it is primarily a reference work, individual entries can be read selectively to learn about a discrete topic, event, law, person, or concept. To the extent possible, this volume is intended to be a dispassionate exploration of its subjects rather than a commentary. The authors have attempted to avoid editorializing the various issues addressed in the pages herein, in the hope that sufficient information on the given topic to allow the reader to draw his or her own conclusions or pursue further inquiry. The entries/essays in the book are arranged alphabetically. If the reader has a particular topic in mind (e.g., treason or seditious conspiracy or why people were not prosecuted for treason for the American Civil War), the reader can turn directly to that entry in the book. Thus, individual topics can be read selectively based upon the reader’s individual interests and intellectual curiosity. At the end of each entry, a “See Also” section directs the reader to related entries, allowing for appreciation of a broader topical context. Each entry concludes with a “Resources” section that both identifies sources we used in creating the entries and suggests further reading for the reader’s independent research and inquiry. Finally, the detailed index at the end of the book is another way in which entries and topics are cross-referenced, and further allows the reader to find topics, theories, persons, concepts, events, laws, and other details mentioned in the text, but that may not have their own separate entry. These various aids should help the reader to connect the dots on sometimes seemingly unrelated topics and to find a host of information on interrelated topics.

In discussing Plato's *Laws,* Harvard Law Professor Mary Ann Glendon once noted Plato's observations on the value and wisdom of learning from the successes and failures from the past and from other rulers (and other Greek City States). Glendon wrote, "since the city [Athens, a Greek city-state] must constantly be re-examining and revising its laws, its Guardians [i.e., rulers] would do well, he [Plato] advises, to send out mature citizens to study especially good laws elsewhere, and to seek assistance from wise persons wherever they may be found, even in ill-ordered cities" (Glendon 1987, 6). This is what is attempted here. Though we do not travel from city to city or seek out "mature citizens to study especially good laws," we do engage in a sort of time travel in this book, visiting different episodes of American history, and studying the laws—good and bad—as they have evolved over time, sometimes even conversing with the dead. It is not only a study of what laws and practices appeared to have worked, but also those that did not.

Discussions of contemporary events like the Capitol Insurrection on January 6, 2021, or the indictment of former President Donald Trump for violating the Espionage Act of 1917 (the first indictment of a president in US history) inevitably lead to broader questions beyond the specifics of that event. Prosecution of some Capitol Insurrection participants for seditious conspiracy invokes questions about the difference between treason and seditious conspiracy and why treason has not been prosecuted more frequently in US history. How far does the freedom of speech and to protest the government extend? In a time of peril, can speech and actions be curtailed to protect government institutions or even the nation itself? What laws has the government put into place to protect itself against further attacks on its sovereignty? Did January 6th have historical analogs? And why did former President Trump's mere possession of classified documents after he left office lead to an indictment for violating the same federal statute under which notorious spies like Aldrich Ames and Robert Hanssen have been prosecuted?

For readers wishing to understand contemporary actions against the government and how the government may lawfully respond, this book provides relevant historical and contemporary illustrations. As such, the goal of this book is to arm the reader with information that will "cut through the noise" of the internet, social media, and broadcast media, and help the reader to (1) learn how to differentiate between sedition, insurrection, treason, domestic terrorism, espionage, and other acts meant to injure or overthrow the government; (2) gain a deeper understanding of laws, policies, and events that have aroused violent or nonviolent opposition; (3) better comprehend the perspectives and motivations of those who commit crimes against the state; and (4) evaluate various state responses to these challenges and threats, from martial law–style crackdowns to new laws and reforms. We hope the study of crimes against the state in our nation's past—whether it is a study of persons, concepts, events, laws, or judicial cases—will help protect and preserve the state in the future.

Resources

Coate, Bill. 2007. *Shocking Secrets & American History*. New York: MJF Books, IX.

Eisenhower, Dwight. 1953. *The White House: Statement by the President*. Dwight David Eisenhower Presidential Library, February 11, 1953. Accessed October 30, 2023. https://www.eisenhowerlibrary.gov/sites/default/files/file/Rosenberg_3a.pdf.

Glendon, Mary Ann. 1987. *Abortion and Divorce in Western Law: American Failures, European Challenges*. Cambridge, MA: Harvard University Press, 6.

Timeline of Major Events Involving Crimes against the State

Note: See individual entries for an in-depth description of those events.

1676 First major armed rebellion or insurrection by American colonists against their own government in New World occurs in Bacon's Rebellion. The leader of the rebellion, Nathanial Bacon, is one of the very first people accused of treason in the New World.

1735 The trial and acquittal of John Peter Zenger for charges of seditious libel illustrate early American intolerance of seditious libel as a crime against the state or an act punishable by the state.

1775 First shots of the American Revolution are fired on April 19, in Lexington, Massachusetts. In June 1775, British General Thomas Gage announces that all colonists in arms are "rebels and traitors, and as such to be treated." During the years of the Revolution (1775–83), tens of thousands of colonists commit open hostility and levy war upon Great Britain and are thus guilty of treason, though few if any are prosecuted by Great Britain. Likewise, thousands of individuals who remain loyal to the Crown find themselves in a position of committing treason against the revolutionary colonies, and during the Revolution scores of such persons are prosecuted for treason by the colonies. The American Revolution and the American Civil War constitute two monumental events involving hundreds of thousands of acts of treason.

1776 American Colonies formally assert independence by delivering to King George a Declaration of Independence, penned by Thomas Jefferson, Benjamin Franklin, John Adams, Robert R. Livingston, and Roger Sherman.

1780 Benedict Arnold engages in an espionage and treason plot for the British government. Arnold commits one of the most notorious acts of treason and espionage against nascent United States by conspiring to sell the fortifications of West Point, New York, to the British.

1786–7 Shay's Rebellion takes place. It is the first of three major anti-taxation rebellions in the United States following independence (*see also* Whiskey Rebellion in 1794 and Fries's Rebellion in 1798–9), but the only major anti-taxation rebellion to occur before the adoption of the United States Constitution. Shay's Rebellion is the first instance wherein hundreds of Americans are charged and convicted of treason for a single series of events.

1789 Ratification of United States Constitution, Article III of which detailed the elements and proof required for treason, the only crime specified in the Constitution. The offense of treason was not previously delineated in the Articles of Confederation (1781–8).

1790 The first Congress passes the Crimes Act of 1790, officially titled "An Act for the Punishment of Certain Crimes Against the United States." It was the US government's first codification of crimes, including crimes against the state, including treason, perjury, bribery, and counterfeiting federal securities or money.

1791 Ratification of the Bill of Rights as the first ten amendments to the United States Constitution, including the First Amendment's guarantee of freedom of speech and of the press and the right to peaceably assemble and petition the government for redress.

1792 Under Congress's Article I, Section 8, power to "provide for calling forth the Militia to execute the Laws of the Union, suppress Insurrections and repel Invasions," Congress first enacted the Militia Act (significantly amended and renamed as the Insurrection Act in 1807).

1794 Government uses military force to suppress the Whiskey Rebellion. The Whiskey Rebellion is the second of three major anti-taxation rebellions in the United States following independence (*see also* Shay's Rebellion in 1786–7 and Fries's Rebellion in 1798–9), and the first instance of treason convictions under the new United States Constitution. Congress calls out the Army under the recently enacted 1792 Militia Act.

1795 A federal trial court discusses the treason indictment of one of the defendants stemming from conduct occurring during the Whiskey Rebellion in *United States v. Mitchell.*

1798 Congress passes four separate laws all dealing with national security of the new nation; these four laws collectively become known as the Alien and Sedition Acts. Among other things, the laws allow for the immediate deportation of aliens deemed "dangerous" to the United States or an "enemy" of the United States and make it a crime to criticize the government, make any statement that would bring the Congress or the President "into contempt or disrepute."

1798–9 Fries's Rebellion takes place. Fries's Rebellion is the third major anti-taxation rebellion after Revolutionary War (*see also* Shay's Rebellion in 1786–7 and Whiskey Rebellion in 1794). Participants are indicted and tried for treason, and other crimes including sedition, insurrection, and rioting. It is the second incident (after the Whiskey Rebellion) where the federal government convicted individuals of treason since the ratification of the constitution in 1789. President John Adams invokes the Insurrection Act and the Militia is again called out to quell the rebellion.

1800 Gabriel's Rebellion, sometimes referred to as the Virginia Plot of 1800, is thwarted. Gabriel's Rebellion involves a plot of thousands of enslaved Black Americans to overthrow the institution of slavery in Virginia and institute a new government in Virginia.

1801 The Sedition Act of 1798 expires as Thomas Jefferson takes office as President. Jefferson pardons all convicted under the Sedition Act during the John Adams administration.

1807 Former Vice President Aaron Burr and his accomplices are put on trial for treason. See *United States v. Burr* (1807). *See also* federal trial court's decision regarding accomplices in *Ex Parte Bollman* (1807).

1807 Congress enacts the Insurrection Act (an amendment to the earlier Militia Act of 1792), authorizing the President to use federal military forces to suppress insurrections or rebellions. Though amended several times, the Insurrection Act is still in effect today.

1808 Federal trial court decides *United States v. Hoxie*, an important early case describing limitations in the application of the "levying war" provision of the Treason Clause in the United States Constitution, and also in dismissing attempts to inculcate the English concept of "constructive treason" into American law. The *Hoxie* case establishes that even armed resistance to the authority of the federal government, without treasonous intent, does not amount to the act of "levying war" and treason.

1812 The War of 1812 is the United States' first war after the ratification of Constitution and therefore is the first instance of the country grappling with whether dissidence during wartime might constitute treason. Unlike the American Revolutionary War, which itself constituted treason against Great Britain, the War of 1812 occurs between sovereign nations. Some New England states contemplate secession or entering into their own peace treaties with Great Britain.

1814 In *New York v. Lynch*, New York prosecutes defendants for treason against the state government, stemming from conduct that took place during the War of 1812.

1822 The second of four plots to overthrow the institution of slavery in North America prior to the American Civil War takes place in Vesey's Rebellion. (*See also* Gabriel's Rebellion in 1800, Nat Turner's Rebellion in 1831, and John Brown's Raid in 1859.)

1831 Nat Turner's Rebellion takes place in Virginia. Nat Turner's Rebellion is the third of four major slave rebellion plots in North America prior to the American Civil War (*see also* Gabriel's Rebellion in 1800, Denmark Vesey's Rebellion in 1822, and John Brown's Raid in 1859).

1837 John Brown begins his campaign to end slavery, an effort that reaches its apotheosis in his 1859 raid on the United States Armory and Arsenal at Harpers Ferry, Virginia.

1841–4 Thomas Wilson Dorr unsuccessfully attempts to supplant the government in Rhode Island that had been in existence since 1663 and seize the Rhode Island state arsenal in an uprising called Dorr's Rebellion. Dorr's Rebellion marks the first instance of a successful prosecution and conviction for treason against a state government (Rhode Island). In 1849, in *Luther v. Borden*, the United States Supreme Court upholds Rhode Island's right to use military force to suppress rebellion against it.

1847 The federal government exercises extraterritorial jurisdiction over Mexican citizen Hipolito Salazar and prosecutes, convicts, and executes him for treason against the United States.

1849 Henry David Thoreau pens his famous essay *On the Duty of Civil Disobedience.*

1851 The Christiana Revolt occurs, leading to the unsuccessful attempted federal prosecution of dozens of individuals for treason for failing to adhere to the federal Fugitive Slave Act of 1850. The Christiana Revolt is a violent confrontation between citizens, fugitive slaves, slave catchers, and a deputized federal marshal. The incident also gives rise to an important judicial pronouncement by a federal trial court on what constitutes "leying war" against the United States in *United States v. Hanway.*

1856 Radical abolitionist John Brown leads several abolitionists to question several settlers near the Pottawatomie River in Kansas regarding their views on slavery. Brown and his men gruesomely murder several men, in what becomes known as the Pottawatomie Massacre.

1859 John Brown and a band of twenty-one men attack the United States Armory and Arsenal at Harpers Ferry, Virginia, attempting to destroy the institution of slavery in Virginia. Virginia prosecutes John Brown and six accomplices for treason against the Commonwealth of Virginia, murder, and insurrection. John Brown's Raid constitutes the last of the major slave rebellion plots in North America prior to the American

Civil War (*see also* Gabriel's Rebellion in 1800, Vesey's Rebellion in 1822, and Nat Turner's Rebellion in 1831).

1861–5 Southern states secede and hundreds of thousands of Southerners take up arms against the federal government between 1861 and 1865 in the American Civil War.

1861 Congress criminalizes seditious conspiracy for the first time, making it a lesser alternative to a treason charge.

1862 Military trial and execution of William Bruce Mumford for a minor infraction/violation of the prevailing martial law in New Orleans, Louisiana.

1864 Supreme Court decides *Ex Parte Vallandigham*. The Court determines it did not have jurisdiction to review an appeal from a military commission. The Supreme Court's decision is momentous in ensuring the military's ability to try and sentence civilians and military members without appellate review, though the Court later reverses itself on that question.

1865 John Wilkes Booth, Mary Surratt, and others attempt to overthrow the federal government through an assassination plot. The conspiracy involves assassinating the President, Vice President, Secretary of State, and the General-in-Chief of the Union Army. President Abraham Lincoln is assassinated.

1865 The American Civil War ends with the South's defeat. President Andrew Johnson issues the first of multiple presidential pardons providing amnesty to large segments of the population who engaged in the Civil War against the federal government.

1865 Confederate veterans seeking to use intimidation and violence to prevent exercise of civil and political rights by newly freed Black Americans form the Ku Klux Klan, the first of several such organizations created to preserve White power and privilege in the South.

1866–8 Attempting to hold Southerners legally accountable for the American Civil War, the federal government unsuccessfully prosecutes the Confederacy's highest-ranking official, ex-Confederate President Jefferson Davis, for treason against the United States.

1866 The Supreme Court decides *Ex Parte Milligan*. The Court addresses two fundamental legal issues: (1) whether a civilian has the right to seek review of his military detention through the principle of habeas corpus; and (2) whether the President has authority to detain noncombatants as part of a war effort.

1867 President Andrew Johnson issues second presidential pardon providing amnesty to those engaged in hostilities against the federal government during the Civil War.

1868 President Andrew Johnson issues final proclamation providing "a full pardon and amnesty for the offences of treason against the United States, or of adhering to their enemies during the late civil war" for all persons.

1868 Fourteenth Amendment ratified. Among other provisions, the Fourteenth Amendment guarantees equal protection and due process of law to all and provides for the disqualification for federal office of anyone who takes an oath to support the Constitution and then engages in insurrection or rebellion against the United States (Disqualification Clause).

1869 In *Texas v. White,* the Supreme Court holds that state governments lack the legal authority to unilaterally withdraw from the Union.

1870–1 Congress passes three "Enforcement Acts," also known as the Force Acts, one of which is known as the Ku Klux Klan Act, to enforce the Civil War Era Constitutional Amendments (i.e., Thirteenth, Fourteenth, and Fifteenth Amendments).

1872 In *Carlisle v. United States*, the United States Supreme Court holds that an alien resident (non citizen) could commit the offense of treason against the United States.

1873–4 In the wake of dissatisfaction with Reconstruction and the results of the 1872 election, attempts to overthrow duly elected government officials with large-scale violence occur throughout the South. One of the violent confrontations results in the Colfax Massacre (1873), which culminates in the "Battle of Liberty Place" (1874). *See also* Eufaula Election Massacre and Spring Hill Insurrections (1874). The Eufaula Election Massacre and Spring Hill Riot are perpetrated by armed White supremacists determined to retake control of government. The White supremacists' success in violent insurrections aimed at the electoral process leads to the domination of state and local government and decades of Jim Crow laws throughout the South.

1876 In *United States v. Cruikshank*, the Supreme Court overturns the convictions of several individuals involved in the Colfax Massacre. The Court takes a very narrow view of the Enforcement Acts and the Enforcement Clauses of the Thirteenth and Fourteenth Amendments.

1886 Pro-labor and anarchy forces clash with police in Chicago, Illinois, in an event called the Haymarket Affair.

1898 White supremacists violently overthrow the elected government of Wilmington, North Carolina, in the Wilmington Insurrection of 1898.

1901 Assassination of President McKinley by an anarchist, who is subsequently tried, convicted, and executed.

1903 The Militia Act of 1903 formally organizes militias under state control into what are today known as state Army National Guard and Air National Guard units.

1912–21 The West Virginia Coal Wars, a series of labor disputes between miners and mining companies from 1912 to 1921. Multiple West Virginia governors declare martial law to address the breakdowns of local government during the hostilities. The fighting culminates with the Battle of Blair Mountain, which requires the mobilization of 2,500 troops from two infantry divisions of the United States Army to quell and is the largest (by number of participants) insurrection in United States history other than the American Civil War.

1917 The United States enters the First World War (1914–18). American involvement in the First World War brings thousands of anti-war protestors, dissidents, and anarchist protestors on the home front. Congress passes the Espionage Act of 1917. The Espionage Act criminalizes obtaining, conveying, transmitting, receiving, or failing to protect information relating to national defense with intent to injure the United States or aid a foreign nation (*any* foreign nation, not just enemies).

1917 Green Corn Rebellion takes place in Oklahoma. Anti-conscription, anti-war, and pro-labor individuals protest and rebel against the draft and the war and meet with violent resistance from town. In the aftermath, nearly 500 protestors/rebels are arrested, and 192 federally prosecuted. The protestors are initially charged with treason, but officials at the Department of Justice in Washington convince the prosecutor to instead test the prosecutorial viability of the recently enacted Espionage Act of 1917.

1918 As the First World War wages on, Congress passes amendments to the Espionage Act that are sometimes informally referred to as the Sedition Act of 1918 (Sedition Act). As has been the case with the Sedition Act of 1798 (one of the Alien & Sedition Acts), the Sedition Act of 1918 is intended to suppress wartime dissent and is Congress's first foray into this area since it enacted the Sedition Act of 1798. In addition to criminalizing anti-war speech, Congress criminalizes disrespecting the American flag or displaying the flag of an enemy.

1919–20 In the wake of the successful Bolshevik seizure of the Russian government in 1917 and end of the First World War, many Americans transfer their First World War distrust of Germans to a distrust of Communists, Bolsheviks, and anarchists after the war in a period known as the "First Red Scare." The First Red Scare leads to rampant civil rights abuses, including the Palmer Raids.

1919 During the First Red Scare, the Supreme Court upholds the conviction of socialist leader Eugene Debs for charges brought under the Espionage Act of 1917 and Sedition Act of 1918 in *Debs v. United States* and upholds government authority to limit critical speech in other cases such as *Schenck v. United States* and *Abrams v. United States*.

1921 Nationwide attention on the successful state prosecution of two anarchists in the Sacco and Vanzetti case.

1925 Supreme Court decides *Gitlow v. New York*. It is the first time the Supreme Court holds that the First Amendment of the United States Constitution restricts state government, not only the federal government. *Gitlow* is another case in which the Supreme Court upholds the ability of government to "protect itself" by restricting speech that might undermine security or the existence of government itself.

1927 Supreme Court decides *Whitney v. California*, in which it rejects the argument that California's criminal syndicalism statute violates the defendant's rights to free speech, expression, and association. In a concurring opinion, Justice Louis Brandeis authors an impassioned defense of a more libertarian view of free speech rights that is vindicated four decades later in *Brandenburg v. Ohio* (1969).

1931 In the case of *Near v. Minnesota*, the United States Supreme Court sets forth for the first time the doctrine that the First Amendment does not permit prior restraint or censorship of speech or publications by the government except in exceedingly rare circumstances.

1937 Supreme Court decides *DeJonge v. Oregon*, holding that "peaceable assembly for lawful discussion cannot be made a crime."

1940 Supreme Court decides *Minersville School District v. Gobitis*, upholding a local school board's requirement that all students salute the national flag as part of a daily school exercise (see Flag Disrespect as Crime against the State).

1941–5 American involvement in the Second World War. Dozens of treason prosecutions take place, including radio propagandists from both the European and Pacific Theatres.

1942 In *Ex Parte Quirin*, the Supreme Court allows the execution of German saboteurs caught in the United States. The Supreme Court affirms the President's authority for military tribunals under the Articles of War and the international law of war.

1943 The Supreme Court reverses course from its 1940 *Gobitis* opinion, ruling in *West Virginia State Board of Education v. Barnette* that states cannot compel school children to salute the flag.

1943 In *Hirabayashi v. United States* and *Yasui v. United States*, the Supreme Court upholds the constitutionality of a curfew imposed only on persons of Japanese ancestry, regardless of United States citizenship.

1944 In the notorious case of *Korematsu v. United States*, the Supreme Court visits the question of the President's authority to detain Japanese Americans (United States citizens) not engaged in combat for alleged violations of orders issued by the military to control civilians during a time of war.

1945 In *Cramer v. United States*, the Supreme Court of the United States decides a case involving a treason conviction for the first time where the offense of treason is the central issue in the case. *Cramer* represents the Supreme Court's first interpretation of the Treason Clause's requirement of an "overt act." The Court also provides its first interpretation of the phrase giving "aid and comfort" to the enemy in the context of a treason conviction.

1946 In the "Battle of Athens," a large group of veterans recently returned from service in the Second World War uses armed force to overthrow elected politicians the veterans deem to be corrupt and engaged in election fixing, raising fears around the nation that veterans might tend toward violent revolution.

1947 In *Haupt v. United States*, the United States Supreme Court explicitly upholds a treason conviction for the first time, affirming the conviction by an eight to one vote. The majority of the Supreme Court upholds the treason conviction of the father of one of the German saboteurs at issue in *Ex Parte Quirin*.

1948 Mildred Gillars, known as "Axis Sally," becomes the first woman in United States history to be convicted of treason for her pro-Nazi radio broadcasting efforts during the Second World War.

1949 Martin Monti is the only person to plead guilty to the offense of treason, and the only US military officer convicted of treason, in United States history.

1949–50 Espionage and perjury prosecution of Alger Hiss.

1950s During the Early Cold War, a "Second Red Scare" engulfs the nation, with the loyalty investigations by Senator Joseph McCarthy known as "McCarthyism" embodying paranoia and resulting in the trampling of civil and political rights.

1950 Congress passes The Internal Security Act of 1950 and the Subversive Activities Control Act, designed to control "subversive activities" and empower the President to prevent espionage or sabotage through broad detention powers.

1950 Puerto Rican Nationalist Party begins its insurrection with a series of attacks against local police and towns in Puerto Rico. The day following the defeat of the Nationalist Party's uprising in Puerto Rico, two members of the party attempt to assassinate President Harry Truman at Blair House, the home where he is staying in Washington, DC, while the White House is being renovated.

1951 The Supreme Court upholds multiple convictions of members of the Communist Party of the United States for violations of the Smith Act in *Dennis v. United States*.

1951–3 Trial, conviction, and execution of Julius and Ethel Rosenberg for espionage and conspiracy to commit espionage.

1952 The Supreme Court affirms a treason conviction for the last time (as of 2024) in *Kawakita v. United States*.

1953 Four members of the Puerto Rican Nationalist Party attack the United States Capitol, opening fire on the House floor where more than 240 members of Congress are voting, wounding five.

1954 Congress passes the Communist Control Act of 1954 (CCA), purporting to outlaw the Communist Party of the United States (Communist Party).

1956 In *Pennsylvania v. Nelson*, the United States Supreme Court holds that states cannot criminalize crimes against the national government where the federal government has already criminalized such activities, but may criminalize crimes against state government.

1957 Prosecution of Rudof Abel for espionage providing intelligence to Soviet Union.

1957 In *Yates v. United States*, the Supreme Court begins narrowing the types of expressive activities that could be punished under the Smith Act.

1967 Supreme Court decides *Keyishian v. Board of Regents*, striking down as unconstitutional holding a New York state law enacted in 1917 that declared that "the utterance of any treasonable or seditious word or words or the doing of any treasonable or seditious act" was grounds for dismissal of employees from the public school system.

1968 Supreme Court decides *United States v. O'Brien*, upholding the constitutionality of a federal statute that, among other things, criminalized forging, altering, destroying, or mutilating a draft card.

1969 In *Brandenburg v. Ohio*, the Supreme Court reverses a state conviction for incitement of violence, holding "that the constitutional guarantees of free speech and free press" prohibited a state from inhibiting calls to use force or violate a law unless the call is "directed to inciting or producing imminent lawless action and is likely to incite or produce such action." The Court thus overturned the decades-long "clear and present danger test."

1969–80 The Weather Underground (also known as the Weathermen, Weatherman, Weatherman Underground, and Weather Underground) terrorizes the country in a bombing campaign meant to overthrow the government of the United States and the overthrow of the capitalist system.

1971 The Supreme Court decides *New York Times v. United States* (the Pentagon Papers case) regarding the powers (or lack thereof) of the government to prevent publication of information that might be damaging to national security versus the rights of newspapers and the media under the First Amendment.

1972 In *United States v. U.S. District Court* (also known as the "*Keith* case"), the Supreme Court unanimously holds that the Fourth Amendment's warrant requirement applies equally to criminal investigations and intelligence gathering, as both risk infringing constitutionally protected liberties.

1974–84 Fuerzas Armadas de Liberacion Nacional (FALN), an even more violent offshoot of the Puerto Rican Nationalist Party, perpetrates a staggering 130 bombings in support of its separatist ideology.

1978–95 The "Unabomber," Ted Kaczynski, terrorizes the country with sixteen separate bombings spanning seventeen years and the continental United States.

1982 Congress enacts the "Intelligence Identities Protection Act" to protect American covert intelligence agents.

1985 Year of the Spy. Considered to be one of the most damaging years to the United States as it relates to espionage, including convictions of American turncoats like John Anthony Walker and Ronald Pelton.

1989 Supreme Court decides *Texas v. Johnson*, holding that burning a flag is expressive conduct protected by the First Amendment. At the time it invalidates Texas's law, forty-seven states had similar flag desecration laws. The Court's decision outrages many Americans and Congress soon thereafter adopts the Flag Protection Act, hoping that a federal law protecting the flag from desecration would be viewed differently by the Court.

1990 In *United States v. Eichman*, the Supreme Court strikes down Congress's attempt to prevent flag desecration, concluding the Flag Protection Act violated the First Amendment.

1992 Clash between citizens and federal law enforcement at Ruby Ridge, Idaho, which plants the seeds for a virulent anti-government militant movement and the Sovereign Citizens Movement.

1993 Series of events that takes place at a religious compound located outside of Waco, Texas, between citizens and federal law enforcement between February and April 1993, culminates in the deaths of over eighty individuals and multiple federal agents. Ruby Ridge and Waco further anger and radicalize perpetrators of the Oklahoma City Bombing.

1993 The first terrorist bombing attack on the World Trade Center occurs. The attack kills six and injures over a thousand individuals, and is, up to that point in time, the deadliest act of terrorism on United States soil.

1994 Aldrich Ames pleads guilty to espionage and agrees to a life sentence without the possibility of parole. Ames was a spy/mole in the Central Intelligence Agency.

1994 Congress enacts a "Material Support" statute, which criminalizes the material support of terrorism or designated terrorist organizations.

1995 The Murrah federal building in Oklahoma City is destroyed by a truck bomb, resulting in the death of 168 individuals, making it the deadliest terror attack on United States soil prior to September 11, 2001.

1995 The Unabomber Ted Kaczynski is apprehended after a seventeen-year bombing campaign.

1996 Congress passes the Anti-Terrorism and Effective Death Penalty Act on the one-year anniversary of the Oklahoma City Bombing. This legislation is designed to increase tools available to law enforcement and prosecutors.

2001 An orchestrated terror attack on New York City and Washington, DC, occurs. Approximately 3,000 individuals perish, making it the deadliest terror attack on United States soil, and forever changing the nation.

2001 Congress passes the USA PATRIOT Act shortly after the 9/11 attack, increasing law enforcement powers particularly as it relates to criminal investigations and surveillance.

2001 Shortly after 9/11, multiple letters are sent in the United States Postal Mail service containing Anthrax, killing and injuring people across multiple locations. The attacks cause the closure of two of three federal branches of government for a time.

2001–2 Federal Bureau of Investigation agent Robert Hanssen pleads guilty to thirteen counts of espionage, one count of attempted espionage, and one count of conspiracy to commit espionage, in a plea bargain that allows Hanssen to avoid the death penalty. Hanssen is sentenced to fifteen consecutive life sentences without the possibility of parole.

2002 John Walker Lindh, the "American Taliban," pleads guilty to providing military support and resources to terrorist organizations and carrying an explosive device in the commission of a felony.

2002 Congress passes the Homeland Security Act one year after 9/11. The legislation re-structures the federal government in a way not seen for a half century, creates the Department of Homeland Security (DHS), and integrates twenty-two existing federal agencies within DHS.

2004 In *Hamdi v. Rumsfeld*, the United States Supreme Court decides that a United States citizen may be tried as an "enemy combatant."

2004–14 The prosecution and multiple federal appeals of Jose Padilla. Padilla is arrested in Chicago, Illinois, when he disembarks his flight from Pakistan, and the FBI believe Padilla intended to perpetrate a "dirty bomb" attack in the United States.

2006 Federal indictment of Adam Gadahn, nicknamed "Azzam the American," for treason. Gadahn is the first American to be indicted for treason against the United States since the 1950s.

2010 Chelsea (then known as Bradley) Manning, a soldier in the United States Army, leaks hundreds of thousands of classified intelligence documents through WikiLeaks.

2013 Bombing at the finish line of the Boston Marathon by Tamerlan and Dzhokhar Tsarnaev.

2013 Edward Snowden, a contractor working for the National Security Agency, leaks classified information revealing massive surveillance programs conducted by the United States and its allies.

2014–16 The two Bundy Standoffs with federal law enforcement occur in 2014 and 2016 between members of the Bundy family and their supporters and federal and state law enforcement in which the Bundys reject federal jurisdiction over federally owned land.

2021 January 6 Capitol Riot occurs. Protestors attempt to delay the certification of the Presidential Election of 2020. Donald Trump holds a pre-riot rally earlier in the day and attempts to go to the Capitol grounds himself to join the rioters but is prevented by Secret Service agents who take him back to the White House.

2021 Donald Trump impeached by the House of Representatives for his role in allegedly inciting insurrection and violence on January 6, 2021. The Senate votes in favor of the removal of Trump from office in a 57–43 vote but falls short of the two-thirds required for conviction and removal.

2022–3 Multiple convictions for seditious conspiracy of defendants from the Oath Keepers and Proud Boys stemming from the defendants' participation in the January 6, 2021, Capitol Riots. The leader of the Oath Keepers is sentenced to eighteen years imprisonment for his role on January 6 and committing seditious conspiracy. The leader of the Proud Boys receives a twenty-two-year prison sentence for his role in the January 6 turmoil.

2023 Jack Teixeira is the latest of several junior service members/intelligence analysts (like Snowden and Manning before him) to leak massive amounts of secret military intelligence to the public.

2023 Donald Trump federally indicted on thirty-one counts for the mishandling of national security documents under the Espionage Act. Trump also indicted by federal grand jury for conspiracy to obstruct justice.

2023 A federal grand jury in Washington, DC, indicts Donald Trump on multiple counts of obstruction of official proceedings of Congress and conspiracy to defraud the United States regarding the January 6 presidential election certification. Trump is also indicted for committing the offense of conspiracy against rights.

2024 The federal Court of Appeals for the District of Columbia rejected claims of presidential immunity for post-presidency prosecution stemming from actions allegedly committed while in office

A

Abel, Rudolf Ivanovich (1903–71)

In the annals of the history of espionage, Rudolf Abel's case (and his exposure as a spy) remains one of the more unusual and bizarre stories. Abel's prosecution as a spy has sometimes been called the Hollow Nickel Case. Abel was one of the most prominent of the first generation of active Soviet spies during the Cold War, committing espionage against the United States from 1948 until his arrest in 1957. In announcing Abel's indictment, the United States Attorney for the Southern District of New York declared that Abel was "the most important Soviet spy ever caught in the United States" (Murphy 1957, 1).

Abel's parents (Henrich and Lyubov Fisher) were revolutionary Bolshevik activists in Tsarist Russia, and Abel's father was convicted of sedition and sentenced to a three-year sentence. As a term of his punishment, Abel's father fled to the UK in 1901, and Rudolf Abel was born there in 1903 with the given name of William August Fisher. Throughout Abel's life, he went by many aliases including but not limited to Martin Collins, Andrew Kayotis, Emil Robert Goldfus, and Rudolf Ivanovich Abel. While Rudolf Ivanovich Abel was first adopted as his name/alias upon his arrest by the Federal Bureau of Investigation (FBI) in 1957, he used it as his legal name from 1957 until his death in 1971. He was referred to as Rudolf Abel by both the United States and the Soviet Union governments from 1957 onward, including in the 1960 United States Supreme Court decision *Abel v. United States.*

After his capture and conviction, Abel openly admitted to being an officer in the Soviet Union's intelligence branch, the KGB. Upon arrival in the United States in the late 1940s, Abel was assigned the fake identity of Emil Robert Goldfus and was provided with a genuine birth certificate and other legal paperwork. The real Emil Goldfus was born in 1903 and had died early in his childhood. With the fake identity, Abel was tasked by the KGB to help run a network of spies assigned to smuggle United States atomic secrets to the Soviets. Abel's network of spies included couriers also involved with Julius and Ethel Rosenberg. After the arrest of the Rosenbergs, for fear of disclosure of the spy ring, several of the individuals who had worked with both the Rosenbergs and Abel were reassigned outside the country. The Rosenbergs never revealed Abel as a spy for the Soviets. However, this fear of exposure led the KGB to assign Abel a new KGB handler named Reino Hayhanen. Ironically, the assignment of Hayhanen to work with Abel led to Abel's exposure, arrest, and prosecution.

Abel had passed atomic secrets to Hayhanen and then to the Soviets by miniaturizing the documents into tiny microfilms that could be hidden inside common everyday items like cuff links, earrings, bolts and nails, and a hollowed-out pencil, all items found in his apartment when searched by the FBI. Unfortunately for Abel, Hayhanen was known to be a heavy drinker and often lacked the necessary attention to detail to be successful at espionage. Abel had placed microscopic film containing sensitive intelligence into a hollowed nickel that Hayhanen picked up from a drop site. However, in one of the more bizarre twists in the history of espionage, Hayhanen either misplaced or spent the nickel, likely the latter. For the next seven months, this nickel exchanged hands and circulated throughout New

York City, until 1953, when the nickel was given to a thirteen-year-old newspaper boy. In taking his daily earnings out of his pocket, the boy dropped the nickel, which broke in half, revealing a hollowed-out center and the microscopic film. The quick-thinking boy promptly reported it to a New York Police Department officer, who in turn referred it to the FBI.

From 1953 to 1957, the FBI tried but failed to decipher the code contained in the film. However, during the same four years, Hayhanen had begun to provide intelligence to the United States and helped the United States finally decode the secret information. Hayhanen assisted the FBI in providing evidence against Abel and testified against Abel at trial. During his October 1957 trial, Abel openly admitted to being a spy for the Soviet Union and a KGB officer and stated that he was a patriot to his country. After three and a half hours, a federal jury convicted Abel of all three charges: conspiracy to transmit defense information to the Soviets, conspiracy to obtain secret information, and conspiracy to act as an agent for a foreign government. The presiding federal judge sentenced Abel to a thirty-year sentence to be served at a federal penitentiary in Atlanta, Georgia. Abel's case was appealed to the United States Supreme Court, which upheld the constitutionality of the search of his New York apartment in a five to four decision in *Abel v. United States*.

Just over four years into his thirty-year sentence, and only a year after the Supreme Court's affirmation of the sentence, Abel was traded to the Soviets in exchange for the release of captured United States U-2 pilot Francis Gary Powers. Years later, in 2005, the prisoner exchange was portrayed in the American movie entitled *Bridge of Spies*.

See Also: Conspiracy, Criminal; Espionage; Rosenberg, Julius and Ethel; Sedition

Resources

Abel v. United States, 362 U.S. 217 (1960).

Arthey, Vin. 2004. *Like Father Like Son: A Dynasty of Spies*. London: Little Brown.

Donovan, James B. 1964. *Strangers on a Bridge: The Case of Colonel Abel*. New York: Atheneum House.

Murphy, Mildred. 1957. "Russian Colonel Is Indicted Here as Top Spy in U.S." *The New York Times*, August 8, 1957, 1.

Abrams v. United States (1919)

As with *Schenck v. United States* (1919) before it, in *Abrams v. United States*, the United States Supreme Court addressed the constitutionality of the Espionage Act of 1917. The petitioners, five individuals, had been convicted of violating Section 3 by "conspiring … to unlawfully utter, print, write and publish … 'disloyal, scurrilous and abusive language'" about the US government, using "language 'intended to bring the form of Government of the United States into contempt, scorn, contumely and disrepute,'" as well as "language 'intended to incite, provoke and encourage resistance to the United States [in the First World War].'" Finally, the petitioners had been convicted of forming a conspiracy to "unlawfully and willfully, by utterance, writing, printing and publication, … urge, incite and advocate curtailment of production of things and products, to wit, ordnance and ammunition, necessary and essential to the prosecution of the war."

Abrams, like *Schenck*, dealt with printed material in leaflets and their distribution, this time in New York City. The accused distributors were from Russia and had lived in the United States, but none were naturalized citizens. They were purported to have printed and distributed over five thousand leaflets around August 22, 1918. Jacob Abrams had rented different rooms in New York City where the printing of the leaflets was discussed, and he had purchased some printing equipment and set it up in a basement. The printed leaflets were thrown from a building in which one of the defendants was employed. The leaflets had the heading "Revolutionists Unite for Action" printed on them. Some text included: "The Russian Revolution cries: Workers of the World! Awake! Rise! Put down your enemy and mine!"; "Yes! [F]riends, there is only one enemy of the workers of the world and that is CAPITALISM"; and "Workers, Russian emigrants, you who had the least belief in the honesty of *our* Government must now throw away all confidence, must spit in the face the false, hypocritic, military propaganda which has fooled you so relentlessly, calling forth your sympathy, your help, to the prosecution of the war." During the trial, four of the five testified on their own behalf, and of these, three admitted to being "rebels," "revolutionaries," or "anarchists."

Justice John H. Clarke, writing for a seven to two majority and citing *Schenck*, quickly dismissed the claim that the First Amendment protected the speech made by the leafleteers and held that the Espionage Act of 1917 was constitutional under the First Amendment if the speech created or incited actual opposition to the war, without explicitly applying the clear and present danger test. The Court then turned to addressing Abrams' contention that there was insufficient evidence in the record of the leafleteers' *intent* to support a conviction under the Espionage Act. The Court determined that the leaflets were "clearly an appeal to the 'workers' of this country to arise and put down by force the Government of the United States." Justice Clarke then wrote that the "purpose of this was to persuade the persons to whom it was addressed to turn a deaf ear to patriotic appeals … and to cease to render [the Government] assistance in the prosecution of the war." He observed that "the plan of action which they adopted necessarily involved … defeat of the war program of the United States," and that "the obvious effect of this appeal … would be to persuade persons of character such as those they regarded themselves as addressing, not to aid government loans and not to work in ammunition factories, … the use of which would cause the 'murder' of Germans and Russians." Because of the language used in the leaflets, the majority concluded that the goal of the leaflets "was to excite, at the supreme crisis of the war, disaffection, riots, and, as they hoped, revolution, in this country for the purpose of embarrassing and if possible defeating the military plans of our Government in Europe."

The creator of the clear and present danger test, Justice Oliver Wendell Holmes, wrote the main dissent, which Justice Louis Brandeis joined. Holmes advocated for an application of the clear and present danger test that would protect more speech. Justice Holmes believed that the Espionage Act could constitutionally prohibit speech that produced or was intended to produce a clear and imminent danger that the government was constitutionally permitted to prevent, and even agreed that the power was greater in times of war than in times of peace because "war opens dangers that do not exist at other times." However, Justice Holmes noted that while the risk of danger may ebb and flow, "the principle of the right to free speech is always the same." In this case, because Holmes perceived there was no actual danger posed by the "surreptitious publishing of a silly leaflet by an unknown man." Justice Holmes feared where the majority's application of the clear and present danger standard was heading: "[W]e should be eternally vigilant against attempts to check the expression of opinions we loathe and believe to be fraught with death, unless they so imminently threaten immediate interference with the lawful and pressing purposes of the law that an immediate check is required to save the country."

Legal scholars—many years after *Abrams*—argued that Holmes laid the foundation for modern First Amendment jurisprudence; the marketplace of ideas doctrine (which promotes free discourse as a means of revealing truth) would be adopted by the Court in *Brandenburg v. Ohio* (1969), when it walked away from the clear and present danger test.

See Also: *Brandenburg v. Ohio* (1969); Clear and Present Danger Test; Conspiracy, Criminal; Espionage Act of 1917 and Sedition Act of 1918; *Schenck v. United States* (1919)

Resources

Abrams v. United States, 250 U.S. 616 (1919).

O'Neill, Timothy J. n.d. "*Abrams v. United States* (1919)." *The First Amendment Encyclopedia*. Accessed July 14, 2022. https://www.mtsu.edu/first-amendment/article/328/abrams-v-united-states.

Schenck v. United States, 249 U.S. 47 (1919).

Advocacy of Illegal Action

See Brandenburg v. Ohio (1969)

Aid and Comfort (Aid to Enemies of the State)

Treason is the single criminal offense expressly delineated in the United States Constitution. The Treason Clause in Article III, Section 3, provides in part: "Treason against the United States shall consist only in levying war against them, or in adhering to their enemies, giving them aid and comfort." Thus, there are two grounds for the charge of treason. First, a person could "levy war" against the government. Second, a person could provide "aid and comfort" to enemies of the state. These two grounds for treason, "levying war" and "adhering to their enemies, giving them aid and comfort," are distinctive and do not represent identical legal acts. A person could be found guilty of committing treason by committing either of the two definitions of treason contained in Article III. Legal scholars have opined that "levying war" represents an act of treason conducted internally by individuals within the United States and targeted against the government (either state or federal), while providing enemies "aid and comfort" covers acts committed in support of an external war executed against the United States by a foreign enemy or adversary.

Like the term "levying war," the Framers of the United States Constitution borrowed the "aid and comfort" language directly from the English Treason Statute of 1351. Under the reign of Edward III, the English Treason Statute specified that "if a man do levy war against our lord the king in his realm, or be adherent to the king's enemies in his realm, giving them aid and comfort in the realm, or elsewhere," the offense of treason has been committed. Just as a body of case law has developed over time which has defined and evolved the meaning of the term "levying war," the same is true for the Aid and Comfort Clause.

Two key aspects of the Aid and Comfort Clause require further definition and interpretation to properly understand the Clause. First, what exactly does "aid and comfort" connote? What level of assistance given to an enemy meets the definition of providing "aid and comfort"? For instance, would the act of writing a letter of encouragement to the leader of an enemy of the United States constitute providing "aid and comfort"? Did Jane Fonda's 1972 visit to North Vietnam during the Vietnam War offering words of encouragement to the North Vietnamese leadership, which earned her the derogatory nickname "Hanoi Jane" and hatred among many US military members, constitute providing "aid and comfort" to the North Vietnamese government? Second, for purposes of the Treason Clause, how is the term "enemy" defined? Does the United States need to be in open armed conflict or hostilities or a declared war against a foreign entity or power for that entity to be classified as an "enemy" of the United States for purposes of the charge of treason?

What sort of activities have courts considered to have risen to the level of "aid and comfort" needed to satisfy the Treason Clause? On a broad level, in *Rex v. Casement* (1917), a case dealing with treason under the English Treason Statute, the English court broadly defined "aid and comfort" as committing any "act which strengthens or tends to strengthen the enemy." However, this could feasibly include much conduct the Framers never intended to be included as "aid and comfort" under American treason law. Unlike the term "levying war," which was discussed, defined, and redefined by various Supreme Court Justices in a bevy of early treason cases in the United States, there has been a relative paucity of cases discussing what constitutes "aid and comfort." Rather, judicial interpretation and instruction are derived from canvassing and reviewing jury and grand jury instructions issued by presiding trial judges in federal cases from the mid-1800s. In reviewing these jury instructions, the clearest examples of providing aid and comfort to an enemy of the United States are if a person were actively engaged in recruiting people to serve in the forces of a foreign power against the United States or enlisting in the forces of a foreign power themselves. Providing material support also could constitute "aid and comfort," particularly items like ammunition, arms, and military equipment that could be utilized against the United States.

The Supreme Court has indicated that selling or buying even non-military goods and products might be sufficient to meet the "aid and comfort" threshold. For instance, in *Young v. United States* (1877), the Supreme Court held that a person who contracted with North Carolina during the Civil War to transport cotton through the Union coastal blockade gave "aid or comfort to the rebellion." The Supreme Court has also indicated, in *Sprott v. United States* (1874), that the specific intent to aid the enemy by providing resources or support was not required. In *Sprott*, the Court commented that a "case is not relieved of its harsh features by a finding of the court that the claimant did not intend to aid the rebellion, but only to make money." However, the reader should note that neither *Young* nor *Sprott* pertained to treason prosecutions and dealt only with whether the seizure by the federal government of property was proper under separate legislation (1863 Captured and Abandoned Property Act). As such, *Young* and *Sprott* should be distinguished from *United States v. Greathouse* (1863), discussed at the end of this entry.

Furthermore, providing military or tactical intelligence to an enemy power also constitutes another clear example of sufficient "aid and comfort" to support treason charges. In an 1861 federal *Charge to the Grand Jury* by Judge Humphrey H. Leavitt (C.C.S.D., Ohio), 30 Fed. Case No. 18272, a thorough definition of actionable conduct was delineated by Judge Leavitt, including providing of intelligence to enemies:

> Thus, to sell to, or provide arms or munitions of war, or military stores, or supplies, including food, clothing, etc., for use of the enemy … and to hire, sell, or furnish boats, railroad cars, or other means of transportation, or to advance money, or obtain credits, for the use and support of a hostile army is treasonable. It is equally clear that the communication of intelligence to the enemy by letter, telegraph, or otherwise relating to the strengths, movements, or position of the army, is an act of treason.

Also, the publication of troop movements is not protected First Amendment speech, as is addressed in a separate entry in this book on the Supreme Court case of *Near v. Minnesota* (1931).

Finally, there is some legal scholarship suggesting that even the exercise of free speech in advising, encouraging, or persuading others to give aid and comfort to the enemies, or to encourage others to obstruct the US efforts against the foreign power, could in some limited contexts constitute the treasonable offering of "aid and comfort" to the enemy. There is clearly a fine line between the constitutionally protected exercise of free speech and the unprotected advocacy of illegal action against the government. As is explained in the entry in this book on the topic of speech as crime against the state, the mere expression of one's views is protected political speech. As Judge Leavitt stated in his 1861 *Charge to the Grand Jury* referenced above, the "mere expression of opinion indicative of sympathy with the public enemy would not ordinarily involve the legal guilt" of treason. However, incitement to violence, the advocacy of illegal action against the government, and encouraging others to join the enemy's forces or participate in hostile actions against the United States likely constitute sufficient acts of "aid and comfort" under the Treason Clause, and speech that would not be protected by the First Amendment.

After resolving the issue of whether "aid or comfort" has been provided, the second issue that must be resolved is what constitutes being an "enemy" for purposes of the "aid and comfort" prong of the Treason Clause. In *United States v. Burr*, 25 F Cas 55 (Circuit Court, Virginia, 1807), United States Chief Justice John Marshall explained that the meaning of the language in Article III was highly dependent on English interpretation of the meaning of the language employed in the English Treason Statute of 1351. Marshall stated that the terms utilized in Article III, Section 3, of the United States Constitution were also "used in a very old statute of that country whose language is our language, and whose laws form the substratum of our laws. It is scarcely conceivable that the term was not employed by the framers of our constitution in the sense which had been affixed to it by those whom we borrowed it." As such, in looking at English law, eminent British jurists and scholars like William Blackstone (1723–80) and Edward Hale (1609–76) were clear in stating that the term "enemy" for treason purposes did not necessarily need to entail a foreign government in open military conflict or a country in a declared war. Rather, states who displayed active hostility toward England, even though there was no declared war, still constituted "enemies" for the purpose of treason law. Furthermore, enemies do not even need to be an independent sovereign state, but can include "foreign pirates or robbers, who may happen to invade our coasts, without any open hostilities between their nation and our own" for purposes of treason law (Larson 2006, 916). This is persuasive precedent for considering terrorist organizations like Al-Qaeda to be enemies under the Treason Clause, and individuals providing any material support and "aid and comfort" to those terrorist groups would be committing an act of treason, among several other criminal offenses under the United States Code.

Some scholars have argued that the United States must be in open hostility or a declared war for the Aid and Comfort Clause to apply. For instance, these scholars have argued that it was legally impossible to commit treason by providing aid and comfort to the Soviet Union during the Cold War because it was not an open armed conflict or a declared war. Some of these scholars explain that was the reason people like Julius and Ethel Rosenberg were prosecuted and convicted for espionage (or conspiracy to commit espionage) with the Soviet Union, and not treason. However, this interpretation runs contrary to English and American legal precedent. For instance, English jurist Edward Hale indicated in his writings on his interpretation of the English Treason Statute of 1351 that there does not need to be an open war between countries, and a *de facto* relationship of hostility would make governments enemies of each other for purposes of treason. This would be analogous to the relationship between the United States and the Soviet Union during the Cold War. Additionally, early in American history, the United States had what has been described as a "pseudo-war" with France in 1798–9, as the relationship between the two countries has significantly deteriorated, and armed conflict was possible. While there was no open armed hostility or declared war, Attorney General Charles Lee issued an opinion in 1798 that stated that there was a *de facto* state of war between France and the United States. In that legal opinion, Lee wrote: "France is our enemy; and to aid, assist, and abet that nation in her maritime warfare, will be treason in a citizen or any other person within the United States" (Larson 2006, 917). Lee's position was vindicated by the subsequent Supreme Court opinion in *Bas v. Tingy* (1800), where the Court held that the United States was at war with France (even though a non-declared war) and France was an enemy of the United States for purpose of applying relevant maritime salvage laws.

In *United States v. Greathouse* (1863), Supreme Court Justice Stephen J. Field set forth the important principle that acts of rebellion or hostility against one's own government can only be treason if those acts themselves amounted to levying war. The Court held that aiding others in acts of rebellion against the United States cannot be treason under the Aid and Comfort Clause, as the Aid and Comfort Clause is only applicable to *foreign* adversaries who are engaged in open hostilities with the United States. Those rebelling against their own governments are not foreign adversaries under the meaning of the Treason Clause in the Constitution.

While there have been far more cases involving the prong of treason dealing with the act of "levying war," there have been important treason convictions based upon providing "aid and comfort" to the enemy as well, such as *Haupt v. United States* (1947).

See Also: American Civil War and Treason; Conspiracy, Criminal; English Treason Statute of 1351; Espionage; *Greathouse, United States v.* (1863); *Haupt v. United States* (1947); Levying War; Material Support Crimes; *Near v. Minnesota* (1931); Rebellion; Rosenberg, Julius and Ethel; Speech as Crime against the State; Treason

Resources

Jackson, Stephen. 2019. "Treason in the Age of Terrorism: Do Americans Who Join ISIS 'Levy War' against the United States?" *American University National Security Law Brief* 9: 155–221.

Larson, Carlton F. W. 2006. "The Forgotten Constitutional Law of Treason and the Enemy Combatant Problem." *University of Pennsylvania Law Review* 154: 863–926.

Warren, Charles. 1918. "What Is Giving Aid and Comfort to the Enemy?" *The Yale Law Journal* 27 (January): 331–47.

Al-Arian, United States v. (2005)

Doctor Sami Al-Arian, a one-time professor of computer engineering at the University of South Florida (USF), was among several defendants indicted in 2003 by a federal grand jury for alleged involvement in the Palestinian Islamic Jihad (PIJ), an organization designated in 1995 by the United States as a foreign terrorist organization. In addition to teaching at USF, Al-Arian served as an imam at a local mosque and helped found several organizations, including the Islamic Concern Project, which had a committee devoted to raising charity for Palestine, the World and Islam Studies Enterprise (WISE), which served as a think tank that promoted public policy initiatives, and a local religious school. Through Al-Arian's facilitation, WISE and USF formally entered into a cooperation agreement in 1992. WISE published journals, supported graduate student education, and held seminars of American and Middle Eastern scholars.

Ultimately, the United States would allege that Al-Arian was a mastermind of a worldwide terrorism organization, responsible for significant fundraising for the PIJ's terrorist activities, and that his various charitable and academic activities and organizations were fronts for these nefarious purposes. Al-Arian and his seven co-defendants were charged with a variety of crimes, including violations of federal racketeering laws, conspiracy within the United States to kill and maim persons abroad, conspiracy to provide material support and resources to PIJ, conspiracy to violate emergency economic sanctions, engaging in various acts of interstate extortion, perjury, obstruction of justice, and immigration fraud. The indictments were the product of a sweeping investigation by the Federal Bureau of Investigation (FBI) that relied heavily on extensive new authorities and methods granted by the USA PATRIOT Act, passed in the wake of the September 11 terror attacks. Attorney General John Ashcroft praised the extended law enforcement powers under the USA PATRIOT Act when announcing the indictment. The FBI investigation, which had begun well before September 2001, lasted over ten years and involved FBI intercepts of 472,239 phone calls. None of these phone calls included any discussion of an attack against the United States or reflected advanced knowledge of attacks in the Middle East. At the trial, an FBI agent testified that the PIJ had planned an attack inside the United States, but stated he could not provide further details because all information about the plot was classified.

Al-Arian's supporters maintained his innocence and used his case to highlight perceived excesses in law enforcement powers provided by the USA PATRIOT Act. The criminal trial against Al-Arian, and related employment actions taken against him by USF for perceived support of terrorism and the disruption caused by such concerns, also prompted many academics in the United States to decry violations of academic freedom and free speech.

After a trial lasting six months, the jury acquitted Al-Arian of eight of the seventeen charges against him and deadlocked on the other nine, meaning he was not convicted of any of the charges. Prosecutors weighed retrying him on some or all of the remaining nine charges. Eventually, Al-Arian pleaded guilty to one count of conspiracy to contribute services to, or for the benefit of, the PIJ, a designated terrorist organization. Though the United States had alleged far broader activities, Al-Arian essentially admitted only to being associated with the PIJ since the late 1980s and providing "services" for the group, which included filing for immigration benefits for key members, hiding the identities of those men, and lying about his involvement.

He was sentenced to the maximum of fifty-seven months in prison for this one charge. During the sentencing proceeding, the sentencing judge rejected Al-Arian's claims that his fundraising efforts had all been for legitimate charities, stating he believed Al-Arian was an active leader of the PIJ who raised money for suicide bombings in Israel. The judge castigated Al-Arian, noting "Your only connection to widows and orphans was that you create them."

Al-Arian was later jailed for civil contempt of court when he refused to testify before a grand jury in a terrorism investigation in Northern Virginia. In 2015, forty years after he first moved to the United States, Al-Arian was deported to Turkey.

Ultimately, Al-Arian's conviction for conspiracy to provide services to the PIJ meant his "crimes against the state" were helping individuals violate United States immigration laws and supporting an organization whose interests were misaligned with US foreign policy.

See Also: Conspiracy, Criminal; Material Support Crimes; Perjury, False Statements, and Obstruction of Justice; September 11, 2001; Terrorism; USA PATRIOT Act

Resources

Gravois, John. 2005. "Al-Arian Acquitted of 8 Terrorism Charges." *Chronicle of Higher Education*, December 16, 2005.

Lichtblau, Eric, and Judith Miller. 2003a. "Threats and Responses: The Professor, Officials Say Case against Professor Had Been Hindered." *New York Times*, February 22, 2003.

Lichtblau, Eric, and Judith Miller. 2003b. "Threats and Responses: The Money Trail; Indictment Ties U.S. Professor to Terror Group." *New York Times*, January 21, 2003.

"Press Release: Members of the Palestinian Islamic Jihad Arrested, Charged with Racketeering and Conspiracy to Provide Support to Terrorists." United States Department of Justice, February 20, 2003. Accessed June 6, 2023. https://www.justice.gov/archive/opa/pr/2003/February/03_crm_099.htm.

Whoriskey, Peter. 2005. "Ex-Professor Won Court Case but Not His Freedom." *Washington Post*, December 14, 2005.

Alien Act (1798)

The Alien Act was one of the four laws that made up what was collectively known as the Alien and Sedition Acts. Under the threat of a possible war with France, the Federalist-controlled Congress and presidency worked in concert to pass the four acts. While Federalists claimed the laws were needed to protect the national security of the United States, detractors claimed that the real purpose of these laws was to silence critics of the Adams administration and to weaken support for Thomas Jefferson's Democratic-Republican party.

The Alien Act, which went into effect on June 25, 1798, allowed the president to remove from the United States all aliens/foreigners whom he decided were "dangerous to the peace and safety of the United States" or wherein reasonable grounds existed "to suspect are concerned in any treasonable or secret machinations" against the United States. The president was the sole and final arbiter as to the alien's suitability to live within the United States. Since "a number of recent immigrants published newspapers or pamphlets … [t]he law effectively let Adams deport anyone who published anything he did not like" (Maxwell 2004, 1).

While there is no known evidence to suggest that President Adams exercised his authority to remove individuals from the United States under his authority under the Alien Act, the fear caused within the immigrant population "caused some aliens to leave the country and frightened others to refrain from speaking out against the Federalists" (Gordon 1970, 115). Dr. Peter Irons, a noted American legal scholar and Emeritus Professor of Political Science at the University of California, wrote that soon after passage of the law, "two shiploads of French citizens promptly sailed for their homeland to escape jailing and forced deportation" (Irons 1999, 14). And while no actual arrests or deportations were ordered by Adams, historians have argued that these acts supply precedent for similar measures to be adopted in the twenty-first century. Unlike the Alien Enemies Act, the Alien Act was allowed to expire and was not renewed.

See Also: Alien and Sedition Acts (1798); Alien Enemies Act (1798)

Resources

An Act Concerning Aliens. United States Statutes at Large 1 (1798): 570–2. Accessed May 21, 2022. https://www.archives.gov/milestone-documents/alien-and-sedition-acts#alien.

Fehlings, Gregory. 2002. "Storm on the Constitution: The First Deportation Law." *Tulsa Journal of Comparative & International Law* 10: 63–114.

Gordon, Irving L. 1970. *Review of American History*. New York: AMSCO.

Irons, Peter. 1999. *A People's History of the Supreme Court*. New York: Viking.

Maxwell, Bruce. 2004. *Homeland Security: A Documentary History*. Washington, DC: CQ Press.

Alien and Sedition Acts (1798)

During the peak of hostilities and the specter of potential war with France, in June and July 1798, Federalist party adherents in Congress drove through the passage of four separate laws, which collectively became known as the Alien and Sedition Acts. On the surface, the collective legislation, signed into law by Federalist President John Adams, was meant to protect the United States from the threat of anarchy, violence, and domestic upheaval initiated by newly arrived immigrants to America's shores. Among other things, the laws allowed for the immediate deportation of aliens deemed "dangerous" to the United States or an "enemy" of the United States. The law also made it a crime to criticize the government, make any statement that would bring the Congress or the President "into contempt or disrepute," or "to excite against them ... the hatred of the good people of the United States, or to stir up sedition within the United States."

The four separate laws that collectively comprised the Alien and Sedition Acts were the Alien Act, the Alien Enemies Act, the Sedition Act, and the Naturalization Act. The Naturalization Act increased the time needed for immigrants to become American citizens (and to vote) from five to fourteen years. The Alien Act enabled the president to deport any immigrant that the president deemed to be "dangerous." The Alien Enemies Act allowed the president to detain any aliens in time of war. Finally, the Sedition Act imposed fines and incarceration to any person who spoke or wrote "false, scandalous, and malicious" statements against the United States, or even words that could be construed to bring the Congress or the president "into contempt or disrepute."

Federalists claimed the Alien and Sedition Acts were needed to protect the United States against anarchists, revolutionaries, and those inebriated with political violence unbottled by the excesses of the French Revolution. Yet, the Democratic-Republican party (and its leader, Vice President Thomas Jefferson) claimed that the laws were chiefly politically motivated for the following reasons: first, the laws targeted immigrants, a majority of whom associated politically with Thomas Jefferson's political party; second, one of the laws significantly lengthened the time required for immigrants to become citizens (from five to fourteen years), which was advantageous to the Federalist Party as most immigrants tended to support and vote for Democratic-Republican candidates and the law would therefore delay the enlargement of support for the Democratic-Republican Party; third, the laws were enforced and implemented in a very partisan fashion, with most of those who were prosecuted and/or deported being opposed to the Federalist Party or its agenda; and fourth, immigrants from France and Ireland were disproportionally targeted under the laws, while immigrants from Great Britain were largely ignored. This was telling because Federalist Party politics reflected hostilities toward France and Ireland, with Federalists favoring relations with Great Britain.

Through the hindsight of history, two additional factors make clear the partisan nature of this legislation, particularly the Sedition Act. While the Sedition Act made it a crime to criticize the president or Congress (both branches controlled by the Federalist Party), the Act omitted the vice president from its "protection." While Thomas Jefferson served as the vice president to John Adams, Jefferson was also the opposition leader of the rival Democratic-Republican Party. Thus, under the Act, one could criticize, defame, and bring into disrepute the vice president with impunity, while the same language against the president or Congress would land the speaker or writer in jail. Second, the expiration terms of the Sedition Act itself make clear its partisan nature as well. The Sedition Act specified that the "Act shall continue and be in force until the third day of March 1801, and no longer." The expiration of the Act would conveniently arrive immediately upon the inauguration of the next president. Thus, if the next president belonged to the Democratic-Republican Party, all manner of criticisms and vitriolic speech would again be permissible.

While the details of many components of the Alien and Sedition Acts will be discussed elsewhere in this book, it is worth noting that there was a backlash and public dislike of these laws collectively, and the passage of the laws was a factor leading to the election of Thomas Jefferson as president. By its own terms, the Sedition Act expired in 1801 and the Naturalization Act, which did not have a similar expiration date in the Act, was repealed by Congress in 1802. In an 1804 letter Thomas Jefferson penned to Abigail Adams, John Adams' wife and a fervent supporter of the Alien and Sedition Acts, Jefferson wrote:

> I discharged every person under punishment or prosecution under the Sedition Law, because I considered, and now consider, that law to be a nullity, as absolute and palpable as if Congress had ordered us to fall down and worship a golden image; and that is was as much my duty to arrest its execution in every stage, as it would have been to have rescued from the fiery furnace those who should have been cast into it for refusing to worship the image. (Lewis 2007, 20)

But Jefferson's pardon could not save all of those convicted under the Sedition Act. For example, Benjamin Bache, the grandson of Benjamin Franklin, who was bequeathed with Franklin's own printing press and followed in his grandfather's tradition of printing newspapers, was convicted and languished in jail for two years. Jefferson's pardon came too late for Bache, as he died in jail just a few months before Jefferson took office (Coate 2006, 20).

See Also: Alien Act (1798); Alien Enemies Act (1798); Anarchy, Criminal; Jefferson, Thomas; Sedition; Sedition Act of 1798

Resources

The Alien and Sedition Acts. United States Statutes at Large 1 (1798): 570–2, 577–8, 596–7. Accessed May 21, 2022. https://www.archives.gov/milestone-documents/alien-and-sedition-acts.

Bird, Wednell. 2020. *Criminal Dissent: Prosecutions under the Alien and Sedition Acts of 1798.* Cambridge, MA: Harvard University Press.

Coate, Bill. 2006. *Shocking Secrets of American History: 115 Surprising Tales.* New York: MJF Books.

Lewis, Anthony. 2007. *Freedom for the Thought That We Hate: A Biography of the First Amendment.* New York: Basic Books.

Maxwell, Bruce. 2004. *Homeland Security: A Documentary History.* Washington, DC: CQ Press.

Miller, John C. 1957. *Crisis in Freedom: The Alien and Sedition Acts.* Boston: Little, Brown and Company.

Alien Enemies Act (1798)

Drawing on the guise of a potential war with France and harnessing strong public sentiment and the specter of mob violence, the Federalist-controlled Congress and President John Adams promulgated a series of four laws known collectively as the Alien and Sedition Acts. Enacted into law on July 6, 1798, the Alien Enemies Act was one of the four pieces of legislation.

Unlike the other three laws passed as part of the Alien and Sedition Acts, the powers of the federal government afforded by the Alien Enemies Act were only implicated at the time of an actual or threatened war by a foreign nation against the United States. More specifically, "whenever there shall be a declared war between the United States and any foreign nation … or any invasion or predatory incursion shall be perpetrated, attempted, or threatened against … the United States, … and the President … make[s] [a] public proclamation of the event," then the president is imbued with the absolute power of apprehension, restraint, and/or immediate deportation.

Pursuant to the terms of the original statute, there must be an actual declared war or threatened war or invasion of the United States. This fact explains why President Adams never deported any aliens under this statute, as a declared state of war did not exist with France. The president was also required to "make a public proclamation of the event." Under these circumstances, "males of the age of fourteen years and upwards, who shall be within the United States, and not actually naturalized," shall be "liable to be apprehended, restrained, secured and removed, as alien enemies." This law (and power of the president to apprehend and deport) has been one of the longest-standing statutes of the United States, statutory law for over 225 years. The law is currently still titled The Alien Enemy Act and is codified at 50 United States Code Section 21. The only meaningful change in the text of the law is now the law is gender neutral. In 1798, the president was authorized to apprehend "males of the age of fourteen years and upwards," while the current statute applies to any fourteen-year-old or older regardless of gender.

Despite the statute remaining largely unchanged for over 225 years, it is still referenced in litigation and pertaining to deportations made by the President. In *Al-Marri v. Hanft*, 378 F. Supp. 2d 673 (D.S.C. 2005), the issue was raised in litigation as to whether the detainee had any rights under The Alien Enemy Act. However, while suggesting that such rights might exist if the statute was applicable to the litigant's case, the reviewing court determined "the Alien Enemy Act does not have direct application to this case is simply a result of the nature of the war on terrorism, which is not a 'declared war' against a 'foreign nation or government'" and therefore outside the scope and applicability of this several hundred-year-old statute (*Al-Marri v. Hanft*, 679).

See Also: Alien Act (1798); Alien and Sedition Acts (1798); Terrorism

Resources

Al-Massi v. Hanft, 378 F.Supp.2d 673 (DSC 2005)

An Act Respecting Alien Enemies. United States Statutes at Large 1 (1798): 577–8. Accessed May 21, 2022. https://www.archives.gov/milestone-documents/alien-and-sedition-acts#enemies.

Sidak, J. Gregory. 1992. "War, Liberty, and Enemy Aliens." *New York University Law Review* 67: 1402–28.

Vladeck, Stephen J. 2007. "Enemy Aliens, Enemy Property, and Access to the Courts." *Lewis & Clark Law Review* 11: 963–96.

American Civil War—Amnesty and Pardons

Persons guilty of crimes against the state rarely receive pardons for such crimes. However, the single most significant crime against the state in US history—the American Civil War—was ultimately followed by the greatest number of pardons.

From the Crimes Act of 1790 until several months into the Civil War, the only punishment authorized under federal law for treason against the United States was death. Congress ultimately recognized the far-reaching consequences of such a draconian punishment in light of a treasonous rebellion involving hundreds of thousands of people, and anticipated the need to eventually reunify the nation after the rebellion was defeated. Accordingly, in 1862, Congress provided an alternative punishment for those convicted of treason: a minimum of five years imprisonment. Treason was still criminal, but with a far less severe punishment available.

Continuing Congress' recognition that national unity would demand that hundreds of thousands of southerners not live under the cloud of possible treason convictions, President Lincoln's first declaration of amnesty (entitled "Proclamation of Amnesty and Reconstruction") was issued on December 8, 1863, long before the Civil War concluded. The amnesty encompassed most of the southerners who had participated in the rebellion, but excluded several classes of persons, including those who were officers and officials in the Confederacy, those who had left positions in the US government to serve in the Confederate government, and those who had abused prisoners of war. Persons in the excepted classes could still seek pardon but were required to do so on an individual basis rather than through the general amnesty process. All persons who wished to take advantage of the amnesty were required to swear a loyalty oath to the United States.

Following President Lincoln's assassination, President Andrew Johnson issued his own amnesty policy on May 29, 1865. Similar to President Lincoln's amnesty declaration, President Johnson's included several classes of persons who were required to seek individual pardon, notably adding anyone whose taxable property exceeded $20,000 and anyone who had taken the loyalty oath required under President Lincoln's December 1863 amnesty but had later violated it. President Johnson's amnesty included not only exemption from criminal sanction, but protection of civil property ownership, except regarding the ownership of former slaves. Some members of Congress considered President Johnson's amnesty program to be too liberal, even suggesting impeachment charges against President Johnson for "corrupt" use of the pardon power.

In 1867, two years after the Civil War concluded, President Johnson issued another amnesty directive, pardoning all who engaged in the rebellion, but again requiring everyone who wished to be covered by the pardon to swear a loyalty oath. Leaders of the Confederate government and state governments thereunder, high-ranking military officers, those who had abused prisoners of war, and persons in confinement or who had participated in the assassination of President Lincoln were excluded from this general amnesty. A year later, President Johnson issued another declaration of amnesty, offering unconditional pardon to every person who assisted the rebellion, except those then under indictment for a charge of treason or other felony. On December 25, 1868, President Johnson altered this proclamation to include "a full pardon and amnesty for the offences of treason against the United States, or of adhering to their enemies during the late civil war" for all persons. The widespread amnesty offered to participants in the rebellion offered by Presidents Lincoln and Johnson is credited with being a key component of the successful reunification of the United States in the years following the Civil War.

In 1872, in *Carlisle v. United States*, the United States Supreme Court confirmed that the general amnesty granted by President Johnson on December 25, 1868, extended to aliens domiciled in the United States before the rebellion who gave aid and comfort to the rebellion. This conclusion was predicated on the holding that aliens domiciled in the United States owe a local and temporary allegiance to the government of the United States, are bound to obey all the laws of the country not immediately relating to citizenship during their residence in it, were thus potentially guilty of treason against the United States, and therefore were covered by President Johnson's grant of amnesty.

Despite the protection of some of the rebels' personal property interests included in amnesty and pardon, not all civil interests were protected. In *Texas v. White* (1869) and *Hanauer v. Doane* (1870), the United States Supreme Court held that all contracts "made in aid of the late rebellion or in furtherance and support thereof" were void. Thus, persons and business entities who after the war sought to recover damages for contract breaches could not recover if at the time of making the contracts they knew the contracts were for the purpose of supporting the rebellion.

See Also: Aid and Comfort (Aid to Enemies of the State); American Civil War and Treason; Assassination; *Carlisle v. United States* (1872); Crimes Act of 1790; Lincoln Assassination (1865); Rebellion; *Texas v. White* (1869); Treason

Resources

Dorris, Jonathan Truman. 1953. *Pardon and Amnesty under Lincoln and Johnson: The Restoration of the Confederates to Their Rights and Privileges, 1861–1898*. Chapel Hill: University of North Carolina Press.

American Civil War and Treason

The American Civil War represents the single largest example of acts of treason being collectively committed against the United States. Hundreds of thousands took up arms against the federal government between 1861 and 1865. As explained by treason expert Professor Carlton F. W. Larson, "most members of the Confederate army were guilty of treason against the United States of America, but none was ever prosecuted" (Larson 2019, 22). Treason is defined by Article III of the United States Constitution as including levying war against the United States or providing its enemies aid and comfort. As multiple postwar Supreme Court decisions make clear (including cases such as *United States v. Carlisle* [1872] and *Radich v. Hutchins*[1877]), the Supreme Court itself viewed actively supporting the civil war as constituting treason, even as it related to non citizens and nationals in the United States who supported the Confederacy. Furthermore, in another postwar decision by the Supreme Court, in *Texas v. White* (1869), the Supreme Court held that state governments lacked the legal authority to unilaterally withdraw from the Union. As such, the claim that one was merely following the lawful dictates of a seceding state likely would not have been a valid defense in individual prosecutions.

Yet not a single individual was ever successfully prosecuted for treason against the government. There was a litany of reasons why treason prosecutions were not pursued against the rank-and-file Confederate soldiers and politicians following the war. First, in a desire to see a rapid reunification between the North and South after the war, several presidential orders of amnesty and pardon were issued. The first was issued by President Abraham Lincoln in 1863 and the second was issued by President Andrew Johnson in 1865 (see American Civil War—Amnesty and Pardons). The legal effect of the presidential pardons was to annul the criminality of those who engaged in treason against the federal government and bar criminal prosecutions for those who availed themselves of the pardons. As was illustrated in *Carlisle v. United States*, even non-residents were covered under the terms of the presidential pardon.

Second, it would have been logistically impossible to prosecute and incarcerate hundreds of thousands of southerners for actions taken during the Civil War. There simply were not enough courts and jails to process and incarcerate such a vast number of individuals. Third, any such prosecutions would be clouded by legal issues regarding the constitutional right of a state to secede (a constitutional issue not definitively resolved until *Texas v. White* in 1869).

Fourth, in accordance with the Supreme Court's decision in *Ex Parte Milligan* in 1869, any postwar prosecution (again, for those not subject to the presidential pardons) would need to take place in a southern federal court and with a jury composed of southerners, which would have presented yet another practical problem to prosecutors pursuing such a case. And indeed, this was one of the problems in the single unsuccessful treason prosecution that did follow the war, the treason case of the Confederacy's President Jefferson Davis. Except for Robert E. Lee (who was indicted for treason, but never prosecuted), Jefferson Davis provided the clearest and most high-profile case of treason (see Davis, Jefferson). Jefferson Davis was the highest leader of the Confederacy and the potential case against Davis included an abundancy of evidence which supported and corroborated the allegations of Davis's treasonous intent and actions taken in levying war against the Unites States. Yet, "even Jefferson Davis, the most plausible defendant, escaped trial when federal officials concluded that no southern jury could be trusted to convict him" (Larson 2019, 365–6 n6).

Fifth, immediately after the war, there was a common view that the leaders of the Confederacy should be charged before rank-and-file individuals. As just indicated, while Confederate President

Jefferson Davis was indicted for treason, the prosecution in the case stumbled through multiple legal obstacles and the case was dismissed before ever reaching a trial. Sixth, partly because of the failed prosecution of Jefferson Davis, there was a belief that prosecutions would also be legally barred because of the ratification of the Fourteenth Amendment in 1868, which the court in the Davis case concluded might operate as a complete bar to any subsequent treason prosecution the federal government might attempt.

Finally, there was also the strange situation where a southerner who took arms *against* the Confederate States of America might be committing treason against his own *state* government. Most states also had treason clauses in their constitutions or state statutes that included levying war against the state. Indeed, as of 2023, forty-three of the fifty state governments made it a criminal offense to commit treason against the state government. This placed the average military-aged southern white male in a conundrum. To actively oppose the state wherein they resided might constitute treason against the state; yet, following the state government into civil war and taking up arms against the federal government clearly constituted levying war against the United States and treason. Even the action of attempting to form a new state government from within a seceding government, or taking offices and positions within this newly formed government, constituted treason. For instance, the Virginia Code of 1849 (the statute in effect at the time of John Brown's Raid and John Brown's subsequent trial in *Virginia v. Brown* in 1859) defined treason as including not only levying war against Virginia or giving its enemies aid and comfort, but also establishing, without authority of the legislature, any government within its limits separate from the existing government or holding or executing, in such usurped government, any office, or professing allegiance or fidelity to it. An example of this constituting treason against the state can be seen in the 1859 case of *Virginia v. Brown*. Thus, the formation of West Virginia, which became a new state and part of the United States on June 20, 1863, created a very strange scenario. Those who played a role in creating the new state of West Virginia and taking up offices in the state government were committing treason against the Commonwealth of Virginia under Virginia law, while at the same time those fighting in the Army of Northern Virginia against the Union Army and the federal government were committing treason against the United States.

It is against this backdrop and context that the failure to pursue treason charges after the Civil War is best understood. It was not because hundreds of thousands of acts of treason against the United States did not occur, but rather that there existed myriad legal considerations that would have complicated and clouded any treason prosecutions and made extremely difficult the likelihood of obtaining actual convictions.

See Also: Aid and Comfort (Aid to Enemies of the State); American Civil War—Amnesty and Pardons; Brown, John; *Carlisle, United States v.* (1872); Davis, Jefferson; *Ex Parte Milligan* (1866); John Brown's Raid (1859); Levying War; *Texas v. White* (1869); Treason; *Virginia v. Brown* (1859); Whiskey Rebellion

Resources

Blair, William A. 2014. *With Malice toward Some: Treason and Loyalty in the Civil War Era*. Chapel Hill: University of North Carolina Press.

Larson, Carlton F. W. 2019. *The Trials of Allegiance: Treason, Juries, and the American Revolution*. Oxford: Oxford University Press.

McPherson, James. 1988. *Battle Cry of Freedom: The Civil War Era*. Oxford: Oxford University Press.

American Revolution and Treason

The United States was born out of the ultimate crime against the state, as the American Revolution constituted treason against Great Britain. While few, if any, revolutionaries were prosecuted by Great Britain, tens of thousands of colonists committed open hostility and levied war upon Great Britain, and in the practical sense, were guilty of the offense of treason. Conversely, during the Revolution, "thousands of Americans opposed the resistance effort, and many of them took active steps to support the king" (Larson 2019, 43). These individuals "were viewed as perhaps the most dangerous traitors of all, secretly lurking among other Americans, just waiting for the right moment to spring their nefarious plots" (Larson 2019, 43). As such, dozens and dozens of colonists were arrested and prosecuted for treason against the nascent United States by revolutionary American forces, with a handful of colonists suffering the punishment of execution after being found guilty of the crime of treason against the forces in opposition to Great Britain.

The Revolutionary War era was a precarious time for individuals and their vulnerability to treason charges. As explained by one treason scholar, "loyalty to the king was no longer a duty, but a crime—high treason against the nascent American nation [and] [a]s the British and American armies rampaged across the continent, the duty of allegiance imposed by law shifted with them" (Larson 2019, 3). For instance, in contested territories like New York City and Philadelphia, "this duty shifted from George III to the United States, then back to George III during the British occupation … and finally back to the United States when the British army departed" (Larson 2019, 3). Many Americans were simply caught between two sovereigns and had no real choice in committing treason against one side or the other. A clear example of the conflicting and irreconcilable allegiances can be seen in a resolution passed by the 1776 Continental Congress "Committee on Spies." This committee was composed of John Adams, Thomas Jefferson, John Rutledge, and Robert Livingston. The committee, while still lawfully subjects to Great Britain, passed a resolution making it treason to levy war against any of the colonies or give aid or comfort to Great Britain and its war effort. The resolution specified that

> all persons owing allegiance to any of the United Colonies, as before described, who shall levy war against any of the said colonies within the same, or be adherent to the king of Great Britain, or others the enemies of the said colonies, or any of them, within the same, giving to him or them aid and comfort, are guilty of treason against such colony.

King George III declared the American revolutionary leaders to all be traitors and engaged in the act of treason. Even before the Revolution started, and when events like the Boston Massacre and the Boston Tea Party took place, many in England began clamoring for treason prosecutions of the leading insurgents. When the war finally started after years of simmering hostilities, "colonial resistance ripened into full-fledged, indisputable treason" (Larson 2019, 41). On April 19, 1775, the first shots of the American Revolution were fired in Lexington, Massachusetts. In June 1775, British General Thomas Gage announced that all colonists in arms were "rebels and traitors, and as such to be treated" (Larson 2019, 41). Two months later, King George III announced that many American colonists were in rebellion, "traitorously preparing, ordering, and levying war against us" and that loyal British subjects should "bring the traitors to justice" and to help thwart all "treasons and traitorous conspiracies" (Larson 2019, 41). After the Declaration of Independence, it was reported that Great Britain intended to prosecute the leaders of the American Revolution for high treason (Larson 2019, 310 n164). English treason law was governed by the English Treason Statute of 1351, which among other things, considered it a treasonous act to engage in "levying war against the king" or "adhering to the king's enemies" and "giving them aid and comfort." Signers of the Declaration of Independence knew they were committing an act of treason, reputedly prompting Benjamin Franklin to remark "we must all hang together, or assuredly, we will all hang separately." And while Great Britain did not capture and execute any of the fifty-six signers of the Declaration for treason, five of the fifty-six were captured and suffered torture and death at the hands of British authorities. Another twelve had their houses and properties ransacked and destroyed by the British Army and nine fought and died during the Revolutionary War.

While the Declaration of Independence was clearly important in announcing the colonies' severance from Great Britain and the intent to form a new nation, the document also had legal consequences relating to colonists and their new obligations and allegiances to the nascent conglomeration of American states. Per treason expert Carlton F. W. Larson,

> so long as the American colonies remained technically united with Great Britain, the adherents of the king ... could not formally be tried by a jury in a court of law or executed [for treason] ... [t]he Declaration of Independence permitted the full force of the criminal law to be brought upon the Loyalists, and many proponents of the Declaration justified it for precisely that reason. (Larson 2019, 4)

In the ensuing years of the war, multiple colonists were tried and convicted of treason. Some were convicted by so-called committees on safety and some by state-convened juries. Additionally, the military "regularly exercised jurisdiction over its own members for traitorous acts" and many individuals were executed by military authorities (Larson 2019, 299 n205); the exact number remains unclear.

Some of the colonies adopted expansive definitions of treason. For instance, the Pennsylvania Assembly passed a statute defining conduct constituting treason for engaging in any number of activities, including "receiving a commission from the King of Great Britain or from other enemies of Pennsylvania or of the United States," "levying war against the state," "aiding or assisting enemies at open war with the state by joining their armies, or by persuading others to join their armies," "furnishing enemies with arms, ammunition, or other provisions for their aid and comfort," "carrying on a traitorous correspondence with the enemy," forming a "combination, plot, or conspiracy" against the revolution, and "sending intelligence to the enemy." An individual not wishing to run afoul of colonial laws such as this one had no choice but to leave the colony as soon as possible.

How many individuals were prosecuted and/or convicted for treason by the various colonies/ states during the revolutionary war? While concrete numbers are illusive, scores were prosecuted for treason either by the military, committees on safety, or via state jury trials, and likely at least a dozen or so individuals were executed. The data from several states alone indicate the general volume and frequency of treason cases. Between September 1778 and April 1779 in Philadelphia, twenty-three treason jury trials were held. Of those cases, four of the defendants were convicted, and the jury recommended leniency to the governor in three of the four cases (Larson 2019, 7, 123). Beyond Philadelphia, and throughout the entire State of Pennsylvania (and not counting military trials), between September 1778 and September 1782, eighty-seven cases of potential treason were submitted to a grand jury, and at least forty-five individuals were prosecuted for treason. Of those forty-five cases, seven defendants were convicted, four pardoned, and three executed (Larson 2019, 217).

Other colonies prosecuted treason with equal zeal as Pennsylvania, and the overall number of executions remained consistent as between the states. Thus, for instance, in Fall 1778, thirty-five men were prosecuted and convicted of treason in New Jersey, but most were pardoned after conviction and only two were executed (Larson 2019, 218). In Delaware, eight men were convicted of treason in 1780 alone, but all were pardoned. In Frederick, Maryland, in July 1781, seven men were convicted of treason and sentenced to death, by only three of the seven were executed (Larson 2019, 219). In Virginia in 1782, ten men were convicted of treason, but all were pardoned (Larson 2019, 219). Thus, while treason prosecutions in the colonies were not infrequent, the number of executions remained low across the several colonies. Admittedly, colonial judicial records are sparse, and some cases may not have been accurately recorded. Additionally, the military handled its own prosecutions for treason, and the total number of those prosecutions and executions remains unclear, as record-keeping for these cases was poor or nonexistent. Upon the finalizing of the Treaty of Paris on September 3, 1783, which brought about a formal end to the Revolution, all American-prosecuted treason cases ceased. One of the terms of the Treaty of Paris was that all treason prosecutions of loyalists should be terminated, and no further property confiscations should take place (Larson 2019, 224).

Despite the early blustering and threatening of treason by Great Britain against the American colonists, there were little to no recorded cases of colonists being prosecuted and/or executed for the specific offense of treason by Great Britain, although tens of thousands of Americans were guilty of the offense. The lack of British prosecutions is best understood by the maxim that the victors of a conflict are not guilty of treason. As English writer Sir John Harrington once penned in 1591: "Treason doth never prosper: what's the reason? Why, if it prospers, none dare call it treason" (Bartlett 1919, 39). Conversely, the American colonists utilized the criminal offense of treason often. Yet, despite the more frequent usage of the treason charge by the Americans, the American Revolution is notable in that it did not disintegrate into violent and terroristic purges as took place in the French Revolution a few short years later. As scholar Bradley Chapin observed, "there was no reign of terror. The record is one of substantial justice done" (Larson 2019, 251).

See Also: Aid and Comfort (Aid to Enemies of the State); American Civil War and Treason; Conspiracy, Criminal; English Treason Statute of 1351; Jefferson, Thomas; Levying War; Rebellion; Treason

Resources

Bartlett, John. 1919. *Familiar Quotations: Passages, Phrases and Proverbs Traced to Their Sources*. New York: Blue Ribbon Books, Inc.

Fleming, Thomas. 1997. *Liberty: The American Revolution*. New York: Viking.

Larson, Carlton F. W. 2019. *The Trials of Allegiance: Treason, Juries, and the American Revolution*. Oxford: Oxford University Press.

York, Neil L. 2011. "Imperial Impotence: Treason in 1774 Massachusetts." *Law and History Review* 29: 657–701.

Ames, Aldrich Hazen "Rich" (1941–)

Aldrich Ames was a former officer/agent of the United States Central Intelligence Agency (CIA) who was convicted of espionage and sentenced to life imprisonment without the possibility of parole. Ames was responsible for illegally disclosing more classified government operations and the identities of more CIA operatives than any other American in history, only surpassed by the subsequent intelligence breaches of Federal Bureau of Investigation (FBI) Agent Robert Hanssen. Ames disclosed to the Soviet Union an estimated one hundred classified CIA operations and disclosed the identities of at least ten CIA operatives in the Soviet Union who were executed after being betrayed by Ames. At his sentencing hearing in federal court in 1994, Ames estimated that he had compromised "virtually all Soviet agents of the CIA and other American and foreign services" and acknowledged providing a "huge quantity" of intelligence information of the United States. Along with Hanssen, many consider Ames to be one of the most harmful and detrimental spies in the history of the United States.

Ames completed the basic CIA training program in 1968 and became a CIA officer. In many of his assignments between 1969 and 1994, Ames was tasked with trying to turn Soviet intelligence officers and/or convince these officers to provide sensitive Soviet intelligence information to the United States. A vast majority of Ames's career and expertise was in Soviet intelligence gathering and operations. The comprehensive 141-page Senate Select Committee on Intelligence Report on Ames, which chronicles Ames's career and acts of espionage, reveals an employee who received multiple mediocre performance evaluations and verbal reprimands, had problems with over imbibing alcohol, and engaged in multiple extra-marital affairs. The highest rank obtained by Ames was GS-14 (General Services Employee, Level 14), making between $60,000 and $70,000 at the time of his arrest.

Foreshadowing his disregard of the importance of classified security materials, in 1976 Ames left a briefcase containing extremely sensitive operational intelligence materials on a New York City subway car. The briefcase was fortunately retrieved by a Polish émigré and turned in to the FBI several hours after Ames left the briefcase unattended. For this early breach, Ames received only a verbal reprimand. In May 1982, Ames received his highest government rank as a GS-14 employee. He was assigned to the CIA SE Division in Washington, DC, in September 1983. In this position, Ames had access to the most sensitive and highly classified documents of all CIA operations against both the KGB (the chief arm of intelligence activities for the Soviet Union) and the GRU (the Soviet agency responsible for military intelligence).

Ames began illegally providing intelligence materials to the Soviet Union in April 1985. The Soviet Union paid Ames $50,000 for this first act of espionage. Ames later stated that he "crossed a line" and "could never step back." Because of Ames's position in the Washington, DC, office, he could visit and meet openly at the Soviet Embassy in Washington, without drawing the scrutiny of the CIA or FBI. Ames would often have lunch with his contact at the Soviet Embassy and would receive $20,000–$50,000 each time. By the time of Ames's arrest, it was estimated that Ames had received $4.6 million from the Soviet Union in compensation for his espionage.

Because numerous CIA operations were being compromised and multiple CIA human assets inside the Soviet Union had disappeared at a suspiciously rapid pace, the CIA leadership believed there was a "mole" (i.e., a double agent/spy) within the agency. After several unsuccessful investigative efforts, the CIA eventually focused on Ames. With the massive influx of cash, Ames began living ostentatiously and well beyond the means of a typical GS-14 employee. For instance, Ames bought a house in Arlington, Virginia, for $540,000 and paid in cash. Ames also bought an expensive automobile (a Jaguar) and began wearing more expensive apparel. By March 1993, the CIA investigation had identified Ames as the "mole" and Ames was subject to round-the-clock physical and electronic surveillance. In early 1994, Ames was scheduled to attend a meeting in Moscow. As the CIA feared that Ames might use this opportunity to flee the United States, Ames was arrested on February 21, 1994.

Both Ames and his wife, Maria del Rosario Casas Dupuy, were indicted on February 22, 1994, on multiple violations of federal law, including espionage, conspiracy to commit espionage, and tax evasion. On April 28, 1994, Ames pled guilty to espionage and agreed to a life sentence without the possibility of parole. As part of a plea bargain agreement, Ames's wife pled guilty to tax evasion and conspiring to commit espionage and received a five-year sentence. Since Ames's conviction, he has been incarcerated at the Federal Correctional Complex at Terre Haute, Indiana, the same facility where Timothy McVeigh was held until McVeigh's execution in 2001.

See Also: Conspiracy, Criminal; Espionage; Hanssen, Robert

Resources

An Assessment of the Aldrich H. Ames Espionage Case and Its Implications for U.S. Intelligence: Report Prepared by the Staff of the Select Committee on Intelligence, United States Senate [84–046]. 1994. Washington, DC: U.S. Government Printing Office. Accessed June 14, 2022. https://www.intelligence.senate.gov/sites/default/files/publications/10390.pdf.

Earley, Pete. 1997. *Confessions of a Spy: The Real Story of Aldrich Ames*. New York: G.P. Putnam's Sons.

Anarchy, Criminal

The term "anarchy" comes from the ancient Greek word *anarkhia*, which means "without a ruler." "Anarchism" is a term to describe an ideology that prefers anarchy. Discussions of the notion of anarchy are as old as the ancient recorded civilizations, with both ancient Chinese and Greek philosophers having explored the idea of anarchy and the tension between government and individual liberty. As a political philosophy, anarchy is somewhat more modern, tracing its origin to the nineteenth century.

Though outside the United States the term "anarchism" is closely related to, and sometimes used interchangeably with, "libertarianism," in the United States' legal and political traditions, the term has most often been used to refer to the anti-authoritarian ideology of left-leaning libertarians. It is in this context that statutes criminalizing anarchy in the United States arose. In the United States, anarchism as a political movement began with the Industrial Revolution and responding to new organizations of workers who rejected capitalism and hierarchical government structure, instead calling for a more socialist—perhaps even communist—social structure. Some of the leaders of socialist and communist movements called for revolution and toppling of existing regimes. In 1883, Johann Most, who established the International Working People's Association (IWPA), called for "[d]estruction of the existing class rule by all means, i.e., by energetic, relentless, revolutionary and international action" (Fine 1955, 779).

In 1886, eight anarchists, all of whom were members of the IWPA, were convicted of attacking a group of police officers in Haymarket Square, Chicago, with a bomb, killing seven and wounding nearly seventy others. Though many individual anarchists eschewed violence as a method for obtaining non-hierarchical cooperation in society, the so-called Haymarket Riot immediately equated anarchism with violence in the minds of Americans. In 1892, another anarchist shot and stabbed well-known industrialist Henry Clay Frick in a failed attempt to call attention to the wrongs of capitalism and the plight of workers. And in 1901, an anarchist assassinated President William McKinley.

Instances of anarchist violence led to the first iterations of speech as crime against the state, in the form of criminal prohibitions on speech advocating the overthrow of the government. New York passed its Criminal Anarchy Statute of 1902 just months after the McKinley assassination. The Supreme Court would uphold this statute as constitutional in *Gitlow v. New York* (1925).

Notably, criminal anarchy statutes in the United States have typically outlawed advocating or conspiring to overthrow the government by force or violence, without specifying the impermissible ideological motivation behind the overthrowal or the desired end state. Thus, though labeled criminal anarchy statutes, under many such statutes, a perpetrator need not be an actual anarchist, seeking abolition of all government. Rather, one can violate many criminal anarchy statutes regardless of the intent post-overthrow. For instance, advocating for an insurrection which simply aims to overthrow the government to replace it with a similar government composed of different persons would run afoul of some criminal anarchy statutes, though true anarchy is not the goal. In fact, the New York criminal anarchy statute was insignificant as an anti-anarchy measure, resulting in apparently no convictions of anarchists. Indeed, in *Gitlow*, the defendant convicted of violating New York's criminal anarchy statute was an extreme socialist advocating not for the total abolition of government, but rather for a "revolutionary dictatorship of the proletariat," under which a system of communist socialism would replace democratic capitalism. In reviewing the case, noted Justices of the New York Court of Appeals Cuthbert Pound and Benjamin Cardozo observed that advocating a dictatorship of the proletariat was not advocating anarchy. But because the terms of the statute were not specific to anarchy, the New York Court of Appeals and ultimately the United States Supreme Court upheld Gitlow's conviction.

Some criminal anarchy statutes are more specific. For instance, Florida's criminal anarchy statute states that "'Criminal anarchy,' 'criminal Communism,' 'criminal Nazism,' or 'criminal Fascism' are doctrines that existing form of constitutional government should be overthrown by force or violence or by any other unlawful means, or by assassination of officials of the Government of the United States or of the several states." Though this description is arguably inaccurate and unhelpfully groups widely varying political ideologies together, it demonstrates the purpose of the criminal anarchy statute: to outlaw overthrowing the government with the intent to accomplish one of these alternative forms of government. Moreover, the Florida statute demonstrates the broader theme that laws like criminal anarchy statutes that prohibit advocating for certain political ideologies or government systems have often been passed or amended to address the perceived threat of the day. For instance, anarchy was the primary concern at the turn of the twentieth century, replaced in subsequent years by the worry over communism that arose with the Bolshevik Revolution, then an apprehension of fascism and Nazism in the 1930s and 1940s, and again a primary fear of communism during the early Cold War in the era of McCarthyism.

Though the Supreme Court had upheld a criminal anarchy statute against a First Amendment challenge in *Gitlow*, the Court's later decision in *Brandenburg v. Ohio* (1969) established a higher burden for criminalizing political speech. Under *Brandenburg*, criminal anarchy statutes, and similar statutes that ban advocacy for alternative forms of government, are effectively unconstitutional except to the extent that they prohibit advocating for *imminent lawless action*. Nevertheless, several states' criminal anarchy statutes remain in their state codes and even federal law still criminalizes advocacy of anarchy (18 United States Code § 2385). Like related state statutes addressing criminal syndicalism and sedition, the enforceability of state criminal anarchy laws is subject to the restrictions of federal preemption imposed by the United States Supreme Court in *Pennsylvania v. Nelson* (1956).

See Also: *Brandenburg v. Ohio* (1969); Criminal Syndicalism; *Gitlow v. New York* (1925); Haymarket Affair (1886); Insurrection; McKinley Assassination (1901); *Pennsylvania v. Nelson* (1956); Second Red Scare (McCarthyism); Sedition; Speech as Crime against the State

Resources

Fine, Sidney. 1955. "Anarchism and the Assassination of McKinley." *American Historical Review* 60 (July): 777–99.

Vile, John. 2009. "Anarchy Statutes." *The First Amendment Encyclopedia.* Accessed June 29, 2023. https://mtsu.edu/first-amendment/article/1168/anarchy-statutes.

Anthrax Attacks (2001)

In the aftermath of the terrorist attack on September 11, 2001, the United States was almost immediately faced with the specter of a second terrorist attack, but this time involving biological and chemical weapons and not a group utilizing airplanes as missiles. After several decades, it is hard to describe the fear and paranoia that were sweeping through every home throughout the United States in the early autumn of 2001. As individuals were still processing the worst terrorist attack on United States soil in its history, about two weeks after September 11, 2001, the American public began hearing through the media that packages containing highly weaponized grade chemical named *Bacillus anthracis* (commonly known as "anthrax") had been sent through the mail via the United States Postal Service, presumably to terrorize and kill citizens. The first five letters containing anthrax were sent to random news outlets, were all dated September 11, 2001, and contained similar language in the enclosed letter, such as "Death to America." The national paranoia and fear were amplified when it was reported that some of the 9/11 hijackers had attempted to rent crop-dusting planes to distribute biological weapons over United States population centers, causing some to believe that the anthrax mailings might be a second wave of attacks.

In the end, seven letters were sent, killing five individuals and seriously injuring eighteen others. The attack caused the closure of two of three federal branches of government for a period (i.e., the United States Congress and the Supreme Court) and postal operations around the country were adversely impacted. More than 33,000 individuals required post-exposure medical care. Finally, the cleanup costs for those buildings and locations impacted by the handling and processing of these letters were estimated at $30 million. The last letter was sent in October 2001, and the FBI finally closed its investigation in February 2010. It is believed that this attack in September–October 2001 was the first instance of a biological terrorism attack in United States history occurring on its own soil.

The first known fatality from this attack was a 63-year-old worker at American Media Inc., the parent company of the National Enquirer in Boca Raton, Florida. Bob Stevens died on October 4, 2001 (approximately three weeks after 9/11). Investigators found traces of anthrax on his computer keyboard, although it later became clear that his exposure came from a contaminated letter that was delivered to his office, and it was presumed that Stevens was likely to have opened the letter at his desk. While the specific letter to Stevens was never found, investigators later determined that at least five anthrax-laced letters, including one received by Stevens, all had the same postmark of Trenton, New Jersey, dated September 18, 2001. Contaminated letters were sent to ABC News, NBC News, CBS News, the *New York Post*, and the *National Enquirer*.

On October 12, 2001, eight days since the first anthrax exposure and one month after 9/11, a contaminated letter addressed to news anchor Tom Brokaw was opened by a staff member. Thankfully, thinking something was awry with the letter, the staff member immediately dropped the letter into the garbage and sought medical treatment and survived because of her quick thinking. Even with the quick medical treatment and not touching or inhaling the contents of the envelope, this person still developed cutaneous anthrax. Inside the envelope, there was a crude note in capital letters with one sentence per line which read as follows: "09-11-01. THIS IS NEXT. TAKE PENACILIN [*sic*] NOW. DEATH TO AMERICA. DEATH TO ISRAEL. ALLAH IS GREAT." Individuals at both CBS News and ABC News received and handled similar letters and were also exposed to anthrax.

Two additional anthrax letters showing the same Trenton, New Jersey, postmark, dated October 9, 2001, were addressed to United States Senator Tom Daschle and Senator Patrick Leahy. Eleven days after the first exposure and death, Senator Daschle announced that his office had received an anthrax-contaminated letter with the same crude block print lettering with one sentence per line. The letter said: "09-11-01. YOU CANNOT STOP US. WE HAVE THIS ANTHRAX. YOU DIE NOW.

ARE YOU AFRAID? DEATH TO AMERICA." Several victims who died from anthrax exposure were thought to have received mail that just happened to pass adjacent to the contaminated letters as the letters were being processed through the mail sorting system. That is, several of the victims were exposed by microscopic trace amounts of anthrax that happened through a cross-contamination as letters were being sorted in mail facilities. For instance, 61-year-old Kathy Nguyen died from being exposed to cross-contaminated mail that circulated through the mailroom she worked at in Bronx, New York. Further proving the deadly consequences of cross-contamination of mail was the death of 94-year-old Ottilie Lundgren, from Oxford, Connecticut. As she rarely left her house, experts believe mail sent to Ms. Lundgren must have come into contact with the anthrax-laced letters at a central mail processing facility. In total, five individuals died from the anthrax-spiked letters, including Mr. Thomas Morris and Mr. Joseph Curseen, two workers who were employed at the Brentwood Postal Office in Washington, DC. In addition to the five fatalities, at least seventeen others were seriously injured.

Though initially many believed the letters were from a foreign source associated with Al-Qaeda, top American scientists were quickly able to determine that the Anthrax strain contained in the contaminated letters was something called the "Ames Strain" (named after Ames, Iowa, where it was first identified in a laboratory years earlier). Furthermore, this particular strain of Anthrax—even as of 2023—can only be found in a handful of tightly controlled US governmental laboratories. In fact, American intelligence quickly determined that it was highly probable that the letters and anthrax originated from a disgruntled or emotionally unstable scientist at one of these facilities.

As technologies continued to improve between 2001 and 2007, new testing and tracing techniques were developed that led federal law enforcement to the United States Army Medical Research Institute of Infectious Disease at Fort Detrick, Maryland. More specifically, investigators traced some of the mailed anthrax spores to a single flask called RMR 1029 which belonged to Dr. Bruce Edwards Ivins that Ivins used in his laboratory. Upon allegedly learning that criminal charges against him would be filed shortly, Dr. Ivins committed suicide on July 29, 2008. On February 19, 2010, the FBI released a 92-page report summarizing the evidence against Ivins and announced that the criminal investigation has been officially closed.

To this day, there are minority viewpoints that Ivins was not working alone, or that he was sponsored by a foreign adversary, or that he was not even involved. Yet, no credible evidence has emerged in the last two decades to prove any of these theories. Most importantly, the 2001 Anthrax attack stands as a precautionary reminder of the vulnerabilities of America's infrastructure and the need to be vigilant in safeguarding against potential exploitation of those vulnerabilities by adversaries of the United States, be those infrastructures the domestic power grid, mail system, railroad networks, large sporting venues and events, or a host of other "soft targets."

See Also: September 11, 2001; Terrorism; Weapons of Mass Destruction

Resources

Committee on Review of the Scientific Approaches Used during the FBI's Investigation of the 2001 Bacillus Anthracis Mailings; National Research Council. 2011. *Review of the Scientific Approaches Used during the FBI's Investigation of the 2001 Anthrax Letters*. Washington, DC: The National Academies Press.

Federal Bureau of Investigation, Department of Justice. 2010. "Amerithrax Investigative Summary." Accessed April 11, 2023. https://www.justice.gov/archive/amerithrax/docs/amx-investigative-summary.pdf.

Heyman, David. 2002. *Lessons from the Anthrax Attacks: Implications for U.S. Bio-Terrorism Preparedness: A Report on a National Forum on Bio-Defense*. Center for Strategic and International Studies and the Defense Threat Reduction Agency. Accessed March 23, 2023. https://biotech.law.lsu.edu/blaw/anthrax/dtra02.pdf.

Anti-Terrorism and Effective Death Penalty Act (1996)

From the dawn of the founding of the United States until the present, the United States has repeatedly reacted to internal and external threats and attacks to its national security with new laws and legislation designed to prevent those acts or threats from occurring or repeating. Indeed, the passage of America's earliest anti-terrorism and homeland security legislation, the Alien and Sedition Acts, was heavily influenced by the threats raised by the specter of war with France in 1798 and massive discord at home involving that potential conflict. Congress passed the USA PATRIOT Act within forty-five days after the horrific tragedy of September 11, 2001. These are just two examples (of many) of Congress legislating to defend the homeland after a threat has developed or been realized. Similarly, the Anti-Terrorism and Effective Death Penalty Act of 1996 (AEDPA) was in response to two major terrorist attacks upon the United States in the 1990s, namely the World Trade Center Bombing in 1993 and the 1995 attack on the Alfred P. Murrah Building in Oklahoma City (Oklahoma City Bombing). Indeed, on the eve of the one-year anniversary of the attack on the Alfred P. Murrah Building in Oklahoma City, on April 18, 1996, Congress presented the AEDPA for President Bill Clinton's signature. Only five days after the one-year anniversary of the calamity at Oklahoma City, President Clinton signed the AEDPA into law on April 24, 1996. At the signing, President Clinton remarked that the AEDPA "stands as a tribute to the victims of terrorism and to … law enforcement who dedicate their lives to protecting all of us from the scourge of terrorist activities" (Beckman 2002, 31).

While the major momentum in the final passage of the AEDPA was in response to the Oklahoma City bombing in April 1995, President Clinton had presented to Congress proposed anti-terrorism legislation several months before the 1995 attack in Oklahoma City, and this earlier legislation was in response to the 1993 bombing of the World Trade Center in New York City. Seven days after the Oklahoma City bombing, the president re-introduced (on April 26, 1995) a much more ambitious and expanded version of the antiterrorism legislation than that previously submitted and urged immediate passage. The resulting legislation spanned an impressive array of assorted topics—ranging from criminalizing material support provided to terrorist organizations, providing more robust powers to deport individuals deemed dangerous to the national security of the United States, and supplying more tools for law enforcement in dealing with cases of potential terrorism. Like the USA PATRIOT Act passed a few years later, the AEDPA was a massive federal statute, ran over one hundred pages in length, comprised nine separate titles, contained a broad array of individual topics, and revised many existing provisions already located at various locations within the United States Code. While all its various provisions cannot be covered in this entry, the major provisions of the AEDPA will be summarized here.

Importantly for international relations between the United States and other countries, the AEDPA prohibited diverse types of support to countries that sponsored or harbored terrorists. In the "findings" and "preamble" section of the AEDPA, Congress specified that "the President should use all necessary means, including covert action and military force, to disrupt, dismantle, and destroy international infrastructure used by international terrorists, including overseas terrorists training facilities and safe havens." This language was cited as legal justification for the United States to preemptively attack Al-Qaeda training camps in 1998. In referring to the AEDPA, President Clinton's National Security Advisor Sandy Berger stated that such preemptive action was "appropriate" because "under a 1996 statute in Congress, [it was appropriate] for us to try to disrupt and destroy those kinds of military terrorist targets" (White House 1998).

The AEDPA criminalized several activities previously uncovered by federal law. The AEDPA made it a federal crime (subject to ten years imprisonment) to make political donations to a group designated as a terrorist organization by the US Secretary of State. Under this provision, there is no requirement that the person making the donation intended or knew that the donation would be utilized for illegal or non-peaceful purposes by the group. The new law also did not require any knowledge of the terrorist group's specific plans nor whether the supporter had any knowledge of these plans. Phrased differently, the statute criminalized providing financial support and/or donations to a designated terrorist group regardless of the donor's actual intentions as to how the money might be used. The AEDPA also criminalized the use of chemical weapons in the United States and against US citizens abroad and enhanced punishments for crimes relating to the use of chemical weapons and the use of explosive devices.

The AEDPA attempted to frustrate the operation of terrorist organizations, including through provisions that would be expanded further with the passage of the USA PATRIOT Act in 2001. The AEDPA did this in several important ways. It allowed the federal government to deport an individual based solely on his or her membership in a designated terrorist organization, even if there was no evidence that the individual ever actively acted in furtherance of the organization's goals. As discussed, Congress also made it a federal crime to make financial contributions to these terrorism-designated groups. Furthermore, under this provision, the Attorney General was empowered to seek immediate removal of individuals under the AEDPA if removal under the usual sections of federal immigration law "would pose a risk to the national security of the United States." In these deportation proceedings, the AEDPA allowed the government to introduce classified evidence supporting the deportation directly to the court without having to disclose this information to the defendant. The evidence would be examined in private ("in camera") by the court and without the ability of the resident alien (the person subject to deportation) or his or her lawyer to review or challenge the information. In fact, the AEDPA authorized the court to consider otherwise illegally obtained information and, according to the exact language of the AEDPA, "an alien subject to removal under this title shall not be entitled to suppress evidence that the alien alleges was unlawfully obtained." The AEDPA even expanded the grounds of deportation based on crimes of moral turpitude.

The AEDPA, like the USA PATRIOT Act several years later, attempted to provide federal law enforcement new powers to combat or investigate threats of terrorism and/or do so more effectively. Key provisions in the AEDPA relating to the expanded powers of law enforcement included the following: the requirement that federal agents could gain easier access to immigration files for purposes of criminal investigations; increased authority to arrest and detain illegal aliens; that plastic explosives must include chemical marking components to aid federal enforcement to track its origin (both the "point of production" and "point of sale" of the explosives); and additional funding for law enforcement to study various anti-terrorism techniques and strategies. Some provisions dropped from the AEDPA before final passage, such as enhanced wiretapping techniques for phones used by suspected terrorists and increased governmental access to consumer credit and other records of suspected terrorist suspects, would eventually be reintroduced and become federal law with the passage of the USA PATRIOT Act in 2001.

Controversially, the AEDPA also revised and narrowed federal habeas corpus rules (involving the right to challenge the lawfulness of one's detention) and specified a one-year limitation on submitting such petitions. The AEDPA also restricted the use of federal habeas corpus processes for state judicial decisions and limited the ability of a petitioner to submit successive habeas corpus provisions unless the petitioner could show the repetitive petition was based on newly discovered evidence or new Supreme Court precedent developed after the previous habeas corpus petition. Some critics claimed that the limitation of federal habeas corpus procedures in the AEDPA had little to no connection to deterring and preventing terrorist attacks.

Finally, the AEDPA contained several victims' rights-related provisions. For instance, the AEDPA required that perpetrators of terrorist acts be responsible for victim restitution and compensation and required the creation of a crime victim compensation fund. The AEDPA also allowed for the utilization of closed-circuit television for victim participation in trials when the trial and venue occur out of state from that of the victim or farther than 350 miles from the victim's residence.

Unfortunately, legislation is almost always reactive instead of proactive, meaning that new laws are instituted after new threats materialize and new means of accomplishing those acts of terrorism are discovered by law enforcement and communicated to lawmakers. No matter how broad the statute, it is next to impossible for lawmakers to legislate for every permutation of a given problem. As one person wrote shortly before 9/11 in describing the AEDPA, "while the AEDPA is the latest in the long list of legislation in the United States dealing with terrorism, it will doubtfully be the last" (Beckman 2002, 32). Five and a half years after the enactment of the AEDPA, 9/11 occurred, and the horrific events of that day ushered in a new array of legislation like the USA PATRIOT Act of 2001 and the Homeland Security reorganization legislation of 2002, with a bevy of new powers and provisions to deter and combat terrorism. And just like the AEDPA in 1996, more recent legislation in this area will most certainly (and unfortunately) not be the last.

See Also: Alien and Sedition Acts (1798); Homeland Security Act (2002); Material Support Crimes; Oklahoma City Bombing (1995); September 11, 2001; Terrorism; USA PATRIOT Act; World Trade Center Bombing of 1993

Resources

Antiterrorism and Effective Death Penalty Act of 1996. 110 Stat. 1214. Public Law 104–132-Apr. 24, 1996. Accessed June 9, 2022. https://www.govinfo.gov/content/pkg/STATUTE-110/pdf/STATUTE-110-Pg1214.pdf.

Beall, Jennifer A. 1998. "Are We Only Burning Witches? The Antiterrorism and Effective Death Penalty Act of 1996's Answer to Terrorism." *Indiana Law Journal* 73: 693–710.

Beckman, James. 2002. "Antiterrorist Legislation." In *Guns in American Society: An Encyclopedia of History, Politics, Culture, and the Law*, edited by Gregg Carter, vol. 1, 28–32. Santa Barbara, CA: ABC-CLIO.

Smith, Roberta. 1997. "Note: America Tries to Come to Terms with Terrorism: The United States Anti-Terrorism and Effective Death Penalty Act of 1996 v. British Anti-Terrorism Law and International Response." *Cardozo Journal of International and Comparative Law* 5 (Spring): 249–90.

The White House. 1998. Press Briefing by Madeleine Albright and Sandy Berger. M2 Presswire, August 21, 1998. Accessed October 31, 2023. https://link.gale.com/apps/doc/A53003351/GBIB?u=orla57816&sid=bookmark-GBIB&xid=653c56f9.

Arnold, Benedict (1741–1801)

For generations, labeling an individual as a "Benedict Arnold" has meant to brand someone who was a traitor or treasonous in his or her conduct or action. The name Benedict Arnold has resonated through the centuries in the United States as a pejorative term connoting betrayal. The actual Benedict Arnold, who rose to the rank of major general in the American Continental Army before defecting to the British, has been labeled as America's "founding traitor" and "remains the quintessential American traitor, his name synonymous with treason itself" (Larson 2020, Chapter 2). As one of America's leading revolutionary war generals turned turncoat for the British, Benedict Arnold's treachery and betrayal shocked the leadership of the Revolutionary War generation in America. After his defection, Benedict Arnold was commissioned as a British brigadier general and fought against his former American soldiers in Connecticut, Virginia, and elsewhere, but was never given a major command by the British.

Arnold was born in Norwich, Connecticut, and spent his early years before the American Revolution as a businessperson with a penchant for drink. Arnold established an apothecary shop in New Haven, Connecticut, and was involved in maritime commercial transactions. While Arnold served briefly in the French and Indian War (thirteen days), Arnold's military reputation skyrocketed at the onset of the American Revolution. First as the head of a militia company from Connecticut, Arnold participated with his company in the capture of Fort Ticonderoga from the British, although the fame and glory of this early American victory went to military leaders like Ethan Allen and Henry Knox. Arnold then emerged as a brilliant military leader in his own right in the unsuccessful attempt to annex Canada and take the British occupied city of Quebec on December 30, 1775. Though unsuccessful, the military movements leading up to the attack on Quebec involved leading approximately one thousand men on a long, harrowing march through miles of largely impassible terrain during repeated incidents of torrential rainstorms and flooding. Arnold was injured during the attempted seizure of Quebec and was forced to retire from the field. During the subsequent year, Arnold was involved in multiple minor actions and rose to the rank of major general and was one of George Washington's most trusted subordinate officers. On October 7, 1777, as part of the second Battle of Saratoga (the Battle of Bemis Heights), Arnold was able to deflect and push back the British Army led by General John Burgoyne and was largely responsible for the American victory in that battle. Arnold was again grievously wounded, with his left leg almost amputated, and was given the command of Philadelphia in June 1778 after British forces had evacuated that city.

While in Philadelphia, Benedict Arnold wooed and wed Tory loyalist-leaning nineteen-year-old Peggy Shippen as his second wife. Shippen came from an aristocratic family and Arnold struggled to provide a lifestyle to which Peggy Shippen was accustomed (an opulent lifestyle demanded by Shippen's father as a condition of the marriage). Arnold frequently argued with other officers and merchants and made numerous political enemies. Arnold's high style of living and his bellicose personality contributed to the eventual charges of corruption levied against him by his opponents, and he was court-martialed in June 1779. During this period, fueled undoubtedly by his new loyalist-leaning wife, Arnold became increasingly disenchanted, writing George Washington in May 1779, saying in part that "having made every sacrifice of fortune and blood, and become a cripple in the service of my country, I little expected to meet the ungrateful returns I have received of my countrymen, but as Congress have stamped ingratitude as a current coin I must take it" (Philbrick 2016). Arnold's bitterness and resentfulness grew by the day, and he began to correspond with British Major John Andre, a social acquaintance of Peggy Shippen, with whom Arnold would subsequently conspire. The same month Arnold penned his letter to Washington, Arnold first secretly extended an offer of his services to the British.

While acquitted of all the court-martial charges but two minor infractions, Arnold nevertheless received a reprimand from General George Washington who declared Arnold's behavior in Philadelphia to be "imprudent" and "improper." However, having not lost faith with Arnold as a fighting soldier, Washington placed Arnold in charge of the important military garrison at West Point, New York, in 1780. The West Point garrison was considered the heart of George Washington's Hudson Highland defense system and considered vital to the American war strategy. The West Point garrison sat at a bend on the Hudson River approximately fifty miles upriver from New York City. Taking West Point would allow the British control of the Hudson River, cut American supply lines, and drive a wedge between the New England colonies and the rest of the fledgling country. Benedict Arnold secretly plotted with John Andre to sell the West Point defensive position to the British. In August 1780, British General Henry Clinton agreed to pay Arnold twenty-thousand pounds if Arnold's treason led to the capture of the garrison and its troops by the British.

The plot was uncovered when John Andre was stopped by militiamen on September 23, 1780, near Tarrytown, New York. The American militiamen found the incriminating plans hidden in one of John Andre's boots. Arnold immediately fled to British lines and John Andre was hung as a spy. Peggy Shippen, described as "probably the most significant female traitor in American history" (Larson 2020, Chapter 2), rejoined her husband behind British lines. Arnold joined the British Army for the remainder of the American Revolution and participated in military campaigns against his former countrymen, including in his home state of Connecticut and in Virginia. While in Virginia, Arnold's forces nearly captured Thomas Jefferson. Arnold eventually took up residence in London. After the war, Arnold briefly came back to North America (New Brunswick, Canada) from 1785–91 to run a business, but failing at the business, he returned to London until his death in 1801. Arnold was never fully accepted into British society and vilified by his former colleagues and compatriots in America. Arnold died a bitter and unhappy man in Britain on June 14, 1801, at the age of sixty.

See Also: American Revolution and Treason; Conspiracy, Criminal; Jefferson, Thomas; Treason

Resources

Brandt, Clare. 1994. *The Man in the Mirror: A Life of Benedict Arnold*. New York: Random House.

Flexner, James Thomas. 1953. *The Traitor and the Spy: Benedict Arnold and John Andre*. New York: Harcourt Brace.

Larson, Carlton F. W. 2020. *On Treason: A Citizen's Guide to the Law*. New York: Ecco, an imprint of HarperCollins (Kindle Edition).

Philbrick, Nathaniel. 2016. "Why Benedict Arnold Turned Traitor against the American Revolution." *Smithsonian Magazine*, May 2016. Accessed May 21, 2022. https://www.smithsonianmag.com/history/benedict-arnold-turned-traitor-american-revolution-180958786/.

Assassination

Assassination is one of the oldest crimes against the state. The crime entails a perpetrator's attempt to damage a political state or change the course of a government regime's actions by decapitation—removing a political leader (head of government) through homicide. History is replete with examples of assassinations and assassination attempts. For example, the Old Testament of the Bible in 2 Kings 12: 19-21 recounts the assassination of the King of Judah (King Joash) in 796 BCE. Some other well-known examples from antiquity include the assassination of the father of Alexander the Great (Philip II of Macedon) in 336 BCE and the assassination of Roman Emperor Julius Caesar in 44 BCE. The term "assassination" itself first entered the English lexicon around 1600. In an early example of the usage of the term assassination in literature, William Shakespeare utilized the term in his play *Macbeth*, wherein the title character contemplates the murder of King Duncan (in Act 1, Scene 7) to seize power for himself. While Shakespeare helped popularize the term in the English language, some scholars have suggested the term "assassin" has its origins in Arabic from the word "hashshashin," roughly meaning the "eaters of hashish." According to these scholars, there existed a certain Islamic sect "whose members were known for murdering their political opponents after ingesting the drug hashish" (Morgan 2005, 90).

In the United States, the first major assassination was the killing of President Abraham Lincoln in April 1865. A group of dissatisfied ex-Confederates, including actor John Wilkes Booth and Mary Surratt, conspired to kidnap and then kill the president in an attempt to avenge the South, alter the war's ending, and change the federal government's policy of reconstruction of the South following the war. The Lincoln assassination conspiracy involved a plan to decapitate the upper echelon leadership of the federal government, with targets including President Lincoln, Secretary of State William Seward, Vice President Andrew Johnson, and Union General Ulysses S. Grant. Different members of the conspiracy were assigned to kill these individuals. Only Booth was successful in assassination. Secretary of State William Seward was grievously injured by Lewis Powell but survived the attack. The other figures were not attacked as Booth had planned.

In the century following the Lincoln assassination, three other American presidents would die at the hands of assassins, namely James Garfield, William McKinley, and John F. Kennedy. Assassination attempts on other presidents included Theodore Roosevelt, Harry Truman, Gerald Ford, Jimmy Carter, and Ronald Reagan. Other notable political figures such as Attorney General Robert Kennedy and Civil Rights Activist Dr. Martin Luther King were also killed by assassins. Of the presidential assassinations, only those of Lincoln and McKinley were done for clearly discernible political purposes and thus represent true crimes against the state. Other assassinations, or attempted assassinations, were for largely personal reasons apparently unrelated to attacking the state or based on ambiguous or unclear motivations. For example, Lynette "Squeaky" Fromme who was associated with the Manson Family, a cult led by Charles Manson, attempted to assassinate President Ford in 1975. Fromme's motive to kill Ford was not primarily motivated by an attack on the government. Rather, Fromme's actions were driven by her devotion to Manson and the Manson Family's ideologies. She believed that through an act of violence, she would draw attention to Manson and his various cult beliefs. Likewise, John Hinckley Jr.'s attempted assassination of President Ronald Reagan in 1981 was not based on a desire to harm the state. Rather, Hinckley's motivations for the assassination attempt stemmed from a combination of personal, psychological, and delusional factors. Hinckley became obsessed with actress Jodie Foster after watching the movie *Taxi Driver* multiple times and believed that by assassinating Reagan, he would gain Foster's attention and admiration.

Of the various attempted assassinations, the attempt on Harry Truman's life perhaps comes closest to being classified as a crime against the state. As described elsewhere in this book (see Puerto Rican Nationalist Party Revolt), the day following the defeat of the Nationalist Party's uprising in Puerto Rico, two members of the party attempted to assassinate President Harry Truman at Blair House on November 1, 1950. The assassins failed to gain entry to the home, where Truman had been staying while the White House was renovated, and President Truman was not harmed, but one Secret Service member and one attacker were killed. The attack was an attempt to change the policy of the United States in relation to Puerto Rican sovereignty.

In 1965, Congress promulgated the Presidential Assassination Statute, which is codified at 18 United States Code Section 1751. This law makes it a federal offense for any individual to assault, kill, kidnap, or attempt or conspire to do any of these acts as it relates to either the president or vice president of the United States. Violations of Section 1751 can result in life imprisonment or a punishment of death if the president or vice president is killed during the commission of the crime. In 1971, Congress expanded the crime of assassination to cover situations where the targets are members of Congress, the Executive Cabinet, and Supreme Court Justices. The 18 United States Code Section 351(a) makes it a crime to kill "any individual who is a Member of Congress or a Member-of-Congress elect, a member of the executive branch of the Government who is the head … the Director or Principal Director of National Intelligence … or the Director … or Deputy Director of the Central Intelligence Agency, a major Presidential or Vice-Presidential candidate … or a Justice of the United States." The statutory punishment for violations of 18 United States Section 351 is the same as violations of 18 United States Code Section 1751, namely up to life imprisonment or the possibility of the death penalty if the targeted member of government dies in the assassination plot. Finally, since the issuance of Executive Order 12333 in 1981, under Part 2.11, it is also unlawful for "any person employed by or acting on behalf of the United States Government [to] … engage in, or conspire to engage in, assassination."

See Also: Booth, John Wilkes; Conspiracy, Criminal; Lincoln Assassination (1865); McKinley Assassination (1901); Puerto Rican Nationalist Party Revolt; Surratt, Mary E.

Resources

18 U.S. Code Section 351, Congressional, Cabinet, and Supreme Court Assassination, Kidnapping, and Assault; Penalties.

18 U.S. Code Section 1751, Presidential and Presidential Staff Assassination, Kidnapping, and Assault; Penalties.

Heaps, Willard A. 1969. *Assassinations: A Special Kind of Murder*. New York: Meredith Press.

Morgan, Brian I. 2005. "Assassinations." In *Encyclopedia of Genocide and Crimes against Humanity*, edited by Dinah L. Shelton, 90–2. Detroit: Macmillan Reference.

Vlasic, Mark V. 2012. "Assassinations & Targeted Killing—A Historical and Post-Bin Laden Legal Analysis." *Georgetown Journal of International Law* 43: 259–91.

Axis Sally (Mildred Gillars) (1900–88)

Axis Sally was the radio name for Mildred Gillars, an American citizen living in Germany during the Second World War, who committed treason against the United States. In 1948, Gillars was the first women in US history to be convicted of treason. Gillars was convicted for providing "aid and comfort" to enemies of the United States through her anti-American/pro-Nazi broadcasting during the war. While apolitical when she first began broadcasting for Radio Berlin in 1940, Gillars's broadcasts became progressively more antisemitic, and she often attacked President Franklin D. Roosevelt, Great Britain, and individuals of Jewish descent in her broadcasts. Long after her death, Axis Sally has been resurrected and re-popularized by white supremacist and neo-Nazi groups in recent years, often glamorized and glorified in podcasts and internet postings by these groups. She was also the subject of a 2021 dramatized movie entitled *American Traitor: The Trial of Axis Sally*, with her defense counsel played by actor Al Pacino. She was one of the more infamous of the "radio traitors" who spread anti-state propaganda during the Second World War (see Radio Traitors and Anti-State Propaganda during the Second World War).

Mildred Gillars was born in Portland, Maine, and moved to Ohio to attend Ohio Wesleyan University for a couple of years before dropping out of school and moving to New York City in the late 1920s. Unsuccessful in her attempts at theater in New York, Gillars moved in 1931 to Dresden, Germany, to study music. By 1935, Gillars was employed in Berlin, teaching English. In 1940, she was hired by Radio Berlin as a broadcaster and actor, and sometimes went by the name of "Midge at the Mike."

Despite being an American citizen, Gillars chose not to leave Germany when the United States declared war. She had signed an oath of loyalty to Adolf Hitler. Perhaps because of this oath, United States Embassy officials confiscated her passport. Additionally, her fiancé (Paul Karlson), a German citizen, said he would not marry her if she returned to the United States. Whatever the reason, or combination of reasons, Gillars stayed in Berlin and continued to broadcast propaganda for Joseph Goebbels's propaganda machine.

Many of Axis Sally's broadcasts provided brief commentary between big band and jazz music songs. American GIs listened to her broadcasts often just for the lively music. However, intermingled with the music was scripted commentary from Gillars wherein she constantly praised the prowess of the German war machine, declared that fighting against the Germans was useless, and indicated that the German Army was unbeatable. In a sultry sensual voice, Gillars would warn the American Gis that their girlfriends and wives back home were getting lonely and might go astray or leave the soldier for another man during the soldier's absence. Some American servicemembers called her "Axis Sally," while some more caustically called her "the Bitch of Berlin." Gillars's last broadcast took place two days before the German government surrendered in 1945.

Gillars' fiancé died fighting on the Eastern Front and Gillars began a relationship with a married man and fervent adherent to Nazism, Max Otto Koischwitz. Koischwitz had been a professor at Hunter College in the United States until ousted for his radical views on the Nazi ideology and antisemitism. Koischwitz retired to Germany and worked in the German Foreign Affairs Office. Gillars never denounced her citizenship to the United States (like other American ex-patriates living in Germany), and she never became a German citizen. While Koischwitz had promise marriage, he never divorced his wife before his death in 1944. This meant that Gillars was an American citizen fully subject to American treason law.

After the War, Gillars used the assumed name Barbara Mome and worked at a furniture store. Victor Woerheide, the special assistant to the attorney general who was preparing to prosecute Martin James Monti for treason, went to Berlin to find and arrest Gillars. Gillars was arrested and held in several internment camps until she was brought back to the United States in 1948. Gillars was charged with ten counts of treason against the United States (subsequently reduced to eight counts). Two weeks before Gillars's trial, she was scheduled to testify in Martin James Monti's treason case (see *Monti, United States v.*); however, Monti pleaded guilty on the eve of his trial. Gillars' trial would take place only two weeks after Monti's treason conviction, and three months before the treason trial of Tokyo Rose. Of the eight counts of treason submitted to the jury, Gillars was convicted of one count, which dealt with her role in the radio production of a play entitled *Vision of Invasion*. In *Vision of Invasion*, Gillars played a heartbroken Ohio mother who dreamed about her son dying in an American invasion of Germany. The play was designed to play on the emotions of parents and to hopefully convince their sons not to enlist or support the American war effort.

Gillars was sentenced on March 8, 1949, to a prison sentence of ten to thirty years and fined $10,000. Gillars converted to Catholicism while in prison, and she was released in 1961 after serving twelve years of her sentence. She moved to Columbus, Ohio, where she lived until her death in 1988. She kept a low profile and taught at a local convent. Shortly before her death, Gillars showed a neighbor a cup that was supposedly given to her by Heinrich Himmler. Perhaps bearing on Gillars' true loyalties, Gillars described the cup to her neighbor as one of her most cherished possessions.

See Also: Aid and Comfort (Aid to Enemies of the State); *Monti, United States v.* (1949); Radio Traitors and Anti-State Propaganda during the Second World War; Tokyo Rose (Iva Toguri D'Aquino); Treason

Resources

Crofton, Ian. 2009. *Traitors & Turncoats: Twenty Tales of Treason from Benedict Arnold to Ezra Pound.* London: Quercus.

Lucas, Richard. 2001. *Axis Sally: The Voice of Nazi Germany*. Philadelphia: Casemate.

Mansky, Jackie. 2018. "'Axis Sally' Brought Hot Jazz to the Nazi Propaganda Machine." *Smithsonian Magazine*, September 25, 2018.

B

Bacon's Rebellion (1676–7)

Today, Bacon's Rebellion is a largely forgotten event in the history of America. Yet, it might rightly be classified as America's very first significant crime against the state by a mob of Americans acting collectively. A hundred years after the event, American Revolutionary War leaders such as Thomas Jefferson viewed Bacon's Rebellion as one of America's first true revolts against British authorities, a forerunner to the American Revolution, and praised the rebellion (see American Revolution and Treason). In addition to being heralded as a precursor to the American Revolution by revolutionaries two generations removed from the original event, Bacon's Rebellion is considered the first major armed rebellion or insurrection by American colonists against their own government (i.e., against Great Britain and the Virginia colonial government) since its founding in the New World. The level of violence by citizens against their own government was unprecedented at this early stage in the development of colonial America. The insurrectionists who participated in Bacon's Rebellion ransacked, burned, and destroyed the capital city of Jamestown and physically threatened the colonial governor. Hundreds of Native Americans were indiscriminately murdered by the insurrectionists (including women and children). The leader of the rebellion, Nathanial Bacon, is one of the very first people accused of treason in the New World.

Nathanial Bacon was a 29-year-old, well-to-do, Cambridge-educated aristocrat whose father sent him to America in 1674 to escape legal problems in England and to run several plantations in the tidewater region of Virginia. Gifted his father's wealth, he immediately became part of America's burgeoning plantation class and was appointed to the Virginia Governor's council. At this time, planters and farmers were struggling and attempted to augment Virginia's holdings and land to weather the financially challenging times by encroaching on Native American lands to expand their crops. Native Americans naturally resisted and fought to safeguard their ancestral lands. When Virginian landholders requested protection from retaliatory Native American raids and for Governor William Berkeley to finance and support a militia to attack the Native Americans, the Governor refused.

The Governor's refusal enraged a group of Virginia farmers, who decided to take matters into their own hands. The group organized a small army, named Nathanial Bacon as its commander and leader, and began waging war against various Native American groups. Defying Governor Berkeley's orders, Bacon's band of men (numbering approximately 500) proceeded to attack various Native American villages, killing hundreds of innocent people. In just one tragic attack of many, 120 Native Americans were massacred in an event aptly named The Battle of Bloody Run. As scholar Alan Taylor remarked, "Bacon led indiscriminate attacks on the Indians in open defiance of the governor. Bacon demanded that the colonists destroy all Indians in general for … they were all Enemies" (Taylor 2002, 149). Bacon reveled in the bloodshed and "advocated for the removal or wholesale slaughter of the indigenous tribes" (Mark 2021) and "favoured the total extermination of the indigenous population" (Jordan and Walsh 2008, 207). In an egregiously offensive boastful claim, Bacon bragged about how he and his men "fell upon the men, women and children … disarmed and destroyed them all" (Jordan and Walsh 2008, 208).

Governor Berkeley attempted to solve the problem by calling for an election, but Bacon and his supporters were able to secure Bacon a seat in the Virginia House of Burgesses (Henrico County), and then elected Bacon as commander-in-chief of the Henrico County militia. Berkeley had repeatedly denied Bacon's request for a military commission but reluctantly relented after Bacon's election to the House of Burgesses and appointment as county militia commander. However, without Berkeley's approval, Bacon then organized another small army of men and began waging war again against nearby Native Americans, attacking multiple tribes and villages, and not distinguishing his victims by gender or age.

At this point, Governor Berkeley labeled Bacon and his men as rogues and outlaws and proclaimed Bacon to be a traitor. While Berkeley awaited British ships for support to put down the rebellion, he traveled the countryside trying to recruit Virginia supporters to his side. Berkeley arrived at the Virginia colonial capital of Jamestown and again condemned Bacon as a traitor and "declared Bacon guilty of treason" (Taylor 2002, 149). Bacon was outraged and his rogue band rushed to Jamestown in 1676, burning and pillaging the capital upon arrival, and engaging in acts of terrorism to those who were identified as Berkeley supporters. Then Bacon's mob set fire to the entire town, burning it to the ground. Governor Berkeley was forced to flee for his life. Bacon and his council of war claimed that they "decided to burn the place to prevent its affording shelter to the obnoxious royalists" (Ellis 1900, 132), but the separate acts of terrorism committed by Bacon indicate this justification was plainly false. After the destruction of the entire well-populated city, all that remained were "the ruins of the church tower and a few tombstones in the graveyard near-by" (Ellis 1900, 132).

News of the rebellion reached the King of England, Charles II, and he sent a squadron of ships and material support. With the colony now under Bacon's control, the rebel leader withdrew his forces to Green Springs, Virginia, to plan further action. A sudden and fatal illness (believed to be dysentery) cut Bacon's life short, and he died on October 26, 1876. Already without a leader, the rebel forces were dealt another blow when the requested British assistance arrived off the coast of Virginia shortly after Bacon's death. With the assistance of the British Naval vessels, Governor Berkeley quickly defeated the remnants of Bacon's forces. After defeat, Berkeley ordered the execution of the top twenty-three remaining leaders for crimes against the state and disobedience to the colonial authorities. An additional three died in prison awaiting execution, and five individuals condemned to death were able to escape. Berkeley wanted to execute more individuals, but King Charles II ordered a stop to the executions, saying "the old fool [Berkeley] has taken more lives in that naked country [Virginia] then I have done here [England] for the murder of my father" (Ellis 1900, 132). Bacon's Rebellion was a harbinger of things to come in America; it was the first of a long line of rebellions and crimes against the state that has plagued the United States for centuries thereafter.

See Also: American Revolution and Treason; Insurrection; Jefferson, Thomas; Rebellion; Terrorism; Treason

Resources

Ellis, Edward S. 1900. *The History of Our Country from the Discovery of America to the Present Time*. Vol. 1. Cincinnati, OH: The Jones Brothers Publishing Company.

Jordan, Dan, and Michael Walsh. 2008. *White Cargo*. New York: New York University Press, 205–12.

Mark, Joshua J. 2021. "Bacon's Rebellion." *World History Encyclopedia*. Accessed February 17, 2023. https://www.worldhistory.org/Bacon%27s_Rebellion/.

Taylor, Alan. 2002. *American Colonies: The Settling of North America*. New York: Penguin Books.

Battle of Athens, Tennessee (1946)

The "Battle of Athens" occurred in the city of Athens, McMinn County, Tennessee, when a large group of veterans recently returned from service in the Second World War used armed force to fight back against perceived corruption and election fixing by the head of the local political machine, Paul Cantrell.

Cantrell, who was associated with the corrupt statewide political machine run by E. H. Crump, had been serving in the Tennessee legislature, but sought election to replace Pat Mansfield as McMinn County Sheriff. During the Second World War, when 10 percent of the county's residents were away fighting in the war, Sheriff Mansfield and his deputies profited greatly from the payment system for law enforcement then common in Tennessee. Rather than receiving a salary, many law enforcement personnel throughout the state received fees for every person booked, incarcerated, and released, incentivizing unscrupulous law enforcers to conduct large numbers of bogus arrests for profit. For example, in McMinn County, Sheriff Mansfield's deputies routinely boarded buses passing through the county and hauled sleeping passengers to jail, charged them with drunkenness, then released them and collected their fee. During his four years as Sheriff ending in 1946, Sheriff Mansfield is believed to have collected $104,000 (roughly $1.5 million in 2023) in such fees. Unscrupulous sheriffs in McMinn County and elsewhere also augmented their funding with kickbacks to allow roadhouses, prostitution, alcohol sales, and gambling.

McMinn County residents serving overseas in the war began hearing reports of the corruption at home, and a number vowed to address it once the war concluded. In the early months of 1946, recently returned veterans formed a non-partisan political party and fielded or supported candidates to run against the corrupt "establishment candidates" for several offices. In the election for Sheriff, the veterans supported Knox Henry, who had served in the Army Air Corps during the war, against Paul Cantrell. Sheriff Mansfield, who had been installed as sheriff by Cantrell's political machine ten years earlier, supported Cantrell. Fearing fraud, in the days leading up to the election, Henry's supporters directly requested assistance from the state governor and attorney general in ensuring a fair election, but their requests went unanswered.

On Election Day, August 1, 1946, voters turned out in the largest numbers in McMinn County history to that point. Cantrell's partisans controlled the polls in all precincts. Veterans serving as poll watchers began observing election irregularities, including direct payments of cash to adult voters, allowing minors and others whose names did not appear on the voter registration rolls to vote, ostensibly for Cantrell, and even one of Cantrell's men shooting in the back of an elderly Black farmer who was attempting to vote.

As tensions rose throughout Athens, Cantrell loyalists took four veterans (poll watchers) hostage and took them and several ballot boxes to the local jail. Several dozen deputies loyal to Sheriff Mansfield and Cantrell were inside the jail and several hundred veterans surrounded the jail. After a several-hour standoff during which numerous shots were fired by both sides, members of the veterans group began attacking the jail with dynamite. Eventually, the deputies surrendered and handed over the ballot boxes to the veterans.

After ballots were counted, veteran-backed candidates were declared to have won all five elections at issue. On August 4, 1946, Sheriff Mansfield resigned. Neither city police nor sheriff's deputies performed law enforcement duties. Instead, armed veterans patrolled the streets and performed law enforcement functions while preparing for an anticipated assault by Mansfield's men that never came. Eventually, Knox Henry was appointed to serve as interim Sheriff until the end of Mansfield's term and the beginning of Henry's official term, and the veterans ceded control of the town to properly hired law enforcement personnel.

Coming at a time when national sentiment was already wary of returning veterans and the possibility that they may tend toward violence, the national press condemned the veterans' takeover of McMinn County government. Syndicated columnist Robert C. Ruark observed "nothing could be more dangerous both for our liberties and our welfare than the making of the McMinn County Revolution into a habit" (Seiber 1985). A few other armed veterans' groups engaged in similar anti-corruption activities in Tennessee, but after the perceived corrupt political leaders were ousted, those actions also abated. The feared nationwide violence and direct takeover of local governments by the Second World War veterans never materialized and, in fact, the veterans in this case were instrumental in ensuring the sanctity and integrity of the electoral process.

See Also: Insurrection; Sedition

Resources

"Armed Veterans Run Town after Tennessee Bloodshed." *New York Times*, August 3, 1946, 1, 3.

Derose, Chris. 2020a. "'Get the Hell Out of Here and Get Something to Shoot With.'" *Politico*, November 1, 2020.

Derose, Chris. 2020b. *The Fighting Bunch: The Battle of Athens and How WWII Veterans Won the Only Successful Armed Rebellion since the Revolution*. New York: St Martin's Press.

Seiber, Lones. 1985. "The Battle of Athens." *American Heritage*, February/March 1985. Accessed October 23, 2023. https://www.americanheritage.com/content/februarymarch-1985.

Battle of Liberty Place (1874)

The "Battle of Liberty Place," also known as the "Battle of Canal Street," occurred in New Orleans, Louisiana, in 1874, nine years after the end of the American Civil War. White Southerners displeased by the policies of the federal government during the Reconstruction Era viewed the Republican-led state government, which arguably had been installed by federal military force, as part of northern tyranny and sought to overthrow it. Some have characterized Reconstruction and resistance by the South, including the Battle of Liberty Place, as a continuation of the Civil War. The pro-Northern Republican government of Louisiana instituted many policies aimed at providing civil and political rights and economic opportunity to recently freed Black citizens, but which were largely paid for by new property taxes that primarily affected White Louisianians.

Under the Reconstruction Act of 1867, the South was divided into five military districts. United States Army General Philip Sheridan governed the Louisiana District from New Orleans. Under the Reconstruction Act, General Sheridan allowed all males—Black and white—to register to vote, so long as they would take an oath that they had never aided the Confederacy. This policy thereby excluded a large percentage of otherwise eligible adult male voters in Louisiana. The resulting voter rolls skewed Republican, allowing Republican candidates opportunities for statewide office and control of Louisiana government that likely would not have existed had white ex-Confederate males been enfranchised. Two factions of the Republican Party formed, one that was dominated by northern "immigrants" (pejoratively referred to as carpetbaggers) and freed Black men, and another faction that was more traditionally southern in orientation.

In the 1872 Louisiana gubernatorial election, the Republican candidate, William Pitt Kellogg, and the Democratic candidate, John McEnery, both claimed to have won the election. Both candidates held inaugurations and appointed subordinate state officeholders. McEnery was supported by Governor Henry Warmoth. Warmoth was an "anti-Grant Republican" who opposed many of the Reconstruction policies of northern Republicans including President Ulysses S. Grant. Warmoth appointed an election board that declared McEnery the victor, but an alternative board declared Kellogg had won. The Louisiana legislature, dominated at the time by pro-Grant Republicans, impeached Warmoth for election malfeasance, leading to the acting governorship of P. B. S. Pinchback, the second African American to serve as a governor of a state. The federal government certified Kellogg as governor. But Democrats continued to dispute the election, leading to several incidents of violence, including the Colfax Massacre, and culminating in the Battle of Liberty Place.

In 1874, a new paramilitary group known as the White League formed. Comprised primarily of ex-Confederate soldiers and serving as a quasi-military arm of the Democratic Party in Louisiana, the White League's platform was plain: "[W]e enter into and found this league for the protection of our own race against the daily increasing encroachment of the negro, and we are determined to use our best efforts to purge our legislative, judicial, and ministerial offices from such a horde of miscreants as now assume to lord it over us" (Schafer 1994). The White League began threatening Republican officeholders and supporters through low-level violence and intimidation throughout the rural areas of the state, until the only remaining Republican government officials in significant concentration were in state and city government in New Orleans.

The Republican government was largely supported by New Orleans police and the mostly Black state militia, commanded by former Confederate General James Longstreet. When General Longstreet learned that a shipment of weapons to be delivered to the White League had arrived on a steamboat at the end of Canal Street, he ordered the police and militia forces to bar the way to the dock. On September 14, 1874, White League forces under the command of former Confederate General Frederick Ogden entered New Orleans to retrieve the weapons shipment and replace Kellogg with McEnery as governor. The White League's roughly 8,400 troops outnumbered Longstreet's combined forces two to one, and the White League quickly overwhelmed the pro-government forces.

For three days the White League controlled the entire city, including the State House and City Hall, and except the United States Customs House into which Governor Kellogg had retreated. The White League decided not to attack the Customs House as it would unnecessarily involve the federal government. However, shortly after Kellogg telegraphed President Grant for assistance, federal troops arrived in Louisiana and six United States Navy warships anchored in the river at New Orleans. Faced with overwhelming federal force, the White League soon surrendered under an agreement with the commander of the federal forces, General William Emory. The agreement provided that those involved in the uprising would not be arrested or prosecuted and that the state and city governments as constituted before the Battle would resume, including again recognizing Kellogg as governor. By September 21, the White League's surrender was complete, though some White League leaders claimed they no longer regarded Louisiana as a state, but rather as a province without a democratic government.

Like the American Civil War itself, the Battle of Liberty Place is cast by some pro-Southern voices as a valiant and courageous fight against northern oppression. Notorious author and pro-Southern apologist Stuart Omer Landry, known primarily for his post-Second World War book *The Cult of Equality*, in which he defended racially disparate treatment, characterized the Battle as "one of the most glorious events in the history of New Orleans" and a necessary "attempt to restore liberty to their native land" considering the "outrages" suffered by the people of Louisiana (Landry 1955, 3). Some historians note that the White League, despite its name and platform, declared during its brief occupation of New Orleans that the civil and political rights of Blacks would be respected. An editorial in the most prominent New Orleans newspaper of the time urged "Nothing can be more false than to claim [the temporary victory by the White League] as … a race victory. It was simply an uprising of the people against an intolerable oppression and flagrant usurpation … under it the state would have been Africanized. Nothing could have been darker, bleaker, and more hopeless than the prospect of Louisiana under such a government" ("The Revolution of September 14" 1891, 4).

By contrast, Louisiana Attorney General A. P. Field argued that all those who had engaged in armed resistance against the government should be tried and hanged for treason. And General Sheridan urged President Grant to declare the White League participants in the Battle "banditti," suggesting he would try them by military commission for murder. None of these suggested prosecutions occurred.

In 1891 the City of New Orleans erected a monument in Liberty Place "in honor of those who fell in defense of liberty and home rule in that heroic struggle of the 14th of September, 1874." For decades, a parade and wreath laying ceremony conducted by the city occurred every September 14. In 2017, the city removed the monument, along with statues of Confederate General Robert E. Lee and Confederate States President Jefferson Davis.

See Also: American Civil War and Treason; Colfax Massacre (1873); Insurrection; Treason

Resources

Landry, Stuart Omer. 1955 [orig. 1884]. *The Battle of Liberty Place*. Gretna, LA: Pelican.
"The Revolution of September 14." *The Times-Picayune*, September 13, 1891, 4.
Schafer, Judith K. 1994. "The Battle of Liberty Place: A Matter of Historical Perception." Louisiana Cultural Vistas, Spring. Reprinted by *64 Parishes*, available at https://64parishes.org/the-battle-of-liberty-place.
Selk, Avi. 2017. "New Orleans Removes a Tribute to 'The Lost Cause of the Confederacy'—With Snipers Standing By." *Washington Post*, April 24, 2017.
"The White Leaguers Make a Demonstration in New Orleans." *Cincinnati Daily Gazette*, September 15, 1874, 1.

Booth, John Wilkes (1838–65)

John Wilkes Booth was the chief conspirator and perpetrator in the assassination of President Abraham Lincoln. Booth would be the first person to commit the act of assassination against an American head of state. In addition to killing Abraham Lincoln on April 14, 1865, Booth was the chief instigator in the Lincoln assassination plot. The single bullet fired by Booth changed the course of American history and still haunts the United States today. Booth's infamous legacy would be that he was the first of four presidential assassins in US history. After the Lincoln assassination, the assassination of a US president, once thought unfathomable in America, became more conceivable and James Garfield, William McKinley, and John F. Kennedy would all subsequently die at the hands of disgruntled and disaffected assassins.

Ironically, until the last year of his life, and despite his virulent racism and white supremacist worldviews, Booth led a somewhat charmed and successful life as one of America's top actors during his adult years. Booth was born in 1838, the ninth son of Julius Booth, who was himself considered to be one of the top actors in the world at that time. One of John Wilkes Booth's siblings, Edwin Booth, was also a world-famous actor whose acting success surpassed that of his younger brother. Prophetically, shortly after Booth's birth, while sitting by the fireside, his mother prayed for a sign regarding John Wilkes Booth's future, and she claimed to have seen the word "country" spelled out in the flames of the fire. While Booth's mother believed this was a sign that Booth was destined for greatness, Booth's future would bring calamity to the country.

In the mid-1850s, the Maryland-born John Wilkes Booth began his professional acting career in Philadelphia, Pennsylvania. After a year in Philadelphia, Booth moved to Richmond. In November 1859, after John Brown's Raid, Booth borrowed a militia uniform from the Richmond Grays to travel up to Charles Town, Virginia, to assist in guarding the jail and the execution site and to ensure John Brown did not escape the hangman's noose. By this point in his life, it was apparent from his writings that Booth was a virulent white supremacist, viewed slavery as a beneficial institution, and despised abolitionists like John Brown, viewing them as evil. Booth secretly snuck onto a train from Richmond to Charles Town even though the actual members of the Richmond Grays militia did not welcome him and "repeatedly pushed him off the coaches" and Booth "secreted himself in the baggage car" to make the trip to Charles Town (Kimmel 1940, 156). Upon arrival at Charles Town, Brown was "part of the guard of Robert E. Lee, which surrounded the scaffold and saw the Sage of Osawatomie die … [and] Wilkes enjoyed his military role until the trap fell and John Brown's body danged in the air" (Kimmel 1940, 156). At that point, "he became pale and asked for a good stiff drink of whiskey." Later, Booth would brag about playing a role in capturing Brown, but his claimed "vaunted heroism was only a figment of Wilkes' imagination" and overblown sense of self (Kimmel 1940, 156), as Brown was safely behind bars before Booth even left Richmond. While Booth hated Brown, Booth was nevertheless intrigued with Brown and his ability to change history through a single violent act. Brown's act of treason in 1859 and Booth's act of assassination in 1865 stand as crimes against the state bookends to the American Civil War.

By 1862, Booth had become a national star in the acting profession and performed over 167 times in a single year in cities across the country, including St. Louis, Chicago, Boston, Baltimore, Cincinnati, Richmond, Louisville, and Washington, DC. Booth was considered a versatile actor, playing eighteen separate roles in a single year. Booth was so popular that he sometimes made over $1,000 for a single night's performance—the equivalent of over $36,000 in today's monetary value.

While not a member of the Confederate Army, Booth worked for the Confederate underground, and he spied on the Union Army and passed along military intelligence to the Confederacy. He also smuggled medicines across opposing lines and to the South. As the war progressed, Booth became increasingly monomaniacal on southern rights and his seething hatred of Abraham Lincoln. Booth became involved with the Confederate Secret Service and traveled to Montreal, Canada, to meet with confederate agents. Upon his return from Canada, Booth first planned out a kidnapping scheme for Lincoln in 1864 and recruited a cadre of accomplices to accomplish that crime. Some of the planning sessions were held at the boarding house of fellow conspirator Mary Surratt and involved individuals who would be co-conspirators in Lincoln's assassination the following year.

By April 1865, Booth's plan of kidnapping Lincoln was discarded, and he instead vowed the death of Abraham Lincoln, an act he committed on April 14, 1865. After the assassination, Booth rightfully and immediately became a pariah to most Americans, North and South. Shortly before his own death, Booth expressed his bewilderment in his diary as to why he was not viewed with admiration even by many of his fellow southerners. Booth wrote:

> After being hunted like a dog through swamps, woods, and last night being chased by gunboats till I was forced to return wet, cold, and starving, with every man's hand against me, I am here in despair. And why? For doing what Brutus was honored for—what made Tell a hero. And yet I, for striking down a greater tyrant than they ever knew, am looked upon as a common cut-throat. (Kimmel 1940, 238)

After a twelve-day fugitive hunt, Booth was captured and killed in an abandoned barn before he could turn himself in to the authorities. His family portrait was wrapped in linen and hidden away for decades, with family members eventually painting over the portrait altogether, and even his own brother Edwin would never speak his name again.

See Also: Assassination; Brown, John; John Brown's Raid (1859); Lincoln Assassination (1865); McKinley Assassination (1901); Surratt, Mary E.; Treason

Resources

Kimmel, Stanley. 1940. *The Mad Booths of Maryland*. Indianapolis: The Bobbs-Merrill Company.
Swanson, James L. 2007. *Manhunt: The 12-Day Chase for Lincoln's Killer*. New York: Harper Perennial.

Boston Marathon Bombing (2013)

The April 15, 2013, bombing at the finish line of the Boston Marathon provides an excellent example of the sometimes blurry line between crimes against the state, crime generally, and war against a state posed by acts of terrorism.

Tamerlan and Dzhokhar Tsarnaev, naturalized US citizens originally from the Caucasus region, planned and perpetrated the bombing. The brothers detonated two bombs made with consumer pressure cookers near the finish line of the Boston Marathon, killing three people and injuring approximately 265 more, resulting in at least fourteen people requiring amputation. The brothers initially escaped, and the ensuing manhunt terrified the Boston area, with the identity of the attackers initially unknown, and the brothers' whereabouts unknown for nearly four days. On April 19, 2013, Tamerlan was killed in a shootout with law enforcement personnel. Dzhokhar was subsequently apprehended while hiding in a boat parked in a residential back yard in Watertown, Massachusetts.

Evidence later suggested the brothers' initial target was to have been a historically well-attended Fourth of July celebration involving the Boston Pops orchestra, but because they were able to build the bombs more quickly than anticipated, the Boston Marathon—one of the most prestigious marathons in the world, drawing nearly 27,000 participating runners and over half a million spectators in 2013—was a "target of opportunity." Evidence also suggested that after the bombing, the brothers spontaneously decided to drive to New York to detonate more bombs in Times Square, but that plan was thwarted when the driver of the car they carjacked was able to escape and alert law enforcement.

After his capture, Dzhokhar Tsarnaev was charged in federal court with approximately thirty crimes, including use of a weapon of mass destruction, murder (for the killing of a police officer during the brothers' attempted evasion from capture), and malicious destruction of property resulting in death. He pleaded not guilty to all charges. During trial, federal prosecutors portrayed Tsarnaev as engaged in a holy war against the United States, while defense attorneys portrayed him as a follower, subject to his older brother's influence. In 2015, Dzhokhar Tsarnaev was convicted by a jury of all charges and sentenced to death. The death penalty was initially overturned by a federal appeals court but reinstated by the United States Supreme Court. He remains on federal death row as of this publication.

Motive represents an important element of crimes against the state. Actions cannot properly be considered crimes against the state if the state is not an intended victim. In the case of the Boston Marathon Bombing, motive is unclear and journalists and political scientists have offered a variety of explanations for the Tsarnaev brothers' actions, some of which would constitute a crime against the state, and some of which would not.

The most widely circulated explanation for the Tsarnaevs' actions, and the conclusion of the Federal Bureau of Investigation (FBI), was that the brothers were defending Islam against the United States. While hiding in the boat in which he was eventually discovered, Dzhokhar scrawled a note claiming the attacks were "retribution for U.S. military action in Afghanistan and Iraq" and that the victims of the bombing were "collateral damage in the same way innocent victims have been collateral damage in U.S. wars around the world." Some have observed the brothers were unconnected with any avowed terrorist organizations, suggesting that undercuts the "anti-United States terrorism" explanation for the attack. But the FBI's conclusion and Dzhokhar's claimed motivation are supported by evidence that the brothers were readers of *Inspire*, an online magazine produced by Al-Qaeda leader Anwar Al-Awlaki, in which he encouraged extremists to individually attack Western powers without being part of terror groups, and in which he provided specific instructions for making pressure cooker bombs. This explanation of the motivation for the attack comports with a crime against the state theory, as the United States itself was the intended victim.

Others have suggested motives less clearly targeting the US government. For instance, author Masha Gessen (2015) researched the brothers' backgrounds and posited that a more significant underlying motivation for the attack was social isolation and insignificance. The bombing served as an opportunity for "greatness," because otherwise insignificant individuals were able to engage with a great power, especially given the United States' tendency to treat acts of terrorism not just as crimes but as acts of war.

Similarly, some have suggested the incident was more akin to a random mass killing, such as the school shooting in Columbine, Colorado, or the sniper shootings that terrorized the Washington, DC, area in 2002, with an unclear or perhaps nonexistent political terrorist motivation. Early speculation suggested the "Tax Day" date of the bombing indicated an anti-government, libertarian motivation similar to Timothy McVeigh's apparent motivation for the timing of the Oklahoma City Bombing. However, no noteworthy evidence has been discovered supporting this theory.

A mixture of motives has also been suggested. For example, reporting in *The Boston Globe* suggested the brothers' life experiences as immigrants who failed to achieve professional, social, or civic success in the United States primed them to be influenced by an ideology that suggested "the West," rather than just a specific government, was engaged in worldwide suppression of Islam (Benjamin 2014). Under this theory, the attack was perhaps less targeting the government—a crime against the state—than "the West" generally, which would be more a crime against society.

See Also: Oklahoma City Bombing (1995); Terrorism; Weapons of Mass Destruction

Resources

Benjamin, Daniel. 2014. "Motive of Destruction." *The Boston Globe*, January 8, 2014.
Gessen, Masha. 2015. *The Brothers: The Road to an American Tragedy*. New York: Riverhead Books.
Global Staff of the Boston Globe. 2013. "The Fall of the House of Tsarnaev." *The Boston Globe*, December 15, 2013.

Brandenburg v. Ohio (1969)

In the fifty years that followed the Court's decision in *Schenck v. United States* (1919), the "clear and present danger test" formed the primary standard by which courts evaluated First Amendment expressive conduct claims related to so-called subversive speech. But in *Brandenburg v. Ohio*, the Court moved to a new benchmark for evaluating speech advocating potentially illegal conduct, embracing a standard that distinguished between "the mere abstract teaching" of the moral imperative to use violence, and the incitement of violence.

In 1968, Clarence Brandenburg planned a rally of the Ku Klux Klan at a farm in Hamilton County, Ohio. Perhaps for posterity's sake, Brandenburg reached out to a Cincinnati reporter who, together with a cameraman, agreed to observe and film the rally. While there, the two-person crew filmed incendiary remarks made by Brandenburg. Among other remarks, Brandenburg said, "We're not a revengent [*sic*] organization, but if our President, our Congress, our Supreme Court, continues to suppress the white, Caucasian race, it's possible that there might have to be some revengeance [*sic*] taken." Brandenburg also said, "Personally, I believe the n***** should be returned to Africa, the Jew returned to Israel." He also announced that the Ku Klux Klan would be "marching on Congress" and then would divide into two groups to march on St. Augustine, Florida, and into Mississippi.

Films of the event were later broadcast by television stations around the nation. The State of Ohio brought charges against Brandenburg under its criminal syndicalism law for "advocat[ing] … the duty, necessity, or propriety of crime, sabotage, or unlawful methods of terrorism as a means of accomplishing industrial or political reform" as well as for "voluntarily assembl[ing] with any society, group, or assemblage of persons formed to teach or advocate the doctrines of syndicalism." The recorded footage was used by the State as evidence against Brandenburg. He was convicted and sentenced to ten years in prison and ordered to pay a $1,000 fine.

Brandenburg appealed, alleging that the Ohio law violated the First Amendment to the United States Constitution. In a *per curiam* opinion, the Supreme Court reversed the conviction, holding "that the constitutional guarantees of free speech and free press" prohibited a state from inhibiting calls to use force or violate a law unless the call is "directed to inciting or producing imminent lawless action and is likely to incite or produce such action." The Court then continued that "the mere abstract teaching … of the moral propriety or even moral necessity for a resort to force and violence, is not the same as preparing a group for violent action and steeling it to such action." If a law aimed at prohibiting violent action failed to draw this distinction, it intruded on the freedoms guaranteed by the First Amendment. Under this imminent incitement test, the Court found that the Ohio statute violated the First Amendment.

In articulating a new test for evaluating speech advocating illegal conduct, the Supreme Court did not explicitly abolish the clear and present danger test, and in fact cited a case from just seventeen years earlier—*Dennis v. United States*—in which the Court had applied the clear and present danger test and said that legislatures should decide what was "dangerous."

On the other hand, in *Brandenburg* the Supreme Court explicitly overruled *Whitney v. California*, a 1927 decision involving a syndicalism statute like Ohio's. In that case, the Supreme Court had upheld the conviction of Charlotte Anita Whitney for her role in helping establish the Communist Labor Party of America. The Court had determined that Whitney's activities abused free speech because she spoke words that were "inimical to the public welfare, tending to incite crime, disturb the peace or endanger the foundations of organized government and threaten its overthrow." In *Whitney*, Justice Louis Brandeis penned a well-known concurrence—one that read more like a dissent than a concurrence—advocating a nearly absolute right to free speech. Brandeis argued that free speech is the key to democracy and that discussion protects against the "dissemination of noxious doctrine" and is a political duty that is a fundamental principle of American government. Brandeis noted that the Founders "eschewed silence coerced by law," and that the remedy to falsehood and fallacies is "more speech, not enforced silence."

Justice William O. Douglas's concurring opinion in *Brandenburg* observed what he saw as the unfortunate ease with which the clear and present danger standard could be "manipulated to crush … '[t]he fundamental right of free men to strive for better conditions through new legislation and new institutions' by argument and discourse … even in time of war." Quoting from Justice Holmes's dissent in *Gitlow v. New York*, Justice Douglas suggested that the Court's new "imminent incitement" standard did not go far enough in protecting speech: "The only difference between the expression of an opinion and an incitement in the narrower sense is the speaker's enthusiasm for the result." In short, Douglas viewed one's thoughts as "sanctuaries which government could not invade," though it could trespass the sanctuary on rare occasions, the line being between "ideas and overt acts." A broader analysis of speech as a crime against the state is provided elsewhere in this volume.

See Also: Clear and Present Danger Test; Criminal Syndicalism; *Dennis v. United States* (1951); Sabotage; *Schenck v. United States* (1919); Speech as Crime against the State; Terrorism

Resources

Brandenburg v. Ohio, 395 U.S. 444 (1969).

Lewis, Anthony. 2007. *Freedom for the Thought That We Hate: A Biography of the First Amendment.* New York: Basic Books.

Brown, John (1800–59)

Dubbed the "Father of American Terrorism," John Brown was a radical militant abolitionist who in 1837 consecrated his life to the destruction of slavery. Brown and three of his accomplices in the 1859 Harpers Ferry Armory attack (Edwin Coppoc, Albert Hazlett, and Aaron Stevens) have been the only people executed for the crime of treason against a state government in United States' history. Even today, the executions of these individuals comprise only a very small number of individuals who were *executed* based upon a treason conviction (state or federal). While there were a handful of other treason *prosecutions* by state governments, no other American citizens were executed on the state level for treason, and no executions of American citizens have ever occurred on the *federal level* (before or after Brown's 1859 case).

Brown was born on May 9, 1800, in Torrington, Connecticut. Brown was born less than eight miles away from the birthplace of Harriet Beecher Stowe, author of *Uncle Tom's Cabin*. Both Stowe and Brown are considered sparks to the powder keg which ultimately set the country aflame in civil war. Brown spent the first four decades of his life in peripatetic wanderings, at various times living in Connecticut, Ohio, Pennsylvania, New York, Massachusetts, the Kansas territory, and Maryland. For most of his life, Brown was a failed businessman who fathered twenty children with two different wives. Brown hated slavery and in November 1837 arose from the back row of a church in Hudson, Ohio, and proclaimed, "here before God, in presence of these witnesses, I consecrate my life to the destruction of slavery" (McGinty 2009, 33).

From 1837 to 1859, Brown participated in various efforts (some peaceful, some violent) to combat slavery, ranging from his participation in the Underground Railroad, his fighting in "Bleeding Kansas" (a period during which citizens violently clashed over whether Kansas would be a free or slave state) including his mutilation and massacre of five pro-slavery men in the Pottawatomie Massacre, Kansas, in 1856, to his 1859 attack (with twenty-one men) on the United States Armory and Arsenal in Harpers Ferry, Virginia (now West Virginia), now dubbed John Brown's Raid. During his attack on the United States Armory and Arsenal, Brown briefly held both the governmental complex and the surrounding town. Brown also kidnapped several hostages during the attack, including Colonel Lewis Washington (the great-grandnephew of George Washington). Brown then commandeered a sword given to George Washington by Frederick the Great and pistols given to Washington by the Marquis de Lafayette, both of which would be in Brown's possession after his capture on October 19, 1859. Captured by ninety United States Marines led by then brevet Lieutenant Colonel Robert E. Lee (and accompanied by Lieutenant J. E. B. Stuart), Brown was put on trial by Virginia on the charges of murder, attempting a slave insurrection, and treason against the Commonwealth of Virginia (see *Virginia v. Brown*).

Brown's admitted goal in attacking the United States Armory and Arsenal located at Harpers Ferry, Virginia, was to strike in the "mother" of all slave states, seize arms from the Armory and Arsenal, and liberate enslaved individuals in the surrounding counties. Brown envisioned his attack would start a massive slave insurrection throughout Virginia and the South. Brown's subsequent plan was to engage in guerilla warfare from the Blue Ridge Mountains, raiding various Southern plantations and liberating by force those enslaved, thereby severely weakening, and then destroying the institution of slavery, which he called a "sin against God" and the "sum of all villainies." Brown also drafted his own "Provisional Constitution of the United States" (which outlawed slavery, among other things) and intended to set up his own anti-slavery government within the Commonwealth of Virginia. Brown's plan to set up his own government within Virginia violated Virginia's treason statute, which among other things, prohibited "erecting or establishing or causing or procuring to be erected or established, any government separate from, or independent of the government of Virginia, within the limits thereof," "swearing or otherwise solemnly professing allegiance or fidelity to the same," or holding any office in the "usurped government." Brown had named himself Commander-in-Chief in his Provisional Constitution and required his men to swear fidelity to his new government.

As is discussed more fully in the entry *Virginia v. Brown*, Brown was found guilty on all three counts and was sentenced to hang in nearby Charles Town, Virginia (now West Virginia) on December 2, 1859. On the day of his execution, church bells pealed throughout the North in homage to "Old Captain Brown." Many prominent individuals, including Nathaniel Hawthorne, Ralph Waldo Emerson, and Henry David Thoreau, among many others, considered John Brown a hero and gave speeches and penned articles proclaiming him as such. Abraham Lincoln saw it differently, however, stating, "Old John Brown has just been executed for treason against a state. We cannot object, even though he agreed with us in thinking slavery wrong. That cannot excuse violence, bloodshed, and treason. It could avail him nothing that he might think himself right" (Villard 1910, 564).

On the way to the gallows, Brown handed his jailer a note that W. E. B. Du Bois later proclaimed to be "the mightiest abolition document that America has ever known" (Du Bois 1997, 186), which stated: "I, John Brown, am now quite certain that the crimes of this guilty land will never be purged away but with blood; I had, as I now think vainly, flattered myself that without very much bloodshed it might be done" (Villard 1910, 554). At his execution, several thousand militia members and soldiers witnessed the execution, including an actor named John Wilkes Booth, who borrowed a uniform from a Richmond militia unit to witness the execution, and who would himself commit his own act of treason just a few short years later by assassinating President Abraham Lincoln (see Lincoln Assassination).

At the time of Brown's execution in 1859, hundreds of thousands of Americans were going about their daily lives on farms, villages, factories, and in a myriad of other day-to-day activities, oblivious to the fact (as Henry Wadsworth Longfellow wrote in his diary on the day of Brown's execution) that Brown's execution was "sowing the wind to reap the whirlwind" of destruction and devastation that was soon to come in their lives (Longfellow 1891, 396). When the Civil War started eighteen months later, tens of thousands of those individuals wearing the Union Army uniform found themselves marching past "John Brown's Fort" (the site of Brown's capture in 1859) and thousands broke out into song, singing "John Brown's Body" (a popular Civil War song) as they passed by the site. By 1865, hundreds of thousands of those same Americans going about their daily lives in 1859 would be dead on America's sacred fields of battle in a struggle, as Brown predicted, to ultimately purge the crimes of this guilty land with blood.

See Also: American Civil War and Treason; Assassination; Booth, John Wilkes; Coppoc, Edwin; Hazlett, Albert; Insurrection; John Brown's Raid (1859); Lincoln Assassination (1865); Pottawatomie Massacre (1856); Stevens, Aaron; Terrorism; Treason; *Virginia v. Brown* (1859)

Resources

Beckman, James. 2005. "Brown, John (1800–1859)." In *The Greenwood Encyclopedia of African American Literature*, edited by Hans Ostrom and J. David, Macey Jr., vol. I, 199–202. Westport, CT: Greenwood Press.

Chowder, Ken. 2000. "Father of American Terrorism." *American Heritage*, February/March 2000.

Du Bois, W. E. B. 1997 [orig. 1909]. *John Brown, a Biography by W.E.B. Du Bois*. Armonk, NY: M.E. Sharpe.

Longfellow, Samuel. 1891. *The Life of Henry Wadsworth Longfellow: With Extracts from His Journals and Correspondence*. Vol. 2. Boston: Houghton Mifflin Company.
McGinty, Brian. 2009. *John Brown's Trial*. Cambridge, MA: Harvard University Press.
Oates, Stephen. 1984. *To Purge This Land with Blood: A Biography of John Brown*. Amherst: The University of Massachusetts Press.
Villard, Oswald Garrison. 1910. *John Brown 1800–1859: A Biography Fifty Years After.* London: Constable & Co. Ltd.

Bundy Standoffs (2014–16)

The Bundy Standoffs were two confrontations in 2014 and 2016 between members of the Bundy family and their supporters and federal and state law enforcement in which the Bundys rejected federal jurisdiction over federally owned land. The confrontations were the culmination of a long-standing legal battle between the Bundy family and the state and federal government.

For two decades, Cliven Bundy had illegally grazed his cattle on federally owned land without obtaining the required grazing permit or paying the permit fees. Bundy asserted the legal theory, rejected by all courts that have addressed the issue and by most legal practitioners and scholars, that the federal government cannot own land outside Washington, DC, and that land the federal government claims it owns in Nevada is actually owned by the state. Bundy's view of federal lands reflected the "Sagebrush Rebellion" of the 1970s and 1980s, which was not an actual rebellion, but rather an attempt by some lawmakers to transfer large swaths of land owned by the federal government in the western United States to state governments. Bundy's views closely aligned with his adherence to the "sovereign citizen movement," which holds that the federal government has no jurisdiction over their actions and asserts states as supremely sovereign, and the related "county supremacy" ideology, which suggests county sheriffs have authority superior to that of federal or state government law enforcement entities by virtue of their election by local citizens. Unsurprisingly, the FBI considers the sovereign citizen movement a domestic terrorism threat. At its roots, Bundy's ideology was apparently motivated by extremist religious views that the American West was the "promised land of Zion," for the benefit of members of the Church of Jesus Christ of Latter-Day Saints.

By 2014, Bundy's unpaid fees amounted to over $1 million. Acting pursuant to a court order, United States Bureau of Land Management (BLM) personnel attempted to remove Cliven Bundy's cattle from federal land where they were grazing and impound them as payment or security for Bundy's unpaid grazing fee debt. In anticipation of the cattle removal, Bundy rallied support from others in the sovereign citizen and militia movements, including the Praetorian Guard, White Mountain Militia, and the Oath Keepers. Over several days in April 2014, armed Bundy supporters blocked roads and highways and prevented the BLM from removing cattle they had gathered. Fearing violence, the BLM sent rangers and snipers, supported by local law enforcement. Eventually, the BLM yielded, announcing it would suspend the cattle roundup due to safety concerns.

Political reaction to the incident was mixed, with some political leaders referring to Bundy and his supporters as domestic terrorists who flouted the rule of law while others characterized them as patriots who had rightfully stood up to an overreaching federal government. Legal consequences for the Bundy supporters were also mixed. A few lower-level participants in the standoff were convicted and sentenced, but Cliven Bundy, his sons Ammon and Ryan Bundy, and other leaders escaped conviction when the cases against them were dismissed by a federal judge who determined the prosecutors had willfully violated discovery rules in failing to disclose relevant evidence to the defense. While walking out of the courtroom a free man, Cliven Bundy said, "My defense is a 15-second defense: I graze my cattle only on Clark County, Nevada, land and I have no contract with the federal government. This court has no jurisdiction or authority over this matter. And I've put up with this court in America as a political prisoner for two years" (Dougherty 2018).

In 2016, the Bundy family was involved in another armed standoff with the federal government, this time in Oregon. Two men named Dwight and Steven Hammond had been convicted of committing arson on federal lands years earlier. They had served some prison time, been released, but then were set to be rearrested after being resentenced to longer prison terms. Ammon and Ryan Bundy sought to protect the Hammonds from rearrest. Despite the Hammonds' decision that they did not want the Bundys' assistance, the Bundys called on a variety of militia members to come to Harney County, Oregon, to help prevent the Hammonds from being arrested. On January 2, 2016, Ammon told a crowd that he intended to occupy the nearby Malheur National Wildlife Refuge (Malheur NWR) and encouraged others to join him. Later that day, a number of armed individuals occupied the headquarters building of the Malheur NWR. Accounts of the number of militia members ultimately involved vary, from militia leaders' claims of over 150 to journalists' observations that there were roughly twenty to thirty. Among other things, the Bundys demanded that the Hammonds be released, and that the federal government cede ownership of the Malheur NWR. They also said the occupiers would remain in the headquarters building for years, with one occupier declaring the Malheur NWR would never be returned to federal government control.

During the first three weeks of the occupation, federal law enforcement personnel allowed the occupiers to freely come and go from the Malheur NWR. However, upon learning that several leaders would be leaving the park for a speaking engagement, law enforcement attempted to apprehend them. During the attempted arrest, one occupier was shot and killed by police as he attempted to retrieve a loaded pistol from his jacket. By January 29, 2016, most of the occupiers had left the Malheur NWR, leaving only four militants who told the FBI they were planning to remain until their supplies were exhausted. On February 11, the remaining occupiers surrendered to the FBI. Twenty-seven people were criminally charged for their actions, most with a single charge of conspiracy to obstruct federal officers in the performance of their duties. Over a dozen were convicted, many after pleading guilty. However, Ammon Bundy and six other defendants were acquitted after a jury trial. Sentences for those convicted ranged from house arrest and small fines to many months in prison and larger restitution obligations. The cost of the six-week standoff to the federal and state government has been estimated to exceed $9 million.

The Bundy standoffs, though small, constituted two armed insurrections in which participants occupied federal property, flouted the rule of law, and threatened federal employees' safety. And due in part to missteps by federal prosecutors, none of the Bundys have been held criminally responsible for the standoffs. Perhaps most important, the Bundys' actions and rhetoric inspired far-right "patriot movement" and militia members to further acts of contravening law and government authority. As said one former member of the militant group the Oath Keepers, who were at the center of the Capitol Insurrection on January 6, 2021, "My time with the Oath Keepers began back at Bundy Ranch, at that first standoff" (Smith 2022).

See Also: Capitol Insurrection on January 6, 2021; Conspiracy, Criminal; Insurrection; Militia Movement (Modern); Rebellion; Sovereign Citizen Movement; Terrorism

Resources

Dougherty, John. 2017. "Cliven Bundy's Armed Insurrection, Rooted in Religious Extremism, Goes on Trial." *The Revelator*, November 1, 2017.

Dougherty, John. 2018. "Bundy Trial Dismissed: 'A Sad Day for America's Public Lands.'" *The Revelator*, January 9, 2018.

Levin, Sam. 2016. "New Photos of Oregon Wildlife Refuge Reveal Damage Done by Bundy Standoff." *The Guardian*, March 24, 2016.

Smith, John L. 2022. "Bundy Ranch Standoff Provided a Warning of What Was to Come." *The Nevada Independent*, July 17, 2022.
Stack, Liam. 2016. "Wildlife Refuge Occupied in Protest of Oregon Ranchers' Prison Terms." *The New York Times*, January 2, 2016.
Temple, John. 2019. *Up in Arms: How the Bundy Family Hijacked Public Lands, Outfoxed the Federal Government, and Ignited America's Patriot Militia Movement*. Dallas: BenBella Books.

Burr, Aaron (1756–1836)

Aaron Burr was one of American's founding fathers and leaders and would have been held in the pantheon of early American leaders like George Washington, John Adams, Thomas Jefferson, Benjamin Franklin, and Alexander Hamilton, but for a series of highly questionable actions he was engaged in immediately after his deadly dueling confrontation with Alexander Hamilton in 1804. Today, Aaron Burr's federal treason case remains the most important treason case in the history of the United States and still informs practitioners, scholars, judges, and courts on the general meaning of the United States Constitution's Treason Clause, and specifically what is required to be held guilty for "levying war" against the Government. Because of the significance of the federal government's treason prosecution in *United States v. Burr*, described as "the most extraordinary treason trial in United States history" (Larson 2020 Chapter 4). This entry will address who Aaron Burr was and what he did to put himself in legal jeopardy for treason charges in 1807.

Aaron Burr was born in Newark, New Jersey, and graduated from the College of New Jersey. Burr then enlisted as a soldier in the American Revolution. Given that Aaron Burr's treason case against the United States is considered one of the most important in history, it is highly ironic that Burr was first placed under the command of Benedict Arnold (later considered the "father of American treason"). Burr also served under the command of General Washington and General Putnam, rising to the rank of lieutenant colonel. After the war, Burr practiced law in New York, before ascending to a variety of political offices, including New York attorney general (1789–91), United States Senator (1791–7), the New York general assembly (1797–9), the third vice president in US history (1800–4) under President Thomas Jefferson's first term. Burr also suffered several notable political defeats, including his reelection bid to the United States Senate in 1791, his rejection as president of the United States by the House of Representatives in the election of 1800, and his defeat as a candidate for the New York governorship in 1804.

During much of Burr's political career, he battled with Alexander Hamilton and exchanged many incendiary and vitriolic words. Provoked again by accusations and libel claimed by Hamilton, Burr finally challenged Hamilton to a duel. The duel took place on July 11, 1804, on the plains of Weehawken, New Jersey. Hamilton was mortally wounded and died the following day, on July 12, 1804. Burr fled to escape the pro-Hamiltonian mobs and an indictment of possibly murder and eventually made his way westward, only to be embroiled in another controversy that would lead to treason charges against him.

Burr became affiliated with General James Wilkinson. While General Wilkinson was a Revolutionary War era general, he also was a long-time and highly paid spy for the Spanish government and was even known in Spain as agent "Number 13." Wilkinson and Burr entered a conspiracy to either independently raise forces to invade Mexico or use those forces to force the Western States of the United States to secede from the Union and form a separate government, with Burr as its head of state. While both contemplated actions were illegal, the unlawful invasion of Mexico would have constituted a mid-level criminal offense; the forced division of the United States and secession of the western states was "levying war" against the United States, and if true, constituted the offense of treason. General Wilkinson arrested Burr and President Thomas Jefferson subsequently insisted on charging Burr with treason. Scholars have speculated that Wilkinson, as a double agent, decided to turn in Burr and reveal the plot to Jefferson in order to not have his own cover exposed and to keep in Jefferson's good graces.

Just a brief time before, in August 1806, Burr had already assembled hundreds of men and arms on Blennerhassett Island, Virginia (now West Virginia). Burr also contracted for the purchase of fifteen additional keel boats capable of transporting up to an additional 500 soldiers and purchased numerous military supplies and equipment for his men. Evidence cited in the Supreme Court's decision in *Ex Parte Bollman* (1807) put the number of men involved in Burr's treason to be in the thousands.

Since Burr never admitted his intentions, and as the government's chief witness (General Wilkinson) was a double agent (Spanish Agent Number 13), the true goals of the Burr's plot may never be ascertained with certainty. While speculative, renowned American Revolutionary War historian Thomas Fleming's explanation of Burr's plan is likely closest to the truth. Per Fleming, Burr had a "long-standing dream ... of revolutionizing Spain's South American colonies, in particular Mexico, with its supposedly fabulous gold and silver deposits." Fleming further postulated that:

> The separation of the eastern states remained linked to this goal in Burr's mind ... It seemed more than probable, after they got to Mexico City and proclaimed their empire, that those who had stayed behind would rush to join the standard of the American Bonaparte [Burr]. Burr was convinced that this act of secession would trigger New England's withdrawal from the Union, leaving Jefferson incapable of stopping the formation of the new empire ... With Mexican gold and ports, he would be able to build a navy that would dominate the Gulf of Mexico and the Caribbean and defy any attempt to intimidate him. (Fleming 1999, 375)

Whether outright treason or a major international incident involving European Powers, Burr had threatened the viability of the newly founded United States of America. Taken in its most favorable light, Burr assembled a private army with the intent to attack Mexico, seize its assets, and perhaps involve the United States in a war with Spain. Taken in its most unsavory light, Burr was assembling thousands of armed men to attack the American city of New Orleans, use control of the Mississippi River to sever the western United States from the eastern United States, and create a new country with Burr as its leader. Three generals were prepared to testify that Burr intended to divide the union and create an additional territory under this control.

By the fall of 1806, Burr was leading a group of 60–100 well-armed men down the Mississippi to New Orleans. To extricate himself from the plot and save himself (or keep his double agent status secret), General Wilkinson sent correspondence to President Jefferson in Washington, DC, accusing Burr of treason and seeking his immediate arrest. On February 19, 1807, Burr was arrested in Alabama and sent to Richmond, Virginia, to be tried in US federal court.

The subsequent trial was notable in numerous respects, including the heated animosity between the various parties. Chief Justice John Marshall presided over the court in 1807 and tensions between Marshall and President Jefferson were high. Jefferson refused to appear in response to subpoenas from Marshall; this treason case occurred only three years after the standoff between Jefferson and Marshall in *Marbury v. Madison.* The trial of Jefferson's former vice president involved the highest-ranking defendant in a treason case in US history. Historians to this day debate whether Aaron Burr's plan was just an audacious plan to organize, lead, and capture Mexico for the United States, or whether he intended to split the United States in half, and name himself the leader of the territory to the west of the Mississippi. Either way, the resulting case entitled *United States v. Aaron Burr* (see *Burr, United States v.*), in which Judge Marshall dismissed the indictment and Burr was acquitted by the jury, easily established itself as the most important treason case in US history, then or now.

Burr's legal victory did not bring him a change of luck or good fortune. From 1808 to 1812, he exiled himself to Europe, even then still unsuccessfully trying to lobby European powers to meddle in Mexican affairs. Eventually Burr moved back to the United States but used the assumed last name of Edwards. He suffered additional heartache with the death of his only acknowledged grandson, and then the death of his beloved daughter Theodosia, who was lost at sea in 1812. He continued practicing law until his quiet, largely unnoticed death in 1836 on Staten Island, New York.

See Also: American Revolution and Treason; Arnold, Benedict; *Burr, United States v.* (1807); Conspiracy, Criminal; *Ex Parte Bollman* (1807); Jefferson, Thomas; Levying War; Treason

Resources

Fleming, Thomas. 1999. *Duel: Alexander Hamilton, Aaron Burr, and the Future of America*. New York: Basic Books.

Larson, Carlton F. W. 2020. *On Treason: A Citizen's Guide to the Law*. New York: Ecco, an imprint of HarperCollins (Kindle Edition).

Newmyer, R. Kent. 2012. *The Treason Trial of Aaron Burr: Law, Politics, and the Character Wars of the New Nation*. Cambridge: Cambridge University Press.

Burr, United States v. (1807)

It was hard to believe that the third vice president of the United States (Aaron Burr) would be arrested and charged for a plot that entailed attempting to destroy what the constitutional Framers had just put into place a mere decade before. Yet, that is just what happened. Burr had assembled hundreds of men and arms on Blennerhassett Island on the Ohio River between Virginia and Ohio for purposes of an armed invasion of New Orleans and Mexico. Furthermore, by the accounts of many government witnesses, Burr's intention was to set in motion an insurrection that would cut the United States in two, capture New Orleans, make war on Mexico, and set up his own country in the western half of the United States. At the time of his arrest, Burr had assembled armed men waiting on his orders to deploy from Blennerhassett Island. In addition to an array of arms and equipment already acquired, Burr had just contracted for fifteen additional keel boats that could transport an additional 500 men. He also ordered thousands of pounds of arms, equipment, food, and sustenance for his men for a prolonged military expedition.

Burr chose as his leading co-conspirator General James Wilkinson, who happened to be a corrupt general in the western territories and a "double agent" for both Spain and the United States. The Spanish called him "Agent No. 13" in Spanish records and correspondence. Wilkinson must have realized his lot was better with the United States and not with Burr's delusions of grandeur, as Wilkinson ultimately betrayed his allegiance to Burr and reported Burr's treasonous intent and plans to President Thomas Jefferson. Jefferson immediately ordered the arrest of Burr for treason and demanded that Burr be brought in chains to Richmond, Virginia (site of the then sitting United States Circuit Court). Burr was to face a prosecution for treason and a lesser crime of committing a "high misdemeanor" for his scheming war against Mexico. On February 19, 1807, Burr was arrested in Alabama (captured with approximately sixty to ninety men in his company at the time) and sent to Richmond to be tried in US federal court and to face the two charges in March 1807.

On March 30, 1807, Burr appeared at a hearing in front of United States Supreme Court Chief Justice John Marshall (presiding over the case on circuit along with United States District Court Judge Cyrus Griffin). The purpose of this first hearing was to decide whether Burr should be granted bail while the federal grand jury was concurrently considering an indictment for treason. Some of the main arguments that would eventually be made at Burr's subsequent trial were set forth in the bail argument. The prosecutors, led by District Attorney George Hay, argued that documentary evidence existed that established Burr's plan to set in motion insurrection and that he intended to sever the country in two. These documents purported that Burr's intention was to levy war against the United States. The government argued that the assembly of arms, men, weapons, and ammunition purchased and provided by Burr, along with the actual assembly of men on Blennerhassett Island awaiting orders and Burr's stated intentions, were surely sufficient for purposes of denying bail. When asked by Chief Justice Marshall why the original documents attesting to these things could not be produced, two differing responses were provided to the court: first, many of the documents were out in the wilderness of the western states and would take months to track down and procure; and second, and perhaps incongruous with the first explanation, Jefferson did not want to produce certain documents that might expose state secrets under a sort of "Executive Privilege" argument, that presidential communications should remain free from unfettered public exposure. How many documents Jefferson possessed versus those in the "wilderness of the west" was unclear, except to Jefferson.

The defense team focused on the sufficiency (or lack thereof) of the submitted evidence for such a serious charge as treason, arguing that surely the most serious charge possible under United States (or even English) law would not be supported by only second-rate and secondhand information. The government relied only on copies of documents (and no originals) and proffered no witness to corroborate or even attest to the veracity and accuracy of the copies. The defense also made much of President Jefferson's pre-trial statements of Burr's guilt, mirroring today's argument of "undue command influence" in military law cases. Jefferson had said that there could be no doubt that Burr was a traitor. The defense team argued that no man should be adjudged of a serious crime (either for purposes of a bail hearing or at trial) without the ability to examine and confront witnesses and view available documents. Jefferson's comments also clearly tainted the public view of Burr.

At the end of this bail hearing, the defense motion on whether Burr should be held on treason charges without bail pending trial was denied by the court because of the insufficiency of the evidence in front of the court. However, beyond being a foreshadowing of things to come, it was a pyrrhic victory as Burr remained in pre-trial confinement on the other pending charge. That is, while the court did not find probable cause to hold Burr over pending trial for treason, the court did find that probable cause existed that Burr committed a "high misdemeanor" by scheming to start war with Mexico. The court found sufficient evidence did exist on this issue because original evidence was produced to the court by General James Wilkinson. Burr was ultimately indicted for treason on June 24, 1807, and Burr was brought to trial in the United States Circuit Court in Richmond, Virginia, presided over by Supreme Court Chief Justice John Marshall.

Given the previous rocky relationship between Chief Justice John Marshall and President Thomas Jefferson after *Marbury v. Madison* in 1803, the handling of this case involving serious matters of national security infuriated Jefferson. The Burr treason case marked the second time in four years that President Jefferson and Chief Justice Marshall were at a standoff. At least in *Marbury v. Madison*, the case "only" dealt with the Court's power of judicial review and the validity of an order requiring the President and Secretary of State to issue judicial commissions (through a *writ of mandamus*). But, in the Burr case, Marshall was demanding access to papers dealing with sensitive issues of national security. Thus, when President Jefferson received the subpoenas from Marshall, he ignored them and decided that he would not comply with any demand for a personal appearance in front of Marshall. While publicly defiant against Marshall and taunting Marshall to come arrest him, Jefferson worked quietly and diplomatically behind the scenes to reach a satisfactory resolution regarding the requested documentation. Jefferson stated that he "wished to avoid the conflicts to high branches of government" and wished to work with Marshall "in a spirit of conciliation" (Jefferson 1807). The compromise was that Jefferson agreed to have his Secretary of War examine records to see if any documents were responsive to the defense's case, and if so, provide them. Additionally, it was agreed that the court could examine original documents relating to Burr's alleged treason, but only after redactions and recissions were made by the government on matters deemed not essential to the Burr defense and/or the charges of treason. Thus, despite Jefferson's conciliatory words, Jefferson never fully complied with providing all the necessary documents.

After the in-person testimony of Generals James Wilkinson and William Eaton, and the production of the documents referenced above, Aaron Burr was indicted for treason on June 23, 1807. As there were still many unknown features about how American treason law would look in practice (as compared with centuries of treason cases in England), there were two overarching unknown considerations for the court and jury. First, how broadly or loosely should the crime of treason be construed? For centuries in England, one could be found guilty of treason by not only being an active participant of treasonous events, but also for being remotely associated with those who committed treasonous acts. This clearly was an extremely broad application of treason and extended to not only the main actors, but also individuals who may have had some vague knowledge of the pending event but took no action themselves in furtherance of the offense (and often even included relatives, neighbors, and other tangential acquaintances). Conversely, in the newly minted United States Constitution, the act of treason (contained in Article III) narrowly specified that treason is only the act of "levying war" against the government or giving its enemies "aid and comfort." Furthermore, evidence of one's guilt needed to be corroborated by two witnesses in open court, testifying to the same overt act in furtherance of treason. One of the issues for this court and jury would be to see whether the jury opted for the broad English approach, or the newly minted narrow American practice. To litigate these issues, Jefferson's administration would spend over $100,000 to prosecute Burr, an amount equivalent to $2.5 million in 2023.

The prosecutors argued at trial that Aaron Burr levied war against the United States on Blennerhessett Island by assembling men, equipment, and arms. Consistent with the centuries-old common law position in England, prosecutors indicated that, as the orchestrator of the event, Burr could not be absolved from liability simply because he was not physically present when events unfolded. The prosecutors made clear that Burr's men were arrested "arms in hand" and hammered home that Burr was "not physically present, but legally present" for the purpose of the application of treason charges. Lastly, the prosecution relied on an unlikely precedent. In *Ex Parte Bollman* (1807), the United States Supreme Court had just held that Erick Bollman (one of Burr's men) could not be found guilty of treason when his sole "job" in the conspiracy was the recruiting of interested parties to join Burr on Blennerhessett Island. Thus, the defense was surprised when the prosecution relied on the case as support for Burr's guilt. However, the short Supreme Court opinion had one line that supported the prosecutors' case against Burr, namely that "to constitute a levying of war, there must be an assemblage of persons for the purpose of effecting by force a treasonable purpose." The prosecution argued that the assembling and arming of men with treasonous purposes alone was sufficient for a treason conviction in light of *Ex Parte Bollman.*

The defense took a strict and literal reading of the United States Constitution, arguing that the United States is not governed by centuries of English Common Law on treason, but narrowly by the language of Article III of the United States Constitution. For the defense, despite the unfortunate one sentence in the *Ex Parte Bollman* opinion, scheming, plotting, or even assembling was not treason under US law. Article III was clear on this point; participants must be actively "levying war," and an overt act of war is required. Furthermore, Article III of the Constitution requires that at least two witnesses in open court must attest to an overt act in furtherance of the treason. Bad associations or even evil intentions do not suffice; open and active deeds must be proven in open court and proven beyond a reasonable doubt.

Defense attorney Luther Martin (a "founding father" himself and a delegate to the Constitutional Convention of 1787) mocked the prosecution based upon the facts at hand. "If I were to name this, I would call it the Will o' wisp treason … for though it is said to be here and there and everywhere, *yet it is nowhere*." Martin went on to stress that not one single believable witness or independently corroborated document connected Burr to treason beyond a reasonable doubt. Martin quipped, the constitutionally required overt act of treason "only exists in the newspapers and in the mouths of the enemies of the gentleman for whom I appear."

Chief Justice Marshall agreed and dismissed the treason indictment because Marshall determined the indictment itself was faulty. That is, the indictment failed to mention the essential element of an overt act being required for a treason conviction. Nonetheless, Marshall left the jury to finish its business and render a verdict. On September 1, 1807, the jury declared that Aaron Burr was not guilty of treason. Upon learning of the not-guilty verdict, Thomas Jefferson was said to remark that "the jury didn't acquit; Marshall did."

Today, Aaron Burr's federal treason case remains the most important treason case in the history of the United States and still informs practitioners, scholars, judges, and courts on the general meaning of the United States Constitution's Treason Clause, and specifically what is required to be held guilty for "levying war" against the Government. Because of the case of *United States v. Burr*, the law is clear that treason charges are only supported when a defendant is actively engaged in "levying war" or "aiding and abetting" enemies of the United States. The mere planning, assembling of men or supplies, or even the conspiracy to engage in treason, is insufficient for purposes of proving the charge of treason itself. For these reasons, and because this case involved the highest-ranking former government official prosecuted for treason, this case is described as "the most extraordinary treason trial in United States history" (Larson 2020, Chapter 4).

See Also: Aid and Comfort (Aid to Enemies of the State); American Revolution and Treason; Arnold, Benedict; Burr, Aaron; Conspiracy, Criminal; *Ex Parte Bollman* (1807); Insurrection; Jefferson, Thomas; Levying War; Rebellion; Treason

Resources

Buckner, F. Melton Jr. 2001. *Aaron Burr: Conspiracy to Treason*. New York: John Riley & Sons.

Fleming, Thomas. 1999. *Duel: Alexander Hamilton, Aaron Burr, and the Future of America*. New York: Basic Books.

Jefferson, Thomas. 1807. Letter to George Hay. *Founders Online*, National Archives. June 17, 1807. Accessed October 31, 2023. https://founders.archives.gov/documents/Jefferson/99-01-02-5770.

Larson, Carlton F. W. 2020. *On Treason: A Citizen's Guide to the Law*. New York: Ecco, an imprint of HarperCollins (Kindle Edition).

Newmyer, R. Kent. 2012. *The Treason Trial of Aaron Burr: Law, Politics, and the Character War of the New Nation*. Cambridge: Cambridge University Press.

C

Calling Forth Act (Militia Act of 1792)

See Insurrection Act

Capitol Insurrection on January 6, 2021

For over two hundred years, America prided itself on the peaceful transition of power between presidents, no matter how rancorous and bitter the previous election season might have been. That is, until January 6, 2021 (hereinafter January 6), the date of a failed insurrection/rebellion by a group of Donald Trump supporters intending to obstruct the United States Congress in its constitutionally mandated job of certifying the 2020 election of Joseph Biden as president. As explained by House Select Committee Vice Chair Liz Cheney, "every President in our history has defended this orderly transfer of authority, except one. January 6, 2021, was the first time one American President refused his Constitutional duty to transfer power peacefully to the next" (House 2022, xv).

Former Senator and former Vice President Joseph Biden overwhelmingly defeated incumbent President Donald J. Trump in the presidential election of 2020. Biden received 81,283,098 votes across the country (51.3 percent of votes cast), more than any other presidential candidate in American history, easily overcoming Trump who received 74,222,958 votes (46.8 percent of votes cast). In addition to surpassing Trump by more than 7 million votes in the popular vote, Biden also defeated Trump by seventy-four votes in the Electoral College (306 Electoral votes for Biden compared with 232 for Trump). As Benjamin Ginsberg, a longtime Republican elections lawyer, explained to the House of Representatives Select Committee to Investigate the January 6 attack on the Capitol (hereinafter, House Committee), "the 2020 election was not close" (House 2022, 207). In disappointment and frustration at Trump's defeat, and based upon encouragement by Trump himself, thirty to forty thousand of Trump's most vehement supporters descended on Washington, DC, on January 6, with the aim of disrupting the election certification.

In the immediate aftermath of the election, Trump made statements indicating that he knew he lost the election. Speaking to an aide, Trump commented "can you believe I lost to this guy?" When discussing foreign policy with United States Joint Chief of Staff Chairman Army General Mark Milley, Trump commented that upcoming foreign affairs issues were no longer Trump's problem, but now belonged to the incoming president (winner of the election). However, in mid-December 2020, Trump commented to White House Chief of Staff Mark Meadows, "I don't want people to know we lost Mark. This is embarrassing. Figure it out. We need to figure it out. I don't want people to know that we lost" (House 2022, 20). Even in the early days and weeks following the election, close Trump advisors and Department of Justice (DOJ) and Homeland Security advisors told Trump that it was the cleanest (i.e., fraud free) election in history and that there was "zero basis" for claims of fraud.

The United States chief law enforcement officer at the time, Attorney General Bill Barr, a Trump appointee, indicated that purported claims of fraud had no basis in fact and were, in Barr's words at various points, "idiotic," "bullsh**," "crazy stuff," and "complete non-sense," and that bringing up such false claims was doing a "great, great disservice to the country" (House 2022, 219–20). In a deposition to the House Committee, Barr stated that "I made it clear that I did not agree with the idea of saying that the election was stolen and putting out this stuff, which I told the President was bullsh**" (House 2022, 378, 405).

Yet, in an effort to cling to power, Trump began to give speeches and send out messages on social media platforms, repeatedly referencing a "stolen election" and "fraud," with the goal of summoning supporters to Washington, DC. Claims of election fraud were concocted by Trump supporters even *before* people began casting their votes on Election Day in early November 2020. Advisor Steve Bannon commented in October 2019: "He's gonna declare victory. But that doesn't mean he's a winner. He's just gonna say he's a winner ... He's gonna declare himself winner. So, when you wake up Wednesday morning, it's going to be a firestorm .... Also, if Trump, if Trump is losing, by 10 or 11 o'clock at night, it's going to be even crazier. No, because he's gonna sit right there and say 'They stole it. I'm directing the Attorney General to shut down all ballot places in all 50 states' ... If Trump—if Biden's winning, Trump is going to do some crazy sh**" (House 2022, 10–11). Roger Stone, another Trump confidant, was even more blunt, also saying in advance of the election, "I really do suspect it will still be up in the air. When that happens, the key thing to do is to claim victory. Possession is nine-tenths of the law. No, we won. F*** you, Sorry. Over. We won. You're wrong. F*** you." Attorney General Barr commented that Trump had this attitude as well (House 2022, 199–201). Barr stated that "[r]ight out of the box on election night, the President claimed that there was major fraud underway. I mean, this happened, as far as I could tell, before there was actually any potential of looking at evidence" (House 2022, 9).

Initially, even though he was told repeatedly that he lost the election, Trump expressed confidence that he would prevail in litigation in front of judges that he appointed. Yet, in the days between November 6, 2020, and January 6, the Trump legal team filed a total of sixty-two separate lawsuits and lost every case except one (and that one case was of minor import). Per the House Report, "in no instance did a court find that the charges of fraud were real" (House 2022, 210). Many of the five dozen separate cases were presided over by Trump-appointed judges, including a federal district court judge who dismissed a lawsuit, calling it "void of plausible allegations" and "sorely wanting of relevant or reliable evidence" (House 2022, 211). In another judicial opinion written by a Trump appointee, the federal Third Circuit Court of Appeals dismissed Trump's claims, stating that "[c]alling an election unfair does not make it so. Charges require specific allegations and then proof. We have neither here" (House 2022, 212).

Despite losing these lawsuits and ignoring the fact that many of his own associates refuted his claims of fraud, Trump continued to publicly claim that he did not lose the election (House 2022, 1–127). In the weeks leading up to January 6, Trump also attempted to pressure Vice President Mike Pence to reject the certified votes presented in the Senate and to send them back to the states for further action, investigation, deliberation, or to hold another general election altogether. Pence refused and indicated "publicly that he told President Trump there was no basis that the election was stolen" (House 2022, 14). Pence also told a reporter that he told Trump directly "many times" that they lost the election (House 2022, 14). In the words of Bennie Thompson, Chair of the House Committee, when Trump's "scheme to stay in power through political pressure hit roadblocks, he relentlessly pushed ahead with a parallel plan: summoning a mob to gather in Washington, DC, on January 6th" (House 2022, x).

Through inflammatory social media messages, Trump called upon his followers to "Stop the Steal" and summoned tens of thousands of supporters to the Capitol on January 6. In one tweet, Trump wrote "election fraud 'more than sufficient' to swing victory to Trump. Big Protest in DC on January 6. Be there, will be wild!" (House 2022, 55–6). The House Committee compiled hundreds of statements from individuals who traveled to the Capitol (many armed with weapons) on January 6 because they believed the president was telling them it was their duty to be there, that the election was stolen, and that it was their duty to take the country back (House 2022, 3).

Because of the disinformation sent out by Trump and his supporters, many people were convinced that they were robbed of their rights as Americans and that the ideals of democracy were being attacked. Tens of thousands of individuals traveled to Washington, DC, to defend what they perceived as "democratic ideals" or "values" by attending a rally organized by Trump. Twenty-eight thousand rally-goers went through the metal detectors to attend Trump's speech on the Ellipse before marching to the Capitol (which was pre-planned by Trump and his aides); thousands more were not counted because they did not wish to go through the metal detectors, as many had handguns and weapons that they did not wish to surrender (House 2022, 640). While the majority of people in the large crowd were there to assemble and protest peacefully, extremist right-wing groups like the Oath Keepers, Proud Boys, and the Three-Percenters stockpiled weapons directly outside of DC in cars and hotel rooms in the event Trump called on them to intervene with force (House 2022, 515). Leader of the Oath Keepers, Stewart Rhodes, stated that the purpose of the actions on January 6 was to effectuate a "regime change."

According to an analysis by Ari Melber in a Foreword to a published copy of the House Committee January 6 investigative Report, the Trump White House plan at this point boiled down to three action items: "1. Revive the elector fraud plot [already debunked] on the Senate floor; 2. Compel Mike Pence to claim he had the authority to delay or override the certification [Pence already determined he lacked such authority and refused to delay the certification]; and 3. Deploy violence to delay or override the certification" (Melber 2022, XXIV). Plainly put, "the objective was to sabotage the certification in order to keep Trump in power" (Melber 2022, XXXVIII). In his speech, Trump implored the crowd to march to the Capitol and "fight like hell" for the country, promising to go there with them himself. The House Committee investigation revealed that Trump tried to get his Secret Service team to take him to the Capitol with the protestors, but the Secret Service refused and returned Trump to the White House. Some expressed concern that taking Trump to the Capitol would turn the event into a clear insurrection or rebellion against the Government, with Trump leading the mob.

After the president's speech, at least two thousand people, many of them carrying weapons, marched to the Capitol, broke through police barricades, and trespassed onto Capitol grounds, showing little regard for federal law enforcement. The violence quickly intensified, with "protestors" ignoring fenced off areas, climbing walls, smashing windows, and ignoring repeated police officer requests/orders to not enter the Capitol. Various protestors in the crowd assaulted Capitol police officers, threw trash and other objects, sprayed bear repellant and mace, thrust flag poles at police and attempted to stab them with flag staffs, and surged into the Capitol. Multiple police officers were injured in the melee. Eventually, the mob breached both the House and Senate chambers, at one point getting to within forty-to-fifty feet of Vice President Pence and his security detail. Representatives and Senators fled from the mob for their safety. Some hid under desks in darkened locked rooms and in closets; some later testified that they feared for their lives.

At 2:24 p.m., Trump sent out a tweet accusing Pence of cowardice saying "Mike Pence didn't have the courage to do what should have been done to protect our country and our constitution, giving States a chance to certify a corrected set of facts, not the fraudulent or inaccurate ones which they were asked to previously certify. USA demands the truth" (House 2022, 38). Immediately after this tweet, the mob got more violent, some chanting "Bring him out. Bring out Pence. Bring him out." and "Hang Mike Pence. Hang Mike Pence. Hang Mike Pence" (House 2022, 38). At this point, the vice president's Secret Service detail determined they could no longer protect Pence and moved him to a different secured location, missing the violent mob by forty feet (House 2022, 38–9).

One insurrectionist, Richard Barnett, brazenly put his feet up on the Speaker of the House Nancy Pelosi's desk, rifled through files, and left a lewd message on her desk. (Barnett was sentenced to four and half years in May 2023 for his actions on January 6.) Chants of violence and havoc toward Vice President Mike Pence and Speaker of the House Nancy Pelosi could be heard echoing through the halls and the exterior of the Capitol. When protesters heard that Vice President Pence was not going to follow Trump's illegal request, the chants of "Hang Mike Pence" grew louder. Someone erected gallows and a hangman's noose on the lawn outside the Capitol.

The litany of individual crimes committed by members of the mob on January 6 involved a virtual "violent crime spree of trespassing, assault, battery, battery with deadly weapons, threatened assassination, and other attacks to delay the certification, which they did," at least for a few hours (Melber 2022, XXIV). At least five people died on January 6 as a result of the attacks (including a Capitol Police officer). Another Capitol Police officer took his life a short time later, ostensibly because of the trauma he experienced on January 6.

While these actions were transpiring, President Trump rejected multiple pleas for help—from politicians of both parties. During part of the assault, Trump watched the events transpire on television while members of Congress feared for their lives and as grossly outnumbered Capitol police officers were beaten by the mob (House 2022, viii–xii). During the attack, President Trump refused to use his power to deploy the National Guard and other agencies to end the chaos on Capitol Hill, or even to tell "his people" to cease and desist and leave the Capitol until very late in the day. The National Guard was finally sent to the Capitol because the power to call the National Guard was delegated to the Department of Defense (DOD). The Committee did not find any evidence that the DOD intentionally delayed calling the National Guard but did find evidence of Trump refusing to make the call. The Committee noted in its report that it recognized that there were members of the DOD who had a genuine fear and concern over the attack and assumed that there was a possibility that President Trump might be tempted to give an illegal order to utilize the armed forces under the Insurrection Act to support his efforts in overturning the election (House 2022, 6–7).

Shortly after January 6, the House of Representatives pursued the impeachment of President Trump for inciting an insurrection on January 6. The Senate voted fifty-seven to forty-three in favor of convicting and removing Trump from office, falling short of the two-thirds majority needed to do so.

This led to the creation of the Select Committee to Investigate the January 6 attack on the United States Capitol, authorized in House Resolution 503, adopted by the 117th Congress. The duty of this committee was to investigate the facts, circumstances, and causes that led to the domestic terror attack on the Capitol. The bipartisan committee included Representatives Bennie Thompson, Adam Schiff, Zoe Lofgren, Stephanie Murphy, Pete Aguilar, Elaine Luria, Jamie Raskin, Adam Kinzinger, and Liz Cheney. The Committee finished its investigation and submitted its final report in December 2022. Excluding appendices, the Committee produced a 692-page final report that named President Trump as "the center of the first and only effort by any U.S. President to overturn an election and obstruct the peaceful transition of power" (House 2022, 128–30).

As of January 4, 2024, according to the Department of Justice, of the several thousand individuals who entered the Capitol, more than 1,265 individuals from all fifty states have been criminally charged. Of those charged, over 700 individuals pleaded guilty to a variety of federal crimes, while another 139 individuals have been found guilty after contested trials. As of January 2024, approximately 749 federal defendants have had their cases completely adjudicated—from indictment through the imposition of criminal punishments, with still more individuals being identified and prosecuted (Department of Justice 2024). Individuals have been charged with offenses ranging from criminal trespassing, to assaulting a federal officer, to seditious conspiracy. Of those charged to date, approximately 452 defendants have been charged with assaulting or impeding law enforcement. Prison sentences range from a few months to twenty-two years. About a dozen individuals (members of the Oath Keepers and Proud Boys) were indicted for seditious conspiracy, most of them found guilty after trials in 2022 and 2023. In May 2023, Stewart Rhodes, the leader of the Oath Keepers, was sentenced to eighteen years in prison for seditious conspiracy. In September 2023, Enrique Tarrio, the leader of the Proud Boys, was similarly sentenced in twenty-two years in prison for seditious conspiracy. Peter Schwartz, a man who attacked Capitol police with pepper spray and a chair, received a sentence of fourteen years and two months. Thomas Webster, a former police officer and United States Marine veteran, was sentenced to ten years for swinging a metal flagpole at law enforcement and tackling and yanking a gas mask off an officer. Two Florida members of the Oath Keepers (both medical doctors) who attended the events on January 6 and helped stockpile arms and ammunition were sentenced to three and three and a half years, respectively. Still other members of Rhodes's group received sentences ranging from four years to eight years and a half. With the exception of those convicted of seditious conspiracy, Guy Wesley Reffitt has received the longest sentence to date of those who did not enter the Capitol building itself. Reffitt brought a handgun and zip ties to the rally outside the Capitol and was found to have rifles and ammunition stockpiled in his car. Reffitt received a sentence of seven and a half years. Thomas Robertson, a former Virginia police officer and Army veteran, received a sentence of seven years and two months. Robertson used a wooden stick to block law enforcement and then destroyed evidence (his phone) after the event. Before destroying his phone, he posted on social media, saying "If you are too much of a coward to risk arrest, being fired, and actual gunfire to secure your rights, you have no words to speak I value" (Patel 2022).

As the House Committee investigation established, Donald Trump "first sent out the call to turn January 6 into a 'wild' gathering in D.C. Trump pushed, welcomed, and encouraged the attack on the Capitol. It was his plan. He did not take action to stop it as president, and he commended the attackers afterward. After leaving office, he vowed pardons for them," including some convicted of one of the more serious federal offenses, seditious conspiracy (Melber 2022, XXIX). As of the date of this publication, Trump still faces many potential legal problems, has been criminally indicted for ninety-one different criminal offenses, and has multiple criminal trials pending in 2024. One of these pending federal trials deals with Trump's criminal culpability for his role and/or participation in the events on January 6. Some have argued that Trump's pre-insurrection advocacy amounts to the criminal act of inciting, assisting, or aiding an insurrection, an offense under 18 United States Code Section 2383. This law applies to anyone who "incites, sets on foot, assists, or engages in any rebellion or insurrection." Other potential criminal offenses arguably committed by Trump include conspiring to defraud the United States (18 United States Code 371) and to obstruct the lawful function of government (Congress's certification of the presidency in a timely matter) as well as conspiracy to make a false statement (18 United States Code 371, 1001) in supporting others in submitting a false/fake slate of electors. Obstruction of an official proceeding, conspiring to defraud the United States, and engaging in conspiracy against rights are three of the major criminal offenses Trump is currently pending a criminal trial in federal district court in Washington, DC.

See Also: Assassination; Conspiracy, Criminal; Insurrection; Insurrection Act; Perjury, False Statements, and Obstruction of Justice; Rebellion; Sabotage; Sedition; Seditious Conspiracy; September 11, 2001

Resources

House of Representatives. 2022. *Final Report of the Select Committee to Investigate the January 6th Attack on the United States Capitol.* Washington, DC: Government Printing Office.

Melber, Ari. 2022. "Foreword on the Coup Conspiracy." In *Final Report of the Select Committee to Investigate the January 6th Attack on the United States Capitol*, V–XXXII. New York: Harper Publishing.

Patel, Vimal. 2022. "Ex-Police Officer Gets 7 Years in Prison for Role in Jan. 6 Attack." *The New York Times*, August 11, 2022. Accessed October 30, 2023. https://www.nytimes.com/2022/08/11/us/thomas-roberston-jan-6-sentenced.html.

Popli, Nik, and Julia Zorthian. 2023. "What Happened to the Jan. 6 Rioters Arrested since the Capitol Attack." *Time Magazine*, May 26, 2023. Accessed June 26, 2023. https://time.com/6133336/jan-6-capitol-riot-arrests-sentences/.

Carlisle v. United States (1872)

Carlisle v. United States was a United States Supreme Court case that addressed whether an alien resident/non citizen could commit treason against the United States and whether President Andrew Johnson's Proclamation 179 granting full amnesty and pardons for treason against the United States applied to alien residents. The Court held that an alien resident/non citizen could commit the offense of treason against the United States, but also that Proclamation 179 covered and applied to any alien residing in the United States during the American Civil War.

The litigants in *Carlisle* were citizens of Great Britain but resided in the United States before and during the Civil War. In 1861, the litigants began making saltpeter in a cave located outside of Scottsboro, Alabama. Saltpeter is an ingredient needed for gunpowder. During the Civil War, the litigants sold the saltpeter they created to the Confederate government. In 1864, Union forces in Alabama occupied the litigants' plantation and seized sixty-five bales of cotton, valued at $43,232 (the equivalent of over $1.5 million in 2023). In July 1868, Congress enacted legislation allowing aliens to pursue claims against the United States in the United States Court of Claims. On December 25, 1868, President Johnson issued Proclamation 179, which granted full pardons and amnesty for the offense of treason committed during the Civil War. The pardon and amnesty operated not only to release offenders from potential legal punishment for treason, but according to the Court, also "obliterates in legal contemplation the offence itself" and "relieve[s] them from the legal consequences of their participation in the rebellion."

The litigants then brought a claim against the United States for the value of the cotton seized by the Union Army during the Civil War. The United States Court of Claims denied the claim, holding that the confiscation of property was proper because the litigants had given aid and comfort to the Confederacy by providing it with saltpeter. This decision was appealed to the United States Supreme Court and the Supreme Court reversed the decision of the Court of Claims and directed the Court of Claims to enter a judgment in favor of the litigants for the amount claimed.

In a unanimous ruling in favor of the litigants, the Supreme Court held that an "alien, whilst domiciled in the country, owes a local and temporary allegiance, which continues during the period of his residence." As such, "[b]y furnishing materials for the prosecution of the war whilst they were domiciled in the country, knowing the uses to which the materials were to be applied, the claimants became participators in the treason of the Confederates equally as if they had been original conspirators with them." The Court further specified that any party "who, being bound by his allegiance to a government, sells goods to the agent of an armed combination to overthrow that government, knowing that the purchaser buys them for that treasonable purpose, is himself guilty of treason or a misprision thereof. He voluntarily aids the treason."

Despite the determination that the litigants had committed treason against the United States, the Court nevertheless held that the litigants were entitled to compensation for the seizure of their property as the pardon and amnesty also covered "claimants who were aliens domiciled in the country, within its provisions." The Court explained that Proclamation 179, "in its comprehensive terms, includes them and all others in like situation," and that the Proclamation not only granted "a full pardon and amnesty for the offence of treason against the United States," but also allowed for the "restoration of all rights, privileges, and immunities under the Constitution and the laws which have been made in pursuance thereof." Since Congress passed legislation authorizing aliens to pursue claims against the United States in its Court of Claims, the Court concluded that "[t]here is therefore, no impediment to the recovery by the claimants in this case of the net proceeds of their cotton paid into the treasury."

See Also: Aid and Comfort (Aid to Enemies of the State); American Civil War—Amnesty and Pardons; American Civil War and Treason; Rebellion; Treason

Resources

Carlisle v. United States, 83 U.S. 147 (1872).

Chin, Larry Wu-Tai (1922–86)

Larry Wu-Tai Chin was considered one of China's most valuable spies against the United States after the Second World War. Chin became the first American (he was a dual national) convicted of espionage for China when he was convicted of seventeen counts of espionage, conspiracy, and tax evasion, and faced the possibility of two life sentences. Chin was arrested in what has become known as the Year of the Spy. While awaiting sentence a few days after his trial, guards brought food to his cell, only to find Chin dead on the floor with a plastic garbage bag wrapped around his head. He apparently died of asphyxiation.

Larry Wu-Tai Chin had a quiet demeanor, which aided his ability to evade detection for over three decades. Chin began working for the federal government in 1944, first for the United States Army and then for the Central Intelligence Agency (CIA). Chin began spying for China in 1944, the same year he began working for the United States Army. In fact, because of his dual citizenship and his strong English-speaking skills, Chin was recruited by the Chinese communist government to obtain his first job with the US government. Thus, Chin was one of the longer-serving spies, spying for China against the United States from 1944 to 1986.

During the Korean War, Chin served as a translator for the Army. Chin's job was to interrogate captured Chinese soldiers who wished to defect to South Korea. During these interviews, Chin would mispresent the military intelligence elicited from these soldiers to the United States Army, thereby damaging future American military operations and tactic decisions in the region. Chin also provided Chinese authorities with the names of Chinese soldiers who provided intelligence to the Americans or expressed antipathy toward the Chinese communist regime. China demanded the return of these soldiers before China would agree to Armistice talks. The fate of these repatriated soldiers was often death at the hands of the Chinese Government. Chin also allegedly told the Chinese the location of prison camps where Chinese soldiers were being detained by the United States.

After the Korean War, Chin was accepted into the CIA as a Chinese language translator. Through his various postings (Okinawa, Japan in 1952–61; Santa Rosa, California from 1961 to 1971, and Rosslyn, Virginia from 1971 to 1981), Chin was tasked with translating intelligence reports originally written in Chinese, and in so doing, gleaned intelligence details about United States operatives working inside of China. Using Chin's information, China routinely arrested and executed the individuals Chin helped identify. The exact number of betrayed operatives remains unclear to this day. Chin's most damaging act of espionage was revealing to Mao Zedong Richard Nixon's plans and objectives for Nixon's historic trip to China. Armed with this information, Mao Zedong was able to prepare for US demands ahead of time and was able to maintain a strategic advantage during the Chinese-United States diplomatic talks.

It remains unclear exactly how much United States intelligence and/or assets were compromised during Chin's thirty-seven years of espionage. Amazingly, he was not flagged or identified once in his periodical national security clearance investigations over almost forty years. It was only when a high-ranking Chinese official (Yu Qiangsheng) defected to the United States that Chin was identified as a spy. It is unclear how many operatives lost their lives due to Chin's treachery. It is uncertain exactly how much Chin was compensated over the course of his thirty-seven years of espionage (believed to be over $1 million), but given the longevity of his espionage and Chin's increasingly opulent lifestyle (and penchant for gambling huge sums of money), it is believed that Chin was one of the highest-paid spies in American history, along with Aldrich Ames, Robert Hanssen, and John Walker.

See Also: Ames, Aldrich Hanzen "Rich"; Conspiracy, Criminal; Espionage; Hanssen, Robert Philip; Walker, John Anthony, Jr.; Year of the Spy (1985)

Resources

Hofman, Tod. 2008. *The Spy within: Larry Chin and China's Penetration of the CIA*. Hanover, NH: Steerforth Press.

Shannon, Don. 1986. "Chin Convicted as Spy for China: He Faces Possibility of Two Life Sentences." *Los Angeles Times*, February 8, 1986.

Christiana Revolt (1851)

The Christiana Revolt, sometimes referred to as the Battle of Christiana or the Christiana Riot, is a significant but largely forgotten event in the history of United States and resulted in an important federal decision on treason law. The Christiana Revolt was a violent confrontation between members of the Underground Railroad, fugitive slaves, slave catchers, and a deputized federal marshal. The incident took place on September 11, 1851, in the little village of Christiana, in Lancaster County, Pennsylvania. The incident and the resulting federal prosecution for treason are relevant for multiple reasons. First, the incident resulted in the indictment of thirty-eight men for treason against the United States, the largest number of individuals indicted for treason at the same time in the history of the United States (the Whiskey Rebellion resulted in the second largest number of indictments for treason). Second, of the thirty-eight men indicted for treason, thirty-four indicted individuals were African American—the only time in history that a single African American has been indicted for treason against the United States, let alone thirty-four. Third, the ensuing federal prosecution resulted in a vital federal decision helpful in interpreting the parameters of what constitutes treason against the United States and what constitutes "levying war" against the United States under the Treason Clause of the United States Constitution. Finally, the incident contributed to a widening divide between Northern and Southern States regarding the enforcement of the Fugitive Slave Act of 1850 and inched the nation closer to civil war. Ironically, the resulting legal case took place on the second floor of Independence Hall in Philadelphia, Pennsylvania, just above where the Revolutionary War-era revolutionaries struggled to forge independence from Great Britain. This irony was not lost on one African American newspaper at the time which complained that the case was being heard in the same building where the words "all men are created equal" had been adopted (Mires 2002, 94).

The Christina Revolt had its genesis in the attempted enforcement of the federal Fugitive Slave Act of 1850. The issue of slavery bedeviled the United States since its inception. On the first floor of Independence Hall in Philadelphia, delegates wrestled with how to appease Southern slaveholders to achieve the unanimity needed to form a new country. The Fugitive Slave Clause of the United States Constitution is an example of one such appeasement to the southern states. Article IV, Section II, of the United States Constitution specified that "no person held to service or Labour in one State, under the Laws thereof, escaping into another, shall, in Consequence of any Law or Regulation therein, be discharged from such Service or Labour, but shall be delivered up on Claim of the Party to whom such Service or Labour may be due." While the terms "slave" or "slavery" are not expressly mentioned, the absence of the terms was a euphemistic attempt to address the issue without express reference to the ugly and vile term slavery itself. Within four years after the ratification of the Constitution in 1789, Congress promulgated the Fugitive Slave Act of 1793 in the attempt to enforce this provision of the Constitution. The Act empowered federal and state judges to make orders effectuating the removal of fugitive slaves back to the location of their original enslavement. The federal law also allowed for the allocation of fines and fees against those individuals who attempted to help or harbor runaway fugitive slaves. Southern states decried this law as not being sufficiently rigorous and, indeed, many Northern states passed "personal liberty laws" requiring jury trials before a fugitive could be returned to the claimed location of enslavement, and some state personal liberty laws even prohibited state officials from enforcing the return of fugitives or prohibited the utilization of state resources such as jails and courtrooms to facilitate the re-enslavement of fugitives.

Edward Gorsuch was a slave owner and owned a farm in Maryland. The farm was located within a short walking distance from Milton Academy, where one of Gorsuch's sons was attending school with a young John Wilkes Booth. The Gorsuch farm (and Milton Academy) was about twenty-two miles due north of Baltimore, Maryland, and about fifteen miles south of the Maryland-Pennsylvania border. In 1849, Edward Gorsuch realized that four enslaved men who worked on the Gorsuch farm had absconded but had no information on the location of these men until 1851. In August 1851, Gorsuch learned that the escaped individuals were residing in Christiana, Pennsylvania. Shortly thereafter (at some point between late August 1851 and September 11), Gorsuch and several accomplices traveled to Christiana to recapture the men. However, the group realized that their presence had been discovered, and the Gorsuch party returned home to re-group. On September 11, and upon having previously secured warrants for arrest authorized by the Fugitive Slave Act of 1850, Gorsuch increased the size of his group with the addition of two Philadelphia police officers and Deputy United States Marshal Henry H. Kline. The group again attempted to capture the men in the early morning hours of September 11, 1851. The group was led to the house of a formerly enslaved individual named William Parker, who was a participant in the Underground Railroad and leader of the local self-protection society.

According to the recitation of facts published in the 1851 federal decision entitled *United States v. Hanway*, the details of the subsequent melee and confusion are clear. The group had again lost the element of surprise. The blowing of horns and trumpets occurred to alert neighboring friends and members of the self-protection society. By the time Gorsuch's group had reached the main house, a sizeable group of armed African Americans also began congregating on the property. The federal marshal led a group of men inside the house and chased several African Americans up a staircase. According to the facts recited in *United States v. Hanway*, the federal marshal "almost immediately ascertained that a large number [of individuals] were concealed in the upper part" of the house. The federal marshal claimed to have read the arrest warrants three times and then attempted to climb the staircase until "a sharp-pointed instrument was thrust at him, and an axe afterwards thrown down, which struck two of the party below." About this time, the various parties began exchanging gunfire at a steady pace. The firing did stop when occupants in the house asked for time to think over the situation, which was a ruse to buy time for more self-protection supporters to show up to repel the invaders. This trick worked and many additional individuals, including a local white neighbor named Castner Hanway, showed up.

The federal marshal attempted to get Hanway to assist with the situation, but the marshal testified that Hanway refused saying "it is none of your business" and the occupants "had rights and could defend themselves." However, other aspects of the marshal's testimony are questionable, as the court itself referred to the marshal as "this Kline, who was not a person of the best character for veracity." Indeed, Castner Hanway attempted to shield some of the white slavecatchers from violence while telling the slavecatcher to leave, but Hanway himself eventually fled the homestead when the occupants told him that he was risking his own life in trying to shield the Marylanders.

Gorsuch and some of his relatives tried to approach the house again without the marshal when Gorsuch was struck on the head with a club and then shot to death. Dickinson Gorsuch, one of Edward's sons, was also shot at close range with a shotgun. A nephew of Gorsuch tried firing his revolver twice at short range, but the weapon malfunctioned, at which time, he was also "struck down, beaten, and maltreated." Two others of Gorsuch's party were knocked down and one was shot in the wrist, side, and shoulder.

Gorsuch's attempt at re-enslaving the men went abysmally. Gorsuch was dead, and his son and several other men were seriously wounded. Additionally, all the escaped slaves had fled, including William Parker, the owner of the house and the organizer of the self-protection organization. Parker and two others fled to Canada. However, en route to Canada, and while passing through Rochester, New York, William Parker made it a point to stop to visit the famed former slave and famous abolitionist and orator Frederick Douglass and presented Gorsuch's own gun to Frederick Douglass as a gift.

To placate enraged Southerners, President Millard Fillmore instructed United States Attorney John Ashmead to proceed with treason charges against all those arrested at the Parker homestead. While thirty-eight men were indicted for treason, the prosecution made the strange decision to prosecute Castner Hanway first. Hanway had showed up at Parker's farm unarmed, did not fire a shot, or take any forceful action against any in Gorsuch's party, and even tried to protect members of Gorsuch's party from violence. As one expert has written, "he was an odd choice for the first trial ... but the prosecutors seemed to believe that the resistance of the African American community of Christiana to the Fugitive Slave Act must have been inspired by white agitators acting behind the scenes, and Hanway, the first white person to arrive on the scene and one of the few who arrived on horse, seemed a likely suspect" (Larson 2020, Chapter 6).

The trial of Castner Hanway has many intriguing and interesting details and is, of itself, a separate entry elsewhere in this book (see *Hanway, United States v.*). However, a few additional comments are relevant here. The trial of Castner Hanway began on November 24, 1851. It was a jury trial and presided over by two federal judges, United States Supreme Court Justice Robert Grier (hearing the case as part of his Circuit Justice duties) and United States District Court Judge John J. Kane. As Supreme Court Justice Grier admitted in his decision, "the whole country has been agitated by questions as to what in application is 'treason.'" The prosecution rested its whole case on the premise that forcibly resisting the Fugitive Slave Act with the intent of making it inoperable is tantamount to "levying war" against the United States. After witness testimony and evidence, Justice Grier issued his final charge to the jury and jury instructions on December 11, 1851. On the central issue of how to define treason, Justice Grier stated that "the better opinion there at present seems to be that the term 'levying war' should be confined to insurrections and rebellions for the purpose of overturning the government by force and arms." By this definition, Hanway's refusal to help Gorsuch and the federal marshal enforce the Fugitive Slave Act could not be treason. Considering this, the jury acquitted Hanway after only fifteen minutes of deliberation.

After the complete failure in prosecuting the Hanway case, the federal government dropped treason charges against the remaining thirty-seven defendants. While state authorities in Lancaster County looked to prosecute others for lesser offenses, the reality was that all the individuals who had engaged in violence had fled and there was no credible evidence tying crimes to remaining defendants still residing in the area. Hanway was acquitted and there is no record of other defendants subsequently charged or prosecuted on the state or federal level.

See Also: Booth, John Wilkes; *Hanway, United States v.* (1851); Insurrection; Levying War; Rebellion; Riot and Incitement to Riot; Treason; Whiskey Rebellion

Resources

Larson, Carlton F. W. 2020. *On Treason: A Citizen's Guide to the Law*. New York: Ecco, an imprint of HarperCollins (Kindle Edition).

Mires, Charlene. 2002. *Independence Hall in American Memory*. Philadelphia: University of Philadelphia Press.

Slaughter, Thomas P. 1991. *Bloody Dawn: The Christiana Riot and Racial Violence in the Antebellum North*. New York: Oxford University Press.

United States v. Hanway, 26 Fed. Cas. 105 (1851).

Civil Disobedience and Crimes against the State

The practice of civil disobedience of laws is based upon a belief that one should disavow or disobey laws or policies that are unjust, morally wrong, or in conflict with principles of higher law or natural law. In 1849, Henry David Thoreau penned his famous essay *On the Duty of Civil Disobedience*, wherein he argued that if the government pursued unjust actions, conscientious individuals were morally justified in refusing to pay their taxes or otherwise disobeying other unjust government dictates, even if the legal non-compliance meant incarceration. In fact, Thoreau viewed incarceration flowing from civil obedience favorably, stating that "the true place for a just man is … a prison." Henry David Thoreau notably protested the negative treatment of Native Americans, the practice of slavery, and the Mexican American War, by declining to pay taxes for six consecutive years. Thoreau violated taxation laws in a public way to bring attention to the above issues and with the hopes of persuading a majority in society to pursue a different path regarding these issues. Thoreau argued that if the law "requires you to be the agent of injustice to another, then, I say, break the law." Thoreau refused to pay his taxes to "quietly declare war with the State" and described his refusal as "the definition of a peaceful revolution, if any such is possible."

Though non-violence is a central tenet of civil disobedience today, Thoreau condoned the use of violence, at least as it related to the institution of slavery. Slavery was the monstrous injustice of Thoreau's age and he appeared to approve of violence at least as it related to the destruction of slavery. In the aftermath of John Brown's Raid, and in the weeks leading up to Brown's execution, Thoreau gave several speeches strongly in favor of John Brown and his actions. On October 30, 1859, less than two weeks after Brown's attack and capture, Thoreau addressed an audience in Concord, Massachusetts, with a speech titled "A Plea for Captain John Brown." In this speech, Thoreau praised Brown and his methods, going so far to compare John Brown to Jesus Christ: "Some eighteen hundred years ago Christ was crucified; this morning, perchance, Captain Brown was hung. These are the two ends of a chain which is not without its links. He is not Old Brown any longer; he is an angel of light." Thoreau extolled Brown's disobedience of laws in opposition to slavery, saying "he was a superior man. He did not value his bodily life in comparison with ideal things. He did not recognize unjust human laws, but resisted them as he was bid." Thoreau further praised Brown stating:

> No man in America has ever stood up so persistently and effectively for the dignity of human nature, knowing himself for a man, and the equal of any and all governments. In that sense he was the most American of us all. He needed no babbling lawyer, making false issues, to defend him. He was more than a match for all the judges that American voters, or office-holders of whatever grade, can create. He could not have been tried by a jury of his peers, because his peers did not exist.

Thoreau asked his audience in 1859:

> Is it not possible that an individual may be right and a government wrong? Are laws to be enforced simply because they were made? Or declared by any number of men to be good, if they are not good? Is there any necessity for a man's being a tool to perform a deed of which his better nature disapproves? Is it the intention of law-makers that good men shall be hung ever? Are judges to interpret the law according to the letter, and not the spirit? What right have you to enter into a compact

> with yourself that you will do thus or so, against the light within you? Is it for you to make up your mind,—to form any resolution whatever,—and not accept the convictions that are forced upon you, and which ever pass your understanding?

In the early 1900s, Mahatma Gandhi acknowledged the influence of Thoreau on his belief about not abiding an unjust law. However, Gandhi eschewed violence to protest an unjust law. In Gandhi's disciplined practice of civil disobedience and non-violence, he led a successful campaign to overthrow British colonial rule in India. Of note was the organization of thousands of individuals to walk 241 miles (now called the "Salt March") to highlight and change the British law that precluded non-English (i.e., indigenous Indians) from collecting or selling salt. The protesters endured the journey and engaged in civil disobedience despite much violence being exerted against them, including the beating of hundreds of non-violent protesters at a place known as the Dharasana Salt-Works.

Almost twenty-five years after Gandhi's famous 241-mile Salt March, Dr. Martin Luther King, Jr., found inspiration from both Thoreau and Gandhi, in his organization of his 381-day bus boycott in Montgomery, Alabama, in 1955–6. The boycotts resulted in threats of violence, arrests, gunfire, and bombs. In his famous *Letter from a Birmingham Jail*, Dr. King commented that "one has not only a legal but a moral responsibility to obey just laws. Conversely, one has a moral responsibility to disobey unjust laws." Furthermore, "one who breaks an unjust law must do so openly, lovingly, and with a willingness to accept the penalty" (King 1963). Thus, today, "Thoreau, Gandhi, and King are widely considered as the paragons of civil disobedience" (Delmas 2016, 682).

While civil disobedience can be traced to Thoreau's 1849 essay on the topic, modern philosophical formulations on civil disobedience took hold in the 1960s when a generation of scholars and philosophers grappled with exactly how civil disobedience should be defined, when or how it should be pursued, and what sort of actions fall outside the practice of civil disobedience. One modern seminal formulation of civil disobedience was set forth by American philosopher John Rawls. While not the only formulation of civil disobedience, Rawls's definition of civil disobedience as set forth in his seminal book *A Theory of Justice* is widely regarded as one of the most suitable definitions of civil disobedience. Rawls argued that civil obedience has five required elements: (1) the disobedience committed should be conscientious; (2) the disobedience should be public (i.e., not violations of the law committed in secret) with fair notice to authorities, akin to a public speech; (3) the disobedience is politically motivated; (4) the disobedience is non-violent in nature; and (5) the non-violent "breach of the law [is] undertaken in order to persuade the majority to change a law or policy in a nearly just, legitimate society" (Delmas 2016, 681). Ideally, "agents of disobedience are to appeal to the community's shared conception of justice in their pleas, and to demonstrate their overall 'fidelity to law' by accepting, or even seeking out, the legal consequences of their actions" (Delmas 2016, 681; Rawls 1999, 366). By accepting the consequences, actors are demonstrating that while they may have violated a law of some nature, it was done in adherence to greater dedication to the rule of law in society. It also avails the actor to the court system to challenge the legitimacy of the law and gives the actor a forum for expressing their views about the law in question. As Dr. King wrote in his *Letter from a Birmingham Jail*, "I submit that an individual who breaks a law that conscience tells him is unjust, and willingly accepts the penalty by staying in jail to arouse the conscience of the community over its injustice, is in reality expressing the very highest respect for the law" (King 1963).

Having a specific denotation of civil disobedience is important as "many historical and recent forms usually referred to as civil disobedience do not fit the standard philosophical definition of 'civil disobedience'" (Delmas 2016, 681). To the extent the actions are said to have met an agreed-upon definition, "the public typically sees civil disobedience as a morally legitimate form of dissent and civil resistance. Invoking images of Martin Luther King, Jr., Rosa Parks, or Mohandas Gandhi, civil disobedience has a long tradition and tends to trigger sympathetic responses in neutral audiences" (Marcou 2021, 493). Furthermore, "in order for civil disobedience to succeed, it must retain a sufficiently distinct moral status such that society as a whole respects its place in the political order. If civil disobedience loses its clarity, if the sharp edges demarking the firebreak deteriorate, civil disobedience fails in its role, loses its force, and erodes the rule of law" (Hall 2007, 2084). Evidence suggests that a true civil disobedient may enjoy more sympathy with law enforcement organizations and/or with their treatment in the judicial system (Marcou 2021, 493). Actions taken in civil disobedience and in good faith may operate as a *de facto* mitigating circumstance in the imposition of punishment by a court after trial.

The application of Rawls's elements is helpful in determining "good intentioned actors" versus "bad actors" as it relates to claims of civil disobedience. For instance, the first criterion requires that disobedience be motivated by concerns of a conscientious nature and principle, and that disobedience should not be utilized in the search for fame, fortune, or power. Rawls's second criterion that the disobedience or breach of the law be done in open and with notice to the government is meant to ensure that the chief motivation of the disobedience stems from a desire to stir the public debate and discourse surrounding a particular law or policy. For instance, Edward Snowden and Chelsey Manning have both claimed that their actions in violating the Espionage Act by leaking national defense information were actions of civil disobedience. Yet, Snowden and Manning would fail on this second element as their violations of law were completed under a cloak of secrecy and not in public and subject to public scrutiny, with accompanying personal responsibility. The Snowden and Manning leaks would also fail on the fifth criterion, a "fidelity to law," discussed later in this entry. The requirement of the act being public allows the public to witness the disobedience with the goal that witnessing the infraction and subsequent arrest and consequences will raise awareness and create dialogue over the underlying societal issue or law. Also, "fair notice" to government authorities similarly establishes the actor's good faith intent not to escape or allude arrest and/ or other legal consequences, but to make a political statement to advance political dialogue on a certain topic.

Rawls's third element that the legal infractions must be politically motivated relates to the underlying nature and essence of civil disobedience, namely that the breach of law is committed in order to engage in, or spark, or advance a political dialogue with the hope "to persuade the majority to change a law or policy in a nearly just, legitimate society" (Delmas 2016, 381). Furthermore, "civil disobedience does not challenge the legitimacy of the government. Instead, it constitutes protest to a particular law or policy" (Hall 2007, 2086).

The fourth and fifth elements of Rawls's formulation of civil disobedience are widely viewed as critical, namely that the disobedience be non-violent and that the actor committing disobedience be willing to accept the legal consequences of his or her action. According to Rawls, the act of violating the law should be non-violent as "to engage in violent acts likely to injure and to hurt is incompatible with civil disobedience as a mode of address" (Rawls 1999, 366). It is argued that "violence against human beings is always and in principle incompatible with persuasive action and as such can never qualify as civil disobedience. By attacking others, one is shutting them out of political deliberations and discussion" (Marcou 2021, 496). As Candance Delmas explains, violence defeats the very purpose for which disobedience is being conducted in the first place. That is, "to the extent that the goal of civil disobedience is to persuade the public, it must not involve any coercion. Rawls's requirement that the civil disobedience be nonviolent implies three intertwined claims: (a) violence coerces, nonviolence persuades; (b) civil disobedience only aims to persuade and as such excludes coercion, and (c) nonviolence is necessary to the communicativeness of civil disobedience" (Delmas 2016, 683). Thus, actors such as Denmark Vesey, Nat Turner, Ted Kaczynski (the Unabomber), and groups such as the Weather Underground (Weathermen) fail miserably under this criterion. Violent actions do not encourage more political discourse, they stifle it; and violence begets more violence and retribution, not a heightened civility in the hopes of spurring more political discourse in the public arena. There is also a strategic advantage to eschewing the use of force in protesting. Protestors who hold fast to non-violence are often met with a disproportional and violent show of force against them, as was seen in the bloody confrontation between police and civil rights protestors on the Edmund Pettus Bridge on March 7, 1965 (see Civil Rights and Crimes against the State). The optics of this force disparity was powerful and outraged many Americans who watched the events unfold on television broadcasts. For observers witnessing the confrontation, harsh disproportionate treatment of non-violent protestors by the government reinforces that the authorities are comfortable using excessive force to maintain power and an unjust system, while the non-violent protesters are favorably viewed as resisting violence and eager to improve the system of government (Marcou 2021, 495–6). It is widely believed that it is to the advantage of those engaged in civil disobedience to remain peaceful for optimal optics and public reactions.

While the use of force or violence is viewed as antithetical to the classical definition of civil obedience, there is debate about whether violence against property might be allowable in some circumstances. To the extent damage to property occurs, there is general agreement that the violence must be minimal and "bear some relationship to the unjust or policy" (Hall 2007, 2090). For instance, in *United States v. O'Brien*, the violence to property was burning a draft card in protest of the Vietnam War. The burning of the draft card related to the governmental policy being pursued (the war in Vietnam) and the government property destroyed was a draft identification card. Thus, the *O'Brien* case might serve as an example wherein minor damage to property would be acceptable. However, the bombing or sabotage of government facilities to protest a war would be widely viewed as unacceptable force even if only property was damaged.

After non-violence, Rawls's next most essential test of one engaged in civil disobedience (and fifth and final element) is whether the individual displays ultimate "fidelity to law … by the willingness to accept the legal consequences of one's act" (Rawls 1999, 366). As mentioned above, a convincing case where this element would not be met would be Snowden's surreptitious leak of classified documents. Snowden claimed he was engaged in civil disobedience when he leaked National Security Agency documents, but upon release of the classified materials to two newspapers (the *Guardian* and *Washington Post*), Snowden fled to Hong Kong and then to Russia and sought asylum in several Latin American countries. This behavior in circumventing legal proceedings against him illustrates a complete lack of accountability and fidelity to the law and must fall outside of the elements of civil disobedience. Strong examples of cases where the person engaged in disobedience while simultaneously evincing a "fidelity to law" and a willingness to accept legal consequences can be seen in the *Hirabayashi v. United States* (1943) and *Yasui v. United States* (1943) cases discussed below. Comparing the Hirabayashi and Yasui cases with *Korematsu v. United States* (1944) is instructive as to the fifth and final Rawls element, ultimate "fidelity to law."

The Second World War-era cases involving Gordon Hirabayashi, Minoru Yasui, and Fred Korematsu resulted from the curfews and mass evacuations of Japanese Americans from the west coast of the United States and into euphemistically named "relocation centers." These relocation centers were composed of wooden barracks with perimeters secured by barbed wire and armed guards. From Seattle to San Diego, over 110,000 individuals were ordered into these relocation centers for a three-year period simply based upon Japanese ancestry and that the individual resided within the "exclusion zone" on the West Coast (Irons 1999, 349).

Gordon Hirabayashi's family belonged to a pacifist sect that, among other things, rejected military service, and as such, Hirabayashi registered with his draft board as a conscientious objector (Irons 1999, 352). He was living in a YMCA dorm on the University of Washington campus at Seattle when the evening curfew was imposed on all Japanese Americans. Hirabayashi complied with the curfew for over a month, often scrambling at the last minute to get back to his dorm by curfew time. Hirabayashi later recalled his thought process and mindset, thinking to himself "Why the hell am I running back? Am I an American or not? Why am I running back and nobody else is?" (Irons 1999, 352). After about a month, as he recorded in his diary, "I received a lift—perhaps it is a release—when I consciously break the silly old curfew" (Irons 1999, 352). When evacuation orders started arriving, recipients had one week to dispose or store their possessions and report to a relocation center. Hirabayashi helped families pack up their belongings, writing in his journal, "Gosh!—something seems wrong there; helping people to go behind barbed wires and flimsy shacks. What a mixed-up life this is—the American way" (Irons 1999, 352). When Hirabayashi received his own evacuation orders, rather than flee or hide, he went to the Federal Bureau of Investigation (FBI) office in Seattle and declared that he was a "conscientious objector to internment" (Irons 1999, 352). He made a recorded statement saying that he was adhering to the will of God and his own convictions that the evacuation order was unjust. The FBI agent arrested Hirabayashi and placed him in jail pending his trial. After his trial and conviction, it was determined that Hirabayashi could not serve his sentence in Washington state because it was within the exclusion zone, but would rather have to serve it in Arizona. Washington state authorities also told Hirabayashi that they would not transport him to Arizona to begin his court ordered incarceration. So instead of disobeying the trial court's order, he walked and hitchhiked to jail, illustrating an incredibly high fidelity to the rule of law.

Minoru Yasui was born in Oregon and attended the University of Oregon, where he trained under the Army's Reserve Officer Training Program and was subsequently commissioned as an officer in the United States Army. Yasui then attended law school at the University of Oregon and gained employment working for the Japanese Consulate office in Chicago. After Pearl Harbor, and as a Second Lieutenant in the Army, Yasui traveled back to Oregon and received orders to report to Fort Vancouver outside of Portland. However, when Yasui attempted to report for duty in uniform, he was refused entry to the base. Yasui tried returning to base eight more times but was turned away each time because of his race. Then, before he even received his evacuation orders, Yasui resolved to challenge the order as an unconstitutional infringement of his rights as an American. Like Hirabayashi, Yasui went of his own volition to law enforcement in Portland. In fact, he walked up and down the street in Portland after the curfew (8 p.m.) and attempted to get arrested. When no police officer would respond, Yasui later recalled that he had to walk up to a police officer and insist that he be arrested, saying "I pulled out this order that said all persons of Japanese ancestry must be in their place of abode, and I pulled out my birth certificate and said, 'Look, I'm a person of Japanese ancestry, arrest me'" (Irons 1999, 353). Even then, the police officer refused, telling Yasui to "run along home, you'll get in trouble" (Irons 1999, 353). Yasui had to then go to police headquarters and insist repeatedly to a desk sergeant on duty to arrest him. Finally, Yasui was arrested; he was placed in solitary confinement for nine months pending his trial.

Fred Korematsu was born in California and after high school attended welding school in Oakland, California, and then worked as a welder at a local shipyard. Six months before Pearl Harbor, Korematsu attempted to join the Navy, but was turned away for health reasons. When Korematsu's evacuation order arrived, he did not go to law enforcement as Hirabayashi and Yasui did. When his family left for a relocation center, Korematsu stayed behind in Oakland because he hoped to make enough money to move to the Midwest with his girlfriend. According to a statement made by Korematsu after his arrest, he had cosmetic surgery to alter the appearance of his eyes and nose in an attempt to look less Japanese, so he "would not be subjected to ostracism when my girl and I went East" (Irons 1999, 354). He also crudely altered his draft card with a pen and when police officers arrested Korematsu while he was walking down the street, he claimed to be a person named Clyde Sarah, and of Spanish-Hawaiian ancestry (Irons 1999, 353). At the police station, he confessed that he was not Clyde Sarah, and gave his real name at that point, as "one of the girls who worked in the office seemed to recognize me" (Irons 1999, 353).

Hirabayashi, Yasui, and Korematsu were all prosecuted and convicted, and the United States Supreme Court upheld all three convictions in *Hirabayashi v. United States*, *Yasui v. United States*, and *Korematsu v. United States*, respectively. The Supreme Court's rationale for its decision in each of the three cases is discussed elsewhere in this volume, but some basic facts of the cases are recited here to illustrate civil disobedience. All three of the defendants conscientiously disagreed with the exclusion curfew and orders, and none of the three engaged in any violent activity. However, of the three defendants, Korematsu is the weakest example of civil disobedience because his actions (cosmetic surgery and an altered document) suggest he was trying to evade the law rather than breach the law to contest and protest it. In contrast, Gordon Hirabayashi and Minori Yasui engaged in principled and public civil disobedience by openly breaching the registration and internment order (Hirabayashi) and curfew order (Hirabayashi and Yasui). Both Yasui and Hirabayashi intentionally and openly violated curfew, and both went to law enforcement of their own volition, and in Yasui's case, insisted repeatedly on being arrested. Not only did Hirabayashi and Yasui openly breach the law, but both also willingly accepted the legal consequences for the law they protested.

Civil disobedience is not a traditional "crime against the state." The underlying crimes of civil disobedience—often offenses like trespassing, disobeying curfews, violating public demonstration regulations, burning draft cards, or failure to pay taxes—are not direct attacks against the government like treason, insurrection, rebellion, espionage, and sedition. And yet, civil disobedience is intended to change government policy through criminal action. In a sense, unlike traditional crimes against the state, in civil disobedience, government *policy* is the intended victim, not the government itself.

See Also: Brown, John; Civil Rights and Crimes against the State; Espionage; Espionage Act of 1917 and Sedition Act of 1918; *Hirabayashi v. United States* (1943); Insurrection; John Brown's Raid (1859); Kaczynski, Theodore ("Unabomber"); *Korematsu v. United States* (1944); Leaks of National Defense Information; *O'Brien, United States v.* (1968); Rebellion; Sabotage; Sedition; Treason; Turner, Nat; Vesey's Rebellion (1822); Weather Underground

Resources

Delmas, Candice. 2016. "Civil Disobedience." *Philosophy Compass* 11: 681–91.

Department of Justice, United States Attorney's Office District of Columbia. "Three Years since the Jan. 6 Attack on the Capitol." Accessed February 21, 2024. https://www.justice.gov/usao-dc/36-months-jan-6-attack-capitol-0#:~:text=Sentencings%3A ,sentenced%20to%20periods%20of%20incarceration.

Hall, Matthew R. 2007. "Guilty but Civilly Disobedient: Reconciling Civil Disobedience and the Rule of Law." *Cardozo Law Review* 28: 2083–130.

Irons, Peter. 1999. *A People's History of the Supreme Court*. New York: Viking.

King, Martin Luther, Jr. 1963. "Letter from a Birmingham Jail." African-American Studies Center, University of Pennsylvania. Accessed November 19, 2023. https://www.africa.upenn.edu/Articles_Gen/Letter_Birmingham.html.

Marcou, Andreas. 2021. "Violence, Communication, and Civil Disobedience." *Jurisprudence: An International Journal of Legal and Political Thought* 12, no. 4: 491–511.

Rawls, John. 1999. *A Theory of Justice*. Second edition. Cambridge, MA: Harvard University Press.

Thoreau, Henry David. 1859. "A Plea for Captain John Brown." Yale Law School, The Avalon Project: Documents in Law, History, and Diplomacy. Accessed April 22, 2023. https://avalon.law.yale.edu/19th_century/thoreau_001.asp.

Thoreau, Henry David. 1903 [orig. 1849]. *On the Duty of Civil Disobedience*. London: The Simple Life Press.

Civil Rights Movement and Crimes against the State

The modern civil rights era refers to the political, legal, and protest movement that took place in the 1950s and the 1960s to achieve equal treatment of minority groups in the United States, particularly in the attempt to improve the plight of African Americans. The principal organizations attempting to achieve equality during this period were the National Association of Colored People (NAACP), the National Urban League, and the Southern Christian Leadership Conference. These groups engaged in non-violent activities and civil disobedience to protest racist segregationist law (e.g., the requirement that Blacks sit at the back of public transportation buses or to use significantly inferior facilities so-called "separate but equal" accommodations). To the extent members of these civil rights groups violated laws, these were not crimes against the state, and the laws violated were almost exclusively state segregation laws that treated Blacks and other minorities as second-class citizens. The goal of the non-violence in violation of these segregationist "Jim Crow" laws was not to harm or destroy the state but to achieve a more egalitarian society. For example, organized "sit-ins" were conducted in multiple locations, where white and Black protestors sat at lunch counters in violation of segregation of "Jim Crow" laws. Freedom Riders rode buses to protect segregation in interstate travel. As Dr. Martin Luther King, Jr., remarked in his famous *I Have a Dream Speech*, the goal was not to target the American way of life, it was a goal and "a dream deeply rooted in the American dream. I have a dream that one day this nation will rise up and live out the true meaning of its creed: We hold these truths to be self-evident, that all men are created equal." The civil right leaders worked assiduously to achieve some semblance of equality, put an end to segregated facilities, stop extrajudicial killings (lynchings), and advocate for fair rights in employment, housing, and the right to vote.

Given the non-violent methods adopted by mainstream civil rights groups, and the abuse heaped upon them by white supremacists, and with local enforcement often standing by and watching violence unfold, the civil rights movement might be said to be a more apt example of crimes committed *by a state*, instead of crimes committed against the state. The litany of abuses, many with the awareness or participation of local governments, are tragically far too numerous to delineate here. In 1961, civil rights activist James Farmer organized freedom riders in two buses to travel into the south to protest segregation laws. The protesters were attacked in both Rock Hill, South Carolina, and Anniston, Alabama, and jailed, simply for violating state segregation laws. The attackers were not jailed. In Birmingham, Alabama, in televised footage that would shock the nation, police under the notorious police chief Eugene "Bull" Connor harassed and attacked non-violent and unarmed protestors with dogs, knocked scores of protestors down with high-velocity water shot from fire hoses, and beat others with batons and "night sticks." Nine hundred *children* were arrested and brought to jail in their school buses for defying local segregation laws. Protests attempting to march across Edmund Pettis bridge were viciously attacked. Black leaders were murdered, and houses were firebombed without legal repercussions for the offenders. In 1963, NAACP leader Medgar Evers was shot and murdered on his front doorstep, and his killer would not be prosecuted and convicted until February 5, 1994, thirty-one years later. Thus, local law enforcement, through either neglect of duty or active participation, and likely both, were the perpetrators, and not the victims, of crime. Despite this violence, the mainstream civil rights movement amazingly maintained its composure and commitment to non-violent civil disobedience to racist laws and violent police tactics. Dr. Martin Luther King, Jr., was awarded the Nobel Peace Prize in 1964 for leading such a peaceful, non-violent protest and demonstration in the face of such ugly, violent, and disgusting opposition.

Despite the overwhelming actions of non-violence, several splinter groups did emerge in the 1960s who became disenchanted with Dr. King's practice of non-violence and advocated using force to defend themselves. Some of these groups included Elijah Muhammad's Black Muslims, Malcom X's splinter Black Muslims/Black Power movement, and the Black Panther Party (BPP). Many members claimed that they needed to be armed to protect themselves against white terrorist groups like the Ku Klux Klan (KKK). The BPP was a perfect illustration of this goal, which was even reflected in its original name, the "Black Panther Party for Self-Defense." And while these splinter groups did embrace the use of force, the force was not directed at the government per se, but against racist individuals in society or terrorist organizations like the KKK. The Black Panthers established patrols in minority neighborhoods to protect residents and to serve as a counterbalance to acts of police brutality by racist police officers. The Black Panthers had a ten-point platform, and there is no reference in the platform to making the US government or its officials targets of crime or violence, or to attempt regime change or the overthrowing of the United States (unlike some participants in the January 6 Capitol Insurrection). The ten-point platform included the following goals of the group:

> 1) We want freedom. We want power to determine the destiny of our Black Community; 2) We want full employment for our people; 3) We want an end to the robbery by the Capitalists of our Black Community; 4) We want decent housing, fit for shelter of human beings; 5) We want education for our people that exposes the true nature of this decadent American society. We want education that teaches us our true history and our role in the present day society; 6) We want all Black men to be exempt from military service; 7) We want an immediate end to POLICE BRUTALITY and MURDER of Black people; 8) We want freedom for all Black men held in federal, state, county and city prisons and jails; 9) We want all Black people when brought to trial to be tried in court by a jury of their peer group or people from their Black Communities, as defined by the Constitution of the United States; and 10) We want land, bread, housing, education, clothing, justice and peace. (National Archives 2023)

Because these splinter groups openly carried and displayed weapons and vowed to engage to armed self-defense against police, when necessary, the Black Panthers, Malcolm X, and others were targeted by federal and state law enforcement groups. As such, many Americans tended to associate these groups with other domestic terrorist organizations like the Weather Underground. Yet, such comparisons miss the mark. Unlike the Weather Underground, the BPP did not advocate the overthrow of the United States as its principal goal. Rather, the BPP "promoted the development of strong, black-controlled institutions, calling for blacks to work together to protect their rights and to improve their economic and social conditions" (Appiah and Gates 1999, 260). In later years, the BPP welcomed alliance with white activists, such as the Students for a Democratic Society (SDS) and later the Weather Underground. In the later years of the BPP, the organization did grow more violent, in response to police violence against the group. Two leaders of the BPP (Fred Hampton and Mark Clark) were killed in a police raid in 1969. By 1970, an estimated twenty-five BPP members had been killed since its founding in the mid-1960s, and many others BPP members were imprisoned or forced to leave the United States. It is against this backdrop of battling what the BPP believed to be racist and/or corrupt police officers for over a decade, that BPP's later acts of violence against police must be considered.

See Also: Capitol Insurrection on January 6, 2021; Civil Disobedience and Crimes against the State; Weather Underground

Resources

Appiah, Kwame Anthony, and Henry Louis Gates, Jr. 1999. *Africana: The Encyclopedia of the African American Experience*. New York: Basic Civitas Books.

National Archives. 2023. "African American Heritage: The Black Panther Party." Accessed June 5, 2023. https://www.archives.gov/research/african-americans/black-power/black-panthers#bpintro.

Njemanze, Paul Obiyo Mbanaso. 2004. "Civil Rights Movement." In *Affirmative Action, an Encyclopedia*, edited by James Beckman, vol 1: 190–5. Westport, CT: Greenwood Press.

Clear and Present Danger Test

First announced and applied by Justice Oliver Wendell Holmes, Jr., in *Schenck v. United States* (1919), the clear and present danger test was the governing approach for evaluating the criminalization of "subversive speech" for nearly half of the 1900s. "The question in every case," wrote Justice Holmes, "is whether the words used are used in such circumstances and are of such a nature as to create a clear and present danger that they will bring about the substantive evils that Congress has a right to prevent." In many cases, the clear and present danger test was used to conclude that speech against the government was not protected by the First Amendment. Indeed, as applied, the test allowed more government restrictions on speech than the later "imminent incitement" standard, thereby permitting an entire category of "speech crimes" against the state.

In *Schenck* the Supreme Court used the clear and present danger test to uphold the constitutionality of the Espionage Act of 1917, which criminalized interference with military operations and recruitment, promotion of insubordination in the military, and supporting enemies during wartime. The Court elaborated that, when at war, "many things that might be said in time of peace are of such hindrance to [a nation's war] effort that their utterance will not be endured so long as men fight and ... no Court could regard them as protected by any constitutional right." But the Court did not expand on what would constitute a clear and present danger, other than stating that "[i]t is a question of proximity and degree."

The same term it decided *Schenck*, a unanimous Supreme Court decided *Frohwerk v. United States* (1919), again upholding a conviction under the Espionage Act of 1917. This time, the accused had circulated articles in a newspaper that were critical of the United States' involvement in the First World War. The Court then added to what it had said in *Schenck* that: "the First Amendment while prohibiting legislation against free speech as such cannot have been, and obviously was not, intended to give immunity for every possible use of language." Curiously, in writing the opinion in *Frohwerk*, Justice Holmes did not explicitly apply the clear and present danger test he had announced in *Schenck*.

In another case decided the same day as *Frohwerk*—*Debs v. United States* (1919)—the Supreme Court relied on *Schenck* to uphold yet another conviction under the Espionage Act of 1917, though it again failed to explicitly state or apply the clear and present danger test, choosing instead to simply cite *Schenck*. Eugene V. Debs—a prominent figure in both the labor and the Socialist movements in the United States—had been convicted of violating the Espionage Act of 1917 for twice delivering a speech advocating "socialism, its growth, and a prophecy of its ultimate success." But Debs was apparently not arrested for the pro-socialism theme of the speech. Rather he was alleged to have "caused and incited and attempted to cause and incite insubordination, disloyalty, mutiny and refusal of duty in the military and naval forces of the United States." Among his remarks cited in support of the charge was "I might not be able to say all that I think, but you need to know that you are fit for something better than slavery and common fodder."

Debs again reflected the initial unanimity of the Supreme Court in cases that concerned the Espionage Act and free speech. But the Court's unanimity would soon evaporate, as the clear and present danger test was at least applied differently—or, as some would argue, modified or abandoned altogether—in some subsequent cases dealing with prosecutions for what the government charged was seditious behavior, as some Justices found the clear and present danger test inappropriately applied. Among these cases were *Abrams v. United States* (1919), *Schaefer v. United States* (1920), *Gitlow v. New York* (1925), and *Whitney v. California* (1927). In these cases, the Court applied what has been labeled by some as the "bad tendency test," which some view as a variation on the clear and present danger test, and others, including Justice Holmes, viewed as a complete misapplication of the latter test. The bad tendency test considered whether the "natural and probable tendency and effect of the words … are such as are calculated to produce the result condemned by the statute." Under such a standard, even expressions of a preference for peace could be criminalized if the "natural tendency" of such words was to hinder conscription or the war effort. To those objecting to this approach—notably including the original creator of the clear and present danger test, Justice Oliver Wendell Holmes—the bad tendency test tended to allow restrictions on speech that did not approach constituting a "present danger."

In *Abrams v. United States* (1919), a seven to two majority of the Supreme Court again upheld convictions under the Espionage Act. The Court cited *Schenck* and *Frohwerk* to quickly dismiss the claim that the First Amendment protected communications expressed in leaflets for which the leafleteers had been convicted, without explicitly applying the clear and present danger test.

The *Abrams* dissenters—Justices Holmes, who had written the majority opinion in *Schenck*, and Justice Brandeis, who would later author one of the most impassioned opinions regarding free speech ever produced by a Supreme Court Justice in *Whitney v. California*—viewed the criminalization of speech in this case as exceeding the parameters of *Schenck*. Justice Holmes reiterated that the clear and present danger he had articulated in *Schenck* was the correct test and claimed the *Abrams* majority had incorrectly abandoned the approach. To the dissenters, the speech "in no way attack[ed] the form of government of the United States" even if the leaflets "d[id] urge curtailment of production of things necessary to the prosecution of the war." Justice Holmes continued that "only the present danger of immediate evil or an intent to bring it about" would justify congressional regulation—and punishment—of speech. In so doing, Holmes reiterated the clear and present danger test by emphasizing the concept of the immediacy of the danger. The dissent concluded with this caution: "[W]e should be eternally vigilant against attempts to check the expression of opinions we loathe and believe to be fraught with death, unless they so imminently threaten immediate interference with the lawful and pressing purposes of the law that an immediate check is required to save the country."

A year after *Abrams*, the Supreme Court again affirmed convictions under the Espionage Act in *Schaefer v. United States* (1920). Here, the convictions dealt with distorted statements of Wisconsin Senator Robert La Follette's speech: two Philadelphia-based German newspapers (the Philadelphia Tageblatt and the Philadelphia Sonntagsblatt) had produced "false reports and statements of certain news items or dispatches purporting to be from foreign places." Again, the Court dismissed the First Amendment claims under the theory that during wartime, restraints on speech are permissible under the Espionage Act, again using the justification that the statements would obstruct the war effort. Justices Brandeis and Holmes again differed from the majority, arguing: "[The clear and present danger test] is a rule of reason. Correctly applied, it will preserve the right of free speech both from suppression by tyrannous, well-meaning majorities and from abuse by irresponsible, fanatical minorities." To them, the majority had again misapplied the clear and present danger standard and instead "threaten[ed] freedom of thought and of belief." Justices Brandeis and Holmes also noted that "[t]he constitutional right of free speech has been declared to be the same in peace and in war," a view seemingly contrary to that which Holmes himself had expressed in *Schenck*.

In *Gitlow v. New York* (1925), members of the Socialist Party were charged with "criminal anarchy" under New York state law for advocating that an "organized government should be overthrown by force or violence, or by assessination [*sic*] of the executive head or of any of the executive officials of government, or by any unlawful means." The publication, The Left-Wing Manifesto, called for the Socialist Party to follow a more vigorous agenda "through mass industrial revolts developing into mass political strikes." The majority clearly stated that the "bad tendency test" was the appropriate test for laws that made a certain type of speech a crime—in this case criminal anarchy, defined as advocating that the government be overthrown by force or violence. The majority explained that the clear and present danger test applied only "where the statute merely prohibits certain acts involving the danger of substantive evil, without any reference to language itself, and it is sought to apply its provisions to language used by the defendant for the purpose of bringing about the prohibited results." Applying the "bad tendency test," the majority held the "very utterance [of anarchy] endangered the public." Again, Justices Holmes and Brandeis dissented, and Holmes again argued that his clear and present danger test was being misapplied: "If what I think the correct test is applied, it is manifest that there was no present danger of an attempt to overthrow the government by force on the part of the admittedly small minority who shared the defendant's views."

In *Dennis v. United States* (1951), the defendants were convicted of violating provisions of the Smith Act related to overthrowing of the US government. Those charged were members of the Communist Party who claimed they merely wished to educate their membership about aspects relating to governmental overthrow. The Court observed that overthrow of the Government by force and violence is "certainly a substantial enough interest for the Government to limit speech," arguing that "if a society cannot protect its very structure from armed internal attack, it must follow that no subordinate value can be protected." The Court further explained "the literal problem which is presented is what has been meant by the use of the phrase 'clear and present danger' of the utterances bringing about the evil within the power of Congress to punish." The Court said that "the words cannot mean that before the Government may act, it must wait until the [effort to overthrow the government] is about to be executed, the plans have been laid and the signal is awaited." Simply put, the government did not have to wait to be in real peril of overthrow when the mere threat of it was sufficient to sustain the convictions. The Court affirmed the convictions, but in doing so offered a somewhat refashioned clear and present danger test, borrowing language from an opinion by Judge Learned Hand: "In each case [courts] must ask whether the gravity of the 'evil,' discounted by its improbability, justifies such invasion of free speech as is necessary to avoid the danger."

The Court would clearly leave behind the clear and present danger test and bad tendency test in *Brandenburg v. Ohio* (1969). In *Brandenburg*, the Court differentiated "the mere abstract teaching" of the moral imperative to use violence and the provocation of actual violence. This case concerned a speech by Clarence Brandenburg, a member of the Ku Klux Klan of Ohio. Brandenburg made remarks disparaging racial minorities and called on the audience to march on Congress and then to St. Augustine, Florida, and Mississippi. He was charged and convicted under Ohio's Criminal Syndicalism law for "advocat[ing] … the duty, necessity, or propriety of crime, sabotage, or unlawful methods of terrorism as a means of accomplishing industrial or political reform" and for "voluntarily assembl[ing] with any society, group, or assemblage of persons formed to teach or advocate the doctrines of syndicalism." The Court ruled "that the constitutional guarantees of free speech and free press" precluded a State from regulating the type of speech Brandenburg made unless it was "directed to inciting or producing imminent lawless action and is likely to incite or produce such action." The Court elaborated: "the mere abstract teaching … of the moral propriety or even moral necessity for a resort to force and violence, is not the same as preparing a group for violent action and steeling it to such action." If a law did not draw lines between the two, it "intrude[d] upon the freedoms guaranteed by the First and Fourteenth Amendments."

In *Brandenburg*, the Supreme Court introduced a new standard for evaluating speech critical of the government or alleged to incite illegal activity, abandoning the clear and present danger test that had been the foundation of many prosecutions for speech crimes against the state.

See Also: *Abrams v. United States* (1919); Assassination; *Brandenburg v. Ohio* (1969); Criminal Syndicalism; *Debs v. United States* (1919); *Dennis v. United States* (1951); Espionage Act of 1917 and Sedition Act of 1918; *Gitlow v. New York* (1925); *Schenck v. United States* (1919); Smith Act; Speech as Crime against the State; *Whitney v. California* (1927)

Resources

Abrams v. United States, 250 U.S. 616 (1919).
Brandenburg v. Ohio, 395 U.S. 444 (1969).
Debs v. United States, 249 U.S. 211 (1919).
Dennis v. United States, 341 U.S. 494 (1951).
Frohwerk v. United States, 249 U.S. 204 (1919).
Gibson, Tobias T. "Bad Tendency Test." *The First Amendment Encyclopedia.* Accessed June 26, 2023. https://www.mtsu.edu/first-amendment/article/893/bad-tendency-test#.
McGoldrick, James Mearl, Jr. 2021. "'This Wearisome Analysis': The Clear and Present Danger Test from *Schenck* to *Brandenburg*." *South Dakota Law Review* 66: 56.
Schenck v. United States, 249 U.S. 47 (1919).

Colfax Massacre (1873)

After the bitterly contested election of 1872 between rival candidates for Louisiana governor, the Colfax Massacre was one in a series of violent confrontations in Louisiana that culminated in the "Battle of Liberty Place." These violent efforts were not limited to Louisiana. Other examples of overcoming electoral deficits through direct violence include the Eufaula Election Massacre and Spring Hill Insurrection (1874) and the Wilmington Insurrection of 1898. These tactics by White supremacists were a primary mechanism through which the Democratic Party, significantly outnumbered throughout much of the American South by Republicans supported by newly enfranchised Black voters, retook control of state and local governments, enabling decades of Jim Crow laws throughout the South.

In the 1872 Louisiana gubernatorial election, the Republican candidate, William Pitt Kellogg, and the Democratic candidate, John McEnery, both claimed to have won. Both candidates held inaugurations and appointed subordinate state officeholders. Kellogg appointed a slate of Republican officials in Grant Parish who took office in the small courthouse there. A coalition of White Democrats and "liberal Republicans" who opposed the federal government's Reconstruction efforts in the South decided to arm themselves and retake the courthouse from the Republican officeholders, who enlisted the assistance of dozens of recently freed Black Republicans to defend the courthouse.

McEnery had appointed Christopher Columbus Nash as Sheriff of Grant Parish. Nash, a confederate veteran, assembled a white paramilitary group from nearby parishes. On Easter Sunday, April 13, 1873, Nash and his 300 men surrounded the courthouse and ordered the defenders of the Republicans and the courthouse to leave. When they did not, Nash's men opened fire with various firearms including a cannon aimed at the courthouse. As men fled the courthouse under a white flag of surrender, they were brutally massacred. Roughly sixty Republican defenders ran and jumped into a nearby river, where Nash's men killed most of them. Nash then ordered the courthouse roof to be set on fire. Though the defenders surrendered, Nash's men killed unarmed men who were hiding and chased down and killed those attempting to flee on horseback.

The number of men killed is disputed, but a report by federal military personnel who were sent to Grant Parish in the aftermath of the massacre to locate the white paramilitary members identified at least 105 Black men had been killed. A Black Louisiana legislator set the figure at 280. Many had been shot in the back of the head or neck, substantiating claims that Nash's men had executed fleeing and already-captured men.

Attempts by federal prosecutors to bring Nash's men to justice were unsuccessful. In one trial, nine men were either acquitted or a mistrial was declared. In another trial, three men were convicted of multiple charges, but the presiding judge, United States Supreme Court Justice Joseph Bradley who was "riding circuit," dismissed the convictions. The United States appealed, and the United States Supreme Court ultimately decided the case as *United States v. Cruikshank* (1875). The Supreme Court, by then dominated by a majority surprisingly hostile to federal attempts to enforce civil rights for Blacks in the South, ruled that the Enforcement Act of 1870, upon which prosecutions had been based, only addressed actions by the state, and not those of individuals or private groups. Bradley's dismissal of the convictions was upheld.

Nash's "success" in the Colfax Massacre and subsequent legal impunity due to the *Cruikshank* decision emboldened white paramilitary organizations. Nash soon formed the first chapter of the White League, which became the military arm of the Democratic Party in Louisiana. The White League subsequently used violence and intimidation to take control of rural Louisiana political and government positions, and ultimately fought against law enforcement in the Battle of Liberty Place.

The Colfax Massacre, called the Colfax Riot among supporters of Nash and his followers, was celebrated by some, with an official state highway marker that stood for seventy years reading "On this site occurred the Colfax Riot, in which three white men and 150 negroes were slain. This event on April 13, 1873, marked the end of carpetbag misrule in the South."

See Also: Battle of Liberty Place (1874); *Cruikshank, United States v.* (1876); Enforcement Acts (1870–71); Eufaula Election Massacre and Spring Hill Riot (1874); Insurrection; Wilmington Insurrection of 1898

Resources

Foner, Eric. 2014. *Reconstruction: America's Unfinished Revolution, 1863–1877*. New York: Harper Perennial.

Keith, LeeAnna. 2009. *The Colfax Massacre: The Untold Story of Black Power, White Terror, and the Death of Reconstruction*. Oxford: Oxford University Press.

Lewis, Danny. 2016. "The 1873 Colfax Massacre Set Back the Reconstruction Era." *Smithsonian Magazine*, April 13, 2016.

Rubin, Richard. 2003. "The Colfax Riot." *The Atlantic Monthly*, July–August, 2003.

Velez, Denise Oliver. 2020. "The Easter Massacre of 1873—And the Subsequent Supreme Court Decision That Sabotaged Reconstruction." *Daily Kos*, April 12, 2020.

Communist Control Act (1954)

The Communist Control Act of 1954 (CCA) purported to outlaw the Communist Party of the United States (Communist Party). The CCA, passed as part of the post-Second World War anticommunist hysteria known as the Red Scare, declared that "The Communist Party of the United States, though purportedly a political party, is in fact an instrumentality of a conspiracy to overthrow the Government of the United States" and "*should* be outlawed" (emphasis added). Though the Internal Security Act of 1950 had attempted to control communism by requiring members of "communist" organizations to register with the federal government, the CCA went further by stripping the Communist Party's "rights, privileges, and immunities attendant upon legal bodies created under the jurisdiction of the laws of the United States." This meant that the Communist Party could not have bank accounts, sue others in court, enforce contracts, conduct business activities or, importantly, appear on a ballot in an election.

The CCA engendered surprisingly little debate in Congress, passing the Senate by a vote of 79 to 0 and the House by a vote of 265 to 2. The bill was opposed by Federal Bureau of Investigation Director J. Edgar Hoover out of a concern that it would drive communists underground and was also opposed by the American Civil Liberties Union on constitutional grounds. The fact that these unusual allies both opposed the bill had apparently little effect on Congress or President Dwight Eisenhower, who signed the CCA into law.

The primary motivating purpose of the CCA was to reduce the influence communism was having on some labor unions. Some in Congress had attempted to amend the Internal Security Act of 1950 to ban all labor unions. Instead, the CCA allowed labor unions declared by the Subversive Activities Control Board to be "communist-infiltrated" the ability to reorganize free of Communist control. This less extreme alternative to banning labor unions altogether has been offered as an explanation for why more liberal politicians, who might otherwise have been expected to oppose outlawing a political party on constitutional grounds, supported the CCA.

The CCA did not criminalize membership in the Communist Party or make its existence criminal. The CCA did explicitly state that becoming or remaining a member of the Communist Party subjected a person to "all the provisions and penalties of the Internal Security Act of 1950." That act criminalized failure to report one's association with a designated communist organization and actions that would "substantially contribute to the establishment within the United States of a totalitarian dictatorship." Thus, though the CCA purported to "outlaw" the Communist Party, a characterization repeated by President Eisenhower when he signed the bill, the CCA only stripped specific civil rights from the Communist Party.

In 1973 a federal district court decided the CCA's prohibition on the Communist Party appearing on election ballots was unconstitutional, but the Supreme Court of the United States has not ruled on the CCA's constitutionality. Congress has repealed portions of the law and its 1993 repeal of the Internal Security Act of 1950 effectively removed the teeth referred to in the CCA.

See Also: Conspiracy, Criminal; First Red Scare and the Palmer Raids (1919–20); Internal Security Act of 1950; Second Red Scare (McCarthyism)

Resources

Haerle, Paul R. 1955. "Constitutional Law: Federal Anti-Subversive Legislation. The Communist Control Act of 1954." *Michigan Law Review* 53: 1153–65.

Ybarra, Michael J. 2004. *Washington Gone Crazy: Senator Pat McCarran and the Great American Communist Hunt*. Hanover, NH: Steerforth Press.

Conspiracy, Criminal

An agreement among two or more individuals to commit a criminal act, along with an overt act in furtherance of the agreement, can itself be a crime against the state. The crime is forming a mutual agreement to commit an unlawful act against the government, and there is no requirement that the planned result ever come to fruition. Many jurisdictions require an overt act by members of the conspiracy to show proof of the agreement and a seriousness of purpose. The overt act itself does not need to be a major step toward commission of the crime but can be any action in a chain of events that would lead to the planned crime. A conspiracy to commit a crime against the state may be an agreement to commit any number of statutorily defined crimes against the state, including such offenses as espionage, mutiny, sabotage, and preventing federal law enforcement officers from discharging their duties. An agreement to commit treason or to overthrow the government by force is known as a seditious conspiracy and is a separately defined criminal offense under federal law. Just as it relates to conspiracy charges, as of January 2024, approximately fifty-seven individuals have been indicted, pleaded, or been found guilty of conspiracy to commit various criminal offenses related to events which took place as part of the Capitol Insurrection on January 6, 2021, including offenses such as seditious conspiracy, obstruction of Congress, obstruction of an official proceeding, destruction of government property, obstruction of law enforcement during civil disorder, conspiracy to injure a federal officer, and defrauding the United States.

Under federal law codified at 18 United States Code Section 371, "if two or more persons conspire either to commit any offense against the United States, or to defraud the United States, or any agency thereof in any manner or for any purpose, and one or more of such persons do any act to effect the object of the conspiracy, each shall be fined under this title or imprisoned not more than five years, or both." The federal criminal offense of conspiracy constitutes a felony (i.e., subject to potential incarceration of a year or more). If co-conspirators agree to commit a criminal offense under the United States Code that is a misdemeanor defense (i.e., subject to potential incarceration of less than one year), 18 United States Code Section 371 provides that in those circumstances "the punishment for such conspiracy shall not exceed the maximum punishment provided for such misdemeanor." Common examples of cases where individuals are indicted for conspiring to defraud the United States include such offenses as wire fraud, bank fraud, and welfare fraud.

Federal law does not require that multiple people be indicted or tried for conspiracy and a single member of a conspiracy may be charged so long as the government can prove the existence of other co-conspirators and that there was agreement to commit a criminal act and an overt act in furtherance of that agreement. Also, if the underlying criminal offense that was the object of the agreement occurs, under federal law, a defendant may be charged and prosecuted for both the conspiracy and the underlying criminal offense. Phrased another way, the crime of conspiracy does not merge into the completed underlying criminal offense. While a "conspiracy may be the sole object of a prosecution, or it may be joined in a separate count with the prosecution of a substantive offense that is the object of the conspiracy," there is no requirement that the government prosecute individuals for the underlying offense if committed (Surette 2022, §8). It is a frequent practice for the United States Department of Justice to indict individuals for both conspiracy and the underlying criminal offense but accept a plea bargain wherein a defendant pleads guilty to conspiracy in exchange for a dismissal of the indictment for the underlying offense.

A high-profile example of how the crime of conspiracy operates can be seen in the June 8, 2023, federal indictment of Donald Trump for thirty-seven counts of violating federal law regarding the illegal retention and his failure to return classified documents that belonged to the United States. Of the thirty-seven counts, thirty-one counts pertain to Trump's alleged violation of the Espionage Act of 1917. However, count thirty-two of the indictment charges Trump and his valet (Waltine Nauta) with "Conspiracy to Obstruct Justice" in violation of 18 United States Code Section 1512(k). Specifically, page 34 (paragraphs 79–80) of the indictment charges as follows: "From on or about May 11, 2022, through in or around August 2022, in Palm Beach County … the defendants Donald J. Trump and Waltine Nauta, did knowingly combine, conspire, confederate, and agree with each other and with others known and unknown … to engage in misleading conduct toward another person and corruptly persuade another person to without a record, document, and other object from an official proceeding … and to corruptly conceal a record, document, and other object from an official proceeding" with "the purpose of the conspiracy" "was for Trump to keep classified documents he had taken from the White House and to hide and conceal them from a federal grand jury." The trial date for the federal criminal case against Donald Trump for alleged violations of the Espionage Act is likely to occur in 2024.

See Also: Capitol Insurrection on January 6, 2021; Espionage; Espionage Act of 1917 and Sedition Act of 1918; Insurrection; Mutiny; Sabotage; Seditious Conspiracy; Treason

Resources

18 U.S. Code Section 371, Conspiracy to commit offense or to defraud United States.
Surette, Eric C. 2022. "Conspiracy." *American Jurisprudence*. Second edition, vol. 16, sections 1–9.
United States Department of Justice. 2023. "Capitol Breach Cases." Accessed May 24, 2023. https://www.justice.gov/usao-dc/capitol-breach-cases.

Constructive Treason

See Hoxie, United States v. (1808)

Cook, John E. (1829–59)

John E. Cook was one of John Brown's most trusted lieutenants and was one of the twenty-one men who participated in John Brown's Raid in attacking the United States Armory and Arsenal in Harpers Ferry, Virginia (now West Virginia), in 1859. Cook survived the raid and briefly escaped but was recaptured and indicted by the Commonwealth of Virginia for the same charges Brown had faced, namely murder, conspiring to induce slaves to engage in insurrection, and treason. Cook was one of the most hated of Brown's men among the residents of Harpers Ferry because Cook surreptitiously moved into the town in early June 1858, over a year before Brown's eventual arrival and attack. Brown sent Cook to spy and engage in espionage on the townspeople and act as an advanced scout and report back to Brown as many details as possible about how the town and armory and arsenal were defended, which plantations outside of town held enslaved individuals who might be agreeable to joining the insurrection, and other logistical and strategic information. Cook even went as far as to wed a local Harpers Ferry teenager (Virginia Kennedy) in April 1859, six months before the attack on the town and the US installation.

Cook came from a well-connected and wealthy family from Connecticut. At the time of the raid, his brother-in-law, Ashbel Willard, was the sitting governor of Indiana, and Willard used his position to lobby Virginia authorities for more lenient treatment for Cook after his capture. Cook attended Yale University and studied law in New York City before joining Brown in "Bleeding Kansas" (a period during which there were violent clashes between citizens over whether Kansas would be a free or slave state). Cook did not meet Brown until shortly after Brown's horrific Pottawatomie Massacre and was not involved in that aspect of Brown's conduct in Kansas.

During the attack on Harpers Ferry itself, Cook was stationed across the confluence of the Shenandoah and Potomac Rivers from Harpers Ferry, charged with shuttling ammunition and firearms back and forth. The position afforded him a perfect view to gauge the success or failure of the endeavor and to escape if it appeared that Brown's attack failed. When Cook saw that Brown's men were hopelessly surrounded in "a perfect steel trap" (as Frederick Douglass had characterized it two months prior in refusing to join Brown), Cook absconded and made it as far north as Chambersburg, Pennsylvania, meeting up with a handful of other survivors along the way. Yet, Cook was captured several days later when he went into town looking for food. As the whole region was on high alert, it was an audacious and dangerous move on Cook's part, and he was quickly identified as one of the handful of Brown's men who had escaped after the raid. "For a short while, John Cook was one of the two most famous militants in the country, second only to John Brown himself" (Lubet 2012, 77), and "America's most wanted man" at that point in time (Lubet 2012, 133), so it was no wonder he was easily identified.

He was extradited to Virginia, tried, and convicted. At the behest of his brother-in-law, Ashbel Willard, Virginia Governor Henry Wise, and the chief prosecutor, Andrew Hunter, Cook made a detailed twenty-five-page written confession. Hunter had Cook create multiple versions of the confession as Hunter (under direction from Governor Wise) was looking for Cook to implicate prominent Northerners in exchange for a reduced sentence. It was common knowledge that Brown was supported by a group of nationally known and prominent men known as "the Secret Six." Hunter and Governor Wise were convinced there were others and hoped to expand the list of conspirators, holding these unnamed northern leaders responsible as well. To Cook's credit, he never falsely implicated others who were not already known to authorities. For his efforts in making a confession, Cook was rewarded only by being acquitted of the charge of treason but was nevertheless still found guilty of the other two offenses, sentenced to death, and executed on December 16, 1859.

Cook had a realistic chance to escape two nights before his execution. Cook and his cellmate Edwin Coppoc had been loosening bricks and created a way of escaping out of the jail cell. Furthermore, Northerners had worked on escape plans for Brown and others. While Brown rejected the attempts, Cook and Coppoc did not. As part of a pre-planned plot, a northern abolitionist had infiltrated the local militia and was stationed at the exact location where Cook and Coppoc would scale the outer prison wall. However, Cook decided to postpone the planned escape by one night because his brother-in-law (and Governor of Indiana) had visited the jail cell earlier in the evening, and Cook did not wish anyone to accuse the Governor of having anything to do with the escape plans. Unfortunately for Cook and Coppoc, on the next night, a different Virginia militia member was guarding the wall, and the "friendly guard" was off duty. Cook and Coppoc were quickly recaptured.

Cook joined in prison several survivors of Brown's "Army of Liberation" who were captured alive after the Armory attack. Each of these men would be executed after trials for various crimes against Virginia. In addition to John Brown, these men included Edwin Coppoc, Aaron Stevens, Shields Green, Albert Hazlett, and John Copeland. Ironically, when the Civil War started eighteen months later, these men would have patriotically taken up arms to put down the rebellion and been praised in opposing the hundreds of thousands of Southerners committing open acts of treason against the United States (see American Civil War and Treason). Cook's headstone concisely captured his motives: "Died for the Cause of Emancipation and Human Liberty with the Noble Patriot John Brown at Charleston [*sic*], Virginia, December 16, 1859" (Lubet 2012, 302 n4). Had Cook survived the raid and died during the Civil War, the wording of the headstone could very well have remained the same, with only the date of death and location changed.

See Also: American Civil War and Treason; Brown, John; Conspiracy, Criminal; Copeland, John Anthony, Jr.; Coppoc, Edwin; Espionage; Green, Shields; Hazlett, Albert; Insurrection; John Brown's Raid (1859); Pottawatomie Massacre (1856); Rebellion; Stevens, Aaron; Treason

Resources

Hinton, Richard J. 1894. *John Brown and His Men: With Some Account of the Roads They Travelled to Reach Harpers Ferry*. New York: Funk & Wagnalls Company.

Lubet, Steven. 2012. *John Brown's Spy: The Adventurous Life and Tragic Confession*. New Haven, CT: Yale University Press.

Lubet, Steven. 2013. "Busted!: John Brown's Best Spy Escaped Harpers Ferry, but He Could Not Escape Justice." *America's Civil War* 26, no. 6: 48–53.

Copeland, John Anthony, Jr. (1834–59)

John Anthony Copeland, Jr., was one of five African American men who joined John Brown in the invasion of Harpers Ferry, Virginia, in October 1859 in the attempt to overthrow the institution of slavery by force. Copeland, an Oberlin College student, was recruited by his uncle, who was another of Brown's men, Lewis Leary. After Brown's trial and conviction, Copeland was tried and convicted with three other co-conspirators in November 1859 and executed for crimes against the Commonwealth of Virginia in December 1859. Copeland was executed for conspiracy to commit a slave insurrection and murder, but not treason, as the trial court ruled that Copeland could not be charged or convicted of treason given the color of his skin and the infamous decision of *Dred Scott v. Sandford* (1857), just two years before.

Copeland was a freed African American who moved with his family from Raleigh, North Carolina, to Oberlin, Ohio, in 1842, when he was about eight years old. For a time, Copeland was a student at Oberlin College, a progressive racially integrated college located in the strongly abolitionist leaning town of Oberlin, Ohio. Copeland was one of the thirty-seven men involved with the Oberlin rescue of the fugitive slave John Price in 1858, as part of the abolitionist mob that broke Price out of jail. Price was hidden in the home of the President of Oberlin College until he could be moved to Canada.

A year later, during John Brown's raid of the United States Amory and Arsenal at Harpers Ferry, Virginia, in October 1859, Copeland was assigned by John Brown to guard the United States Rifle Factory complex along the Shenandoah River, along with John H. Kagi, and Copeland's uncle, Lewis Sheridan Leary. When the three men were overwhelmed by a local militia, each tried to escape by fleeing across the Shenandoah River. Kagi and Leary were both mortally wounded trying to swim across the river. Copeland was captured by a townsperson who tried to execute Copeland on the spot in the middle of the river, but the person's gun failed to discharge because it had gotten wet. While a mob of townspeople yelled for Copeland to be lynched as he was dragged ashore, he was temporarily saved by a local doctor, Dr. John D. Starry, who shielded Copeland from the angry mob and delivered him to the federal authorities.

After all the prisoners had been arraigned on October 25, 1859, John Brown was tried first and separately. Copeland and three other men (Shields Green, John Cook, and Edwin Coppoc) were all tried together the week after Brown's case was completed in November 1859. As with his fellow conspirator Shields Green, the treason charge against Copeland was dismissed due to the United States Supreme Court's recent ruling in *Dred Scott v. Sandford* (1857), which held that African Americans were not intended by the Constitution to be citizens and that a Black man "had no rights which the white man was bound to respect." Because of this language by the Supreme Court, the lawyers for Copeland and Green argued that it was legally impossible to hold a person guilty of treason when that person was not a citizen and was afforded no rights or obligations under the Constitution. The trial court judge agreed and dismissed the treason charge, although Copeland and Green were nevertheless still found guilty of murder and conspiracy to commit a slave insurrection. Copeland was sentenced to die on December 16, 1859, along with Edwin Coppoc, Shields Green, and John E. Cook.

The trial judge stated Copeland "was the prisoner who impressed me the best … he had been educated, and there was a dignity about him that I could not help liking. He was always manly" (Villard 1910, 684). The main prosecutor, Andrew Hunter, commented that "Copeland was the cleverest of all the prisoners … [and] if I had had the power and could have concluded to pardon any man among them, he was the man I would have picked out" (Villard 1910, 684).

From prison on November 26, Copeland wrote his parents that "his fate as far as man can seal it is sealed, but let this not occasion you any misery for remember the cause in which I was engaged, remember that it was a 'Holy Cause,' one in which men who in every point of view better than I have suffered and died, remember that if I must die I die in trying to liberate a few of my poor and oppressed people" (Villard 1910, 684).

Copeland's execution was set for December 16, 1859, a mere fourteen days after John Brown's execution on December 2, 1859. "Even in death, Virginia demanded strict segregation of the races," as the two Black defendants (Shields Green and Copeland) were ordered to be executed separately from the other two white defendants (John E. Cook and Edwin Coppoc) (Lubet 2013, 1803). After execution, Copeland's body, along with the body of Shields Green, was sent to Winchester Medical College for dissection and display. A professor from Oberlin College (Ohio) traveled to Winchester Medical College on behalf of Copeland's relatives in an unsuccessful attempt to retrieve the bodies for proper burial. In 1865, the town of Oberlin erected a monument to Shields Green, John Copeland, and Lewis Sheridan Leary. The inscription read in part that these "citizens of Oberlin, the heroic associates of the immortal John Brown, gave their lives for the slave." The monument also included a Latin phrase, which translated meant "And now slavery is indeed dead, thanks be to God" (Lubet 2013, 1815).

See Also: Brown, John; Conspiracy, Criminal; Cook, John E.; Coppoc, Edwin; Green, Shields; Insurrection; John Brown's Raid (1859); Treason; *Virginia v. Brown* (1859)

Resources

Lubet, Steven. 2013. "Execution in Virginia, 1859: The Trials of Green and Copeland." *North Carolina Law Review* 91: 1785–815.

McGinty, Brian. 2009. *John Brown's Trial*. Cambridge, MA: Harvard University Press.

Villard, Oswald Garrison. 1910. *John Brown: A Biography Fifty Years After*. Boston: Houghton Mifflin Company.

Coppoc, Edwin (1835–59)

Edwin Coppoc (sometimes spelled "Coppock") was one of John Brown's band of men who participated in the attack on the United States Armory and Arsenal at Harpers Ferry, Virginia (now, West Virginia), in an event now known as John Brown's Raid in 1859. After the initial seizure by Brown's men, Edwin Coppoc survived the subsequent assault by Marines who were retaking the governmental complex. Coppoc was captured and taken to Charles Town, Virginia (now West Virginia) to be put on trial for murder, insurrection, and treason. He was executed along with Shields Green, John Copeland, and John Cook on December 16, 1859. Coppoc was the second person ever executed for treason in the United States (John Brown was the first, a mere fourteen days before Coppoc, on December 2, 1859). While Green, Copeland, and Cook were also executed on December 16, none of these three individuals were executed for treason (for the reasons why, see the individual entries on those individuals in this book). John Brown and Edwin Coppoc remain among less than a handful of Americans ever executed for treason by the Government (state or federal) through the present day.

Edwin Coppoc and Barclay Coppoc were brothers from Iowa, members of the Quaker faith, and both displayed a strong antipathy towards the institutional of slavery and the barbarity of human bondage. Both were known for their intellect, courage, and studious and honorable character. The brothers joined Brown's band of men in early 1859. When their mother learned about her sons' affiliation with Brown, she lamented "I believe you are going with old Brown. When you get the halters around your necks, will you think of me?" To which, Barclay Coppoc responded that "we can not die in a better cause" (Grahame 1928, 391).

During John Brown's raid, the Coppoc brothers split up and were assigned different tasks. Barclay Coppoc was stationed as a guard at Brown's temporary headquarters about five miles from Harpers Ferry, which fortuitously gave him the opportunity to escape the situation and flee North when Brown's forces were subsequently defeated by the United States Marines. Barclay's brother, Edwin, was assigned much more perilous work. Edwin Coppoc, along with Albert Hazlett, was tasked with seizing the unguarded United States Arsenal, where tens of thousands of rifles and muskets were stored. Eventually, Edwin Coppoc was forced to flee the Arsenal complex and take shelter in the Armoy Fire Station (also called the Engine House—where the fire engines were stored—or "John Brown's Fort"—because that was where Brown made his last stand) with John Brown and his few remaining surviving raiders. When the Marines assaulted the Engine House, Coppoc amazingly survived the onslaught of bullets and thrusting bayonets and was captured alive. When questioned immediately after his capture about why he was at Harpers Ferry, Coppoc replied, "I have no apologies for being here. I think it is a good place to be" (Grahame 1928, 399). When Virginia Governor Henry Wise told Coppoc that "you look like too honest a man to be found with a band of robbers," Coppoc retorted, "but Governor, we look upon you as the robbers" (Grahame 1928, 399).

Shortly before his execution, Edwin Coppoc and his cellmate John Cook had a chance to escape. A Northern supporter had infiltrated the militia guarding the prison and would assist in Coppoc and Cook's escape. Cognizant of the plan, Cook and Coppoc removed bricks and made a small opening to exit their cell and get into the adjacent jail courtyard. The plan was to use a makeshift rope and escape unnoticed, with the help of the implanted Northern supporter/guard on duty. Unfortunately, Cook decided to postpone the planned escape by one day so as not to wrongly implicate individuals who had visited them in the cell earlier in the day (including his brother-in-law, the Governor of Indiana).

So, Cook and Coppoc attempted their escape on the next night, but the friendly northerner supporter was no longer on guard duty, and both Cook and Coppoc were quickly apprehended.

Edwin Coppoc's brother, Barclay, died two years later. Barclay Coppoc saw serving in the Union Army as a way to continue the fight he started with John Brown in 1859. On July 31, 1861, he was commissioned a lieutenant in the Third Kansas Volunteer Infantry. He received orders to travel to his hometown in Springfield, Iowa, to secure the enlistment of childhood neighbors and friends. As he traveled back to Springfield by train, the train was crossing a bridge over a river gorge (the Platte River near Saint Joseph, Kansas), the bridge, weakened by previous Confederate sabotage, collapsed under the weight of the train. The train plummeted into the river below killing over one hundred individuals. Incredibly, Barclay Coppoc briefly survived, but succumbed to his injuries in September 1861.

See Also: Brown, John; Conspiracy, Criminal; Cook, John E.; Copeland, John Anthony, Jr.; Green, Shields; Hazlett, Albert; Insurrection; John Brown's Raid (1859); Sabotage; Treason; Turner, Nat; Vesey's Rebellion (1822)

Resources

Grahame, Pauline. 1928. "The Coppoc Boys." *The Palimpsest*, November 1928. Iowa City: The State Historical Society of Iowa, 385–436.

Hinton, Richard J. 1894. *John Brown and His Men: With Some Account of the Roads They Travelled to Reach Harpers Ferry*. New York: Funk & Wagnalls Company.

Corruption of Blood

The term "corruption of blood" is a reference to the ancient English common law practice of precluding family members and descendants from inheriting or receiving property from a person who has been convicted of treason. The underlying idea was that by committing an act of treason, a person's blood was tainted by that misdeed. Under the "pernicious" practice of "corruption of blood," "the person attainted was deemed to have never legally existed [and] his blood had been 'corrupted,' and no person could inherit by descent from his bloodline" (Larson 2020, Chapter 1).

In England, prior to 1870, a person convicted of treason permanently forfeited his or her properties to the State, but a descendant's right of inheritance of land or possessions owned by the perpetrator was also extinguished under the concept of "corruption of blood." This practice, going back well over six centuries and pre-dating the English Treason Statute of 1351, was finally abolished in England by the Forfeiture Act of 1870.

In the United States, the practice was abolished by ratification of the Constitution in 1789. More specifically, the United States Constitution limited this power as compared to old English common law practice. Article III, Section 3, Clause 2, in defining the offense of treason, provides that "Congress shall have Power to declare the Punishment of Treason, but no Attainder of Treason shall work Corruption of Blood, or Forfeiture except during the Life of the Person attainted." Thus, while Congress has the authority to set appropriate punishments for the offense of treason, those punishments may neither include the disenfranchisement of property or belongings of a family member or descendant of a person convicted of treason, nor bar one convicted of treason from the general right of passing one's inheritances to offspring or relatives. As James Madison wrote in Federalist Paper #43, the purpose of the "corruption of blood" provision within the Treason Clause to the Constitution, was in "restraining the Congress … from extending the consequences of guilt beyond the person of its author." In adherence to this limitation, under 18 United States Code Section 2381, Congress has declared that those convicted of treason "shall suffer death, or be imprisoned not less than five years, and fined under this title but not less than $10,000 and shall be incapable of holding office under the United States." Thus, today, there is no encumbrance on the rights of descendants to inherit the property of the person convicted of treason. Demonstrating its disapproval of corruption of blood as a punishment generally, the First Congress prohibited the penalty for all federal crimes in the Crimes Act of 1790.

See Also: Crimes Act of 1790; English Treason Statute of 1351; Treason

Resources

Larson, Carlton F. W. 2020. *On Treason: A Citizen's Guide to the Law*. New York: Ecco, an imprint of HarperCollins (Kindle Edition).

Stier, Max. 1992. "Corruption of Blood and Equal Protection: Why the Sins of the Parents Should Not Matter." *Stanford Law Review* 44, no. 3: 727–57.

Cramer v. United States (1945)

In *Cramer v. United States*, the Supreme Court of the United States decided a case involving a treason conviction for the first time where the offense of treason was the central issue in the case. *Cramer* represented the Supreme Court's first interpretation of the Treason Clause's requirement of an "overt act." Though lower courts had previously attempted to define "overt act," such as in *United States v. Mitchell* (1795), the Supreme Court had made no previous pronouncement on the issue. And though the Supreme Court had tangentially discussed the meaning of the Aid and Comfort Clause in earlier decisions such as *United States v. Greathouse* (1863) and *Young v. United States* (1877), the Court in *Cramer* provided its first interpretation of the phrase giving "aid and comfort" to the enemy in the context of a treason conviction. Importantly, the Supreme Court also addressed whether Congress could create separate laws outlawing treason-like conduct apart from the Constitution's criminalization of treason, which explicitly states the "only" conduct that may for the basis for a treason charge.

Anthony Cramer, born in Germany but a naturalized US citizen, befriended a German living in America named Walter Thiel. Thiel would eventually become one of the "Nazi Saboteurs" whose prosecution and execution the Supreme Court addressed in *Ex Parte Quirin*. However, in June 1942, before Thiel's attempted sabotage efforts, Cramer met with Thiel in various public places in New York City on multiple occasions. Agents of the Federal Bureau of Investigation (FBI) observed two of the meetings but did not overhear the substance of Cramer and Thiel's conversations. FBI agents were able to determine that Thiel gave Cramer a money belt containing over $3,600, of which Cramer kept $200, put aside some for Thiel, and then deposited the rest in a safe deposit box. When confronted by FBI agents, Cramer made false statements regarding his interactions with Thiel.

The Treason Clause states, "Treason against the United States, shall consist only in levying War against them, or in adhering to their Enemies, giving them Aid and Comfort. No Person shall be convicted of Treason unless on the Testimony of two Witnesses to the same overt Act, or on Confession in open Court." Cramer was charged with multiple counts of treason but ultimately convicted based on three acts: his two meetings with Thiel witnessed by the FBI agents, and his false statements to the FBI.

When Cramer's appeal reached the United States Supreme Court, the Justices initially agreed to decide the case based on an evidentiary issue. However, a majority decided they would address the constitutional questions posed by Cramer's appeal. The Court ordered reargument and rebriefing, specifically indicating it wanted to hear the parties' views on the meaning of "treason" and "overt act" and regarding the requirement that overt acts be proved by testimony of two witnesses. Furthermore, the Court heard argument regarding whether the evidence submitted against Cramer at trial met the constitutional requirements.

On the meaning of the "overt act" requirement in the Treason Clause, Cramer argued that the overt act alone must manifest a traitorous intention. The government countered that the overt act requirement required only that the prosecution prove by two witnesses an act, no matter how commonplace or insignificant, that, along with other circumstances, could be used to infer that the overt act was a step toward commission of treason. The Court adopted neither approach, choosing instead to interpret the Treason Clause as requiring that the overt act witnessed by two people must actually give aid and comfort to the enemy, but that the overt act need not itself manifest treasonous intent. The Court found that Cramer's meetings with the enemy (Thiel) were not sufficient evidence of giving the enemy aid and comfort. In writing the opinion for the majority, Justice Robert Jackson, who had just finished serving as the lead prosecutor of Nazi war criminals at the Nuremburg Tribunals, wrote of Cramer's actions that meeting "in public drinking places to tipple and trifle was no part of the saboteurs' mission and did not advance it. It may well have been a digression which jeopardized its success." Jackson further noted there was no evidence that Cramer gave Thiel any information of value, or shelter, or sustenance or supplies, "or even paid for their drinks." The Supreme Court reversed Cramer's conviction.

Before *Cramer*, because of the Constitution's textual prohibition on "treason" constituting anything other than "levying War" against the United States or "adhering to their Enemies, giving them Aid and Comfort," the ability to outlaw "treason-like" actions, arguably circumventing the Treason Clause, was not a certainty. Along with interpreting the Treason Clause for the first time, in *Cramer* the United States Supreme Court signaled that Congress could criminalize acts such as espionage, sedition, trading with the enemy, and other similar acts, even if the prohibited conduct was essentially treason.

Cramer had the effect of making treason charges harder for prosecutors to prove. Because of this, some have attributed to *Cramer* the five decades between the 1950s (Sgt. John Provoo) and 2000s (Adam Gadahn) during which the United States did not charge *anyone* for treason. While this view may have some merit, the several successful treason prosecutions in the years immediately after *Cramer* was decided suggest the explanation for the long absence of treason prosecutions may be more complex.

See Also: Aid and Comfort (Aid to Enemies of the State); Espionage; *Ex Parte Quirin* (1942); Gadahn, Adam Yahiye; *Greathouse, United States v.* (1863); Levying War; *Mitchell, United States v.* (1795); Perjury, False Statements, and Obstruction of Justice; Sabotage; Sedition; Treason

Resources

Cramer v. United States, 325 U.S. 1 (1945).

Crane, Paul T. 2009. "Did the Court Kill the Treason Charge?: Reassessing *Cramer v. United States* and Its Significance." *Florida State University Law Review* 36: 635–96.

Crimes Act of 1790

The Crimes Act of 1790 (Crimes Act), officially titled "An Act for the Punishment of Certain Crimes against the United States," was the US government's first codification of crimes, including crimes against the state. Many of the offenses in the Crimes Act were not what we consider to be "crimes against the state." These included murder and manslaughter occurring on federal property, piracy, larceny, receiving stolen property, and helping prisoners escape. However, several offenses were classic crimes against the state, including treason, perjury, bribery, and counterfeiting federal securities or money.

The Constitution had explicitly defined the crime of treason and specified the proof required for a conviction and penalty (death) upon conviction. So, the Crimes Act simply restated those requirements, codifying them in the federal code. The Crimes Act also outlawed "misprision" (concealment) of treason, imposing a maximum seven-year prison sentence. The Crimes Act provided even greater detail regarding the procedure required for treason cases, including requiring that any person accused of treason had to be provided with a copy of the indictment, a list of the jury and witnesses, the right to defense counsel, and the right to court assistance in compelling defense witnesses. These key procedural rights would ultimately be enshrined for all criminal cases in the Sixth Amendment, but as of 1790, the Sixth Amendment had not yet been ratified.

The procedural rights provided for treason also applied to any capital case. In addition to treason, the Crimes Act imposed the death penalty as the exclusive punishment for murder, piracy, and aiding the escape of a prisoner who had been sentenced to death. The First Congress considered counterfeiting to be a very serious crime against the state, as the death penalty was also the only permitted punishment. Though counterfeiting may have private victims, it is also an important crime against the state because of the significant harm to the government if it lost control of the value of its securities or money or if the full faith and credit of the United States were placed in doubt. The seriousness of counterfeiting as a crime against the state is illustrated by the fact that England including counterfeiting as one of seven activities that constituted treason in the English Treason Statute of 1351. Especially in the United States' infancy, even small losses of control over economic activity or uncertainty regarding the United States' ability to pay its debts could have had disastrous consequences. Today, federal law no longer imposes the draconian death penalty for counterfeiting, but it is still a felony, punishable by up to twenty years imprisonment.

The Constitution had specifically provided Congress authority to define and punish some of the crimes contained in the Crimes Act of 1790, including treason, piracy, counterfeiting, felonies on the high seas, and offenses against "the Law of Nations" (international crimes). An example of a crime against the state that was not explicitly authorized in the Constitution but that the First Congress nevertheless criminalized in the Crimes Act is the offense of bribery. Unlike most offenses identified in the Crimes Act, prison sentences for bribery were left to the "discretion of the court," with no maximum length imposed. The Crimes Act further mandated that bribery offenders would "forever be disqualified to hold any office of honour, trust or profit under the United States," adding to the offenses that prevented subsequent public service already articulated in the Disqualification Clause of the Constitution. The bribery offense in the Crimes Act was narrower than it is today, outlawing only bribery related to the judicial process (i.e., paying to receive a favorable opinion, judgment, or decree from a federal judge). This reflects the First Congress's continuing focus, after the Judiciary Act of 1789 and Process Act of 1789, on establishing, and protecting the integrity of, the new federal judiciary. Today, federal law bans bribery of all public officials.

In addition to the various sentences prescribed and allowed for various offenses, the Crimes Act also outlawed a particular sentence: Corruption of Blood. The United States Constitution already prohibited imposing that penalty for Treason, but the Crimes Act extended that prohibition to all federal crimes.

See Also: Corruption of Blood; Disqualification Clause; English Treason Statute of 1351; Perjury, False Statements, and Obstruction of Justice; Treason

Resources

Crimes Act of 1790.

Currie, David P. 1994. "The Constitution in Congress: Substantive Issues in the First Congress, 1789–1791." *The University of Chicago Law Review* 61: 775.

Criminal Syndicalism

In response to the rise of industrial capitalism in the late 1800s and early 1900s, pro-workers movements began to emerge. The largely impoverished industrial workforce began to coalesce, demanding improved working conditions, pay, and other benefits. The ensuing labor unrest manifested itself in numerous ways, from peaceful work slowdowns to strikes to violent uprisings. These incidents were often of sufficient magnitude that they resulted in significantly increased instances of declarations of martial law to address the labor unrest and use of the federal military to engage in surveillance of union activities.

Workers' movements gained momentum worldwide, including the 1917 Bolshevik Revolution and ultimate installation in Russia of the communist government based on Marxist-Leninist economic and political ideology. Worried about rising economic, social, and political unrest, industrial employers in the United States successfully lobbied federal and state legislatures to enact a wide variety of laws aimed at suppressing the power of unions and workers. In many parts of the country, executive branch officials, including law enforcement, prosecutors, and governors, supported industrial management in the labor upheavals. One such example is that during the first decades of its enforcement, there were more prosecutions of *labor unions* under the Sherman Antitrust Act—an act intended to reduce *corporate* monopolies—than of corporations (White 2006, 667–8).

In the United States, the primary left-leaning organization attracting negative attention for marshalling workers was the Industrial Workers of the World (IWW), founded by Eugene Debs. The IWW advocated for widespread economic and political change, seeking elimination of the hierarchical class structure of the industrialized economy and toppling of political institutions supporting the industrial capitalist system. For several years, the IWW vigorously advocated for "sabotage" of industry to accomplish its aims, though after 1917, the union was more careful to explain that sabotage meant things like work stoppages and strikes, not actual violence or destruction (White 2006, 748–9). The IWW was an openly militant organization, protesting and engaging in free speech battles in localities throughout the nation. Many of these conflicts became violent, often with battle lines drawn with union members on one side and employers, employer-hired security personnel, and law enforcement on the other.

During the first couple decades of the twentieth century, the IWW became the primary target of business interests seeking to suppress worker movements. The IWW's opposition to America's entry into the First World War further enflamed many Americans, allowing industry and government to add patriotic fuel to the anti-IWW fire. During the summer of 1917, the United States Department of Justice openly acknowledged its attempts to destroy the IWW, securing hundreds of indictments and convictions for conspiracy to hinder federal laws relative to the production and distribution of wartime goods and conspiracy to thwart enforcement of the draft and undermine military morale and mobilization efforts. Anti-IWW sentiment was so strong that convictions were often easy for the government to obtain. In one notorious case, an apparently biased jury in Chicago took fifty-five minutes to convict 100 defendants of 400 counts detailing 10,000 allegations of criminal acts (White 2006, 692–4).

One method for repressing the IWW and similar organizations was criminal syndicalism laws, which criminalized accomplishing change in industrial ownership or control or political change through crime, sabotage, violence, or terrorism, and, importantly, outlawed any doctrine or precept advocating, teaching or, aiding and abetting such activities. Though purportedly concerned primarily with criminal acts to change the economic and political landscape, the overwhelming majority of prosecutions for violating criminal syndicalism laws were for alleged *advocacy* of such activities and for mere *membership* in organizations that sometimes advocated for, or engaged in, attempts to empower workers to take control of industry or take power from the "capitalist state." Thousands of members of the IWW were convicted under these laws.

Though the IWW was the initial target that criminal syndicalism laws were enacted to defeat, they were later used against other unpopular groups, including other trade unions, populist farmers organizations, and ultimately socialists and communists. Advocates for criminal syndicalism laws often engaged in hyperbolic rhetoric that asserted all manner of dangers the groups posed to the delicately preserved social, economic, and political order. That said, the primary impetus for enactment of these laws was economic in nature: business owners were the primary champions of enactment and enforcement. In total, twenty-one states and two territories enacted criminal syndicalism statutes, and numerous state supreme court opinions upheld the statutes' constitutionality. However, as the IWW's influence receded in the 1920s, efforts to adopt criminal syndicalism laws in states and in Congress failed more frequently (White 2006, 703–4).

State and federal courts largely upheld criminal syndicalism laws against challenges that they violated free speech, free association, due process, and equal protection rights. The United States Supreme Court upheld California's criminal syndicalism law in *Whitney v. California* (1927). Not until 1969 in *Brandenburg v. Ohio* (1969) did the Supreme Court ultimately declare a state's criminal syndicalism statute to be an unconstitutional violation of free speech and association rights under the First Amendment to the United States Constitution. Like related state statutes addressing criminal anarchy and sedition, the enforceability of state criminal syndicalism laws is subject to the restrictions of federal preemption imposed by the United States Supreme Court in *Pennsylvania v. Nelson* (1956).

See Also: Anarchy, Criminal; *Brandenburg v. Ohio* (1969); *Pennsylvania v. Nelson* (1956); Sabotage; Sedition; Speech as Crime against the State; Terrorism; *Whitney v. California* (1927)

Resources

Brandenburg v. Ohio, 395 U.S. 444 (1969).

Merriam, Eric. 2022. "Necessary Necessity: Courts' Historical Assessment of the Condition Precedent for Martial Law." *Oklahoma Law Review* 75: 649–770.

White, Ahmed A. 2006. "The Crime of Economic Radicalism: Criminal Syndicalism Laws and the Industrial Workers of the World, 1917–1927." *Oregon Law Review* 58: 649–769.

Whitney v. California, 274 U.S. 357 (1927).

Cruikshank, United States v. (1876)

United States v. Cruikshank was a case that arose out of the Colfax Massacre, which, along with the Battle of Liberty Place, was part of a series of violent confrontations following the bitterly contested 1872 Louisiana gubernatorial election. After a Democratic Party-associated white militia killed scores of newly freed Black Republicans during the Colfax Massacre, the federal government prosecuted a small number of members of the white militia, including Cruikshank, with violating the federal Enforcement Act of 1870. The Act contained many provisions, but the provision the defendants were charged with violating prohibited two or more people from conspiring "to violate any provision of this act, or to injure, oppress, threaten, or intimidate any citizen, with intent to prevent or hinder his free exercise and enjoyment of any right or privilege granted or secured to him by the Constitution or laws of the United States." Of the hundreds of whites who participated in the Colfax Massacre, federal investigators identified ninety-six, who were subsequently indicted for violating the Enforcement Act of 1870. Yet, of the ninety-six, only nine stood trial, and six were acquitted. Only three men, William Cruikshank, John Hadnot, and William Irwin were convicted of conspiracy.

The Supreme Court dismantled the convictions of these three defendants in a series of arguments that might strike readers as contrary to modern society's understanding of the reach of constitutional rights. In fact, "[the Court's] opinion rivaled that of Chief Justice Taney in *Dred Scott* in its deliberate misreading of law and history" (Irons 1999, 203). First, the Court noted that some of the convictions charged that the white militia members had hindered the Black Republicans "in the free exercise and enjoyment of their 'lawful right and privilege to peaceably assemble together with each other and with other citizens of the United States for a peaceful and lawful purpose.'" The Court found that the right to peaceably assemble, though protected against federal government interference in the First Amendment, was actually a right that predated the Constitution, and was thus not granted or secured by the Constitution. Furthermore, the Court held that protection of the right was the responsibility of the State government. Interpreting the First, Fourteenth, and Fifteenth Amendments very narrowly, the Court concluded that because the charge alleged hindrance of peaceable assembly for *any lawful purpose*, rather than only for those purposes "connected with the powers or the duties of the national government," it was beyond the federal government's authority to prohibit under the Enforcement Act.

Similarly, the Court rejected convictions based on charges that alleged conspiracy to deny the Black Republicans' their right to bear arms. As it had with supposed First Amendment freedoms, the Court found that the Second Amendment restricted Congress's authority, but not that of the states. Thus, the Second Amendment did not grant or secure a right that the federal government was permitted to protect through the Enforcement Act.

The defendants were also charged with depriving the slain Black Republicans of their lives and liberty "without due process of law," in violation of the Fourteenth Amendment's Due Process Clause. Here, the Court could not rely on the argument that the Fourteenth Amendment only restricted the federal government, because the Fourteenth Amendment had explicitly provided the federal government the authority to enforce the requirement that states not deprive persons of the life, liberty, or property without due process of law. The Court changed tack, and here determined, as it would again in *The Civil Rights Cases* (1883), that the Fourteenth Amendment prohibited only deprivations of life or liberty by state government, not by private individuals not acting or officially employed as state employees or "state actors." The Court similarly disposed of convictions based on the Fourteenth Amendment's Equal Protection Clause.

The Court also rejected convictions on charges alleging the defendants had violated the victims' Fifteenth Amendment right to vote. Relying on similar logic to its analysis regarding First and Second Amendment rights, the Court held that the Fifteenth Amendment did not guarantee an absolute right to vote, but rather guaranteed only a right to be free from discrimination on the basis of race in the exercise of the right to vote. Because the right to vote came from the states and state citizenship, it did not fall within the federal government's authority to enforce.

The Court finally rejected convictions based on charges that had alleged the defendants conspired to hinder the victims' free exercise and enjoyment of the rights, privileges, immunities granted them as citizens of the United States and Louisiana and the rights guaranteed by the Constitution and laws of the United States. Here, rather than finding the federal government lacked constitutional authority to prohibit such actions, the Court found the charges were too vague and overbroad.

In *Cruikshank*, the United States Supreme Court rejected the federal government's ability to punish the perpetrators of the Colfax Massacre who had engaged in a successful insurrection to overthrow local government. Instead, the Court left that authority to the state of Louisiana, which did nothing. More broadly, the Court eviscerated the federal government's general ability to enforce civil rights and even rights most people today consider to be constitutional rights. Just as the apparent "success" of the Colfax Massacre had emboldened white paramilitary groups to further violence, the *Cruikshank* decision provided legal encouragement to such actors, ensuring they need worry only about state prosecutions. In states where their actions were widely praised by the controlling white majority, this was no worry at all. As one constitutional scholar has aptly written, "the Supreme Court's decision in *United States v. Cruikshank* handed down in 1876, simply underscored the fact that no branch of the federal government would offer southern blacks any protection from the reign of terror that swept the region" (Irons 1999, 206). Because of the lack of protection, "the South were able to terrorize and murder blacks with virtual impunity" (Irons 1999, 206).

The *Cruikshank* decision was one in a series of post-American Civil War cases (including *The Slaughterhouse Cases* [1873], *The Civil Rights Cases*[1883], and *Plessy v. Ferguson* [1896]) in which the Court severely limited the reach and applicability of the newly ratified Fourteenth and Fifteenth Amendments and the federal government's ability to enforce those Amendments to protect constitutional, civil, and political rights. In leaving these police powers to the states, the Court both restrained the federal government's authority to define and punish new crimes against the state and enabled states to disregard the rights of newly freed Black Americans for decades to come. Put bluntly, the "Court's decision [in these cases] slammed the door on federal protection of blacks against terrorist attacks" (Irons 1999, 213).

See Also: Battle of Liberty Place (1874); Colfax Massacre (1873); Conspiracy, Criminal; Enforcement Acts (1870–71); Insurrection

Resources

Foner, Eric. 2014. *Reconstruction: America's Unfinished Revolution, 1863–1877*. New York: Harper Perennial.
Irons, Peter. 1999. *A People's History of the Supreme Court*. New York: Viking.
United States v. Cruikshank, 92 U.S. 542 (1876).

Cybersecurity

As James Clapper, Director of National Intelligence, stated on March 12, 2013: "In some cases, the world is applying digital technologies faster than our ability to understand the security implications and mitigate potential risks" (Clapper 2013). Indeed, if one was asked in the 1990s about the topic of cybersecurity, the questioner would likely have gotten a response about stolen credit card numbers, individual financial fraud from some on-line consumer purchase, or perhaps the latest e-mail received from a Nigerian prince in need of a quick payment to regain his throne and free-up his frozen assets. And certainly, one could (and still can) commit a plethora of such computer-related offenses (called cybercrimes). Yet, as abundant as cybercrimes have become, this entry is not about cybercrimes, but rather cybersecurity. Cybersecurity, in the context of this book, entails the protection of the state from damage by malevolent individuals wishing to target the state or the state's ability to do its duties and functions by disrupting computer operations for which the state has increasingly relied upon in modern times. While one nation may commit cyberattacks against another nation, this facet of cybersecurity is largely outside the scope of this book (except by way of explaining technology which has been used to threaten a state which might also be employed by individuals).

Cybersecurity involves protecting the state against crimes and threats that can damage its institutions or the country itself. In the past, the biggest threat to a state in terms of cyberactivity or cyberattacks might be if a hacker defaced the home page of a government agency website, as happened in May 2001 to the home pages for the United States Senate and the Federal Bureau of Investigation (FBI). Activists, who were responding to the federal government's treatment of a Houston hacker, displayed a mocking message for the FBI and an obscene image that took the Senate the weekend to take down. Another cyberattack practice is known as a "denial-of-service attack," wherein a governmental website is overwhelmed by repeated requests, blocking users and causing the website to crash. While temporarily damaging and criminal in nature, the effects of these older types of attacks were typically minimal and could be fixed in short order. As late as 2008, when Russia was engaged in hostilities with Georgia, Russia employed hackers to engage in cyberattacks against Georgia that took the form of website defacement and denial-of-service attacks.

Then, in 2010, the field of cyberattacks and cybersecurity changed, and the world took notice of that dramatic change. The Israelis and Americans had developed a malware code named Stuxnet that had massive adverse repercussions on the Iranian nuclear program. Malware code are lines of computer script (sometimes a handful of computer command lines among thousands) that trick a computer into operating in a fashion different than how it was originally programed to operate. The infected code is unknowingly introduced into a system by an employee clicking on a phishing email or infected file (which injects altered command code language into the system and overrides the regular computer programing), by using an infected USB flash drive, or visiting a malicious website. Once the infected code is introduced into a computer, it operates like a human virus and infects the system. In the 2010 case of Stuxnet and the Iranian reactors, the malware operated to alter the appropriate speed by which a nuclear centrifuge is required to spin. The centrifuge must spin at a precisely calibrated rotational speed to create uranium suitable for use at the nuclear power facility. The Stuxnet malware altered the original computer code to cause the centrifuge to spin at an inappropriate (and damaging) rate of rotation. More deviously, the malware allowed the system operators to see a false report suggesting that everything in the system was running properly, so no one was alerted to a problem. The Stuxnet malware set the Iranian nuclear program back at least two years, and it was found in nuclear reactors in several other Middle Eastern countries. Stuxnet ushered the world into a new era of cyberattacks that could threaten a nation's national security and well-being and the safety of its citizens.

Stuxnet ushered in an era of digital wars conducted by cyberattacks wherein catastrophic results could occur with the alteration of a few simple lines of computer code. As one expert has stated, "but for people who worry about the security of critical U.S. facilities, Stuxnet represented a nightmare: a dangerous computer worm that in some modified form could be used to attack an electric or telecommunications grid, an oil refinery or a water treatment facility in the United States" (Gelten 2011). In a written statement by the Department of Homeland Security, officials noted "attackers could use the increasingly public information about the [Stuxnet] code to develop variants targeted at broader installations of programmable equipment in control systems" (Zetter 2011). Michael Assante, former security chief for a private cybersecurity company commented, "It's just a matter of time. Stuxnet taught the world what's possible, and honestly it's a blueprint" (Gelten 2011).

For years, intelligence figures such as former Central Intelligence Director R. James Woolsey and former Counterterrorism Czar Richard Clarke have been warning Americans that a cyberattack against America's infrastructure is possible and would be devastating, unless major changes are made to better protect it. Malware may be injected into a system but lay dormant for years, until someone decides to activate it and potentially bring computer networks that operate power grids or water systems to a standstill.

In 2012, another virus was identified called FLAME. "While Stuxnet was meant to destroy things, Flame's purpose was merely to spy on people" and allow for espionage without the human element (Kushner 2013). With a few lines of computer code, "most impressively, Flame could exchange data with any Bluetooth-enabled device. In fact, the attackers could steal information or install other malware not only within Bluetooth's standard 30-meter range but also farther out" (Kushner 2013). According to cybersecurity experts, "once Flame had compromised a machine, it could stealthily search for keywords on top-secret PDF files, then make and transmit a summary of the document—all without being detected" (Kushner 2013). These cyberattacks revolutionize the way espionage is conducted against the State.

In December 2015, Russia graduated from low-level cyberattacks and engaged in the world's first cyberattack targeting an electrical grid (Ukraine's). In the opening phases of its invasion of Ukraine in 2022, Russia again employed cyberattacks to eliminate basic infrastructure facilities (gas, power, water, electricity). According to a 2021 federal grand jury indictment of six Russian officers in the United States, Russia has launched some of "the world's most destructive malware to date" (Office of Public Affairs 2020).

This begs the question of what can be done to defend the homeland from cyberattacks against the State. Billions of individuals post content to the internet, and a mind-boggling amount of information is transmitted at nearly instantaneous speeds around the globe, within which a few lines of malicious code must be identified and thwarted.

In 2011, then Deputy Secretary of Defense William Lynn admitted that the United States starts with a disadvantage in cyberspace: "The internet was designed to be open, transparent, and interoperable. Security and identity management were secondary objectives in system design. This lower emphasis on security in the internet's initial design … gives attackers a built-in advantage" (William J. Lynn Remarks 2011). This "built-in advantage" for attackers can be overcome, but only through adequate resources and vigilance. While more money and resources have been expended to protect federal computer programs, local-level systems remain vulnerable. Thus, "[t]hreat actors who ultimately have their sights set on federal targets might begin their attack by going after lower level of government. The latter's more limited resources can mean weaker defenses, giving attackers easier initial entry points before they move through intergovernmental connections to reach their true targets" (Pattison-Gordon 2023).

More robust resources and training for lower-level governments are an essential aspect of a solid cybersecurity plan. The ability to protect against cyberattacks also preserves the operational function of government from attacks from within by individuals desiring to harm the government and state.

See Also: Espionage

Resources

Clapper, James R. 2013. "Worldwide Threat Assessment of the US Intelligence Community, Statement for the Record to the Senate Select Committee on Intelligence." *National Security Archive*, March 12, 2013. Accessed October 31, 2023. https://nsarchive.gwu.edu/media/21491/ocr.

Fadilpasic, Sead. 2023. "Cyberattacks on Governments Saw a Huge Increase in the First Few Months of 2023." *MSN*. Accessed May 12, 2023. https://www.techradar.com/news/cyberattacks-on-governments-saw-a-huge-increase-in-the-first-few-months-of-2023.

Gelten, Tom. 2011. "Stuxnet Raises 'Blowback' Risk in Cyberwar." *National Public Radio*, November 2, 2011. Accessed May 12, 2023. https://www.npr.org/2011/11/02/141908180/stuxnet-raises-blowback-risk-in-cyberwar.

Kushner, David. 2013. "THE REAL STORY OF STUXNET: How Kaspersky Lab Tracked down the Malware That Stymied Iran's Nuclear-fuel Enrichment Program." *IEEE Spectrum*, February 26, 2013. Accessed May 12, 2023. https://spectrum.ieee.org/the-real-story-of-stuxnet#toggle-gdpr.

Office of Public Affairs, U.S. Department of Justice. 2020. "Six Russian GRU Officers Charged in Connection with Worldwide Deployment of Destructive Malware and Other Disruptive Actions in Cyberspace." October 19, 2020. Accessed October 30, 2023. https://www.justice.gov/opa/pr/six-russian-gru-officers-charged-connection-worldwide-deployment-destructive-malware-and#:~:text=Their%20computer%20attacks%20used%20some,Destroyer%2C%20which%20disrupted%20thousands%20of.

Pattison-Gordon, Julie. 2023. "What's Top of Mind for State, Local Govt Cybersecurity?" *Government Technology*, May 9, 2023. Accessed May 12, 2023. https://www.govtech.com/security/whats-top-of-mind-for-state-local-govt-cybersecurity.

Porter, Christopher. 2023. "Washington Must Take Cybersecurity Efforts Seriously." *The National Interest*, May 6, 2023. Accessed May 12, 2023. https://nationalinterest.org/blog/washington-must-take-cybersecurity-efforts-seriously-206456.

Smith, Zhanna L. Malekos. 2022. "Critical Questions and Answers: Emerging Cyber Threats: No State Is an Island in Cyberspace." *Center for Strategic and International Studies*, March 23, 2022. Accessed May 12, 2023. https://www.csis.org/analysis/emerging-cyber-threats-no-state-island-cyberspace#:~:text=The%20U.S.%20intelligence%20community%20(IC,%2C%20Iran%2C%20and%20North%20Korea.

William J. Lynn Remarks on the Department of Defense Cyber Strategy [Transcript]. 2011. Department of Defense Cyber Strategy. Accessed May 12, 2023. https://www.securityweek.com/william-j-lynn-remarks-department-defense-cyber-strategy-transcript/.

Zetter, Kim. 2011. "DHS Fears a Modified Stuxnet Could Attack U.S. Infrastructure." July 26, 2011. Accessed May 12, 2023. https://www.wired.com/2011/07/dhs-fears-stuxnet-attacks/

D

Davis, Jefferson (1808–89)

Had the American Civil War not occurred and had Jefferson Davis not cast his lot with the Confederacy as its first and only president, his legacy might have been one of the country's great leaders. By 1860, Davis had completed a variety of impressive accomplishments, placing him in the upper echelon of America's nineteenth-century leaders. A graduate of the United States Military Academy at West Point, Davis served honorably in the United States Army, including service in the Mexican American War, and was wounded in the Battle of Buena Vista. After his service in the Mexican War, Davis courted and married his first wife, who was the daughter of Zachary Taylor. General Taylor, nicknamed "Old Rough and Ready," saw service in the War of 1812, the Black Hawk War, the Second Seminole War, and was one of America's two top military leaders in the Mexican American War. Shortly after the conclusion of the Mexican American War, Taylor would be elected president in 1849. In his own right, until the Civil War, Davis had an illustrious governmental career, serving as a member of the United States House of Representatives, a United States Senator from Mississippi, and the United States Secretary of War in the administration of President Franklin Pierce.

Yet, when Davis was elected president of the Confederate States of America, his lifetime of service to the US government and his legacy of service were destroyed. In fact, "a fair argument can be made that Jefferson Davis was the greatest traitor in American history" (Larson 2020, Chapter 9), rivaling Benedict Arnold for that ignoble accolade.

Carlton Larson, a professor of constitutional law at the University of California, argued that even under the most sympathetic interpretation of southern motivations and intentions and giving those individuals every benefit of the doubt, the Confederate Army and Government (and those who offered the Confederacy aid and comfort) clearly levied war against the United States. Larson characterized the rebellion as "the most widespread act of treason in the history of the United States, with hundreds of thousands of people engaged in open warfare against their own government" (Larson 2020, Chapter 9). Thus, every confederate participant could have been prosecuted and convicted of treason against the United States. Yet, this did not occur, which begs the question of why (see American Civil War and Treason)? First, both the common law English practice of treason prosecutions and early American treatment of treasonous events (such as the Whiskey Rebellion, Fries's Rebellion, Shay's Rebellion, and others) were to hold the top leaders responsible for treason while offering pardons or non-prosecutions to lower echelon participants. Second, a month and a half after the assassination of President Lincoln in 1865, President Andrew Johnson began proclaiming amnesty and pardon, pardoning any former Confederate participant who would swear renewed allegiance to the United States. Participants ranging from low-level privates to high-ranking generals like Joseph E. Johnson and James Longstreet took advantage of this amnesty. Robert E. Lee was indicted for treason but never ultimately tried or pardoned before his death.

Yet, for many Northerners, Jefferson Davis was the head of the snake and not suitable for amnesty or pardon. Veterans from the North vociferously clamored for Davis to be executed for treason, calling him the greatest American traitor, and saying things such as: "hang him! Hang him! Yes I say HANG him twenty times … treason must be made odious; traitors must be punished and impoverished! … I would arrest them, I would try them, I would convict them, and I would hang them!" (Winik 2001, 171). Even the popular song "John Brown's Body"—soon to be repurposed as the Battle Hymn of the Republic—contained a line that promised to "hang Jeff Davis to a tree."

After Davis's capture by federal troops in Georgia as he tried to escape the United States in April 1865, President Johnson was faced with three alternatives: one, issue an outright pardon for Davis, which would offend hundreds of thousands of veterans, Northerners, and those next of kin of those who made the ultimate sacrifice to preserve the Union; two, prosecute Davis by a military tribunal; or three, indict and try Davis in a civilian court for treason. None of these options were ideal. A pardon would be seen as letting the chief culprit and head of the confederacy off without any accountability. Similarly, a prosecution by a military tribunal was problematic because the hostilities were over and civilian courts were again in operation, and the use of a military tribunal might give the appearance of an unfair swift "victor's justice" and might lack proper jurisdictional authority as well (as the justification for wartime measures had lapsed; see *Ex Parte Milligan*). Lastly, the seemingly best option, a formal accusation and trial in civilian court, was fraught with peril, as the case would be decided by a southern jury, one sympathetic to Davis and the Southern cause, potentially resulting in an acquittal and outright vindication of Davis (and perhaps the Confederacy as well). In the end, President Johnson opted for a civilian jury trial and attempted to have Davis prosecuted and convicted for treason by a jury of his southern peers.

In addition to several notable legal problems with the prosecution's case (discussed later in this entry), the prosecution was also handicapped by an unlikely alliance of Northern supporters for Davis, individuals who funneled money and support to Davis for his defense. Some of the surprising Northern supporters of Davis included notable Americans such as Cornelius Vanderbilt (who had a son die during the Civil War), Horace Greeley (a radical Republican serving in Congress during the war), Gerrit Smith (one of John Brown's "Secret Six," financial supporters in Brown's attempt to overthrow the institution of slavery), and Thaddeus Stevens (one of the most zealous radical Republicans in Congress and who had previously defended Castner Hanway in 1851 for Hanway's role in the Christiana Riot). In addition to this strange cabal of supporters, the subsequent treason case would be presided over by United States Supreme Court Justice Salmon P. Chase (along with United States District Court Judge John C. Underwood), who still harbored presidential ambitions and viewed this case as one that could undercut his political viability regardless of the ultimate outcome, alienating potential voters in the North or South, depending on Chase's rulings in the case. In the end, Chase's political ambitions may have played a role in the favorable outcome in the case for Davis.

All told, from start to finish, Jefferson Davis would spend 720 days (about two years) in confinement at Fort Monroe, Virginia, pending the resolution of his case (and raising the additional problem of violating Davis's constitutional right to a "speedy trial"). While the case started off in a seemingly expeditious fashion, it soon disintegrated into delays spanning years (several of which Davis spent in military pre-trial confinement at Fort Monroe under military guard). Within a month and a half of the end of the Civil War, in May 1865, and in a foreshadowing of many delays to come, a federal court in Virginia charged Davis with treason, but the indictment was lost, could not be found, and has to this day never been recovered. As a result of the "lost" indictment, another Washington, DC, court issued another indictment, only to have this indictment quashed because the court concluded that the trial should take place where the treason was committed, namely in one of the eleven confederate states, and not in Washington, DC. Thus, on January 6, 1866, United States Attorney General James Speed issued a pronouncement that Davis would subsequently be tried for treason in a civilian court in a state where his treasonous crimes were perpetrated, namely Virginia. Yet, despite this pronouncement, the year 1866 came and went without Davis facing a trial. In May 1867, after several years of confinement at Fort Monroe, Virginia, Davis was eventually transferred to civilian control and granted bail pending his trial, which would never take place.

Davis was again indicted for treason in March 1868. This indictment superseded the previous indictment. The grand jury was the first federal grand jury in American history to be racially integrated, with three African Americans serving as grand jury members. As the year 1868 came to an end and the Davis case appeared to be finally moving toward trial, the court (presided over by two judges) was split on a motion to dismiss the case on the grounds that the prosecution was constitutionally barred. Then, likely influenced by the specter of another constitutional impediment in the prosecution of Davis, President Andrew Johnson capitulated and announced that Davis would be given amnesty. On December 25, 1868, President Andrew Johnson released an amnesty proclamation for all Confederates not covered by previous amnesty proclamations. One of the few people covered by this proclamation was Jefferson Davis. Thus, for the first time since his capture, Davis was free from fear of federal prosecution, conviction, and potential execution for treason.

The significant delays and foot dragging by the federal courts illustrate real problems lurking behind the scenes in the treason prosecution of Jefferson Davis. There were numerous legal problems and technical problems that would have likely precluded a guilty verdict even if Jefferson Davis were put on trial for treason. First, the case would have been immediately bogged down into a legal post-mortem analysis of whether state governments had a constitutional right of secession, a question practically resolved by the force of arms during the Civil War and answered in part through the spilling of over 600,000 Americans' blood. Davis's case would have deteriorated into a convoluted academic debate about the right of secession because Davis's lawyers suggested that it was legally impossible for Davis to have committed treason against the United States, as he claimed he was a citizen and head of a foreign state of the lawfully constituted Confederate States of America. The success of this argument would obviously hinge on whether the act of secession was constitutionally permissible. The Supreme Court did not definitively answer this constitutional question until its decision in *Texas v. White* (1869).

Second, and related to the above, Davis's lawyers planned to argue that, as head of the Confederacy from 1861to 1865, Davis owed the United States no loyalty or allegiance. This had been a leading argument and defense by defendants in multiple treason cases from the 1840s and 1850s, including the federal treason prosecution of Hipolito Salazar in 1847 and Virginia's prosecution of John Brown for treason in 1859. And Davis had strong precedent on his side. United States Supreme Court Chief Justice John Marshall, writing thirty years earlier for the majority in the Supreme Court case titled *United States v. Wiltberger*, stated that "treason is a breach of allegiance, and can be committed by him *only* who owes allegiance (to the sovereign) either perpetual or temporary." Further, eminent English common law jurist William Blackstone explained that treason "imports a *betraying*, treachery, or *breach of faith*" (Blackstone 1769, 75). Davis's lawyers intended on arguing that Davis's allegiance and loyalty to the United States ended when he joined the Confederacy and was elected its first and only president.

To muddy the waters further, Chief Justice Chase (as one of the two presiding judges over the pending prosecution) indicated to the defense late in 1868 (shortly after the Fourteenth Amendment was enacted) that the Disqualification Clause in Section Three of the Fourteenth Amendment might operate as an absolute bar to the prosecution of Davis for treason. The purpose of Section Three of the

Fourteenth Amendment, ratified just a few months before Davis was finally scheduled to go on trial, was to ban former Confederate officials from holding any public office. Specifically, Section Three of the Fourteenth Amendment provided in part that

> "no person shall … hold any office … who having previously taken an oath, as a member of Congress, or as an officer of the United States, or as a member of any State legislature, or as an executive or judicial officer of any state, to support the Constitution of the United States, [who] shall have engaged in insurrection or rebellion against the same, or given aid and comfort to the enemies thereof."

It became apparent in Chase's handling of a pre-trial defense motion that Chase viewed this Fourteenth Amendment language as the *exclusive* punishment set forth and intended by Congress for cases of treason committed by former US officials during the Civil War. Phrased another way, because Davis was punished for his treason by being barred from future public office, additional prosecution of Davis for treason would be unconstitutional and akin to double jeopardy.

While there is nothing in the legislative history of the Fourteenth Amendment to suggest that the drafters of the Amendment intended it to serve as the sole and exclusive remedy to "punish" those who committed treason during the Civil War, Davis's defense team immediately filed a motion to dismiss the case in late 1868 on just those grounds. The judges split over whether to grant the motion. Chase was in complete agreement with the defense's argument and granting the motion would allow Chase a way to finally rid himself of the troubling Davis case to the extent Chase was still harboring presidential ambitions; yet the other trial judge (United States District Court Judge Underwood) did not agree with Chase. Judge Underwood was persuaded by the prosecution's argument that Section Three provides no textual evidence it was intended to exempt former Confederates from treason or any other criminal prosecutions. As the prosecution argued "probably nothing would more surprise the people of the United States than to learn that by adopting Amendment XIV, they had repealed all the penalties against treason, insurrection, or rebellion" ("Case of Jefferson Davis" 1876, 101–2).

Thus, the bench was equally split over the constitutionality of continuing with Davis's prosecution considering Section Three of the Fourteenth Amendment. This division spelled the end of the prospect of holding Davis accountable for treason because the issue would be appealed to the Supreme Court, with Chief Justice Salmon Chase presiding over the appeal and subtly directing its outcome at the Supreme Court. As explained by Professor Carlton Larson, "the bottom line for the Johnson administration, however, was clear—the chief justice of the United States had stated in open court that the treason prosecution of Jefferson Davis was unconstitutional" (Larson 2020, Chapter 9). Thus, on December 25, 1868, President Johnson finally put an end to the saga of Davis treason proceedings by issuing a final amnesty proclamation which, while in general language pardoned anyone not previously subject to amnesty, in reality was a pardon for just one man, Jefferson Davis. Not one individual of the hundreds of thousands who participated in the Civil War would be held legally accountable for the offense of treason—not Jefferson Davis, not Robert E. Lee (indicted for treason, but never tried), and not the hundreds of thousands of foot soldiers who levied war against the United States.

See Also: Aid and Comfort (Aid to Enemies of the State); American Civil War—Amnesty and Pardon; American Civil War and Treason; Arnold, Benedict; Brown, John; Christiana Riot; Disqualification Clause; *Ex Parte Milligan* (1866); Fries's Rebellion (1799); *Hanway, United States v.* (1851);

Insurrection; Levying War; Rebellion; Salazar, Hipolito; Shay's Rebellion (1786–7); *Texas v. White* (1869); Treason; Whiskey Rebellion

Resources

Blackstone, William. 1769. *Commentaries on the Laws of England.* Vol. 4. Oxford: Clarendon Press.

"Case of Jefferson Davis." 1876. *Reports of Cases Decided by Chief Justice Chase in the Circuit Court of the United States for the Fourth Circuit, during the Years 1865–1869.* New York: Diossy & Co.

Larson, Carlton F. W. 2020. *On Treason: A Citizen's Guide to the Law*. New York: Ecco, an imprint of HarperCollins (Kindle Edition).

Nicoletti, Cynthia. 2017. *Secession on Trial: The Treason Prosecution of Jefferson Davis*. New York: Cambridge University Press.

Winik, Jay. 2001. *April 1865: The Month that Saved America.* New York: Perennial.

Debs v. United States (1919)

In *Debs v. United States*, a unanimous Supreme Court upheld the conviction of socialist leader Eugene Debs for charges brought under the Espionage Act of 1917 and Sedition Act of 1918. Debs was arrested for comments he made during a speech to a general audience of over 1,000 people in Canton, Ohio, following a visit to some socialists imprisoned for violating the Sedition Act. Among the several thousand Debs supporters, a handful of undercover Department of Justice agents milled about in the crowd, tasked with shadowing Debs across the country and writing down his words in the hopes of finding some words that might be actionable in prosecuting Debs.

One person, E. R. Sterling, recorded Deb's words verbatim, using shorthand. Debs was aware that he was being followed by federal agents and that they were transcribing his words, saying "I realize that, in speaking to you this afternoon, there are certain limitations placed upon the right of free speech. I must be exceedingly careful, prudent, as to what I say, and even more careful and more prudent as to how I say it." Debs continued that "I may not be able to say all that I think [crowd laughter noted by Sterling in his notes]; but I am not going to say anything that I do not think [Sterling noted laughter and applause]. But, I would rather a thousand times be a free soul in jail than a sycophant and coward on the streets [Sterling noted applause and shouts]."

Debs was charged with inciting insubordination, disloyalty, mutiny, and refusal of duty in the military and naval forces of the United States and with intent so to do delivered, to an assembly of people, a public speech, set forth and that in making the speech he obstructed the recruiting and enlistment service of the United States.

In his speech, Debs praised socialism, praised specific socialists who were then in prison for violating the Sedition Act as "paving the way to better conditions for all mankind," and argued that "the master class has always declared the war and the subject class has always fought the battles" and that "the subject class has had nothing to gain and all to lose, including their lives; that the working class, who furnish the corpses, have never yet had a voice in declaring war and never yet had a voice in declaring peace." In his speech, Debs also expressed his disgust that a woman (Rose Pastor Stokes) received a ten-year prison sentence for stating: "I am for the people and the government is for the profiteers." Reaching a crescendo, Debs thundered that "the United States, under the rule of the plutocracy, is the only country that would send a woman to the penitentiary for ten years for exercising her constitutional right of free speech. If this be treason let them make the most of it." Debs concluded his speech by telling listeners "Don't worry about the charge of treason to your masters; but be concerned about the treason that involves yourselves."

Debs objected to his conviction on two primary grounds. First, he argued the Espionage Act of 1917 and Sedition Act of 1918 were unconstitutional infringements on his right to free speech under the First Amendment. Second, Debs argued that none of his specific comments explicitly incited insubordination in the military or obstructed recruiting and enlistment. The Supreme Court rejected Debs's First Amendment argument, relying on its just-announced decision in *Schenck v. United States* (1919) that the Espionage Act did not violate the First Amendment. The Supreme Court also found the underlying intent and meaning of Debs's speech were sufficient to convict, even though he had not explicitly encouraged resistance to the draft.

The Supreme Court's decisions in *Schenck* and *Debs* are widely considered the low point in protection of political speech under the First Amendment. Though the wartime context of the speech leading to convictions in both cases likely affected the Supreme Court's view of the danger of the speech, *Schenck* and *Debs* remained good law for many decades to come.

See Also: Espionage Act of 1917 and Sedition Act of 1918; Mutiny; *Schenck v. United States* (1919); Speech as Crime against the State; Treason

Resources

Debs v. United States, 249 U.S. 211 (1919).

Rabban, David M. 1997. *Free Speech in Its Forgotten Years*. New York: Cambridge University Press.

Stone, Geoffrey R. 2004. *Perilous Times: Free Speech in Wartime from the Sedition Act of 1798 to the War on Terrorism*. New York: W.W. Norton and Co.

DeJonge v. Oregon (1937)

Oregon's criminal syndicalism statute defined criminal syndicalism as "the doctrine which advocates crime, physical violence, sabotage or any unlawful acts or methods as a means of accomplishing or effecting industrial or political change or revolution." The criminal syndicalism statute prohibited a variety of acts related to disseminating and advocating for criminal syndicalism.

Dirk DeJonge was convicted of violating Oregon's criminal syndicalism statute and sentenced to seven years imprisonment. He was convicted for assisting the conduct of a meeting which was called under the auspices of the Communist Party, an organization that advocated criminal syndicalism. DeJonge admitted his participation in the meeting, and that it was held under the auspices of the Communist Party but objected that neither criminal syndicalism nor any unlawful conduct was taught or advocated at the meeting. When DeJonge appealed, the Oregon Supreme Court upheld the conviction because the meeting was held under the auspices of the Communist Party, and even though no such advocacy or discussion occurred at the specific meeting DeJonge helped conduct, the Communist Party at large sometimes advocated criminal syndicalism.

The United States Supreme Court unanimously reversed the Oregon Supreme Court and overturned DeJonge's conviction. The Court reiterated what it had said in *Gitlow v. New York* (1925), that the freedom of speech and right to assemble were guaranteed against abridgment by state government through the Fourteenth Amendment's Due Process Clause. The Court recognized the great importance of "safeguarding the community from incitements to the overthrow of our institutions by force and violence." But it held that as that interest grew in importance, so too did the rights of free speech, free press, and free assembly so that government would be responsive to the will of the people and that changes, if desired by the people, could be accomplished by peaceful means. In other words, protecting speech and assembly guards against lawless or violent government overthrow.

Ultimately, the United States Supreme Court held that "peaceable assembly for lawful discussion cannot be made a crime." The Court explained that "[t]he holding of meetings for peaceable political action cannot be proscribed. Those who assist in the conduct of such meetings cannot be branded as criminals on that score. The question, if the rights of free speech and peaceable assembly are to be preserved, is not as to the auspices under which the meeting is held, but as to its purpose; not as to the relations of the speakers, but whether their utterances transcend the bounds of the freedom of speech which the Constitution protects."

Further, the Court made clear that "[I]f the persons assembling have committed crimes elsewhere, if they have formed or are engaged in a conspiracy against the public peace and order, they may be prosecuted for their conspiracy or other violation of valid laws. But it is a different matter when the State, instead of prosecuting them for such offenses, seizes upon mere participation in a peaceable assembly and a lawful public discussion as the basis for a criminal charge." Notably, the Court did not declare that Oregon's criminal syndicalism statute was unconstitutional in all situations, but rather that it was unconstitutionally applied to DeJonge's actions in conducting a meeting where no advocacy of crime, violence, sabotage, or other unlawful acts took place.

See Also: Criminal Syndicalism; *Gitlow v. New York* (1925); Sabotage; Speech as Crime against the State

Resources

DeJonge v. Oregon, 299 U.S. 353 (1937).

Dennis v. United States (1951)

In 1940, Congress enacted the Alien Registration Act, more popularly known as the Smith Act. In 1948, after what was at the time the longest federal trial in United States history (nine months), Eugene Dennis and several other leaders of the Communist Party of the United States (also known as the Communist Political Association) were convicted of violating the Smith Act for conspiring "(1) to organize … a society, group and assembly of persons who teach and advocate the overthrow and destruction of the Government of the United States by force and violence, and (2) knowingly and willfully to advocate and teach the duty and necessity of overthrowing and destroying the Government of the United States by force and violence."

Before Dennis's appeal reached the United States Supreme Court, the Second Circuit Court of Appeals had found sufficient evidence that leaders of the Communist Party were "unwilling to work within our framework of democracy" and intended to initiate a violent revolution when the opportunity arose. Dennis and others disputed this, contending they had communicated only that Marxist-Leninist doctrine taught that force and violence would be necessary to achieve a Communist form of government in an existing democratic state because the ruling classes of that state would never allow the transformation. The defendants in *Dennis* also argued that the Smith Act was an unconstitutional restriction on free speech under the First Amendment because it prohibited even academic discussion of Marxist ideas. At the Second Circuit, famed jurist Judge Learned Hand observed that the clear and present danger test lacked a fixed standard by which courts could determine when a danger is "clear" or when it is "present." He summarized the question posed by the clear and present danger test in the context of an alleged conspiracy as how long a government had to wait to act after discovering a conspiracy. He concluded, "In each case [courts] must ask whether the gravity of the 'evil,' discounted by its improbability, justifies such invasion of free speech as is necessary to avoid the danger." In this case, Judge Hand agreed the gravity of the evil was sufficient to sustain the convictions.

A splintered Supreme Court also upheld the convictions but demonstrated widely diverging views on the proper application of the clear and present danger test. Indeed, the Supreme Court's divided views of the *Dennis* case demonstrated the difficulty with the test. Four Justices adopted the "gravity of the evil" test articulated by Judge Hand. Two more Justices concurred, favoring deference to the legislature (Congress, which had enacted the Smith Act). Though concurring, Justice Robert Jackson also noted the inadequacy of the clear and present danger test.

Dissenting, Justice Hugo Black complained, "These petitioners were not charged with an attempt to overthrow the Government. They were not charged with overt acts of any kind designed to overthrow the Government. They were not even charged with saying anything or writing anything designed to overthrow the Government. The charge was that they agreed to assemble and to talk and publish certain ideas at a later date." Black argued that the Smith Act posed an unconstitutional prior restraint on speech. The other dissenting Justice, William O. Douglas, similarly argued the defendants were being punished for their beliefs rather than for actual advocacy of rebellion.

In 1957, in *Yates v. United States*, the United States Supreme Court would begin to narrow the types of expressive activities that could be punished under the Smith Act. And the Supreme Court's decision in *Dennis* would be implicitly overruled in *Brandenburg v. Ohio* (1969), when the Court implemented the "imminent lawlessness test," thereby abandoning the "gravity of the evil" approach to the clear and present danger test.

See Also: *Brandenburg v. Ohio* (1969); Clear and Present Danger Test; Conspiracy, Criminal; Smith Act; *Yates v. United States* (1957)

Resources

Dennis v. United States, 341 U.S. 494 (1951).

Gorfinkel, John A., and Julian W. Mack Jr. 1951. "*Dennis v. United States* and the Clear and Present Danger Rule." *California Law Review* 39: 475–96.

Walker, James L. n.d. "Dennis v. United States (1951)." *The First Amendment Encyclopedia*. Accessed July 15, 2022. https://www.mtsu.edu/first-amendment/article/190/dennis-v-united-states.

Disqualification Clause

The Disqualification Clause of the Fourteenth Amendment to the United States Constitution does not proscribe crimes against the state, but rather prescribes an *effect* of committing specific crimes against the state: disqualification from federal office. Included in the Fourteenth Amendment ratified just after the American Civil War, the Disqualification Clause was intended to prevent military officers and others who participated in, or supported, the Confederacy from serving in certain positions of responsibility in the US government. Specifically, the Disqualification Clause states, "No person shall be a Senator or Representative in Congress, or elector of President and Vice-President, or hold any office, civil or military, under the United States, or under any State, who, having previously taken an oath, as a member of Congress, or as an officer of the United States, or as a member of any State legislature, or as an executive or judicial officer of any State, to support the Constitution of the United States, shall have engaged in insurrection or rebellion against the same, or given aid or comfort to the enemies thereof. But Congress may by a vote of two-thirds of each House, remove such disability." Note that the Disqualification Clause lists triggering offices—the offices someone must have held prior to engaging in the listed offenses—and banned offices—the offices a disqualified person may not hold. Furthermore, the only disqualifying crimes against the state are explicitly identified: insurrection, rebellion, or giving aid and comfort to the enemies of the United States.

Given the paucity of cases applying the Disqualification Clause, questions abound. What does "engaged in" mean? What is the definition of an insurrection for the purposes of the Disqualification Clause? Does "aid or comfort to the enemies" mean the same thing in the Disqualification Clause as the similar phrase in the Constitution's Treason Clause? Are the offices of president and vice president included as banned offices? *Electors* for those offices are specifically identified, but not the offices themselves. On the other hand, the presidency certainly seems to be contemplated as "any office, civil or military, under the United States." Similarly, are judicial positions included? "Judicial officers of any State" are specifically identified in the list of triggering offices, but not explicitly identified in the list of banned offices. Who decides the answers to these questions?

Though there have been few disqualification cases, there have been some. In 1867, the House of Representatives refused to seat John Young, who had been elected to represent Kentucky, because the House found he had given aid and comfort to the enemy during the Civil War by providing information to Confederates that led to the capture of Union soldiers and by calling for Abraham Lincoln to be hanged. Left undecided by the House of Representatives in Young's case was whether words of encouragement alone could constitute "aid and comfort." The House answered that question the next year when it refused to seat John Young Brown, also of Kentucky, finding he had provided "aid and comfort" to the Confederacy by publicly advocating for anyone who joined the Union Army to be shot. Civil War-related cases ended once Congress granted amnesty to former Confederates in 1872, thus removing the disqualification "disability," as the Disqualification Clause's final sentence allows. However, a later case, in which Victor Berger, a socialist elected from Wisconsin to the United States House of Representatives, demonstrated the Disqualification Clause did not die with the Civil War amnesty. Berger spoke out against American involvement in the First World War while a sitting Congressman. The House subsequently voted 311–1 to exclude Berger from the House for giving aid and comfort to America's enemies.

A significant question related to the Disqualification Clause involves who is empowered to enforce it. As noted above, Congress has exercised the ability to enforce disqualification by refusing to seat members in the House of Representatives and Senate under Article I, Section 5, Clause 1 of the

Constitution. But what about persons subject to the Disqualification Clause who are not part of Congress? After the Civil War, Congress passed the Ku Klux Klan Act, part of the Enforcement Acts, directing district attorneys to petition courts for writs "*quo warranto*" that would allow courts to remove unauthorized officeholders. After Congress repealed the Ku Klux Klan Act, the statutory basis for district attorneys to petition courts no longer exists, but the *quo warranto* procedure still exists in District of Columbia law, which may apply to federal officeholders with offices in Washington, DC. Some commentators have called on Congress to reenact the Ku Klux Klan Act's procedure for disqualifying insurrectionists and rebels in federal court, especially after the Capitol Insurrection on January 6, 2021.

Beyond *quo warranto* procedures, some have suggested Congress should pass legislation that specifically bars individuals or classes of individuals from holding office and that such a law could extend to offices in any branch of the federal government. But others have argued such a statute is unnecessary or might constitute an unconstitutional bill of attainder, which bars the government from punishing an individual or group without a trial and by one's name or group status alone. Additionally, numerous states have variations of the writ *quo warranto*, but those generally apply only to state officeholders, who are also subject to the federal Constitution's Disqualification Clause.

Many have considered the Disqualification Clause's applicability to participants in the Capitol Insurrection on January 6, 2021, including political officials alleged to have encouraged or aided in the insurrection. Though a small subsection of the overall number of participants on January 6, several members of the mob who forced their way into the Capitol held "triggering offices" under the Disqualification Clause, including a state legislator and some former military officers. Beyond that, several members of Congress were alleged to have aided those who participated in the insurrection or encouraged others to overturn the election. In a challenge to the eligibility for office of Congresswoman Marjorie Taylor Greene, a judge opined that "[m]erely disloyal sentiments or expressions" would not constitute "engagement" for purposes of the Disqualification Clause, but that "marching orders or instructions to capture a particular objective, or to disrupt or obstruct a particular government proceeding, would appear to constitute engagement." Nevertheless, the judge ultimately ruled there was insufficient evidence to establish that Greene "engaged in insurrection or rebellion against the same, or [gave] aid or comfort to the enemies thereof" (*Green v. Raffensperger*, Civil Action No. 22-CV-1294-AT (2022)). Similar challenges to Arizona Representatives Paul Gosar and Andy Biggs also failed. A federal lawsuit also was filed by North Carolina Representative Madison Cawthorn seeking to block the North Carolina Board of Elections from disqualifying him from office based on his alleged participation in the January 6 insurrection. While the District Court issued a preliminary injunction in favor of Cawthorn on the alleged grounds that the Amnesty Act of 1872 applied to those involved in the January 6 insurrection, the United States Court of Appeals for the Fourth Circuit reversed this ruling, setting precedent that the 1872 Amnesty for ex-confederates did not protect the January 6, 2021, insurrectionists. However, the case was dismissed as moot when Cawthorn lost his seat in Congress and the subsequent primary election.

At the time of this writing, it is unknown whether former President Donald J. Trump will face a similar effort under the Disqualification Clause to prevent his taking office again as president. As of late 2023, numerous lawsuits have been filed across multiple states to keep Trump off state primary ballots based upon a plain reading of the disqualification clause. These cases (or the appeal from trial court rulings) are still pending in 2024. In February 2024, the Supreme Court heard oral arguments in *Trump v. Anderson*, a case which deals with whether a state can remove a candidate from a primary ballot for the presidency, a claim ultimately rejected by the Court in a 9-0 decision. Such challenges would need to determine whether Trump's efforts to overturn the 2020 election constituted insurrection, rebellion, or giving aid and comfort to America's enemies. Trump was impeached for incitement of insurrection, and the January 6th Committee also concluded Trump incited insurrection. Whether *inciting* an insurrection constitutes *engaging* in an insurrection sufficient to trigger the Disqualification Clause is uncertain. President Trump's invitation to supporters to protest at the Capitol on January 6th and his command to the assembled crowd to "fight like hell" arguably constituted incitement of a violent uprising (insurrection) or "words of encouragement" from "one occupying an influential position" (aid and comfort). But, as noted, it is not entirely certain whether the offices of President and Vice President are subject to the Disqualification Clause at all.

See Also: Aid and Comfort (Aid to Enemies of the State); American Civil War and Treason; Capitol Insurrection on January 6, 2021; Enforcement Acts (1870–71); Insurrection; Rebellion; Treason

Resources

Baude, William, and Michael Stokes Paulsen. 2024. "The Sweep and Force of Section Three." *University of Pennsylvania Law Review* 174: 1–126.

Elsea, Jennifer K. 2022. "The Insurrection Bar to Office: Section 3 of the Fourteenth Amendment." *Congressional Research Service*, LSB10569, September 7, 2022.

Hemel, Daniel J. 2021. "Disqualifying Insurrectionists and Rebels: A How-To Guide." *Lawfare*, January 19, 2021. Accessed June 12, 2023. https://www.lawfareblog.com/disqualifying-insurrectionists-and-rebels-how-guide.

Hempowicz, Liz, David Janovsky, and Norman Eisen. 2022. "The Constitution's Disqualification Clause Can Be Enforced Today." *Project on Government Oversight*, November 14, 2022.

Magliocca, Gerard. 2021a. "Amnesty and Section Three of the Fourteenth Amendment." *Constitutional Commentary* 36: 109–10.

Magliocca, Gerard. 2021b. "The 14th Amendment's Disqualification Provision and the Events of Jan. 6." *Lawfare*, January 19, 2021. Accessed June 12, 2023. https://www.lawfareblog.com/14th-amendments-disqualification-provision-and-events-jan-6.

Dorr's Rebellion (1841–2)

Dorr's Rebellion refers to Thomas Wilson Dorr's failed attempts to: supplant the existing government in Rhode Island in 1841–2; seize the Rhode Island state arsenal (located in Providence) in May 1842; and lead approximately 140 men in armed opposition against the state government in June 1842. After fleeing the state, Dorr was indicted for treason against the state of Rhode Island in August 1842. Upon Dorr's return to Rhode Island in October 1843, he was at once detained and subsequently stood trial in state court on the charge of treason against the state in April 1844. He was found guilty and was sentenced to life imprisonment at hard labor. While Dorr would be released from prison after a year, his case was significant as it was the first time since the ratification of the United States Constitution in 1789 that a state government was able to successfully prosecute and convict a defendant for treason against that government. The next time this would occur would be when the Commonwealth of Virginia successfully oversaw the trial, conviction, and execution of abolitionist John Brown for treason against Virginia in 1859 in *Virginia v. Brown.*

Thomas Dorr was an attorney and the leader of a popular sovereignty movement in Rhode Island, a group that sought to create a written constitution for Rhode Island by circumventing the Rhode Island General Assembly. The Rhode Island General Assembly, which had the legal authority to call for a constitutional convention, had refused to do so. The Rhode Island General Assembly was a Charter government that had been in continuous operation since 1663 and was left intact until the 1840s. The Charter operated in lieu of a state constitution, and under the Charter, only the Rhode Island General Assembly had the authority to call for an amendment of the Charter, or substitution with a new state constitution. In response to the General Assembly's refusal to call for a constitutional convention, Dorr and his supporters played a significant role in convening an assembly to draw up a new constitution. This assembly, called the Rhode Island Suffrage Convocation, was described as "peaceful revolution ... by ignoring the constituted authorities" (Lawson 1914, 7). At this convention, Dorr helped draft a new constitution called The People's Constitution, which widened the pool of eligible voters in the state. Dorr was then elected as governor under this larger pool of eligible voters. However, under the original (and then still binding) Rhode Island Royal Charter, voters instead elected Samuel King as governor. Thus, for a time, Rhode Island had two people claiming to be the governor of the state.

To solidify power, Dorr and his supporters (called Dorrites) unsuccessfully attempted to seize arms stored at the Rhode Island state arsenal in Providence in May 1842. This attempt failed almost immediately, as the cannon Dorr and his supporters attempted to use was doused with a pail of water and would not ignite. In fear of arrest, Dorr fled to New York; however, Dorr returned in June 1842 upon hearing that supporters were gathering to march on the government. But upon returning to lead this uprising, Dorr discovered that hardly any defensive earthworks had been erected and only 140 men were assembled on Dorr's behalf. In response to Dorr's threats, Governor Samuel King had declared martial law and called out the state militia, reported to be more than four thousand soldiers. Facing such an overwhelming force arrayed against him, Dorr again fled the state. His trial for treason commenced in April 1844.

At the time of Dorr's indictment for treason, there were two Rhode Island state laws in effect that criminalized treason against the state. The first state law (passed in 1838) defined treason as consisting "only in levying war" against the state, "or in adhering to the enemies thereof, giving them aid and comfort." The second treason law (passed in 1842) after the People's Constitution was put into effect and Dorr elected as governor, specified that treason within the state also included holding any high office in a newly established government within the state. The prosecution claimed that Dorr levied war against the government by attacking the state arsenal in May 1842 and attempting to lead forces against the existing government in June 1842. Dorr unabashedly held high office (governor) in a newly established government (under The People's Constitution). Dorr's counsel argued that all of Dorr's actions were valid as the elected governor of Rhode Island, that Rhode Island lacked the ultimate authority to try a defendant for treason against the state, and that treason could only be committed against the United States. The trial court ruled against Dorr as to these defenses (as a matter of law) and advised the jury that those defenses were improper. More specifically, the court instructed the jury that Dorr was not the duly elected lawful governor of Rhode Island and that Rhode Island had the right to defend its sovereignty through the use of treason laws and charges.

In instructing a grand jury in 1842, Justice Joseph Story set forth the meaning of treason law that probably guided the jury in Dorr's case. Story stated that "[t]o constitute an actual levy of war, there must be an assembly of persons met for the treasonable purpose, and some overt act done, or some attempt made by them with force to execute, or towards executing, that purpose. There must be a present intention to proceed in the execution of the treasonable purpose by force." Justice Story further explained that if these above conditions are met, no actual blows are needed for treason.

With not a single "Dorrite" serving on the jury and having been instructed that Dorr's main arguments were inadmissible, the jury "immediately" returned a guilty verdict; as one jury member stated, "there was nothing for us to do, the Court made everything plain for us" (Lawson 1914, 164). Dorr was sentenced to life imprisonment and subject to hard labor. About a year later, the Rhode Island General Assembly enacted a law authorizing Dorr's release from prison. The United States Supreme Court in *Luther v. Borden* (1849) refused to rule on which state government in 1842 was legitimate and held that such a decision was a "political question" best left to other branches of the government and the political process.

See Also: Aid and Comfort (Aid to Enemies of the State); Brown, John; John Brown's Raid (1859); Levying War; *Luther v. Borden* (1849); Marital Law; Treason; *Virginia v. Brown* (1859)

Resources

Lawson, John D., ed. 1914. "The Trial of Thomas Wilson Dorr for Treason, Rhode Island, 1844." *American State Trials* 2: 5–170. Accessed May 24, 2022. https://ia800304.us.archive.org/6/items/americanstatetr04howagoog/americanstatetr04howagoog.pdf.

McConkie, J. Taylor. 2013. "State Treason: The History and Validity of Treason against Individual States." *Kentucky Law Journal* 101: 281–336.

E

Ellsberg, Daniel

See Pentagon Papers and Trials of Daniel Ellsberg and Anthony Russo

Enforcement Acts (including the "Ku Klux Klan Act") (1870–71)

After the American Civil War ended, three key constitutional amendments—sometimes called "the Civil War Amendments"—were ratified. The Thirteenth Amendment abolished slavery, the Fourteenth Amendment guaranteed, among other things, equal protection and due process of law by state governments, and the Fifteenth Amendment protected against denying the right to vote based on race, color, or previous condition of servitude. Despite—or perhaps, because of—these Civil War Amendments, significant attempts were made by groups, particularly in the former Confederate States, to deny Black Americans their rights as citizens, especially including the right to vote. Formed in 1865 by Confederate veterans, the Ku Klux Klan (KKK) was the predominant group attempting to use intimidation and violence to prevent citizenship and voting by Black Southerners. The extent and effect of the violence in some places resembled continued rebellion or insurgency against the government and Constitution of the United States. In some places, the Klan openly refused to submit to elections that did not result in exclusively white-dominated government. The Klan targeted not only Black Americans, but also white Republicans viewed as supporting the rights of Black Americans.

Finding the Civil War Amendments insufficient to ensure Black Southerners' effective participation in voting and government, Congress passed three "Enforcement Acts," also known as the Force Acts, between 1870 and 1871. The first Enforcement Act criminally prohibited "force, bribery, threats, intimidation, or other unlawful means" to obstruct or prevent voting. The second Enforcement Act gave the federal government, especially federal judges and US marshals, significant authority to supervise federal elections in Southern states. The third Enforcement Act, also known as the Ku Klux Klan Act, criminalized a wide variety of activities, including conspiracies to overthrow the government of the United States or by force, intimidation, or threat to prevent, hinder, or delay the execution of the laws of the United States. Additionally, the Ku Klux Klan Act made it a federal crime to use "force, intimidation, or threat" to infringe on people's rights to vote, hold office, or serve on a jury. Importantly, the third Enforcement Act modified the Insurrection Act by authorizing the president to use the military to suppress any insurrection, domestic violence, unlawful combination, or conspiracy that obstructed or hindered the execution of the law so as to deprive people of any rights, privileges, or immunities identified in the Constitution. Finally, the third Enforcement Act authorized the President to suspend the privilege of the writ of habeas corpus when in a state or part of a state an unlawful combination was so numerous and powerful as to be able to overthrow or defy state and federal authorities.

The Enforcement Acts thus provided the federal judiciary and president with significant tools to enforce voting rights and the law of the United States and to thwart organizations attempting to overthrow or defy the US government and Constitution. The third Enforcement Act was particularly effective in diminishing its primary intended target, the KKK. At President Ulysses S. Grant's direction, the federal military participated in arrests of suspected Klansmen throughout the south. In South Carolina, President Grant declared martial law and suspended habeas corpus, causing the Klan to largely disband and end its activities there. By 1873, federal prosecutors had obtained more than 1,000 convictions for Enforcement Act violations. By 1873, the KKK was largely decimated, and would not reemerge as a significant organization in the United States until forty years later.

Though initially enacted to address problems of Reconstruction in the South following the Civil War, the language of the Enforcement Acts applies beyond Reconstruction. Many of the Enforcement Acts' provisions remain law today, empowering the federal judicial and executive branches to defeat groups engaged in criminal activity against the government or against individual rights. Perhaps the most important of these is 42 United States Code § 1983, which allows individuals to sue government officials for civil rights violations. The Act was cited in lawsuits against former President Donald J. Trump, alleging conspiracy to overturn the results of the 2020 presidential election and conspiracy to incite violence resulting in the Capitol Insurrection on January 6, 2021.

Less well known than § 1983 is another provision of the Enforcement Act of 1870 still in the federal criminal code that criminalizes "conspiracy against rights." Passed in response to persistent violent attacks against newly freed Black Americans, the provision criminalized conspiracies between two or more persons "to injure, oppress, threaten, or intimidate any person in any State, Territory, Commonwealth, Possession, or District in the free exercise or enjoyment of any right or privilege secured to him by the Constitution or laws of the United States." Importantly, the provision applies not only to government officials, but to private actors.

In an early test of the conspiracy against rights provision, in *United States v. Cruikshank* (1876), the United States Supreme Court overturned convictions under the provision of perpetrators of violence in the Colfax Massacre. In *Cruikshank*, the Court found that none of the rights alleged to have been interfered with arose under the United States Constitution or federal law, and thus the conspiracy against rights provision did not apply. However, the Supreme Court has since upheld convictions under the provision, including in situations involving both violent and non-violent rights oppression. Many conspiracy against rights prosecutions have focused on suppression of voting rights arising under the United States Constitution and federal statute. In 2023, former President Donald Trump was indicted under the provision. Federal prosecutors alleged that Trump's attempts to overturn the 2020 presidential election that he lost constituted a conspiracy with others to interfere with "the right to vote, and to have one's vote counted," but did not allege specifically whose rights had been infringed. That prosecution is pending trial as of the date of publication.

See Also: American Civil War and Treason; Capitol Insurrection on January 6, 2021; Colfax Massacre (1873); Conspiracy, Criminal; *Cruikshank, United States v.* (1876); Insurrection; Insurrection Act; Martial Law; Threats against Government Officials

Resources

Cresswell, Stephen. 1987. "Enforcing the Enforcement Acts: The Department of Justice in Northern Mississippi, 1870–1890." *Journal of Southern History* 53: 421–40.

D'Andrea, Jason, and Kai Wiggins. 2023. "Three Questions about Section 241, the Conspiracy against Rights Statute." *Lawfare*, August 16, 2023. Accessed November 15, 2023. https://www.lawfaremedia.org/article/three-questions-about-section-241-the-conspiracy-against-rights-statute.

Foner, Eric. 2020. *The Second Founding: How the Civil War and Reconstruction Remade the Constitution.* New York: W.W. Norton & Co.

Klarman, Michael. 2004. *From Jim Crow to Civil Rights: The Supreme Court and the Struggle for Racial Equality*. Oxford: Oxford University Press.

Trickey, Erick. 2021. "The 150-Year-Old Ku Klux Klan Act Being Used against Trump in Capitol Attack." *The Washington Post*, February 18, 2021.

English Treason Statute of 1351

Nothing illustrates the ancient nature and meaning of American treason law better than its textual mooring to the English Treason Statute of 1351. The two core verbal formulations of American treason law and the two key treason offenses ("levying war" against the government or providing "aid and comfort" to its enemies) were crafted by English lawmakers less than a decade after the Bubonic Plague first began decimating Europe in the 1340s.

The English Treason Statute of 1351 covered six distinct categories of conduct that would constitute "high treason," most of which were clearly archaic and inapplicable to the United States 436 years later when delegates met in Philadelphia to draft the new United States Constitution in the summer of 1787. The original 1351 text of the English Treason Statute classified the following as treasonous conduct: first, when a person "doth compass or imagine the death" of the king, the queen, or the eldest son and heir of the king or queen; second, if a man "do violate" (i.e., have sexual relations) the wife of the king, the king's eldest unmarried daughter, or the wife of the king's eldest son; third, "if a Man do levy War against … the King in his Realm"; fourth, being "adherent to the King's Enemies in his Realm, giving to them Aid and Comfort in the Realm, or elsewhere"; fifth, committing the offense of counterfeiting; and sixth, killing "the Chancellor, Treasurer, or the King's Justices" and judges. Only two of the six grounds for treason ("levying war" and giving "Aid and Comfort" to enemies of the government) were thought to be applicable and relevant to the concept of treason in the new American Republic. While the delegates to the Constitutional Convention viewed counterfeiting as a serious offense, it was viewed as a lesser crime, and thus the delegates authorized Congress to set forth punishments for counterfeiting outside of the contours of treason. The delegates of course viewed the killing of government officials as serious as well, but normal state murder statutes and laws would be sufficient to cover those egregious acts.

Legislators and legal scholars in the subsequent centuries praised the English Treason Statute as an example of limiting and narrowing the scope of an arguably amorphous and potentially politically manipulative criminal charge. United States Supreme Court Justice Joseph Story, in his famous book on the Constitution of the United States, explained that the history of treason in England prior to the 1351 Treason Statute was "full of melancholy instruction on this subject" and "became but too often the instruments, in its hands, of injustice" (Story 1871, 240). Story elaborated that in the hands of "tyrannical princes, they had abundant opportunities to create constructive treasons; that is, by forced and arbitrary constructions, to raise offences into the guilty and punishment of treason, which were not suspected to be such" (Story 1871, 240). According to Justice Story, the potential of abuse "of these constructive treasons was so enormous" that it "so often weighed down the innocent, and the patriotic" (Story 1871, 240). As such, by adopting the 1351 Treason Statute, "the sober sense of the nation has generally abrogated [constructive treasons] or reduced their power within narrow limits" (Story 1871, 240).

The statute also limited those cases that would be subject to one's forfeiture of his or her property to the state under the legal doctrine of Corruption of Blood. One of the greatest of England's common law jurists and scholars, Sir Edward Coke, argued that the greatness of the English Statute of Treason was second only to that of the venerable Magna Carta. James Wilson, the delegate to the United States Constitutional Convention most attributed to the drafting of the Treason Clause in Article III of the Constitution, stated in 1790 that he specifically utilized several key provisions from the English Statute on Treason as it was "like a rock, strong by nature, and fortified … and impregnable by all the rude and boisterous assaults … [and] it may well be styled the legal Gibraltar of England"

(McCloskey 1967, 663–5). Justice Story characterized the English Treason Statute as "the pole star of English jurisprudence upon this subject" (Story 1871, 240). Finally, judges and justices in famous American treason cases ranging from *Aaron Burr v. United States* in 1807 to *Cramer v. United States* in 1945 have favorably endorsed the language from the half millennium old English statute on Treason as continuing to be pertinent and relevant to modern cases. And in each subsequent case from *Aaron Burr v. United States* in 1807 to *Cramer v. United States* in 1945, American judges continue to struggle with the meaning of these seemingly simple words and their application to a drastically different world. As the Supreme Court stated in the *Cramer* decision (in speaking about the English Treason Statute of 1351): "We can read this statute only as our forebears read it—through the eyes of succeeding generations of English judges, to whom it has been the core of all decision, and of common-law commentators, to whom it has been the text."

See Also: Aiding and Comfort Clause (Aid to Enemies of the State); *Burr, United States v.* (1807); Corruption of Blood; *Cramer v. United States* (1945); Levying War; Treason

Resources

Bellamy, John G. 1970. *The Law of Treason in England in the Later Middle Ages*. Cambridge: Cambridge University Press.

Larson, Carlton F. W. 2006. "The Forgotten Constitutional Law of Treason and the Enemy Combatant Problem." *University of Pennsylvania Law Review* 154: 863–926.

McCloskey, Robert Green, ed. 1967. *Of Crimes, Immediately against the Community, in Works of James Wilson*. Cambridge, MA: Harvard University Press.

Story, Joseph. 1871. *A Familiar Exposition of the Constitution of the United States*. New York: Harper & Brothers.

Treason Act 1351. 25 Edw. 3 Stat 5, c.2 §2 (Eng.). Accessed June 29, 2023. https://www.legislation.gov.uk/aep/Edw3Stat5/25/2/contents.

Espionage

Broadly speaking, espionage refers to acts committed in the passage of secret or classified information from an individual or individuals from one country to another country via clandestine and secretive activities. Often, the information transited by one engaged in espionage deals with governmental secrets of a scientific, diplomatic, or military nature. The motivation of individuals committing the offense of espionage is wide-ranging, from acting out of ideological beliefs (like in the cases of Julius and Ethel Rosenberg and Alger Hiss), to monetary compensation or feeling unappreciated by their own government (like in the cases of Aldrich Ames and Robert Hanssen).

The practice of espionage is as old as the existence of nations. For instance, there is evidence that an extensive network of spies was employed by the pharaohs in Egypt roughly four thousand years ago (Samuels 2005). Spying also played a prominent role in the American Revolution. Benedict Arnold was a turncoat during the Revolution and earned the epithet America's Founding Traitor by attempting to sell military secrets to the British during the war. George Washington was considered an expert in espionage operations, and his spies were essential in enabling him to win important victories at Trenton and Princeton (Fleming 1997, 309). One of Washington's spies, a hulking Irish American named Hercules Mulligan, fed Washington invaluable intelligence about British operations in New York. Mulligan also warned Washington about a British plot to kidnap Washington in 1780, a plan that would have been undoubtedly damaging to the American war effort had it been successful. Throughout the twentieth century and the course of the First and Second World Wars, all the warring countries of Europe (and the United States) employed vast spying networks. Concerns over espionage in the First World War led the United States Congress to pass the Espionage Act of 1917, still the chief governing federal law pertaining to espionage in the twenty-first century. Espionage has occurred in every US war and conflict, and in times of peace as well, and unfortunately continues through the present, as illustrated in the June 8, 2023, federal indictment of former President Donald Trump for thirty-one separate violations of the Espionage Act for the willful illegal retention of National Defense Information (18 United States Code Section 793e).

The Espionage Act of 1917 can be found at 18 United States Code Chapter 37, Sections 792–9. The Act makes criminal the passage of any information deemed national defense information in a wide variety of contexts, including the gathering, transmitting, improperly retaining, or losing defense information (Section 793) and gathering or delivering defense information to aid foreign governments (Section 794) to the photographing of defense installations (Sections 795–7) and the simple intentional or unintentional disclosure of classified information (Section 798).

Recent criminal investigations and/or prosecutions of low-level individuals for violation of the Espionage Act of 1917 include Edward Snowden, Julian Assange, Chelsea/Bradley Manning, and Jack Teixeira (see Leaks of National Defense Information). At the highest level, former President of the United States, Donald Trump was federally indicted for thirty-one counts of the Espionage Act in early June 2023 for his alleged mishandling of classified documents which were found at his estate at the Mar-a-Lago Club in Palm Beach, Florida. This prosecution against Trump is still pending as of February 2024.

See Also: Ames, Aldrich Hazen "Rich"; Arnold, Benedict; Capitol Insurrection on January 6, 2021; Espionage Act of 1917; Hanssen, Robert Philip; Hiss, Alger; Leaks of National Defense Information; Mutiny; Rosenberg, Julius and Ethel; Sabotage; Seditious Conspiracy; Treason

Resources

18 U.S. Code Chapter 37. 2022. *Espionage and Censorship.* Sections 792–99.

Becket, Henry S. A. 1986. *The Dictionary of Espionage: Spookspeak into English.* New York: Stein and Day.

Fleming, Thomas. 1997. *Liberty: The American Revolution.* New York: Viking.

Hitz, Frederick P. 2004. *The Great Game: The Myth and Reality of Espionage.* New York: Knopf Publishing.

Samuels, Richard J., ed. 2005. "Espionage." *Encyclopedia of United States National Security.* Vols. 1–2. SAGE Publications, Inc. Accessed November 10, 2023. https://doi.org/10.4135/9781412952446.

Espionage Act of 1917 and Sedition Act of 1918

Two months after the United States declared war with Germany in April 1917, Congress passed the Espionage Act of 1917 (Espionage Act). The Espionage Act criminalized obtaining, conveying, transmitting, receiving, or failing to protect information relating to national defense with intent to injure the United States or aid a foreign nation (*any* foreign nation, not just enemies). It further criminalized inducing, or conspiring with, others to commit such acts. Additionally, the Espionage Act prohibited making false statements with intent to interfere with the success of the military or to promote the success of its enemies and also outlawed causing, or attempting to cause insubordination, disloyalty, mutiny, refusal of duty, in the military or obstructing the recruiting or enlistment service of the United States (see Perjury, False Statements, and the Obstruction of Justice).

In 1918, as the First World War waged on, Congress passed amendments to the Espionage Act that are sometimes informally referred to as the Sedition Act of 1918 (Sedition Act). As had been the case with the Sedition Act of 1798 (one of the Alien and Sedition Acts), the Sedition Act of 1918 was intended to suppress wartime dissent and was Congress's first foray into this area since it enacted the Sedition Act of 1798. The 1918 Sedition Act expanded the types of speech that were prohibited under the Espionage Act, adding "disloyal, profane, scurrilous, or abusive language" about "the form of government of the United States, or the Constitution of the United States, or the military or naval forces of the United States, or the flag of the United States, or the uniform of the Army or Navy of the United States." The Sedition Act also outlawed interfering with the sale of government war bonds or making of loans to the government, teaching or inciting resistance to the United States, and even displaying the flag of an enemy of the United States. Though many Senators opposed the bill on free speech grounds, it passed the Senate forty-eight to twenty-six and sailed through the House of Representatives 293 to one.

Thousands of people were successfully prosecuted for violations of the Espionage Act and Sedition Act (the Acts) during the First World War. In a typical example, a minister in Vermont was prosecuted under the 1918 Sedition Act for telling his Bible study class that "a Christian can take no part in the war" and "Don't shed your precious blood for your country" (Lewis 2007, 103). The jury concluded that the minister's words violated the law because his words illustrated an intent to "cause insubordinate, disloyalty, or refusal of duty" (Lewis 2007, 103). The minister was sentenced to fifteen years in jail for those words uttered in his Bible study class. The Sedition Act was passed only a few months before the First World War concluded, and by its terms was operative only during wartime, so there were fewer convictions under the Sedition Act than the original Espionage Act. Persons prosecuted often challenged the Acts as violating the First Amendment right to free speech, but the United States Supreme Court repeatedly upheld the constitutionality of the Acts and the underlying convictions. For example, the Acts were found not to violate the right to free speech in *Schenck v. United States* (1919), *Frohwerk v. United States* (1919), *Debs v. United States* (1919), and *Abrams v. United States* (1919), all cases involving speech critical of the government, its wartime policies, and capitalism. Though the Acts were upheld as constitutional in those cases, since the Supreme Court's decision in *Brandenburg v. Ohio* (1969), it is unlikely that the portions of the Acts prohibiting speech merely criticizing the government would be considered constitutional.

The Sedition Act was repealed by Congress in the early 1920s as part of its repeal of a number of wartime laws. However, most of the Espionage Act remains in force today. The Espionage Act has been amended several times. For instance, the Internal Security Act of 1950, passed during the Second Red Scare, amended the Espionage Act to make "mere retention" of certain national defense information a crime, regardless of intent to harm the United States or aid another country.

The Espionage Act is still used today to prosecute dissemination of classified national defense information. Some such prosecutions are for traditional "spying," where the defendants intended to harm the United States and/or benefit other countries. For instance, the prosecution of Julius and Ethel Rosenberg relied on the Espionage Act, as did several of the prosecutions related to the Year of the Spy, and the prosecutions of notorious modern spies Aldrich Ames and Robert Hanssen. But in the second fifty years of the Espionage Act's existence, it has also been used to prosecute release of national defense information to the public by persons who many view not as spies, but rather as "whistleblowers" providing a public service by releasing the information. For instance, though the charge was later dismissed, Daniel Ellsberg was initially charged with violating the Espionage Act for his role in leaking the Pentagon Papers to the *New York Times* and *Washington Post*. And alleged perpetrators of other Leaks of National Defense Information, including Julian Assange, Edward Snowden, Chelsea Manning, Reality Winner, and Jack Teixeira, have been charged with, or convicted, of violating the Espionage Act.

The Espionage Act has long had many critics. The prosecution of "whistleblowers" has caused some to call for revision of the Espionage Act to exclude such situations. Defenders of the law counter that it is simply too dangerous to allow individuals to determine in advance and by themselves what it is in the national interest to publicly reveal. The Federal Bureau of Investigation's investigation into former President Donald Trump's apparent retention of classified information at his home in Florida after his presidency concluded, which potentially violated the Espionage Act as amended by the Internal Security Act of 1950, has also prompted proposals to revise the Espionage Act to no longer criminalize mere retention of information without intent to harm the United States or aid foreign nations. In Trump's case, as of June 2023, according to the federal indictment released on June 8, 2023, he has provided no explanation or justification as to why he retained 102 documents marked "Confidential," "Secret," or "Top Secret," especially when previously advised to return those documents to the federal government. The federal grand jury indicted Trump for thirty-one separate counts of violating the Espionage Act, specifically in the unlawful willful retention of National Defense Information (18 United States Code Section 793e), despite multiple attempts by the federal government to get the documents back and because of Trump's obstruction and refusal to cooperate with the federal government in retrieving those documents. The first ever trial of a former United States' president for alleged violations of the Espionage Act of 1917 is pending at the time of this writing. And finally, as was the case when it was first enacted, many today argue the Espionage Act inappropriately—and perhaps unconstitutionally—suppresses valuable speech.

See Also: *Abrams v. United States* (1919); Ames, Aldrich Hazen "Rich"; Alien and Sedition Acts (1798); *Brandenburg v. Ohio* (1969); *Debs v. United States* (1919); Flag Disrespect as Crime against the State; Hanssen, Robert Philip; Internal Security Act of 1950; Leaks of National Defense Information; Mutiny; Pentagon Papers and Trials of Daniel Ellsberg and Anthony Russo; Perjury, False Statements, and Obstruction of Justice; Rosenberg, Julius and Ethel; *Schenck v. United States* (1919); Second Red Scare (McCarthyism); Sedition Act of 1798; Speech as Crime against the State; Year of the Spy (1985)

Resources

Abrams v. United States, 250 U.S. 616 (1919).

Barnes, Julian E. 2022. "What Is the Espionage Act and How Has It Been Used?" *The New York Times*, August 15, 2022.

Brandenburg v. Ohio, 395 U.S. 444 (1969).
Debs v. United States, 249 U.S. 211 (1919).
Espionage Act of 1917.
Frohwerk v. United States, 249 U.S. 204 (1919).
Lewis, Anthony. 2007. *Freedom for the Thought that We Hate: A Biography of the First Amendment*. New York: Basic Books.
Rehnquist, William H. 2001. *All the Laws but One*. New York: Knopf, Chapter 14.
Schenck v. United States, 249 U.S. 47 (1919).
Sedition Act of 1918.
Stone, Geoffrey R. 2004. *Perilous Times: Free Speech in Wartime from the Sedition Act of 1798 to the War on Terrorism*. New York: W.W. Norton and Co.

Eufaula Election Massacre and Spring Hill Riot (1874)

After emancipation and ratification of the Fifteenth Amendment, the newly enfranchised Black electorate had a significant impact on elections throughout the American South. In the early 1870s, Republican candidates supported by Black voters won many elections. These candidates tended to support policies of Reconstruction and civil rights for Black citizens. White supremacist-backed Democrats fought back in a variety of ways, the most effective of which was employment of violence and physical intimidation. One such incident occurred in Eufaula, Alabama, on election day, November 3, 1874.

Four years before the massacre, newly enfranchised Black voters had helped Republicans elect Elias Keils to the position of city judge. Judge Keils was a white Southerner who supported the federal government's Reconstruction policies, earning him (and other Southerners like him) the epithet "scalawag." In 1874, Keils' bid for reelection caused a backlash among white Democrats, who began threatening violence and engaging in other intimidation tactics in the lead-up to election day. Some circulated false rumors that large groups of Black residents of Eufaula were planning election day violence. Some members of the White League, an armed white supremacist group associated with the Democratic Party throughout the south, created a weapons cache outside the town.

On election day, White League members and supporters gathered in Eufaula and attempted to intimidate Black voters who were marching to the polls in large groups. Someone fired a gun (accounts differ as to whether the shooter was white or Black). After that, a large group of white men retrieved their stockpiled weapons and began firing upon the crowd of Black voters, most of whom were unarmed. Six to eight Black voters were killed and up to eighty injured. Most fled, among them an estimated 500 Black voters who had not yet voted.

Later the same day, a mob of white men attacked a different polling place in nearby Spring Hill, Alabama. The election supervisor at that location was Judge Keils, whose requests in advance of the election to state and federal officials for security assistance had been denied. The mob broke open the ballot box, burned the ballots, and killed Judge Keils's sixteen-year-old son.

Though Republican voters outnumbered Democrats two to one in the county, after the violence and ballot burning, Democrats won all the elections in the county that day. But the effects of the massacre lasted much longer than one election. After the intimidation and threats of physical violence leading up to the election were followed by actual physical violence, Black residents stopped voting. Roughly 1,200 Black Eufaula residents voted in the 1874 election on the day of the massacre (ostensibly before the massacre began); ten Black residents cast ballots in the 1876 election. In 1904, in downtown Eufaula where Blacks were shot and killed for voting, the city of Eufaula erected a towering Confederate monument donated by the United Daughters of the Confederacy. Upon its unveiling, a confederate soldier who allegedly witnessed (and perhaps participated in) the massacre was asked to be a keynote speaker. The monument stood on this spot and was still standing as late as November 2022. In December 2022, the Eufaula City Council passed a resolution authorizing the relocation of the 35-foot monument, citing the need to move it "from its present high traffic area for safety reasons and future public transportation system projects" (City of Eufaula 2022).

Despite a Congressional investigation and numerous eyewitnesses identifying various individuals in the White League who participated in the Eufaula and Spring Hill violence and insurrection, none were ever charged or convicted. Thirty years after the massacre, Braxton Bragg Comer, one of the leaders of the attack on the polling place in Spring Hill, would be elected governor of Alabama.

As with the Colfax Massacre (1873), the Battle of Liberty Place (1874), the Wilmington Insurrection of 1898, and others, the Eufaula Election Massacre and Spring Hill Riot were perpetrated by armed white supremacists determined to retake control of government. And the white supremacists' success in violent insurrections aimed at the electoral process led to the domination of state and local government and decades of Jim Crow laws throughout the South.

See Also: Battle of Liberty Place (1874); Colfax Massacre (1873); Insurrection; Wilmington Insurrection of 1898

Resources

Carter, Dan T. 1995. *The Politics of Rage: George Wallace, the Origins of the New Conservatism, and the Transformation of American Politics*. New York: Simon & Schuster, 36–7.

City of Eufaula, Alabama. 2022. Resolution 108–2022. Accessed October 31, 2023. https://www.eufaulaalabama.com/DocumentCenter/View/1725/108-2022–Resolution-RE-Broad-Barbour-Eufaula-Avenue-Intersections.

Owen, Harry P. 1963. "The Eufaula Riot of 1874." *Alabama Review* 16 (July): 224–7.

"Reconstruction in America: Racial Violence after the Civil War, 1865–1876." *Equal Justice Initiative*. Accessed June 29, 2023. https://eji.org/report/reconstruction-in-america/.

Ex Parte Bollman (1807)

Ex Parte Bollman (1807) was an important early Supreme Court opinion that delineated the narrow scope and parameters of treason law under the United States Constitution. The Court's decision in *Ex Parte Bollman* precluded the possibility of individuals being convicted for treason based only upon the conspiracy to engage in levying war against the government. Phrased another way, merely conspiring to engage in treason or having the intention to levy war against the United States (without overt actions in furtherance of the plans) is not treason under Article III of the United States Constitution. The *Ex Parte Bollman* decision influenced and foreshadowed the outcome in the subsequent prosecution of Aaron Burr for treason a brief time later in *United States v. Burr* (1807).

The Supreme Court's opinion in *Ex Parte Bollman* resulted from the attempt to prosecute for treason two of Aaron Burr's co-conspirators, Erick Bollman and Samuel Swartwout. It was alleged that Bollman and Swartwout assisted Burr with the recruitment of men needed for Burr's treasonous plans (see Burr, Aaron and *Burr, United States v.*). Bollman was also promised an ambassadorship by Burr should Burr's plans succeed. Bollman and Swartwout were arrested in New Orleans before Burr was captured, and incriminating evidence was found on both individuals. Bollman and Swartwout were transferred to the nation's new capital, to be put on trial in the District of Columbia (DC). Shortly after Bollman and Swartwout's arrival in DC, on February 5, 1807, counsel for the two defendants requested that the United States Supreme Court review the pre-trial detention of Bollman and Swartwout. In granting the defendants' petition for *habeas corpus* and ordering the defendants' release, the Court explained its rationale in the *Ex Parte Bollman* decision.

In a decision authored by Chief Justice John Marshall, the majority held that "to constitute a levying of war, there must be an assemblage of persons for the purpose of effecting by force a treasonable purpose. Enlistments of men to serve against government is not sufficient." This meant Bollman and Swartwout were free men. For a brief time after the *Ex Parte Bollman* decision and until Aaron Burr was acquitted of treason charges a short time later, it was unclear whether the assembly of persons alone could constitute treason. Prosecutors in the *Burr* case focused on the one sentence in the *Ex Parte Bollman* ruling that specified that there "must be an assemblage of persons for the purpose of effecting by force a treasonable purpose." The faulty reliance by the Burr prosecutors on only the first part of this sentence ("that there must be an assemblage of persons") would be explained by Chief Justice Marshall (as the presiding judge) in the subsequent trial of Aaron Burr as being insufficient in and of itself for purposes of determining that the defendant had levied war against the United States. That is, in *United States v. Burr*, Chief Justice Marshall would make clear that assembly alone cannot constitute levying war and treason. There must be an assemblage of forces and actual armed hostile actions taken against the government.

See Also: Burr, Aaron; *Burr, United States v.* (1807); Conspiracy, Criminal; Levying War; Treason

Resources

Colunga, Isaac J. 2006. "Ex Parte Bollman: Revisiting a Federalist's Commitment to Civil Liberty." *Thomas M. Cooley Law Review* 23: 429–42.

Ex Parte Bollman (1807), 8 U.S. (Cranch) 75–137.

Passos, John Dos. 1966. "The Conspiracy and Trial of Aaron Burr." *American Heritage*, February 1966. Accessed May 23, 2022. https://www.americanheritage.com/conspiracy-and-trial-aaron-burr.

Ex Parte Milligan (1866)

Ex Parte Milligan involved a Confederate sympathizer during the American Civil War named Lambdin Milligan. Milligan was an Indiana resident, US citizen, attorney, and political candidate representing an extreme faction of the Democratic Party. Milligan joined a secret organization—the "Sons of Liberty"—that was hostile to the national government and sympathetic to the "states' rights" argument made by the secessionist Confederate States of America. Apparently, Mr. Milligan was not in any way associated with the Confederate Army or acting at the direction of the Confederacy; he was merely sympathetic to the Confederate cause of states standing up to federal government power.

The United States Army was sufficiently concerned about the Sons of Liberty that it placed undercover spies in the organization. When a large number of weapons and ammunition were discovered in a warehouse owned by one of the Sons of Liberty's leaders, a plot to attack a Union armory and use the weapons obtained at the armory to free Confederate prisoners from a nearby Union prison was uncovered. Though the Civil War was raging at the time, the armory Milligan and other Sons of Liberty plotted to attack was nowhere near any military conflict. Nevertheless, United States Army officers ordered various leaders of the Sons of Liberty, including Milligan, arrested by military authority. Ultimately, Milligan was convicted by a military commission of violation of the laws of war, treason, and conspiracy.

At the time of Milligan's arrest and conviction by a military tribunal, the civilian criminal courts were still functioning in Indiana. A civilian grand jury had been sitting in the jurisdiction where Milligan would have been tried in civilian court, but it failed to return an indictment against him before he was brought before the military tribunal. Though Milligan was found guilty and sentenced to be hanged, the execution was not carried out immediately. Once the war ended, some Indiana *Republicans* successfully lobbied President Andrew Johnson to commute Milligan's sentence to life in prison. Milligan challenged his detention, conviction, and sentence in a case that reached the United States Supreme Court.

In *Ex Parte Milligan*, the Supreme Court addressed two fundamental legal issues: (1) whether Milligan had the right to seek review of his detention through the principle of habeas corpus; and (2) whether the president had authority to detain noncombatants as part of a war effort. The Supreme Court ultimately determined that Milligan had the right to use the habeas corpus process to challenge his detention. More importantly for understanding of how crimes against the state may be prosecuted, in *Milligan* the Supreme Court held that the president—and the military acting under his command—did not have the authority to try Milligan before a military commission under the circumstances, because he was a US citizen and the civilian courts were open and functioning, and the alleged crimes and the court were outside the war zone. Though the Supreme Court ultimately split on whether Congress could have granted the president such authority, it had not, and so the Court concluded Milligan's detention, conviction, and arrest were without authority.

Ex Parte Milligan was the first significant Supreme Court decision regarding military commissions. In agreeing with Milligan's claim that the military commission was unlawful, the Supreme Court observed that Congress had not authorized military commissions to try civilian citizens who were not combatants in the military conflict and where the civilian courts were open and functioning outside the theater of war. The majority also suggested that Congress could not have authorized a military commission under such circumstances, though concurring Justices believed Congress could have authorized a tribunal, but simply had not. Importantly, the Court found that the "laws of war" for which Milligan was tried were irrelevant in the case, because they can "never be applied to citizens in states which have upheld the authority of the government, and where the courts are open and their process unobstructed .... [N]o usage of war could sanction a military trial there for any offense whatever of a citizen in civil life, in nowise connected with the military service." The Court's unwillingness to allow military tribunals to substitute for available civilian courts rests in large part on the persistent concern that military commissions are anathema to liberty:

> When peace prevails ... there is no difficulty of preserving the safeguards of liberty ... but if society is disturbed by civil commotion—if the passions of men are aroused and the restraints of law weakened, if not disregarded—these safeguards need, and should receive, the watchful care of those intrusted with the guardianship of the Constitution and laws .... [Martial law] destroys every guarantee of the Constitution, and effectually renders the "military independent of and superior to the civil power"—the attempt to do which by the King of Great Britain was deemed by our fathers such an offense, that they assigned it to the world as one of the causes which impelled them to declare their independence.

Milligan's actions call to mind another famous attempted attack on a US armory. But John Brown's Raid went far beyond the planning stage, came far closer to being "successful" than Milligan's effort, and was motivated by nearly the opposite intention. And the protagonists of each saga met far different fates. John Brown was convicted of treason against the Commonwealth of Virginia and executed. On the other hand, Milligan's conviction by military commission was overturned by the Supreme Court, and though a federal grand jury in Indianapolis indicted Milligan for conspiracy to overthrow the government, the United States attorney did not pursue the case. In fact, Milligan "successfully" sued the United States Army officers who had arrested and convicted him, though the jury awarded Milligan only $5.

Ex Parte Milligan, which suggests that US citizens cannot be tried by military commission when civilian courts are open and functioning, even for crimes targeting the military, would be called into question in the Second World War case of *Ex Parte Quirin*, and again later in *Hamdi v. Rumsfeld* (2004) and other cases arising during the "war on terror" following the 9/11 terror attacks.

See Also: American Civil War and Treason; Conspiracy, Criminal; *Ex Parte Quirin* (1942); *Hamdi v. Rumsfeld* (2004); John Brown's Raid (1859); Martial Law; Treason

Resources

Merriam, Eric, and Douglas B. McKechnie. 2021. *National Security Law.* St. Paul: West Academic, 233–4, 254–5.

Towne, Stephen. n.d. "Lambdin P Milligan and Dissent in the Civil War." *State of Indiana*. Accessed June 29, 2023. https://www.in.gov/history/about-indiana-history-and-trivia/annual-commemorations/civil-war-150th/hoosier-voices-now/lambdin-p-milligan-and-dissent-in-the-civil-war/.

Ex Parte Quirin (1942)

The *Ex Parte Quirin* case involved Germany's attempt to infiltrate and sabotage military-related targets in the continental United States during the Second World War. Code named "Operation Pastorius," Germany's plan sought to attack production facilities like aluminum plants and raw materials processing factories for aluminum, necessary for manufacturing aircraft. Additionally, waterways and rail lines would be targeted throughout the northeast and Midwest. The plan was to land saboteurs on US beaches by U-boat (German submarine) every six weeks. Germany had a ready supply of saboteurs who could blend in the United States, as thousands of Germans who had lived for a long time in the United States and could speak English had returned to Germany.

In June 1942 during the early months of the United States' participation in the Second World War, eight German nationals came to the United States to engage in sabotage. All eight had been born in Germany but had previously lived in the United States. Two of the eight—Herbert Haupt, son of Hans Max Haupt, who would later be prosecuted in *Haupt v. United States* (1947), and Ernest Burger—were dual citizens of the United States and Germany. Under the cover of darkness, the saboteurs arrived by U-boat on two Atlantic beaches—one on Long Island, New York, and the other near Jacksonville, Florida. After arriving in uniform, the Germans changed into civilian clothes and began preparations to sabotage manufacturing plants, freight rails, and other key infrastructure. An unarmed Coast Guard patrolman approached the Long Island group, and then pretended to accept a $260 bribe from them to remain quiet. He promptly returned to his base and sounded the alarm, but by the time a search patrol arrived, the four had left the beach and escaped by train to New York City. Two of the saboteurs—George Dasch, who had previously served in the United States Army, and Ernest Burger—soon had a change of heart and alerted the Federal Bureau of Investigation (FBI) of their plans before any acts of sabotage were executed or even attempted. All eight saboteurs were quickly apprehended.

Postwar debriefing of German personnel confirmed that these two failed missions initiated with submarine landings were the only such attempts by Germany during the Second World War. According to the FBI, although it investigated many allegations of sabotage in the United States during the Second World War, not one instance was found of enemy-conducted sabotage. Every suspect act was traced to some other motive, such as "vandalism, pique, resentment, a desire for relief from boredom, the curiosity of children 'to see what would happen,' or other personal motive" (Federal Bureau of Investigation 2023).

Less than a week after the would-be saboteurs were captured, President Franklin D. Roosevelt established a military commission to try "all enemies who have entered upon the territory of the United States as part of an invasion or predatory incursion" and who under enemy states' direction, committed acts of sabotage, espionage, or "violations of the law of war" (Federal Bureau of Investigation 2023). Two days later, on July 4, 1942, a military tribunal convened. After a trial that lasted nearly three weeks, and included Dasch and Burger testifying against their fellow saboteurs, the saboteurs' military defense counsel, Colonel Kenneth Royall, challenged the lawfulness of the military tribunal by demanding a writ of habeas corpus from a federal district court, and appealed lower courts' denials all the way to the United States Supreme Court in a blisteringly fast matter of days.

Citing *Ex Parte Milligan*, the saboteurs' counsel argued that the beaches where the eight had come ashore could not be considered "zones of military operation" as there was no combat there, and that because the civil courts were still functioning in the United States, they—not military tribunals—were the appropriate venue for charges against the eight to be tried. On July 29, 1942, the Supreme

Court met in special session (because the Court's term for the year had concluded), and on July 31 orally issued its unanimous opinion that the military commission was lawful because the men were enemy belligerents. And because they were *unlawful* enemy combatants, they were not entitled to immunity from prosecution ordinarily afforded prisoners of war.

On August 3, the seven members of the military commission found all eight men guilty and recommended they be executed, though the commission noted the assistance Dasch and Burger had provided in the apprehension of the teams and by testifying for the prosecution during the trial, recommending their death sentences be commuted to life in prison. President Roosevelt agreed with the military commission's recommendations, and on August 8, the six were executed by electric chair. Dasch and Burger were sentenced to confinement and hard labor for life, though they were ultimately deported to Germany following the war.

The Supreme Court did not issue its written opinion in the case until October 29, 1942, months after the men had been executed. The Supreme Court found the president had authority for the military tribunals under the Articles of War (the system of military justice that predated the Uniform Code of Military Justice) and the international law of war. Importantly, the status of two of the saboteurs as dual United States citizens did not exempt them from military tribunals as unlawful enemy combatants.

Understanding how *Milligan* and *Quirin* relate to each other is important. In *Milligan*, the Supreme Court held that a US citizen in the United States and not in a war zone *could not* be tried by a military commission while the civilian courts were still open and functioning. In *Quirin*, the Court effectively held that US citizens (Haupt and Burger) in the United States and not in a war zone *could* be tried by a military commission even though the civilian courts were still open and functioning. The Supreme Court in *Quirin* found a difference between the facts of the cases to be significant: *Milligan* was a civilian and the *Quirin* defendants were belligerents. Indeed, the *Quirin* defendants were uniformed soldiers of an enemy state. It was the *Quirin* defendants'—including the two US citizens'—status as admitted enemy belligerents that changed the result. Importantly, the Court in *Quirin* did not articulate a standard for when a US citizen will be considered a belligerent or sufficiently associated with an enemy military to be susceptible to trial by military commission, but that is likely because it was obvious in *Quirin* and the US citizens did not challenge their status as belligerents.

Quirin seemed destined for the pile of obsolete precedent until the terror attacks of September 11, 2001. *Quirin* then played a meaningful role in several subsequent Supreme Court opinions regarding the lawfulness of military tribunals, including *Hamdi v. Rumsfeld* (2004), *Hamdan v. Rumsfeld* (2006), and *Boumediene v. Bush* (2008).

See Also: Espionage; *Ex Parte Milligan* (1866); *Hamdi v. Rumsfeld* (2004); *Haupt v. United States* (1947); Sabotage; September 11, 2001

Resources

Buttaro, Andrew. 2006. "Ex Parte *Quirin*: The Nazi Saboteur Case and the Tribunal Precedent." *American University Law Brief* 6: 37–65.

Ex Parte Quirin, 317 U.S. 1 (1942).

Federal Bureau of Investigation. "Nazi Saboteurs and George Dasch." Accessed June 29, 2023. https://www.fbi.gov/history/famous-cases/nazi-saboteurs-and-george-dasch.

Merriam, Eric, and Douglas B. McKechnie. 2021. *National Security Law.* St. Paul: West Academic, 237–40, 279–80.

Ex Parte Vallandigham (1864)

During the American Civil War, President Lincoln declared martial law, giving subordinate military commanders authority to carry it out. In April 1863, Major General Ambrose Burnside, commander over Military District of Ohio, issued General Order Number 38, declaring that all persons found within his jurisdiction who committed "acts for the benefit of the enemies of our country, should be tried as spies or traitors, and if convicted should suffer death" and also prohibiting "declaring sympathies for the enemy."

Clement Vallandigham was a former Democratic Congressman from Ohio who was pro-Confederate, pro-slavery, and against the Civil War. He was the leader of the pro-Confederate group of northerners known as Copperheads and had participated in the interrogation of John Brown after John Brown's Raid of the southern federal armory and arsenal in 1859. After losing in the 1862 Congressional election, in 1863, Vallandigham began a campaign for governor of Ohio as an anti-war candidate. On May 1, 1863, just weeks after General Burnside's order, Vallandigham gave a public speech in which he argued that the Civil War was "a wicked, cruel, and unnecessary war, one not waged for the preservation of the Union, but for the purpose of crushing out liberty and to erect a despotism; a war for the freedom of the blacks and the enslavement of the whites; and that if the administration had not wished otherwise, that the war could have been honorably terminated long ago." He exhorted supporters of the war, "Defeat, debt, taxation [and] sepulchers—these are your trophies." Vallandigham characterized General Order Number 38 as "a base usurpation of arbitrary authority," urging his listeners to resist martial law, exclaiming "the sooner the people inform the minions of usurped power that they will not submit to such restrictions upon their liberties, the better" (Swisher 1974, 925).

A few days after his speech, Vallandigham was apprehended by military officials and charged with "having expressed sympathies for those in arms against the government of the United States, and for having uttered, in a speech at a public meeting, disloyal sentiments and opinions, with the object and purpose of weakening the power of the government in its efforts for the suppression of an unlawful rebellion." Vallandigham was tried by a military commission (a trial by military officers appointed by their commander rather than a civilian court). He denied the jurisdiction of the military commission and initially refused to enter a plea. Nevertheless, Vallandigham ultimately participated in the trial by military commission, with the benefit of counsel. He was convicted and sentenced to be imprisoned for the duration of the war.

Vallandigham's trial and conviction unleashed a furor of criticism by Democrats and even some Republicans. In defending Vallandigham's conviction for his speech, President Lincoln asked, "Must I shoot a simple-minded soldier boy who deserts, while I must not touch a hair of the wily agitator who induces him to desert?" (Swisher 1974, 928). But the political fallout of the conviction was such that Lincoln felt he had to take action, so he banished Vallandigham to the Confederacy, sending him behind enemy lines to Tennessee.

Vallandigham appealed his conviction and sentence, arguing the military commission did not have jurisdiction to try civilians under the circumstances. In *Ex Parte Vallandigham*, the United States Supreme Court determined it did not have jurisdiction to review an appeal from a military commission. The Supreme Court's decision was momentous in ensuring the military's ability to try and sentence civilians and military members without appellate review, though the Court would later change its mind on that question (for instance, two years later in *Ex Parte Milligan*, the Court determined it did have jurisdiction to review—and overturn—the military detention and prevent the military commission of a civilian). Moreover, in deciding it did not have jurisdiction to review the case, the Supreme Court sidestepped the serious constitutional question of whether mere speech that is critical of a war effort or that supports ending the war, without action, can be criminalized as a crime against the state.

See Also: American Civil War and Treason; Brown, John; *Ex Parte Milligan* (1866); John Brown's Raid (1859); Martial Law; Speech as Crime against the State

Resources

"Clement Laird Vallandigham." *American History Central*. Accessed June 29, 2023. https://www.americanhistorycentral.com/entries/vallandigham-clement/.

Ex Parte Vallandigham, 68 U.S. 243 (1864).

Swisher, Carl B. 1974. *The Taney Period, 1836–64. Vol. 5 of History of the Supreme Court of the United States.* New York: Macmillan Publishing.

F

First Red Scare and the Palmer Raids (1919–20)

The first Red Scare Era (1919–20) following the First World War, not to be confused with the Second Red Scare Era (1946–60) following the Second World War, involved a mixture of both very real threats to the United States' homeland security, and hysteria, xenophobia, antisemitism, racism, and other ugly human tendencies. The Palmer Raids (1919–20), named after United States Attorney General A. Mitchell Palmer, were an attempt to combat perceived threats to the country in 1919 and 1920, and resulted in the arrest and deportation of persons deemed undesirable. While the public viewed the raids as an unqualified success at the time, through the hindsight of history, the raids are today remembered for the rampant civil rights abuses and constitutional law violations that occurred to thousands of innocent Americans.

The Red Scare (and the resulting Palmer Raids) had its genesis in the period immediately following the end of the First World War and the Bolshevik seizure of the Russian government in 1917. Many Americans transferred their the First World War distrust of Germans, fueled by United States government propaganda during the First World War, to a distrust of Communists, Bolsheviks, and anarchists after the war. The general fear was that Bolshevik-inspired revolution and violence might be exported to the United States. Economically, some historians traced the growing hysteria and alarm over communist and socialist threats within the United States to the Seattle General Strike (February 6, 1919–February 11, 1919). The Seattle General Strike involved a work stoppage of approximately 315,000 individuals (roughly the population of Seattle at that time) and 25,000 union members who also went on strike and joined 35,000 shipyard workers already also on strike. This massive labor strike is said to be the catalyst that set in motion the onset of the Red Scare Era of 1919–20.

Additionally, several significant terrorist events occurred in late April 1919 and June 2, 1919, that further heightened the public hysteria. This terrorism drastically increased the public distrust of foreigners, extending it beyond socialists and communists to many eastern European immigrants, including immigrants of Jewish and Italian descent.

In April 1919, anarchists (mostly Italian immigrants known as "Galleanists" because they followed the beliefs of anarchist Luigi Galleani) mailed thirty-six booby-trapped packages to prominent political and business leaders, including Congressmen, Senators, John D. Rockefeller, J. P. Morgan, Supreme Court Justice Oliver Wendell Holmes Jr., and Attorney General A. Mitchell Palmer. Each package contained dynamite and was designed to detonate when the package was opened after delivery on May 1 (May Day), which had special meaning to the International Workers Union and is known as International Workers Day. Fortunately, only one of the thirty-six boxes was opened, injuring the wife and a domestic servant of a United States Senator, and no-one was killed in the bombing attempt. On June 2, 1919, the anarchists mailed nine additional bombs to be detonated simultaneously in eight separate cities. These packages each contained twenty-five pounds of explosives. One bomb prematurely exploded outside the home of Judge Charles Cooper Nott Jr., in New York City, killing the two people who were planting it.

Public hysteria and the "Red Scare" reached a fevered pitch in response to the bombings, prompting the Attorney General to adopt an aggressive approach to combat this group of anarchists. On August 1, 1919, Palmer named a 24-year-old protégé, J. Edgar Hoover, to lead the new division of the Justice Department's Bureau of Investigation. Hoover previously worked for the New York Public Library and helped develop a comprehensive card catalogue system while working for the library. Hoover used this specific skill set for Attorney General Palmer in 1919–20, when Hoover developed intelligence cards (containing biographical and personal information) on a little over a half-million Americans for Palmer. Sixty thousand individuals were targeted for surveillance and/or arrest by Palmer and his forces. Over the course of Hoover's long subsequent law enforcement career until his death in 1973, he would maintain and expand his card database on hundreds of thousands of average Americans.

Over the course of a couple of months at the end of 1919 and the beginning of 1920, Palmer authorized a series of law enforcement raids across the country attempting to flush out and arrest suspected subversive aliens and communists. Many teachers and civil activists were targeted, despite having no affiliation with the Communist Party or anarchists. As an illustration of the overbroad dragnet nature of these raids, on one day alone, November 7, 1919, raids were conducted in twelve cities across the United States, and upwards of 10,000 individuals were arrested without judicial warrants. Government officials claimed that the raids netted thousands of individuals who were suspected of fomenting riots, advocating the overthrow of the government, and violating immigration laws. Of the 650 individuals arrested in New York City, forty-three were eventually deported (approximately 6 percent). Although most of those arrested were innocent of the charges levied against them, hundreds were tried, found guilty, and sentenced to deportation. In December 1919, a ship carrying approximately 250 deportees left the United States for Russia. Historians estimate that across the country over 75 percent of the arrestees were released after arrest without any charges or judicial processing, but some only after significant detention without trial. In Hartford, Connecticut, for example, one hundred individuals were held for five months, during which time they were not allowed lawyers and were not informed of the charges. On another single night of raids, January 2, 1920, thirty cities in twenty-three states were targeted. Of the approximately 10,000 arrested, 3,500 were held in detention without charge, and of those, 556 were eventually deported under the Immigration Act of 1918. The most famous of the individuals deported as part of the Palmer Raids was Emma Goldman, the noted political activist and author. Later, Attorney General Palmer reported to the United States Senate that his department had amassed 60,000 names for purposes of subsequent surveillance, undoubtedly the names contained on J. Edgar Hoover's surveillance cards, a catalogue that would only grow in number in subsequent years.

The consensus of many today is the Palmer Raids cast its net far too widely, leading to the detention and arrest of many thousands of innocent people, often in violation of those individuals' constitutional rights. As commented by Professor Jay Shafritz, "thousands of citizens and laborers were arrested without specific charges. The raids were noted for their lack of due process and violation of civil liberties" (Shafritz 1988, 468). According to Bruce Maxwell, "[m]any of those arrested were not communists; the authorities frequently made arrests without search or arrest warrants; and the civil liberties of those arrested—such as the right to counsel—were routinely violated" (Maxwell 2004, 19). Even J. Edgar Hoover later admitted that "clear cases of brutality" were committed by agents during the Palmer Raids. According to the Federal Bureau of Investigation (FBI) on its official website in 2022, the FBI admitted that the Palmer Raids were not "ideal," saying: "The 'Palmer

Raids' were certainly not a bright spot for the young Bureau. But it did gain valuable experience in terrorism investigations and intelligence work and learn important lessons about the need to protect civil liberties and constitutional rights."

The period of the first Red Scare and Palmer Raids involved genuine threats to homeland security (a total of forty-five highly explosive bombs sent to prominent politicians and business leaders) intermixed with public hysteria feeding on the worst elements of human nature such as xenophobia, antisemitism, and racism. One positive consequence of these events is that they led to the creation of the American Civil Liberties Union (ACLU) in 1920.

In June 1920, Massachusetts District Court Judge George Anderson ordered the discharge of several defendants who were rounded up during the Palmer Raids and powerfully noted: "A mob is a mob whether made up of Government officials acting under instructions of the Department of Justice, or of criminals and loafers and the vicious classes" (Congressional Record 1940, 7279).

See Also: Anarchy, Criminal; Espionage Act of 1917 and Sedition Act of 1918; Riot and Incitement to Riot; Second Red Scare (McCarthyism); Terrorism

Resources

Congressional Record: Proceedings and Debates of the 76th Congress (Third Session). 1940. Vol. 86 (Part 7): 7279. Washington, DC: United States Government Printing Office.

Federal Bureau of Investigation. 2022. "History: Famous Cases & Criminals: Palmer Raids." Accessed May 21, 2022. https://www.fbi.gov/history/famous-cases/palmer-raids.

Maxwell, Bruce. 2004. *Homeland Security: A Documentary History*. Washington, DC: CQ Press.

Murray, Robert K. 1964. *Red Scare: A Study in National Hysteria, 1919–1920*. New York: McGraw Hill.

Shafritz, Jay M. 1988. *The Dorsey Dictionary of American Government and Politics*. Chicago: The Dorsey Press.

Shepley, Nick. 2015. *The Palmer Raids and the Red Scare: 1918–1920: Justice and Liberty for All*. Luton, England: Andrews UK Limited.

Flag Disrespect as Crime against the State

The American flag is the supreme symbol of the United States to Americans and non-Americans alike. It is the primary subject of the National Anthem, is worn on the uniforms of its servicemembers and drapes their caskets, was planted on the moon by the first human visitor to its surface, is present at most sporting events, and is flown twenty-four hours a day at the White House. Revered by some with great pride and patriotism and reviled by others with great enmity, no national icon conjures stronger emotion. Because of that important sentiment, numerous states and the federal government have attempted to protect the flag by making disrespect or desecration a crime against the state.

Efforts to "protect the flag" during the early twentieth century and into the First World War initially involved state laws criminalizing flag desecration. One such law was sanctioned by the United States Supreme Court in *Halter v. Nebraska* (1907), when the Court unanimously upheld a beer company's conviction for including an image of the American flag on its beer bottle labels. The Court determined that the Nebraska law did not conflict with any federal laws and that states had the right to protect the flag "as an emblem of National power and National honor." In the Sedition Act of 1918, Congress followed suit and criminalized at the federal level disrespecting the American flag or displaying the flag of an enemy.

Decades later in *Minersville School District v. Gobitis* (1940), the United States Supreme Court upheld a local school board's requirement that all students salute the national flag as part of a daily school exercise. The Court held that the requirement violated neither the student's freedom of religion nor freedom of speech. The majority observed that local government had the "right to select appropriate means" for attainment of "national cohesion" and that "National unity is the basis of national security."

Perhaps emboldened by the Supreme Court's *Gobitis* opinion, and during the Second World War, a number of states enacted "flag salute laws," which in some instances mandated saluting the flag and in other instances prohibited even advocating against saluting the flag. In 1943, the Supreme Court reversed course from its *Gobitis* opinion, ruling in *West Virginia State Board of Education v. Barnette* that states could not compel school children to salute the flag. The Court found that such laws violated the First Amendment. In a stinging rebuke to the argument that all Americans should revere and salute the flag, Justice Robert Jackson, writing for the majority, wrote that "compulsory unification of opinion achieves only the unanimity of the graveyard." And Justice Jackson famously concluded, "If there is any fixed star in our constitutional constellation, it is that no official, high or petty, can prescribe what shall be orthodox in matters of politics, nationalism, religion, or other matters of opinion[,] or force citizens to confess by word their faith therein." Also in 1943, in *Taylor v. Mississippi*, the Court invalidated a Mississippi law that criminalized helping "create an attitude of stubborn refusal to salute, honor or respect the flag or government of the United States, or of the state of Mississippi."

During the controversial Vietnam War and turbulent Civil Rights Movement of the 1960s, the American flag again became a flashpoint, with some burning or otherwise desecrating the flag as a form of protest against the United States and its policies. In its 1969 decision in *Street v. New York*, the Supreme Court overturned the conviction of Sidney Street for what was arguably civil disobedience. In New York City, Street protested the shooting of civil rights leader James Meredith by setting an American flag on fire while saying "If they did that to Meredith, we don't need an American flag" and "We don't need no damn flag." A New York state statute criminalized desecration of the American flag, including speaking contemptuous words about the flag. In a five to four opinion, the Court found that the New York statute's prohibition of disrespectful words violated the First Amendment, but the Court did not decide whether burning the flag was also protected. Five years later, in *Spence v. Washington* (1974), the Court reversed the conviction under Washington state law of a college student who had attached a peace symbol to the American flag and then publicly displayed the flag hanging upside down. The Court held that the student's actions constituted protected symbolic speech.

Twenty years after its opinion in *Street v. New York*, the Supreme Court finally directly addressed the question of whether burning the flag constitutes protected speech. Gregory "Joey" Johnson protested at the Republican National Convention in Dallas by setting an American flag on fire. Johnson was prosecuted under Texas's flag desecration law and sentenced to a year in jail. In *Texas v. Johnson* (1989), the Supreme Court held that burning the flag is expressive conduct protected by the First Amendment. At the time that the Court invalidated Texas's law, forty-seven states had similar flag desecration laws. The Court's decision outraged many Americans, and Congress soon thereafter adopted the Flag Protection Act, hoping that a federal law protecting the flag from desecration would be viewed differently by the Court. However, in *United States v. Eichman* (1990), the Supreme Court again struck down Congress's attempt to prevent flag desecration, concluding the Flag Protection Act violated the First Amendment. Numerous efforts since that time to protect the American flag with a constitutional amendment have failed.

The power and importance of the American flag have generated many efforts to protect it through laws criminalizing flag desecration and disrespect. But over the past half-century, the Supreme Court has consistently, if narrowly, held that this particular speech as crime against the state itself violates the Constitution.

See Also: Civil Disobedience and Crimes against the State; Espionage Act of 1917 and Sedition Act of 1918; Speech as Crime against the State

Resources

Flag Protection Act. Public Law 101–131; 103 Stat. 777.
Goldstein, Robert J. 2000. *Flag Burning and Free Speech.* Lawrence: University Press of Kansas.
Sedition Act of 1918. Public Law 65–150; 40 Stat. 553 (enacted May 16, 1918; repealed December 30, 1920).
Stone, Geoffrey. 1989. "Flag Burning and the Constitution." *Iowa Law Review* 75: 111–24.

Fries's Rebellion (1799)

Fries's Rebellion, named after its leader John Fries, was a movement in 1798–9 to protest property taxes that were being levied to finance the build-up of federal military forces needed to face a potential military confrontation with France. The group led by Fries never numbered more than a couple hundred individuals. Most of its activities involved harassing federal tax collectors, not paying assessed taxes, and protesting taxes through assembly meetings and speeches. No shots were fired during the "rebellion" and no federal officials were seriously injured, as supporters of Fries's movement focused on preventing federal tax authorities from counting windows and measuring the size of windows in their houses. (The number and size of windows in a home dictated the amount of taxes to be paid.) Despite the lack of violence compared with the Whiskey Rebellion, Fries and a number of his accomplices were indicted for treason for levying war against the United States.

In preventing federal authorities from doing their job, "women set dogs on the assessors, and poured scalding water on them when attempted to measure the windows" (Harley 1896, 23). Tax accessors were also chased out of towns when they counted windows and measured windows. One tax collector was doused with the contents of farmer's chamber pot. In March 1799, when Fries learned that twenty people were being held in a jail in Bethlehem, Pennsylvania, for not cooperating with federal authorities, Fries led 130–150 men to the jail to demand the release of the prisoners. After hours of negotiation between Fries's forces and federal marshal William Nichols, and as tensions mounted and the likelihood of violence began to escalate, the outnumbered Nichols agreed to release all the prisoners, reporting them as "stolen" even though John Fries offered to post bond/bail for each of them. Within minutes, "all parties dispersed, the streets emptied, and the 'horrible' Fries's Rebellion peacefully concluded ... [and] following the 'rebellion' the participants returned to their everyday activities, confident that their actions would not merit a government reprisal" (Newman 1995, 58).

At worst, it would seem, Fries's group was guilty of kidnapping and rioting, or interference with federal officials in doing their business. Weeks later, however, federal military forces appeared at the homes of John Fries and his men and arrested thirty-one of them for various crimes. Fries and two accomplices were indicted and tried for treason; other followers were indicted for lesser crimes against the state, including sedition, insurrection, and rioting. After two trials, John Fries, George Getman, and Frederick Heaney were convicted of treason—only the second time (after the Whiskey Rebellion) the federal government convicted individuals of treason since the ratification of the Constitution in 1789.

As the United States seemed on a military collision course with France in 1798–9, Congress passed legislation called the Direct Tax Act. The legislation was passed to allow the federal government to levy taxes on land, houses, and slaves, to fund the nation's first standing Army and bolster its fledgling defenses. Five days later, President John Adams signed the Direct Tax Act into law, the same day he signed the Alien and Sedition Acts. German American immigrants in eastern Pennsylvania, many of whom had French leanings over the British, viewed the laws with distrust and questioned the timing of both the tax law and the Alien & Sedition Acts being signed by Adams on the same day. While many of Fries's followers donned French caps and even the tripartite French flag, many were also US revolutionary war veterans and intensely patriotic. Many of Fries's followers believed that the Direct Tax Act was unconstitutional and a violation of their property rights. Indeed, John Fries, the leader of the movement, was a revolutionary war veteran and even responded to George Washington's call for service to put down the Whiskey Rebellion, serving as a militia captain, a mere five years earlier.

During many of the assembly meetings with supporters, Fries and his men called for the lawful repeal of the laws that they deemed to be disagreeable.

Perhaps because Fries's Rebellion was the third major uprising in Pennsylvania in thirteen years (Shay's Rebellion occurred in 1786–7 and the Whiskey Rebellion occurred in 1794), the federal government was understandably anxious. However, these anti-taxation rebellions were not equal. Shay's Rebellion, the first resistance or rebellion against the federal government, involved rebel forces led by Daniel Shay, who led an army of appropriately 2,000 soldiers and attempted to seize the United States Armory and Arsenal at Springfield, Massachusetts. The Whiskey Rebellion, which resulted in the first treason convictions under the newly ratified Constitution, had a rebel force of 15,000 individuals at one point, and necessitated President George Washington calling up a 13,000-member militia. Fries's Rebellion, by contrast, never employed more than forty to sixty men at any given time, and the most egregious activities of Fries's group were assaulting tax collectors and negotiating the release of twenty men from temporary pre-trial detention. Nevertheless, the federal military (over five hundred federal soldiers and a contingency of cavalry) were called out to capture John Fries and his men, most of whom were at home toiling on their farms and fields.

On April 12, 1799, a federal grand jury indicted Fries, Getman, and Heaney. During the nine-day trial, lawyers for the defense argued that while lesser crimes might have been committed (e.g., rioting), the defendants did not levy war against the federal government and were merely engaged in challenging laws they viewed to be unconstitutional. However, the presiding judge (Judge James Iredell) rejected the defense's argument and advised the jury as a matter of law that "if the intention was to prevent by force the execution of any act of the congress of the United States altogether, any forcible opposition calculated to carry that intention into effect, was a levying of war … and of course an act of treason." This was the exact same interpretation of the meaning of "levying war" under the Treason Clause that Judge William Patterson articulated in the Whiskey Rebellion treason prosecutions just five years before. While not the law today, taken broadly, this early interpretation of treason law would have made any defendant's actions in preventing the execution of federal law to be a treasonable act. The resulting verdict was a finding of guilt.

One of the two presiding judges, Judge Peters, presciently stated how treason law would be defined in the twentieth century. According to a summary of Judge Peters's jurisprudence by a famous American treason expert, Peters's view on levying war under the Treason Clause could only be one of three things:

> (1) arraying a body of armed men in the martial manner with a view toward ending the existence of government; (2) a throwing off of allegiance by one part of the Union from the other part; and (3) taking possession of the legislative or executive authority by force of arms to compel either of the departments of government to act in a particular way. (Larson 2006, 906)

A few days later, on April 29, 1800, a new trial was ordered because the defense had learned that a jury member (before the start of the first case) had stated that Fries was guilty and ought to be hung. Although the trial was repeated, the jury again returned a verdict of guilty. The presiding judge of the second case, Samuel Chase, consistent with Judge Iredell, also instructed the jury that it would be "equally treason if the intention is by force to prevent the execution of any one or more of the general laws of the government, or to resist the exercise of any legitimate authority of the government in its sovereign capacity." After their treason conviction on May 9, Judge Samuel Chase ordered that the three defendants be executed by hanging on May 23.

President John Adams, ignoring the unanimous views of his cabinet that Fries should be executed, pardoned Fries, Getman, and Heaney on May 21. Like George Washington five years before, it is possible that Adams did not want to be the first sitting president to oversee the execution of a defendant for violations of the country's new treason laws, the scope and the wording of which were still very much open for debate and subsequent refinement. In predicting the evolution of treason law by at least a half-century, Adams decided to pardon the defendants for treason because he viewed it as an overexpansive interpretation of what it meant to "levy war" against the government. Adams wrote that Fries's Rebellion was no more "than a riot, highhanded, aggravated, daring, and dangerous indeed [but hardly treason] … Is there not great danger in establishing such a construction of treason as may be applied to every sudden, ignorant, inconsiderable heat among a part of the people wrought up by political dispute?" (Smith 1962, 1033).

See Also: Alien and Sedition Acts (1798); Insurrection; Levying War; Rebellion; Riot and Incitement to Riot; Sedition; Shay's Rebellion (1786–7); Treason; Whiskey Rebellion

Resources

Harley, Lewis R. 1896. "Fries's Rebellion: Treason. Misdemeanor." *The American Historical Register and Monthly Gazette of the History, Military and Patriotic-Hereditary Societies of the United States of America* 4 (March): 19–28.

Larson, Carlton F. W. 2006. "The Forgotten Constitutional Law of Treason and the Enemy Combatant Problem." *The University of Pennsylvania Law Review* 154 (April): 863–926.

Newman, Paul Douglas. 1995. "Fries's Rebellion and American Political Culture, 1798–1800." *The Pennsylvania Magazine of History and Biography* 119 (January–April): 37–73.

Smith, Page. 1962. *John Adams, Volume II: 1784–1826.* Garden City, NY: Doubleday & Company, Inc.

Fuchs, Klaus (1911–88)

Klaus Fuchs, born in 1911, fled Nazi Germany in 1933 and became a British national. He earned his doctorate from Bristol University in 1936 and took up laboratory work under the supervision of Oxford University Professor Dr. Rudolf Peierls. Dr. Peierls was considered the British Father of the Atomic Bomb and, along with Fuchs, traveled to the United States to contribute to the United States' Second World War Manhattan Project. Unbeknownst to his fellow scientists (including his mentor, Rudolf Peierls), Fuchs had been engaged in espionage with the Soviet Union for fourteen years before his arrest in 1950. In fact, British authorities had first identified Fuchs as a spy in the highly classified VENONA Cables; Fuchs' code name in the top-secret cables was "Rest." The earliest British intelligence on Fuchs indicated that he was staunchly anti-Nazi, was on the Gestapo "hit list," and was a student activist and a member of the Communist Party. Between 1942 and 1944, British intelligence reported that Fuchs passed British nuclear secrets to the Soviets on at least five separate occasions.

Despite the negative British intelligence (not shared with the Americans), Fuchs and a team of British scientists were sent to the United States in 1943 to work on the American atomic nuclear weapons program and to conduct work as part of the Manhattan Project. Fuchs was one of the first British scientists transferred to the United States for this important secret work (Gibbs 2010, 559). For a brief time after the Second World War, Fuchs was assigned to work at the Los Alamos National Laboratory, another American nuclear weapon and energy facility. He returned to England in 1946 to work at the British main nuclear weapon facility, the Atomic Energy Research Establishment at Harwell—just outside Oxford, England. However, in 1949, Fuchs was apprehended for his continued acts of espionage and pleaded guilty in British Crown Court to four counts of espionage and violating the Official Secrets Act by "communicating information to a potential enemy." Fuchs agreed to a fourteen-year prison sentence but was released in 1959 for good behavior. Fuchs moved to East Germany, where he died in 1988. Although Fuchs was not prosecuted for a crime against the United States (his criminal case took place in England), his actions clearly constituted a crime against the United States.

Fuchs' treachery cannot be overstated. He "admitted to passing the Soviets substantial secret material over an eight-year period, including 'the full design of the atom bomb'" (Gibbs 2010, 564). Fuchs's espionage enabled the Soviet Union to acquire the technology years ahead of when it would have developed atomic weapons on its own. Furthermore, Fuchs's behavior sowed seeds of distrust and discord for years to come after his espionage. Fuchs was "described as the most important of the British atom spies [and] Fuchs' actions had a hugely detrimental effect on Anglo-American relations and 'led to a crisis in the Special Relationship'" (Kassimeris and Price 2023, 2). Furthermore, "the exposure of Fuchs' espionage contributed to the rise of McCarthyism" (Kassimeris and Price 2023, 2). "In America these fears resulted in a witch hunt led by Senator Joe McCarthy and many individual scientists, most notably J. Robert Oppenheimer, were subjected to an extreme level of public scrutiny and shaming" (Kassimeris and Price 2023, 27). Fuchs's espionage also contributed to the downfall of Julius and Ethel Rosenberg:

> [T]he discovery of Fuchs' espionage had huge repercussions in America. Investigations following his conviction led to the discovery of his Soviet intelligence contact in Santa Fe, Harry Gold. After confessing his own involvement, Gold informed the FBI about a further Soviet agent in the Manhattan Project, David Greenglass. In the

> summer of 1950, Greenglass led the FBI to his brother-in-law, Julius Rosenberg, the leader of a Soviet spy ring in New York. Rosenberg and his wife, Ethel, were convicted of espionage and executed in June 1953. (Kassimeris and Price 2023, 2, n3)

See Also: Espionage; Rosenberg, Julius and Ethel; Second Red Scare (McCarthyism)

Resources

Close, Frank. 2010. *Trinity: The Treachery and Pursuit of the Most Dangerous Spy in History*. London: Penguin Books.

Gibbs, Timothy. 2010. "Catching an Atomic Spy: MI5 and the Investigation of Klaus Fuchs." In *The Oxford Handbook of National Security Intelligence*, 555–67. Oxford: Oxford University Press.

Goodman, Michael S. 2005. "Who Is Trying to Keep What Secret from Whom and Why?" *Journal of Cold War Studies* 7, no. 3 (Summer): 124–46.

Kassimeris, George, and Oliver Price. 2023. "'What Did You Do to Them Klaus?': The Klaus Fuchs Atomic Espionage Case and Its Impact on the Scientific Community in the Early Cold War Britain." *British Century British History* 34, no. 2: 1–29.

Fuerzas Armadas de Liberacion Nacional (FALN)

A more recent violent revolutionary group and offshoot of the Puerto Rican Nationalist Party (Nationalist Party) Revolt was a group in the 1970s called Fuerzas Armadas de Liberacion Nacional (FALN). The FALN continued the work of revolution and independence sought by the National Party but adopted a distinctive Marxist ideology and intensified the violence committed by the group. For example, from its founding in 1974 until its disbandment in 1984, the FALN was responsible for a staggering 130 bombings. The FALN was one of the best-organized and well-trained domestic terrorism organizations within the United States during that period.

Like the Irish Revolutionary Army on the British Isles, the FALN believed that the group could force Puerto Rican independence through bombings and other violent acts. In the early 1970s, the Federal Bureau of Investigation reported that "by 1973, 135 Puerto Rican radicals had received 'extensive instruction in guerrilla war tactics, preparation of explosive artifacts and sophisticated methods of sabotage' within Cuba itself" (Dorfman 2017). In January 1975, FALN bombed the historic Revolutionary era Fraunces Tavern in New York City, resulting in the death of four, the wounding of sixty-three, and considerable damage to this historical building. In one day in October 1975, FALN was responsible for detonating ten bombs in a one-hour period in three different cities and causing one million dollars in property damage. In August 1977, FALN planted numerous bombs in Manhattan, New York, prompting 100,000 workers to evacuate their offices, and killing one person and injuring six due to the detonation of one of the bombs. In 1979, FALN threatened to blow up a nuclear power point north of New York City. In 1980, FALN members broke into a Carter-Mondale election headquarters in Chicago, and a George H. W. Bush headquarters in New York, temporarily holding campaign workers as hostages. In 1981, FALN plotted the kidnapping of Ron Reagan, President Reagan's son.

The FALN ceased operations after the federal government was able to infiltrate, arrest, and prosecute most of its membership. By 1984, the FALN was defunct. A couple of years before FALN disbanded, one of its top leaders, Oscar Lopez, was arrested in a routine traffic stop in 1981. He was arrested with an illegal handgun (filed-down serial number of the weapon) and fake identification. A subsequent search of his apartment yielded what one person called a "bomb-making factory," replete with bags of dynamite, a FALN bomb-making manual, blasting caps, a bomb timer, and an automatic weapon, among other things. Lopez was accused of training FALN members to use bombs and being involved in the planning of both FALN robberies and bombings. He was tried and convicted on various charges, including seditious conspiracy, attempted armed robbery, explosives possession, and weapons violations. Lopez received a 55-year sentence, but his sentence was extended an additional fifteen years behind bars when Lopez conspired with two individuals from the Weather Underground (Weathermen) to attempt a violent escape from prison, a plan which included "flying a helicopter stocked with machine guns and explosives … [and] riddl[ing] guard towers with rounds from automatic weapons, and throw[ing] grenades into the path of those who pursued" the convicts (Dorfman 2017). In one of President Obama's last acts of president, Lopez's sentence was commuted in January 2017. Lopez's served thirty-six years in person, the longest any person convicted of seditious conspiracy has served.

The commutation of Lopez's sentence by President Obama was not the only presidential intervention. Approximately eighteen years before, President Bill Clinton offered to commute the sentences of sixteen FALN members (including Lopez) so long as they each acknowledged in writing that they were "renouncing the use or threatened use of violence for any purpose" (Department of Justice

1999). Under Clinton's proposal, two FALN members (including Lopez) would not be released but would only have their sentences reduced, with additional time to serve. In Lopez's case, his seventy-year sentence would have been reduced to about forty-four and a half years, which would permit him to exit prison in 2025. Fourteen of the sixteen FALN members accepted Clinton's commutation. Lopez refused, in part, because he would not renounce violence. Just a few years prior, Lopez had given an interview saying the FALN cause was "a just struggle, and because it's a just struggle, we have the right to wage it by any means necessary, including armed struggle … we can anticipate more violence" (Dorfman 2017). After an additional eighteen years behind bars, Lopez was finally freed on the condition he return to Puerto Rico.

See Also: Puerto Rican Nationalist Party Revolt; Sabotage; Seditious Conspiracy; Terrorism; Weather Underground

Resources

Bauer, Shane. 2014. "This Man Is Serving 75 Years for 'Seditious Conspiracy.' Is He a Danger to Society?" *Mother Jones*, May 29, 2014. Accessed May 29, 2023. https://www.motherjones.com/politics/2014/05/oscar-lopez-rivera-75-years-seditious-conspiracy/.

Department of Justice. 1999. "News Advisory." August 11, 1999. Accessed October 31, 2023. https://www.justice.gov/archive/opa/pr/1999/August/352dag.htm.

Dorfman, Zach. 2017. "Why Did Obama Free This Terrorist? Oscar Lopez Was One of the Most Violent Extremists of His Time. The Fact That Obama Commuted His Sentence Doesn't Speak Well of U.S. Politics." *Politico*, January 24, 2017. Accessed May 10, 2023. https://www.politico.com/magazine/story/2017/01/oscar-lopez-commutation-barack-obama-214685/.

G

Gabriel's Rebellion (1800)

Gabriel's Rebellion, sometimes referred to as the Virginia Plot of 1800, involved an effort by upward of 10,000 Black Americans to overthrow the institution of slavery in Virginia and institute a new government in Virginia devoid of slavery with many revolutionary Black leaders in charge. The rebellion, thwarted on the eve of its planned commencement, has been described as "the most sophisticated and politicized of all North American slave conspiracies" (Egerton 1998, 354). If successful, the governor of Virginia (James Monroe) would have been taken hostage, the state's arsenal of thousands of arms seized, and the Capitol Square taken over and fortified by a rebel army. "A small number of city leaders were to die, but most would live as hostages in order to force the Virginia elite to grant the slaves' demands, which included their freedom and an equitable division of city property" (Egerton 1998, 354). Gabriel's followers justified their plans under Thomas Jefferson's oft-quoted belief that the oppressed were justified to "endeavor to secure relief by refreshing the tree of liberty occasionally with the blood of their oppressors" (Carroll 2004, 48).

The plan's chief goal was the eradication of slavery, the re-distribution of property among the enslaved, and that some of the rebellion's leaders (like Gabriel) would assume leadership roles in Richmond. Beyond that, there did not appear to be any elaborate plans for the reconfiguration of Virginia's government. Simply put, "when all the whites were dead, Gabriel was to be crowned King of Virginia, with Richmond as the capital" (Carroll 2004, 50). Gabriel's lieutenants were to be named "princes, governors, and councilors" under his new revolutionary regime, and Gabriel hoped a "white flag" of truce could be raised with white merchants, ushering in an alliance between the Black revolutionaries and the white merchants of town. Under Gabriel's plan, all white individuals were to be killed except "the French, the Quakers, and the Methodists, who were to be spared because they were believers in liberty" (Carroll 2004, 50). "Poor white men who held no slaves were to be spared" as well because Gabriel believed that these individuals would join in the criminal conspiracy (Carroll 2004, 50).

Gabriel (with no known first name) was born into slavery in 1776 and spent his short life enslaved outside of Richmond, Virginia. He was noted for his courage, intellect, charisma, and knowledge of military tactics. Like Nat Turner and Denmark Vesey (in Vesey's Rebellion) in the decades which followed, Gabriel viewed himself as a man of destiny and sanctioned by God's will to conduct his actions. Gabriel planned the operation for months and held many meetings under the guise of religious celebrations and under the guise of assembling for religious worship. While exact numbers are hard to accurately report, Gabriel claimed he had about 10,000 supporters. On the eve of the commencement of activities, on August 30, 1800, Gabriel had one thousand men recruited from Richmond, six hundred from a place called Ground Squirrel Bridge, four hundred from Goochland, and six thousand from Caroline County. It will never be known exactly how many conspirators participated in Gabriel's Rebellion.

Just before its commencement, two of Gabriel's men alerted authorities to the impending rebellion. This allowed Governor James Monroe to call out Virginia armed forces and guard all the places Gabriel intended to attack (Capitol Square, city arsenal, city warehouse district, etc.). The city of Richmond took on the appearance of a military "training camp" and "it was said that City of Richmond resembled a town under siege" (Carroll 2004, 53). Then, a freak torrential rainstorm hit the area that further delayed Gabriel's actions. The rain was described as "one of most extraordinary falls of rain ever known in the country" and "roads and plantations were submerged, bridges were carried away, and fords were rendered wholly impassable" (Carroll 2004, 51).

At this point, Gabriel's Rebellion disintegrated, and the conspirators (including Gabriel) fled. The organizers and leaders were slowly captured and executed for committing crimes against Virginia. Before Gabriel's capture, eleven of Gabriel's men were executed. After eleven days, Gabriel was captured on September 24, 1800, convicted on October 3, and executed on October 10. On the day of Gabriel's conviction, ten other men were executed. Gabriel was found guilty of conspiracy and instigating an insurrection. He was executed at the town gallows near the present location of 15th and Broadstreet in Richmond. At Gabriel's execution, fifteen other men were executed alongside him. Then, a few days after Gabriel's execution, another four men were executed. Thus, Gabriel and about forty of these top lieutenants were executed in the two months following the thwarted rebellion. Given the scope of the participation of the planned rebellion, countless others faced lesser punishments such as corporal punishment, reduced rations, and other inhuman punishments. One scholar commented that "for so many slaves were involved in the conspiracy that, if all guilty persons had been arrested and executed, a large percentage of the total Negro population of the state would have been annihilated" (Carroll 2004, 54).

The alleged crimes against the state in Gabriel's Rebellion, Nat Turner's rebellion, Denmark Vesey's Rebellion, and John Brown's Raid all have in common that the participants were motivated by the inhuman and unjust practices of the state itself. Phrased another way, the state brought evil upon itself. Unlike events like Waco, Ruby Ridge, and the Oklahoma City Bombing, the participants in these crimes against the state were motivated to wage war against a colossal state immoral practice. As stated by one author, "slavery is a monster,—most horrible of all monsters,—tyranny, excepted. Democracy, therefore, in Virginia is like virtue in Hell" (Carroll 2004, 54). "But the truth is, the secret of the Insurrection lay deeper. It rested in the eternal injustice of slavery. General Gabriel like Nat Turner and Denmark Vesey, merely embodies the love of liberty" (Carroll 2004, 56). Phrased yet another way, legitimate and American principles of "liberty and equality had brought the evil upon the state" and "this doctrine of equality … cannot fail in producing either a general Insurrection or a general emancipation" (Carroll 2004, 56). These crimes against the state are the most understandable and relatable to those who believe in an America that stands for equality and equal justice for all under the law. In acknowledgment of this, in August 2007, Virginia Governor Tim Kaine pardoned Gabriel and his followers, saying that Gabriel's motivation had been "his devotion to the ideals of the American revolution—it was worth risking death to secure liberty" (Associated Press 2007).

See Also: Conspiracy, Criminal; Insurrection; Jefferson, Thomas; John Brown's Raid (1859); Oklahoma City Bombing (1995); Rebellion; Ruby Ridge (1992); Turner, Nat; Vesey's Rebellion (1822); Waco (1993)

Resources

Associated Press. 2007. "Slave Who Led Failed Revolt in 1800 'Pardoned.'" *NBC News*, August 31, 2007. Accessed October 31, 2023. https://www.nbcnews.com/id/wbna20536296.

Carroll, Joseph Cephas. 2004 [orig. 1938]. *Slave Insurrections in the United States 1800–1865*. Mineola, NY: Dover Publications, Inc.

Egerton, Douglas R. 1998. "'Gabriel' and 'Gabriel's Rebellion'." In *Macmillan Encyclopedia of World Slavery*, edited by Paul Finkelman and Joseph C. Miller, vol. 1: 353–5. New York and London: Macmillan Reference USA, Simon & Schuster Macmillan, and Simon & Schuster and Prentice Hall International.

Gadahn, Adam Yahiye (1978–2015)

Adam Gadahn, nicknamed "Azzam the American" by his Al-Qaeda confederates, was born Adam Pearlman in Oregon in 1978. Gadahn's only real significance was that in 2006 he was the first American to be indicted for treason against the United States since the 1950s. The Gadahn indictment illustrated that the treason charge was still a viable option for prosecutors in the twenty-first century.

After spending his childhood on the west coast of the United States, Gadahn converted to Islam in 1995 and emigrated to the Middle East. After September 11, 2001, Gadahn became affiliated with Osama Bin Laden and produced and directed several anti-American and Al-Qaeda propaganda videos. Many of his recordings called for death and destruction of US individuals and properties. On October 11, 2006, a federal grand jury from the Southern Division of the United States District Court for the Central District of California indicted Gadahn for treason against the United States, the first known treason indictment in a US court since October 27, 1954. The last indictment for treason was a Second World War case involving Sergeant John Provoo, who allegedly offered his services to the Japanese while being held as an American prisoner of war (*United States v. Provoo*, 17 F.R.D. 183, 184 [D. Md. 1955]). Provoo was indicted and convicted of treason, but his conviction was overturned by an appellate court. He was re-indicted on October 27, 1954, but this indictment was dismissed by the trial court because Provoo's constitutional right to a speedy trial had been denied.

The main accusation against Gadahn was that he afforded "aid and comfort" to the enemies of the United States, namely Al-Qaeda. More specifically, the indictment charged that Adam Gadahn had "knowingly adhered to an enemy of the United States, namely al-Qaeda, and gave al-Qaeda aid and comfort within the United States and elsewhere, with the intent to betray the United States."

The treason case against Gadahn never proceeded beyond the indictment stage, as Gadahn was killed in a drone strike in Pakistan on January 19, 2015. His death was confirmed by Al-Qaeda on June 25, 2015. Had he not been killed, and his case proceeded to trial, there was ample evidence and legal precedent to support the treason charge that Gadahn was guilty of rendering "aid and comfort" to the enemies to the United States. Numerous propagandists were tried and convicted of treason during the Second World War (both in the United States and the UK) for spreading false information and propaganda that tended to demoralize and damage the fighting spirit of soldiers in the American armed forces. Perhaps the most notable case involved Iva Toguri D'Aquino, dubbed "Tokyo Rose," who was tried and convicted for treason against the United States in 1949, and served three decades in prison until her sentence was eventually commuted by President Gerald Ford in the 1970s.

See Also: Aid and Comfort (Aid to Enemies of the State); Levying War; September 11, 2001; Tokyo Rose (Iva Toguri D'Aquino); Treason

Resources

Kash, Douglas A. 2009. "The United States v. Adam Gadahn: A Case for Treason." *Capital University Law Review* 37: 1–25.

Khatchadourian, Raffi. 2007. "Azzam the American: The Making of an Al-Qaeda Homegrown." *The New Yorker*, January 22, 2007.

Larson, Carlton F. W. 2020. *On Treason: A Citizen's Guide to the Law*. New York: Ecco, an imprint of HarperCollins (Kindle Edition).

Unsealed Indictment. 2005. *United States of America v. Adam Gadahn* (October 2005 Grand Jury Indictment), SA CR 05-254(A). Accessed May 4, 2022. https://www.justice.gov/archive/opa/documents/adam_indictment.pdf.

Gitlow v. New York (1925)

Benjamin Gitlow was a member of the Left Wing Section of the Socialist Party, a dissenting branch of the party opposing the mainstream Socialist Party's more moderate positions. Gitlow arranged for 16,000 copies of the Left Wing Section's "Manifesto" to be printed and mailed. The Manifesto condemned "moderate Socialism" for its acceptance of the necessity of the democratic parliamentary state and repudiated moderate Socialism's policy of introducing Socialism by legislative measures. The Manifesto argued instead for accomplishing the "Communist Revolution" by a militant and "revolutionary Socialism," based on class struggle and mobilizing the "power of the proletariat in action," through mass industrial revolts developing into mass political strikes and "revolutionary mass action" for the purpose of conquering and destroying the parliamentary state. The Manifesto further predicted that once the parliamentary state was destroyed, and through a "revolutionary dictatorship of the proletariat," the system of Communist Socialism would be established in its place. The Manifesto urged that revolutionary Socialism must use these mass industrial revolts to broaden the strike, make it general and militant, and develop it into mass political strikes and revolutionary mass action for the annihilation of the parliamentary state. There was no evidence of any effect resulting from the publication and circulation of the Manifesto.

For his role in writing and distributing the Manifesto, in February 1920, Gitlow was convicted of violating New York's anarchy statute, which criminalized advocacy of "criminal anarchy." The statute was passed in the wake of the Palmer Raids and the Red Scare Era, during which there were multiple bombing attempts by anarchists. The statute allowed prosecution of any person who:

> 1. By word of mouth or writing advocates, advises or teaches the duty, necessity or propriety of overthrowing or overturning organized government by force or violence, or by assassination of the executive head or of any of the executive officials of government, or by any unlawful means; or, 2. Prints, publishes, edits, issues or knowingly circulates, sells, distributes or publicly displays any book, paper, document, or written or printed matter in any form, containing or advocating, advising or teaching the doctrine that organized government should be overthrown by force, violence or any unlawful means.

Gitlow unsuccessfully argued that New York's anarchy statute violated his right to free speech. He was sentenced to five-to-ten years imprisonment. On appeal, the Supreme Court upheld Gitlow's conviction in a seven to two ruling. He was subsequently pardoned and released from prison in 1925.

Gitlow is an important case for two reasons. First, it was the first time the United States Supreme Court held that the First Amendment of the United States Constitution—which states that "*Congress* shall make no law … abridging the freedom of speech, or of the press; or the right of the people peaceably to assemble"—also restricts *state* governments' ability to limit speech and assembly (see Speech as a Crime against the State). In *Gitlow*, the Court held that this right, previously applicable only to federal government actions, was "incorporated" against the states through the Due Process Clause of the Fourteenth Amendment. Over the subsequent decades, the Supreme Court would apply this doctrine of incorporation to other rights contained in the Bill of Rights.

Second, *Gitlow* represented another case in which the United States Supreme Court upheld the ability of government to "protect itself" by restricting speech that might undermine security or the existence of government itself. Noting that freedom of speech is not absolute, the Court held that a state may "punish utterances endangering the foundations of organized government and threatening its overthrow by unlawful means." Thus, despite finding that the First Amendment applied to states through the incorporation doctrine, the Court nevertheless found no violation of the First Amendment.

As in several other cases during this decade addressing similar free speech arguments, including *Abrams v. United States* (1919) and *Whitney v. California* (1927), Justices Oliver Wendell Holmes, Jr., and Louis Brandeis dissented. They argued that, when properly applied, the clear and present danger test first articulated in *Schenck v. United States* (1919) required a level of present danger that did not exist in this case. The majority had found that the Manifesto's closing line, which declared "The proletariat revolution and the Communist reconstruction of society—*the struggle for these*—is now indispensable .... The Communist International calls the proletariat of the world to the final struggle!" was not prediction of future events, but rather constituted direct incitement. The dissenters disagreed, believing there was little chance the Left Wing Section's Manifesto posed any threat whatsoever to the government. Acknowledging that "[e]loquence may set fire to reason," Justice Holmes contended that in this case the communication "had no chance of starting a present conflagration."

See Also: *Abrams v. United States* (1919); Anarchy, Criminal; Clear and Present Danger Test; First Red Scare and the Palmer Raids (1919–20); *Schenck v. United States* (1919); Speech as a Crime against the State; *Whitney v. California* (1927)

Resources

Gitlow v. New York, 268 U.S. 652 (1925).

Greathouse, United States v. (1863)

United States v. Greathouse (1863) is a treason case arising from the American Civil War. The *Greathouse* case set forth the important principle that acts of rebellion or hostility against one's own government can only be treason if those acts themselves amounted to levying war. The court in *Greathouse* held that aiding others in acts of rebellion against the United States cannot be treason under the Aid and Comfort Clause, as the Clause is only applicable to foreign adversaries who are engaged in open hostilities with the United States. Those rebelling against their own governments are not foreign adversaries under the meaning of the Treason Clause in the Constitution.

On March 15, 1863, United States officers seized a schooner named the *J. M. Chapman* in the harbor off the coast of San Francisco, California. The *J. M. Chapman* was fitted out as a privateer and received a letter of marque and reprisal from Confederate President Jefferson Davis (see Davis, Jefferson). Letters of marque and reprisal were written authorizations from the government to vessels to prey on the commerce of foreign adversaries, and privateer vessels were merchant vessels fitted with armaments needed to attack other vessels. The leaders of the *J. M. Chapman* were attempting to interfere with "the commerce of the United States" by intercepting mail shipments. There were also plans to capture the federal military installation at Alcatraz. Ridgeley Greathouse and multiple other sailors on board the *J. M. Chapman* were charged with committing treason. The indictment against the defendants alleged:

> (1) The existence of a rebellion against the United States, their authority and laws; (2) That the defendants traitorously engaged in, and gave aid and comfort to, the same; (3) That in the execution of their treasonable purposes, they procured, fitted out and armed a vessel to cruise in the service of the rebellion, on the high seas, and commit hostilities against the citizens, property and vessels of the United States; and that the vessel sailed on such cruise.

Supreme Court Justice Stephen Johnson Field, acting as a Circuit Justice, instructed the jury that defendants charged with treason for assisting others in rebellion against the United States should only be charged and, if appropriate, convicted, of levying war against the United States, and not adhering to its "enemies, giving them aid and comfort." Justice Field held that a treason charge based upon providing aid and comfort to an enemy of the United States only applies if the aid and assistance was rendered to a "foreign power in a state of open hostility" with the United States. Justice Field ruled, in part, as follows: "[t]he term enemies, as used in the second clause, according to its settled meaning, at the time the constitution was adopted, applies only to the subjects of a foreign power in a state of open hostility with us." Justice Field indicated that the Aid and Comfort Clause in treason cases "does not embrace rebels in insurrection against their own government. An enemy is always the subject of a foreign power who owes no allegiance to our government or country."

In a separate opinion rendered by federal district court judge Ogden Hoffman, presiding alongside Field, the judge instructed the jury that he concurred with Justice Field's analysis and that Justice Field's opinion should be "exclusively received as the opinion and instructions of the court." However, Judge Hoffman also made clear that, in hearing the evidence, his "individual opinion" was also that the second clause of the treason provision in the Constitution should "apply only to cases of adhering, and giving aid and comfort to, foreign public enemies. It was therefore held that an indictment charging the defendant with having given aid and comfort to domestic rebels was bad, and that the acts should be charged as a levying of war against the United States."

See Also: Aid and Comfort (Aid to Enemies of the State); American Civil War and Treason; Davis, Jefferson; Insurrection; Levying War; Rebellion; Treason

Resources

Jackson, Stephen. 2019. "Treason in the Age of Terrorism: Do Americans Who Join ISIS 'Levy War' against the United States?" *American University National Security Law Brief* 9: 155–221.

United States v. Greathouse, 26 F. Cas. 18 (C.C.N.D. Cal. 1863).

Green Corn Rebellion (1917)

In the early 1900s, socialism and workers' rights movements were especially strong in Oklahoma. For instance, in the 1916 presidential election, the Socialist Party earned more than a quarter of the votes cast in some counties, even though President Woodrow Wilson's proclaimed anti-war stance drew away many socialists who voted for him and the Democratic Party. Another labor organization, formed to represent poor tenant farmers, was called the Working Class Union (WCU). The WCU was racially diverse, composed of Black, Native American, and white tenant farmers. Though not directly affiliated with the Industrial Workers of the World (IWW), which barred tenant farmers from its membership, or the Socialist Party, the WCU embraced a similar ideology to those groups: pro-worker, pro-union, and anti-industrial capitalism. Unlike the Socialist Party and IWW, the WCU was a secret society, willing to use violence to accomplish its aims. The WCU engaged in physical intimidation and beatings of tenant farmers who refused to join or support the organization, and when an unpopular cattle disease control regimen was imposed in Oklahoma, WCU members dynamited disease control facilities and burned the barns of supporters of the program.

When the First World War began, anti-conscription and anti-war sentiment became a core WCU tenet. Nationwide, many working-class people viewed the war as being fought to benefit industrial capitalists: "Rich man's war. Poor man's fight." In the summer of 1917, weeks after the initial draft selection under the Selective Service Act of 1917 had taken place, hundreds of WCU men in southeast Oklahoma decided to rebel against the draft and the war. Believing they would be joined by groups with similar ideologies nationwide, they planned to march from Oklahoma to Washington, DC, to force President Wilson to end the war with Germany. They planned to eat roasted "green corn" (unripe corn) along the way to Washington. Not all members of the WCU supported the plan for armed resistance. A group that would become known as the "Jones Family" separated themselves from the WCU's efforts, choosing not to join in an armed revolt, but instead to simply help some draft resisters hide from the government. In late July 1917, they were discovered and arrested.

On July 27, 1917, a local Socialist and WCU member named John Spears raised red flags over his farm along a river, signaling WCU members to gather there to begin their planned revolt. By midnight on August 3, 1917, approximately 800 to 1,000 WCU members had assembled on Spears's farm and began their rebellion. Some men were armed with weapons, though many had no weapons and had been told to use stones, clubs, or take weapons from their adversaries. Some men left to dynamite railroad trestles and bridges and cut telegraph wires, but the majority remained at Spears's farm. Someone tipped off the local authorities, who organized a posse of townspeople who armed themselves with weapons from a nearby National Guard armory. When the posse arrived at Spears's farm, a few shots were fired, but when the rebels saw their foes were not the National Guard, but rather their fellow townspeople with whom they had no quarrel, they retreated and disbanded. In the following days, posses of townspeople arrested nearly 500 men who had been associated with the short-lived rebellion.

Of the nearly 500 rebels arrested, authorities released 266 due to insufficient evidence, and 192 would ultimately face trial in federal district court. W. P. McGinnis, the local United States Attorney, initially announced he would try the men for treason, but officials at the Department of Justice in Washington convinced him to instead test the prosecutorial viability of the recently enacted Espionage Act of 1917, which forbade "causing, or attempting to cause insubordination, disloyalty, mutiny, refusal of duty, in the military or obstructing the recruiting or enlistment service of the United States." In a series of trials, several WCU leaders faced serious charges under the Espionage Act, but most only faced charges of personally resisting the draft. Most defendants pleaded guilty, though several did not. The federal judges presiding over the trials imposed wide-ranging sentences on those convicted. Ultimately, thirty-six men were sentenced to be incarcerated at the federal government's prison in Leavenworth, Kansas, for terms ranging from one to ten years. Twenty-three were sentenced to shorter terms at local federal jails, and thirty-four served short sentences at the state penitentiary. During the trials it became apparent that many of the participants had been duped regarding the likely success of the rebellion and the extent to which they would be joined by others from around the nation.

Likely at the behest of the Justice Department, the prosecution in the Green Corn cases attempted to connect WCU members to the much larger IWW, against which the Department of Justice was waging a nationwide campaign. Though that effort failed in the trials of Green Corn Rebellion participants, the prosecution's overall success in the Green Corn and Jones Family cases served as the blueprint for the federal government's nationwide Espionage Act-based prosecutions against other groups, including the IWW and Socialist Party, and in cases such as *Schenck v. United States* (1919), *Frohwerk v. United States* (1919), *Debs v. United States* (1919), and *Abrams v. United States* (1919). In 1919, Oklahoma would become one of twenty-nine states to pass criminal syndicalism laws, which criminalized advocating violence to accomplish political goals.

See Also: *Abrams v. United States* (1919); Criminal Syndicalism; *Debs v. United States* (1919); Espionage Act of 1917 and Sedition Act of 1918; Rebellion; *Schenck v. United States* (1919); Treason

Resources

Burbank, Garin. 1977. *When Farmers Voted Red: The Gospel of Socialism in the Oklahoma Countryside, 1910–1924*. Westport, CT: Praeger.

Sellars, Nigel. 2002. "Treasonous Tenant Farmers and Seditious Sharecroppers: The 1917 Green Corn Rebellion Trials." *Oklahoma City University Law Review* 27: 1097.

"Working Class Union." n.d. *Encyclopedia of Oklahoma History and Culture, Oklahoma Historical Society*. Accessed October 18, 2023. https://www.okhistory.org/publications/enc/entry?entry=WO021.

Green, Shields (1836–59)

Shields Green, nicknamed "the emperor" because of his self-confident and aristocratic bearing, was one of five African American men who joined John Brown in the invasion of Harpers Ferry, Virginia, in October 1859 in an attempt to overthrow the institution of slavery by force. After Brown's trial and conviction, Green was tried and convicted with three other co-conspirators in November 1859 and executed for crimes against the Commonwealth of Virginia in December 1859. Green was executed for conspiracy to commit a slave insurrection and murder, but not treason, as the trial court ruled that Green could not be charged or convicted of treason given the color of his skin and the infamous decision of *Dred Scott v. Sandford* (1857), decided just two years before.

Earlier in his life, Green had escaped enslavement from Charleston, South Carolina, and served as Frederick Douglass's personal attendant and footman. John Brown met multiple times with Frederick Douglass in an attempt to convince Douglass to join Brown and his men in the invasion and seizure of the Harpers Ferry United States Arsenal and Armory. Green was present at several of these meetings. Most notably, Brown's last surreptitious meeting with Douglass occurred just two months before the Harpers Ferry invasion. In mid-August 1859, Brown met with Douglass and Green at an abandoned quarry in Chambersburg, Pennsylvania, a mere fifty-six miles from the targeted United States Armory and Arsenal at Harpers Ferry, Virginia. At this meeting, Brown tried desperately to get Douglass to join him, saying that "I will defend you with my life," that he needed Douglass "for a special purpose," and "when I strike, the bees will begin to swarm, and I shall want you to help me hive them" (Villard 1910, 413). Douglass refused to join Brown saying that an attack on the federal government would "array the whole country" against him and that Brown "was going into a perfect steel-trap and that once in he would never get out alive" (Villard 1910, 413). At the end of this meeting and before departing, Douglass asked Green what he wanted to do. Green simply responded, "I b'lieve I'll go wid de ole man" (Villard 1910, 413), and Green joined Brown and his men.

During the invasion of the federal installation, Green helped capture several hostages (including Lewis Washington, a grand nephew of President George Washington), shot and killed a townsperson, and fought alongside Brown and his men until his final capture by United States Marines on October 18, 1859. After Green's capture, he was taken with his surviving compatriots (John Brown, Aaron Stevens, Edwin Coppoc, and John Copeland) to Charles Town, Virginia, to await arraignment and trial. All five men were arraigned on October 25, 1859. Brown was tried first and separately, with Green and the other three men tried the week after Brown's case was completed. At Green's trial, his defense counsel successfully argued that the treason charge against him must be dismissed considering the United States Supreme Court's recent ruling in *Dred Scott v. Sandford* (1857). In the infamous *Dred Scott* ruling, the Supreme Court had held that African Americans were not intended by the Constitution to be citizens and that a Black man "had no rights which the white man was bound to respect." Because of this language by the Supreme Court, Green's lawyer argued that it was legally impossible to hold a person guilty of treason when that person was not a citizen and was afforded no rights or obligations under the Constitution. The trial court judge reluctantly agreed with this argument and dismissed the treason charge, although Green was still found guilty of murder and conspiracy to commit a slave insurrection and on November 10, 1859, was sentenced to death by hanging.

The execution was set for December 16, 1859, a mere fourteen days after John Brown's execution. "Even in death, Virginia demanded strict segregation of the races," as the two Black defendants (Shields Green and John Copeland) were ordered to be executed separately from the other two white defendants (John E. Cook and Edwin Coppoc) (Lubet 2013, 1803). After execution, Green's body, along with the body of John Copeland, was sent to Winchester Medical College for dissection and display. A professor from Oberlin College (Ohio) traveled to Winchester Medical College in an unsuccessful attempt to retrieve the bodies for proper burial. The professor wrote that he was moved by the tragedy and pathos of seeing the body of Green, noting Green's "unclosed, wistful eyes staring wildly upward, as if seeking, in a better world, for some solution of the dark problems of horror and oppression so hard to be explained in this" (Lubet 2013, 1814).

See Also: Brown, John; Conspiracy, Criminal; Cook, John E.; Copeland, John Anthony, Jr.; Coppoc, Edwin; Insurrection; John Brown's Raid (1859); Stevens, Aaron; Treason; *Virginia v. Brown* (1859)

Resources

Lubet, Steven. 2013. "Execution in Virginia, 1859: The Trials of Green and Copeland." *North Carolina Law Review* 91: 1785–815.

McGinty, Brian. 2009. *John Brown's Trial*. Cambridge, MA: Harvard University Press.

Villard, Oswald Garrison. 1910. *John Brown: A Biography Fifty Years After*. Boston: Houghton Mifflin Company.

Greenwood, New York, Insurrection (1882)

In 1872, the town of Greenwood, New York, population roughly 1,400, was one of several small towns that borrowed money to pay for a proposed twenty-mile-long railway through several communities in western New York. Commissioners in Greenwood issued a $30,000 bond and contributed the borrowed funds to a private rail company to build the railway from Hornell, New York, to the border with Pennsylvania, including through Greenwood. Ultimately, though some grading was completed, the company became insolvent and did not build the railway. Nevertheless, the bond had to be repaid.

As part of a plan to repay the bond, a special tax of $8,000 was issued upon the townspeople of Greenwood that required individual taxpayers to pay a pro rata share of the special tax. Many townspeople objected, claiming they had been "defrauded and robbed" and they should not have to pay taxes to which they did not agree, to pay for a railway that was not built. They challenged the legality of the initial bonds in court. Though their legal claims were vindicated in a victory before a New York state appellate court, ultimately the New York legislature passed a bill confirming the legality of the bonds.

When the townspeople still refused to pay the special tax, a tax collector began forced sales of their personal property and real estate. On multiple occasions, the tax collector attempted to conduct auctions, but groups of townspeople and sympathizers showed up in large groups, sometimes armed with clubs, and on at least one occasion, with military fife and drum musical accompaniment. Because potential buyers were intimidated—and apparently on at least one occasion physically assaulted—the tax collector was prevented from completing sales and collecting proceeds to pay the tax. Though occasionally aided by deputies and accompanied by posses of dozens of men, the county sheriff was unable to cause the crowds to disperse so that the forced tax sales could be accomplished. In February 1882, the sheriff sought assistance from the governor of New York. Governor Alonzo Cornell declared the town of Greenwood to be in a state of insurrection, ordered residents to stop preventing officials from engaging in their lawful activities and to disperse and remain in their homes, and authorized activation of the militia to support the sheriff's efforts.

After the governor's declaration, the tax collector and sheriff were able to successfully conduct the tax sales sufficient to satisfy the $8,000 debt. In June 1882, the governor declared the insurrection over. In 1896, a different rail company finally provided the people of Greenwood with rail service.

See Also: Insurrection

Resources

"Trouble in Steuben." *Buffalo Weekly Express* (Buffalo, NY), February 16, 1882.

H

Hamdi v. Rumsfeld (2004)

Yaser Hamdi, a US citizen by virtue of his birth in Louisiana, was raised in Saudi Arabia. In Summer 2001, Hamdi, aged twenty, ran away from home and trained at a Taliban camp in Afghanistan. In November 2001, Hamdi was captured in Afghanistan along with hundreds of Taliban fighters by the Northern Alliance, an Afghan group that fought against the Taliban. The Northern Alliance transferred Hamdi to the US military. He was initially detained at the United States' recently built detention facility at Guantanamo Bay, Cuba, but upon learning he was a US citizen, the military transferred Hamdi to the Hanahan Naval Brig in Charleston, South Carolina. The Bush administration claimed that despite Hamdi's US citizenship, he was an "enemy combatant" because he was caught with the Taliban, with which the United States was at war, and therefore subject to indefinite detention.

Hamdi, who claimed he was a relief worker, not a Taliban fighter, challenged his detention. The United States Supreme Court ultimately heard the case. Justice Sandra Day O'Connor's plurality opinion found there was sufficient statutory authority from the 2001 Authorization for the Use of Military Force (AUMF) to allow the government to detain enemy combatants, even if they were also US citizens. The Court acknowledged that the AUMF did not reference "detention" specifically, but that the AUMF did give the president power to use "all necessary and appropriate" force, which includes detention for the purpose of preventing captured individuals from "returning to the field of battle and taking up arms once again." In reaching its judgment, the Supreme Court recognized the status of "enemy combatant" for persons who wage war against the United States and explicitly permitted that status to be conferred regardless of the citizenship of the combatant who has associated himself with an enemy military.

In the view of the dissenting Justices, because Hamdi was a citizen, historic precedent—especially *Ex Parte Milligan* (1866)—mandated only two options for the government to detain Hamdi: (1) Congress must suspend the right to *habeas corpus*; or (2) Hamdi must be tried under civilian criminal law in civilian courts. Another American captured the same day as Hamdi, John Walker Lindh, was tried for civilian criminal offenses in federal court, and not treated as an enemy combatant. The dissenters noted that in *Milligan*, the Supreme Court had prohibited military detention of Americans without appeal or writ of *habeas corpus* as long as civil courts were functioning. The plurality looked instead to *Ex Parte Quirin* (1942) for the proposition that "capture, detention, and trial of unlawful combatants" are "important incidents of war," and that "[t]here is no bar to this nation's holding one of its own citizens as an enemy combatant." The Hamdi plurality noted that *Quirin* was a unanimous opinion that post-dated *Milligan*, and that if *Milligan* once could have been viewed as standing for the proposition that the military does not have the authority to detain and try an American citizen accused of spying against his country during wartime, "*Quirin* makes undeniably clear that that is not the law today."

Adding up the votes from several plurality opinions issued in the *Hamdi* case can be confusing, but the web of opinions can be distilled to a few key points. First, the idea that US citizens can be detained by the military under certain circumstances garnered five votes, a majority. Six Justices agreed the Executive Branch does not unilaterally have the power to hold US citizens indefinitely without providing some due process and judicial review and that US citizens must be accorded due process when determining whether they are enemy combatants. Only four Justices—a plurality—agreed that the 2001 AUMF authorized the detention of Hamdi under the circumstances.

After *Hamdi*, extended detention of US persons requires statutory authority and individualized assessment of the factual basis for detention (due process). However, *Hamdi* left open some important questions, one of which was whether the US military has authority to detain indefinitely a US citizen not apprehended on the battlefield. A federal court of appeals would attempt to answer that in *Padilla v. Hanft* (2005).

A few months after the Supreme Court issued its opinion in his case, the US government released Hamdi and deported him via United States Air Force C-17 to Saudi Arabia, where he had been raised, on the condition that he renounce his US citizenship and commit to travel restrictions. Though he was detained for five years for his actions in waging war against the United States, the United States never charged Hamdi with a crime.

See Also: *Ex Parte Milligan* (1866); *Ex Parte Quirin* (1942); *Padilla, United States v.* (2004–2014)

Resources

Bartelme, Tony. 2009. "Hanahan Brig: The Next Guantanamo?" *The Post and Courier*, March 15, 2009.

Merriam, Eric, and Douglas B. McKechnie. 2021. *National Security Law*. St. Paul, MN: West Academic, 329–31.

Hanssen, Robert Philip (1944–2023)

Robert Hanssen was a former Federal Bureau of Investigation (FBI) agent who committed numerous acts of espionage for the Soviet Union (and then Russia) from 1979 until his arrest in 2001. The United States Department of Justice (DOJ), in the unclassified portion of its report mandated by the Senate Select Committee on Intelligence and by the United States Attorney General, described Hanssen's espionage as "possibly the worst intelligence disaster in U.S. history." The DOJ Report also concluded that "Hanssen was the most damaging spy in FBI history, and he betrayed some of this nation's most important counterintelligence and military secrets, including the identities of dozens of human assets, at least three of whom were executed." After a 25-year career at the FBI, and just two months before his retirement from the FBI, Hanssen was arrested in February 2001 after attempting to pass the last bundle of top-secret government documents to the Soviets at a pre-arranged location. Hanssen was the subject of an intense three-month investigation and constant surveillance leading up to his arrest. Hanssen pled guilty to thirteen counts of espionage, one count of attempted espionage, and one count of conspiracy to commit espionage, in a plea bargain that allowed Hanssen to avoid the death penalty. He pleaded guilty in July 2001 and was sentenced in May 2002 to fifteen consecutive life sentences without the possibility of parole.

After a brief stint as a Chicago police officer, Hanssen became an FBI agent in 1976. According to the DOJ Report on Hanssen, he "was a mediocre agent who exhibited strong technical abilities but had weak managerial and interpersonal skills." One supervisor said Hanssen was the "strangest person" he had encountered in the FBI and was "a kind of cipher who was rigid, dour, and a religious zealot." Within three years, by 1979, Hanssen began spying for the Soviet Union. Hanssen intermittently engaged in espionage with the Soviets throughout the next two decades. During his career, Hanssen committed several significant security breaches known to the FBI. On one occasion, he passed sensitive classified material to a Soviet defector. On another occasion, Hanssen installed a password de-encryption program on his computer, which allowed him to hack into various FBI databases to monitor various FBI investigations and to ensure he was not being investigated as a spy. Hanssen was questioned but not disciplined for these breaches of security. Hanssen spent most of his time on Soviet Counterintelligence assignments in New York City and Washington, DC. Counterintelligence operations involve efforts to thwart the intelligence collection efforts of foreign adversaries. Ironically, Hanssen was assigned responsibility for curtailing Soviet spying efforts against the United States. He also had assignments at the State Department and FBI Headquarters in the 1980s and 1990s and had unfettered access to a wide array of top-secret materials from a variety of federal agencies. Over the course of years engaged in espionage, in return for a treasure trove of top-secret material, the Soviets paid Hanssen more than $1.4 million dollars and a few diamonds.

While many of the details of Hanssen's espionage and the damage done remain unknown to the public (the full 674-page DOJ report on Hanssen is classified as Top Secret and the abridged 383-page DOJ report on Hanssen, with sensitive sources redacted, is classified as Secret), the unclassified executive summary of the DOJ report reveals that Hanssen was responsible for giving the Soviets thousands of pages of extremely sensitive intelligence. Some of the materials Hanssen provided the Soviets detailed US strategies if a nuclear war were to occur, continuity of government details in the event of an attack, information on the identities of dozens of FBI and Central Intelligence Agency (CIA) assets/sources (some of whom were subsequently executed by the Soviets), and active open operational FBI and CIA cases against the Soviets. On two occasions, Hanssen gave the Soviets a complete list of every American double agent. According to David Vise, in his book *The Bureau and the Mole*, Hanssen's espionage may have also ultimately aided Osama bin Laden because Hanssen provided the Soviets sophisticated software programs that were being utilized by the United States to track security threats. According to Vise, these programs were sold by someone in Russia to Al-Qaeda, and possession of this material by Al-Qaeda may have enabled Bin Laden to avoid surveillance by the United States prior to 9/11. Hanssen also disclosed to the Soviets a multi-million-dollar surveillance tunnel constructed by the FBI under the Soviet Embassy in Washington, DC, making it inoperable.

The discovery of Hanssen as a spy was delayed for several reasons: first, CIA officer Aldrich Ames was spying for the Soviets at the same time and some of Hanssen's stolen intelligence information was attributed to Ames's espionage; second, Hanssen hacked into various FBI databases and monitored ongoing investigations about finding spies within the CIA/FBI and altered his activities accordingly; and third, according to the unclassified DOJ report, "Hanssen escaped detection not because he was extraordinarily clever and crafty, but because of longstanding systemic problems in the FBI's counterintelligence program and a deeply flawed FBI internal security program." However, Hanssen's crimes were eventually discovered when the FBI paid $7 million to an agent of the Soviet security agency Komitet Gosudarstvennoy Bezopasnosti (KGB) for a dossier containing evidence that implicated Hanssen. Hanssen was then put under surveillance and assigned an aide, Eric O'Neill, who was an undercover FBI surveillance specialist. O'Neill was able to obtain Hanssen's Palm III PDA (a personal handheld electronic organizer popular at that time). The FBI was able to copy and decode its contents and discovered a plethora of additional damning evidence against Hanssen, including where he was going to make his last "drop" of intelligence to the Soviets. Hanssen was arrested when attempting to make that last "drop." Between Ames and Hanssen, every American human source/asset was disclosed to the Soviets, thousands of pages of top-secret information were passed onto the Soviets, and the two individuals irreparably damaged the national security of the United States for years and years to come. Hanssen was incarcerated in a federal supermax facility and kept in solitary confinement twenty-three hours a day. He was found dead in his cell on June 5, 2023.

See Also: Ames, Aldrich Hazen "Rich"; Conspiracy, Criminal; Espionage

Resources

Department of Justice, Office of the Inspector General. 2003. "A Review of the FBI's Performance in Deterring, Detecting, and Investigating the Espionage Activities of Robert Phillip Hanssen: Unclassified Executive Summary." August 14, 2003. Accessed July 2, 2022. https://oig.justice.gov/sites/default/files/archive/special/0308/index.htm.

Vise, David. 2002. *The Bureau and the Mole: The Unmasking of Robert Philip Hanssen, the Most Dangerous Double Agent in FBI History*. New York: Atlantic Monthly Press.

Vise, David. 2003. *Spy: The Inside Story of How the FBI's Robert Hanssen Betrayed America*. New York: Random House Trade Paperbacks.

Hanway, United States v. (1851)

Castner Hanway was indicted for treason against the United States for his involvement in the Christiana Revolt of 1851. The Christiana Revolt involved a bloody confrontation between several slave catchers, a deputized federal marshal, and a few escaped slaves and members of the underground railroad. During an attempt to capture several alleged escaped slaves, the chief slave owner (Edward Gorsuch) was killed. During the ensuing melee, Castner Hanway, a neighbor of the house where escaped slaves were staying, arrived unarmed on horseback. According to multiple accounts, Castner Hanway attempted to convince the slave catchers to leave and even shielded some of these men from violence. During this process, Henry Kline, the deputized federal marshal attempting to enforce the Fugitive Slave Act of 1850 (and a man the federal court went out of its way to describe as "not a person of the best character for veracity"), pleaded with Hanway to assist them in subduing the runaway slaves and argued that Hanway was obligated to help Kline and his slave catching party under the terms of the federal Fugitive Slave Act of 1850. Hanway refused, telling Kline that the African Americans "had a right to defend themselves" and that "it was none of your [Kline's] business."

Thirty-eight individuals were indicted by the United States Attorney for treason in resisting the attempted enforcement of the Fugitive Slave Act. Despite Hanway's non-central role in the direct aiding and harboring of runaway slaves, committing no acts of violence, and even showing up to the property once the confrontation between the opposing groups was already underway, the prosecutor made the unconventional decision to prosecute Castner Hanway first. The treason charge against Hanway was based upon Hanway's refusal to participate in the execution/enforcement of the Fugitive Slave Act of 1850. More specifically, the bill of indictment for treason charged Hanway with "wickedly intending and devising the peace and tranquility of the United States to disturb, and prevent the execution of the laws [the Fugitive Slave Act] … [and therefore] wickedly and traitorously intend[ed] to levy war against the United States." Hanway's charged act of treason was that he, along with a larger group of persons, refused to help a deputized federal marshal (Klein) enforce the federal law, and that Hanway was in a crowd of people, some of whom were armed and violently resisted Kline's efforts. Hanway was not armed and there was no evidence he committed any act of violence against any federal official.

The legal case itself had several interesting details. First, the case was heard in United States District Court in Philadelphia, which at that time was then holding court on the second floor and above Independence Hall, where American Revolutionary War delegates to the Continental Congress famously debated and asserted the Declaration of Independence, which posited that "all men are created equal." Second, the jury pool was summoned by United States Marshal Anthony Roberts, who owed his position to radical abolitionist and antislavery politician Thaddeus Stevens. This prompted at least one legal historian to write that "southerners would later argue that the entire process of jury selection had been tainted" in favor of the abolitionists (Larson 2020, Chapter 6). Additionally, Marshal Roberts was responsible for securing the presence of two prominent African American witnesses, "who mysteriously escaped and never heard from again" (Larson 2020, Chapter 6). Finally, Thaddeus Stevens himself would serve as Castner Hanway's chief defense attorney.

The federal prosecution of Castner Hanway began on November 24, 1851. It was a jury trial and presided over by two federal judges, United States Supreme Court Justice Robert Grier (hearing the case as part of his circuit duties) and United States District Court Judge John J. Kane. Despite the chaotic and riotous events that took place on September 11, 1851 (which became known as the Christiania Revolt), Castner Hanway's role in the event was not subject to much dispute.

Violence and refusal to adhere to the Fugitive Slave Act had certainly transpired, and one man lay dead and several injured at the end of the confrontation between the opposing groups. But the prosecution of these types of events typically is handled through more run-of-the-mill criminal law charges like murder, battery, obstruction of justice, etc. Yet, Hanway was charged with treason because, according to the prosecutors, his presence at the scene and his refusal to assist in the enforcement of the federal law constituted "levying war" against the United States.

The prosecution rested its case on the premise that resisting the Fugitive Slave Act with the intent of making it inoperable is equivalent to "levying war" against the United States. Thus, the case was more about the meaning of federal law (i.e., the Treason Clause and the concept of "levying war") and less (or not at all) about questions of fact. After the testimony of witnesses and the closing arguments of both sides, Justice Grier issued his jury instructions. On the crucial issue of how to define treason, Justice Grier stated that "the better opinion there at present seems to be that the term 'levying war' should be confined to insurrections and rebellions for the purpose of overturning the government by force and arms." By this meaning, Hanway's refusal to help the slave owner and the federal marshal enforce the Fugitive Slave Act, absent additional facts, simply could not be treason. As a result, Hanway was acquitted after only fifteen minutes of jury deliberation.

The Hanway prosecution also resulted in a federally reported judicial opinion which is quite valuable for readers and scholars interested in learning more about the evolution and changing connotations of the term "levying war" as contained in the Treason Clause in the United States Constitution. After the first seven pages of the decision (dealing exclusively with issues of jury qualifications to sit on treason cases), and after a recitation of the facts leading up to the prosecution, the second half of the federal decision delineates the historical origin, evolution, and changing meaning of the "Levying War" Clause for purposes of treason law. In its decision, the court admitted that in England, which also defines treason in part as "levying war" against the government, that "many of the English cases, then considered good law and quoted by the best writers as authorities, have since been discredited, if not overruled." The older meanings attributed to "levying war" against the government equated the disobedience or violent resistance to the law as being akin to treason, which the court stated should "perhaps now be treated merely as aggravated riots or felonies." The court said the better approach is that "'levying war' should be confined to insurrections and rebellions for the purpose of overthrowing the government by force and arms," and not merely a refusal to follow or adhere to the law. The court concluded that "when the object of an insurrection is of a local or private nature, *not having a direct tendency to destroy <u>all</u> property and <u>all</u> government, by numbers and armed force, it will <u>not</u> amount to treason*" (emphasis added).

See Also: American Revolutionary War and Treason; Christiana Revolt (1851); Insurrection; Levying War; Perjury, False Statements, and Obstruction of Justice; Rebellion; Riot and Incitement to Riot; Treason

Resources

Larson, Carlton F. W. 2020. *On Treason: A Citizen's Guide to the Law*. New York: Ecco, an imprint of HarperCollins (Kindle Edition).

Slaughter, Thomas P. 1991. *Bloody Dawn: The Christiana Riot and Racial Violence in the Antebellum North*. New York: Oxford University Press.

United States v. Hanway, 26 F. Cas. 105 (1851).

Hasan, Nidal (1970–)

On November 5, 2009, Nidal Hasan, a service member assigned at Fort Hood, Texas, yelled "Allahu Akbar" (Arabic for "God is Great") and opened fire on people at a Readiness Center (where soldiers and their families prepare for servicemember deployment), killing thirteen people (and an unborn child), and injuring more than thirty other individuals. It was the worst mass murder to occur on a US military base. In a subsequent report by the United States Senate, Hasan's murderous rampage was described as "the worst terrorist attack on United States soil since September 11, 2001." Hasan's mass murder is a crime against the state and distinguishable from other horrendous mass murders because Hasan's intention was to injure and wage war against the United States. At his criminal trial (court-martial) on August 6, 2013, Hasan stood up in court and told the jury panel that he "switched sides" and viewed himself as a Mujahideen waging "jihad" (waging a holy war) against the United States.

Hasan was a physician (psychiatrist) in the Army and held the rank of major immediately before his murderous rampage. Some early red flags of his radicalization as an alleged adherent to the teaching of radical Islam were missed by authorities because Hasan claimed that he was doing research to relate to his Muslim service member patients who were allegedly struggling with being a devout Muslim and yet fighting wars in Afghanistan and Iraq. Thus, when the Federal Bureau of Investigation (FBI) initially flagged e-mail communications with the late Iman Anwar al-Awlaki, a radical Islamic cleric with ties to Al-Qaeda, the FBI determined (before the shooting) that the communications were part of Hasan's professional research to help him better understand his patients. Intelligence agencies monitoring radical Islamic websites believe Hasan posted under the screenname "NidalHasan," and posted about suicide bombings. But these postings were never acted upon by the FBI or other government agencies.

Throughout his early military career, Hasan's colleagues described him as extremely difficult to work with, and workers often complained about his instability and emotional outbursts. His co-workers described him as frequently agitated, often arguing with soldiers. His last officer evaluation before arriving at Fort Hood indicated "poor performance" in his job. Soldiers reported that Hasan often made bizarre comments during public presentations. For instance, in a talk entitled "The Quranic World View as It Relates to Muslims in the U.S. Military" at Walter Reed, Hasan argued that Muslim soldiers should be given conscientious objectors status and that the failure of the military to do this could lead soldiers to snap and refuse deployment, commit acts of espionage, or kill fellow soldiers.

Some suggest Hasan's final breaking point was when he received orders to report to Afghanistan on November 28, 2009. He told acquaintances that he did not want to deploy, which would require him to fight or kill fellow Muslims. On November 5, 2009, Hasan decided to take his war against the United States to innocent soldiers going about their daily business on post at Fort Hood. Thanks to the heroic actions of two Army police officers (Kimberly D. Munley and Mark Todd), Hasan's murderous rampage was stopped after about ten minutes. But for the actions of Munley and Todd, the death toll would have been much higher. Munley was shot in the leg twice as she continued to distract Hasan, and Mark Todd shot Hasan and then kicked the gun out of Hasan's hand and handcuffed him.

At trial (a military court martial), Hasan insisted on representing himself. Hasan was charged with thirteen counts of premeditated murder and thirty-two counts of attempted murder. After months of pre-trial haggling between the government lawyers and Hasan's advisor counsel, the first day of trial commenced on August 6, 2013. Representing himself, within hours, Hasan had admitted that he was the attacker and killed the victims, that "he switched sides," and that he was waging "jihad" against the United States. Despite Hasan's multiple admissions of guilt, the prosecutors presented a mountain of evidence against Hasan, including the testimony of ninety witnesses over an eleven-day period (with Hasan refusing to cross-examine the witnesses). A mountain of forensic evidence was also admitted, leaving absolutely no doubt as to Hasan's guilt. On August 23, 2013, the military court-martial panel convicted Hasan of all charges. After listening to a bevy of aggravating circumstances, the jury recommended that Hasan be sentenced to death. To this day, Hasan is incarcerated at Fort Leavenworth, Kansas, awaiting the imposition of the death penalty. However, the US military has not executed a service member for a court martial conviction since 1961, so many are skeptical that the death penalty will ever be implemented. Given Hasan's many inflammatory statements, his connections with known Al-Qaeda operatives, the overwhelming evidence in the case, Hasan's own admissions, and a host of factors indicating Hasan viewed himself at war with the United States, many individuals have questioned why the government did not charge Hasan with terrorism or treason.

Noted terrorist and Al-Qaeda spokesperson Adam Yahiye Gadahn posted a message praising Hasan in 2010, saying in part, that the "Mujahid brother … [has] shown us what one righteous Muslim with an assault rifle can do for his religion and brothers in faith … and yearns to discharge his duty to Allah and play a part in the defense of Muslims against the savage, heartless, and bloody Zionist Crusader assault on our religion, sacred places, and homelands" (Gadahn 2010).

On November 14, 2009, *The New York Times* stated the harm facing the United States: "Major Hasan may be the latest example of an increasingly common type of terrorist, self-radicalized with the help of the internet, [who] wreaks havoc without support from overseas networks and without having to cross a border to reach his target" (Scott and James 2009).

See Also: Capitol Insurrection on January 6; Espionage; Gadahn, Adam Yahiye; Insurrection; September 11, 2001; Terrorism; Treason

Resources

Federal Bureau of Investigation. 2012. "FINAL REPORT of the WILLIAM H. WEBSTER COMMISSION on The Federal Bureau of Investigation, Counterterrorism Intelligence, and the Events at Fort Hood, Texas, on November 5, 2009." Accessed May 9, 2023. https://www.hsdl.org/c/view?docid=717443.

Gadahn, Adam. 2010. "A Call to Arms." *Central Intelligence Library*. Accessed October 31, 2023. https://www.cia.gov/library/abbottabad-compound/4B/4BD3A76FADAFF0C98CE2BD51584C899A_A_Call_To_Arms.pdf.

Scott, Shane, and Dan James. 2009. "Investigators Study Tangle of Clues on Fort Hood Suspect." *The New York Times*, November 22, 2009.

United States Senate Committee on Homeland Security and Governmental Affairs. 2011. "A Ticking Time Bomb: Counterterrorism Lessons from the U.S. Government's Failure to Prevent the Fort Hood Attack." Accessed May 9, 2023. https://www.hsgac.senate.gov/wp-content/uploads/imo/media/doc/Fort_Hood/FortHoodReport.pdf.

Haupt v. United States (1947)

In *Haupt v. United States*, the United States Supreme Court sustained a treason conviction for the first time, affirming the conviction by an eight to one vote. Hans Max Haupt was a naturalized US citizen, born in Germany. Haupt was the father of Herbert Hans Haupt, one of several German saboteurs executed for espionage after conviction by military tribunal, which was upheld by the Supreme Court in *Ex Parte Quirin* in 1942. Hans Haupt was sentenced to life imprisonment after being convicted of multiple counts of treason for various activities in support of his son's espionage and sabotage efforts on behalf of the German Reich during the Second World War.

In 1939, Hans's son Herbert, who also had been born in Germany and was apparently a naturalized citizen, worked for the Simpson Optical Company in Chicago, Illinois, where Hans also lived. Simpson Optical manufactured lenses for instruments, including parts for the Norden bomb sight, an important technology allowing the United States to conduct daytime bombing activities from high altitudes. In the spring of 1941, Herbert went to Germany to work for the German government. He was trained in sabotage work and was brought into the Operation Pastorius sabotage program. In June 1942, Herbert returned to the United States, arriving on a Florida beach at night by submarine. His mission was to act as a secret agent, spy, and saboteur for the German Reich. He was instructed to return to Chicago, acquire an automobile, and become reemployed by the Simpson Optical Company, where he was to gather information about the plant that would be used to guide the saboteurs.

In June 1944, Hans Haupt was convicted of various treasonous acts, including aiding Herbert's sabotage efforts by giving him a place to stay, helping him acquire an automobile, and assisting him in being rehired by Simpson Optical. In appealing his conviction, Hans Haupt challenged both that the acts alleged were not treasonous and that the evidence was constitutionally insufficient.

The majority of the Supreme Court dismissed the argument that sheltering an enemy saboteur, or helping him purchase a car, or helping him obtain employment at the target of his sabotage operation were insufficient to constitute treason, finding instead that the acts were of aid and comfort to Herbert Haupt in his mission of sabotage. "In light of this mission and his instructions, they were more than casually useful; they were aids in steps essential to his design for treason."

Because the Constitution's Treason Clause requires that "No person shall be convicted of treason unless on the testimony of two witnesses to the same overt act," the Court spent a considerable portion of its opinion demonstrating how two witnesses testified to the same overt acts that formed the basis for the treason charge.

The Supreme Court agreed with the trial judge's instructions to the jury that if they found Haupt's actions were merely giving aid to his son as an individual, rather than for the purpose of helping his son aid the German Reich or injure the United States, they could not convict. In upholding the jury's conviction despite Haupt's argument to that effect, the Supreme Court noted that the jury may have been influenced by Haupt's own prior statements that after the war he intended to return to Germany, that the United States was going to be defeated, that he would never permit his boy to join the American Army, and that he would kill his son before he would send him to fight Germany. Importantly, the Supreme Court held that the constitutional requirement of two witnesses to the same overt act or confession in open court does not exclude confessions or admissions made out of court, so long as a legal basis for the conviction has been established by the testimony of two witnesses and such out-of-court confessions or admissions are merely corroborative.

The Supreme Court distinguished Haupt's case from *Cramer v. United States*, in which the Court had overturned a treason conviction because the overt acts the two witnesses saw could not be said to have given "assistance or comfort." However, some view the Court's decision in *Haupt* as a departure from *Cramer*, rather than being consistent with it. In fact, in *Haupt*, Justice Douglas authored a separate opinion highlighting that the Court's decision in that case validated his prior dissent in *Cramer*.

Worried primarily about the danger of treason prosecutions as a convenient tool of oppression, especially during war, Justice Murphy, the lone dissenter in the *Haupt* case, preferred a stricter rule for what constitutes a treasonous overt act. In notes on a prior version of his opinion that were ultimately not included in the published version, Justice Murphy advocated limiting treason to those "acts which are completely inconsistent with non-treasonous motives," thereby "removing the crime from the realm of war-hysteria." To illustrate, he observed that the act of supplying a military map to a saboteur "for use in the execution of his nefarious plot" is an overt act of treason because it excludes all possibility of having been motivated by non-treasonable considerations. He contrasted this with providing a meal to an enemy agent who also happens to be one's son, where the act may have been motivated by some "non-treasonable basis."

Recognizing that the "law of treason makes, and properly makes, conviction difficult, but not impossible," the Supreme Court held that Haupt's "acts aided an enemy of the United States toward accomplishing his mission of sabotage. The mission was frustrated, but defendant did his best to make it succeed. His overt acts were proved in compliance with the hard test of the Constitution."

Hans Haupt was one of six of Herbert Haupt's relatives ultimately prosecuted for treason in connection with Herbert's sabotage efforts as part of Operation Pastorius. Upon Hans Haupt's conviction, he lost his US citizenship. In 1957, Haupt was deported to Germany after President Dwight Eisenhower granted clemency, under the condition that if Haupt returned to the United States, his clemency would be revoked and he would be returned to prison.

See Also: Aid and Comfort (Aid to Enemies of the State); *Cramer v. United States* (1945); Espionage; *Ex Parte Quirin* (1942); Sabotage; Treason

Resources

Crane, Paul T. 2009. "Did the Court Kill the Treason Charge?: Reassessing Cramer v. United States and Its Significance." *Florida St. Law Review* 36: 635.

Haupt v. United States, 330 U.S. 631 (1947).

Haymarket Affair (1886)

The Haymarket Affair, also known as the "Haymarket Riot," occurred on May 4, 1886, in Chicago's Haymarket Square. Initially, the incident began days before when thousands of workers across the country went on strike and attended rallies to demand an eight-hour workday. On May 3, Chicago police killed several workers striking at the McCormick Reaper Works. Labor leaders quickly called for a rally the following day, with one well-known labor leader, August Spies, distributing a flier exhorting workers: "Workingmen Arm Yourselves and Appear in Full Force!" Multiple leaders associated with the pro-labor anarchy movement at the time, including August Spies, addressed the rally attendees while standing on a hay wagon. The event was sufficiently peaceful that the mayor of Chicago, who had attended the rally hoping that his presence would help keep the peace, left early. However, as the rally was nearing its conclusion, a large group of Chicago police officers arrived to disperse the crowd. An unidentified individual then threw a bomb into the group of police officers. The bomb exploded, killing at least one police officer and wounding at least sixty. In the ensuing gunfire, several more police officers and a few civilians were killed.

Eventually, eight men who were members of the International Working People's Association and labeled as anarchists were charged with the bombing and indicted for murder. Many observers have suggested their subsequent trial, which resulted in all eight being convicted of murder on less than clear evidence of their connection to the bombing, was biased and unfair. This allegation was in part because of the fear of anarchists and the labor movement that had swept the country. Moreover, much of the evidence offered by prosecutors was made up of the defendants' pre-event speeches and writings. In denying the defendants' subsequent appeal of their convictions, the Illinois Supreme Court, in *Spies v. Illinois* (1887), upheld this use of speech as evidence, concluding "It was a question for the jury, whether, with the evidence before them, the attack upon the police at the Haymarket 'was so connected with the inflammatory language used, that they can not be separated by time or other circumstances.'" Seven of the eight defendants were sentenced to death. Four were hanged, one committed suicide on the eve of his scheduled execution, and successive Illinois governors pardoned, or commuted the sentences of, the remaining defendants.

The Haymarket Affair had wide-ranging consequences. The killing of police officers was widely portrayed in the national media as the result of violent, pro-labor, anarchists, dealing a blow to the general labor movement, causing widespread fear and suspicion of anarchists, and leading to the First Red Scare. In fact, the violent incident was one of several around the turn of the twentieth century that led to criminal anarchy statutes, which were ultimately upheld as constitutional by the United States Supreme Court in *Gitlow v. New York* (1925). By contrast, the incident, including the perceived injustice of the subsequent trial in which eight men were convicted for the bombing, is said to have inspired some to join the anarchy movement, including important anarchist leaders Emma Goldman and Alexander Berkman. The international "May Day" movement, which celebrates workers' rights every May 1st, was largely inspired by the Haymarket Affair.

See Also: Anarchy, Criminal; First Red Scare and the Palmer Raids (1919–20); *Gitlow v. New York* (1925)

Resources

Avrich, Paul. 1984. *The Haymarket Tragedy*. Princeton, NJ: Princeton University Press.

Foner, Philip S. 1986. "The First May Day and the Haymarket Affair." In *May Day: A Short History of the International Workers' Holiday, 1886–1986*, 27–39. New York: International Publishers.

Green, James. 2006. *Death in the Haymarket: A Story of Chicago, the First Labor Movement and the Bombing That Divided Gilded Age America*. New York: Pantheon Books.

"Haymarket Riot." *History.com*, May 1, 2020. Accessed November 19, 2023. https://www.history.com/topics/19th-century/haymarket-riot.

Hazlett, Albert (1837–60)

Albert Hazlett was a mystery man, at least to Virginia authorities in 1859. Hazlett was one of the group of men that participated in John Brown's Raid. While only four or five of the twenty-one who attacked the United States Armory and Arsenal had escaped, there was a general fear that other Brown supporters might be lurking about in the area. Virginia encouraged vigilantism by offering an award of $1,000 (a value of approximately $36,000 in 2023 currency) to anyone who could identify any of Brown's surviving men, escaped or otherwise. Hazlett was able to escape the "perfect steel trap" of Harpers Ferry (Frederick Douglass's words [Villard 1910, 413]), on October 18, 1859, only to be captured in Pennsylvania on October 22. He was using the alias William Harrison and was pulled off a train in Carlisle, Pennsylvania, four days after the military defeat of John Brown at Harpers Ferry some eighty miles away. He was ordered extradited back to Virginia on November 5, and arrived on November 8, less than a month after the attempted treason and insurrection.

Hazlett was born on September 21, 1837, and was just thirty-three when he joined John Brown's Provisional Army. Like many passionate Northern youths of that era, Hazlett had volunteered to go to "Bleeding Kansas" (a term referring to a period during which there were violent clashes over whether Kansas would be a free or slave state) to wage war against the dreaded pro-slavery Border Ruffians. He was just twenty when he joined a militia company. In the latter half of 1858, Hazlett joined John Brown and his men and participated in a raid organized by Brown in Missouri, helping to free an enslaved family. In early 1859, with a bounty on the head of old Captain John Brown, Hazlett went to Ohio for work and then back to his home state of Pennsylvania. In September 1859, Hazlett had joined Brown's Provisional Army (as it was called) and spent the month of September and the first half of October in the Kennedy Farmhouse, a building in Maryland about five miles outside of Harpers Ferry. Brown's men waited at the Kennedy farmhouse for recruits, money, and arms to arrive.

Despite being a man of sleight build and muscle, Hazlett was tall at five feet, eleven inches tall, and described by Annie Brown (John Brown's daughter) as "a bright, kindly, obliging young man." On the evening of October 16 and morning of October 17, Hazlett was tasked to take and guard the United States Arsenal along with Edwin Coppoc, Shields Green, and Osbourne Anderson. Anderson would be the only one of these three men to escape Harpers Ferry, survive the American Civil War, and live until 1871. When militia and United States forces began outnumbering Brown's meager "army," the Hazlett, Coppoc, and Anderson saw their chance to escape and took it. Coppoc was captured several days later in Chambersburg, Pennsylvania, and Hazlett in Carlisle. Shields Green decided to stay in Harpers Ferry and fight with Brown as Brown made his last stand at the Armory Engine house/Fire station (now called John Brown's Fort).

As the most high-profile defendant, John Brown was tried first and executed on December 2, 1859. Next came the trials of Edwin Coppoc, John Copeland, John Cook, and Shields Green, all found guilty and executed on December 16, 1859. This left just Aaron Stevens and Hazlett in custody. Aaron Stevens was being held in jail while negotiations were ongoing as to whether he would be turned over to the federal government for treason charges and for wider federal subpoena power to learn about Brown's famous Northern supporters. Hazlett was held in pre-trial confinement for 140 days, not as a bargaining chip (like in the case of Stevens), but because Hazlett claimed he was William Harrison, and authorities could not prove, beyond a reasonable doubt, his identity. Finally, Hazlett was tried in March 1860 and even then, the government could conjure up only one witness that Harrison was Hazlett. The witness, Joseph Barry, lived through John Brown's Raid and the Civil War in Harpers Ferry, wrote about his experiences, and became the town's first chronicler and author. The first history book on Harpers Ferry by Barry is *The Strange Story of Harpers Ferry*, wherein Barry clearly identifies Albert Hazlett/William Harrison as one of Brown's men. Hazlett was convicted of treason, insurrection, and conspiracy to incite a slave revolt.

Thus, while Brown was the first person to ever be executed for treason in the United States (and by a state government no less), Albert Hazlett, Aaron Stevens, and Edwin Coppoc hold the dubious distinction of being executed by Virginia for treason as well. Aaron Stevens and Albert Hazlett, executed at the same time in March 1860, are the last people executed for treason in the United States (their executions occurred approximately four months after Brown's). The day before Hazlett's execution, he wrote "I am willing to die in the cause of liberty. If I had 10,000 lives, I would willingly lay them down for the same cause" (Villard 1910, 682).

See Also: American Civil War and Treason; Brown, John; Conspiracy, Criminal; Cook, John E.; Copeland, John Anthony, Jr.; Coppoc, Edwin; Green, Shields; Insurrection; John Brown's Raid (1859); Stevens, Aaron; Treason

Resources

Hinton, Richard J. 1894. *John Brown and His Men: With Some Account of the Roads They Travelled to Reach Harpers Ferry*. New York: Funk & Wagnalls Company.

Sadler, Spencer. 2020. *Absalom Hazlett: A Loyal Soldier in John Brown's Army*. Mount Pleasant, SC: Arcadia/ America through Time.

Villard, Oward Garrison. 1910. *John Brown: 1800–1859: A Biography Fifty Years After*. New York: Houghton Mifflin.

Hess v. Indiana (1973)

During the Vietnam War, students protested against the war at many colleges and universities throughout the United States. In May 1970, in the wake of the killing of four students by National Guardsmen at Kent State University, students at Indiana University protested against the war and against the university administration for not adequately opposing (in the students' view) President Nixon's policies. During the protest, a police car drove up a street full of protestors, causing the protestors to step back onto the sidewalk. While doing so, one student protestor named Gregory Hess shouted "We'll take the f***ing street again" toward no one in particular. Unbeknownst to Hess, the county sheriff was standing immediately behind him as he yelled. The sheriff then jumped on Hess's back and immediately arrested him for disorderly conduct. Hess and five others charged with disorderly conduct were convicted and fined $1.00 each.

Represented by professors from Indiana University's law school, Hess appealed his conviction on several grounds, one of which was that his speech was protected by the First Amendment. The Indiana Supreme Court disagreed, upholding Hess's conviction. Citing the United States Supreme Court's recent decision in *Brandenburg v. Ohio* (1969), the Indiana Supreme Court held that "[t]he trial court was justified in finding that the statement was intended to incite further lawless action on the part of the crowd in the vicinity of appellant and was likely to produce such action," and as such fell into the category of unprotected speech under the First Amendment. Hess appealed to the United States Supreme Court, which, in a six to three decision, overturned the conviction. The majority concluded that it was unclear whether Hess intended to incite lawlessness at all, given that his statement could have been construed as a plea for the crowd to back away. Furthermore, the majority held that even if "take the street again" was intended to incite some lawless action, Hess's utterance "amounted to nothing more than advocacy of illegal action at some indefinite future time." That is, because it was not inciting *imminent* lawlessness, the speech was protected. *Hess* has been cited by courts numerous times for the requirement that the illegality must be clear and the timeframe of the encouraged illegal acts imminent, not at some indefinite future time. Speech cannot be a crime against the state, even when criticizing the state, when not intended to produce imminent lawless action.

See Also: *Brandenburg v. Ohio* (1969); Speech as Crime against the State

Resources

Hess v. Indiana, 414 U.S. 105 (1973).

"Hess v. Indiana Revisited: A Panel Discussion with Case Participants (video)." *Indiana University Law School*. Accessed June 14, 2023. https://www.youtube.com/watch?v=TTgzLVlGN1Q.

Hirabayashi v. United States (1943)

In *Hirabayashi v. United States*, the Supreme Court assessed whether a curfew imposed only on persons of Japanese ancestry was constitutional. Roughly ten weeks after Japan attacked the United States in Pearl Harbor, Hawaii, President Franklin D. Roosevelt signed Executive Order 9066, an order that declared the Japanese race to be an "enemy race." The order authorized the Secretary of War and subordinate military commanders to impose curfews on people of Japanese ancestry in, and ultimately exclude such people from, areas designated by the military as exclusion zones. Subsequently, General John DeWitt of the United States Army issued an order that all persons of Japanese ancestry within the designated military area (most of the West Coast of the United States) "be within their place of residence between the hours of 8 p.m. and 6 a.m." More notoriously, General DeWitt's order included an exclusion of all persons of Japanese dissent—including United States citizens—from the West Coast and forced relocation to internment camps. This exclusion and internment would be the focus of *Korematsu v. United States* (1944).

In an act of civil disobedience, Gordon Hirabayashi, an American citizen and student at the University of Washington, chose to disobey the curfew and exclusion order. (Though Hirabayashi would ultimately be convicted of violating the exclusion and internment order, the Supreme Court assessed only the curfew in his appeal.) After not being caught for these violations for some time, Hirabayashi turned himself in to the Federal Bureau of Investigation. He was arrested and jailed for five months awaiting trial. At his trial, the jury deliberated just ten minutes before finding him guilty. After his trial and conviction, it was determined that Hirabayashi could not serve his sentence in Washington state because it was within the exclusion zone; he would have to be confined in Arizona. Washington state authorities told Hirabayashi that they would not transport him to Arizona, so he walked and hitchhiked his way from Washington to the prison camp in Arizona where he served his sentence.

Although it recognized that the curfew targeted only one race of individuals, the Supreme Court unanimously upheld the military's authority to impose the curfew. The Court determined that however "odious to a free people" racism was, the curfew was relevant to the nation's safety. Three Justices initially drafted dissenting opinions, but ultimately concurred, with their concurrences reading more like dissents.

The day it decided *Hirabayashi*, the Supreme Court announced its decision in a companion case, *Yasui v. United States*. Minoru Yasui, born in Oregon, became a commissioned officer in the United States Army. Yasui then attended law school at the University of Oregon and gained employment working for the Japanese Consulate office in Chicago. After Pearl Harbor, and as a Second Lieutenant in the Army, Yasui traveled back to Oregon to serve, but was refused entry numerous times to his assigned base due to his race. Like Hirabayashi, Yasui self-reported his violation of the curfew to law enforcement. He walked up and down the street in Portland after the curfew, telling one police officer "Look, I'm a person of Japanese ancestry, arrest me." After that officer refused to arrest him, Yasui went to police headquarters and insisted he be arrested. Yasui got his wish and was placed in solitary confinement for nine months pending his trial. The Court considered the *Hirabayashi* and *Yasui* cases together because they both involved a curfew, with the primary difference between the cases being the *Yasui* trial judge's determination that Yasui had lost his US citizenship when he worked for the Japanese Consulate. With little analysis, and primarily relying on its opinion in *Hirabayashi*, the Court unanimously upheld Yasui's conviction.

The object of Hirabayashi's and Yasui's crimes was the racially predicated policy of the United States they believed to be unconstitutional. Both maintained they were loyal US citizens.

In 1986, forty-three years after the Supreme Court had upheld it, a federal district court judge in Seattle vacated Hirabayashi's wartime conviction. The conviction was overturned on the basis of later-discovered evidence that the Solicitor General had presented fabricated evidence to the Supreme Court during oral argument on his appeal during the Second World War. Specifically, the Solicitor General repeated the military's claimed threat of invasion of the West Coast by Japanese forces that the military knew was insignificant. Surprisingly, the Department of Justice appealed the district court's ruling vacating Hirabayashi's conviction to the Ninth Circuit Court of Appeals. During oral arguments to the Ninth Circuit, lawyers for the government were asked why the government had not moved to vacate the convictions on its own. With Hirabayashi still alive and present, the government lawyer unbelievably answered, "we didn't think there was anyone out there who cared." In a unanimous ruling by the Ninth Circuit vacating Hirabayashi's conviction, federal judge Mary Shroeder wrote: "A United States citizen who is convicted of a crime on account of race is lastingly aggrieved." In May 2011, Acting Solicitor General Neal Katyal acknowledged and apologized for his predecessor's lapse. In 2012, President Barack Obama posthumously awarded Hirabayashi the Presidential Medal of Freedom.

See Also: *Korematsu v. United States* (1944); Civil Disobedience and Crimes against the State

Resources

Hirabayashi v. United States, 320 U.S. 81 (1943).

Irons, Peter. 1999. *A People's History of the Supreme Court*. New York: Viking.

Kastenberg, Joshua, and Eric Merriam. 2016. *In a Time of Total War: The Federal Judiciary and the National Defense—1940–1954*. New York: Routledge.

Katyal, Neal. 2011. "Confession of Error: The Solicitor General's Mistakes during the Japanese-American Internment Cases." *United States Department of Justice*, May 20, 2011. Accessed June 14, 2023. https://www.justice.gov/archives/opa/blog/confession-error-solicitor-generals-mistakes-during-japanese-american-internment-cases.

Yasui v. United States, 320 U.S. 115 (1943).

Hiss, Alger (1904–1996)

Alger Hiss was a high-ranking official in the United States State Department who was accused of being a spy for the Soviet Union in the 1930s and was the subject of two sensational trials that revolved around allegations of perjury and espionage. The federal prosecution of Alger Hiss is considered among the great trials of American legal history, and Hiss was the most famous example of espionage after Julius and Ethel Rosenberg. The Alger Hiss case also had far-reaching political ramifications, including injecting a relatively obscure California Congressman Richard Nixon into the public spotlight and serving as the launching pad for Joseph McCarthy's claims of communist infiltration of the government (see Second Red Scare [McCarthyism]).

In 1948, Whittaker Chambers was a former member of the Communist Party and an editor at *Time* magazine. Despite his communist past (he quit the Communist Party in 1938), Chambers came to view communism as a danger to the United States and a threat to national security. On August 3, 1948, Chambers testified in front of the United States House of Representatives Un-American Activities Committee (HUAC). During this testimony, Chambers accused Alger Hiss of being a spy and committing espionage for the Soviet Union between 1933 and 1938. Hiss, a Harvard-educated lawyer who had once clerked for Supreme Court Justice Oliver Wendell Holmes, Jr., was a high-ranking employee in the State Department and had served as one of the chief American negotiators at the Yalta Conference in 1945 at which the United States, UK, and Soviet Union had discussed the postwar reorganization of Germany and Europe. Chambers testified that he had stayed at Hiss's residence in the 1930s, knew the floorplan and layout, the types and style of furniture, and Hess's habits, nicknames, and pets. Chambers knew other obscure details, such as Hiss's hobby as a amateur ornithologist and sighting of a rare "Prothonotary Warbler" on an early morning on the Potomac River with his wife, Priscilla. After Chambers' initial HUAC testimony, Hiss sent a telegram to HUAC denying that he had been a member of the Communist Party and claimed that he did not "know Mr. Chambers and, so far as I am aware, have never laid eyes on him." Hiss offered to provide his own testimony to HUAC in response, which he did on August 5, 1948. Hiss denied ever being a member of the Communist Party and again denied knowing Chambers.

President Truman pressured the HUAC to drop the investigation of Hiss, calling it "a red herring." Congressman Richard Nixon, then a junior member of the HUAC, believed Chambers and thought Hiss's testimony to be "condescending," "insulting," and "insolent," and therefore pressed his colleagues on the HUAC to continue the investigation. The HUAC formed a subcommittee, chaired by Nixon, which was charged with determining who was telling the truth and who was lying. A turning point in the credibility of the witnesses occurred when Nixon asked Hiss what hobbies he had, if any. Hiss responded that his hobbies included tennis and being an amateur ornithologist. Another HUAC member, Congressman John McDowell, immediately interjected and asked, "did you ever see a Prothonotary Warbler?" Hiss excitedly responded, "I have, right here on the Potomac, do you know that place?" It seemed implausible to some HUAC members that Chambers could have produced details such as Hiss seeing a Prothonotary Warbler on the Potomac River unless Chambers and Hiss did know each other.

At this point, Hiss changed his testimony from denying he "ever laid eyes upon" Chambers to claiming that he may have met Chambers previously, but that Chambers went by the name "George Crosley" and was a reporter investigating a story about Hiss's work in government. The committee confronted Hiss with other evidence that corroborated Chambers's claim that he knew Hiss, such as Hiss leasing an apartment to Chambers in the 1930s and signing over a title of Hiss's 1929 Ford automobile to Chambers. The subcommittee concluded its work with a report that classified Hiss's testimony as "vague and evasive" and Chambers's testimony as "forthright and emphatic." Hiss responded with a fourteen-page letter attacking the congressional committee and its work.

Hiss then brought a lawsuit against Chambers for defamation. During the discovery phase of the lawsuit, Hiss's lawyers asked if Chambers could produce any correspondence from Alger Hiss. In response, Chambers produced sixty-five pages of re-typed State department documents and four handwritten notes by Alger Hiss. Chambers subsequently lead two HUAC investigators out to a pumpkin patch on his farm and produced five rolls of 35-mm film containing pictures of Navy and State Department documents from a hollowed-out pumpkin. They became known as "the pumpkin papers." Chambers claimed he did not provide these documents earlier because he wanted to spare Hiss unnecessary embarrassment, but it is likely Chambers viewed these documents as incriminating himself with espionage as well.

Chambers's testimony to the HUAC, Hiss's "vague and evasive" testimony, and the "pumpkin papers" all strongly corroborated that Hiss and Chambers did indeed know each other. The unresolved question became whether Hiss committed espionage. Fortunately for Hiss, at the time, the statute of limitations for espionage was five years, and even the most recent of the "pumpkin papers" was from a decade earlier. However, armed with the HUAC testimony and the "pumpkin papers," a federal grand jury indicted Hiss for two counts of perjury for lying to HUAC. One count of perjury was based upon Hiss's statement to HUAC that he never knew or "laid eyes upon" Chambers. The second count of perjury was based upon Hiss's denial that he ever transferred documents to Chambers.

At Hiss's first perjury trial starting in May 1949, Chambers was the lead witness and testified that Hiss would bring home state department documents, retype them, and pass them on to his Soviet handler. Chambers's wife Ester also testified to their close relationship with Alger and Priscilla Hiss and described visits and social interactions with them. A former State department colleague of Hiss testified that Hiss often took State Department documents home with him. A Federal Bureau of Investigation (FBI) analyst testified that the various documents found in the pumpkin patch were typed with the same Woodstock typewriter owned by Hiss. Hiss's defense team attacked Chambers character as morally bankrupt, claiming that Chambers was a blasphemer of Christianity, an avowed former communist party member, and that Chambers may have frequented a prostitute. Hiss also claimed that the typewriter in question had been given away before the documents were allegedly typed by him. Hiss also had several well-known individuals serve as character witnesses for him, including two United States Supreme Court Justices, a former United States Solicitor General, a former presidential nominee (John Davis), and a future presidential nominee (Adlai Stevenson).

In July 1949, the case was given to the jury. The jury came back twice indicating that they were hopelessly deadlocked and could not reach a consensus. The federal judge eventually declared a mistrial, and Hiss was tried a second time for perjury. The second trial was largely a repeat of the first, except that Hiss's defense now claimed that someone must have obtained Hiss's typewriter to frame him. On January 20, 1950, the jury found Hiss guilty on both counts of perjury, and Hiss was sentenced to a five-year sentence. The verdict was upheld on appeal by the United States Court of Appeals for the Second Circuit, and the United States Supreme Court denied a request to review the case. Hiss served forty-four months of the sentence before being released for good behavior.

The Hiss case had far-reaching implications. Joseph McCarthy gave his first speech about communists infiltrating the government two weeks after the Hiss conviction, commonly considered the start of the McCarthyism era. In 1952, Richard Nixon was elected to serve as vice president under President Eisenhower. Also in 1952, Chambers authored a book entitled *Witness*, which many consider to be one of America's great autobiographies. President Ronald Reagan claimed that

Chambers's book influenced his decision to switch from a New Deal Democrat to a Republican. On March 20, 1984, President Reagan awarded Chambers the Presidential Medal of Freedom. In 1988, Hiss wrote his autobiography, entitled *Recollections of a Life*, wherein he continued to maintain his innocence, which he continued to do until his death in 1996. After the end of the Cold War, intelligence community documents (called the Venona Cables) delineating communications between various Soviet actors were declassified. Many have argued that the documents refer to Hiss and provide proof that Hiss was a Soviet agent and committed espionage at the Yalta Conference. Since the end of the Cold War, multiple former members of the Soviet Union intelligence community also alleged that Hiss was a Soviet agent.

See Also: Espionage; Perjury, False Statements, and Obstruction of Justice; Rosenberg, Julius and Ethel; Second Red Scare (McCarthyism)

Resources

Shelton, Christina. 2012. *Alger Hiss: Why He Chose Treason*. New York: Threshold Editions.
Tanenhaus, Sam. 1997. *Whittaker Chambers: A Biography*. New York: Random House.

Holder v. Humanitarian Law Project (2010)

See Material Support Crimes

Homeland Security Act (2002)

Throughout its history and since its genesis, the United States has promulgated a variety of laws meant to protect the homeland from threats and violence against the state. One of the earliest attempts were the 1798 Alien and Sedition Acts, which were passed to curtail perceived threats of terrorism and attacks on the government by French immigrants and opponents of the reigning Federalist party. Toward the latter half of the First World War, Congress passed the Espionage Act of 1917 to protect governmental secrets from being transmitted to foreign powers. After the bloody engagement at Waco in 1993 and the 1995 Oklahoma City Bombing, Congress passed the Anti-Terrorism and Effective Death Penalty Act of 1996. And in the immediate aftermath of September 11, 2001, Congress enacted the USA PATRIOT Act. While all designed to protect the homeland, each of these laws was piecemeal in nature and did not comprehensively address the issue of homeland security or engage in large-scale transformation of how the federal government was structured in order to systematically protect the country better from threats. A year after the deadly attacks on September 11, 2001, and the subsequent passage of the USA PATRIOT Act in October 2001, Congress enacted its most sweeping legislation in this area in the country's history with the passage of the Homeland Security Act of 2002.

The Homeland Security Act was a voluminous legislative act spanning 484 pages. It created the Department of Homeland Security (DHS) and restructured and integrated twenty-two existing federal agencies into the newly founded department. The creation of the DHS and reorganization of agencies under DHS auspices were the most comprehensive and widespread restructuring of the federal government in over a half century, a vast transformation not seen since President Truman signed legislation creating the Department of Defense in 1947. The main mission of DHS, as stated in Section 101(b)(1) of the Homeland Security Act, is to reduce the United States' vulnerabilities to terrorist attacks, prevent acts of terrorism, and ensure the overall economic security of the United States is not diminished by homeland security measures. Additionally, DHS is responsible for ensuring that each of the twenty-two agencies transferred under DHS oversight continue to carry out the original planned functions of each agency, including acting as the lead in responding to disasters (manmade or acts of nature) and emergency planning and preparedness. The transfer of these agencies under the integration and supervision of a single cabinet level department (DHS) also was intended to ensure the uniform cooperation of the various agencies, the free flow of intelligence across agencies, and to ensure that the various agencies were not acting at cross-purposes.

As of 2023, the Department of Homeland Security employed approximately 240,000 employees and is one of the largest federal agencies within the federal government. Existing federal agencies moved under DHS include Customs and Border Patrol Protection, Secret Service, Coast Guard, and the Federal Emergency Management Agency. The DHS also oversees airport security through the Transportation Security Administration, an agency created a year prior to the DHS in November 2001.

See Also: Alien and Sedition Acts (1798); Anti-Terrorism and Effective Death Penalty Act of 1996; Espionage Act of 1917 and Sedition act of 1918; Oklahoma City Bombing (1995); September 11, 2001; Terrorism; USA PATRIOT Act; Waco (1993)

Resources

Domestic Security: Homeland Security Organization. 2023. 6 U.S. Code Sections 101–677.
Homeland Security Act. 2002. Pub. L. No. 107–296, 116 Stat. 2135.
"U.S. Department of Homeland Security." 2013. In *Health Care and Travel: Gale Encyclopedia of Everyday Law*, edited by Donna Batten, vol. 2: 927–30. Detroit: Gale.
Zusman, Lynne K., and Neil Helfand. 2004. "Department of Homeland Security Act (2002)." In *Major Acts of Congress*, edited by Brian K. Landsberg, vol. 1: 202–8. New York: Macmillan Reference.

Hoxie, United States v. (1808)

In this early important federal case, the court vigorously disagreed with and dismissed the Jefferson administration's position of classifying violations of a federal statute by American citizens as acts of treason. The decision in *United States v. Hoxie* is important because it articulated limitations in the application of the "levying war" portion of the Treason Clause in the United States Constitution, and in dismissing attempts to inculcate the English concept of "constructive treason" into American law. The court expressly declared that "it is more safe, as well as more consonant to the principles of our constitution, that the crime of treason should not be extended, by construction, to doubtful cases." The *Hoxie* case established that even armed resistance to the authority of the federal government, without treasonous intent, did not amount to the act of "levying war" and treason.

The *Hoxie* case had its origins in Congress's passage of the Embargo Act (1807–9), which prohibited American vessels from sailing to any foreign port and barred American exports to all foreign countries. The Embargo Act completely banned all foreign commerce and only permitted US merchants to engage in US coastal trading. Furthermore, the Act authorized the Navy and Revenue Cutters to enforce this federal law. Consequences for violations of the Embargo Act included forfeiting of the ship and cargo and fines ranging from $1,000 to $20,000, depending on the severity of the violation. The Jefferson administration promoted the Embargo Act as necessary to potentially influence English and French foreign policy as it related to the United States. Thomas Jefferson erroneously believed that the United States could force those countries to change their maritime policies toward the United States by depriving them of American commerce and produce.

In 1808, Frederick Hoxie was contracted to deliver a raft packed with cut timber from Vermont to Canada by way of Lake Champlain. Hoxie was to be paid $800 at the conclusion of this job. However, the Embargo Act clearly prohibited this activity—the transferring of American produce (cut timber) from the United States to Canada. A US federal official seized the raft near the Canadian border, and a US soldier was assigned to guard the raft. A brief time later, Hoxie appeared with approximately sixty men armed with muskets and clubs, retook the raft, and sailed north toward Canada. Hoxie's men were then met by federal troops and a brisk gun battle took place between Hoxie's men and the federal troops, although amazingly no one was injured or killed. Hoxie was arrested and put on trial for treason.

Acting as a Circuit Justice, United States Supreme Court Justice Henry Brockholst Livingston presided over the trial. Through his instructions to the jury, Livingston excoriated the Jefferson administration's position that an armed violation in protest or non-adherence to a specific law of the United States (sometimes referred to as "constructive treason") could of itself be treason. Judge Livingston rejected the assertion that non-adherence to federal law (or even armed violations of federal law) could be treason, holding that such conduct, in and of itself, did not constitute "levying war" against the government, and therefore did not constitute treason against the United States. Justice Livingston's opinion, which was his legal instructions to the jury on treason before submitting the case for their decision, all but directed the jury to return a verdict of not guilty. Livingston instructed the jury that "it has already been observed, that, taking the constitution as our guide, not a doubt can be entertained of the prisoner's innocence of treason."

The court in *Hoxie* was cognizant that, only a few years before, defendants were prosecuted and convicted for treason for actions taken during the Whiskey Rebellion (1794) and Fries's Rebellion (1799) for engaging in armed resistance to the enforcement of taxation laws. However, Livingston distinguished these cases from Hoxie's case in several respects. First, Hoxie had no desire to overturn the Embargo Act by force (but simply to transport a raft of timber from Vermont to Canada), while the main actors in the Whiskey Rebellion and Fries's Rebellion were motivated by the desire to make certain federal taxation laws ineffective and unenforceable. The court concluded that Frederick Hoxie simply did not have any treasonous intent (even under the nebulous doctrine of "constructive treason"), while the main actors in the Whiskey Rebellion and Fries's Rebellion were acting in part to hopefully see the wholesale reversal of certain federal taxation laws. Second, Livingston in the *Hoxie* decision distinguished the slight use of force and goals in the case (the seizure of one single raft) compared to the actions in the Whiskey Rebellion and Fries's Rebellion "which threatened the existence of government, were well calculated to intimidate the legislature, and for a time actually suspended the operation of certain laws which were deemed obnoxious in a large district of [the] country." The court simply concluded that none of this was the case with Hoxie's actions. Unlike the Whiskey Rebellion and Fries's Rebellion, the court in Hoxie concluded that Hoxie's "offense laid, stripped of its artificial dress, and technical appearance, is nothing more than the forcible rescuing of a raft from the custody of a military guard placed over it by a collector."

Today, the Hoxie decision is instructive and an important early judicial precedent for what constitutes "levying war" under the Treason Clause of the United States Constitution. In the *Hoxie* decision, the court indicated that the "levying of war ... would seem to be nothing short of the employment, or at least the embodying of a military force, armed and arrayed, in a warlike manner, for the purpose of forcibly subverting the government, dismembering the Union, or destroying the legislative functions of congress. These troops should be so armed, and so directed, as to leave no doubt, that the United States, or their government, were the immediate object of their attack." Later in the *Hoxie* opinion, Justice Livingston discussed the case of *Ex Parte Bollman* (1807), which he described as "the only occasion on which the supreme court of the United States has delivered any opinion on the doctrine of treason." Then, the *Hoxie* court went on to quote the following language from *Ex Parte Bollman*: first, "[t]o constitute this crime [treason], war must actually be levied against the United States. However flagitious may be the crime of conspiring to subvert by force the government of our country, such conspiracy is not treason;" and second, "there must be an actual assemblage of men, for the purpose of executing a treasonable design."

See Also: Conspiracy, Criminal; *Ex Parte Bollman* (1807); Fries's Rebellion (1799); Levying War; Treason; Whiskey Rebellion

Resources

Mashaw, Jerry L. 2007. "Reluctant Nationalists: Federal Administration and Administrative Law in the Republican Era." *The Yale Law Journal* 116: 1636–740.

Simpson, B. Mitchell III. 2018. "Treason and Terror: A Toxic Brew." *Roger Williams University Law Review* 23: 1–53.

United States v. Hoxie, 26 Fed. Cas. 397, no. 15,407 C.C.D. Vt. (1808).

I

Imminent Incitement Test

See Brandenburg v. Ohio (1969)

Insurrection

The term "insurrection" is defined by the *Oxford English Dictionary* as "the action of rising in arms or open resistance against established authority or government restraint" (OED 2022). The first instance where the term is referenced in the English language was in 1459 in the Rolls of Parliament, with the annotation: "He [Jack Cade] … wrote letters to many Citees [*sic*] … to have made a comon [*sic*] insurrection" (OED 2022). In the antebellum era within the United States, the term "insurrection" was often used in association with slave rebellions. There is ambiguity as to how large a force must be (if at all) to qualify as an insurrection under this definition. While the "action of rising in arms" suggests at least two people are involved (because of the plural of "arms"), even this is not altogether clear. In the Bundy Standoff, Cliven Bundy, a rancher, mounted an armed standoff with his son, Ammon Bundy, against the federal government in 2014 and 2016. This could be classified as an insurrection under this definition. In US history, there have been numerous insurrections even though many of these events are called "rebellions." Armed open resistance constituting an insurrection can be seen from the very earliest days of the country's history, in events like the Whiskey Rebellion and Fries's Rebellion. Both the United States Constitution and the United States Code use the terms "insurrection" and "rebellion" (often in the same provision in each legal source); yet the actual legal difference in meaning (if any) remains undefined, ambiguous, and subject to individual interpretation.

In the Constitution, the term "insurrection" is expressly used four times, once in the main text (Article I, section 8) and three times in the Fourteenth Amendment (see clauses 3–4). Article I, Section 8 of the Constitution gives Congress the power "to provide for calling forth the Militia to execute the Laws of the Union, suppress Insurrections and repeal Invasions." Under the Fourteenth Amendment (clause 3), referred to as the Disqualification Clause, an individual who "engaged in insurrection or rebellion" against the United States is disqualified from holding any public office. Similarly, the terms "insurrection or rebellion" are used twice more in the Fourteenth Amendment in clause 4, which provides that "the validity of the public debt of the United States, authorized by law, including debts incurred for payment of pensions and bounties for services in suppressing insurrection or rebellion, shall not be questioned." Furthermore, "neither the United States nor any State shall assume or pay any debt or obligation incurred in aid of insurrection or rebellion against the United States, or any claim for the loss or emancipation of any slave; but all such debts, obligations and claims shall be held illegal and void."

Under federal criminal law, Congress has made criminal both "rebellion" and "insurrection." Under 18 United States Code Section 2383, "Whoever incites, sets on foot, assists, or engages in any rebellion or insurrection against the authority of the United States or the laws thereof, or gives aid or comfort thereto, shall be fined under this title or imprisoned not more than ten years, or both; and shall be incapable of holding any office under the United States."

Finally, under Congress's Article I, Section 8, power to "provide for calling forth the Militia to execute the Laws of the Union, suppress Insurrections and repel Invasions," Congress enacted the Insurrection Act. Amended multiple times over the years and spanning several sections, the Insurrection Act authorizes the president to deploy military forces inside the United States to suppress insurrections and rebellions. As described more completely in the next entry (see Insurrection Act), military force has been frequently utilized under the Insurrection Act in responding to a variety of different insurrections and rebellions over the years.

See Also: Bundy Standoffs (2014–16); Disqualification Clause; Fries's Rebellion (1799); Insurrection Act; Rebellion; Whiskey Rebellion

Resources

Morris, Seren. 2021. "What Does Insurrection or Sedition Mean? Definition of Words Used to Describe Capitol Riot." *Newsweek*, January 7, 2021. Accessed June 18, 2023. https://www.newsweek.com/what-does-insurrection-sedition-mean-definition-capitol-riot-1559745.

Oxford English Dictionary. 2022. "Insurrection." Oxford: Oxford University Press. OED.com

"Rebellion or Insurrection," 18 United States Code Section 2383.

Insurrection Act

The Insurrection Act permits the president of the United States to use the US military domestically against Americans in case of insurrection. The Constitution explicitly authorizes Congress to "provide for calling forth the Militia to execute the Laws of the Union, suppress Insurrections and repel Invasions." The Insurrection Act is Congress's effort to provide for a military response to suppress insurrections or rebellions.

The "Insurrection Act" is actually an amalgamation of acts and amendments throughout the US history that touch on the ability to use the military in domestic law enforcement operations. Most use the term to refer to the Insurrection Act of 1807 and subsequent amendments, though its roots can be traced to the earlier Militia Act of 1792 (also known as the Calling Forth Act). In fact, the first two presidents each invoked the Militia Act to use militias to suppress domestic insurrection. President George Washington used it to suppress the Whiskey Rebellion, and President John Adams used it to put down Fries's Rebellion. When the third President, Thomas Jefferson, asked Congress to also authorize the use of federal military forces, not just militias, to repress insurrections, the "Insurrection Act of 1807" was enacted. Jefferson initially wanted the authority to use federal troops to address Aaron Burr's Conspiracy, and Jefferson eventually used the Insurrection Act to have the federal military stop violations of the Embargo Act of 1807 in Vermont.

Because the Insurrection Act does not define what constitutes an "insurrection," the meaning of the term has been the subject of long-standing debate and controversy. Throughout early US history, the term was often used to refer to fears of slave uprisings, but it encompasses much more than that. Broadly defined, an insurrection is a violent uprising against government authority, but the permanence of the outcome sought or the extent to which government authority is undermined is not precise. For example, the perpetrators of the Wilmington Insurrection of 1898 sought not to abolish Wilmington's government altogether, but rather to replace democratically elected officials with preferred individuals. Moreover, though some level of violence is generally required for an attempt to usurp government authority to be considered an insurrection, the extent of such violence is not clear. For instance, some debate whether the Capitol Insurrection on January 6, 2021, involved sufficient violence to be a true insurrection.

By not defining the term, the Insurrection Act seems to leave to the president the choice of deciding whether an act constitutes an insurrection. The United States Supreme Court upheld this view in its 1827 decision in *Martin v. Mott*, in which the Court unanimously held "that the authority to decide whether the exigency [sufficient to call out the militia] has arisen belongs exclusively to the President, and … his decision is conclusive upon all other persons …. He is necessarily constituted the judge of the existence of the exigency, in the first instance, and is bound to act according to his belief of the facts."

Presidents have invoked the Insurrection Act at least thirty times, most often related to post-Civil War violent uprisings and labor disputes. Many invocations of the Insurrection Act have involved situations with a racial or racist component. President Abraham Lincoln's invocation of the Act was in response to secession by southern states. President Ulysses Grant's several uses of authority under the Act involved suppression of white supremacist groups, including the Ku Klux Klan (KKK), in the aftermath of the Colfax Massacre, the Vicksburg Massacre, and the Battle of Liberty Place. President Grover Cleveland twice used the Act to quell racially motivated riots in the Seattle area. President Franklin Roosevelt invoked the Act to address rioting over racial tensions during the Second World War in Detroit. And several presidents would invoke the Act during the Civil Rights era.

President Dwight Eisenhower used federal troops to enforce the Supreme Court's 1954 *Brown v. Board of Education* school desegregation decision in Arkansas, and President John F. Kennedy used the federal military for similar purposes. President Lyndon Johnson used the Insurrection Act to protect civil rights marchers in Selma, Alabama, to put down violent racially motivated rioting in Detroit, and to quell unrest across the nation after the assassination of Dr. Martin Luther King, Jr. Most recently, the Insurrection Act was employed by President George H. W. Bush to address civil unrest in Los Angeles after four white police officers were acquitted for beating Black motorist Rodney King. In 2020, Donald Trump publicly considered invoking the Insurrection Act to suppress protests in the wake of a white police officer killing a Black man, George Floyd, in Minneapolis, but ultimately elected not to. In the waning days of the Trump administration, some Trump advisors purportedly encouraged him to consider invoking the Insurrection Act to delay the certification of Joseph Biden as the next president of the United States.

President Trump's contemplated invocation of the Insurrection Act is important due to another option that apparently was also under consideration by his administration, an option that is often confused with invoking the Insurrection Act: martial law. Martial law has never been conclusively defined, but generally it refers to use of the military to carry out some or all the functions of civil government by displacing, replacing, or subordinating civil government, its laws, and its functions, rather than merely assisting civil government. Thus, martial law involves acting *outside* the legal framework to use the military. Because the Insurrection Act and equivalent state laws authorize commanders-in-chief to employ the military to quell insurrections and other violent disorders within legal boundaries, such actions are not "martial law."

The Insurrection Act has been modified and amended a number of times. Three key modifications are discussed here: the Enforcement Act of 1871, the Posse Comitatus Act of 1878, and the 2006 and 2008 Amendments.

Targeting the violence perpetuated by the KKK and similar white supremacist groups during Reconstruction, the Enforcement Act of 1871 allowed the president to use the military when domestic violence or an insurrection resulted in the denial of citizenship rights or equal protection conferred on citizens by the new Fourteenth Amendment. Critics argued this modification extended presidential power too far, allowing the president to impose the military not just to respond to insurrection, but also for less severe civil unrest.

The Posse Comitatus Act of 1878 was intended to serve as a check on using military forces for law enforcement purposes. Introduced by southern members of Congress seeking to limit federal military power during Reconstruction, the Posse Comitatus Act stated, "it shall not be lawful to employ any part of the Army of the United States as a posse comitatus, or otherwise, for the purpose of executing the laws, except in such cases and under such circumstances as such employment of said force may be expressly authorized by the Constitution or by act of Congress." The Posse Comitatus Act thus attempted to cabin the president's authority that had been arguably expanded with the Enforcement Act, and the Act limits one way in which the government might otherwise seek to prevent or respond to crimes against the state.

In 2005, President George W. Bush considered using federal military forces to intervene in Louisiana after the federal and state governments' disastrous response to Hurricane Katrina and the widespread lawlessness that ensued. In 2006, an unidentified Congressperson added to the National Defense Authorization Act a provision that amended the Insurrection Act to allow military intervention in state affairs without state request or consent when "as a result of a natural disaster, epidemic, or other serious public health emergency, terrorist attack or incident, or other condition in any State or possession of the United States, the President determines that: 1) domestic violence has occurred to such an extent that the constituted authorities of the State or possession are incapable of maintaining public order; and 2) such violence results in a condition that so hinders the execution of the laws of a State or possession … that any part or class of its people is deprived of a right, privilege, immunity or protection named in the Constitution and secured by law." Thus, the federal military was authorized to enforce *state* law. After fifty state governors unanimously issued a statement condemning the 2006 Amendment, the changes were repealed in 2008.

Today, the Insurrection Act has three key components. Section 251 allows the president to deploy troops if a state's legislature or governor requests federal aid to suppress an insurrection in that state. Sections 252 and 253, which derive in part from the Enforcement Act of 1871, allow the president to deploy troops without a request from the affected state and even over the state's desire. Section 252, permits federal military deployment in order to "enforce the laws" *of the United States* (as opposed to state laws) or to "suppress rebellion" whenever "unlawful obstructions, combinations, or assemblages, or rebellion" make it "impracticable" to enforce federal law in that state by the "ordinary course of judicial proceedings." Section 253 allows the president to use the military in a state to suppress "any insurrection, domestic violence, unlawful combination, or conspiracy" that "so hinders the execution of the laws" that inhabitants are deprived of a constitutional right or in a state that "opposes or obstructs the execution of the laws of the United States or impedes the course of justice under those laws."

Critics of the current form of the Insurrection Act observe that the law is so broad and vague that the president has nearly limitless discretion to use federal military forces in nearly any case of civil unrest, regardless of whether that unrest rises to the level of a true "insurrection." Calls for a more precise definition of insurrection or other triggering events continue. As it stands, the Insurrection Act is a powerful tool given to the president to respond to the potential crimes against the state.

See Also: American Civil War and Treason; Assassination; Battle of Liberty Place (1874); Burr, Aaron; *Burr, United States v.* (1807); Capitol Insurrection on January 6, 2021; Colfax Massacre (1873); Enforcement Acts (1870–71); Fries's Rebellion (1799); Insurrection; Jefferson, Thomas; Martial Law; Rebellion; Whiskey Rebellion; Wilmington Insurrection of 1898

Resources

10 U.S.C. §§ 251–55.

Allan, Hawa. 2022. *Insurrection: Rebellion, Civil Rights, and the Paradoxical State of Black Citizenship.* New York: W.W. Norton.

Hauser, Christine. 2020. "What Is the Insurrection Act of 1807, the Law Behind Trump's Threat to States?" *The New York Times*, June 2, 2020.

Merriam, Eric. 2023. "Necessary Necessity: Courts' Historical Assessment of the Condition Precedent for Martial Law." *Oklahoma Law Review* 75: 191.

Merriam, Eric, and Douglas B. McKechnie. 2021. *National Security Law.* St. Paul, MN: West Academic, Chapter 19.

Nunn, Joseph. 2022. "The Insurrection Act Explained." *Brennan Center for Justice*, April 21, 2022. Accessed June 14, 2023. https://www.brennancenter.org/our-work/research-reports/insurrection-act-explained.

Intelligence Identities Protection Act (1982)

The Intelligence Identities Protection Act (IIPA) was enacted in 1982 as an amendment to the National Security Act of 1947. Proponents in Congress were concerned about a perceived "systematic effort" by some Americans to disclose the names of covert intelligence agents during the Cold War. These Americans included former Central Intelligence Agency (CIA) officers who became disillusioned with the agency and endeavored to take it down. Among them, in the late 1970s, Philip Agee and Lewis Wolf produced books and other publications in which the names of thousands of CIA officers were disclosed. The bill's primary sponsor was Senator (later President) George H. W. Bush, who had previously served as the Director of Central Intelligence.

The IIPA criminalizes the intentional, unauthorized disclosure of information identifying a covert agent, when the discloser knows the information identifies a covert agent as such and knows the United States is concealing the covert agent's foreign intelligence relationship to the United States. Covert agents include officers and employees of any US intelligence agency, including military officers assigned to an intelligence agency, whose identities are classified and who are serving or have served within the last five years outside the United States, as well as those who act as an informant, agent, or source to any intelligence agency, and whose relationship with the US government is classified. The IIPA prescribes increasingly severe punishments according to the level of access to classified information the offender exploited. Offenders who lack access to classified information can also be subject to criminal liability, but only if they participated in a "pattern of activities intended to identify and expose covert agents" and with "reason to believe that such activities would impair or impede the foreign intelligence activities of the United States."

While under consideration, some members of Congress raised concerns that the IIPA might violate the First Amendment and create another form of speech as crime against the state. For instance, Senator (later President) Joseph Biden published an article in which he asserted "The language [of the IIPA] is so broadly drawn that it would subject to prosecution not only the malicious publicizing of agents' names but also the efforts of legitimate journalists to expose any corruption, malfeasance, or ineptitude occurring in American intelligence agencies" (Biden 1982, 26). Nevertheless, the Congressional Conference Committee countered that the "gratuitous listing of agents' names in certain publications goes far beyond information that might contribute to informed public debate on foreign policy or foreign intelligence activities." The Committee concluded that the IIPA would impose

> criminal penalties only in very limited circumstances to deter those who make it their business to ferret out and publish the identities of agents. At the same time, it does not affect the First Amendment rights of those who disclose the identities of agents as an integral part of another enterprise such as news media reporting of intelligence failures or abuses, academic studies of U.S. government policies and programs, or a private organization's enforcement of its internal rules.

To date, the United States Supreme Court has not opined on the IIPA's constitutionality, perhaps because so few prosecutions have relied on it. Though a number of persons have been convicted of crimes involving identifying covert agents, few have been convicted under the IIPA. Most such cases, including those involving Aldrich Ames and Robert Hanssen, have instead resulted in convictions under the Espionage Act of 1917. However, at least two persons have been convicted of violating the IIPA. During the Year of the Spy (1985), Sharon Scranage, a former CIA clerk, pleaded guilty to disclosing the identities of covert agents to a Ghanaian intelligence operative with whom she had become romantically involved. Scranage first came under suspicion after failing a routine polygraph examination administered to those with access to classified information. She then agreed to help the Federal Bureau of Investigation (FBI) lure the Ghanaian operative to the United States. He was successfully apprehended and ultimately traded to Ghana for some of the spies Scranage's disclosure had outed. Scranage was ultimately sentenced to two years in prison. In 2012, former CIA officer John Kiriakou pleaded guilty for violating the IIPA. In 2007, Kiriakou, who had led the team that captured high-level Al-Qaeda operative Abu Zubaydah, gave an interview to ABC News in which he described an interrogation technique known as "waterboarding" as necessary torture. When reporters investigating the CIA's interrogation program subsequently reached out to Kiriakou for more information, he disclosed to two journalists the names of two other covert agents employing "enhanced interrogation techniques" of terrorist suspects. He was sentenced to thirty months incarceration.

The IIPA took prominence in the political scandal during the George W. Bush administration known as the "Plame Affair." During the lead-up to the Iraq War in 2003, as justification for the coming invasion, President Bush asserted in a speech to Congress that Iraq had attempted to purchase a large quantity of uranium from Africa. After the invasion, former diplomate Joseph Wilson, who prior to President Bush's speech had been asked by the CIA to go to Africa to investigate whether Iraq had in fact attempted to purchase uranium, participated in a series of op-eds in which he challenged the bases for the invasion. In one such piece in the *New York Times* titled "What I Didn't Find in Africa" (July 6, 2003), Wilson asserted that he had discovered no evidence Iraq had attempted to purchase uranium and that President Bush's claim to the contrary was therefore a misrepresentation. Eight days later, journalist Robert Novak wrote about Wilson's trip to Africa and asserted "Wilson never worked for the CIA, but his wife, Valerie Plame, is an agency operative on weapons of mass destruction" (Novak 2003). Some asserted that the leak of Plame's identity was part of a White House effort to smear Wilson for criticizing the war. Without acknowledging whether Plame was in fact a covert agent, Wilson himself later argued "Naming her this way would have compromised every operation, every relationship, every network with which she had been associated in her entire career. This is the stuff of Kim Philby and Aldrich Ames" (Corn 2003). Novak admitted the CIA had asked him not to publish Plame's identity, but denied knowing that Plame was a *covert* agent, asserting he never would have named her had he known. Novak further denied that anyone in the Bush administration had asked him to leak her identity.

At the CIA's request, the Department of Justice (DOJ) initiated an investigation into how Plame's identity was leaked and ultimately appointed a special counsel. The subsequent grand jury investigation led to no indictments for the leak itself (i.e., for the act that might have violated the IIPA). As part of the investigation, Vice President Dick Cheney's Chief of Staff, Lewis "Scooter" Libby, was indicted for perjury, false statements, and obstruction of justice for testimony he provided to the grand jury and FBI investigators. Libby's sentence was commuted by President Bush, and Libby was later pardoned altogether by President Donald Trump. Richard Armitage, a member of the Bush administration, later acknowledged he released Plame's identity to Novak, but also insisted he did not know she was a covert agent.

Involving several presidents, the history of the IIPA is one of political intrigue but uncertain consequences. In insulating itself against disclosure of identities of some government employees, the government has attempted to protect itself from the potentially disastrous consequences of such disclosures. But the law itself, and thus the crime against the state it creates, has led to few actual prosecutions, and the consequences of the disclosures in those specific cases were less than disastrous.

See Also: Ames, Aldrich Hazen "Rich"; Espionage Act of 1917 and Sedition Act of 1918; Hanssen, Robert Philip; Perjury, False Statements, and Obstruction of Justice; Speech as Crime against the State; Year of the Spy (1985)

Resources

Biden, Joseph R. 1982. "A Spy Law That Harms National Security." *Christian Science Monitor* 74, no. 91: 26.

Corn, David. 2003. "A White House Smear." *The Nation*, July 16, 2003. Accessed November 1, 2023. https://www.thenation.com/article/archive/white-house-smear/.

Elsea, Jennifer K. 2013. "Intelligence Identities Protection Act." *Congressional Research Service* 21636, April 10, 2013.

Isikoff, Michael, and David Corn. 2006. *Hubris: The Inside Story of Spin, Scandal, and the Selling of the Iraq War*. New York: Crown Publishers.

Novak, Robert D. 2003. "Mission to Niger." *The Washington Post*, July 14, 2003, A21.

Internal Security Act of 1950

The Internal Security Act of 1950 (ISA), also known as the McCarran Act (after Senator Pat McCarran, who introduced the bill) and the Subversive Activities Control Act, was designed to control "subversive activities" and empower the president to prevent espionage or sabotage through broad detention powers. The sweeping bill was introduced by Senator McCarran, a supporter of McCarthyism in the late 1940s and 1950s.

The ISA had six main components. First, it created the Subversive Activities Control Board, which could order organizations determined to be communist to register with the Department of Justice. Individual members of such organizations were also required to register their affiliations with such organizations. The ISA thus made it a crime against the state to fail to report one's political affiliation, but only if that affiliation was with a communist organization. Second, the ISA criminalized a variety of actions, including any act that would "substantially contribute to the establishment within the United States of a totalitarian dictatorship," conveying classified information to any member of any communist organization, and seeking employment by the United States or at a US defense facility without disclosing membership in a communist organization. Third, the ISA prohibited members of communist organizations from obtaining US passports, effectively barring their travel abroad. Fourth, the ISA criminalized violations of orders or regulations issued by military officials for the protection of military assets and installations. Fifth, the ISA reiterated that certain groups of aliens, including anarchists and members of communist organizations, were prohibited from entering the United States or remaining in the United States. Sixth, the ISA authorized the president to detain any person who "probably will conspire with others to engage in, acts of espionage or of sabotage" in the event of invasion, declaration of war, insurrection, or a "state of internal security emergency" declared by the president. Though the justifications for this final provision mentioned communism and totalitarian dictatorship, the authorized detentions were not limited to persons advancing only those causes. This provision enabled the Executive Branch to detain indefinitely any "subversives" without any of the constitutional requirements and protections for detention.

The preventive detention portion of the ISA was not originally offered by Senator McCarran but was included as an amendment by opponents of the ISA, who hoped the draconian provision would make the bill impossible to pass. This turned out to be a miscalculation, and the bill was passed with the detention provision intact. President Harry S. Truman vetoed the ISA, arguing it was "the greatest danger to freedom of speech, press, and assembly since the Alien and Sedition [Acts] of 1798," and a "mockery of the Bill of Rights" (Truman 1950). The House and Senate promptly overrode President Truman's veto.

The Supreme Court initially supported the ISA. In 1954, in *Galvan v. Press*, the Court upheld the deportation of a Mexican alien on the grounds that he briefly had been a member of the Communist Party. And in 1961, in *Communist Party of the United States v. Subversive Activities Control Board*, the Court upheld the legality of requiring the Communist Party to register with the Subversive Activities Control Board. Justice Felix Frankfurter, writing for the five to four majority, opined that the right to free association under the First Amendment can be trumped when the right conflicts with national security. Interestingly, only one of the four dissenters, Justice Hugo Black, relied on the First Amendment right to find the ISA unconstitutional. The other three dissenters concluded that the ISA's registration requirement violated the Fifth Amendment right against self-incrimination.

Eventually, the Court began chipping away at the ISA. In 1964 in *Aptheker v. Secretary of State*, the Court declared unconstitutional the provision barring members of a communist organization from obtaining passports. In 1965, the court invalidated the ISA's requirement that members of communist organizations register with the Department of Justice on the grounds that, because being a member of the Communist Party of the United States was a crime under the Smith Act, the ISA violated members' Fifth Amendment right against self-incrimination. And in 1967, in *United States v. Robel*, the court invalidated the provision banning members of communist organizations from working for the federal government as a violation of their First Amendment right to free association.

Congress itself also chipped away at the ISA's provisions. In 1971 Congress passed the Non-Detention Act (NDA) to repeal the Executive Branch's authority under the ISA to detain United States citizens. The NDA was supported in large part by those citing the noxious Internment of Japanese Americans (Second World War). In fact, President Richard Nixon noted that historical context when signing the NDA into law. In 1972, Congress cut the Subversive Activities Control Board's budget and no funds were allocated for it in President Nixon's 1973 budget. The Board ceased operating that year. The provision criminalizing violations of military orders and regulations for the protection of military assets and infrastructure remains in effect and is still relied upon by the military today.

See Also: Alien and Sedition Acts (1798); Communist Control Act (1954); Espionage; Insurrection; Rebellion; Sabotage; Second Red Scare (McCarthyism); Smith Act

Resources

Bickel, Alexander M. 1968. "Supreme Court: Internal Security Cases." *New Republic*, January 6, 1968, 21–2.
Izumi, Masumi. 2005. "Prohibiting 'American Concentration Camps.'" *Pacific Historical Review* 74: 165–94.
Truman, Harry. 1950. "Veto of the Internal Security Bill." *The American Presidency Project*. Accessed November 1, 2023. https://www.presidency.ucsb.edu/documents/veto-the-internal-security-bill.
Trussell, C. P. 1950. "Red Bill Veto Beaten, 57–10, By Senators." *New York Times*, September 24, 1950.
Ybarra, Michael J. 2004. *Washington Gone Crazy: Senator Pat McCarran and the Great American Communist Hunt*. Hanover, NH: Steerforth Press.

J

Jefferson, Thomas (1743–1826)

Though all US presidents have had to concern themselves with crimes against the state, perhaps no president took a more visible role in both committing and rejecting crimes against the state than the nation's third president, Thomas Jefferson.

Jefferson believed in a right of revolution, famously asserting that the oppressed could "endeavor to secure relief by refreshing the tree of liberty occasionally with the blood of their oppressors." Accordingly, Jefferson likely did not view his actions in penning the Declaration of Independence or the colonial rebellion as treason. Nevertheless, he took on an outsized role in the first significant act of collective treason against Great Britain when he served as the primary author of the Declaration of Independence. Jefferson, who praised earlier attempts to reject British tyranny such as Bacon's Rebellion, penned words not only declaring independence from the mother country, but also articulating a list of grievances and explaining precisely why Americans would engage in treason to establish their independence. In the Declaration of Independence, Jefferson argued it was not only right, but a duty, to break free from an unjust ruler, writing "[b]ut when a long train of abuses and usurpations, pursuing invariably the same Object evinces a design to reduce them under absolute Despotism, it is their right, it is their duty, to throw off such Government, and to provide new Guards for their future security." Furthermore, "[t]hat whenever any Form of Government becomes destructive of these ends, it is the Right of the People to alter or to abolish it, and to institute new Government, laying its foundation on such principles and organizing its powers in such form, as to them shall seem most likely to effect their Safety and Happiness."

Later, at the onset of the American Revolutionary War, Jefferson served on the Continental Congress's "Committee on Spies," which passed a resolution declaring it to be treason to levy war against any of the colonies or give aid or comfort to Great Britain and its war effort. This despite the fact that all members of the committee were, at the time, lawfully subjects of Great Britain.

Other than the Declaration of Independence, Jefferson's most prominent contribution to our understanding of crimes against the state occurred in his response to the Alien and Sedition Acts of 1798, enacted by Congress with staunch support of the John Adams administration. The Alien Act granted the president unilateral authority to deport non citizens who were subjects of foreign enemies, and the Sedition Act undercut what is understood today to be a core element of free speech and a free press—the right to criticize the government. The Sedition Act criminalized criticism of the resident (at the time, Federalist John Adams) but not criticism of the vice president (at the time, political archrival, Democratic Republican Jefferson). Advanced by the Federalists as necessary to keep public order and ensure domestic homeland security in light of a potential war with France, Jefferson and his fellow Democratic Republicans viewed the Alien and Sedition Acts as primarily an attempt by the Federalists to limit support for Democratic Republicans and quell dissent and eliminate any subversive activities antithetic to the Federalist agenda.

Specifically, Jefferson claimed the Alien Act and associated Naturalization Act intentionally targeted immigrants, a majority of whom associated politically with Jefferson's political party; significantly lengthened the time required for immigrants to become citizens (from five to fourteen years), which was advantageous to the Federalist Party as most immigrants tended to support and vote for Democratic Republican candidates; and were enforced and implemented in an unequal and partisan fashion, with immigrants from France and Ireland disproportionally targeted under the laws, while immigrants from Great Britain, who largely supported Federalist Party politics, were largely overlooked.

The partisan nature of the Sedition Act was readily apparent from its explicit "sunset provision," which specified that the "Act shall continue and be in force until the third day of March 1801, and no longer." The expiration of the Act thus conveniently arrived immediately upon the inauguration of the next president, Thomas Jefferson. Jefferson's substantive argument against the Sedition Act of 1798 included articulation of a more libertarian view of individual speech rights that generally opposed speech as crime against the state. More than twenty-five prominent newspaper editors and some prominent politicians were immediately indicted and prosecuted under the Sedition Act, most of which were put on trial during the Adams-Jefferson campaign election season. Several prominent Jefferson-aligned politicians were prosecuted, and at least four Democratic-Republican newspapers closed. In response, Democratic Republicans urged state governments to condemn the Alien and Sedition Acts or assert that they would not follow the law. Jefferson personally authored one such law, the Kentucky Resolution of 1798, which declared that the Alien and Sedition Acts are "not laws," are "altogether void," "utterly void," and "of no force."

Though he was a vehement opponent of the Alien and Sedition Acts, Jefferson likely benefitted from them politically. Backlash and public disfavor for the laws was a significant factor in Jefferson's electoral defeat of Adams for President. When Jefferson took office, he allowed the Sedition Act to lapse rather than attempt to extend it and use it to prosecute and persecute his political opponents as Adams had done. Jefferson pardoned all those convicted under the Sedition Act, later explaining to John Adams's wife Abigail:

> I discharged every person under punishment or prosecution under the Sedition Law, because I considered, and now consider, that law to be a nullity, as absolute and palpable as if Congress had ordered us to fall down and worship a golden image; and that is was as much my duty to arrest its execution in every stage, as it would have been to have rescued from the fiery furnace those who should have been cast into it for refusing to worship the image. (Lewis 2007, 20)

Jefferson's argument against the Sedition Act planted a seed that would eventually bloom into the Supreme Court's modern free speech jurisprudence and our modern understanding of the right to criticize government, but not before a century and a half of the Court generally allowing government to criminalize speech. Because Jefferson allowed the Sedition Act to lapse, its constitutionality was never assessed by the Supreme Court, though in dicta (in comments without legal bearing) in *New York Times v. Sullivan* (1964), the Court finally suggested the Sedition Act unconstitutionally infringed on rights protected by the First Amendment.

Later in his administration, Jefferson took a more favorable view of asserting government power to repress dissension. When he asked Congress to authorize use of federal military forces, not just militias, to repress insurrections occurring in the nation, Congress enacted the Insurrection Act of 1807, a law still in effect today. Jefferson initially sought the authority to use federal troops to address

Aaron Burr's Treasonous Conspiracy, and Jefferson eventually relied on the Insurrection Act to use the federal military to curb violations of the Embargo Act of 1807 in Vermont. In a related case, the Jefferson administration argued that those in Vermont engaged in armed non-adherence to federal law were engaged in "constructive treason," a view firmly rejected by the court in *United States v. Hoxie* (1808).

See Also: Alien Act (1798); Alien and Sedition Acts (1798); American Revolution and Treason; Bacon's Rebellion (1676–7); Burr, Aaron; *Burr, United States v.* (1807); *Hoxie, United States v.* (1808); Insurrection Act; Rebellion; Sedition Act of 1798; Speech as Crime against the State; Treason

Resources

Levy, Leonard. 1960. *Legacy of Suppression: Freedom of Speech and Press in Early American History.* Cambridge, MA: Harvard University Press.

Levy, Leonard. 1963. *Jefferson and Civil Liberties: The Darker Side.* Cambridge, MA: Belknap Press (of Harvard University).

Levy, Leonard. 1985. *Emergence of a Free Press.* Oxford: Oxford University Press.

Lewis, Anthony. 2007. *Freedom for the Thought That We Hate: A Biography of the First Amendment.* New York: Basic Books.

John Brown's Raid (1859)

In October 1859, John Brown and a band of twenty-one men entered Virginia with the goal of attacking the United States Arsenal and Armory at Harpers Ferry, Virginia (now West Virginia), to seize weapons and cause a widespread slave rebellion. Brown's plan was to seize the weapons from the United States Arsenal and Armory where tens of thousands of muskets and rifles were stored, free enslaved individuals from local plantations willing to join his "army," and flee to the adjacent Blue Ridge Mountains with his new recruits and weapons to wage war on the institution of slavery. Brown's plan hinged on arming the enslaved individuals he was convinced would rally to him in Harpers Ferry, telling Frederick Douglass that he needed Douglass to "hive the bees" when "they came swarming." Then, with arms and men, Brown's plan was to use the mountains as his base of operations to engage in guerilla warfare throughout Virginia and the South, swooping down out of the mountains to raid and attack plantations and liberate the enslaved. Brown drafted a new provisional constitution for the United States meant to govern his new state, a constitution devoid of slavery. Brown's men came from all walks of life, including freed slaves, a schoolteacher, a lawyer, two Quaker brothers, a couple of college students from Oberlin College, and a former United States Army Dragoon.

Calling the event "John Brown's Raid" is a bit of a misnomer. The term "raid" is a curious term to describe the violent attack resulting in the deaths of at least fourteen people (and six more in subsequent executions by Virginia). People began using the term raid in the twentieth century to describe the incident, perhaps to downgrade the significance of the event. At the time, however, the event was not commonly called a raid, a term which connotes a minor incursion. Within a month following the attack, a Baltimore newspaper had a bevy of articles about the Virginia violence at Harpers Ferry. "The most common words were 'insurrection,' 'rebellion,' 'uprising,' and 'invasion.' Further down the list appeared 'war,' 'treason,' and 'crusade.' There were twenty-six terms [utilized] in all. 'Raid' was not among them" (Horowitz 2011, 4). Southerners viewed Brown's attack as nothing short of war or rebellion. Generations of Southern whites had lived in fear of another slave rebellion like those that occurred in Virginia in Gabriel's Rebellion (1800) and Nat Turner's Rebellion (1831), and Vesey's Rebellion (1822) in South Carolina. Many in Harpers Ferry recalled the bloodletting that took place in Nat Turner's Rebellion, which occurred just twenty-eight years before Brown's attack.

Brown had funding to take "his war to Africa" (as he called the Harpers Ferry attack) from some of the most well-known Americans of the nineteenth century. Called the Secret Six, his supporters included Gerrit Smith (largest landowner in America), educator Samuel Gridley Howe (husband of Julia Ward Howe—noted abolitionist in her own right and author of the *Battle Hymn of the Republic*), well-known abolitionist and minister Theodore Wentworth Higginson, clergy member Theodore Parker, reporter and author Frank Sanborne, and industrialist George Sterns. Brown also met and spoke somewhat frequently with civil rights leaders like Frederick Douglass (and even stayed in Douglass's house while Brown drafted his "Provisional Constitution for the United States"), Harriett Tubman, and Martin Delaney (medical doctor and first Black officer in Army during the Civil War) and tried unsuccessfully to convince them to join in his attack. Of all the leaders of the antebellum slave rebellions, John Brown was best funded and best known across the country. Many abolitionists in the North deferentially referred to Captain John Brown (although he never held that military rank or served in the military) or Osawatomie Brown, in reference to his defense of abolitionists in "Bleeding Kansas" (a period of violence in the fight to determine whether Kansas would be a free or slave state), including his role in the Pottawatomie Massacre. Of Brown's army of twenty-one at Harpers Ferry, sixteen were white and five were Black.

After secretly encamping at the Kennedy Farmhouse about five miles outside of Harpers Ferry from July 1 to October 16, 1859, waiting for reinforcements, equipment, and money to arrive from the "Secret Six," Brown determined it was finally time to act. Late in the evening of October 16, Brown and his men proceeded to Harpers Ferry, leaving several behind to guard supplies. The attack initially went well. Brown's men seized the bridges spanning the Shenandoah and Potomac Rivers that surround the town on two of the three sides, rounded up hostages (including a relative of George Washington), temporarily "freed" several of the hostages' slaves, and successfully seized all the major government works, including the Arsenal, the Rifle Factory, and the Armory. One of Brown's men even began carting weapons away from the Armory to a storage area a few miles away.

Then things started to go awry. The first person Brown and his men killed on their war to liberate the country of slavery was Hayward Shepherd, a free Black man living in town. Only a handful of slaves joined John Brown, and Brown was convinced they just needed more time. The lack of participation by the local Black population was likely because the date of the attack was kept secret. Brown had also changed the date of the attack on at least two occasions, leaving the local population confused as to when the rebellion was to take place.

By far, Brown's biggest mistake was that he lingered in town too long. Brown could have left and declared victory with the few individuals who had joined him and a cache of additional weapons. (Brown was already well-stocked with Sharpe Rifles and 1,000 pikes to arm the newly freed individuals.) Brown's delay left time for militias to arrive from neighboring towns, retake the bridges, and cut off Brown's modes of escape from the town. More catastrophically for Brown, he left time for a contingent of Marines (sent by President James Buchanan) to travel from the Washington, DC, Naval Yard and arrive at Harpers Ferry by the evening of October 17, 1859. Thus, when Brown and his surviving men looked out over the armory grounds through the haze of the morning mist in the early morning hours on October 18, they saw the glistening bayonets and blue uniforms of ninety United States Marines, commanded by Lieutenant Colonel Robert E. Lee. At that point, Brown was trapped, and Harpers Ferry turned into a "perfect steel trap … that once in he would never get out alive" that Frederick Douglass had warned Brown about just two months prior, in August 1859 (Villard 1910, 413).

Throughout the day on October 17, local militias took pot-shots at Brown's men, killing several, and Brown's men killed several townspeople, including the mayor. Then on the morning of October 18, Lee ordered Lieutenant J.E.B. Stuart to demand Brown's unconditional surrender. When Brown refused, Stuart gave a pre-arranged signal, and a detachment of Marines stormed the Armory Fire Engine house (today called "John Brown's Fort") where Brown and his men were making their last stand. The first Marine into the Engine house, Private Luke Quinn, was killed and is buried in Harpers Ferry. Another Marine was seriously injured. But the Marines were able to make quick business in the capture of Brown and his few remaining men. The Marine Lieutenant in charge of the storming party, Israel Green, attempted to run his sword through Brown's chest. But in an ironic twist, Green forgot to exchange his parade sword for his combat sword before leaving for Harpers Ferry. When the flimsy dress sword struck something in Brown's breast pocket, the sword doubled in half. So Brown survived, and Green had to subdue Brown by beating him over the head with his bent and damaged sword. Had Brown died on the Engine House floor, he might not have become the martyr to the North (and the world) that he became as a result of his profuse letter writing from jail and his public statements made during his trial (see *Virginia v. Brown*), both reported in papers around the globe.

Between his capture on October 18, and his execution on December 2, even international figures like French writer Victor Hugo wrote letters pleading for John Brown's pardon and/or release from jail.

The Marines' attack on the Engine House and their defeat of Brown's forces took less than three minutes. Brown's war to free the slaves lasted thirty-six hours. No hostages were injured, and no slaves were liberated. Ten of Brown's twenty-one men (including two of Brown's sons) lay dead in the streets and alleys. One of Brown's men was executed by a mob of townspeople on a bridge, with his body thrown off the bridge and into the river, where townspeople used his corpse for target practice for several days. One of the first of Brown's men to die was Dangerfield Newby, a man who joined Brown because he was trying to free his wife and children from bondage. In his breast pocket was found a note from his wife, dated August 1859, where she pleaded with her husband to come get her and their children because she feared they were going to be sold to a plantation owner in the deep South. After Newby was killed, enraged townspeople mutilated his body, and cut off body parts for souvenirs. Several townspeople were killed as well, along with a Marine and the town's mayor. Brown and five of his men (Shields Green, John Copeland, Aaron Stevens, Edwin Coppoc, and Albert Hazlett) were captured alive and sent to a neighboring town eight miles away (Charles Town), the seat of County government, to stand trial. No major slavery uprising occurred, and it looked like Brown had failed. Or had he?

Through a mistake by Lieutenant Green, Brown survived—allowing him to turn this tactical defeat into a major strategic victory. Brown sat in jail awaiting his execution scheduled for December 2, 1859, and wrote hundreds of letters that galvanized the North. Prominent American thinkers like Ralph Waldo Emerson and Nathaniel Hawthorne liken John Brown to Jesus Christ in public addresses. Henry David Thoreau gave an impassioned speech for Brown entitled "A Plea for Captain John Brown," a speech so popular it was printed and distributed throughout the North. Even Victor Hugo, one of Europe's most celebrated writers of the age, pleaded with American authorities in a letter to spare Brown's life and prophetically stated: "In killing Brown, the Southern States have committed a crime which will take its place among the calamities of history. The rupture of the Union will fatally follow the assassination of Brown" (Villard 1910, 569). On November 1, 1859, while Brown sat in jail, Wendell Phillips, the grand abolitionist (called the "Golden Trumpet") and noted pacifist, wrote: "The lesson of the hour is insurrection … We seem to be entering on a new phase … Virginia is a pirate ship and John Brown sails the seas as a Lord Admiral of the Almighty, with his commission to sink every pirate he sees … Harpers Ferry is the Lexington of today" (Oates 1984, 318). Did John Brown fail? Consider that the American Civil War started a mere eighteen months after Brown's attack. Within two years of Brown's raid, Harpers Ferry and Virginia were occupied by tens of thousands of Union soldiers, thousands singing "John Brown's Body"—the chorus of the song which says, "John Brown's Body lies a moldering in the grave, but his soul goes marching on." And in time, "John Brown's Body" would be transformed into one of America's most patriotic songs, the *Battle Hymn of the Republic*. On the way to the gallows, Brown handed his jailer a note, which said "I, John Brown, am now quite certain, that the crimes of this guilty land will never be purged away but with blood; I had, as I now think vainly, flattered myself, that without very much bloodshed, it might be done" (McGinty 2009, 271). By the end of the American Civil War, a little more than six years later, the institution of slavery had been destroyed, as Brown had predicted, purged away with copious amounts of blood spilt on the sacred fields of Antietam, Gettysburg, Fredericksburg, and hundreds of other locations.

See Also: American Civil War and Treason; Brown, John; Cook, John E.; Copeland, John Anthony, Jr.; Coppoc, Edwin; Gabriel's Rebellion (1800); Green, Shields; Hazlett, Albert; Insurrection; Oklahoma

City Bombing; Pottawatomie Massacre (1856); Rebellion; Stevens, Aaron; Treason; Turner, Nat; Vesey's Rebellion (1822); *Virginia v. Brown* (1859)

Resources

Documents Relative to the Harpers Ferry Invasion. 1859. *His Soul Goes Marching On: The Life and Legacy of John Brown.* West Virginia Archives and History. Accessed November 1, 2023. http://129.71.204.160/history/jbexhibit/virginiadocuments.html.

Douglass, Frederick. 1881. *John Brown: An Address by Frederick Douglass at the Fourteenth Anniversary of Storer College, Harper's Ferry, West Virginia, May 30, 1881.* Dover, NH: Morningstar.

Horwitz, Tony. 2011. *Midnight Rising: John Brown and the Raid that Sparked the Civil War*. New York: Henry Holt & Company.

McGinty, Brian. 2009. *John Brown's Trial.* Cambridge, MA: Harvard University Press.

Oates, Stephen B. 1984, *To Purge This Land with Blood: A Biography of John Brown.* Second edition. Amherst: The University of Massachusetts Press.

Villard, Oward Garrison. 1910. *John Brown: 1800–1859: A Biography Fifty Years After*. New York: Houghton Mifflin.

K

Kaczynski, Theodore ("Unabomber") (1942–2023)

When Theodore "Ted" Kaczynski's acts of violence and terrorism first came to the attention of the Federal Bureau of Investigation (FBI), he was given the code name "Unabomber" because of Kaczynski's penchant for targeting universities and airlines. (The "UN" in Unabomber referenced universities, the "A" referenced airlines, and the rest of the code name was "bomber.") In time, most of the country would know Kaczynski better by his code name than his given name and refer to him as such. Kaczynski's goal through a decades-long campaign of bombings was to overthrow the industrialized and technologically reliant United States and do so through violence, killing, and revolution. Kaczynski's attack on universities and airlines was part of an effort to bring about a revolution in the United States not only against industry and education, but the state itself which supports and enables this technology. Kaczynski's campaign of violence was meant to cripple the government by striking at its educational and technological base. Ultimately, he was for the rejection of any government that supported, enabled, or relied on industrialization and technology. In Kaczynski's view, nothing short of a revolution against the government was needed. The entire system (education, technology, industrialization, and government) needed to be eradicated and a new system set up in its place.

Kaczynski terrorized the country for seventeen years (1978–95) with sixteen separate bombings spanning the continental United States. Had all these bombings succeeded as planned, Kaczynski would have been one of the deadliest terrorists and serial killers in the US history. For instance, in one of his sixteen bombings, Kaczynski planted a bomb on American Airlines Flight 444 on November 15, 1979, with seventy-two passengers and six crew members aboard. The bomb did not cause as much damage as anticipated, and the plane was able to safely land without any fatalities and with only twelve passengers suffering from smoke inhalation. Numerous other bombs were planted at universities and could have also involved a great loss of life had they exploded in a crowded room as opposed to a secretary or faculty member's office. Fortunately, in Kaczynski's sixteen bombings spanning seventeen years, the fatality count was amazingly low at three, but at least twenty-three others were seriously wounded. Kaczynski's terrorism plans entailed the sabotage and disruption of businesses and universities, and caused the complete closure of Los Angeles International Airport (LAX) on June 28, 1995, due to the fear of a Kaczynski-planted bomb on a plane. Kaczynski was not interested in peaceful advocacy for change or civil disobedience. In his published manifesto, Kaczynski unambiguously stated: "In order to get our message before the public with some chance of making a lasting impression, we've had to kill people" (Thomas and Weiser 1996, A1).

Kaczynski was an unconventional candidate to become one of America's most violent and dangerous terrorists. He finished high school in three years and earned a full academic scholarship to Harvard in 1950 at sixteen. With a recorded IQ of 167, Kaczynski excelled academically, and upon graduation from Harvard, enrolled as a doctoral student at the University of Michigan, studying Theoretical Mathematics. He completed his Ph.D. in just four years (1962–6). Kaczynski then accepted an assistant professor position at the University of California at Berkeley in 1966 but resigned in 1972 to move to a small cabin in the rural area of Lincoln, Montana. When his department chair asked why Kaczynski was throwing his academic career away, Kaczynski reportedly responded that he stayed in the position just long enough to earn enough money to buy a small cabin and land and that he never believed all the "crap" being dispensed at universities. Kaczynski rejected the industrial-technological culture that he believed had ruined America, and he felt that corporations and the government had too much power over the lives of American citizens.

During the first few years living as a hermit in a ten-by-fourteen-foot cabin with no electricity, Kaczynski began plotting how to overthrow the current system by revolution. He began keeping a secret coded journal that would eventually grow to over 22,000 pages. During this period, Kaczynski stated he "was working at paying back the system. Revenge" (Traub 2023, A1). He also engaged in local criminal acts of sabotage by destroying his neighbor's sawmill machinery by dumping sand and dirt into it. After being upset by noise made by another neighbor, Kaczynski took an axe and destroyed the inside of the neighbor's cabin.

Kaczynski despised modern corporate and industrialized America, stating that "the main thing is to get rid of the industrial system by whatever means may be necessary." Kaczynski believed that "the system could not be reformed in such a way to reconcile freedom with technology, the only way out is to dispense with the industrial system altogether" (Engelhart 1998). He clearly condoned and encouraged violence saying "it would be better to dump the whole stinking system and take the consequences. We therefore advocate a revolution against the industrial system" (Unabomber Manifesto 1995). He also desired to set the standard for others saying, "if I could be used as a symbol for promoting revolutionary activity, that's fine with me" (Slade 2022a).

Kaczynski began his decades-long bombing campaign in 1978 when he planted a bomb at Northwestern University in Chicago, which detonated on May 25, 1978. A year later, on May 25, 1979, he again bombed an office at Northwestern University. In his secret coded journal, he noted after this bombing that "I had hoped that the victim would be blinded or have his hands blown off or be otherwise maimed" (Slade 2022b).

Kaczynski also had a fascination with plans to blow up a plane in flight or at least target selected airline executives. Thus, six months after his second bombing at Northwestern University, Kaczynski had a bomb placed in mail aboard American Airlines Flight 444. The bomb was designed to denote when the plane reached a certain altitude. The bomb detonated in flight as planned, blowing a small hole in the outer shell of the plane. Fortunately, the plane landed safely despite the damage caused by the bomb. Perhaps out of frustration, Kaczynski's next target was an executive at United Airlines, with a bomb placed in a hollowed-out book and sent to the victim at his residence in Lake Forest, Illinois. The bomb detonated on June 10, 1980, injuring its target. It was Kaczynski's fourth bombing in two years. Kaczynski never gave up on his plans for sabotaging airplanes. Much later, on June 28, 1995, Kaczynski sent a threat to local newspapers saying that he was planning to blow up an airliner in the next six days. His threat (and some intelligence leads) caused Los Angeles International Airport (LAX) to be completely shut down for an entire day while airport personnel scrambled to ensure no bombs were planted on board a plane at LAX.

Over seven years after his second bombing of Northwestern University in 1980, Kaczynski planned and planted eight separate bombs. Of the eight, seven detonated and seriously injured or killed people, while one of the bombs was successfully defused before exploding. Bombs were sent to the University of Utah (1981), Vanderbilt University (1982), the University of California at Berkeley (1985), a psychologist's office in Salt Lake City, Utah (1985), a business executive in

Ann Arbor, Michigan (1985), and another business executive in Salt Lake City (1987). Kaczynski's 1987 bombing was significant in that an eyewitness saw a man with a sweatshirt hoodie and wearing aviator sunglasses place the bomb by the business. The sketch artist rendering of Kaczynski was circulated nationwide and the sketch became ubiquitously associated with the Unabomber.

By 1987–8, Kaczynski became one of the most wanted men in America. The FBI launched one of the largest task forces in its history to identify and capture the culprit with 150 FBI agents assigned to the case. It was described as the largest fugitive hunt in American history and one of the most expensive investigations in FBI history, costing approximately fifty million dollars. Perhaps because of the intensive nationwide attention, Kaczynski was dormant for about five years, with some believing the suspect had died or been imprisoned on unrelated criminal offenses. However, Kaczynski reemerged in 1993–4, with three additional bombings.

On June 22, 1993, Charles Epstein, one of the country's foremost geneticists (specializing in advanced studies in attempting to find a cure for Down's Syndrome), was significantly injured when a letter bomb from Kaczynski was delivered to Epstein's office at the University of California at San Francisco. Only two days later, on June 24, 1993, another letter bomb detonated in the office of computer science professor at Yale University, seriously injuring the professor. Finally, this wave of bombings ended with the bombing and killing of a senior public relations executive at Exxon. The victim, Thomas Mosser, opened the package in his kitchen, and the bomb was so powerful that, according to Mosser's widow, only the victim's two feet were identifiable after the denotation. Despite the horrendous nature of Mosser's murder, Kaczynski recorded in his secret journal that the bombing was a "totally satisfactory result" (Johnson 1998, A1). Before his capture, Kaczynski's last two bombings occurred on April 24, 1995, and April 26, 1995. The first bomb was sent to a timber/ lumber industrial lobbyist, seriously injuring the victim. The second was sent to an executive with the Timber Association of California, killing the victim.

In addition to the 22,000-page journal of his ramblings, Kaczynski also produced a separate 35,000-word manuscript intended to be distributed to newspapers around the country, and subsequently known as the Unabomber Manifesto. Kaczynski wrote two letters to the *New York Times* (1993 and 1995) indicating that the bombings and killings would continue if the newspaper did not print his manuscript "advocating the destruction of the worldwide industrial system." In these letters, Kaczynski claimed to be a member of the "Freedom Club," which he claimed was a group of economic anarchists. Six major newspapers published Kaczynski's manifesto in full and without any editing. Ironically, the publication of this manifesto was what led authorities to Kaczynski as the culprit.

Largely based on suspect profiling techniques, the FBI developed a list of 2,417 individuals who might meet the characteristics of the bomber, and amazingly, Kaczynski was the second *last* ("suspect number 2,416") most viable name on the list. It was the published manifesto that tipped off Ted Kaczynski's brother, David Kaczynski, and subsequently made Ted Kaczynski the FBI's prime suspect. At the time, Kaczynski's mother was ill, and in cleaning out his mother's house, David Kaczynski found a twenty-three-page document Ted Kaczynski had sent to his mother years earlier. Comparing the language in the document with the Unabomber Manifesto, David Kaczynski realized that the wording was similar (and sometimes verbatim) between the two. David Kaczynski immediately called the police, and Ted Kaczynski was finally arrested on April 3, 1996.

Kaczynski was indicted on ten separate criminal counts, including three counts of homicide. Kaczynski's defense lawyers wanted to raise the insanity defense on his behalf, but Kaczynski refused, arguing that he wanted the world to know that he was sane, and that it was the world that was insane in its embrace of technology and industry. Kaczynski's rejection of the insanity defense brought comparisons with radical abolitionist John Brown, who rejected the insanity defense in

Virginia v. Brown because he did not want those who were against slavery and acted against the institution to be viewed as insane. However, the comparisons between Kaczynski and Brown end there. Kaczynski engaged in indiscriminate murder and violence, while Brown eschewed violence when possible and advised his men on the eve of John Brown's Raid to take life only when necessary to defend themselves or when fired upon and to hold "the lives of others as dearly as you hold yours." When Kaczynski was asked about the comparison, he reputedly responded that he did not know about John Brown, did not care about him, and was not influenced by him.

After Kaczynski's lawyers indicated that they would not represent him absent the insanity defense, Kaczynski tried to fire them and represent himself. The trial judge denied the request and ruled that it was too late in the process to switch attorneys and represent himself. That night, Kaczynski tried to kill himself in his jail cell. Later, Kaczynski went into court and pleaded guilty, resulting in multiple life sentences. His guilty plea was conditioned on the avoidance of the death penalty. He received eight life sentences to be served at the federal supermax penitentiary in Florence, Colorado. Early in his incarceration, Kaczynski made friends with Ramzi Yousef (perpetrator of the 1993 World Trade Center Bombing) and Timothy McVeigh (perpetrator of 1995 Oklahoma City bombing).

Throughout his writings, Kaczynski expressed a complete lack of remorse for the deaths and maiming of individuals. The re-occurring theme in his pages was "anger and revenge." Indeed, it has been argued that several of the targeted individuals may have had some previous interaction with Kaczynski, and that Kaczynski may have remembered and targeted them. Attacks based on anger and revenge have little to do with his claimed goal of ushering in a revolution that would cast off the country's reliance on technology and industry. Regardless, Kaczynski seemed to justify his blood lust in that it allowed him to force the publication and furtherance of his views.

While in prison, Kaczynski continued to write and publish his anti-technology and anti-industrial viewpoints and declare the need for a revolution. At one point, Kaczynski suggested that like-minded anarchists in the United States should consider joining forces with terrorist groups like Al-Qaeda. Kaczynski has been depicted in popular culture in songs, clothing, movies, and television shows. Much more troubling, "he has influenced many other radical actors and movements" in recent years (Fleming 2021, 207), and individuals inspired by Kaczynski continue to embrace appear in nihilist, anarchist, and eco-extremist movements (Richardson 2018, 63). Kaczynski committed suicide in his prison cell on June 10, 2023.

See Also: Anarchy, Criminal; Brown, John; Civil Disobedience and Crimes against the State; John Brown's Raid (1859); Oklahoma City Bombing (1995); Sabotage; Terrorism; *Virginia v. Brown* (1859); World Trade Center Bombing of 1993

Resources

A Chronology of the UNABOM investigation. 1998. *Cornell Law*. Accessed March 23, 2023. https://www.law.cornell.edu/background/unabom/history.html.

Engelhart, L. Kurt, ed. 1998. "Unabomber Manifesto (Condensed)." Accessed November 1, 2023. http://lkengelhartassoc.org/unabombr.htm#:~:text=The%20only%20way%20out%20is,in%20the%20nature%20of%20society.

Fleming, Sean. 2021. "The Unabomber and the Origins of Anti-Tech Radicalism." *Journal of Political Ideologies* 27, no. 2: 207–25.

Johnson, David. 1998. "In Unabomber's Own Words, A Chilling Account of Murder." *The New York Times*, April 29, 1998, A1.

Mello, Michael. 1998. "Raising Holy Hell: John Brown's Trial Lawyers (and Ted Kaczynski's Lawyers) and the Politics of the Insanity Defense." *Criminal Law Bulletin* 34: 279.

Richardson, John H. 2018. "Children of Ted Two Decades after His Last Deadly Act of Ecoterrorism, the Unabomber Has Become an Unlikely Prophet to a New Generation of Acolytes." *New York Magazine*, December 11, 2018. Accessed March 23, 2023. https://nymag.com/intelligencer/2018/12/the-unabomber-ted-kaczynski-new-generation-of-acolytes.html.

Slade, Theo. 2022a. "Does the Unabomber Have Any Relevance to Anarchism?" *The Ted K Archive*. Accessed November 1, 2023. https://www.thetedkarchive.com/library/does-the-unabomber-have-any-relevance-to-anarchism.

Slade, Theo. 2022b. "Ted Kaczynski's Journal of Early Crimes." *The Ted K Archive*. Accessed November 1, 2023. https://www.thetedkarchive.com/library/ted-kaczynski-s-journal-of-early-crimes.

Thomas, Pierra, and Benjamin Weiser. 1996. "Reputed 'Manifesto' Recovered." April 13, 1996, A01.

Traub, Alex. 2023. "Ted Kaczynski, 'Unabomber' Who Attacked Modern Life, Dies at 81." *The New York Times*, June 10, 2023, A1.

Unabomber Manifesto. 1995. "The Unabomber Trial: The Manifesto." *The Washington Post*, September 22, 1995 (special section published at direction of FBI).

Wiehl, Lis. 2020. *Hunting the Unabomber: The FBI, Ted Kaczynski, and the Capture of America's Most Notorious Domestic Terrorist*. Nashville, TN: Nelson Books.

Kawakita v. United States (1952)

Kawakita v. United States is the last time the Supreme Court affirmed a treason conviction. The case is a helpful demonstration of a key condition necessary for the crime of treason that is not mentioned in the Treason Clause of the United States Constitution: that the offender owes an allegiance to the United States.

Tomoya Kawakita was born in California, giving him US citizenship, but he was also a Japanese citizen because his parents were Japanese. In 1939, two years before the Japanese attack on Pearl Harbor that dragged the United States into the Second World War, Kawakita moved from California to Japan, where he enrolled in university and formally registered as a Japanese national. During the war, Kawakita worked at a nickel mine and processing plant that became a prisoner of war (POW) work camp for American POWs. As POWs would later testify at his trial, Kawakita beat prisoners and sometimes caused them to beat each other.

After Japan lost the war, Kawakita renounced his Japanese citizenship, and renewed his US passport, stating under oath at the American consulate in Yokohama, Japan, that he was a US citizen and had not done various acts amounting to expatriation. Kawakita then returned to the United States where he enrolled in the University of Southern California. When a former POW from Kawakita's camp recognized him in a Los Angeles store, the POW informed the Federal Bureau of Investigation. Kawakita was subsequently arrested and charged with fifteen counts of treason.

At trial, the defense acknowledged that Kawakita had engaged in some abusive conduct but urged that his actions could not constitute treason against the United States because he had lost his US citizenship when he registered as a Japanese citizen. The trial judge instructed the jury that under US law, "any American citizen of alien parentage may, on becoming of age, renounce his American citizenship and thus become a citizen of only the country of his parents" and "an American citizen cannot owe `permanent allegiance' to more than one country at any given time. That is to say, it is legally impossible for any American citizen to owe conflicting allegiance to any other country so long as he or she remains a citizen of the United States." The judge further instructed the jury that if it determined Kawakita genuinely believed he was no longer a United States citizen when he committed the charged acts, he lacked the requisite treasonous intent and could not be convicted of treason. Ultimately, the jury convicted Kawakita of eight of the original fifteen counts of treason. He was sentenced to death and, perhaps ironically, his conviction for treason permanently cost Kawakita his US citizenship, citizenship he disclaimed during the war, then reclaimed after it.

In announcing his decision to impose the death sentence, the judge made an observation to those assembled in the court that is helpful in understanding how crimes against the state differ from other crimes:

> As I view this matter, it is not a question of whether the defendant kicked some American prisoner of war or a dozen of them. His crime might be briefly put in two sentences. He said that from 1943 on he did everything he could to help the Japanese Government win the war. The jury found that he owed a duty of loyalty at that time to the United States. So, his crime cannot be considered … in terms of beating up someone, no matter how brutal. His crime is a crime against the country of his birth. His crime is not against a few American prisoners of war. His crime is against the whole people of this country where he was born and where he was fed and where he was educated.

> Throughout history treason has always been the crime most abhorred by English-speaking peoples. The traitor has always been considered even worse than a murderer. And the distinction is based upon reason: for the murderer violates at most only a few, while the traitor violates all the members of his society, all the members of the group to which he owes his allegiance.

When upholding Kawakita's conviction and death sentence, the United States Supreme Court agreed with the trial judge that whether Kawakita had renounced his American citizenship was for the jury to determine and that Kawakita's assertion of the rights of citizenship of one country (Japan) did not by itself mean he had renounced the citizenship of another (the United States). Furthermore, the Court opined that a person can be punished for acts of treason even if they are of dual nationality because they still owe an allegiance to the United States. The Court also noted that the Treason Clause contains no territorial limitation and thus treasonable acts can be committed by American citizens living outside the United States.

The case demonstrated that an offender must owe an allegiance to the state, either by virtue of citizenship or by virtue of having a temporary presence in the state at the time the treasonous acts were committed, as a condition for the crime of treason. In several earlier treason cases, citizenship was held not to be a requirement, only that the offender owed the sovereign some allegiance through temporary residence or other minimum contacts with the state at the time of the treasonous conduct. For instance, in the 1820 case of *United States v. Wiltberger*, United States Supreme Court Chief Justice John Marshall stipulated the pre-requisites for a proper treason charge as follows: "treason is a breach of allegiance, and can be committed by him only who owes allegiance (to the sovereign) either perpetual or *temporary*" (emphasis added). In *Virginia v. Brown* (1859), the Virginia state trial court (in a decision affirmed on appeal) deemed John Brown's brief presence in Virginia to be sufficient for purposes of treason charges, even though John Brown was not a citizen or resident of Virginia. Common law writers like Edward Coke and William Blackstone also stressed that citizenship or temporary presence in the state would equally suffice to establish a person's owed allegiance to the State. In the *Kawakita* case, the issue was whether he still owed the United States allegiance by virtue of his citizenship (citizenship allegedly revoked by his claimed Japanese citizenship), despite having no other contacts or presence with the United States during the time in question. For whatever reason, the Court did not discuss whether a temporary presence in the state might equally suffice for purposes of treason law, and simply held that, at a minimum, citizenship alone (even without presence in the country) establishes the allegiance necessary for treason laws to apply.

In 1953, President Dwight D. Eisenhower commuted Kawakita's death sentence to life imprisonment, which Kawakita initially served at the Alcatraz Federal Penitentiary. A decade later, President John F. Kennedy ordered Kawakita released, deported from the United States, and banned for life. In requesting his release, Kawakita argued that after sixteen years in prison, he had been incarcerated longer than any other person in Japan charged with wartime offenses. Indeed, he had been in prison over twice as long as had fellow traitor Tokyo Rose (Iva Toguri D'Aquino).

See Also: Brown, John; Tokyo Rose (Iva Toguri D'Aquino); Treason; *Virginia v. Brown* (1859)

Resources

Kawakita v. United States, 343 U.S. 717 (1952).
United States v. Tomoya Kawakita, 96 F. Supp. 824 (S.D. Cal. 1951).

Kentucky Resolution of 1798

See Jefferson, Thomas

Keyishian v. Board of Regents (1967)

New York law, initially enacted in 1917 during the First Red Scare, declared that "the utterance of any treasonable or seditious word or words or the doing of any treasonable or seditious act" was grounds for dismissal of employees from the public school system. Furthermore, New York law disqualified from the civil service and from employment in the educational system "any person who advocates the overthrow of government by force, violence, or any unlawful means, or publishes material advocating such overthrow, or organizes or joins any society or group of persons advocating such doctrine." State University of New York trustees also imposed a requirement that employees in the university system certify that they were not members of the Communist Party. A group of academic employees at State University of New York at Buffalo sued when they were terminated or threatened with termination for failing to sign the certification.

The United States Supreme Court, which had upheld New York's laws just fifteen years earlier during the Second Red Scare (in *Adler v. Board of Education* [1952]), this time struck down the laws as unconstitutional. The Court held that the law banning uttering treasonable or seditious words or committing such acts was unconstitutionally vague, because no teacher could know what constitutes the boundary between seditious and non-seditious utterances and acts. Furthermore, the Court concluded that provisions prohibiting the employment of one who advocates doctrine abstractly, without any attempt to incite others to action, might be unconstitutionally construed to cover mere expression of belief. The Court noted that academic freedom is a special concern of the First Amendment, which does not tolerate laws that cast a "pall of orthodoxy over the classroom." In light of this concern, the Court found the New York laws could stifle the "free play of the spirit which all teachers ought especially to cultivate and practice."

In addition to speech and academic freedom, the Court also focused on associational freedom. The Court held that the New York law that made Communist Party membership a sole ground for disqualification from employment was "overbroad," and therefore unconstitutional. The Court repeated its earlier pronouncement (in *Elfbrandt v. Russell* [1966] and other cases) that mere membership in an organization, without a specific intent to further any unlawful aims of that organization, is not a constitutionally adequate basis for imposing sanctions, even if the member knows the organization or some within it have such unlawful goals.

Known primarily for its bold assertion of constitutional protection for academic freedom, the *Keyishian* case was also an important limitation on speech as a crime against the state after decades of contrary jurisprudence.

See Also: First Red Scare and the Palmer Raids (1919–20); Second Red Scare (McCarthyism); Sedition; Speech as Crime against the State; Treason

Resources

Keyishian v. Board of Regents, 385 U.S. 589 (1967).

Korematsu v. United States (1944)

In the notorious case of *Korematsu v. United States*, the Supreme Court visited the question of the president's authority to detain US citizens not engaged in combat for alleged violations of orders issued by the military to control civilians during a time of war. Roughly ten weeks after Japan attacked the United States in Pearl Harbor, Hawaii, President Franklin D. Roosevelt signed Executive Order 9066, which authorized the Secretary of War and subordinate military commanders to remove people of Japanese ancestry from areas designated by the military as exclusion zones. Subsequently, General John DeWitt of the United States Army issued a Civilian Exclusion Order requiring all persons of Japanese descent to leave a large area of the West Coast of the United States. Pursuant to this order, more than 120,000 persons, two-thirds of whom were US citizens, were relocated from the West Coast of the United States to concentration camps (often euphemistically referred to as the internment of Japanese Americans to relocation centers during the Second World War). Most of these individuals were subsequently detained in internment camps throughout the western and midwestern United States. One such citizen, Fred Korematsu, decided not to comply with the Civilian Exclusion Order. He was arrested and appealed his subsequent conviction to the Supreme Court.

The government's claimed justification for the exclusion of US citizens was military necessity. A majority of the Supreme Court deferred to this judgment and the assertion made by the military that a danger of sabotage and espionage existed. Specifically, the Supreme Court noted, "we cannot reject as unfounded the judgment of the military authorities and of Congress that there were disloyal members of that population, whose number and strength could not be precisely and quickly ascertained." The majority determined the prevention of espionage and sabotage was a proper exercise of the Legislative and Executive Branches' war powers. Justice Felix Frankfurter issued a concurring opinion suggesting the government's action was constitutional because of the total war in which the United States was involved, while acknowledging the action might have been unlawful in peacetime.

Three important dissents highlighted some of the contentious issues raised by the *Korematsu* case. Justice Frank Murphy argued that though deference to the military is important, there must be limits to military discretion, "especially where martial law has not been declared." Murphy's suspicion of the exclusion order was well-placed, as we now know there was significant influence on General DeWitt's decision to issue the order that had nothing to do with military necessity. For instance, California businesses looking to eliminate competition pressured authorities to exclude Japanese persons from the region. And the United States Department of Justice and Solicitor General subsequently suppressed knowledge of possible falsehoods in the "Final Report of General DeWitt" that undercut the military necessity claim. For example, Solicitor General Charles Fahy hid from the Supreme Court a military report that concluded very few persons of Japanese descent posed a risk and almost all who did were already in custody when Executive Order 9066 was enforced. The faulty military intelligence prompted Murphy to lament that the military position was "largely an accumulation of much of the misinformation, half-truths and insinuations that for years have been directed against Japanese Americans by people with racial and economic prejudices."

Justice Murphy also addressed the racism involved in the case. He saw the exclusion of persons of Japanese ancestry as falling "into the ugly abyss of racism" and ironically resembled "the abhorrent and despicable treatment of minority groups by the dictatorial tyrannies which this nation is now pledged to destroy."

In another dissent, Justice Robert Jackson argued the Supreme Court should not decide the case at all, because a judicial order would unnecessarily constitutionalize the order. Jackson's view suggests the military's "extra-constitutional" behavior may be acceptable within the proper military sphere: "When an area is so beset that it must be put under military control at all, the paramount consideration is that its measures be successful rather than legal." Justice Jackson essentially conceded that the order and Korematsu's arrest were unconstitutional, but that the Court should not sanction what was unconstitutional. Instead, the Court should stay out of the matter and let the political process deal with unconstitutional behavior. Jackson also complained of the racist impact of the majority's opinion, asserting "here is an attempt to make an otherwise innocent act a crime merely because this prisoner is the son of parents as to whom he had no choice, and belongs to a race from which there is no way to resign." Jackson also remarked that the majority opinion in *Korematsu* would be "a loaded weapon ready for the hand of any authority that can bring forward a plausible claim of an urgent need."

Justice Owen Roberts also dissented, characterizing the case as one of "convicting a citizen as a punishment for not submitting to imprisonment in a concentration camp, based on his ancestry, and solely because of his ancestry, without evidence or inquiry concerning his loyalty and good disposition towards the United States."

In essence, in *Korematsu*, the Supreme Court deferred to the Executive Branch's determination of military necessity. Korematsu's alleged "crime against the state" was interfering with the national security of the United States during wartime by remaining in an area of the country where the military had decided he should not be. But this was only a crime because of his ancestry; a citizen of non-Japanese heritage could not commit a crime against the state under the same circumstances. Writing for Supreme Court majority years later in *Adarand v. Constructors, Inc., v. Pena* (1995), Justice Sandra Day O'Connor criticized the deference the Supreme Court gave to the military's racial classification in *Korematsu* and warned that the failure of the Supreme Court to strictly scrutinize and rigorously analyze the clearly "racially discriminatory" government order in *Korematsu* "can only increase the risk of another such error occurring in the future."

The *Korematsu* case highlights the perils of justifying unequal treatment of certain racial or ethnic backgrounds based on alleged threats to national security posed by members of those groups. Indeed, many believe the only offense in this case was the one committed *by* the state, rather than any crime committed against it. The Supreme Court has never formally overturned its *Korematsu* decision, though in 2018 a majority of the Court in *Trump v. Hawaii* did state that *Korematsu* had been wrongly decided. A majority of the Court in *Adarand v. Constructors, Inc., v. Pena* in 1995 had previously stated that the government's actions in *Korematsu* to be "racially discriminatory," but did not overturn the decision as precedent. Korematsu's conviction was overturned in 1983 when a federal district court judge agreed the original conviction was so tainted by prosecutorial misconduct it should be void. In a ceremony at the White House in January 1998, President Bill Clinton presented Fred Korematsu with the Presidential Medal of Freedom, saying that Korematsu conducted himself with "quiet bravery" during those perilous times.

See Also: Espionage; *Ex Parte Milligan* (1866); *Hirabayashi v. United States* (1943); Internal Security Act of 1950; Martial Law; Sabotage

Resources

Kastenberg, Joshua, and Eric Merriam. 2016. *In a Time of Total War: The Federal Judiciary and the National Defense—1940–1954*. New York: Routledge.

Katyal, Neal. 2011. "Confession of Error: The Solicitor General's Mistakes during the Japanese-American Internment Cases." *United States Department of Justice*, May 20, 2011. Accessed June 14, 2023. https://www.justice.gov/archives/opa/blog/confession-error-solicitor-generals-mistakes-during-japanese-american-internment-cases.

Korematsu v. United States, 323 U.S. 214 (1944).

Korematsu v. United States, 584 F. Supp. 1406 (N.D. Cal. 1984).

Merriam, Eric, and Douglas B. McKechnie. 2020. *National Security Law*. St. Paul: West Academic, 322–3.

Rostov, Eugene V. 1945 "The Japanese-American Cases—A Disaster." *Yale Law Journal* 54: 489.

Koresh, David

See Waco

L

Leaks of National Defense Information

The Espionage Act of 1917 (Espionage Act) criminalizes disseminating national defense information. The Espionage Act is used primarily to prosecute traditional "spying," where the purpose is to harm the United States and/or benefit other countries. For instance, several of the prosecutions related to the Year of the Spy relied on the Espionage Act, as did the prosecutions of notorious modern spies Aldrich Ames and Robert Hanssen. But the Espionage Act has also been used to prosecute release of information to the public by persons who many view not as spies, but as "whistleblowers" who are providing a public service by releasing the information. For instance, the quintessential "whistleblowing leaker," Daniel Ellsberg, was initially charged with violating the Espionage Act for his role in leaking the Pentagon Papers, though the charge was later dismissed. Leaking national defense information is considered by the government to be a crime against the state due to the potential national security implications of such actions. But many view the types of leaks discussed here as having significant public policy value, protected by the First Amendment. Ellsberg's actions are discussed in detail in a separative entry. Other illustrative modern leaks of national defense information include those by Julian Assange, Chelsea Manning, Edward Snowden, Reality Winner, and Jack Teixeira.

Julian Assange was a successful Australian computer hacker and security expert who helped found WikiLeaks, an international organization devoted to divulging information that governments and organizations attempt to keep secret. Inspired by Daniel Ellsberg's Pentagon Papers release, Assange created WikiLeaks in part to shorten the time between a leak and its publication (in the Pentagon Papers case, the delay was two years).

Though the US government was neither the first nor only target of WikiLeaks's disclosure efforts, Assange's most notorious leaks of information occurred in 2010 when WikiLeaks released hundreds of thousands of classified Department of Defense and Department of State documents and other media provided by Chelsea Manning. Assange was alleged to have encouraged Manning to leak the documents. Investigated repeatedly for years, Assange was ultimately indicted by a federal grand jury in 2018. He was charged in that matter with hacking into US government computers. In 2019, Assange was also indicted on seventeen additional charges under the Espionage Act, including conspiracy to obtain and disclose national defense information, obtaining national defense information, and disclosure of national defense information. Assange was indicted in absentia due to his asylum in an Ecuadorian embassy in Great Britain, followed by his imprisonment in Great Britain. Since 2019, Assange has been contesting his extradition in the British court system and, as of the time of publication, his extradition is still pending. Assange also allegedly helped Russia meddle in the 2016 US presidential election, though that claim has not yet yielded any publicly known indictments.

Assange's indictment raises the thorny issue of whether his actions in publishing classified documents differ, in kind or degree, from traditional media's similar disclosures. For instance, *The*

New York Times published many of the same documents WikiLeaks made available. Some argue that Assange's and WikiLeaks solicitations and publication of information—in essence actively encouraging or assisting government employees to steal information and then making no effort to verify or to avoid harm that disclosure may cause—differ from decisions made by traditional media outlets to publish national defense information they are provided. But under the Espionage Act, the legal distinction is slight, as it is the dissemination itself, not the motivation or mechanism, that is prohibited. In fact, concern over the implications for freedom of the press, a right protected by the First Amendment, apparently prevented the Obama administration from seeking an indictment of Assange. Many see the possible prosecution of Assange as a threat to press freedom more broadly. Indeed, though many traditional journalists and news organizations have distanced themselves from Assange, arguing he is not a journalist due to his methods, some of the same journalists and organizations oppose his prosecution due to concerns over chilling the press.

Assange's and WikiLeaks's biggest leak involved disclosing information provided to them by United States Army soldier Chelsea (then known as Bradley) Manning. While deployed to Iraq, Specialist Manning, an intelligence analyst, had access to classified network and communications systems. Over several days in January 2010, Manning downloaded nearly 500,000 documents from the system, burning them on a CD and smuggling them out of the secured facility in which she worked. When she returned to the United States, she offered the material to *The New York Times* and *Washington Post.* In February 2010, after neither paper expressed interest, Manning passed the information to WikiLeaks. After returning to Iraq, Manning found on an Army judge advocate's network folder a video of a US helicopter attacking Baghdad that included the killing of civilians. Manning passed the video to WikiLeaks and Assange released the video, which he titled "Collateral Murder" in late February 2010. In March and April 2010, Manning downloaded 250,000 diplomatic cables and uploaded them to a WikiLeaks dropbox. Manning confided in a well-known hacker who alerted authorities. Manning was arrested in May 2010. Later that year, WikiLeaks and three newspapers, including *The New York Times*, began publishing the other documents.

Manning was charged with a variety of crimes under the Uniform Code of Military Justice, including aiding the enemy and failure to obey regulations, and of violating the Espionage Act and related Computer Fraud and Abuse Act. At her 2013 court-martial, Manning initially pleaded guilty to some of the charges, but not to the charge of aiding the enemy or espionage. Prosecutors elected to go forward on the remaining charges. Manning was ultimately convicted of nineteen of twenty-two charges, including six counts of violating the Espionage Act, but acquitted of the charge of aiding the enemy. During sentencing, Manning apologized, saying "I am sorry that my actions hurt people. I'm sorry that they hurt the United States. I am sorry for the unintended consequences of my actions. When I made these decisions I believed I was going to help people, not hurt people." The military judge sentenced Manning to thirty-five years confinement.

Manning appealed her conviction and sentence, arguing the Espionage Act was too vague to provide fair notice of the criminal nature of disclosing classified documents and that her actions were protected by the First Amendment. But the United States Army Court of Criminal Appeals upheld Manning's conviction, opining that the facts of the case left "no question as to what constituted national defense information. Appellant's training and experience indicate, without any doubt, she was on notice and understood the nature of the information she was disclosing and how its disclosure could negatively affect national defense." The court also rejected Manning's First Amendment claim. The United States Court of Appeals for the Armed Forces declined to review the Army Court of Criminal Appeals' decision. In January 2017, days before he left office, President Barack Obama commuted Manning's sentence to seven years confinement, and she was released in May 2017. Like many others involved in leaking national defense information, Manning has been vilified by some and lionized by others for her actions.

In 2013, while serving as a contractor for the National Security Agency (NSA), Edward Snowden leaked classified information revealing massive surveillance programs conducted by the United States and its allies. Though estimates vary, Snowden is believed to have obtained over one million files, including tens of thousands of files from Australia and Britain, but claimed to have personally reviewed every document before disclosing it to others.

The surveillance activities revealed by Snowden included PRISM, under which the US government could access Americans' email accounts, a secret court order under which Verizon turned over millions of Americans' phone records, and the tapping of undersea communications cables to access information from hundreds of millions of Google and Yahoo account holders. Snowden's revelations also included the NSA's "black budget," under which the NSA was paying private tech companies for access to their networks and vast spying activities by the United States against countries and world leaders, including allies Britain, Germany, and France. Many government officials have observed that Snowden's disclosures revealed to terrorists and foreign adversaries precisely how to avoid detection.

Not long after he began disclosing information, Snowden moved to Hong Kong. And days after media organizations began publishing documents he had leaked, Snowden fled Hong Kong to Russia, ostensibly on his way to Ecuador, which would give him asylum. This plan had been arranged and paid for by WikiLeaks and Julian Assange. However, after arriving in Russia, Snowden was unable to leave because the United States had revoked his passport. Snowden requested asylum from nearly two dozen countries, but ultimately remained in Russia. In 2013, Snowden was charged with theft of government property and two counts of violating the Espionage Act of 1917.

Some political figures have expressed nuanced views of Snowden's actions. President Obama acknowledged some good in raising public awareness of mass surveillance, while condemning Snowden's methods, saying "the benefit of the debate he generated was not worth the damage done, because there was another way of doing it" (Myre 2019). In 2015, United States Senator Bernie Sanders stated that "Snowden played a very important role in educating the American public" (Democracy Now 2015) and that although Snowden should not go unpunished for breaking the law, "that education should be taken into consideration before the sentencing" (Democracy Now 2015). In 2016, former United States Attorney General Eric Holder said that Snowden "performed a public service by raising the debate that we engaged in and by the changes that we made," but that Snowden's actions were nevertheless inappropriate and illegal (Jaffee 2016).

In August 2020, despite his 2013 comments that Snowden was a traitor who should be executed, President Donald Trump stated he would consider issuing Snowden a pardon. Trump's suggestion caused an uproar and objection by many in government, including Trump's Attorney General, William Barr, who asserted that Snowden was a traitor who greatly hurt the safety of the American people.

Daniel Ellsberg called Snowden's release of NSA material the most significant leak in US history. Snowden argued he was compelled to leak classified information because the only established whistleblowing options involved reporting misdeeds directly to those responsible for them. He also claims to have been motivated solely by a desire to "inform the public as to that which is done in their name and that which is done against them," arguing government should be more transparent (Greenwald 2013). Some have defended Snowden's leak as an act of civil disobedience, while others have rejected this argument as Snowden fled the jurisdiction of the American judicial system, displayed no willingness to be held accountable for his actions, and showing no underlying fidelity to the rule of law in society. In 2022, Snowden became a citizen of Russia.

In 2017, Reality Winner was an intelligence contractor working for the NSA when she came across a report attributing efforts to compromise the 2016 election to Russia's GRU military intelligence agency. She printed a copy of the report and smuggled it out of the facility in which she worked, and then mailed it to *The Intercept*. When *The Intercept* showed a copy of the report to an NSA official while attempting to verify its authenticity, it inadvertently revealed the leaker to be Winner. When arrested, she told agents of the Federal Bureau of Investigation (FBI) that she "wasn't trying to be a Snowden or anything." She later explained that she leaked the report because she thought Americans were being intentionally misled by the Trump administration about Russia's attempts to influence the 2016 US presidential election. Winner pleaded guilty to violating the Espionage Act and was sentenced to sixty-three months in prison. Prosecutors claimed her sentence was the longest ever imposed in federal court for an unauthorized release of government information to the media.

The latest major leak of national defense information occurred in late 2022 when 21-year-old United States Airman Jack Teixeira purportedly leaked classified information on an online gaming chat room site called "Discord." Teixeira posted a message to a member of the online group acknowledging that Teixeira was posting classified information and claimed "idgaf," short for "I don't give a [expletive]." From there, online members reposted the materials to other websites, and someone even distributed the information to the Russian media. According to the Department of Justice (DOJ), during Teixeira's pre-trial confinement hearing, the damage Teixeira caused "to the U.S. national security is immense" and the further damage he "is still capable of causing is extraordinary."

When the FBI arrested Teixeira at his parent's home, a cache of weapons and ammunition (including high-capacity semi-assault weapons) was discovered. In his pre-trial confinement hearing, prosecutors revealed that Teixeira had used his government computer to research past mass shootings in the United States and armed stand-offs with federal agents, including the search terms "Ruby Ridge," "Las Vegas shooting," "Mandalay Bay shooting," "Uvalde," and "Buffalo tops shooting" (the last one a reference to a racially motivated mass shooting in Buffalo, NY, in 2022). Prosecutors indicated that Teixeira also stated on social media that he would like to "kill a [expletive] ton of people" if he had his way, because it would be "forcibly culling the weak minded," and "I hope isis goes through with their attack plan and creates a massacre at the World Cup." Another person reported to the FBI that Teixeira said he was tempted to convert a mini-van into an "assassination van." In court filings, the Department of Justice (DOJ) indicated that Teixeira was suspended from his high school when he was overheard discussing weapons and making racist comments. According to prosecutors, his firearm applications were twice denied before he joined the National Guard "due to the concerns of the local police department over the Defendant's remarks at his high school."

Teixeira joined the Massachusetts Air National Guard right after high school in 2019. Within two years, he had a Top-Secret Security clearance and access to very sensitive intelligence materials. On at least three previous occasions, Teixeira was caught by his supervisors trying to access intelligence information that was unrelated to his job responsibilities and each time was told to "cease and desist." After his arrest, many questioned how someone with Teixeira's background could so easily obtain a Top-Secret Security clearance, why someone as junior and new as Teixeira had access to so many sensitive documents, and why Teixeira was not better supervised. The Biden administration announced that it was in the process of limiting access to certain classified information moving forward.

Teixeira has been charged with six counts of violating the Espionage Act, specifically by retaining and transmitting national defense information without authorization (18 United States Code Section 793) and in the unauthorized removal and retention of classified information (18 United States Code Section 1924). Teixeira pleaded "not guilty" at his arraignment in June 2023, and has not provided any explanation for his conduct. He has been held in confinement since his arrest in April 2023, and he ultimately pleaded guilty to all six counts of the indictment in March 2024.

Cases like those discussed in this entry nearly always engender public debates about the advisability and constitutionality of prosecuting persons who claim to be acting in the public interest under the same statute used to prosecute traditional spies. The Espionage Act has most often been used to prosecute spies: individuals with access to classified information who make it available to foreign agents and foreign agents who obtain classified information. But as noted by the Congressional Research Service, "the United States has also prosecuted individuals claiming an altruistic desire to expose protected information to the public based on their belief that the public good favors transparency into particular government activities" (Congressional Research Service 2023).

Those critical of such prosecutions claim they are unjust because they wrongly target whistleblowers, because the Espionage Act affords whistleblower defendants little meaningful defense, and because they unconstitutionally suppress speech. Whistleblowers' backers observe that the United States prosecutes individuals for leaking but never traditional news organizations for receiving and publicizing leaked information. The argument that whistleblower defendants have little defense points to the fact that under the Espionage Act, motive behind the disclosure of national defense information is irrelevant to the crime. Thus, defendants are not permitted to explain the reasons for their actions or raise issues like over-classification of documents. The idea that defendants are unable to defend based on the claimed public interest motivation for their actions draws empirical support. Though not every prosecution against an alleged "whistleblower" has been successful, no individual has been acquitted of an Espionage Act charge on the grounds that the public interest in the leaked information was so significant as to justify an otherwise unlawful disclosure. Daniel Ellsberg has argued "the current state of whistleblowing prosecutions under the Espionage Act makes a truly fair trial wholly unavailable to an American who has exposed classified wrongdoing," and advocated for the United States Supreme Court to find the use of the Espionage Act overbroad and unconstitutional "in the absence of a public interest defense" (Ellsberg 2014). Finally, many have recognized the First Amendment concerns involved, both for the free speech of the leaker and freedom of press for the publisher of the leaked information. And yet, First Amendment concerns must be weighed against the real danger that exposure of protected information may harm US national security.

See Also: Ames, Aldrich Hazen "Rich"; Espionage; Espionage Act of 1917 and Sedition Act of 1918; Civil Disobedience and Crimes against the State; Conspiracy, Criminal; Hanssen, Robert Philip; Pentagon Papers and Trials of Daniel Ellsberg and Anthony Russo; Ruby Ridge (1992); Speech as Crime against the State; Year of the Spy (1985)

Resources

Brandon, Russell. 2018. "Reality Winner Accepts Guilty Plea for 63 Months in Prison on Espionage Charge." *The Verge*, June 26, 2018.

Congressional Research Service. 2023. *Criminal Prohibitions on Leaks and Other Disclosures of Classified Defense Information.* May 11, 2023. CSR R41404.

Democracy Now. 2015. "Is Snowden a Hero or Traitor? Democrats Debate Whether NSA Whistleblower Should Face Jail Term." October 14, 2015. Accessed November 1, 2023. https://www.democracynow.org/2015/10/14/is_snowden_a_hero_or_traitor.

Ellsberg, Daniel. 2014. "Daniel Ellsberg: Snowden Would Not Get a Fair Trial—and Kerry Is Wrong." *The Guardian*, May 30, 2014. Accessed November 1, 2023. https://www.theguardian.com/commentisfree/2014/may/30/daniel-ellsberg-snowden-fair-trial-kerry-espionage-act.

Espionage Act of 1917.

Greenwald, Glenn, Ewen MacAskill, and Laura Poitras. 2013. "Edward Snowden: The Whistleblower behind the NSA Surveillance Revelations." *The Guardian*, June 11, 2013. Accessed November 1, 2023. https://www.theguardian.com/world/2013/jun/09/edward-snowden-nsa-whistleblower-surveillance.

Jaffee, Matthew. 2016. "Eric Holder Says Edward Snowden Performed a 'Public Service.'" *CNN*, May 31, 2016. Accessed November 1, 2023. https://www.cnn.com/2016/05/30/politics/axe-files-axelrod-eric-holder/index.html#:~:text=%E2%80%9CWe%20can%20certainly%20argue%20about,University%20of%20Chicago%20Institute%20of.

Mulligan, Stephen P., and Jennifer K. Elsea. 2023. "Criminal Prohibitions on Leaks and Other Disclosures of Classified Defense Information." *Congressional Research Service* 41404, May 11, 2023: 1–31, 14.

Myre, Greg. 2019. "In 'Permanent Record,' Edward Snowden Says 'Exile Is an Endless Layover.'" *National Public Radio*, September 13, 2019. Accessed November 1, 2023. https://www.npr.org/2019/09/13/759833071/in-permanent-record-edward-snowden-makes-his-case-against-mass-surveillance#:~:text=President%20Barack%20Obama%20has%20criticized,that%20spied%20were%20once%20executed.

Stuart, Tessa. 2021. "'Bitter,' 'Angry,' 'Enraged': Reality Winner Blasts the Intercept after 4 Years in Jail." *Rolling Stone*, November 24, 2021.

Levying War

Levying war against the government has been considered one of the most serious crimes against the state that a person could commit. The act of levying war against the government was classified as an act of treason by the English Statute on Treason of 1351, which specified that "levying war against the king in his realm" was grounds for the charge of treason. The Framers of Article III of the United States Constitution, influenced by the wording of the English Treason Statute of 1351, incorporated the concept of "levying war against the United States" as one of the grounds for treason.

The definition of what constitutes levying war has evolved over time. United States Chief Justice John Marshall wrote in the court's opinion in the Aaron Burr prosecution, that levying war was a "technical term. It is used in a very old statute of that country whose language is our language, and whose laws form the substratum of our laws. It is scarcely conceivable that the term was not employed by the framers of our constitution in the sense which had been affixed to it by those whom we borrowed it." The early understanding of "levying war" under US law was heavily informed and influenced by early English cases involving treason. The most obvious example of levying war involved armed attacks or insurrections aimed at overthrowing the monarch. However, under English law, armed attacks against the government with the purpose of making law or laws ineffectual also was included under the notion of levying war. This was sometimes referred to as a "constructive" act of levying war against the government or "constructive treason."

Early American jurisprudence tracked the early English interpretation of levying war under the 1351 treason statute. That is, levying war included both armed attempts to overthrow the government as well as armed attempts at making US law ineffectual. The best early example illustrating those armed attempts at overthrowing the government that constituted levying war and treason can be seen in *United States v. Burr* in 1807. In that case, Chief Justice Marshall wrote in part that "[a]ll those who perform the various and essential military parts of prosecuting the war … may with correctness and accuracy be said to levy war." Similarly, in a separate treason prosecution in *United States v. Hoxie* (1808), Supreme Court Justice Henry Livingston explained that levying war embodied "a military force, armed and arrayed in a warlike manner, for the purpose of forcibly subverting the government, dismembering the Union, or destroying the legislative functions of congress. These troops should be so armed, and so directed, as to leave no doubt that the United States, or their government, were the immediate object of their attack."

However, one can also see early examples of "constructive" levying of war in the Whiskey Rebellion in 1794 and Fries's Rebellion in 1799. In both instances, there was an armed rebellion and resistance to the application of certain taxation laws. Neither the rebels in the Whiskey Rebellion nor in Fries's Rebellion sought to overthrow the US government; rather, in both instances, those in rebellion sought to make certain taxation laws ineffectual. Thus, United States Supreme Court Justice William Patterson, as the presiding judge in the prosecution of defendants in the Whiskey Rebellion, instructed the jury in *United States v. Mitchell* (1795), that if the intention of the defendants "was to suppress the excise offices, and to prevent the execution of an act of Congress, by force and intimidation," then the act of levying war and treason had occurred. Likewise, Supreme Court Justice Samuel Chase, presiding over the prosecution involving Fries's Rebellion, wrote in the *Case of Fries* (1800) that "any such insurrection or rising to resist or prevent by force or violence, the execution of any statute of the United States … is a levying of war against the United States."

By 1851, US law was evolving to a more restrictive interpretation of levying war than those earlier cases. This evolution can be seen in the prosecution of Caster Hanway, the first defendant tried after the Christiana Revolt. Hanway was prosecuted for failing to follow the Fugitive Slave Act of 1850 and for actively thwarting the enforcement of this law relating to a group of escaped slaves. Supreme Court Justice Robert Grier, charging the jury in *United States v. Hanway* (1851), indicated that many of the English cases relied on as precedent by American judges in the criminal prosecutions stemming from Whiskey Rebellion and Fries's Rebellion "have since been discredited, if not overruled in that country." Justice Grier went on to explain that "levying war" ought to be "confined to insurrections and rebellions for the purpose of overthrowing the government by force and arms."

The restrictive view on what constitutes levying war was reaffirmed on the state level in 1922 in the most recent case to discuss the concept of levying war. *State of West Virginia v. William Blizzard* involved the prosecution of a group of men who had led thousands of fellow coal miners in the attempt to end martial law and to release a group of miners who were being held in custody. The defendant in this case was involved in the Battle of Blair Mountain (see West Virginia Coal Wars). The presiding West Virginia state judge explained that levying war should be confined to those instances where there is a specific "design against the sovereignty of the State" and that there was the plan "by force and violence to commit some act or some acts, which, if successful, will subvert the Government in whole or in part."

Finally, the crime of treason by levying war cannot be committed unless there is an application or use of force and with the imminent ability to effectuate the use of that force. Additionally, levying war cannot occur without accomplices. As Chief Justice Marshall explained in the Aaron Burr treason prosecution, "[w]ar can only be levied by the employment of actual force. Troops must be embodied, men must be assembled, in order to levy war" and there must be "a warlike assemblage, carrying the appearance of force, and in a situation to practice hostility."

See Also: Burr, Aaron; *Burr, United States v.* (1807); Christiana Revolt (1851); English Treason Statute of 1351; Fries's Rebellion (1799); *Hanway, United States v.* (1851); *Hoxie, United States v.* (1808); Insurrection; Martial Law; *Mitchell, United States v.* (1795); Treason; West Virginia Coal Wars; Whiskey Rebellion

Resources

Larson, Carlton F. W. 2006. "The Forgotten Constitutional Law of Treason and the Enemy Combatant Problem." *University of Pennsylvania Law Review* 154: 863–926.

Larson, Carlton F. W. 2020. *On Treason: A Citizen's Guide to the Law*. New York: Ecco, an imprint of HarperCollins (Kindle Edition).

Lincoln Assassination (1865)

The most infamous example of the crime of assassination in the United States and an attack that also constituted a crime against the state was the murder of President Abraham Lincoln on April 14, 1865. While three American presidents (James Garfield, William McKinley, and John F. Kennedy) were assassinated in the years since the killing of Abraham Lincoln, only the McKinley assassination mirrored the Lincoln assassination in that it was also motivated to harm the country and government as a whole. For the purposes of this book, an assassination or attempted assassination plot is not considered a crime against the state if the perpetrator attempts the assassination for wholly personal reasons independent of a desire to harm the government or nation as a whole. For example, Lynette "Squeaky" Fromme, who was associated with the Manson Family, a cult led by Charles Manson, attempted to assassinate President Gerald Ford in 1975; however, Fromme's actions were driven by her desire to impress Manson, not to harm the nation or government. Although clearly a violation of federal law and subject to prosecution and conviction, Fromme's crime was not a crime against the state.

The Lincoln assassination plot was particularly notable for several reasons. First, never in the history of the United States did a group of conspirators come as close to executing multiple leaders in the upper echelon of the federal government. While Abraham Lincoln was the prime target of the conspiracy and the only immediate targeted fatality, other prominent federal leaders were targeted as well, a fact reflected in the indictments of the conspirators to the crime. While each indictment varied slightly in language (based upon each person's participation), the indictments generally provided that the defendants "maliciously, unlawfully and traitorously in aid of the existing rebellion ... combining, confederating and conspiring together to kill and murder Abraham Lincoln, the late President; Andrew Johnson, Vice President; William H. Seward, Secretary of State; Ulysses S. Grant, then in command of the Army of the United States." While John Wilkes Booth was able to assassinate Abraham Lincoln, if the rest of the conspiracy had succeeded, the conspiracy plot would have decapitated the federal government. Second, the killing of Abraham Lincoln was the first time in US history wherein a president of the United States was the victim of assassination, a crime many in the United States previously thought unfathomable. Reflecting this naivete that the American experience was insulated from such a base and vile crime against the state, William Seward wrote as late as 1862 that political murders were alien to the American experience, and that "Assassination is not an American practice or habit, and one so vicious and desperate cannot be engrafted into our political system. This conviction of mine has steadily gained strength since the civil war began. Every day's experience confirms it" (Swanson 2007, 99).

Ironically, many scholars have argued that the plan to assassinate Lincoln and other top Northern leaders had its genesis in 1864 in a northern military operation against the Confederate government. The Kilpatrick-Dahlgren raid (February–March 1864) was a plot concocted by Union Brigadier General Judson Kilpatrick to attack the lightly guarded Confederate capitol, free Union prisoners of war being held in Richmond, set fire to Richmond, and kill Confederate President Jefferson Davis and his cabinet. When the attack was thwarted by the Confederates and Colonel Ulric Dahlgren was killed, Confederates found on Dahlgren's body detailed plans to burn the city and assassinate Jefferson Davis and his cabinet. It is not clear how widely known this plot was, and scholars still argue whether Secretary of War Edwin Stanton or President Abraham Lincoln himself approved or had knowledge of the details. What is clear, however, is that the discovered Dahlgren papers enraged the

South, and southern leaders began considering and planning attacks against the North and Abraham Lincoln in retaliation.

Immediately after the papers' discovery, Confederate Robert E. Lee asked that they be published in various newspapers throughout the South, so that "our people & the world may know the character of the war our enemies wage against us, & the unchristian & atrocious acts they plot & perpetrate" (Hanchett 1991, 70). After the Lincoln assassination, in trying to explain some seemingly delusional statements made by Jefferson Davis in the last few days of the war in claiming that the South could still win when it was clearly decimated, former Confederate Vice President Alexander Stephens speculated that Davis "might have been relying on something I and world generally knew nothing about" and that perhaps Davis was referring to Confederate Secret Service plans then afoot in Canada which might bring about "either the uprising of the people of the North or the abduction of the heads of their government" (Hanchett 1991, 71). On May 2, 1865, United States President Andrew Johnson issued a proclamation declaring the assassination plot had been "incited, concerted, and procured" by Confederate political leaders and the Confederate Secret Service in Canada (Hanchett 1991, 28). The historical record makes clear that Jefferson Davis transferred a million dollars to Confederate Secret Service agents in Canada to engage in "black flag" operations. Many members of the Lincoln assassination plot communicated frequently with the Confederate operatives in Canada, and some, including Booth, visited those agents in Canada. Furthermore, several members of the Confederate Secret Service (e.g., Confederate General Bradley T. Johnson and Confederate spy Thomas N. Conrad) wrote later accounts admitting to having the approval and cooperation of the Confederate government in Richmond. As historian William Hanchett has speculated, "If Davis, like Lee and others believed Lincoln had contemplated Davis's capture or death, why should Davis not have contemplated Lincoln's?" (Hanchett 1991, 70). And while there is convincing evidence that the Confederate Secret Service communicated and coordinated with Booth and his accomplices to kidnap Lincoln in 1864–5, the true connection and complicity of the Confederate Government in the Lincoln assassination will never be known, absent the discovery of some long misplaced and forgotten historical document pointing to such involvement.

In 1864, John Wilkes Booth and a group of men at first planned to kidnap President Lincoln and hold him hostage for the release of Union prisoners of war; this plan appeared to have the support of the Confederate Secret Service. Virtually all of Booth's subsequent co-conspirators in the assassination were involved in the planning and near kidnapping of Lincoln in 1864. Claims made by some of Booth's assassination conspirators (e.g., Mary Surratt, Samuel Mudd, etc.) that they did not know Booth (or knew him only in passing) seem disingenuous in retrospect when these individuals were involved in meetings with Booth about the kidnapping plans a year before the assassination took place. George Atzerodt (a co-conspirator in the Lincoln assassination), shortly before his execution in July 1865, told Union authorities that there was another Confederate plan to blow up the White House (and its occupants) in the early months in 1865.

After the Army of Northern Virginia surrendered at Appomattox on April 9, 1865, there were massive celebrations in the North. After four long years of war, Lincoln decided to spend a relaxing night watching a play at Ford's Theatre. On the morning of the assassination, April 14, 1865, Booth, who was still despondent over the defeat of the Confederacy, learned that he had his long-awaited chance to kill the president at Ford's Theatre that evening. Quickly communicating with his co-conspirators, Booth laid out his plans to assassinate President Lincoln, Vice President Andrew Johnson, and Secretary of State William Seward. Booth had hoped to kill Ulysses Grant as well, but Grant left Washington, DC, earlier in the day. Booth assigned himself to kill Lincoln, assigned the hulking Lewis Powell (aka Lewis Paine) to attack William Seward, and tasked George Atzerodt with killing Vice President Johnson. None but Booth's assassination of Lincoln was successful. Atzerodt got cold feet sitting in a tavern, never bothered to even approach Johnson, and left Washington, DC, in the hopes of distancing himself from the conspiracy (and the arrest that was sure to come). Powell invaded Seward's home and stabbed him numerous times with a knife, but Seward miraculously survived the attack.

Only Booth succeeded in his dastardly deed. At Ford's Theatre (a place Booth knew intimately because of his time as an actor performing in the building), Booth made his way to the private box in which Lincoln and his wife, Mary Todd Lincoln, were watching the play with two guests. Lincoln's box was unguarded, and Booth effortlessly entered the private box, placed a.44 caliber revolver to the back left side of Lincoln's head, and pulled the trigger. The round entered the skull and lodged behind Lincoln's right eye. After being taken to the Peterson boarding house across the street from Ford's Theatre, Lincoln finally succumbed to his injuries and died on the morning of April 15, 1865, at 7:22 a.m.

What followed was one of the largest manhunts in American history. Authorities caught up to Booth in a dilapidated barn in Virginia on April 26, 1865, where he was shot and killed by a US soldier. His death at the hands of a Union soldier, despite an order by Secretary of War Stanton to take Booth alive, prevented the government from interrogating Booth and deprived the country and posterity from ever definitively knowing whether the Confederate government and leadership was complicit in the plot to assassinate Lincoln.

Eight of Booth's co-conspirators and accomplices were tracked down and arrested for Lincoln's murder. These individuals included David Harrod, Lewis Powell, George Atzerodt, Mary Surratt, Samuel Mudd, Michael O'Laughlen, Samuel Arnold, and Edman Spangler. Many of these individuals were intimately involved in the earlier planning and at least one thwarted attempt to kidnap Lincoln. Several planning sessions took place at Mary Surratt's boarding house in Washington, DC.

Some apologists for conspirators like Mary Surratt and Samuel Mudd argue that the murder/assassination charges are unsupported or incorrect because these people were only tangentially involved with the main perpetrators of the assassination. But those critics have not considered the common law English Doctrine that was explicitly referenced and used in criminal cases in that period, namely the common law doctrine of Accomplice Liability. Accomplice Liability is a common law rule/doctrine that specifies that if you have knowledge of a criminal enterprise and take steps in furtherance of that enterprise (even minor steps in assistance—such as providing weapons, facilitating an escape route, etc.), it is as if you committed the crime yourself. If you load a weapon and hand it to an accomplice, who aims, fires, and kills another, you have aided and abetted the killing of another. During common law, and indeed today, there is no "aiding and abetting murder," just "murder." If one has knowledge of the criminal enterprise and commits acts in furtherance of that enterprise, no matter whether he or she was present on the spot or a mile off, the party is equally guilty of the underlying offense. Mary Surratt allowed the use of her boarding house for meetings with conspirators, and the day before the assassination, she dropped off weapons and field glasses to be picked up by Booth at the Surrattsville tavern immediately after the assassination occurred and Booth was making his escape from Washington, DC. Samuel Mudd was intimately involved in earlier kidnapping schemes involving Lincoln and introduced John Wilkes Booth to several confederate operatives, including John Surratt, Jr., in 1864. He also procured a horse for Booth and introduced Booth to confederate sympathizers who would help Booth make his escape.

Of the surviving co-conspirators, Lewis Powell, George Atzerodt, David Herold, and Mary Surratt were hanged at the gallows, on the present location of Fort McNair, on July 7, 1865, shortly before 1:00 p.m. Samuel Mudd, David Herod, Michael O'Laughlen, Samuel Arnold, and Edman

Spangler received lesser sentences. The most lenient sentence was for Edman Spangler, whose sole participation in the event was procuring someone to hold John Wilkes Booth's horse when Booth was inside Ford's Theatre committing his act of assassination. One Northern newspaper captured the mood of the entire country immediately after the execution of the four co-conspirators on July 7, 1865, when it proclaimed that "we wish to hear their names no more … and to be permitted to think of our dead president only as a great and good man and patriot gone to his rest, without associating his name with the names of the wretches who have paid the penalty of their crimes with their worthless lives" ("The Last Act of the Tragedy" 1865, 274). The Lincoln assassination altered the course of the nation for decades to come, illustrating the devastating impact a crime against the state can have not only on citizens at the time the crime occurs, but for future generations of Americans as well.

See Also: Assassination; Booth, John Wilkes; Conspiracy, Criminal; McKinley Assassination (1901); Surratt, Mary

Resources

Hanchett, William. 1986. *The Lincoln Murder Conspiracies*. Urban: University of Illinois Press.

Hanchett, William. 1991. "Who Helped Booth Murder Lincoln? An Expert Raises Questions." *Civil War Times Illustrated* (November): 28–35, 70–1.

Leonard, Elizabeth D. 2004. *Lincoln's Avengers: Justice, Revenge, and Reunion after the Civil War*. New York: W.W. Norton & Company.

Lewis, Lloyd. 1929. *The Assassination of Lincoln: History and Myth*. New York: Harcourt Brace.

Swanson, James L. 2007. *Manhunt: The 12-Day Chase for Lincoln's Killer*. New York: Harper Perennial.

"The Last Act of the Tragedy." *The Frank Leslie's Illustrated Newspaper* 20, no. 510 (July 22, 1865): 274.

Lindh, John Walker (1981–)

Dubbed the "American Taliban," John Walker Lindh gained instant notoriety in December 2001 when his capture and subsequent questioning was broadcast on CNN (Cable News Network). After the September 11, 2001, attacks, and in the newly launched War on Terror, Lindh was the first American captured abroad who was accused of being affiliated with, and fighting for, Al-Qaeda. Lindh's capture, questioning, and subsequent indictment in United States District Court for the Eastern District of Virginia were widely covered in the media. The media depictions of Lindh ranged from Lindh being a terrorist and a traitor to just being a misinformed and misguided American youth who was in the wrong place at the wrong time. Many argued that Lindh should be charged with treason against the United States. Ultimately, Lindh pleaded guilty to two counts (supplying services to the Taliban and carrying an explosive device during the commission of a felony) as part of plea deal.

Lindh lived the first ten years of his life in a Washington, DC, suburb, and then subsequently moved with his parents and siblings to an affluent community outside of San Francisco, California. As a twelve-year-old, Lindh reportedly gained a keen interest in Islam after watching the 1992 Spike Lee film *Malcolm X*. By age sixteen, in 1997, Lindh converted to Islam. During this period, he reportedly participated in online chatroom conversations under the assumed name "Brother Mujahid" and called himself Suleyman al Faris. By age seventeen, he obtained his parents' permission to travel to Yemen to study Arabic but stayed in Yemen less than a year and returned to the United States in 1999. After staying in the United States for eight months, he traveled back to Yemen and then to Pakistan, where he began training with a jihadist group with ties to the Taliban and Al-Qaeda. Lindh then traveled to Afghanistan to fight with the Taliban, and in May 2001, spent six weeks training at the Al-Qaeda Al Forouq training camp, where he met with Osama bin Laden on at least one occasion.

From September to November 2001, Lindh fought with the Taliban in Afghanistan against the Northern Alliance (NA). The NA, acting with the support and assistance of the United States, was a loose coalition of forces in northern Afghanistan that forcibly resisted Taliban rule through a series of armed engagements. On November 24, 2001, the Taliban forces with whom Lindh was fighting surrendered to the NA and were detained by the NA at the nineteenth-century Qala-i-Jangi fortress. On December 10, 2001, Lindh and others were brought outside to a courtyard to be questioned by United States Central Intelligence officers Johnny Michael "Mike" Spann and Dave Tyson. In an interaction recorded on video, Lindh can be seen being asked several questions by Spann and Tyson. In this interaction, Lindh stayed silent and did not speak; minutes later, a violent prisoner uprising occurred, resulting in the death of Michael Spann and numerous other NA members. The death of Spann would be the first known US fatality in the War on Terror in Afghanistan. After several days of fighting, Lindh was captured and transferred to US custody and then held at Camp Rhino, Afghanistan. After capture, Lindh made multiple statements, some captured on video by a CNN reporter. According to Attorney General John Ashcroft, Lindh chose to waive his right to an attorney both orally and in writing to the FBI (Federal Bureau of Investigation), was given *Miranda* warnings, and then made multiple statements about his involvement with the Taliban.

In January 2002, Lindh was transported back to the United States to face criminal charges in federal court. Lindh was indicted and charged with ten counts, offenses ranging from conspiracy to kill US nationals overseas to providing material support and resources to a US-designated terrorist group. While Lindh initially submitted a not-guilty plea, a plea bargain was offered wherein Lindh would plead guilty to two offenses, and the federal government would drop the remaining eight charges. Lindh pleaded guilty to the offense of supplying services to the Taliban and carrying an explosive device (two grenades) during the commission of a felony. Lindh was sentenced to twenty years, ten years for each of the two counts, to be served consecutively. As part of the plea deal Lindh waived all claims against the United States stemming from his time in custody before trial. Lindh was released in May 2019, serving seventeen years of twenty-year sentence.

See Also: Conspiracy, Criminal; Material Support Crimes; September 11, 2001; Terrorism; Treason

Resources

de Luce, Dan, Robbie Gramer, and Jana Winter. 2017. "John Walker Lindh, Detainee No. 001 in the Global War on Terror, Will Go Free in Two Years. What Then?" *Foreign Policy*, June 23, 2017.
Lipton, Adam. 2007. "John Walker Lindh's Buyer's Remorse." *New York Times*, April 23, 2007.
Pelton, Robert Young. 2006. "The Truth about John Walker Lindh." February 2006. Accessed May 22, 2022. https://web.archive.org/web/20060325105219/http://www.honormikespann.org/pdfs/pelton_feb2006.pdf.
Roche, Timothy, Brian Bennett, Hilary Berryman, Hilary Ayton, Siobhan Morrissey, and Amang Radwan. 2002. "The Making of John Walker Lindh." *Time*, October 2, 2002.

Luther v. Borden (1849)

In 1841, a large group of Rhode Islanders held a convention, drafted a new state constitution, and elected a new state legislature and governor, Thomas W. Dorr. The pre-existing charter government, which had been established in 1663 by Charles the Second, opposed the purported new government, declared martial law, and quelled the rebellion (see Dorr's Rebellion).

One of the insurgents, Martin Luther, later brought a civil suit against several members of the state charter's military forces, including Luther Borden, who had entered his dwelling and arrested him during the rebellion. Borden and the other defendants justified their actions on the state charter government's purpose of putting down an attempted coup by military force, arguing that the rebels were levying war upon the state. Martin Luther claimed the charter government had been displaced by the new constitution, and thus lacked authority.

In *Luther v. Borden*, the United States Supreme Court decided two issues. First, it concluded that whether the charter government or the Dorr government was legitimate was not a decision for the federal courts but rather for the political branches of the federal and state governments. Under the Guarantee Clause of the United States Constitution, the United States is required to guarantee to each State a republican form of government. Luther argued that the charter government in Rhode Island was not a republican government, and therefore its actions were void. But the Supreme Court determined that Congress, not the federal courts, must necessarily decide whether a government established in a state constitutes a republican form of government, and because Congress had neither repudiated the charter government nor embraced the Dorr government, the court had no authority to decide otherwise.

The United States Supreme Court also addressed whether the defendants were justified in entering Luther's house. The Court held that, though a military government established as the permanent government of the State would not be a republican government, martial law had been established in Rhode Island only to meet the peril in which the existing (charter) government was placed by the "armed resistance to its authority." The Court further held that "unquestionably a State may use its military power to put down an armed insurrection too strong to be controlled by the civil authority. The power is essential to the existence of every government, essential to the preservation of order and free institutions, and is as necessary to the States of this Union as to any other government." Holding that Rhode Island was in a state of war, the Supreme Court found the defendants had reasonable grounds to act as they had.

Luther v. Borden provides strong support for the idea that state governments determine for themselves what is the lawful government, subject to the national government's constitutional responsibility to guarantee to all states a republican form of government. The unwillingness of the federal judiciary to intervene in such matters eroded some in the intervening decades, especially after the American Civil War and the Fourteenth Amendment, which established additional federal authority. The opinion in *Luther v. Borden* also provides strong support for the right of individual states to suppress rebellion, including through martial law. Again, however, in the century following this decision, the United States Supreme Court retreated from its unqualified stance in *Luther v. Borden* that a decision by a state to engage in martial law is not reviewable by the courts, engaging repeatedly in such reviews in martial law cases arising from Texas, Oklahoma, and elsewhere.

See Also: Dorr's Rebellion (1841–42); Insurrection; Levying War; Martial Law; Rebellion

Resources

Luther v. Borden, 48 U.S. 1 (1849).

Merriam, Eric. 2022. "Necessary Necessity: Courts' Historical Assessment of the Condition Precedent for Martial Law." *Oklahoma Law Review* 75: 199–202.

M

Manning, Chelsea/Bradley

See Leaks of National Defense Information

Martial Law

Martial law is relevant to consideration of crimes against the state in two ways. First, martial law is a potential *response* to significant crimes against the state. Second, imposition of martial law could theoretically *be* a crime against the state committed by the executive imposing it.

As the Supreme Court observed in *Duncan v. Kahanamoku* (1946), "the term 'martial law' carries no precise meaning. The Constitution does not refer to 'martial law' at all and no Act of Congress has defined the term. It has been employed in various ways by different people and at different times." Though the term "martial law" has not been conclusively defined, it generally refers to use of the military to carry out some or all functions of civil government by displacing, replacing, or subordinating civil government, its laws, and its functions, rather than merely *assisting* civil government. Thus, martial law involves using the military outside the existing legal framework.

In 2005, in a now-defunct Department of Defense (DOD) regulation (32 Code of Federal Regulations Section 501.4), the DOD provided the following guidance which may still illuminate contemporary thinking on the subject:

> Martial law depends for its justification upon public necessity; necessity gives rise to it creation; necessity justifies it exercise; and necessity limits its duration. The extent of the military force used, and the actual measures taken, consequently, will depend upon the actual threat to order and public safety which exists at the time. In most instances, the decision to impose martial law is made by the President … However, the decision to impose martial law may be made by the local commander on the spot if the circumstances demand immediate action, and time and available communications facilities do not permit obtaining prior approval from a higher authority.

While no longer in force, this DOD regulation illustrates how martial law might be viewed within the military, both in 2005 and today.

It is important to note that using the military to augment or aid civil government, rather than replace or subordinate it, is not martial law and, assuming prescribed procedures are followed, is typically legal. For instance, the Insurrection Act and equivalent state laws authorize commanders in chief to employ the military to quell insurrections and other violent disorders within specified legal boundaries.

Scholars and jurists debate whether martial law can ever be lawful or consistent with the rule of law. Those who argue that there are instances where martial law *can* be considered lawful generally agree that the condition precedent for lawful martial law is *necessity*. That is, the extreme option of imposing martial law can only be acceptable when it is necessary because no other solution can adequately address the situation. Such circumstances have typically involved violence on a scale that overwhelms civilian law enforcement and other government functions such as the court system. In his concurring opinion in *Youngstown Sheet & Tube Co. v. Sawyer* (1952), Justice Robert Jackson remarked that the Framers made no express provision for exercise of extraordinary authority because of a crisis, except "as in a very limited category by itself, the establishment of martial law."

Though there have been no instances of a president or governor imposing martial law in over half a century, martial law was more common during earlier periods of US history. In one of the earliest instances, Rhode Island was subjected to martial law in response to the establishment of a rival state government during the Dorr Rebellion. In *Luther v. Borden* (1849), the United States Supreme Court upheld the imposition of martial law and did so in expansive terms that suggested broad discretion on the part of government, especially executives, to determine the propriety of imposing martial law. In the late 1800s and early 1900s, governors in several states availed themselves of this discretion to impose martial law to address violence and uprisings related to labor disputes.

During the most significant of the labor uprisings leading to martial law, the West Virginia Coal Wars, the West Virginia Supreme Court upheld the governor's decision to impose martial law, finding that the level of violence amounted to *war*. A lone dissenting Justice argued that violence between strikers and mine owners could never amount to war because the government was not the target of the violence. Nevertheless, most courts have considered insurrection or rebellion to be a sufficient justification for imposing martial law, though not all have agreed what facts constitute an insurrection or rebellion.

What no court has considered a sufficient justification for martial law is an executive's dissatisfaction with another government entity's actions. Perhaps surprisingly, more than one executive has attempted to implement martial law due to his dissatisfaction with the actions of another government official or agency. For example, when in 1931 the Texas governor was dissatisfied with decisions of the Texas Railway Commission regarding oil and gas production in the state and federal district court decisions on the same topic, he imposed martial law to override those government entities' actions. The United States Supreme Court struck down this use of martial law in *Sterling v. Constantin* (1932). A few years later, the governor of Oklahoma imposed martial law when the Oklahoma City Council refused to institute a racially segregated zoning ordinance. The state supreme court rendered the governor's action unlawful. In what may be the most shocking use of martial law to attempt to override the actions of other government entities, in 1939, the governor of Georgia imposed martial law in his attempt to replace a lawfully appointed chairman of the State Highway Board failed. The governor used martial law to subvert Georgia law regarding appointments to the State Highway Board, to attempt to defeat the appointed chairman's decision not to leave his appointment, and, most brazenly, to "obstruct and prevent the execution of the judgments" of the state court regarding the issue. Unsurprisingly, the federal district court addressing this matter struck down the governor's attempted usurpation of multiple government units through martial law. Following the 2020 presidential election, several senior advisors to President Donald Trump recommended he declare martial law and seize voting machines to implement recounts or revotes in states that had voted for Trump's opponent, Joe Biden. Had Trump followed this suggestion, such a declaration of martial law may itself have constituted an unlawful insurrection. To date, no chief executive has faced criminal sanction for an imposition of martial law later determined to be unjustified or unlawful, but an attempted use of martial law to usurp a government function or constitutional process in such a way could constitute sedition or insurrection.

See Also: Insurrection Act; Dorr's Rebellion (1841–42); Insurrection; *Luther v. Borden* (1849); Rebellion; West Virginia Coal Wars

Resources

Merriam, Eric. 2023. "Necessary Necessity: Courts' Historical Assessment of the Condition Precedent for Martial Law." *Oklahoma Law Review* 75: 191.

Merriam, Eric, and Douglas B. McKechnie. 2021. *National Security Law*. St. Paul: West Academic.

Nunn, Joseph. 2020. "Martial Law in the United States: Its Meaning, Its History, and Why the President Can't Declare It." *Brennan Center for Justice*, August 20, 2020. Accessed June 15, 2023. https://www.brennancenter.org/our-work/research-reports/martial-law-united-states-its-meaning-its-history-and-why-president-cant.

Material Support Crimes

After the World Trade Center Bombing of 1993, Congress enacted the first material support statute making it a crime to "provide material support or resources" to another "knowing or intending that they are to be used in preparation for, or in carrying out" specific acts of terrorism. This enactment is located at 18 United States Code Section 2339A. While a powerful statute, some in Congress were concerned that prosecutions under Section 2339A might be difficult because it would be hard to show beyond a reasonable doubt that a defendant specifically knew or intended that the aid or support would be used in a specific terrorist act. Thus, after the 1995 Oklahoma City Bombing, Congress enacted the Anti-Terrorism and Effective Death Penalty Act (1996), which, among other things, amended federal criminal law to include an additional material support statute prohibiting "providing material support or resources to designated foreign terrorist organizations." This second material support crime (providing support or resources to a designated foreign terrorist organization [FTO]) was codified at 18 United States Code Section 2339B. Section 2339B became operational in October 1997, when the United States announced the first twenty-nine designated FTOs. Engaging in fund raising operations in the United States for any designated FTO constitutes a federal criminal offense under Section 2339B. Unlike Section 2339A, Section 2339B only requires a defendant to know that the group for which the material support or aid was intended was a designed FTO or was an organization engaged in terrorism.

Prosecutions were slow in the first few years after enactment of Section 2339B and the Secretary of State's designation of the first FTOs. While several individuals were indicted for violations of Section 2339B, there were no recorded Section 2339B convictions before 2002. This lethargy would end because of September 11, 2001, and Congress's subsequent enactment of the USA PATRIOT Act. One of the many provisions of the Patriot Act allowed for the cross-sharing of intelligence information between US intelligence agencies and domestic law enforcement. When domestic law enforcement began receiving foreign intelligence on terrorism operations (including intelligence on those who might be providing support to designated terrorist groups), federal prosecutions rapidly increased.

The floodgates opened further in the aftermath of the John Walker Lindh prosecution. Federal prosecutors believed a treason indictment against Lindh was problematic because there were no two witnesses who could testify in open court to the same overt acts of treason (a requirement of the United States Constitution). Thus, the prosecutors needed to charge Lindh differently. One charge eventually levied against Lindh was his violation of Section 2339B. More specifically, prosecutors argued that Lindh provided material support to an FTO (Al-Qaeda) by volunteering his own services or, rather, "personnel." This charge was contested by Lindh's defense team, but the United States District Court agreed with the prosecution's argument and ruled that providing one's own body in service to an FTO could constitute providing "personnel" under the meaning of the Section 2339B. The importance of this ruling was explained by one former federal Department of Justice prosecutor who commented that "this might seem like small potatoes, but it was a watershed event for §2339B enforcement and counterterrorism cases, just as much as the PATRIOT Act information-sharing changes" (Breinholt 2016). Now, prosecutors could use 2339B to not only charge individuals who raise funds or financial support for an FTO, but also those individuals who were attempting to provide "personnel" to an FTO through their own physical participation. By this interpretation, "Section 2339B became more than just a white-collar crime. It could be used to incapacitate bomb-throwers as well" (Breinholt 2016). Consequently, "most new terrorism indictments you read about these days include a 'material support' charge" (Breinholt 2016). Congress subsequently amended the definition section of "material support or resources" to indicate that "personnel" under the statute included "one or more person who may be or include oneself."

In the years following, prosecutions spread and soon numbered well over three hundred cases. One early example of such a prosecution involving the fund raising efforts of an individual in the United States for an FTO can be seen in *United States v. Al-Arian* (2005). Prosecutors have used Section 2339B charges to successfully prosecute individuals in sleeper cells in the United States under the argument that those training or attempting to provide one's own services to an FTO constitute offering or providing "personnel." This has enabled the federal government to break up terrorism cells in Pennsylvania (the so-called Lackawanna defendants), Oregon (so-called Portland jihad cell), Florida (so-called Liberty City Six), and Virginia (so-called Virginia jihad network or the Virginia Paintball group), and prosecute the individuals involved in these groups under Section 2339B.

While the statutory punishment for violation of Sections 2339A or 2339B was initially set at up to ten years imprisonment, Congress has amended the statutes to allow for longer punishments. Today, a person convicted for violating Sections 2339A or 2339B, or conspires with another to do so (see Conspiracy, Criminal), "shall be fined under this title or imprisoned not more than 20 years, or both, and, if the death of any person shall be imprisoned for any term of years or for life." In 2004, Congress amended Section 2339B to allow for "extraterritorial jurisdiction" (18 United States Code §2339B(d)), which means that person can be successfully prosecuted in the United States for this offense even though the underlying conduct may not have occurred in the United States and the person may not have other connections with the United States. Phrased another way, "prosecutors can now prosecute §2339B defendants who have never set foot in the U.S. before their arrest and extradition" (Breinholt 2016). Finally, the United States Supreme Court rejected claims of the unconstitutionality of Section 2339B. More specifically, in *Holder v. Humanitarian Law Project* (2010), the Supreme Court ruled that Section 2339B was not insufficiently vague as it related to terms such as "expert advice," "training," "service," and "personnel," and that the statute did not violate a person's freedom of speech or associational rights under the First Amendment. The Court opined that the government has a compelling interest—national security and preventing the country from terrorism—in preventing support to foreign terrorist groups, and thus the content-based restriction on speech satisfied strict scrutiny. The Court further determined that the law did not prohibit "mere association," which could violate the First Amendment, but prohibited material support, which was more than simple association.

See Also: *Al Arian, United States v.*; Anti-Terrorism and Effective Death Penalty Act (1996); Conspiracy, Criminal; Lindh, John Walker; Oklahoma City Bombing (1995); September 11, 2001; Speech as Crime against the State; Terrorism; Treason; USA PATRIOT Act; World Trade Center Bombing of 1993

Resources

18 United States Code Sections 2339A (Providing Material Support to Terrorists) and 2339B (Providing Material Support or Resources to Designated Foreign Terrorist Organizations).

Breinholt, Jeff. 2016. "Material Support: An Indispensable Counterterrorism Tool Turns 20." *War on the Rocks: Texas National Security Review*. Accessed April 29, 2023. https://warontherocks.com/2016/04/material-support-an-indispensable-counterterrorism-tool-turns-20/.

Doyle, Charles. 2016. "Terrorist Material Support: An Overview of 18 U.S.C. §2339A and §2339B." *Congressional Research Service*. 7-5700, Report R41333. Accessed April 29, 2023. https://crsreports.congress.gov/product/pdf/R/R41333.

Rufener, P. Scott. 2010. "Prosecuting the Material Support of Terrorism: Federal Courts, Military Commissions, or Both?" *University of Massachusetts Law Review* 5, no. 1 (January): 151–87.

McKinley Assassination (1901)

While any assassination of a sitting government official can constitute a crime against the state, not all are intended to harm the state itself. For instance, the attempted assassination of President Ronald Reagan was the product of a deranged man intending to impress a celebrity actress whom he did not know. The assassination of President William McKinley, however, was intended as a political statement by an avowed anarchist, Leon Czolgosz, and had significant consequences for the anarchy movement and law attempting to protect against anarchy.

Czolgosz embraced anarchism after losing his job in a labor dispute in 1893. He had several encounters with famed anarchist Emma Goldman, who did not advocate violence, but whose words favoring anarchism had a great influence on Czolgosz. In September 1901 when President McKinley visited Buffalo, New York, where Czolgosz was living at the time, Czolgosz decided he should assassinate McKinley. As Czolgosz later told police, "It was in my heart, there was no escape for me. I could not have conquered it had my life been at stake. There were thousands of people in town on Tuesday. I heard it was President's Day. All those people seemed bowing to the great ruler. I made up my mind to kill that ruler." On September 6, 1901, Czolgosz shot McKinley while he was attending the Pan-American Exposition in Buffalo. Though it initially appeared to doctors that McKinley might survive the shooting, he succumbed on September 14, 1901. Czolgosz was quickly tried, convicted, and executed.

Some have speculated that Czolgosz's assassination of McKinley had more to do with mental infirmity than anarchism. Whatever Czolgosz's mental state and intent, the successful assassination was viewed by the public as a prime example of the threat posed by anarchism and anarchists, whom the public believed regarded assassination and violence as a legitimate means to destroy government and authority. Around the country, numerous anarchists, including Emma Goldman, were subsequently arrested and charged with having conspired to assassinate President McKinley. When police could produce no evidence of such a conspiracy, the anarchists were released. But the assassination turned anarchism and anarchists—even those who were merely ideological or philosophical anarchists, with no record of advocating for violence to achieve anarchical aims—into the target of widespread American fear and disapprobation.

Theodore Roosevelt, who became president because of McKinley's death, argued in his first message to Congress as president that "we should war with relentless efficiency not only against anarchists, but against all active and passive sympathizers with anarchists," whom Roosevelt described as a "body of criminal who object to all governments, good and bad alike." He argued that all apologists for anarchism were "morally accessory to murder before the fact."

Congress was inundated by legislative proposals related to the assassination and anarchy. Some proposed new penalties for assassinations and attempts and conferred jurisdiction on federal courts for the same. Though the House of Representatives and Senate were unable to agree on many of the proposals, one thing upon which they could agree was to stop the flow of anarchist immigrants from entering the country. Congress passed a bill preventing immigrants who were opposed to organized government, or associated with organizations teaching such views, from entering or remaining in the United States or become US citizens. This bill would eventually be upheld as constitutional by the United States Supreme Court in *United States ex rel Turner v. Williams*, despite a vigorous argument by famed attorney Clarence Darrow that excluding persons from the country because of their views alone violated principles of free speech and due process. Writing for the majority, Chief Justice Melville Fuller noted that in passing the law, "Congress was of opinion that the tendency of the general exploitation of such views is so dangerous to the public weal that aliens who hold and advocate them would be undesirable additions to our population."

In addition to federal law, McKinley's assassination inspired some states to pass criminal anarchy statutes. These statutes banned not only acts, but mere advocacy of overthrow of the government. The first of these statutes, New York's criminal anarchy statute, was passed within months of McKinley's assassination and later upheld as constitutional in *Gitlow v. New York* (1925). Some state criminal syndicalism statutes also trace their origins to post-McKinley assassination furor. During the First Red Scare in the years following the Bolshevik Revolution in Russia, worries over anarchism, and laws used to address it inspired by McKinley's assassination, would be transferred to the even greater fear of communism.

See Also: Anarchy, Criminal; Assassination; Criminal Syndicalism; First Red Scare and the Palmer Raids (1919–20); *Gitlow v. New York* (1925)

Resources

Fine, Sidney. 1955. "Anarchism and the Assassination of McKinley." *American Historical Review* 60 (July), 777–99.

Miller, Scott. 2011. *The President and the Assassin*. New York: Random House.

McVeigh, Timothy

See Oklahoma City Bombing

Militia Act of 1792

See Insurrection Act

Militia Movement (Modern)

The modern militia movement refers to a collection of discrete extremist groups that, though not centrally organized, have some ideological similarities. Most such groups oppose government power generally (and especially federal government power), engage in paramilitary training and activities, strongly support unlimited gun rights, are premised on one or more conspiracy theories, believe they are defending what they believe to be a historically correct understanding of the United States Constitution, and are generally united by a desire to preserve or protect supposed traditional American values. Most groups regularly engage in "field training exercises," wear military-style uniforms, and employ loose military-like hierarchical rank structures. There are some significant differences among groups, too. For instance, some are associated with white supremacy, while others oppose racism. Some are strongly opposed to law enforcement, while others view themselves as law enforcement partners when those agencies are perceived to be protecting shared values, such as Customs and Border Patrol (CBP) officers controlling immigration or police cracking down on protests by perceived left-wing demonstrators.

Though a small number of modern militia groups date back to the 1950s, the modern militia movement primarily traces its roots to the reaction to incidents in the early 1990s at Ruby Ridge and Waco, in which federal law enforcement power was perceived to encroach on individual liberties, and at a time when significant federal gun control legislation, including the assault weapons ban, was in force. However, after it was revealed that the 1995 Oklahoma City Bombing was perpetrated by Timothy McVeigh and Terry Nichols, both of whom had been previously associated with the "Michigan Militia," militia groups receded from the public eye and decreased significantly in number. The Southern Poverty Law Center estimated that there were nearly 400 militia groups in the United States in 1996, but that number dwindled to fewer than seventy by 1999. The modern militia movement was reenergized by the 2008 election of President Barack Obama, when the number of militia groups in the United States nearly tripled in one year. This can be attributed to several factors, including militia groups' concerns over Democratic Party policies on gun control and immigration, white supremacist militia members' reaction to the election of the nation's first Black president, and the emergence of a popular right-wing mainstream political movement (embodied by the "Tea Party") that publicly articulated many of militias' tenets, providing legitimacy to those views.

As of 2023, several hundred militia groups existed throughout the United States, some intertwined with the Sovereign Citizens Movement. A few large nationwide militia organizations were prominent, including the Oath Keepers, Proud Boys, and Three Percenters, each of which participated in the Capitol Insurrection on January 6, 2021, leaders of which have been convicted of seditious conspiracy.

However, most militia organizations are small and local in orientation, and even the nationwide organizations are comprised of local chapters that are not completely unified.

Some have criticized the use of the term "militia" to describe groups of the modern militia movement, noting that legitimate militias have a long-standing and important role in the United States and referring to non-sanctioned military-like groups by the same term legitimizes them and risks confusion. Indeed, legitimate militias were an important part of the American Revolution and references to militia appear in multiple places in the Constitution. And early presidents used militias to suppress insurrectionist movements such as the Whiskey Rebellion and Fries's Rebellion. The Militia Act of 1903 formally organized militias under state control into what are today known as state Army National Guard and Air National Guard units. By contrast, militias in the modern militia movement are not state-sanctioned or recognized by the government, and indeed many engage in illegal activities. Opponents of the term militia suggest some groups are more accurately labeled insurrectionists or domestic terrorist organizations.

Militia groups have engaged in overtly illegal activities involving violence, use of force, or illegal confrontation with government forces. For example, militia groups resisted federal law enforcement in the Bundy Standoffs. A small militia group known as the Wolverine Watchmen plotted to kidnap Michigan Governor Gretchen Whitmer. Other instances not detailed in this book include an apparent plot to kidnap the governor of Virginia, a plot to bomb a mosque, and the illegal detention of immigrants by a militia group purporting to be "assisting" CBP with border patrol activities. Beyond these illegal acts, the very existence of paramilitary organizations and military training violate many state laws. Dozens of states outlaw paramilitary or private armies, paramilitary training, or both. However, law enforcement and prosecutors have been largely unwilling to prosecute groups that have been perceived to be largely harmless (until they engage in illegal acts) out of concern for violating free speech, associational rights, Second Amendment claims, and fear of provoking violent confrontation or increasing support for militia organizations, as happened following confrontations with law enforcement at Ruby Ridge and Waco. One researcher who studies militias summarized many prosecutors' attitudes, saying "If these militias are just running around the woods with guns, most states don't really care."

See Also: Bundy Standoffs (2014–16); Capitol Insurrection on January 6, 2021; Fries's Rebellion (1799); Insurrection; Oklahoma City Bombing (1995); Ruby Ridge (1992); Seditious Conspiracy; Sovereign Citizens Movement; Terrorism; Waco (1993); Whiskey Rebellion; Wolverine Watchmen

Resources

Doxsee, Catrina. 2021. "Examining Extremism: The Militia Movement." *Center for Strategic & International Studies*, August 12, 2021. Accessed June 15, 2023. https://www.csis.org/blogs/examining-extremism/examining-extremism-militia-movement.

"Militia Movement." *Southern Poverty Law Center*. Accessed June 15, 2023. https://www.splcenter.org/fighting-hate/extremist-files/ideology/militia-movement.

Rathod, Sara. 2016. "Why the Law Turns a Blind Eye to Militias." *Mother Jones*, October 25, 2016. Accessed June 15, 2023. https://www.motherjones.com/politics/2016/10/paramilitary-militia-laws-training/.

Salehyan, Idean. 2020. "Why We Shouldn't Call Militias, 'Militias.'" *Political Violence at a Glance*, October 19, 2020. Accessed June 15, 2023. https://politicalviolenceataglance.org/2020/10/19/why-we-shouldnt-call-militias-militias/.

Mitchell, United States v. (1795)

United States v. Mitchell was an early federal opinion examining how treason was defined under the brand-new United States Constitution, a document ratified a mere five years before the prosecution of John Mitchell for his conduct during the Whiskey Rebellion. The underlying trials of John Mitchell and Philip Vogel took place in western Pennsylvania (Federal Circuit for Western Pennsylvania) and the case was presided over by Supreme Court Justice William Paterson and a local federal judge. Justice Paterson wrote the court's decision.

The prosecution was one of only two prosecutions for treason stemming from the Whiskey Rebellion. The legal questions before the court were twofold. First, did the suppression of taxation efforts of the government, the prevention of execution of government laws, and compelling a US official to resign his commission under threat of violence constitute levying war against the government and therefore treason under the Constitution? Second, the Treason Clause of the Constitution requires two separate witnesses to testify to an overt act of treason in open court. Was testimony of two witnesses who observed that the defendant "marched as a volunteer with arms and in a military array with a party which actually used force to prevent the execution of an act" sufficient to satisfy this two-witness rule when the defendant was observed at separate locations by each witness?

The most obvious example of "levying war" against the government for treason purposes (and as concisely stated by the court in its ruling) is "exciting internal, or waging external, war against the state." Yet, the court also reluctantly concluded that it was bound by the now obsolete view that levying war included "raising a body of men to obtain, by intimidation or violence, the repeal of a law, or to oppose and prevent by force and terror, the execution of a law, is an act of levying war as well."

This now obsolete view of levying war, known as "constructive" or "interpretative" treason, had its early proponents, including President Thomas Jefferson. However, federal courts began routinely rejecting this view as early as 1808 in *United States v. Hoxie*. By 1851 it was well-settled law that disobeying the law or ignoring government authority did not constitute treason. For example, in *United States v. Hanway* (1851), Supreme Court Justice Grier commented that the term "'levying war' should be confined to insurrections and rebellions for the purpose of overturning the government by force and arms." Even the judges in *United States v. Mitchell* indicated that they were applying the old rule reluctantly. Justice Paterson acknowledged the danger of expansively defining levying war as constituting any governmental disobedience and stated that "constructive, or interpretative treason, must be the dread and scourge of any nation that allows" it in the future. And while the judges "acquiesce[d] in the decision that has already taken place, [they] furnish[ed] a strong caution against too easy admission of future cases." Finally, expressing his displeasure with the application of treason laws in this case, Justice Paterson commented "an attempt to defeat or destroy [the government] must be treason." However, ignoring the laws, or a "flagrant attempt to obstruct the legitimate operations of government, to prevent the execution of its laws … must no longer be regarded as high treason." Then, commenting on the recently convicted co-defendant, Paterson wrote "Vogel, who has been convicted, ought to have been acquitted, and all the prisoners committed upon the same charge, ought to be released. But this doctrine and its consequences will not be found compatible with our constitution and cannot receive the continence of a court of justice."

As to the issue of the "necessity for two witnesses to an overt act of treason," the court stated "it is not the power of judges or juries to dispense" with this rule and the court construed this element broadly in Mitchell's case. The court concluded that "it is not required that every witness should have seen him at the same spot, at the same moment, and in the same act; but if they see him at the place and time of rendezvous, exhibiting the same species of traitorous conduct, the law is satisfied." The conclusion of the court's ruling on the two-witness rule now also represents an outdated view, and the reader should consult the entry on *Cramer v. United States* (1945) for a more up-to-date analysis of this constitutional requirement.

John Mitchell and Philip Vogel were found guilty of treason and sentenced to death by hanging. However, President Washington intervened and pardoned both men in November 1795, believing one to be a mere "simpleton" and the other to be "insane."

See Also: *Cramer v. United States* (1945); *Hanway, United States v.* (1851); *Hoxie, United States v.* (1808); Insurrection; Jefferson, Thomas; Levying War; Rebellion; Treason; Whiskey Rebellion

Resources

Hurst, William. 1945. "Treason in the United States." *Harvard Law Review* 58: 806–47.
United States v. Mitchell, Case No. 15,788, 26 Fed. Cas. 81, 2 Dall. 348 (1795).

Monti, United States v. (1949)

Martin Monti is the only person in US history to plead guilty to the offense of treason. Monti is also the only US military officer convicted of treason in US history. While Benedict Arnold was one of America's highest-ranking traitors (a Major General during the American Revolution), his acts of treason predated the formation of the United States and its Constitution. In 1949, Monti pleaded guilty to twenty-one counts of treason and was sentenced to prison for twenty-five years. Monti was charged with stealing a P-38 plane from the United States Army Air Corps and turning it over to the German government, offering his services to the German military, making several Nazi propagandist broadcasts (including with Axis Sally), serving with a German Waffen-S.S. unit, and aiding in the German war effort between October 1944 and May 1945. Monti's acts of treason were very unusual and "can only be described as bizarre" (Policano 1963, 17).

Monti was a Second Lieutenant in the United States Army Air Corps and was stationed in India (now Pakistan). He stowed away on a military transport plane to North Africa and then made his way to an American airbase in Southern Italy, where he stole a P-38 plane and flew it to Naples, Italy, then occupied by German forces. Upon arriving, he turned the intact plane over to the Germans and immediately requested asylum and disappeared behind enemy lines. He reappeared in Berlin and made several broadcasts with Axis Sally (also known as Mildred Gillars). His on-air alias was Martin Wiethaupt. He then joined the German S.S. and helped drop Nazis propaganda leaflets on ally forces. After V-E Day, Monti turned himself in to American forces still wearing a German Waffen-S.S. uniform. According to the court transcript for the treason charges, it was established that Monti was originally interrogated as a German prisoner of war and did not initially disclose that he had stolen a plane, delivered to the Germans, and then defected. After further questioning, Monti claimed he was wearing the S.S. uniform as a disguise to secure safe passage back to American lines. He also admitted to stealing the airplane but claimed this was only because he was bored and wanted to fight the Germans himself. Apparently initially believing this story, Monti was court-martialed but charged only with the theft of the airplane and being absent without leave. The fifteen-year recommended sentence was rescinded by Presidential Order, and Monti was allowed to reenlist as a private, rising to the level as a non-commissioned officer (rank of Sergeant). Upon Monti's discharge in 1947, he was immediately arrested by the Federal Bureau of Investigation, who had by this time pieced together Monti's actual activities during the waning days of the Second World War.

Monti pleaded guilty in 1949 to twenty-one counts of treason and received a twenty-five-year sentence and was fined $10,000. Several years into his prison sentence, while incarcerated at Fort Leavenworth, Kansas, Monti unsuccessfully tried to rescind his guilty plea, claiming ineffective assistance of counsel and that his lawyers misled him and coerced him into pleading guilty. Monti was granted parole in 1960. In 1963, out on parole, Monti again petitioned the government to have his treason conviction invalidated, claiming that he never admitted in 1949 that he had any intent to betray the United States. In this 1963 petition, Monti claimed "that his only reason for going to Germany was to assassinate Hitler and end the war" (Policano 1963, 17). This petition was denied as well. Monti faded into obscurity and died in 2000 aged seventy-eight.

See Also: Arnold, Benedict; Axis Sally (Mildred Gillars); Radio Traitors and Anti-State Propaganda during the Second World War; Treason

Resources

Cooperman, Jeannette. 2020. "How a North County Boy Became the First U.S. Military Officer Ever to Be Convicted of Treason." *St. Louis Magazine*, December 2020. Accessed July 11, 2022. https://www.stlmag.com/longform/the-first-traitor-north-county-world-war-II/.

Policano, Joseph. 1963. "Traitor Seeks Sentence Reversal." *The Record.* Hackensack, New Jersey. July 26, 1963.

United States v. Monti, 100 F.Supp. 209 (U.S. Dist. Ct. E.D. NY, 1951).

Werrell, Kenneth. 2020. "Turncoat and Traitor? Lt. Martin Monti (USAAF)." *Air Power History* 67, no. 3 (Fall): 33–42.

Mumford, William Bruce (1819–62)

The trial and execution of William Bruce Mumford illustrates how treason and related charges can be misused to punish unpopular symbolic speech and actions. Mumford committed an offense that could be described as minor, an infraction against prevailing martial law. Mumford removed a US flag from atop a government facility in New Orleans, Louisiana, in 1862, and his actions resulted in a conviction for violation of marital law, for which he was executed a brief time later. Serving as a stark reminder and admonishment of the overextension of charges like treason and sedition to cover less serious criminal offenses, the incident also reinforces the importance of protecting free speech that touches on national security issues (see Flag Disrespect as Crime against the State). Typically, statutory laws pertaining to flag burning and destruction are justified on national security grounds (e.g., the Supreme Court case of *Texas v. Johnson* [1989]), and such laws even extend to activities like burning draft cards (e.g., *United States v. O'Brien* [1968]). The Mumford case illustrates the need for Congress and the federal courts to stay vigilant in avoiding the overly broad extension of criminal charges to those offenses not originally intended by the constitutional Framers when they enshrined the offense of "high crimes and misdemeanors" in the Treason Clause in Article III of the United States Constitution.

William Mumford was a Southerner from North Carolina and was living in New Orleans at the time of the charged offense of treason. He was a veteran of both the Seminole and the Mexican American Wars. Several days before the Union forces landed in force to occupy the City of New Orleans, Union Admiral Farragut ordered US flags flown atop several government buildings, including the United States Mint building. An ardent confederate, at the end of April 1862, Mumford pulled down the flag several days before occupying forces landed in New Orleans. As one of his court defenders remarked, "Mumford was an unresisting and non-combative captive," and committed no overt act of violence.

On May 1, 1862, Union forces led by General Benjamin "Beast" Butler landed and occupied New Orleans. Shortly thereafter, Butler had Mumford arrested and charged with "high crimes and misdemeanors against the laws of the United States." On June 5, 1862, General Butler issued General Order 70, authorizing the execution of Mumford, and Mumford was executed in the courtyard of the United States Mint building, in the shadow of the building's top that had once flown the flag that Mumford had taken down. It was also reported that the scaffolding for Mumford's hanging was made from parts that were utilized just a few days earlier to hoist the flag that Mumford took down.

The Mumford case stands as one of the only examples wherein taking down a flag constituted "high crimes and misdemeanors against the laws of the United States." While Mumford certainly was violating martial law by disobeying military authority (a military authority that had not even arrived in the city yet), most would argue that the termination of Mumford's life for this infraction is clearly an excessive and disproportionate sentence and should not be utilized as legitimate precedent in the support of charges related to symbolic speech in contemporary society.

See Also: American Civil War and Treason; Flag Disrespect as Crime against the State; Levying War; Martial Law; *O'Brien, United States v.* (1968); Sedition; Treason

Resources

Broadwater, Robert P. 2005. "William B. Mumford Became a Southern Hero for Defying Union Sailors in New Orleans." *America's Civil War* 18, no. 5 (November): 20.

The New York Times. 1862. "The Case of Mumford—The Occupation of New Orleans." December 29, 1862.

Mutiny

Many believe that the offense of mutiny is a by-gone vestige of maritime law from the 1800s, and the term conjures up images of sailors conspiring to overthrow the officers and captain of a ship and commandeering the vessel. While the crime of mutiny did (and still) applies to rebellions by a ship's crew on the high seas and against the ship's organizational leadership, the crime is still relevant today and covers any situation where more than one person in concert attempts to usurp and overthrow their command structure or violates direct orders and engages in insubordination through violence. Mutiny can occur on both land and sea.

While the offense of mutiny covers a wide variety of situations on land and sea, the United States Code still maintains a separate offense for the classical historical scenario of a revolt or mutiny of sailors occurring on the high seas. "Revolt or Mutiny of Seaman," 18 United States Code Section 2193, makes mutiny an offense separate from the crime of mutiny contained in the Uniform Code of Military Justice. Section 2193 deals specifically with a member of "the crew of a vessel of the United States, on the high seas, or on any other waters within the admiralty and maritime jurisdiction of the United States." This section makes it a crime punishable by a sentence of up to ten years to do the following: "unlawfully and with force, or by fraud, or intimidation, usurps the command of such vessel from the master or other lawful officer in command thereof, or deprives him of authority and command on board, or resists or prevents him in the free and lawful exercise thereof, or transfers such authority and command to another not lawfully entitled" to such command.

More broadly, Article 94 of the Uniform Code of Military Justice (UCMJ), 10 United States Code Section 894(a)(1), specifies that any military member from any branch of the service who "with intent to usurp or override lawful military authority, refuses, in concert with any other person, to obey orders or otherwise do his duty or creates any violence is guilty of mutiny." Additionally, this section makes it a crime if a person "fails to do his utmost to prevent and suppress a mutiny or sedition being committed in his presence, or fails to take all reasonable means to inform his superior commissioned officer or commanding officer of a mutiny … which he knows or has reason to believe is taking place, is guilty of a failure to suppress or report a mutiny or sedition."

Thus, under Article 94 of the UCMJ, a service member may commit mutiny by collective insubordination (i.e., two or more individuals), by acting in concert, and disobeying orders with the intent to usurp or override lawful military authority. This is typically charged as "Mutiny by Refusing to Obey Orders or to Perform Duty." Another variation of the mutiny charge is when two or more service members employ violence with the intent to usurp or override proper military authority. This is typically charged as "Mutiny by Creating Violence or Disturbance." Finally, as specified by the language in Section 894(a)(3), it is also a crime to prevent or suppress a mutiny and/or notify his or her superior officer of a planned mutiny. This is typically charged as "Failure to Prevent and Suppress a Mutiny" and "Failure to Report a Mutiny."

In the United States, the charge of mutiny has been levied and prosecuted with success by the government on numerous occasions. In an early classical example of mutiny, in 1842, a small group of sailors plotted a mutiny on board the USS Somers. The plot was discovered, and three sailors were convicted of conspiring to commit mutiny and were executed. In the twentieth century, three notable large-scale mutinies occurred, the Townsville Mutiny (1942), the Port Chicago Mutiny (1944), and the Presidio Mutiny (1968), all of which occurred on land.

The Townsville Mutiny involved about 600 African American service members from the United States Army Corps of Engineers who were stationed in Townsville, Australia. The men were part of a labor battalion tasked with manual labor and construction projects and were ill-treated by white officers. In May 1942, attempting to kill the white commander, a few of the Black service members fired machine guns into the tents of white officers, and an eight-hour firefight ensued, resulting in at least one death and numerous injured. The incident (and the resulting disciplinary punishments for those involved) was hidden from the media and public for seventy years and was only discovered by a researcher in 2012. Future President Lyndon B. Johnson was a Lieutenant Commander stationed in Townsville at the time and was given a detailed account about the mutiny and violence. Johnson suppressed the distribution of the incident to the media and the public and wrote in his military report at the time that "one of the biggest stories of the war which cannot be written and which shouldn't be written, of course—is the mutiny among American Negro troops which took place near Townsville on May 22" ("Negro Servicemen Riot" 2020).

The Port Chicago Mutiny was another massive mutiny by African American soldiers in August 1944. A total of 258 African American service members refused to load ammunition onboard ships three weeks after a horrific explosion (called the Port Chicago disaster) killed 322 individuals (202 of whom were Black) and injured another 390 military members and civilians. Despite fears of another explosion, men were ordered to again start loading powerful explosives onboard ships. After they were threatened with mutiny charges, all but fifty of the African American service members agreed to start loading ammunition and explosives on the boats. These men were punished for their initial disobedience of orders by losing three months' pay. By contrast, the fifty men who continued to refuse to load explosives were charged with mutiny and court-martialed. The trial took twelve days and future Supreme Court Justice Thurgood Marshall, then chief counsel for the NAACP (National Association for the Advancement of Colored People), was detailed to monitor the case and sat through all twelve days of the trial. Marshall declared the trial to be unfair and that while the men might be guilty of insubordination, they should not have been charged with mutiny as none intended to usurp or overturn the military leadership. In October 1944, after eighty minutes of deliberation, the military jury found all fifty defendants guilty of mutiny (including one defendant who had a broken wrist and a cast on the wrist at the time he was supposed to load explosives and two others who had medical reasons excusing them from loading ammunition). All fifty men received fifteen-year sentences, although the Navy reduced the sentences to eight years the following year. Then, in October 1945, all the sentences were reduced to two years (for those with good behavior) and three years (for those with bad conduct during incarceration). By January 1946, the Navy released forty-seven of the fifty men (one remained incarcerated for bad conduct and two were in a Navy hospital). After release, all men received Honorable Discharges.

A third major mutiny case called the Presidio Mutiny involved a group of twenty-seven soldiers who became known as the Presidio 27. These soldiers conducted a sit-down protest of the Vietnam War at the Presidio (then an active military base) in California in October 1968. After the peaceful protest where the soldiers sang "We Shall Overcome," and ignored an order to disperse and re-join their units, they were arrested and charged with mutiny. During pre-trial confinement, three of the defendants escaped and fled to Canada, one of whom remained a fugitive until 1980 and was not released from jail until 1985. After conviction, the court handed down severe sentences ranging from fourteen to sixteen years at hard labor, which drew harsh criticism from the international community. On appeal, the Army Court of Criminal Appeals rescinded the long sentences for mutiny to much shorter sentences (one to three years) for willful disobedience of a superior officer (for ignoring the command to disperse and rejoin their formations), and Gerald Ford dropped the mutiny charges in 1975. The Presidio Mutiny and the Presidio 27 gained national and international attention; it was one of the first examples of resistance of military members to the Vietnam War.

Mutiny remains a serious crime against the state. For instance, several legal commentators have stated that any service members actively participating in the Capitol Insurrection on January 6, 2021, faced the possibility of being tried for mutiny.

See Also: Capitol Insurrection on January 6, 2021; Insurrection; Rebellion

Resources

10 U.S.C. §894 and 18 U.S.C. §2193.

Allen, Robert. 1994. "Injustice Upheld in Port Chicago Mutiny Trial." *The Black Scholar* 24: 56–9.

Allen, Robert. 2006. *The Port Chicago Mutiny: The Story of the Largest Mass Mutiny Trial in U.S. Naval History*. Berkeley, CA: Heyday Books.

Froeba, Kristine. 2021. "Oldest Living WWII Veteran, 112, Wants to Be Remembered as 'Good Soldier.'" *The Tampa Bay Times*, November 11, 2021. Accessed July 3, 2022. https://www.tampabay.com/news/military/2021/11/11/oldest-living-wwii-veteran-112-wants-to-be-remembered-as-good-soldier/.

"Negro Servicemen Riot at the Upper Ross, Townsville on 22 May 1942." *Australia at War*. 2020. Accessed November 1, 2023. https://www.ozatwar.com/ozatwar/riotupperross.htm.

N

Near v. Minnesota (1931)

In the case of *Near v. Minnesota* (1931), the United States Supreme Court set forth the doctrine that the First Amendment does not permit the government to impose prior restraint or censorship of speech or publications except in exceedingly rare circumstances.

In 1925, Minnesota enacted a statute entitled "Public Nuisance Law," which allowed the courts to issue injunctions to halt the publication of any "malicious, scandalous and defamatory newspapers." While the statute did provide that a newspaper could protect itself by proving that the published articles were true, this defense of truth in the contents of a publication was only applicable if the author had published the materials "with good motives and for justifiable ends." In 1927, Jay M. Near, an avowed antisemite, published a weekly paper called the *Saturday Press*. The newspaper contained numerous statements alleging that various politicians and leaders in Minnesota were corrupt and in collusion with Jewish gangsters. After nine such publications, Minnesota requested an injunction against Near to prevent his publication of any further newspapers, a request which was granted by a Minnesota trial court under the 1925 Public Nuisance Law. Near appealed the ruling to the Minnesota Supreme Court, which rejected Near's appeal and upheld the Minnesota law. Near then appealed to the United States Supreme Court, which overturned the Minnesota law as unconstitutional.

In a five to four ruling, the Supreme Court held that the Minnesota Public Nuisance Law violated the First Amendment. In an opinion authored by Chief Justice Charles Evan Hughes, the majority held that the government may not prevent, restrain, or censor speech before it has occurred, a doctrine now referred to as the doctrine or rule against prior restraint. The Court found that if a newspaper did publish factually incorrect and defamatory statements, the newspapers could be sued for libel and damages after publication.

The Court did acknowledge, however, that the rule prohibiting prior restraint was not absolute and exceptions might exist in very narrow and extreme circumstances. The Court specified that "[n]o one would question but that a government might prevent actual obstruction to its recruiting service or the publication of the sailing dates of transports or the number and location of troops" and "[t]he security of the community life may be protected against incitements to acts of violence and the overthrow by force of orderly government." This narrow rule potentially allowing prior restraint or censorship has been referred to as the "Near Exception" and obviously applies in cases dealing with national security.

In allowing the publication of the Pentagon Papers and denying the federal government's request for an injunction in *New York Times v. United States* (1971), the Supreme Court, citing *Near v. Minnesota*, held that "any system of prior restraints of expression comes to this Court bearing a heavy presumption against its constitutional validity." The Court also noted in the *New York Times* case that the government "thus carries a heavy burden of showing justification for the imposition of such a restraint," and "that the Government had not met that burden." According to Pulitzer Prize-winning author and journalist Anthony Lewis, "*Near v. Minnesota* was and remains a bulwark of American press freedom. Because of that decision, it is very difficult to persuade a judge to issue a prior restraint on the press" (Lewis 2007, 46).

See Also: *New York Times v. United States* (1971); Pentagon Papers and Trials of Daniel Ellsberg and Anthony Russo; Speech as Crime against the State

Resources

Friendly, Fred W. 1981. *Minnesota Rag: The Dramatic Story of the Landmark Supreme Court Case that Gave New Meaning to Freedom of the Press*. New York: Random House.

Lewis, Anthony. 2007. *Freedom for the Thought That We Hate: A Biography of the First Amendment*. New York: Basic Books.

Near v. Minnesota, 283 U.S. 697 (1931).

New York Times v. United States (1971)

Often referred to as the Pentagon Papers case, *New York Times v. United States* (1971) was a seminal decision regarding the powers of the government to prevent publication of information that might be damaging to national security versus the rights of newspapers and the media under the First Amendment to inform the public of important governmental policies and decisions. The core of the case was whether any prior restraint (i.e., pre-publication censorship) on speech or publication by the government can be justified under the First Amendment, even in areas concerning national security.

On June 13–14, the *New York Times* began publishing portions of 7,000 pages of classified materials (referred to as the Pentagon Papers) that were leaked to it by Daniel Ellsberg, an ex-Department of Defense employee. United States Attorney General John Mitchell first demanded that the *New York Times* cease publication of the top-secret materials as Mitchell contended that it was a clear violation of the Espionage Act of 1917. When the *New York Times* failed to respond to Mitchell's demand, on June 15, 1971, the federal government filed an injunction in federal district court in New York preventing the publication of any further information. On Wednesday, June 16, the United States District Court for the Southern District of New York (Judge Murray Gurfein) granted a temporary injunction precluding the publication of further information, the first time in American history an order of this nature had been made by a court. As soon as the *New York Times* stopped publishing articles because of the injunction, the *Washington Post* began publishing articles about the Pentagon Papers on June 18. The federal government rushed to file an injunction against the *Washington Post* the very same day, but federal district court Judge Gerhard Gesell refused to grant a temporary injunction on June 18, concluding that the government could not substantiate irreparable harm to national security. The federal government immediately appealed Gesell's ruling and was granted an injunction the next day (June 19) by the United States Court of Appeals for the District of Columbia.

On June 19, in New York, Judge Gurfein wrote an opinion dissolving the temporary restraining order he had issued to the *New York Times* three days before but ruled that the injunction was subject to continuation "until such time during the day as the Government may seek a stay from the Federal Circuit Court of Appeals for the Second Circuit," which the government did immediately, and the Second Circuit issued an injunction against further publication by the *New York Times*. Thus, the federal government had temporarily stopped the publication of the Pentagon Papers by either the *New York Times* or *Washington Post* through temporary injunctions by two federal courts of appeals. By the following week, the Court of Appeals for the Second Circuit (covering New York) ruled that the case should be remanded to Judge Gurfein for hearings to determine whether the government could substantiate that the documents should be withheld from publication on the grounds that the publication would pose "grave and immediate danger" to national security. The *New York Times* immediately appealed this ruling to the Supreme Court arguing that any restraint "imposes an insupportable burden on a free press" and "urgent issues of overriding public importance were involved."

Conversely, the Court of Appeals for the District of Columbia upheld the denial of an injunction by the trial judge and ruled in favor of the *Washington Post*. In its ruling, the court found that "the government's proof, judged by the standard suggested in *Near v. Minnesota* … does not justify an injunction." The Supreme Court case of *Near v. Minnesota* (1931) put forth the doctrine that no prior restraint or censorship by the government is permissible except in rare circumstances. The Supreme Court in *Near v. Minnesota* gave an example of when rare circumstances supporting an injunction might exist, namely the "publication of the sailing dates of transports or the number and locations of troops." The government promptly appealed this ruling to the Supreme Court, and the Supreme Court granted reviews in both cases and consolidated the cases for purposes of review. The Supreme Court granted review of the lower court cases on June 25, 1971, a mere twelve days after the first publication of information in the *New York Times*. The Court agreed to an expedited review with oral arguments to occur the very next day, on June 26, 1971, and the Supreme Court would ultimately issue its ruling four days after oral arguments, on June 30, 1971.

The Supreme Court, in a six to three ruling, held that pre-publication censorship, or "prior restraints" could not be justified regarding the publication of the Pentagon Papers. In a short *per curiam* opinion (i.e., an opinion not signed by the specific Justices), the Court, citing *Near v. Minnesota*, held that "any system of prior restraints of expression comes to this Court bearing a heavy presumption against its constitutional validity." The Court then noted that the government "thus carries a heavy burden of showing justification for the imposition of such a restraint," and the Court agreed "that the Government had not met that burden." While six Justices could agree with the decision and the broad principle noted above, the brief opinion masked underlying divergent views of the various Justices as to what should be the precise standard for determining when prior restraint may be permissible, if at all. Each of the nine Justices wrote concurring or dissenting opinions in the case.

The case is heralded as one of the Supreme Court's landmark decisions and one of the most important First Amendment cases in the Court's history. The Court's decision stands as precedent for the principle that the federal government does not have unfettered powers of censorship in the name of national security. The decision also empowered the media to serve as a check against government secrecy.

See Also: Espionage Act of 1917 and Sedition Act of 1918; *Near v. Minnesota* (1931); Pentagon Papers and Trials of Daniel Ellsberg and Anthony Russo; Speech as Crime against the State

Resources

New York Times v. United States, 403 U.S. 713 (1971).

Oakes, James L. 1982. "The Doctrine of Prior Restraint since the Pentagon Papers." *University of Michigan Journal of Law Reform* 15: 497–519.

Rudenstine, David. 1998. *The Day the Presses Stopped: A History of the Pentagon Papers Case*. Berkeley, CA: University of California Press.

Sims, John Cary. 1993. "Triangulating the Boundaries of the Pentagon Papers." *William & Mary Bill of Rights Journal* 2: 342–453.

New York v. Lynch (1814)

During the War of 1812 between the United States and Great Britain, several citizens of the state of New York, including Mark Lynch, provided food to "British subjects"—presumably British Royal Navy sailors—aboard the HMS *Bulwark*, a seventy-four-gun British Royal Navy warship. According to the indictment against Lynch and the other defendants, they delivered "fifty barrels of beef, fifty barrels of pork, fifty hams, one hundred pounds weight of butter, and thirty cheeses" to the *Bulwark*. For providing "aid and comfort" to the enemy, the defendants were charged in New York state criminal court with treason against the state of New York and treason against the United States.

In *New York v. Lynch* (also known as *People v. Lynch*), the New York Supreme Court of Judicature removed the case from the trial court to decide two important legal questions raised by the treason charges. First, whether the facts amounted to treason against the state. Second, whether New York state courts had jurisdiction to decide cases involving allegations of treason against the United States.

In answering the first question, the Court noted the existence of a New York statute that criminalized treason against the state, defined as "levying war, against the people of this state, within the state, or adhering to the enemies of the people of this state, giving to them aid and comfort in this state, or elsewhere." The prosecution argued that if the statute did not apply in cases like the one before the court, the statute was "nugatory" (meaningless). The Court rejected this argument, and noted that treason against the state could occur, for example, in an "open and armed opposition to the laws of the state, or a combination and forcible attempt to overturn or usurp the government." The Court also allowed for the possibility that a state could be engaged in a war with a foreign enemy. However, the Court concluded that neither of these situations existed in this case. "Great Britain cannot be said to be at war with the state of New York ... as an independent government, and, therefore, [is] not an enemy of the state .... The people of this state, as citizens of the United States, are at war with Great Britain, in consequence of the declaration of war by [C]ongress. The state, in its political capacity, is not at war. The subjects of Great Britain are the enemies of the United States of America, and the citizens thereof, as members of the union, and not of the state of New York."

Having determined that the facts did not amount to treason against the state of New York, the Court turned to the question of whether state courts could have jurisdiction over charges of treason against the United States. The Court noted that under the United States Constitution, "the judicial power of the United States extends to all cases arising under the constitution and laws of the United States." The Court further observed that the federal Judiciary Act of 1789 had given federal "circuit courts [jurisdiction], exclusive of the courts of the several states, of all crimes and offenses cognizable under the authority of the United States." Thus, the Court held, only federal courts could have jurisdiction over charges of treason against the United States. Accordingly, the Court said the indictments could not be supported and ordered Lynch and the other defendants released.

Prosecutions of individuals for treason against states have been rare in the United States, but *New York v. Lynch* is not the only such case. For instance, Thomas Wilson Dorr was convicted of treason against Rhode Island in relation to his activities in orchestrating Dorr's Rebellion. And the famed John Brown's Raid in Harpers Ferry, Virginia, led to *Virginia v. Brown* (1859), in which John Brown was convicted of treason against the Commonwealth of Virginia and then executed.

See Also: Aid and Comfort (Aid to Enemies of the State); Brown, John; Dorr's Rebellion; John Brown's Raid (1859); Levying War; Treason; *Virginia v. Brown* (1859)

Resources

People v. Lynch, 11 Johns. 549 N.Y. (1814).

Nichols, Terry

See Oklahoma City Bombing

O

O'Brien, United States v. (1968)

In 1965 during the Vietnam War, Congress passed an amendment to the Selective Service Act that, among other things, criminalized forging, altering, destroying, or mutilating one's Selective Service registration certificate ("draft card"). In Spring 1966, David O'Brien and a few others burned their draft cards in front of a courthouse in Boston, Massachusetts, to protest the draft and the war. At his trial, O'Brien testified that he burned his draft card "so that other people would reevaluate their positions with Selective Service, with the armed forces, and reevaluate their place in the culture of today." O'Brien was convicted and sentenced to six years of confinement. He appealed his conviction, arguing that his expressive conduct was protected by the First Amendment. O'Brien's case is sometimes cited as an example of civil disobedience in protesting the draft and the war in Vietnam.

In *United States v. O'Brien*, the Supreme Court upheld the constitutionality of the prohibition on destroying draft cards. The Court rejected O'Brien's argument that the law violated the First Amendment and articulated a new test for when infringements on "expressive conduct" would be constitutional:

> We think it clear that a government regulation is sufficiently justified if it is within the constitutional power of the Government; if it furthers an important or substantial governmental interest; if the governmental interest is unrelated to the suppression of free expression; and if the incidental restriction on alleged First Amendment freedoms is no greater than is essential to the furtherance of that interest.

Applying its newly articulated test to the facts of the case, the Supreme Court determined that the law was constitutional. First, the Court found the law was within Congress's power to enact because of its power under Article I of the Constitution to "raise and support armies" by "classify[ing] and conscript[ing] manpower for military service." Second, the Court found that issuing draft cards was a "legitimate and substantial administrative aid" in the effective functioning of the draft system. Third, the Court determined that the registration and raising of troops were unrelated to the suppression of speech, even though during the debate over the law, some Congresspersons had argued that the law would be an effective way to limit one avenue anti-war protestors were using to express their views. Finally, the Court saw "no alternative means" by which the government could ensure that draft cards would continue to be available than a law that prohibited their willful destruction. Thus, burning a paper form issued by the government was upheld as a constitutional crime against the state. Two decades later, in *Texas v. Johnson* (1989), the Supreme Court would reach the opposite conclusion regarding the constitutionality of a law that prohibited burning the US flag. Factual differences between the cases may partially explain the different outcomes: in *Texas v. Johnson*, the property being destroyed was a privately owned flag, not a government-owned draft card, and the national security issues such as raising an army present in *O'Brien* were not at issue in *Texas v. Johnson*. Moreover, *O'Brien* was decided during wartime, while *Texas v. Johnson* was not.

See Also: Civil Disobedience and Crimes against the State; Flag Disrespect as Crime against the State; Speech as Crime against the State

Resources

McGoldrick, James M., Jr. 2006. "United States v. O'Brien Revisited: Of Burning Things, Waving Things and G-Strings." *University of Memphis Law Review* 36: 903–49.

United States v. O'Brien, 391 U.S. 367 (1968).

Oklahoma City Bombing (1995)

At 9:02 a.m. on April 19, 1995, a massive explosion ripped through an otherwise tranquil morning in Oklahoma City, Oklahoma. The blast, heard and felt up to fifty-five miles away, killed 168 people including 19 children, injured 680 more, destroyed the nine-story Alfred P. Murrah federal building, and damaged 324 additional buildings. The bombing is the deadliest act of domestic terrorism in United States history and was the most lethal terrorist attack on US soil until the attacks on September 11, 2001.

The extraordinary carnage in Oklahoma City was the result of an enormous bomb containing 7,000 pounds of explosives constructed in the cargo area of a rented box truck parked next to the Murrah building and detonated by Timothy McVeigh. McVeigh, aged twenty-seven at the time of the attack, had served in the United States Army during the Gulf War. During his military basic training, McVeigh met his future Oklahoma City Bombing co-conspirator, Terry Nichols. After an honorable discharge, McVeigh moved to multiple locations, failing to hold a steady job, and becoming an increasingly radicalized opponent of government, taxes, and gun control. For a time, McVeigh lived with Nichols on Nichols's family farm in Michigan, where Nichols and his brother taught McVeigh how to build explosive devices. During this time, McVeigh and Nichols frequently traveled to gun shows around the country, selling military surplus and weapons. Like McVeigh, Nichols's post-military life involved increasingly radical anti-government views. Nichols became interested in the militia movement and was an adherent of the sovereign citizen movement, even attempting to renounce his US citizenship and claiming the government and its courts had no jurisdiction over him.

During the fifty-one-day standoff and siege by federal and state law enforcement of the compound belonging to the religious cult known as the Branch Davidians in Waco, Texas, McVeigh drove to Waco to show support for the besieged cult members and to protest against the law enforcement officials conducting the siege. McVeigh eventually returned to the Nichols farm in Michigan and, on April 19, 1993, exactly two years before the Oklahoma City Bombing, McVeigh and Nichols watched the culmination of the Waco siege on television, becoming enraged at federal government power and vowing to exact revenge for the siege that killed scores of Branch Davidians and for an earlier siege by the federal government at Ruby Ridge in 1992.

McVeigh carefully and intentionally selected both the target and date of the bombing. After considering a variety of federal government targets, including an assassination campaign against specific individuals he thought responsible for Waco and Ruby Ridge, McVeigh decided to attack a federal government building because, in his view, federal agents had become "soldiers" and he should strike their command centers. He ultimately chose the Murrah building because it housed several federal agencies. The building contained regional offices for the Drug Enforcement Administration (DEA), the Bureau of Alcohol, Tobacco, and Firearms (ATF), the United States Secret Service, the Department of Veterans Affairs, the Social Security Administration, the U.S. Department of Housing and Urban Development, and recruiting offices for the US military. The building also housed a children's day care, which McVeigh later claimed not to have known about. McVeigh chose the date of the attack to coincide with the second anniversary of the fiery end of the Waco siege. April 19, the date of the Patriots Day holiday in New England, is also cherished among many members of the extreme right who hail the date as the start of the American Revolution, when individuals stood against tyranny.

In Fall 1994, McVeigh and Nichols began purchasing and stealing the supplies necessary to construct the truck bomb, including ammonium nitrate, nitromethane, Tovex (a dynamite alternative), blasting caps, and fuses, storing the supplies in several rented storage units. Nichols has claimed he did not know the ultimate intended target of the bomb, but he nevertheless provided significant assistance to McVeigh, including mixing the ingredients of the bomb and helping McVeigh preposition a getaway vehicle in Oklahoma City just days before the attack.

On the Morning of April 19, 1995, as he drove the truck bomb to its target, McVeigh wore a T-shirt on which was printed two slogans. On the front, "Sic semper tyrannis," meaning "thus always to tyrants," which is supposedly what Brutus proclaimed as he assassinated Julius Caesar and what John Wilkes Booth said immediately after the Lincoln assassination. The back of McVeigh's shirt proclaimed Thomas Jefferson's famous assertion that "The tree of liberty must be refreshed from time to time with the blood of patriots and tyrants." McVeigh parked the truck directly in front of the children's daycare in the building, started the bomb's two-minute timed fuse, locked the truck, and walked toward his getaway car, dropping the truck keys along the way. McVeigh was stopped and arrested less than two hours later when an Oklahoma State Trooper noticed his car had no license plate and eventually determined McVeigh also possessed an illegal firearm. McVeigh was still in local custody for these violations three days later when the Federal Bureau of Investigation (FBI) identified him as the prime suspect in the bombing and he was transferred to federal custody. Nichols was at home with family when the bomb exploded.

The FBI's investigation of the bombing was, to that point, the largest criminal investigation in US history, involving over 28,000 interviews, 1,400 investigators, 238,000 photographs (print, not digital), three tons of evidence, and nearly one billion pieces of information. McVeigh was ultimately tried in federal court, convicted of eleven counts of murder and conspiracy, and sentenced to death. Nichols was tried in both federal and state court. In federal court, he was found guilty of conspiring to build a weapon of mass destruction (WMD) and eight counts of involuntary manslaughter of federal officers and was sentenced to life without parole. Dissatisfied with that sentence, the State of Oklahoma subsequently prosecuted Nichols and a jury convicted him of 161 counts of first-degree murder. After the jury deadlocked on the death penalty, the judge sentenced him to 161 consecutive life terms without the possibility of parole. McVeigh was executed in 2001, the first execution by the federal government in thirty-eight years. Nichols is incarcerated at the federal Supermax Prison in Florence, Colorado, where he has shared a cell block (known as "bombers row") with Ramzi Yousef (World Trade Center Bombing of 1993), Eric Rudolph (1996 Olympic Park and other bombings), and Theodore Kaczynski ("Unabomber").

In the wake of the Oklahoma City Bombing, Congress passed the Anti-Terrorism and Effective Death Penalty Act (1996), a massive bill that, among other things, criminalized providing material support to terrorist organizations, provided more robust powers to deport individuals deemed dangerous to the national security of the United States, and supplied more tools for law enforcement in dealing with cases of potential terrorism. Congress also separately revised federal criminal law relating to WMD by criminalizing threats of use of WMD.

The bombing caused a decade-long recruiting and enrollment setback to the militia movement, as negative press associated with McVeigh's and Nichols's prior participation in militia groups in Michigan decreased support for such groups nationwide. But commentators have drawn a direct line between the bombing and the resurgence of radical right-wing ideology and tactics that undergirded the Bundy Standoffs and the Capitol Insurrection on January 6, 2021.

See Also: Anti-Terrorism and Effective Death Penalty Act (1996); Assassination; Bundy Standoffs (2014–16); Capitol Insurrection on January 6, 2021; Conspiracy, Criminal; Jefferson, Thomas; Kaczynski, Theodore ("Unabomber"); Lincoln Assassination (1865); Material Support Crimes;

Militia Movement (Modern); Ruby Ridge (1992); Rudolph, Eric Roberts; September 11, 2001; Sovereign Citizen Movement; Terrorism; Waco (1993); Weapons of Mass Destruction; World Trade Center Bombing of 1993

Resources

Federal Bureau of Investigation. n.d. "The Oklahoma City Bombing: 20 Years Later." Accessed June 26, 2023. https://stories.fbi.gov/oklahoma-bombing/.

Michel, Lou, and Dan Herbeck. 2001. *American Terrorist: Timothy McVeigh and the Oklahoma City Bombing*. New York: Harper.

Toobin, Jeffrey. 2023. *Homegrown: Timothy McVeigh and the Rise of Right-Wing Extremism*. New York: Simon & Schuster.

Olympic Bombings, 1996

See Rudolph, Eric

P

Padilla, United States v. (including *Padilla v. Rumsfeld* and *Padilla v. Hanft*) (2004–14)

In May 2002, the Federal Bureau of Investigation (FBI) arrested Jose Padilla in Chicago, Illinois, when he disembarked his flight from Pakistan. The FBI believed Padilla intended to perpetrate a "dirty bomb" attack in the United States. He was initially arrested by FBI agents on a material witness warrant, which allows the government to hold a person sufficiently long for that person to provide information relevant to another criminal action or case without the person fleeing or disappearing, though Padilla was eventually transferred to military detention and his status changed to "enemy combatant."

A US citizen, Padilla was born in Brooklyn, New York, but raised in Chicago. While serving a jail sentence for aggravated assault and manslaughter, he converted to Islam, and when released he moved to the Middle East. Padilla trained in Afghanistan with Al-Qaeda, allegedly learning to build and detonate radiologic "dirty bombs." He also apparently served as an armed guard at a Taliban outpost. Because the Taliban controlled the government of Afghanistan at the time, Padilla's actions made him not only a member of the terrorist organization Al-Qaeda, but an affiliate of an enemy state as well.

Padilla challenged his military detention (*Padilla v. Rumsfeld*). In late 2002, the District Court for Southern New York ruled that the president of the United States, as Commander-in-Chief, had the authority to designate an American citizen captured on US soil as an enemy combatant and detain him for the duration of the conflict with Al-Qaeda. The Second Circuit Court of Appeals subsequently reversed that ruling, holding that "The President lacked inherent constitutional authority as Commander-in-Chief to detain American citizens on American soil outside a zone of combat." Additionally, the court held the 2001 Authorization for the Use of Military Force (AUMF) did not provide authorization for detention incident to war because the AUMF authorized only detention of enemies "arrayed against us in the field of battle," which was not Padilla's situation when he was detained. The court also noted that the federal statute known as the Non-Detention Act requires a clear statement of law to support detention of US citizens captured on US soil. Finally, the court relied on the case of *Youngstown Sheet & Tube Co. v. Sawyer* (1954), in which the United States Supreme Court ruled that President Harry Truman could not use his position and power as Commander-in-Chief to seize the nation's steel mills on the eve of a nation-wide steelworkers' strike.

The District Court also determined that under the Constitution, extraordinary government power to curb civil rights and liberties during crises such as times of war lies with Congress, not the president. For instance, Article I, Section 9, Clause 2, of the United States Constitution grants Congress, not the president, the power to suspend the right of habeas corpus during a period of rebellion or invasion. The government appealed the Second Circuit ruling to the Supreme Court of the United States, which remanded because it found the Second Circuit did not have jurisdiction over Padilla's case because

Padilla was no longer detained in New York, within the jurisdiction of the Second Circuit, since the government had moved him to the Naval Brig in Charleston, South Carolina.

When Padilla again challenged his detention, this time in the District of South Carolina, his case was eventually decided by the Fourth Circuit Court of Appeals in 2005 (*Padilla v. Hanft*). Between the Second Circuit and Fourth Circuit decisions in Padilla's case, the Supreme Court had decided *Hamdi v. Rumsfeld* (2004), which significantly impaired Padilla's claim that the President could not militarily detain US citizens. Relying on factual similarities between the *Padilla* and *Hamdi* cases, the Fourth Circuit determined that the AUMF authorized his detention because, although he was captured in the United States, he had previously been training and traveling with Al-Qaeda and the Taliban during military operations. The Fourth Circuit found that in *Hamdi* the Supreme Court had made no distinction between enemy combatants captured on the battlefield and those captured in the United States after they fled the battlefield.

Padilla appealed the Fourth Circuit's ruling to the Supreme Court of the United States. On the eve of the Supreme Court of the United States' decision regarding whether to hear the case, President George W. Bush ordered Padilla to be removed from military custody and returned to civilian custody. Apparently concerned the Supreme Court might overturn the Fourth Circuit's ruling favorable to the government, the government terminated the military detention it had contended was imperative for national security and that had lasted three and a half years. Padilla's transfer to civilian custody rendered his challenge to his military detention, including his appeal to the Supreme Court of the United States, moot.

Ultimately, Padilla was charged in federal court with conspiracy to commit murder, kidnapping, providing material support to terrorists and terrorist organizations, and maiming of persons *overseas* (*United States v. Padilla*). He was never charged for the alleged dirty bomb plot in Chicago that had been the basis for his years-long military custody. In 2014 he was ultimately sentenced to twenty-one years in prison and is expected to be released from the ADX Florence "Supermax" prison in 2026.

See Also: Conspiracy, Criminal; *Hamdi v. Rumsfeld* (2004); Material Support Crimes; Rebellion; Terrorism

Resources

Merriam, Eric, and Douglas B. McKechnie. 2021. *National Security Law.* St. Paul: West Academic, 332–3.

United States Department of Justice Office of Public Affairs. 2014. "Jose Padilla Re-sentenced to 21 Years in Prison for Conspiracy to Murder Individuals Overseas, Providing Material Support to Terrorists." September 9, 2014. Accessed May 14, 2023. https://www.justice.gov/opa/pr/jose-padilla-re-sentenced-21-years-prison-conspiracy-murder-individuals-overseas-providing.

Pelton, Ronald William (1941–)

Ronald Pelton was a National Security Agency (NSA) communications specialist from 1965 to 1979 and engaged in espionage with the former Soviet Union. Pelton was arrested in November 1985, dubbed the Year of the Spy because of numerous high-profile espionage cases, including Larry Wu-Tai Chin (a Central Intelligence Agency officer who provided Top Secret information to the Chinese), Jonathan Pollard (a Navy analyst who provided Top Secret information to Israel), and John A. Walker, Jr. (a Navy Chief Warrant Officer who provided Top Secret information to the Soviet Union). Pelton was the most high-profile case involving espionage and the NSA until Edward Snowden.

Pelton did not begin spying for the Soviet Union until after his resignation from the NSA in 1979. In 1980, in need of money to pay his homeowners association fees and repairs, Pelton visited the Soviet Embassy in Washington, DC, and offered his knowledge of highly classified information. Pelton received a modest $35,000 from the Soviets. In turn, Pelton provided the Soviet Union with sensitive signal intelligence information from the NSA. Pelton was responsible for disclosing the details of Operation Ivy Bells to the Soviets. Operation Ivy Bells was a signal intelligence operation that allowed the United States to surveil Soviet communications between Soviet military bases that were transmitted via deep sea communication cables. Listening devices were attached to the cables that allowed the United States to monitor and collect intelligence. The devices were designed to detach from the cable and fall to the ocean floor undetected if the Soviet Union attempted to repair cables or investigate the security of the cables. Because of Pelton's espionage, the United States was forced to abandon Operation Ivy Bells in 1981.

Pelton was prosecuted and convicted for violations of the Espionage Act of 1917 and was sentenced to three life terms (to run concurrently) plus ten years. Pelton was released from prison on parole in November 2015.

See Also: Chin, Larry Wu-Tai; Espionage; Espionage Act of 1917 and Sedition Act of 1918; Pollard, Jonathan Jay; Walker, John Anthony, Jr.; Year of the Spy (1985)

Resources

Aftergood, Stephen. 2015. "Soviet Spy Ronald W. Pelton to Be Released from Prison." *Federation of American Scientists*. Accessed July 25, 2022. https://fas.org/blogs/secrecy/2015/11/pelton-release/.

Burgess, Christopher. 2021. "After 15 Years at the NSA, Russian Linguist Flips His Espionage Switch and Gets Prison Time." *Clearance Jobs*. Accessed July 25, 2022. https://news.clearancejobs.com/2021/12/06/after-15-years-at-the-nsa-russian-linguist-flips-his-espionage-switch-and-gets-prison-time/.

Pennsylvania v. Nelson (1956)

Steve Nelson, the Chair of the Communist Party of Western Pennsylvania, was convicted in Pennsylvania state court for advocating the overthrow of the government of the United States, in violation of the Pennsylvania Sedition Act. The Pennsylvania Sedition Act outlawed speech or conduct that was intended to encourage or incite anyone to overthrow the government of the United States or the State of Pennsylvania.

Nelson successfully argued that the Smith Act, a federal law that outlawed sedition, preempted state laws outlawing the same conduct. Engaging in federal preemption analysis that is beyond the scope of this book, the Supreme Court found that Congress had "occupied the field to the exclusion of parallel state legislation." The Court found this to be the case even though the Pennsylvania Sedition Act predated the federal legislation and even though the federal legislation had explicitly stated "Nothing in this title shall be held to take away or impair the jurisdiction of the courts of the several States under the laws thereof." The United States Supreme Court agreed with the Pennsylvania Supreme Court, which had overturned Nelson's conviction, opining "Sedition against the United States is not a local offense. It is a crime against the Nation. As such, it should be prosecuted and punished in the Federal courts."

In this case, Nelson had been charged with sedition against the United States, not against Pennsylvania. The United States Supreme Court took care to observe that it was not declaring state sedition laws to be unconstitutional when the state government is the target of the seditious activity or speech. The Court explicitly said that states could protect *themselves* from sedition, but could not attempt to protect the United States from sedition when the federal government had laws attempting to do the same. Thus, all state criminal anarchy, criminal syndicalism, treason, and sedition laws must be analyzed considering the Supreme Court's federal preemption holding in *Nelson.*

The Supreme Court's opinion in *Pennsylvania v. Nelson* occurred in the midst of the Second Red Scare. This context led some to believe the Court chose federal preemption as the mechanism for overturning Nelson's conviction rather than relying on First Amendment principles because the Court was concerned about public backlash had it overturned the conviction based on a broader statement restricting prosecutions of speech as crime against the state. Indeed, it would be another thirteen years before the Court, in *Brandenburg v. Ohio* (1969), would retreat from its prior jurisprudence broadly allowing criminalization of speech critical of the government.

See Also: Anarchy, Criminal; *Brandenburg v. Ohio* (1969); Criminal Syndicalism; Second Red Scare (McCarthyism); Sedition; Smith Act; Speech as Crime against the State; Treason

Resources

Foster, James C. "Pennsylvania v. Nelson (1956)." *The First Amendment Encyclopedia.* Accessed June 15, 2023. https://www.mtsu.edu/first-amendment/article/637/pennsylvania-v-nelson.

Pennsylvania v. Nelson, 350 U.S. 497 (1956).

Pentagon Papers and Trials of Daniel Ellsberg and Anthony Russo

The Pentagon Papers refers to a voluminous top secret United States Department of Defense (DOD) study entitled *United States-Vietnam Relations 1945–1967* that was surreptitiously released to certain members of Congress and then leaked to various newspapers, most notably the *New York Times* and the *Washington Post*. The documents were released by a former DOD employee, Daniel Ellsberg, whom Henry Kissinger dubbed "the most dangerous man in America." Upon its release in 1971, the Pentagon Papers represented the most gigantic leak of top-secret documents up until that point in time in the history of the United States. In total, the Pentagon Papers spanned forty-seven volumes and over 7,000 pages of top-secret documents, including 4,000 pages of primary/original documents and 3,000 pages of contemporaneous analysis and assessments of the Vietnam War. All 7,000 pages were classified as secret, top secret, or top secret-sensitive. The Pentagon Papers revealed the secret history of the Vietnam War spanning four presidential administrations, containing a massive amount of information that had been intentionally hidden from the public, the media, Congress, the international community, and international allies. The impact of the Pentagon Papers cannot be overstated. The release of the Pentagon Papers led to one of the most famous Supreme Court cases in history (*New York Times v. United States*), strengthened the press as a check on governmental abuses, fueled the antiwar movement regarding Vietnam, increased cynicism of the public towards the government, placed a check on government secrecy based upon national security justifications, and may have contributed indirectly to the resignation of Richard Nixon.

The origins of the Pentagon Papers stem from DOD Secretary Robert McNamara's heightened disenchantment and disillusionment with the Vietnam War and his desire to document and analyze the war and determine what had gone wrong and why. In 1967, McNamara assigned a team of researchers (including Ellsberg) from the Pentagon and RAND Corporation (a non-profit organization created to research and analyze issues for the US military) to comprehensively study the Vietnam War from its inception through the present (1967). The result was a massive report that was filled with damning information illustrating a cavalcade of incidents of deception, miscalculations, manipulation of information, and in many instances, a wanton disregard for morality and humanity.

The Pentagon Papers revealed that, despite public claims to the contrary, US military involvement in Vietnam did not begin with the Gulf of Tonkin incident in 1964 but went back to 1950. The Pentagon Papers revealed active military operations of sabotage and warfare against North Vietnam as early as 1954. The Pentagon Papers also revealed that President Lyndon Johnson deceived the public and the Congress regarding the Gulf of Tonkin incident to receive carte blanche military authorization for an expanded war in Vietnam through the Gulf of Tonkin Resolution. Some have suggested the intentional omission of essential details of the Gulf of Tonkin incident may have impacted the vote on the congressional resolution authorizing the use of force in Vietnam.

The Pentagon Papers also revealed the concealment of the magnitude of air strikes being conducted against North Vietnam (air strikes which were ongoing before the Gulf of Tonkin incident in August 1964) and the strength and number of South Vietnamese forces and need for larger numbers of US ground troops in Vietnam. The Pentagon Papers also revealed a complicity in, or at least ambivalence to, the possible assassination of South Vietnamese President Ngo Dinh Diem (who was assassinated in 1963) and displayed pessimism about Saigon being able to sustain itself. Finally, instead of what the public was being told about why the United States was fighting in Vietnam, one McNamara document contained in the Pentagon Papers listed what DOD considered to be the actual goals of the war: "70% to avoid a humiliating U.S. defeat; 20% to keep South Vietnam territory from Chinese hands; [and only] 10 % to permit the people of South Vietnam to enjoy a better, freer way of life. Also to emerge from crisis without unacceptable taint from methods used."

In coordination with a former RAND employee, Anthony Russo, Ellsberg began surreptitiously copying hundreds of pages each evening. Ellsberg rented a Xerox machine and an office from a friend in Los Angeles and would sneak documents out of the RAND offices at the end of each workday; Ellsberg and Russo would spend each evening for four months copying the documents. Ellsberg also involved his two teenage children in copying the materials. After copying the 7,000 pages, Ellsberg first released the Pentagon Papers to several Senators and Congressmen who he believed were sympathetic to ending the war in Vietnam. In March 1971, once Ellsberg had determined that these Senators and Congressman were not going to act, he leaked the papers to *New York Times* reporter Neil Sheehan. For several months, a team of *New York Times* reporters secretly reviewed the materials in a suite of rooms at the New York Hilton while the newspaper's lawyers argued about whether to publish the papers. The outside counsel for the *New York Times* advised not to publish the materials and return them to the government because its continued unauthorized possession and contemplated distribution would violate the Espionage Act of 1917. However, in-house counsel, James Goodale, advised the paper that it had a right and a duty to the public to publish the papers.

On Sunday, June 13, 1971, the *New York Times* published the first batch of reports from the Pentagon Papers in a massive 486-page Sunday edition. The second set of disclosures was published on Monday, June 14. That evening, John Mitchell, the United States Attorney General, sent the *New York Times* a telegram that advised that the paper was publishing documents bearing "a top secret classification" and that the "publication of this information is directly prohibited by the provisions of the Espionage Law." Mitchell then demanded that the *New York Times* "publish no further information of this character" and to advise him that arrangements had been made to deliver the documents back to the DOD. On Wednesday, June 16, the United States District Court for the Southern District of New York granted a temporary injunction precluding the publication of further information, the first time in American history an order of this nature had been made by a federal court.

Just as the *New York Times* stopped publishing articles because of the injunction, the *Washington Post* started publishing articles about the Pentagon Papers on June 18. The government rushed for another temporary injunction from the United States District Court for the District of Columbia (DC). The federal district court judge in Washington, DC, refused to grant a temporary injunction, and so the federal government immediately appealed and was granted an injunction the next day by the United States Court of Appeals for the District of Columbia. However, in the meantime, articles started appearing around the country in papers such as the *Boston Globe*, the *Chicago Tribune*, the *Los Angeles Times*, and others. Ellsberg had released the materials to over seventeen different papers. Furthermore, on June 15, the *Washington Post* secretly delivered a set of the Papers to Michael Gravel, a junior United States Senator from Alaska, who began reading the papers as part of his filibuster in an empty Senate subcommittee meeting on June 29. Exhausted, and in the early hours of the morning, Gravel made a motion to have the complete set of the Pentagon Papers entered into the Congressional Record. Since he was the only person in the room, he indicated that since there was no objection, it was ordered into the public record without objection. Gravel's actions became the subject of a criminal investigation and resulted in the Supreme Court case *Gravel v. United States* (1972).

During the month of June, the legal challenges to the publication of the Pentagon Papers had made their way up to the United States Supreme Court. On June 30, 1971, the Court, in a six to three decision, issued its landmark ruling in *New York Times v. United States*, holding that the government had not met its burden of showing justification for the pre-publication censorship of the materials, and the media could continue to publish the Pentagon Papers.

Despite the landmark ruling in *New York Times v. United States*, the federal government was pursuing criminal charges against both Russo and Ellsberg for multiple violations of the Espionage Act. Russo was facing potential incarceration of up to thirty-five years for various charges under the Act and Ellsberg was facing up to 115 years of incarceration. Mid-trial, federal district court Judge William M. Byrne, Jr. declared a mistrial after learning that the Federal Bureau of Investigation (FBI) had illegally utilized a wiretap to eavesdrop on conversations between the defendants and their attorneys. The trial judge impaneled a new jury, and a second prosecution was attempted. Judge Byrne again concluded that the government had corrupted the case because, in addition to the illegal wiretaps, White House Counsel John Ehrlichman had ordered a covert operation involving Nixon's "plumbers' unit" to break into Ellsberg's psychiatrist's office and steal his patient records. This would be the same group that would break into the Watergate complex a short time later. Ehrlichman also met privately with the judge during the trial and suggested the possibility that the judge could be appointed as the next FBI director. On May 11, 1973, Judge Byrne declared a second mistrial and dismissed the charges with prejudice because of "improper government conduct."

See Also: Espionage Act of 1917 and Sedition Act of 1918; *New York Times v. United States* (1971)

Resources

Ellsberg, Daniel. 2003. *Secrets: A Memoir of Vietnam and the Pentagon Papers*. New York: Penguin Books.

New York Times v. United States, 403 U.S. 713 (1971).

Sheehan, Neil, et al. 2017. *The Pentagon Papers: The Secret History of the Vietnam War*. New York: Racehorse Publishing.

United States-Vietnam Relations, 1945–1967: Study Prepared by the Department of Defense. 1971. Washington, DC: United States Government Printing Office.

Perjury, False Statements, and Obstruction of Justice

The offense of perjury is considered a crime against the state as it adversely affects the ideal smooth administration of the criminal justice system and court proceedings. One might conceptualize perjury as a cog or impediment in the wheels of justice. Committing perjury may also lead to unfair and/or incorrect judicial disposition of cases, and often may adversely impact criminal investigations on issues pertaining to national security. It is common for individuals who have committed offenses against the government to also be charged with the offense of perjury, making a false statement, or obstructing an investigation by providing misleading and untruthful information to investigators. While the offenses of perjury, making false statements, and obstruction of justice all have the telling of a lie as one of the components of the offense, each of the three offenses is distinct and has different requirements.

When it comes to a person lying as part of a criminal investigation or court proceeding, the offense of perjury frequently is the first offense that comes to mind for many individuals. Included in the Crimes Act of 1790, perjury was outlawed by the federal government as a crime against the state quite early in US history. Today, under 18 United States Code Section 1621, perjury is defined as when a person "willfully and contrary to [an] oath states or subscribes any material which he does not believe to be true." For charges of perjury to be applicable, the federal perjury statute requires that a person be under oath when the statement was made. The oath, however, is not limited to testimony in court after being sworn in as a witness. Any oath required by any "competent tribunal, officer, or person, in any case in which a law of the United States authorizes an oath" is sufficient to satisfy the requirements of the statute. Thus, the oath required for perjury may occur in other settings beyond actual trials, in forums such as depositions, administrative hearings, arbitration, and other settings. Additionally, a written document that one signs under "penalty of perjury" constitutes an oath for purposes of the statute. While this certainly includes an affidavit or sworn written statement, it also includes statements made on any governmental forms when the signatory of the document affirms the truthfulness of the document's contents under "penalty of perjury."

It should be noted that for the perjury prosecution to be successful, the government must show beyond a reasonable doubt that (1) the statement (either oral or in writing) was under oath, (2) there was a material misrepresentation of facts, and (3) the defendant made such statements "willfully," meaning he knew the statement to be false when stated. A material misrepresentation means that the untruthful statement or declaration must pertain to a meaningful aspect of the investigation or grounds for questioning, and not a trivial detail not relevant to the circumstances being investigated. According to the Supreme Court, "a material statement" is any information which *may* have bearing on the governmental decision or outcome. Furthermore, the decision of what is a "material" statement is a decision of fact made by the jury and based upon the particular facts of the case. A prime example of a person being charged and convicted of perjury while being investigated for a crime against the state (i.e., espionage) can be seen in the Alger Hiss case. While under oath, Hiss lied about whether he had ever met or knew his accuser and whether Hiss had given classified information to that individual. Hiss denied both facts as being false, but independent evidence subsequently established them to be true.

The penalty for a perjury conviction under federal law is up to five years imprisonment for each count or instance of lying. In the Hiss case referenced above, Hiss was charged with one count of lying to congressional investigators about knowing a person and charged with a second count of lying to investigators about whether he disclosed classified information to that person. Found guilty on both counts, Hiss was sentenced to the maximum sentence of five years for each of the two counts, with the punishments to run concurrently. Finally, convincing another person to commit perjury (called "subornation of perjury"), is a separate criminal offense under 18 United States Code section 1622. Section 1622 specifies that "whoever procures another to commit any perjury is guilty of subornation of perjury, and shall be fined under this title or imprisoned not more than five years, or both."

Unlike the offense of perjury, the crime of making a false statement (i.e., lying) to a government official on a matter they are investigating requires no oath or sworn statement to be found in violation. This means that lying to a federal law enforcement officer who is questioning a witness about a case constitutes a criminal offense of making "false statements." The federal statute covering "false statements" is incredibly broad and gives expansive authority to prosecutors to pursue a wide variety of cases whereby a person makes material misstatements of facts and/or lies to an investigating federal agent or officer. The crime of making "false statements" is covered in 18 United States Code Section 1001, which specifies that it is a criminal offense if a defendant "knowingly and willfully ... makes any materially false, fictitious, or fraudulent statement or representation" during "any matter within the jurisdiction of the executive, legislative, or judicial branch" of the federal government. This means it is a violation of US criminal law to answer any question asked of you by federal law enforcement falsely during their investigation. If a person is uncertain as to the truth or falsity of the statement, he should clearly state that he is uncertain of the answer or just decline to answer the question.

Like perjury, the "false statement" offense applies to statements made orally and in writing. But the key difference is that 18 United States Code section 1001 does not require the false statement to be made under oath for it to be a crime. Any false statements made on government documents or in response to questions by government agents as to any material fact would constitute a crime. The statutory punishment for violating section 1001 is imprisonment for not more than five years or, if the offense involves international or domestic terrorism, imprisonment for not more than eight years.

A clear illustration of this crime can be seen in the criminal prosecution of President Donald Trump's first National Security Advisor, Michael Flynn (in *United States v. Flynn*). Flynn was questioned by FBI (Federal Bureau of Investigation) agents about what contacts he may have had with Russian officials before the end of President Obama's administration. While not under oath, Flynn gave misleading and incorrect answers to several of the questions posed to him. Flynn also failed to disclose on his security clearance application payments he received for speaking engagements in Russia during the waning days of the Obama administration. As a result, Flynn resigned as Trump's National Security Advisor after a mere twenty-four days in office, making his tenure the shortest ever in the history of that office (the average tenure is two to three years). Flynn was charged and pleaded guilty to one felony count of "willfully and knowingly making materially false statements and omissions to the Federal Bureau of Investigation" about conversations with the Russian ambassador to the United States in violation of 18 United States Code Section 1001. Flynn was pardoned by Trump for the crime in the last two months of the Trump presidency.

Another example can be seen in the federal indictment issued on June 8, 2023, concerning Trump's mishandling of classified, secret, and top-secret documents he kept at Mar-a-Lago, Florida. In addition to thirty-one separate counts of violating the Espionage Act of 1917, Trump was also indicted in Count 37 of the indictment for making "false statements and representations" in violation of 18 United States Code Section 1001. Specifically, Trump certified to the FBI through his representatives that a comprehensive search for classified documents was conducted on the grounds at Mar-a-Lago and that they have returned all required documents to the FBI. According to the Indictment (Page 42, paragraph 92 of the Indictment), "the statements and representations set forth above were false, as Trump knew, because Trump had directed that boxes be removed from the Storage Room" and moved elsewhere within Mar-a-Lago before his own attorneys could access what needed to be returned to the FBI (Trump Indictment 2023, 40). Trump is awaiting a federal criminal trial for this alleged violation of federal law as of early 2024.

Finally, a criminal offense related to perjury and false statements is the offense of obstruction of justice. It is a criminal offense, per 18 United States Code Section 1505, for a person who "corruptly … obstructs, or impedes or endeavors to influence, obstruct, or impede the due and proper administration of the law under which any pending proceeding is being had before any department or agency of the United States." For purposes of this criminal offense, the term "corruptly" is defined as "acting with an improper purpose, personally or by influencing another, including making a false or misleading statement." A defendant may find himself afoul of this criminal statute in combination with either the perjury statute or the making of false statements statute as well. That is, if a defendant willfully lies about a material fact to a government official during an investigation, there is a clear violation of 18 United States Code Section 1001. However, if the person lies with the intent to "influence, obstruct, or impede" the investigation, a violation of 18 United States Code Section 1505 has occurred as well. If the defendant made the material misrepresentation under oath, perjury charges would then apply as well. A violation of Section 1505 carries a maximum potential sentence of no more than five years imprisonment per count, or eight years per count if the offense involves international or domestic terrorism investigations.

An illustration of the offense can be seen in the prosecution of Vice President Dick Cheney's Chief-of-State I. Lewis "Scooter" Libby. Libby had improperly disclosed the identity of a Central Intelligence Agency operative (Valerie Plame Wilson) in speaking to National Broadcast Company's Tim Russert. In the ensuing federal investigation, Libby denied disclosing Wilson's identity as a CIA agent to Russert. As a result, in June 2007, a federal jury found Libby guilty on a count of obstruction of justice, two counts of perjury, and one count of making false statements (see Intelligence Identities Protection Act). Libby was sentenced to thirty months in jail, a $250,000 fine, two years of supervised release, and 400 hours of community service. This sentence was commuted in part by George W. Bush in July 2007, and Libby was pardoned by Donald Trump in 2018. Similarly, Donald Trump was indicted by a federal grand jury for conspiracy to obstruct justice in allegedly conspiring with a co-defendant to "engage in misleading conduct toward another person and corruptly persuade another person to withhold a record, document, and other object, from an official proceeding," and "corruptly conceal[ing] a record, document, and other object, form an official proceeding" (Trump Indictment 2023, 34).

See Also: Conspiracy, Criminal; Crimes Act of 1790; Espionage; Espionage Act of 1917 and Sedition Act of 1918; Hiss, Alger; Intelligence Identities Protection Act; Terrorism

Resources

Doyle, Charles. 2018. "False Statements and Perjury: An Overview of Federal Criminal Law." *Congressional Research Service*, May 11, 2018. Accessed July 7, 2022. https://sgp.fas.org/crs/misc/98-808.pdf.

Murillo, Helen Klein. 2017. "The Law of Lying: Perjury, False Statements, and Obstruction." *Lawfare*, March 22, 2017. Accessed July 7, 2022. https://www.lawfareblog.com/law-lying-perjury-false-statements-and-obstruction.

United States of America v. Donald J. Trump and Waltine Nauta Indictment (Trump Indictment). 2023. Criminal Indictment. Case 9:23-cr-80101-AMC (United States District Court, Southern District of Florida), June 8, 2023. Accessed June 16, 2023. https://d3i6fh83elv35t.cloudfront.net/static/2023/06/trump-indictment.pdf.

Pollard, Jonathan Jay (1954–)

Most American spies convicted of espionage have been found guilty of providing information to America's adversaries. A vast majority of American espionage cases since the Second World War were cases involving the Soviet Union and/or Russia. Jonathan Pollard, a civilian analyst for the Navy, was arrested in 1985 (the Year of the Spy) and pleaded guilty in 1987. He is unique in that he pleaded guilty for spying for Israel, a country considered to be a close ally of the United States. He also only pleaded guilty to a single count under Section 794 of the Espionage Act of 1917, which involved a "conspiracy to deliver national defense information to a foreign government." Pollard's case is also considered somewhat unusual in that he was sentenced to the maximum possible sentence (life imprisonment) and incarcerated far longer than other spies who pleaded guilty, even those found guilty of multiple counts of violating the Espionage Act of 1917 for espionage on behalf of an adversary as opposed to an ally. That is, Pollard is the only person sentenced to life imprisonment for passing classified information to an *ally* and without the alleged intent to harm the United States. The reasons for this harsher punishment have to do with the volume of intelligence passed (tens of thousands of documents), the fact that he and his wife reportedly conspired to have evidence destroyed after he was questioned, his alleged propensity for duplicity, and that he violated instructions of the court while his plea deal was being finalized, including speaking to media and the press on multiple occasions.

Pollard, born in 1955, graduated from Stanford University with a degree in Political Science in 1976. Pollard's reputed propensity for stretching the truth or telling outright lies was exhibited during his time at Stanford. College acquaintances remembered Pollard for telling extravagant stories, such as being employed by Israel's Mossad, saying that he obtained the rank of Colonel, and killed a person while on guard duty. There is no evidence that any of this was true. From 1976 to 1979, Pollard attended several graduate programs, but did not graduate from any of the schools. He then applied for a job at the Central Intelligence Agency (CIA) in 1979 but was not offered a position because he reportedly told CIA administrators during a pre-employment polygraph test that he had taken large quantities of illicit drugs in the mid-1970s. He was then offered an intelligence analyst position with the United States Navy Field Operational Office in September 1979. This position did not require a polygraph as a condition of employment and Pollard allegedly lied about several material issues both during his interview and in subsequently attempting to secure a Top Secret/ Sensitive Compartmentalized Information (TS/SCI) security clearance, a requirement for the job. Some of the issues Pollard allegedly lied about include his drug usage in the mid-1970s, as well as reputedly misrepresenting his language-speaking skills and educational accomplishments. He also allegedly stated on numerous occasions that his father was a CIA operative (his father was a college professor at the University of Notre Dame), and there is no evidence of his father's alleged work with the CIA.

In his early years with the Navy (1979–84), Pollard was re-assigned multiple times while issues with his security clearance were sorted out. The CIA reportedly advised the Navy that Pollard was an intelligence risk and that he should not be utilized in any intelligence collection operations. While undergoing a Navy polygraph test, Pollard admitted to his prior drug use, making false statements, and having contacts with representatives of foreign governments. During the polygraph test, Pollard became disruptive, "shouting and shaking and making gagging sounds as if he were going to vomit," which caused the test administrator to recommend against Pollard be granted the security clearance he was seeking (Olive 2006, 20–2). As a result of his behavior, Pollard was ordered to see a psychiatrist. He saw the psychiatrist as ordered, but also filed a grievance against the Navy seeking a higher security clearance. After the psychiatrist cleared Pollard for return to duty, and after Pollard had several positive evaluation reviews, Pollard finally obtained his Top Secret/SCI security clearance. In October 1984, Pollard accepted a job as an intelligence analyst for the Naval Intelligence Command. By this time, he had already begun spying for Israel, passing along intelligence information to an Israel officer starting in June 1984.

As a rationale for his espionage, Pollard claimed that he was upset that the United States was withholding intelligence information from an ally. Pollard claimed to the judge during his sentencing that payment was forced on him, implying he would have done the spying without compensation. During questioning, Pollard reluctantly acknowledged that "I did accept money for my services," but quickly qualified that statement by saying that he only took money "as a reflection of how well I was doing my job." Later, Pollard alleged that he was going to repay the money he received from Israel. Despite Pollard's claim that he was not spying for the money, a government investigation after his arrest determined that Pollard was paid handsomely. He received a lump sum of $10,000 and several rare jewels when he first began spying. By the time of his arrest in 1985, Pollard was receiving $2,500 a month from the Israeli government (equivalent of $7,048 a month in 2023). Pollard also received thousands of dollars in cash payments to pay for various hotel stays and meals. And despite Pollard's claim that he spied for Israel because of his close affinity with Jewish culture, during his prosecution, evidence was introduced that showed that Pollard either passed, or attempted to pass, classified material to other countries as well, including South Africa, Pakistan, and Australia. The Federal Bureau of Investigation uncovered evidence that suggested that Pollard was also using classified documents to broker arms deals between a range of countries, including South Africa, Argentina, Taiwan, Pakistan, and Iran.

The full extent of documents passed to Israel has still not been officially ascertained. In a memorandum provided by Secretary of Defense Caspar Weinberger to the presiding judge, it was alleged that among the items copied was a top secret ten-volume manual which comprehensively delineated America's international electronical surveillance networks at the time. Pollard had also filled a large suitcase with around seventy pounds of classified materials (which was turned over to authorities by a neighbor). US officials believe Pollard passed tens of thousands of highly sensitive defense documents. Part of the reason the exact amount of material has never been definitively determined is because Pollard called and tipped off his wife (Anne Pollard) within a few hours of when he was first questioned, using a code word in the call to alert his wife he had been caught, and that indicated she should start destroying evidence. His wife also met with Pollard's Israeli contacts, all of whom fled the country within twenty-four hours of Pollard's initial questioning. Anne Pollard was arrested the very next day (November 22, 1985). As part of Jonathan Pollard's plea bargaining, he indicated he would cooperate if his wife were given a more lenient sentence. Ultimately, Anne Pollard was sentenced to a five-year prison sentence but was paroled after three and half years due to health issues.

As part of his plea agreement, Pollard was required not to discuss or speak publicly about his case, cooperate fully with the government's investigation, and not disclose any additional classified security information. Yet, both Jonathan and Anne Pollard disregarded these conditions and defiantly gave several media interviews. The government subsequently alleged that Pollard engaged in further "unauthorized disclosure of classified information" while answering questions from reporter Wolfe Blitzer, then a reporter with the *Jerusalem Post*. The Pollards gave another interview on *60 Minutes* where Anne stated, "I feel my husband and I did what we were expected to do, and what our moral obligations was as Jews, what our moral obligation was as human beings, and I have no regrets about that" (Black 2002). During sentencing, the prosecutor argued that the Pollards had violated numerous orders of the court and concluded by saying: "In combination with the breadth of this man's knowledge, the depth of his memory, and the lack of honor that he has demonstrated in these proceedings, I suggest to you, your honor, he is a very dangerous man." The judge gave Jonathan Pollard the maximum sentence of life imprisonment.

Pollard's actions strained relations between the United States and Israel. The Israeli government apologized to the United States for its role in 1987 but did not admit to paying Pollard for the intelligence until 1998. In May 1998, Israeli Prime Minister Benjamin Netanyahu admitted Pollard was a paid Israeli spy. After serving thirty years of his life sentence, Pollard was released on parole on November 20, 2015. Though Pollard or his representatives had sought his release many times over the years through political and diplomatic channels, his release came about by simple adherence to applicable federal parole guidelines. On December 30, 2020, Pollard and his second wife (Pollard had divorced his first wife, Anne) moved to Israel and are both Israeli citizens.

The last chapter of this story took place on Donald Trump's last day in office. Years prior, the main Israeli handler for Pollard, Aviem Sella, was indicted in the United States on three counts of espionage. Israel refused to make Sella available for interviews unless he was granted immunity, and Israel refused to extradite Sella to the United States. On January 20, 2021, in one of his last acts as president, Trump granted a full pardon to Sella. The Israeli government, led by Prime Minister Benjamin Netanyahu, requested the pardon from Trump.

See Also: Espionage; Espionage Act of 1917 and Sedition Act of 1918; Year of the Spy (1985)

Resources

Black, Edwin. 2002. "Why Jonathan Pollard Is Still in Prison?" *Forward*, June 29, 2002. Accessed November 1, 2023. https://web.archive.org/web/20060107223010/http://www.forward.com/issues/2002/02.06.28/news.pollard.html.

Hersh, Seymour M. 1999. *Annals of Espionage: The Traitor. The New Yorker*, January 18, 1999, 26–33.

Olive, Ronald J. 2006. *Capturing Jonathan Pollard: How One of the Most Notorious Spies in American History Was Brought to Justice*. Annapolis, MD: Naval Institute Press.

United States Central Intelligence Agency. 1987. "The Johnathan Jay Pollard Espionage Case: A Damage Assessment." Foreign Denial and Deception Analysis Committee (for Director of Central Intelligence), October 30, 1987. Accessed May 20, 2023. https://www.archives.gov/files/declassification/iscap/pdf/2007-010-doc1.pdf.

United States Government Department of Justice. 1987. "Government's Reply to Defendant's Sentencing Memorandum." *United States of America v. Jonathan Jay Pollard*, Criminal No. 86-0207, March 3, 1987. Accessed May 20, 2023. https://nsarchive.gwu.edu/document/20615-national-security-archive-doc-09-government-s.

Pottawatomie Massacre (1856)

The Pottawatomie Massacre was one of the infamous brutal acts of violence in "Bleeding Kansas" (a period during which citizens clashed over whether Kansas would become a slave or free state) and a nineteenth-century act of domestic terrorism (an act of mass violence committed upon a civilian population to achieve political goals). On the night of May 24, 1856, radical abolitionist John Brown and a group of seven other men visited multiple settler cabins located on the Pottawatomie River in Kansas. Brown and his men forced their way into each cabin and questioned the male occupants on their views pertaining to slavery. By the end of the night, Brown and his men had murdered five proslavery men. The murders were committed in an especially brutal fashion, with Brown's men hacking the limbs off several of the victims with broadswords. Several of the victims also had their skulls split in half. Brown planned and led his men to commit these acts of bloodshed at Pottawatomie in response to the general harassment of anti-slavery settlers in Kansas, including the Border Ruffians' (i.e., Missourians sympathetic to slavery) burning of many free-state buildings and residences in Lawrence, Kansas. Brown believed that it was time "to fight fire with fire" and "to strike terror into the heart of all proslavery people" (Oates 1984, 133). Brown achieved his goal as "the midnight mass murder sent a chill of horror through Kansas" (Abels 1971, 65).

As a result of the Pottawatomie Massacre, President James Buchanan offered a reward for John Brown's capture. Brown derisively responded by offering two dollars and fifty cents for the arrest of Buchanan. Brown went into hiding and left Kansas. After freeing eleven enslaved individuals from two homesteads in Missouri in 1858 and escorting them hundreds of miles to the Canadian border, Brown moved east and openly raised funds to "carry this war into Africa" (Oates 1984, 171). Brown reappeared in 1859, attacking the federal Armory and Arsenal at Harpers Ferry, Virginia (John Brown's Raid), with the goal of overthrowing the institution of slavery by force.

See Also: Brown, John; John Brown's Raid (1859); *Virginia v. Brown* (1859); Terrorism

Resources

Abels, Jules. 1971. *Man on Fire: John Brown and the Cause of Liberty*. New York: The Macmillan Company.

Oates, Stephen. 1984. *To Purge This Land with Blood*. Second edition. Amherst: The University of Massachusetts Press.

Prize Cases (1862)

The *Prize Cases* was a civil war-era Supreme Court decision dealing with the constitutionality of actions by President Abraham Lincoln to suppress domestic rebellion and insurrection. In a closely divided five to four opinion, the Court upheld Lincoln's view that the president could utilize the constitution's "war power" to suppress a domestic rebellion in advance of Congressional legislation authorizing the action.

Shortly before and after Lincoln's inauguration in March 1861, several southern states seceded from the Union. In April 1861, and while Congress was in recess, Lincoln called for 75,000 volunteers to enlist in various state militias to defend the Union, suspended the writ of habeas corpus, and ordered the naval blockade of southern ports. In a message to Congress in 1861, Lincoln explained that his unilateral exercise of the country's "war power" was necessary to suppress the rebellion and insurrection. Lincoln stated that he had little choice "but to call out the war power of the Government and so to resist force employed for its destruction by force for its preservation" and with "deepest regret" the duty of exercising the "war power in defense of the Government forced upon him" (Fisher 1985, 289). When Congress came back into session, Lincoln sent a note to the Congress explaining further that his actions "whether strictly legal or not, were ventured upon under what appeared to be a popular demand and a public necessity, trusting then, as now, that Congress would readily ratify them" (Fisher 1985, 289). Congress subsequently did just that, passing an act "approving, legalizing, and making valid all the acts, proclamations, and orders of the President, etc., as if they had been done under the previous express authority and direction of the Congress of the United States" (Fisher 1985, 289).

The resulting *Prize Cases*, involving the seizure of four different ships pursuant to the federal blockade, were consolidated into one case for purposes of the Supreme Court's review. The ship *Amy Warwick* was transporting coffee and was seized enroute to Richmond; the ship *Hiawatha* was a British ship in port in Richmond when the blockade began and was captured a few days after leaving port; the ship *Crenshaw* was captured taking tobacco enroute from Richmond to England; and the *Brilliante* was a Mexican ship that was captured after departing New Orleans. The Supreme Court upheld the seizure and condemnation of all four of these vessels.

While the Supreme Court ruled on several different technical issues in its decision, the underlying thread in all four cases was the constitutional question of whether the President had the unilateral power to order a blockade of southern ports without Congressional authorization and in absence of a declared war. In a war with another nation, the president would have authority as part of the executive's powers as Commander-in-Chief. However, in times of peace, the authority to regulate interstate commerce between the states resides with the Congress under the Interstate Commerce Clause under Article I, Section 8, of the United States Constitution. Additionally, the power to declare war is vested in Congress under Article I, Section 8, as well. The Lincoln administration wished to utilize executive powers that the president typically could utilize in times of war, but without acknowledging that there was an international conflict with another sovereign nation. Phrased another way, the Lincoln administration did not wish to acknowledge or accept that the Confederate States of America was a sovereign independent nation state who was engaged in belligerencies against the United States. Lincoln claimed southern secession attempts were not valid and that it was a large-scale domestic rebellion against federal authority. The owners of the ships claimed that "justify the exercise of this right, and legalize the capture of a neutral vessel for violating it, a state of actual war must exist, and the neutral must have knowledge or notice that it is the intention of one belligerent to blockade the ports of the other," and that this could not occur in absence of congressional action.

In upholding the seizures, the majority held that "the present civil war between the United States and the so-called Confederate States has such character and magnitude as to give the United States the same rights and powers which they might exercise in the case of a national or foreign war, and they have, therefore, the right *jure bello* to institute a blockade of any ports in possession of the rebellious States." In so holding, the Court determined that it was not necessary to be at war with an independent power, indicating that "a civil war exists, and may be prosecuted on the same footing as if those opposing the Government were foreign invaders, whenever the regular course of justice is interrupted by revolt, rebellion, or insurrection, so that the Courts cannot be kept open." The Court held that the state of conflict and war may exist without any formal declaration of war by either party, the executive could indicate such a conflict exists, and the resident "was the proper person to make such notifications." The Court also determined that all persons in the southern states "are liable to be treated as enemies, though not foreigners." In defining what exactly is an enemy under international law at the time, the Court provided as follows: "[w]hen the party in rebellion occupy and hold in a hostile manner a certain portion of territory; have declared their independence; have cast off their allegiance; have organized armies; have condemned hostilities among their foreigner sovereign; the world acknowledges them as belligerent and the contest a war."

However, the Court also made clear that neither defining who is an "enemy" for purposes of the confiscation of vessels at issue in the *Prize Cases* nor the Court's affirmation of Lincoln's efforts at blockading Southern ports could transform a domestic rebellion into a war or alter the legal obligation of those "enemies" to adhere to US laws. The Court stated that "insurgents who have risen in rebellion against their sovereign, expelled her Courts, established a revolutionary government, and commenced hostilities, are not enemies because they are traitors, and a war levied on the Government by traitors, in order to dismember and destroy it, is not a war because it is an insurrection."

Making clear that the *Prize Cases* did not alter existing treason law in the United States, seven months after the *Prize Cases,* Supreme Court Justice Stephen Field advised a jury on the law in *United States v. Greathouse* (1863). Field stated that

> [t]he term "enemies," as used in the second clause [of the Treason Clause], according to its settled meaning, at the time the constitution was adopted, applies only to the subjects of a foreign power in a state of open hostility with us. It does not embrace rebels in insurrection against their own government. An enemy is always the subject of a foreign power who owes no allegiance to our government or country.

The Lincoln administration's defense in the *Prize Cases* was bolstered by the fact that Congress did in fact authorize all the president's actions as soon as Congress reconvened. As such, "the theory of the war accepted in this case implied that other actions by the president, including the Emancipation Proclamation and the suspension of habeas corpus, were also constitutionally permissible, especially when supported by subsequent congressional approval" (Finkleman 1992, 681).

See Also: American Civil War and Treason; *Greathouse, United States v.* (1863); Insurrection; Rebellion; Treason

Resources

Finkleman, Paul. 1992. "Prize Cases." In *The Oxford Companion to the Supreme Court of the United States*, edited by Kermit Hall, 681. Oxford: Oxford University Press.
Fisher, Louis. 1985. *Constitutional Conflicts between Congress and the President*. Princeton, NJ: Princeton University Press.
Prize Cases. 1862. 67 U.S. 635.

Puerto Rican Nationalist Party Revolt

The Puerto Rican Nationalist Party (Nationalist Party) Revolt was a series of actions taken against the governments of Puerto Rico and the United States in pursuit of independence from the United States. Since shortly after its acquisition by the United States as part of the Spanish American War, the territory of Puerto Rico has operated with a local civilian government, but under the control of the US government. Puerto Rico's semi-autonomous status as neither state nor independent nation has left it ripe for secessionist sentiment.

The Puerto Rico Nationalist Party formed in 1922 in response to what it perceived as colonial occupation by the United States. By the 1930s, the party was advocating for independence through armed conflict against the United States. The party was led for decades by Pedro Albizu Campos, Puerto Rico's first Harvard Law School graduate, who adopted Puerto Rican independence as his life's work. In 1934, he led a large agricultural strike that caught the attention of the Federal Bureau of Investigation and US military. In response, the United States appointed a military governor who militarized the Puerto Rican police force. Albizu Campos also organized a young people's military organization, Los Cadetes de la República, which trained for the eventual armed revolt for independence. In 1936, two cadets were executed for assassinating a police official and Albizu Campos was convicted of sedition.

After spending nearly two decades in US federal prisons, Albizu Campos was released. The long-time pro-US governor of Puerto Rico had instituted a gag law that allowed imprisonment of anyone who publicly expressed pro-independence views and even banned the Puerto Rican flag. Albizu Campos determined to rise up against the pro-US government and the United States itself. In October 1950, Albizu Campos and the Nationalist Party began its insurrection with a series of attacks against local police and towns. Albizu Campos's forces had some early successes, capturing two small towns. But the governor, whose own home was the target of some of Campos's attacks, successfully used federal and local forces to return control of the towns to the government. The Puerto Rican Air National Guard strafed one of the towns Albizu Campos controlled, marking the first time US military forces launched an air attack against US citizens. Albizu Campos's secessionist actions did not end there. The day following the defeat of the Nationalist Party's uprising in Puerto Rico, two members of the party attempted to assassinate President Harry Truman at Blair House, the home where he was staying in Washington, DC while the White House was being renovated. This plot failed before the men gained entry to the home but resulted in the deaths of one Secret Service member and one attacker. Albizu Campos was subsequently sentenced to eighty years in but in September 1953, Albizu Campos was pardoned by the Puerto Rican governor.

In October 1953, Congress overwhelmingly approved Puerto Rico's status as an unincorporated US territory, a "Commonwealth" of the United States. Seeing this development as a significant threat to eventual independence, four members of the Nationalist Party attacked the US Capitol. They smuggled pistols into the building, entered the visitors' gallery above the House of Representatives, and opened fire on the House floor, where more than 240 members of Congress were voting. They wounded five members of Congress, all of whom recovered. Albizu Campos publicly praised the attack and was suspected of having planned it. The governor revoked his pardon and Campos was reimprisoned. In 1965, Albizu Campos was pardoned a second time and died shortly after leaving prison. He remains a folk hero among some in the Puerto Rican community, with schools, streets, and other buildings named in his honor in Puerto Rico, Chicago, and New York City.

A more recent violent revolutionary group called Fuerzas Armadas de Liberacion Nacional (FALN) was founded in the 1970s. The FALN continued the work of revolution and independence of their predecessors, but adopted a Marxist ideology and escalated the violence significantly. For example, from its founding in 1974 until its disbandment in 1984, the FALN was responsible for a staggering 130 bombings. FALN was one of the best-organized and well-trained domestic terror organizations within the United States during that period.

See Also: Assassination; Fuerzas Armadas de Liberacion Nacional (FALN); Insurrection; Rebellion; Sedition

Resources

Anderson, Jon Lee. 2017. "The Dream of Puerto Rican Independence, and the Story of Heriberto Marín." *New Yorker*, December 27, 2017.

Denis, Nelson A. 2015. *War against All Puerto Ricans: Revolution and Terror in America's Colony*. New York: Nation Books.

Smith, Harrison. 2020. "Rafael Cancel Miranda, Puerto Rican Nationalist Who Opened Fire on U.S. Capitol, Dies at 89." *Washington Post*, March 3, 2020.

"Truman Plotter Freed in San Juan; Albizu, 73, Pardoned—Led Assassination Plan in '50." *New York Times*, November 16, 1964, 19.

R

Radio Traitors and Anti-State Propaganda during the Second World War

During the Second World War, several American citizens engaged in propaganda efforts against the United States on behalf of enemies Germany, Italy, and Japan. The propagandists who received the most attention primarily used a relatively new media form that had captured the world's interest: radio. Two of the most notorious and effective anti-US radio propagandists during the Second World War—"Axis Sally" (Mildred Gillars) and "Tokyo Rose" (Iva Toguri D'Aquino)—are detailed separately in this book. Several additional "radio traitors" are profiled here. The propagandists' efforts to undermine American resolve in its fight against the Axis powers during the Second World War were marginal, but actions that may have constituted protected criticism of the government and policy during peacetime were viewed by the US government and courts as treasonous efforts to aid its enemies during the war (see Aid and Comfort).

In 1942, during the early days of America's involvement in the Second World War, President Roosevelt and Federal Bureau of Investigation (FBI) Director J. Edgar Hoover agreed that something should be done about Americans who were spreading propaganda on behalf of enemy governments. In 1943, the ensuing FBI investigation led to seven American citizens being indicted for treason because of their radio work broadcasting propaganda against the United States and its allies: Ezra Pound, Fred W. Kaltenbach, Robert H. Best, Douglas Chandler, Edward L. Delaney, Constance Drexel, and Jane Anderson. Of these seven, only two ultimately stood trial for treason.

Ezra Pound, born in 1885 in Idaho Territory, was the most well-known of the seven Americans indicted in February 1943. He was an important modern poet and, as an editor, helped discover and promote several literary giants, including T. S. Eliot, James Joyce, and Ernest Hemingway. During the Second World War, Pound lived in Italy and wrote and recorded hundreds of radio broadcasts for the Italian government. In these broadcasts, Pound expressed support for Benito Mussolini, Adolf Hitler, and fascism. As with many other radio traitors, Pound verbally attacked the United States, Great Britain, President Roosevelt, international weapons manufacturers, and the Jewish people. A few days after Mussolini was shot, Pound was captured and turned over to the United States. After several months of incarceration in a prison camp in Italy, Pound was escorted back to the United States for trial. After his arraignment in late 1945, the judge presiding over the case ordered Pound to be confined to a psychiatric ward. Several psychiatrists evaluated him, with differing diagnoses and opinions on whether he was fit to stand trial. Pound remained in psychiatric confinement until 1958, when he was released, and he moved to Italy. Pound died in 1972, having never stood trial for treason.

Fred W. Kaltenbach was one of several Americans accused of treason due to his broadcasts of Axis propaganda that reached into the United States via shortwave radio. Born in Iowa to a German citizen who had emigrated to the United States, Kaltenbach was on a post-high school graduation cycling tour of Germany with his brother in 1914 when the First World War erupted. The Kaltenbach boys were arrested by Germany on suspicion of espionage but released a few months later. Despite this experience, Kaltenbach loved Germany and thought of it as home. Nevertheless, Kaltenbach returned to the United States and accepted a commission in the United States Army just as the First World War was ending. Kaltenbach eventually became a teacher in Iowa, but during the period between the two world wars, concerned by the growth of "Bolshevism," he embraced fascism. In 1935 he formed a high school student group that bore a strong resemblance to aspects of the Nazi Hitler Youth program in Germany, including dressing in brown military-style uniforms, secret initiation rituals, and going on weekend group hikes. Kaltenbach was dismissed from his teaching position, and he returned to Germany where he married a German woman. The newlyweds then took a honeymoon to the United States with funds provided by the German Ministry of Propaganda. Shortly before Germany invaded Poland in 1939, the Kaltenbachs returned to Germany, where Fred began his radio broadcasts.

Germany's radio propaganda broadcasts were the brainchild of Joseph Goebbels, who believed the broadcasts could erode American popular support for involvement in the war and thereby curtail US support to Britain. Kaltenbach's first radio addresses were in the form of a program he called "Letters to Iowa," in which he praised Germany and the German war effort, supported American isolationism, and urged Americans to not let Britain "drag America" into the Second World War. In mid-1940, Kaltenbach added additional programs that were broadcast into the United States. Eventually, his broadcasts could be heard throughout America on Monday and Saturday evenings and Thursday and Friday afternoons. Though Kaltenbach's pro-Germany, anti-American broadcasts were initially considered protected free speech, once the United States entered war against Germany on December 11, 1941, his propaganda supporting Germany legally transformed into treason. After he learned of his indictment for treason, Kaltenbach insisted in a broadcast that he was guilty of "treason to Roosevelt and his warmongers, but not to the American people." Kaltenbach protested that he assisted the Third Reich "out of a genuine desire to promote good relations between Germany, the land of my father, and America, the land of my birth." He closed that broadcast quoting Patrick Henry: "If that be treason, make the most of it" (Laurie 1994). After the fall of Berlin in 1945, United States Army officials were on their way to Kaltenbach's Berlin home when Soviet agents swooped in and took Kaltenbach into custody. For months, American military requests to the Soviet Union to produce Kaltenbach were met with resistance and denials about his whereabouts. Eventually, the Soviet Union announced that Kaltenbach had died in Soviet captivity in October 1945, an assessment with which the United States eventually agreed. The United States District Court dismissed the indictment against him in April 1948.

Robert H. Best was one of several experienced journalists who would become radio traitors during the Second World War. Best was born in South Carolina, but after graduating from the Columbia University School of Journalism in 1922, he toured Europe and settled in Vienna where he served as a freelance correspondent, contributing articles to the *New York Times*, *Chicago Daily News*, *Time*, and *Newsweek*. Ironically, when the United States declared war on Germany on December 11, 1941, Best was arrested by German authorities on suspicion of espionage and detained at a German internment camp for a few months. Best told his German captors he did not wish to be exchanged along with other American journalists back to the United States, and instead volunteered his services for German State Radio. Broadcasting as "Mr. Guess Who," Best's invective against Germany's enemies largely focused on, and promoted, anti-Semitism rhetoric. In one such broadcast, which was played for the jury at his eventual trial for treason, Best congratulated listeners for writing "letters to their members of Congress demanding that 'they impeach funny Frankie and purge the White House of the stain and curse he has brought upon it with his shame trust of Jews and Jewocrats'" ("Best's Jury" 1948). In January 1946, Best was arrested by British forces in Austria and returned to the United States. In April

1948, he was convicted of twelve counts of treason and sentenced to life in prison. He died in federal custody in December 1952.

Born in Chicago, Douglas Chandler served in the United States Navy during the First World War and then became a writer for the *Baltimore Sunday American* newspaper. Following financial ruin in 1929, Chandler moved to Germany, where he worked as a freelance journalist whose articles painted an idealized portrait of Nazi Germany, including contributions to *National Geographic* magazine. After the perceived failures of Kaltenbach and Delaney to generate a sufficient audience in the United States, Chandler was trotted out by the Goebbels propaganda machine. Broadcasting as "Paul Revere," Chandler's broadcasts began with the melody of Yankee Doodle and the clip-clop of horse hooves. Broadcasting six nights each week, Chandler urged his fellow Americans to throw off the tyranny of "Roosevelt and his Jews," who were his frequent targets. Chandler's broadcasts eventually demonstrated he knew of, and supported, Hitler's "Final Solution" to eradicate Judaism, and he urged it be adopted in the United States. After his indictment in 1943, his broadcasts grew somewhat less vitriolic, often featuring classical music and poetry. Chandler was arrested by United States Army personnel in May 1945 and later flown to the United States to stand trial. Over his lawyers' objections that his broadcasts had been merely an exercise of his First Amendment rights, and despite an insanity defense, in June 1947, Chandler was convicted of ten counts of treason and sentenced to life imprisonment. Twenty witnesses testified against him, including sixteen former German colleagues. In 1963, when Chandler was the last of the radio traitors still imprisoned, President John F. Kennedy commuted Chandler's sentence on the condition he immediately leave the United States. Chandler returned to Germany, where he lived at least until the 1970s. The time, location, and circumstances of his death are not publicly known.

Edward Delaney was born in Illinois. He was an actor, theatrical manager, and author. In December 1939, he moved to Italy, where he was recruited to Berlin to create a series of pro-German broadcasts for German State Radio. He began broadcasting on German radio in 1940, using the pseudonym E. D. Ward. His broadcasts primarily featured news favorable to Germany and contained less invective against the United States than some other radio traitors' transmissions. Apparently, Delaney made no broadcast recordings after the United States declared war on Germany on December 11, 1941, and he left German State Radio and Berlin in 1943. In May 1945, Delaney was arrested in Prague by Czechoslovak police and turned over to the United States. He was returned to the United States in 1947, but the Department of Justice (DOJ) soon thereafter dropped charges against him, finding that it was not worthwhile to continue to investigate him in light of the "very few wartime recordings made by him" (Department of Justice 1946). Delaney died in 1972.

Another American indicted for treason in 1943, but who never faced trial due to lack of evidence, was Constance Drexel. Born in Germany and naturalized, she first achieved notoriety for falsely claiming to belong to the famous Drexel family of Philadelphia. She completed her education at the Sorbonne in Paris and then bounced back and forth between the United States and various European countries, serving as a correspondent covering a wide variety of political issues, including women's suffrage and the League of Nations. In 1939, Drexel settled in Germany. After Germany's 1939 invasion of Poland, Drexel wrote stories for American newspapers, including *The New York Times*, that were uniformly positive regarding Nazi Germany and its impact on Europe. In one such piece, she praised the German Anschluss in Austria as saving Austrians from certain starvation. However, rather than politics or international relations, Drexel's radio broadcasts on Nazi channels usually featured positive accounts of Germany's art, music, food, fashion, and culture. After the war, Drexel was arrested and detained by the United States, then returned to Ellis Island, New York. During proceedings to determine whether she could enter the United States or had forfeited her citizenship, the DOJ conceded that prosecution for the indicted treason charge was no longer possible because it had failed to collect sufficient evidence. Moreover, investigators conceded that Drexel's broadcasts were not "political in nature" (Department of Justice 1946). The treason charges against Drexel were dropped. Drexel died in August 1956, as she was preparing to move from the United States to Switzerland.

Like Edward Delaney and Constance Drexel, Jane Anderson was indicted for treason in 1943 but never tried, also due to lack of evidence. Anderson was a war reporter during the Spanish Civil War who became an evangelist for Francisco Franco and other far-right figures and causes. While working for the Spanish Ministry of Propaganda, she was recruited by German State Radio in 1940. Broadcasting from Berlin under the name "The Georgia Peach," Anderson's programs featured praise for Hitler and condemnation of Roosevelt and Churchill. Her broadcasts typically began and ended with her slogan "Always remember progressive Americans eat Kellogg's Corn Flakes and listen to both sides of the story" (Department of Justice 1946). As with Drexel and Delaney, though Anderson had been indicted in 1943 and arrested after the war and turned over to the United States, DOJ dropped the charges due to lack of evidence regarding broadcasts after the United States entered the war against Germany. She did not return to the United States and died in Spain in 1972.

Though not among those originally indicted in absentia in 1943, Herbert John Burgman was another American citizen ultimately convicted of treason against the United States for his anti-US broadcasts from Germany. Originally from Minnesota, in 1921 Burgman joined the State Department as a clerk in the United States Embassy in Berlin. Rather than return to the United States during the Second World War, Burgman chose to remain in Berlin, where he became a broadcaster for "Radio Debunk, the Voice of All Free America," using the pseudonym Joe Scanlon. Like other propagandists, Burgman's primary targets were President Roosevelt, Jews, and Communists. He claimed that Britain and the Soviet Union were in collusion against the United States, echoing a theme of several radio traitors who attempted to undercut popular support for the American war effort. Burgman also attempted to erode support for American servicemen, claiming prostitution and sexually transmitted diseases were rampant among US military personnel stationed overseas. After the United States defeated Germany in 1945, Burgman was arrested by American soldiers and eventually returned to the United States to stand trial for treason. Evidence against him included recordings of his broadcasts and accounts of two German women who testified that Burgman had boasted about how his broadcasts hurt the United States. In December 1949, Burgman was convicted of thirteen counts of treason and sentenced to imprisonment for six to twenty years. He died in federal prison in December 1953.

Donald Day was another radio traitor who was not indicted in 1943 with the other propagandists profiled here but was detained for a time after the war with Herbert Burgman and Mildred Gillars ("Axis Sally"). Born in Brooklyn, Day served in the United States Navy during the First World War and became a journalist. He lived in Riga, Latvia, and reported on the Soviet Union for nearly two decades, leaving after the Soviets invaded Latvia in 1940. Day relocated to Sweden, then Finland, and eventually to Germany. Day's experiences reporting on the Soviet Union led him to believe the West needed to defend against dangerous Communist expansion, and he came to believe Nazi Germany was the West's best hope. Day broadcast radio programs to the United States and to American forces in Europe from August 1944 until April 1945, denouncing the Soviet Union and President Roosevelt's alliance with Stalin and vigorously promoting anti-Semitic ideology. Day was arrested by US forces in May 1945, then conditionally released in December 1946. Day was rearrested in January 1949 to be charged with treason, but the DOJ soon dropped the case despite possessing evidence against Day similar to that used in its successful prosecutions of Best, Chandler, and Gillars. Moreover, DOJ had previously concluded Day had committed treason, leaving speculation as to why the case against Day was dropped. Some have contended it was not due to insufficient evidence, but rather because other agencies of the US government believed Day possessed information about the Soviet Union valuable to the United States. Others have speculated that by 1949, sufficient time had elapsed since the end of the war that prosecution for treason during the war was no longer considered important.

See Also: Aid and Comfort (Aid to Enemies of the State); Axis Sally (Mildred Gillars); Espionage; Tokyo Rose (Iva Toguri D'Aquino); Treason

Resources

"Best's Jury Hears His Talk for Nazis." *The New York Times*, April 3, 1948, 6.

"Burgman Guilty of Treason; Jury out Nearly Five Hours." *The Washington Post*, November 16, 1949.

Childs, Harwood, and John B. Whitton, eds. 1942. *Propaganda by Shortwave*. Princeton, NJ: Princeton University Press.

Department Of Justice. 1946. "Office Memorandum; Subject: Treason Cases." June 14, 1946. Accessed November 1, 2023. https://www.justice.gov/sites/default/files/criminal/legacy/2010/04/11/ezra-pound-p4.pdf, 15.

Edwards, John Carver. 1991. *Berlin Calling: American Broadcasters in Service to the Third Reich.* Westport, CT: Praeger.

Laurie, Clayton D. 1994. "Goebbels's Iowan: Frederick W. Kaltenbach and Nazi Short-Wave Radio Broadcasts to America, 1939–1945." *Annals of Iowa* 53: 219–45. Accessed November 1, 2023. https://usgerrelations.traces.org/kaltenbach.html.

Shirer, William L. 1943a. "The American Radio Traitors." *Harper's Magazine*, October 1943, 397.

Shirer, William L. 1943b. "The Propaganda Front." *The Washington Post*, February 14, 1943.

Strochlic, Nina. 2017. "The Nazi Who Infiltrated National Geographic." *National Geographic*, April 27, 2017.

Tully, Andrew. 1949. "Another Accused Traitor in Dock." *The Pittsburgh Press*, October 14, 1949.

"*United States v. Best*." *The American Journal of International Law* 42 (July 1948): 727–9.

Wilkes, Donald E. 1995. "Jane Anderson: The Nazi Georgia Peach." *The Athens Observer*, May 18, 1995, 5.

Rahman, United States v. (1999)

See Seditious Conspiracy

Rebellion

The term "rebellion" in common vernacular generally means an open, organized, and armed uprising against one's own government. The Civil War was the most significant rebellion in US history (see American Civil War and Treason). Numerous other examples throughout American history include Bacon's Rebellion, Fries's Rebellion, Shay's Rebellion, the Whiskey Rebellion, Gabriel's Rebellion, Vesey's Rebellion, Dorr's Rebellion, and the Green Corn Rebellion. The term "rebellion" is distinguishable from the term "revolution." Thomas Jefferson spoke of the right to revolution, and the United States has its genesis in the American Revolution (see American Revolutionary War and Treason). Whether an armed uprising against one's own government is labeled a rebellion or revolution seems to depend on the overall outcome of the event: "The ability of those fighting to overthrow a government to sustain their cause ultimately affects whether history calls them revolutionaries or rebels—as the Confederate states discovered when they lost the American Civil War" (Shafritz 1988, 478). Additionally, the term "rebellion" is often used along with the term "insurrection" both in the Constitution (see, e.g., Fourteenth Amendment, clause 3) and in federal statutory law (see, e.g., 18 United States Code Section 2383).

In the Constitution, the term "rebellion" is expressly referenced several times, once in the main text (Article I, Section 9) and four times within the Fourteenth Amendment (see clauses 2–4). Article I, Section 9 deals with the power of the Congress to suspend the writ of habeas corpus and provides that "the Privilege of the Writ of Habeas Corpus shall not be suspended, unless when in Cases of Rebellion or Invasion the public Safety may require it." Under the Disqualification Clause of the Fourteenth Amendment (clause 3), an individual who "engaged in insurrection or rebellion" against the United States is disqualified from holding any public office. Similarly, the terms "insurrection or rebellion" are both used together in the Fourteenth Amendment, clause 4, which provides that "the validity of the public debt of the United States, authorized by law, including debts incurred for payment of pensions and bounties for services in suppressing insurrection or rebellion, shall not be questioned." Finally, the "representation clause" of the Fourteenth Amendment (clause 2), provides "representatives shall be apportioned among the several States according to their respective numbers … except for participation in rebellion, or other crime, the basis of representation."

Under federal law (18 United States Code Section 2383), Congress has criminalized both "rebellion" and "insurrection": "Whoever incites, sets on foot, assists, or engages in any rebellion or insurrection against the authority of the United States or the laws thereof, or gives aid or comfort thereto, shall be fined under this title or imprisoned not more than ten years, or both; and shall be incapable of holding any office under the United States."

Finally, under Article I, Section 8, the power to "provide for calling forth the Militia to execute the Laws of the Union, suppress Insurrections and repel Invasions," Congress enacted the Insurrection Act. Amended multiple times over the years and spanning several sections, the Insurrection Act authorizes the president to deploy military forces inside the United States to suppress rebellions. For example, 10 United States Code Section 252, part of the Insurrection Act, provides:

> Whenever the President considers that unlawful obstructions, combinations, or assemblages, or rebellion against the authority of the United States, make it impracticable to enforce the laws of the United States in any State by the ordinary course of judicial proceedings, he may call into Federal service such of the militia of any State, and use such of the armed forces, as he considers necessary to enforce those laws or to suppress the rebellion.

See Also: American Civil War and Treason; American Revolution and Treason; Bacon's Rebellion (1676–7); Disqualification Clause; Dorr's Rebellion (1841–42); Fries's Rebellion (1799); Gabriel's Rebellion (1800); Green Corn Rebellion; Insurrection; Insurrection Act; Jefferson, Thomas; Shay's Rebellion (1786–7); Vesey's Rebellion (1822); Whiskey Rebellion

Resources

"Rebellion or Insurrection," 18 United States Code Section 2383.
Shafritz, Jay. 1988. *The Dorsey Dictionary of American Government and Politics*. Chicago: The Dorsey Press.
"Use of Militia and Armed Forces to Enforce Federal Authority." 10 United States Code Section 252.

Riot and Incitement to Riot

The offense of riot or incitement to riot is a criminal offense at both the state and federal levels. At common law and pursuant to many state statutes, the offense of riot is typically defined as a boisterous disturbance of the peace by several people or a group of people collectively committing an act (lawful or unlawful) in a violent or turbulent fashion. The essential components of the offense of riot in most jurisdictions are threefold: first, some assemblance of persons; second, the use of force or violence or threat of force or violence by words or action; and third, the ability to immediately and imminently effectuate force or violence. Many jurisdictions specify that the group involved must consist of at least three individuals for the offense of riot to be applicable.

The difference between a lawful assembly and exercise of freedom of speech (however offensive) under the First Amendment and the offense of riot is often a fine line and depends on whether the speakers or actors in the group are capable of effectuating immediate or imminent violence. In *Brandenburg v. Ohio* (1969), the United States Supreme Court held "that the constitutional guarantees of free speech and free press" prohibited the government from criminalizing speech calling for violence unless the speech or action is "directed to inciting or producing imminent lawless action and is likely to incite or produce such action."

An example of the prosecution for the offense of inciting a riot can be seen in a 2002 New York case entitled *People v. Upshaw*. In this case, a group of five defendants were prosecuted for "inciting to riot" for approaching a crowd in New York City in the days following September 11, 2001, and yelling out inflammatory language indicating that they supported the attacks and were disappointed that the carnage was not greater. They also threatened the crowd with violence. Some of the inflammatory remarks included: "ITS GOOD THAT THE WORLD TRADE CENTER WAS BOMBED. MORE COPS AND FIREMEN SHOULD HAVE DIED. MORE BOMBS SHOULD HAVE DROPPED AND MORE PEOPLE SHOULD HAVE BEEN KILLED. WE'VE GOT SOMETHING FOR YOUR ASSES" (*People v. Upshaw,* 706) (capitalization of words in original). In denying the defendants' claim that their actions were protected under the First Amendment (specifically, the rights of assembly and freedom of speech), the trial court held that "viewed in context, the defendant's words … were plainly intended to incite the crowd to violence, and not simply to express a point of view." The court further explained that the defendants "accosted people in the crowd and shouted a threat—WE'VE GOT SOMETHING FOR YOUR ASSES—directly into the faces of some of the onlookers …. [t]his conduct went well beyond protected speech and firmly into the realm of criminal behavior" (*People v. Upshaw*, 708–9).

Congress criminalized the offense of riots during the anti-war and racial protests in the 1960s. The federal offense is defined at 18 United States Code Section 2101 and criminalizes riots wherein one "travels in interstate commerce … or uses any facility of interstate or foreign commerce, including, but not limited to … the mail, telegraph, telephone, radio, or television." One is guilty of violating this statute if, in addition to travel or use of interstate commerce, the person has the "intent (1) to incite a riot; or (2) to organize, promote, encourage, participate in, or carry on a riot; or (3) to commit any act of violence in furtherance of a riot; or (4) to aid or abet any person in inciting or participating in or carrying on a riot or committing any act of violence in furtherance of a riot." The federal statute further defines a riot as "a public disturbance," involving "an act or acts of violence," wherein the act of violence is committed by at least one person who is part of a group of three or more individuals. Defendants found guilty of violating this federal statute "shall be fined … or imprisoned not more than five years, or both."

The United States Department of Justice (DOJ) has prosecuted individuals under the Riot Act in recent years. Two notable cases illustrating the continued viability of the federal criminal offense can be seen in the United States Fourth Circuit Court of Appeals case entitled *United States v. Miselis*, 972 F.3d 518 (4th Cir. 2020) (involving defendants from the white supremist Rise Above Movement who traveled from California to participate in the notorious "Unite the Right" demonstration in Charlottesville, Virginia) and the United States District Court decision in *United States v. Betts*, 509 F. Supp. 3d 1053 (C.D. Ill. 2020) (involving a defendant who posted threats of rioting on social media for a specific date and then participated in rioting and looting a short time later). Yet, despite the continued prosecution of defendants by the DOJ for violating the Riot Act in recent years, none of the over one thousand charged individuals involved in the Capitol Insurrection on January 6, 2021, were indicted or charged with violation of this statute, despite many of the charged individuals meeting the statutory elements of the offense. Donald Trump's role in inciting the Capitol riot has been the subject of much scrutiny (see, e.g., Conklin 2022).

See Also: *Brandenburg v. Ohio* (1969); Capitol Insurrection on January 6, 2021; Insurrection; September 11, 2001

Resources

18 U.S. Code Section 2101–2102. Domestic Security: Homeland Security Organization. 2023. 6 U.S. Code Sections 101–677.

Conklin, Michael. 2022. "Capitol Offense: Is Donald Trump Guilty of Inciting a Riot at the Capitol?" *University of St. Thomas Journal of Law & Public Policy* 15: 483–97.

People v. Upshaw. 190 Misc. 2d 704–9 (March 19, 2002).

Wright, R. George. 2021–2022. "Re-Reading the Riot Act." *Alabama Civil Rights & Civil Liberties Law Review* 13: 79–117.

Rosenberg, Julius, and Ethel

The 1951 case of Julius and Ethel Rosenberg for conspiring to pass atomic secrets to the Soviet Union is one of the most sensational, controversial, famous, and significant espionage cases in American history. Even after the Rosenbergs' conviction, controversy continued to swirl around the case and the imposition of the death sentence. There were mass protests around the world. J. Edgar Hoover characterized it as the "crime of the century," while French philosopher and Nobel Prize recipient Jean-Paul Sartre described the case and the execution as "a legal lynching which smears with blood a whole nation." Approximately 3 million letters were sent to the White House requesting clemency for Ethel Rosenberg, including letters from Albert Einstein and Pope Pius XII. Refusing to pardon the conviction or commute the sentence for either Julius or Ethel Rosenberg, President Dwight Eisenhower remarked that the "nature of the crime for which they have been found guilty and sentenced far exceeds that of the taking of the life of another citizen; it involves the deliberate betrayal of the entire nation and could very well result in the death of many, many thousands of innocent citizens." Eisenhower then added "by immeasurably increasing the chances of atomic war, the Rosenbergs may have condemned to death tens of millions of innocent people all over the world" (Falcoff 2002, 57). And for the next half-century, many would continue to hotly debate whether the Rosenbergs were guilty of espionage, whether the trial errors led to a massive injustice, or whether either party was deserving of punishment. Only in the last several decades has definitive evidence emerged to answer some of these long lingering questions.

In 1949, US spy planes detected elevated levels of radioactivity over Siberia, demonstrating the Soviet Union was testing newly developed atomic weaponry. At the same time, US intelligence officers had deciphered encrypted Soviet communications that revealed the Soviets had infiltrated America's nuclear weapons program and had operatives inside US installations like Los Alamos, New Mexico. For US defense officials, the infiltration and espionage explained how a country they perceived as an industrially backward nation could so quickly develop a sophisticated nuclear arsenal, and only four years after the United States had done so through its Manhattan Project. During the heightened investigations that followed, the US and British intelligence apprehended Klaus Fuchs, who admitted to transmitting atomic secrets to the Soviets while working at the Los Alamos facility. Fuchs received the maximum sentence permitted by British law at the time, but he also gave up sources, which led US investigators to Harry Gold, and then to David Greenglass, both Los Alamos workers. During interrogation by the FBI, Greenglass, a 28-year-old living in New York City, admitted to being a Soviet spy and said that he had been recruited by his brother-in-law, Julius Rosenberg, and sister (Rosenberg's wife), Ethel.

The Rosenbergs, along with a third co-defendant named Martin Sobell, were charged with conspiracy to pass atomic secrets to the Soviets to aid in their building of a bomb and also in violating the Espionage Act of 1917. David Greenglass (and another accomplice named Harry Gold) pleaded guilty and provided testimony against both Julius and Ethel Rosenberg. As prosecutors later admitted, they hoped the charges (and threat of the death penalty) would get Julius and Ethel to name other members of the spy ring. In documents that were later declassified, it became clear that US intelligence had intercepted Soviet communications that indicated the involvement of numerous individuals in espionage activities. Not wanting to reveal to the Soviets that their communications had been compromised, the United States preferred to identify spies through the people like the Rosenbergs as part of their criminal confessions.

The Rosenbergs' trial began on March 6, 1951, in United States District Court in New York, and lasted three weeks. David Greenglass and his wife, Ruth, were the main witnesses. They were able to provide crucial testimony that they were recruited into the Soviet spy ring by Julius Rosenberg and present at meetings with Julius and Ethel where espionage issues were being discussed and notes from documents were typed up for their Soviet intelligence handler. Greenglass also gave damaging testimony that Julius Rosenberg had arranged for Greenglass to give Harry Gold the design of the atomic weapon utilized by the United States Army at Nagasaki, Japan, during the Second World War. The design of the bomb used at Nagasaki differed significantly from the one used at Hiroshima, information the Soviets lacked. When Harry Gold testified, he named Soviet KGB officer Anatoli Yakovlev as their initial contact, thereby establishing the former connection between Gold, Greenglass, and Rosenberg with Soviet Union Intelligence Services. Decades later, Julius Rosenberg's own Soviet handler, Alexander Feklisov, recounted that he met Julius Rosenberg over fifty times to transfer documents. Feklisov also claimed that Rosenberg passed "some 9,000 pages of secret documents relating to 100 different programs in the planning stage, half of which were deemed 'very valuable' by the KGB … [and] even brought him an actual fuse-proximity detonator" (Falcoff 2002, 55).

While the above information from Julius Rosenberg's Soviet handler did not become public until over a half-century later, after a three-week trial, the jury believed it had sufficient information to convict both Julius and Ethel Rosenberg for conspiracy to commit espionage after about eight hours of deliberation, and the Rosenbergs were found guilty at the end of March 1951. The execution date was set for May 26, 1951, but the appellate process took approximately two years, so the Rosenbergs were not executed until Friday, June 19, 1953. The execution by electric chair took place on the Rosenbergs' fourteenth wedding anniversary. Julius and Ethel Rosenberg repeatedly denied being Soviet spies up through their executions.

For a half century, many legal scholars and historians have pointed out blatant errors in the trial process (e.g., *ex parte* communications between the prosecutor and the judge) and that there was insufficient information to establish that the Rosenbergs were in fact Soviet spies. However, during this same time period, the dissolution of the Soviet Union occurred, and with the declassification of once Top-Secret US government documents, it is now quite clear that Julius Rosenberg was not only a Soviet spy but the leader of a spy network in the United States who recruited others to spy for the Soviet Union. Evidence of Julius Rosenberg's guilt has come from a variety of sources. Former Soviet Secretary General, Nikiti Khrushchev, in his 1990 published memoir (and comments made on audio tapes for the book), stated that he overheard Joseph Stalin remarking that the "Rosenbergs provided very significant help" (Khrushchev 1990, 194). Then, in 1995, the United States declassified intercepted communication cables known by the code name Venona or Venona Cables. Julius Rosenberg's name appears numerous times in these secret Soviet communications, and he had several code names (including "Liberal" and "King") that are also frequently mentioned. One report refers to Ethel Rosenberg as "Liberal's wife, Ethel." Julius Rosenberg's brother-in-law is referred to by the code name "Caliber." Julius Rosenberg's handler, Alexander Feklisov, is mentioned often in the cables alongside references to Julius Rosenberg, and Feklisov asserts within the documents that Rosenberg had been helpful in passing US military information to the Soviets. Finally, in 2008, Martin Sobell (a co-defendant with Julius and Ethel Rosenberg in the 1951 trial), and a life-long friend of Julius Rosenberg, admitted that both he and Julius were Soviet spies. Thus, despite the legal irregularities of the trial, Julius Rosenberg was indeed engaged in massive espionage for the Soviet Union and recruited other individuals to spy.

The more puzzling question is whether Ethel Rosenberg was wrongly convicted. A former KGB agent turned historian claimed in 1995 that in going through Soviet archives he found references to both Julius and Ethel as Soviet spies/assets. Ethel Rosenberg was also mentioned in the Venona Cables, but never with a code name, and only as the "Liberal's wife." Most historians (and even Ethel's oldest son, Michael Meeropol) have stated that Ethel Rosenberg knew about and supported Julius's actions, agreed with his politics (both were long-time Communist Party members), and may have recruited others into the spy ring, including her sister-in-law and brother. However, to be guilty of conspiracy to commit espionage, it would be insufficient that Ethel Rosenberg knew of Julius Rosenberg's criminal enterprise and plans, or that she supported such endeavors. Rather, the government must prove that there was an agreement among the participants as to the purpose plus some overt act (however small) in furtherance of the criminal conspiracy. The primary evidence that ensured Ethel Rosenberg's conviction at trial was testimony from her sister-in-law Ruth Greenglass that Ethel typed notes for Julius Rosenberg to pass along to his Soviet handlers. The timing of this crucial information is curious as Ruth Greenglass offered this information to the government only weeks before the start of the trial, and after Ethel Rosenberg refused to give names or testify against her husband.

This was the most damning evidence against Ethel Rosenberg because it was the only evidence the government had of an overt act in furtherance of the conspiracy—and it was likely untrue. Without this evidence, the government lacked a case against Ethel Rosenberg. Indeed, the prosecutor dramatically invoked this testimony twice to the jury, and reminded the jury that the courtroom testimony was that Ethel Rosenberg on many occasions "sat at that typewriter and struck the keys, blow by blow, against her own country and in the interests of the Soviets." However, David Greenglass later recanted any knowledge of Ethel Rosenberg typing notes, and claimed before his death that he did not remember Ethel being in the room, but that he was told that was what happened by his wife, Ruth, and did not want to contradict his wife. Furthermore, recently released grand jury testimony revealed that Ruth Greenglass told multiple lies in her grand jury testimony and that there were many factual inconsistencies with her later statements. Unfortunately, the defense was not privy to that information at the time of the trial. Many historians have since argued that Ruth Greenglass typed the notes that sent Ethel Rosenberg to the electric chair and that David Greenglass protected his wife over his sister. David Greenglass agreed to plead guilty and testify for the government in exchange for a fifteen-year sentence and under the condition that Ruth Greenglass not be prosecuted. Thus, Ruth Greenglass was the only one of the four not prosecuted or punished (despite her knowledge of, and likely involvement in, the espionage activities). Morton Sobell received a thirty-year sentence.

Ironically, the government may not have wanted to execute the Rosenbergs, preferring that the couple supply valuable information about their espionage activities: "Had Julius and Ethel been willing to talk, Eisenhower was fully prepared to commute their sentence to life imprisonment. Even that would never have been served to term, for under federal law, as the President himself pointed out, 'if they do not go to the chair, they will be released in fifteen years'" (Falcoff 2002, 58). Even assuming their guilt, no civilian court before 1953—or since—imposed a death sentence for espionage. The Rosenbergs were the first and last executed in America for conspiracy to commit espionage.

See Also: Conspiracy, Criminal; Espionage; Espionage Act of 1917 and Sedition Act of 1918; Fuchs, Klaus

Resources

Falcoff, Mark. 2002. "Observations: Retrying the Rosenbergs (Again)." *Commentary* (March): 54–8.
Feklisov, Alexander, and Sergei Kostin. 2001. *The Man behind the Rosenbergs*. New York: Enigma Books.
Khrushchev, Nikita. 1990. *Khrushchev Remembers*. Boston: Little, Brown.
Roberts, Sam. 2011. "1951: The Rosenberg Trial." *The New York Times Upfront Magazine*.
Rosenberg v. United States, 346 U.S. 273 (1953).
Schneir, Walter. 2016. *Final Verdict: What Really Happened in the Rosenberg Case*. Brooklyn, NY: Melville House.

Ruby Ridge (1992)

The incident at Ruby Ridge, Idaho, in 1992, planted the seeds that would germinate and sprout into a virulent anti-government militant movement. Ruby Ridge caused many Americans to distrust the government and especially federal law enforcement agencies such as the Bureau of Alcohol, Tobacco, and Firearms (ATF) and the Federal Bureau of Investigation (FBI). The event also enraged and further radicalized many people who already distrusted and/or hated the government, people like Timothy McVeigh, who pointed to the government misconduct at Ruby Ridge as a factor in his decision to perpetrate the Oklahoma City Bombing in 1995. Three decades after the tragic events, the name Ruby Ridge still evokes strong emotions. The incident is not only a crime against the state (as federal laws and federal authority were willfully ignored and a US federal Marshal was killed), but also illustrates egregious government misconduct in the attempt to enforce laws.

At its core, Ruby Ridge entailed a stand-off between Randy Weaver and his family and federal law enforcement (ATF, FBI, and the United States Marshals Service). As a result of a number of mistakes made by law enforcement during the stand-off, two members of Randy Weaver's family were killed. His son (Sammy) was shot in the back, and his wife (Vicki) was shot in the face when opening a door to their cabin. United States Marshal William Degan was killed as well. The family dog, a golden Labrador named Striker, was killed by federal agents after they provoked it into a chase.

The ten-day standoff and multiple fatalities followed Randy Weaver's alleged violation of the National Firearms Act of 1934 (NFA). Weaver allegedly attempted to sell a shotgun with a barrel fewer than eighteen inches long, a category of firearm that must be registered with the ATF (with taxes paid) under the terms of the NFA. However, some Weaver supporters claimed he was targeted by the ATF after he refused to serve as a confidential informant against the Aryan Nation, a white supremacist group.

Randy Weaver was a Vietnam-era Army veteran who served stateside on active duty at Fort Bragg, North Carolina. He was trained as a Green Beret and reached the rank of sergeant before leaving the military. After attending the University of Northern Iowa, he and his wife Vicki began adhering to a religion with unorthodox tenets (e.g., that women were unclean during their menstrual period each month and should be isolated and that the world was coming to an end). The Weavers also believed that God mandated that their children should be homeschooled, a practice not permitted in Iowa, where they were living at the time. Thus, the Weavers moved to Idaho in 1983 and bought an isolated cabin in the woods. Randy Weaver also began attending Aryan Nation meetings, although he never became a member. Through the Aryan Nation meetings, Weaver met a person who agreed to help him sell shotguns with sawed-off barrels to make money. The Aryan Nation contact was in fact an undercover ATF agent.

Weaver was indicted on January 17, 1991, for violations of the NFA. On his way back to his cabin one day, Randy Weaver stopped to help people he believed were stranded motorists with car trouble. The "stranded motorists" were ATF agents using the ruse to apprehend Weaver before he made it back to his property. Upon his arrest, Weaver swore to the agents that he would never be tricked like this again. During his subsequent interrogation by law enforcement, ATF agents suggested Weaver could avoid prosecution on the NFA gun charges if he would serve as a confidential informant for the ATF and gather information about Aryan Nation activities. Weaver refused and then told alleged members of the Aryan Nation that they were under investigation by ATF.

Weaver's trial date was set for February 20, 1991. However, his probation officer told Weaver that his trial would commence on March 20, 1991. When Weaver did not appear in court on February 20,

1991, the judge issued a bench warrant for Weaver's arrest. From this point onward, Weaver refused to leave his mountaintop cabin, and after several months, the United States Marshals Service began surveilling the property (at a cost of $13,000 per week), hoping to arrest Weaver if or when he left his property.

On August 21, 1991, six heavily armed federal Marshals were testing the adequacy of Weaver's home surveillance and his perimeter surveillance by throwing pebbles onto the property to see if that would alert the Weaver family. This alerted the Weaver dog, Striker, and Striker began chasing the Marshals through the woods. Randy Weaver's son, Sammy, and family friend, Kevin Harris, grabbed their firearms and started following Striker, thinking Striker was chasing a deer. Striker, Sammy Weaver, and Kevin Harris caught up with the Marshals and a firefight ensued. The agents shot and killed Striker, who they claimed was attacking an agent. Sammy allegedly screamed and started running back to the cabin whereupon he was fatally shot in the back. Harris later claimed that, on discovering that Sammy had been shot, he began indiscriminately firing his weapon into the wooded area, killing United States Marshal William Degan. Federal agents claimed that Sammy Weaver was shot in the back by his own father (Randy Weaver) by mistake and that Harris intentionally aimed at, shot, and killed federal Marshal Degan. The FBI was called in, and because tensions were running high, the Governor of Idaho declared a state of emergency for the state of Idaho.

The tragic events unfortunately did not end on August 21. The FBI provided its agents a set of Rules of Engagement for the situation that allowed for the use of deadly force if any agent saw a person with a firearm on their person or in their possession (regardless of whether the firearm was being pointed or used in some fashion). Unbeknownst to the Weavers and Harris, a team of FBI snipers had set up a perimeter around the Weaver property. On August 22, Randy Weaver, his daughter Sara, and Harris went to an outbuilding to pray over the deceased body of Sammy Weaver. When the group came into sight, an FBI sniper (Lon Horiuchi) fired, hitting Randy Weaver under his arm. When this occurred, Vicki Weaver was in the main cabin, holding her ten-month-old child. When she heard the shot, Vicki Weaver opened the kitchen door and yelled for everyone to get back into the cabin. Randy Weaver, Sara Weaver, and Kevin Harris ran to the cabin and entered the open door. FBI sniper Horiuchi fired another shot, which he claimed was aimed at Harris. However, the shot struck Vicki in the head, with the bullet penetrating her temple, mouth, tongue, shattering her jawbone, and severing her carotid artery. When Vicki Weaver collapsed to the floor, she was still holding the ten-month-old baby. The velocity and caliber of the shot were so powerful (from a.308 caliber rifle) that the same round continued and struck Harris in the arm and chest cavity. The FBI sniper later claimed that he did not see Vicki Weaver at all, only Keven Harris.

After these killings, a ten-day standoff took place. Decorated Vietnam veteran Colonel James Bo Gritz attempted to serve as an intermediary. Gritz was a famed Green Beret, decorated sixty-two times for valor in Vietnam, and at the time, a cultural folk hero for many people in anti-government religious and survivalist movements. Gritz recorded a message for Randy Weaver, but the FBI refused to play it. When Gritz arrived at Ruby Ridge, the FBI denied Gritz entrance. Eventually, the FBI reluctantly allowed Gritz to serve as a go-between, and the family retained the services of renowned attorney Gerry Spence. Spence negotiated the surrender of Harris on August 30 and Randy Weaver on August 31.

Weaver and Harris were indicted by a federal grand jury for murder of a federal agent, aiding and abetting a murder, conspiracy, and assault. The trial began on April 14, 1993 (five days before the horrific events at Waco, Texas), and the case was submitted to the jury on June 15, 1993. The jury deliberated for close to a half month, finally returning a verdict on July 1, 1993. Harris was acquitted of all charges and released from jail (his pre-trial confinement). Weaver was acquitted of all the charges stemming from the events of August 21–30 as well. He was found guilty only on the charges of failing to appear for trial for his original NFA firearm charge and for violating the terms of parole for which he was subject. Weaver was sentenced to eighteen months and ordered to pay a fine of $10,000. Because Weaver already had time served because of his pre-trial confinement, he was released from jail on December 18, 1993, six months after the jury returned its verdict.

However, the Ruby Ridge saga was still far from over. The Department of Justice (DOJ) Office of Professional Responsibility issued a scathing 542-page report detailing governmental mishandling of the incident. While the report was meant to be kept secret, a copy was leaked and circulated on the internet.

In August 1994, Gerry Spence filed two lawsuits on behalf of Harris (alleging deprivation of civil rights) and Weaver (deprivation of civil rights and wrongful death). In 1995, the federal government settled with Weaver and paid $3.1 million in compensation for the deaths of Randy Weaver's son and wife but denied any wrongdoing in the incident. In 2000, Harris received $389,000 in compensation. The FBI disciplined twelve employees for their conduct. The FBI Assistant Director who approved the Rules of Engagement that led to the deaths of Randy Weaver's son and wife had a letter of censure placed in his personnel file.

In 1997, an Idaho county state prosecutor attempted to bring manslaughter charges against Lon Horiuchi, the FBI sniper. The DOJ contested the legitimacy of a state prosecution against a federal official for actions taken during the scope of his federal employment. In June 2000, in a six to five decision in *Idaho v. Horiuchi*, the United States Court of Appeals for the Ninth Circuit held that "when federal officers violate the Constitution, either through malice or excessive zeal, they can be held accountable for violating the state's criminal laws" and subject to state level prosecutions. Despite the green light for prosecution given by the federal court, in 2001 a newly elected prosecutor for Boundary County, Idaho, dropped the charges, saying that the state would have difficulty proving guilt beyond a reasonable doubt.

Ruby Ridge remains a lightning rod for many people. The actions of Randy Weaver could be argued as a crime against the state because he willfully failed to submit to federal authority and comply with United States' laws and a highly decorated United States Marshal was killed in the line of duty. Yet, for others, the incident at Ruby Ridge illustrates a state appearing to be at war with its citizens. Undoubtedly, having a sawed-off shotgun is a felony under the NFA, and it is not prudent to disregard a court date or a bench warrant. The United States Marshal's Service was certainly authorized and justified to apprehend Weaver as a fugitive and someone subject to an outstanding bench warrant. However, the use of deadly force by law enforcement was not appropriate in this situation. The Supreme Court settled this issue in its seminal ruling in *Tennessee v. Garner* (1985). The Court in that case invalidated the old "fleeing felon" rule, determining that law enforcement could not use deadly force to capture a fleeing felon absent the likelihood of imminent bodily harm to others or the imminent commission of a violent felony by the fleeing individual. After *Garner*, shooting a suspect in the back who is not an immediate threat to another or about to commit an imminent felony is beyond reasonable law enforcement behavior and can constitute its own criminal offense. Sammy Weaver (shot in the back) and Vicki Weaver (holding a child) posed no imminent risk to another, nor did Randy Weaver and Kevin Harris as they fled into the cabin. As was powerfully stated by the leaked internal DOJ task force report (and quoted in part in the dissenting opinion in a related federal case):

> Besieged by a platoon of FBI agents with high-powered rifles, two armored vehicles and a helicopter, the suspects at Ruby Ridge posed

> no immediate danger. There was no chance they could escape and take hostages. There was time to call out a warning, and there were many occasions to give the suspects a chance to surrender. Instead, FBI Agent Lon Horiuchi shot and killed Mrs. Weaver. (*Idaho v. Horiuchi* 2000, 997)

Randy Weaver failed to obey the rule of law, but so did the government. The federal misconduct at Ruby Ridge is a reminder that, just as the average citizen's conduct can cross over to illegality, law enforcement and the government can exceed its legal authority. One does not justify the other; and both are equally undesirable and antithetical to a peaceful democracy premised on adherence to, and respect for, the rule of law.

See Also: Conspiracy, Criminal; Oklahoma City Bombing (1995); Sovereign Citizens Movement; Waco (1993)

Resources

Bock, Alan. 1996. *Ambush at Ruby Ridge: How Government Agents Set Randy Weaver Up and Took His Family Down.* New York: Berkley Publishing.

Idaho v. Horiuchi, 215 F.3d 986, 997 (9th Cir. 2000) (Kozinski, J, dissenting).

United States Department of Justice Office of Professional Responsibility. 1994. "Ruby Ridge Task Force Report: Internal Investigation of Shootings at Ruby Ridge, Idaho during Arrest of Randy Weaver." Accessed May 7, 2023. http://law2.umkc.edu/faculty/projects/ftrials/weaver/dojruby1.html.

Walter, Jess. 1996. *Every Knee Shall Bow: The Truth and Tragedy of Ruby Ridge and the Randy Weaver Family*. New York: Harper Publishing.

Rudolph, Eric Roberts (1966–)

Eric Rudolph, sometimes referred to as the 1996 Olympic Park Bomber or the 1990s abortion clinic bomber, is a textbook example of a homegrown American domestic terrorist. After his last known bombing on January 29, 1998, Rudolph went into hiding and was a fugitive from justice for approximately five years, from 1998 to 2003. During those five years, he was one of the Federal Bureau of Investigation (FBI)'s Ten Most Wanted Fugitives.

Rudolph was indicted in the Northern District of Georgia for the bombing attack at Centennial Olympic Park on July 27, 1996, which killed Alice Hawthorne and seriously injured more than 100 other people; the bombing attack on a Sandy Springs, Georgia, family planning abortion clinic on January 16, 1997, which injured more than fifty people; and the bombing attack on an Atlanta nightclub, the Otherside Lounge, on February 21, 1997, which injured five people. Rudolph was also indicted in the Northern District of Alabama for the bombing attack on a Birmingham family planning clinic on January 29, 1998, which killed Birmingham Police Officer Robert Sanderson and critically injured nurse Emily Lyons. According to the Department of Justice (DOJ), "Rudolph agreed to plead guilty to the three Atlanta bombings and the Birmingham bombing and agreed to waive all appeals. The plea agreements provide for multiple life sentences for Rudolph without the possibility of parole" (Department of Justice 2005). In total, Rudolph agreed to four consecutive life sentences to avoid the death penalty.

While not convicted of domestic terrorism (the federal criminal offense of domestic terrorism was not available until after the passage of the USA PATRIOT Act in 2001), Rudolph clearly meets the federal statutory definition of being a domestic terrorist. The Patriot Act amended 18 United States Code 2331 to criminalize the following: (1) an act dangerous to human life that is a violation of the criminal laws of the United States or of any State; (2) appears to be intended to intimidate or coerce a civilian population, or to influence the policy of a government by intimidation or coercion, or to affect the conduct of a government by mass destruction, assassination, or kidnapping; and (3) occurs within the territorial jurisdiction of the United States.

In a wandering statement as to why he bombed the Olympic Park in 1996, Rudolph admitted that it was meant to influence the policy of the United States by intimidation or coercion. After vaguely asserting that the bombing was "to celebrate the ideals of global socialism" and "promote the values of global socialism," Rudolph stated, in much clearer language: "The purpose of the attack on July 27 was to confound, anger and embarrass the Washington government in the eyes of the world for its abominable sanctioning of abortion on demand" (National Public Radio 2005). Thus, applying the clear federal statutory language of what constitutes a domestic terrorist, Rudolph admitted that he was a domestic terrorist. He bombed the Park in order to "influence the policy of a government by intimidation or coercion." Rudolph's bombing of the abortion clinics, which appears to have the same motive, could also fit within the federal statute for terrorism. Rudolph's negative views about the government and its policies, coupled with his violent actions directed toward the state, transform and elevate what might otherwise be considered ordinary criminal offenses into crimes against the state.

During his guilty plea, Rudolph tried to deny government authority over him, stating that by pleading guilty, he had effectively "deprived the government of its goal of sentencing me to death," and "the fact that I have entered an agreement with the government is purely a tactical choice on my part and in no way legitimates the moral authority of the government to judge this matter or impute my guilt." While Rudolph may have earnestly believed that the government had no authority to find him guilty, he has been incarcerated at the ADX Florence Supermax facility since August 22, 2005. In 2021, Rudolph unsuccessfully tried to have part of his sentence vacated.

See Also: Assassination; Sovereign Citizens Movement; Terrorism; USA PATRIOT Act

Resources

Department of Justice. 2005. "Eric Robert Rudolph to Plead Guilty to Serial Bombing Attacks in Atlanta and Birmingham; Will Receive Life Sentences as Part of Plea Agreement, Rudolph Disclosed Locations of Hidden Bomb and Dynamite." April 8, 2005. Accessed May 15, 2023. https://www.justice.gov/archive/opa/pr/2005/April/05_crm_176.htm.

National Public Radio. 2005. "Full Text of Eric Rudolph's Confession." April 14, 2005. Accessed May 15, 2023. https://www.npr.org/templates/story/story.php?storyId=4600480.

Rudolph v. United States, 551 F. Supp. 3d 1270 (N.D. AL 2021).

S

Sabotage

The crime of sabotage against the State may occur during wartime or peacetime. Sabotage entails doing damage or destruction to some aspect of the country's national defense systems, defense premises or fortifications, military equipment and armament, or the communication and transportation infrastructure that facilitates the national defense. The Sabotage Act, codified at 18 United States Code Section 2151–2156, is the main federal law governing the crime of sabotage, although sabotage is covered elsewhere in the United States Code as well. The Sabotage Act was first enacted during the First World War, has existed since 1918, and was amended during the Second World War. Of the five distinct categories of sabotage contained within the Sabotage Act, two cover acts of sabotage committed during time of war or national emergency, and consequently carry the potential of much more significant punishments than convictions for sabotage committed during peacetime.

The term "sabotage" has wide popular usage in the English vernacular. People may speak of sabotaging a personal relationship or sabotaging a job opportunity. In a business and labor context, the term might be used, for example, in reference to sabotaging a negotiation. Indeed, some scholars have suggested that the word "sabotage" is derived from the French word "sabot," meaning wooden shoe, potentially a reference to a French labor strike, during which workers hurled their wooden shoes into combines and threshing machines to make the machines inoperable and protest increasing industrialization. While sabotage as a crime against the state most frequently describes destructive actions taken against the military or military infrastructure to impede its operation, economic sabotage can also constitute a crime against the state. The offense of criminal syndicalism applies to cases involving labor-related sabotage.

Under the Sabotage Act, the general definition of sabotage is damaging, destroying, or adversely impacting military assets and infrastructure with the specific intent to impede or hinder the ability of the United States to protect its national security, prepare for possible military activities, or participate in military actions. The damaged infrastructure runs the gamut from physical damage to a bridge, a plane, or a bomb, to things like hacking into a computer system, database, or program and damaging or altering the computer code of the system.

A range of actions are covered under the statute. First, under 18 United States Code Section 2152, anyone who interferes with, injures, damages, or destroys governmental installations, fortifications, harbor defenses, and coastal defense areas is guilty of sabotage with a punishment of up to five years imprisonment. Second, 18 United States Code Section 2153 applies when the United States is at war, or in times of national emergency as declared by the president or by the Congress. In those circumstances, if a person specifically intends to injure, interfere with, or obstruct the defensive activities of the United States, or willfully injures, damages, or destroys any war material, he or she is guilty of sabotage and subject to potential imprisonment up to thirty years. Third, like the previous section, in times of war or national emergency, 18 United States Code Section 2154 specifies that any intentional interference or damage or destruction to war materials, or intentional production of defective war materials, is subject to up to thirty years' incarceration. Fourth, during peacetime, under 18 United States Code Section 2155, destroying or contaminating materials to be utilized in national defense constitutes sabotage with potential incarceration of up to twenty years. However, if a death results because of the damaged war material, the statute authorizes up to life imprisonment. Finally, fifth, 18 United States Code Section 2156 covers those situations where businesses and employees intentionally produce defective national defense materials. A violation of this statutory provision can result in up to ten years' incarceration.

A classic example of attempted wartime sabotage can be seen in *Ex Parte Quirin* (1942). The defendants in that case were German saboteurs who were assigned to infiltrate and sabotage military-related targets in the United States during the Second World War in an operation named "Operation Pastorius." Operation Pastorius was designed to land saboteurs on US beaches by U-boat (German submarine) every six weeks. Germany's plan was to have the saboteurs damage or destroy wartime production facilities like aluminum plants. Additionally, waterways and rail lines would be targeted throughout the northeast and Midwest. However, this German sabotage operation was thwarted by a single unarmed Coast Guard lookout guard, who observed the first group of men landing and notified military authorities. The men were captured and prosecuted by a military tribunal, and six of the eight were executed (two individuals received a reduced sentence for cooperating with US authorities upon their detention). Additionally, the father of one of the saboteurs, Hans Max Haupt, was later prosecuted for aiding his son (Herbert Hans Haupt), and the father's case resulted in the Supreme Court ruling of *Haupt v. United States* (1947).

In 1961, in the attempt to protect important US infrastructure pertaining to communication, the Congress passed 18 United States Code Section 1362, which provides criminal penalties as follows: "Whoever willfully or maliciously injures or destroys any … cable, line … or other means of communication, operated or controlled by the United States, or used or intended to be used for military or civil defense functions of the United States." This language was not previously covered under the Sabotage Act. However, federal courts have specified that the Sabotage Act is a precursor to Section 1362 (and the protection of communication infrastructure). As the United States Court of Appeals for the Fourth Circuit wrote in *United States v. Turpin* (1995), "Congress explicitly amended §1361 in 1961 to extend the protection for communication facilities that already existed under the Sabotage Acts during wartime or in cases of specific intent to injure national defense." Thus, in *United States v. Turpin*, the convictions of two defendants for stealing copper wiring (used for communication) along a railroad track that was utilized occasionally by the military was upheld by the federal Fourth Circuit. The fact that the defendants stole the copper wiring simply to make money and not with the intention to injure US national defense had no applicability or relevancy to the guilt of the defendants under 18 United States Code Section 1362. The court did explain that had the act occurred during wartime and there was evidence of intent to impede the national defense of the United States, the defendants would have been charged and convicted for violations of the Sabotage Act and been subject to a more onerous punishment and prosecuted under 18 United States Code Section 1362 and/or 18 United States Code Section 2153.

An interesting modern case involving peacetime sabotage occurred in July 2012. Three defendants (an eighty-two-year-old nun and two Army veterans, ages fifty-seven and sixty-three) wished to engage in civil disobedience and protest the use of nuclear weapons. They used bolt cutters to cut through four layers of fencing, successfully evaded security, and made it to the building where enriched uranium was stored. Once in the room, the three threw blood and spray-painted antiwar slogans on the walls. The trio also hung yellow crime scene tape, wrote biblical verses on the walls, and sang hymns. When the security guards arrived, the group read a statement and peacefully surrendered to the guards. For these actions, the three were prosecuted and convicted of two main charges. First, the group was charged with destroying government property and trespass—which the defendants readily conceded at trial and on appeal. However, the defendants' "act of civil disobedience" was also prosecuted as an act of sabotage, and a jury convicted the three. The sabotage charge alone carried a sentence of up to twenty years imprisonment. The district court sentenced the nun to three years in prison and the other two accomplices to five years. The defendants were charged with a violation of 18 United States Code Section 2155, which provides that a defendant is culpable for sabotage if he or she acted "with intent to injure, interfere with, or obstruct the national defense." The case garnered nationwide attention and the convictions were appealed. On appeal, in *United States v. Walli, et al.*, the United States Court of Appeals for the Sixth Circuit overturned the convictions finding that the defendants' "lacked the intent necessary to violate the Sabotage Act." Although the defendants' acts of civil disobedience could be successfully prosecuted for trespass on government property (18 United States Code Section 2278a [c]) and damage to government property (18 United States Code Section 1361), a conviction for sabotage in peacetime could not stand, absent proof of actual damage to US national security or military operations.

See Also: Civil Disobedience and Crimes against the State; Criminal Syndicalism; *Ex Parte Quirin* (1942); *Haupt v. United States* (1947)

Resources

The Sabotage Act, 18 U.S.C. Sections 2151–6.

United States v. Walli, Nos. 14-52220/5221/5222, United States Court of Appeals for the Sixth Circuit, May 8, 2015.

Warner, Sam Bass. 1941. "The Model Sabotage Prevention Act." *Harvard Law Review* 54 (February): 602–31.

Sacco–Vanzetti Case (1921)

The prosecution of Nicola Sacco and Bartolomeo Vanzetti for double homicide and robbery in the summer of 1921 was no different than hundreds of thousands of other criminal prosecutions across the United States, then or now. There was nothing novel or significant about the crime, no unique legal issues, nothing overly unusual about the victims, or even the accused, for that matter. Yet, in a 1992 book entitled *Famous American Trials*, the Sacco–Vanzetti case was described "as the most celebrated case in America in the last fifty years" (Busch 1992, 53). Although at first glance it appeared to be a simple criminal trial, the Sacco–Vanzetti trial turned into a public spectacle lasting seven years.

Why did the case captivate the country and attract international attention? Undoubtedly, for many Americans, it epitomized the type of crime sweeping the United States during the early-twentieth-century anarchy and anti-capitalist movement, perceived as also embracing acts of terrorism and criminal syndicalism. The crime and prosecution also occurred right in the middle of the hysteria surrounding the First Red Scare and Palmer Raids. Average Americans saw the defendants Sacco and Vanzetti as anarchists who engaged in violence as a broader attack against the legitimacy of the government of the United States. Supporters of Sacco and Vanzetti claimed that the defendants were being framed by the authorities for a crime they did not commit and that the prosecution of the two men was an example of heavy-handed treatment by the police, often unfairly employed against anarchists in America. When Sacco and Vanzetti were found guilty after an extensive trial, acts of violence occurred against government offices and residences around the world.

Sacco and Vanzetti were avowed anarchists who avoided service in the First World War, leading many in the country to believe that they were guilty of murder simply because of their political leanings. The trial of Sacco and Vanzetti started under heavy security in May 1921 in Braintree, Massachusetts, the birthplace of Presidents John Adams and John Quincy Adams. Because of fears of violence and attempted jailbreaks, extra guards were provided, and in an age before metal detectors and courtroom security screening, people entering the courtroom were searched for concealed weapons and explosives. The facts of the crime leading to the prosecution of Sacco and Vanzetti were straightforward. Two men murdered a paymaster and his bodyguard as the two victims were walking down a street and attempting to deliver a payroll. Only Sacco and Vanzetti were identified by some of the eyewitnesses to the crime. Sixty-one witnesses testified for the prosecution (twenty-one who were eyewitnesses to the crime), and 107 witnesses testified for the defense (twenty-eight who were eyewitnesses to the crime). With so many eyewitnesses, the jury was tasked with sifting through a bevy of often conflicting accounts and information. The trial record was over 2,100 printed pages. The defendants were found guilty on July 14, 1921, and the sentence of death was administered on August 23, 1927.

After the guilty verdict, there were frequent acts of violence targeting governmental offices and places associated with the government's case. In France, the American Ambassador's house in Paris was bombed. In a protest meeting in Paris, a grenade was thrown into the crowd of protestors, and another bomb was detonated in Marseilles. After the Supreme Judicial Court of Massachusetts denied the defendants' appeals in 1926, a bomb was detonated in the United States Embassy in Buenos Aires. Two weeks later, the home of a prosecution witness was bombed. Two days after that, the United States Embassy at Montevideo was bombed. A bomb was detonated at the American Consulate in Nice, Italy, and the Washington Monument in Buenos Aires was destroyed. In 1932, thirteen years after the conviction of Sacco and Vanzetti, the residence of the original trial judge was bombed and demolished.

Sacco and Vanzetti took on a folk-hero-type status among the anti-government/anarchy movement in the United States. Famous songwriter and singer Woody Guthrie wrote a song about Sacco and Vanzetti entitled "Two Good Men (a Long Time Gone)." The song was a folk ballad popularizing the lives of Sacco and Vanzetti and postulated that they were heroes in the fight against corrupt capitalism in the United States. Because of favorable popular depictions of Sacco and Vanzetti, they served as martyrs and role models to anti-government radicals in the 1930s. If there was any doubt about Sacco's complicity with the anarchist movement, it seemed to have been eliminated at his execution, when Sacco yelled his last words, "Long Live Anarchy!" (Russell 1962, 110).

See Also: Anarchy, Criminal; Criminal Syndicalism; First Red Scare and Palmer Raids (1919–20); Terrorism

Resources

Busch, Francis X. 1992. *Famous American Trials*. New York: Barnes & Noble Books, 53–141.

Russell, Francis. 1962. "Sacco Guilty, Vanzetti Innocent?" *American Heritage* 13, no. 4 (June): 4–9, 110–1.

Wayman, Dorothy G. 1959. "Sacco-Vanzetti: The Unfinished Debate." *American Heritage* 11, no. 1 (December): 89–93.

Salazar, Hipolito (1817–47)

The trial and execution of Hipolito "Polo" Salazar has been described as "one of the worst miscarriages of justice in the history of the United States" (Larson 2020a, Chapter 8). The Salazar case stands today as the only instance wherein the US federal government executed a non-United States citizen for treason, when the non citizen owed the United States no loyalty or allegiance and the breach of such a loyalty is considered an essential element to the charge of treason. Furthermore, Salazar is the only person in US history ever executed for treason by the federal government's civilian judicial system. While military authorities executed William Mumford for violation of martial law in 1862, Hipolito Salazar was convicted of treason by a civilian court. Salazar was not a US citizen at the time of his trial and conviction but of Mexican nationality. In fact, Salazar had never set foot in the United States. Furthermore, his trial did not take place on US soil but in the Republic of Mexico. As Professor of Law Carlton F. W. Larson explained, "the horrific consequence was that the only treason execution under federal authority rested on a legal error—the government had executed a legally innocent man" (Larson 2020a, Chapter 8).

The trial of Hipolito Salazar (and multiple other compatriots of Salazar) has its origins in the United States–Mexican War (1846–8). As a result of this war, the first war the United States had fought chiefly on foreign soil, the United States cut the Republic of Mexico in half, seizing huge swaths of land comprising parts of the present states of Arizona, California, Colorado, Nevada, New Mexico, and Utah. However, before the Treaty of Guadalupe Hidalgo was signed in 1848, all this land still belonged to the Republic of Mexico, and it was a foreign country and foreign territory as far as US jurisdiction was concerned.

Understandably, still at war with the United States in 1846–7, many inhabitants of the Republic of Mexico denied the claimed authority of the United States and took up arms. In one of several locations of violent uprisings against the United States in Taos, New Mexico, the territorial governor of New Mexico was killed along with numerous American settlers from adjacent settlements. In response to what was known as the "Taos Revolt," the US military not only quelled the uprising but killed several hundred Mexican citizens in the process. And if the United States' armed response was not sufficient, the newly appointed attorney general for the territory, a young 26-year-old named Francis Blair, decided that it was his responsibility to zealously prosecute all the surviving insurgents for treason.

Approximately one hundred miles away, Blair began his campaign of treason prosecutions in Santa Fe, Mexico (now, New Mexico). There, Blair sought grand jury treason indictments for twenty-nine individuals, but the grand jury declined to indict twenty-five of the twenty-nine men. Only four were indicted for treason. Of these four individuals, only one person was convicted, Antonio Maria Trujillo, who was sentenced to death. However, Trujillo was seventy-six years old, nearing the end of his years, and all the members of the prosecution team (and the jury and several presiding judges) signed a petition for clemency, which was subsequently granted by President James K. Polk in 1847.

Hipolito Salazar and his compatriots from Taos, Mexico, were not so fortunate. While the prosecutor initially sought over fifty treason indictments in Toas, only five individuals were indicted for treason, one being Salazar. Of these five men, the prosecutor subsequently decided not to prosecute three of the five and the fourth individual was acquitted. That left just Hipolito Salazar, who was tried, convicted, and sentenced to death for treason against the United States. Salazar was scheduled to die on April 9, 1847. Along with him on the execution scaffolding were five other Mexican defendants who had been convicted of homicide and condemned to be executed on the same day. Despite clear legal error in Salazar's case, there were no petitions for commutation or pardon as had been the case for 76-year-old Antonio Maria Trujillo, and Salazar died by hanging on April 9, 1847.

The court's position in the Salazar case was clearly a legal error in accordance with well-established United States Supreme Court precedent and well-known common-law doctrines going back a century before Salazar's trial. Twenty-seven years before Salazar's conviction and execution, United States Supreme Court Chief Justice John Marshall, writing for the majority of the Court in *United States v. Wiltberger*, set forth the prerequisites for a proper treason charge (and conviction) as follows: "treason is a breach of allegiance, and can be committed by him *only* who owes allegiance (to the sovereign) either perpetual or temporary." Furthermore, eminent English common-law jurist William Blackstone explained that treason "imports a *betraying*, treachery, or *breach of faith*" (Blackstone 1769, 75).

The Hipolito Salazar case was largely forgotten until several years ago when it was uncovered by Professor Carlton F. W. Larson. As Professor Larson persuasively argues in describing his research of the case, even in other trials occurring contemporaneously with the Salazar trial in Mexico in 1847, American lawyers representing Mexican defendants charged with treason were effectively arguing that Mexican citizens were not citizens of the United States and could not therefore be guilty of treason against the United States, having owed the United States no allegiance or loyalty. Salazar owed the Republic of Mexico his loyalty, and he was a combatant actively fighting for his country's defense against the United States.

See Also: Levying War; Martial Law; Mumford, William Bruce; Treason

Resources

Blackstone, William. 1769. *Commentaries on the Laws of England*. Vol. 4. Oxford: Clarendon Press.

Larson, Carlton F. W. 2020a. *On Treason: A Citizen's Guide to the Law*. New York: Ecco, an imprint of HarperCollins (Kindle Edition).

Larson, Carlton F. W., 2020b. "Treason, the Death Penalty, and American Identity." *History News Network*. Accessed May 6, 2022. https://historynewsnetwork.org/article/177832.

Schenck v. United States (1919)

In *Schenck v. United States*, a unanimous Supreme Court upheld the convictions of Charles Schenck and Elizabeth Baer for charges brought under the Espionage Act of 1917. Schenck was a US citizen who served as the general secretary of the Socialist Party, and Baer was another member of the Socialist Party. They were accused of distributing leaflets promoting anti-war propaganda, targeting those drafted under the Selective Service Act of 1917.

In 1917, the United States decided to openly enter the First World War. To further the war effort, the Congress enacted the Espionage Act of 1917. The Congress' goal was to prevent interference with military operations or recruitment, insubordination in the military, and the support of hostile enemies during wartime. The Espionage Act criminalized spreading information that would cause insubordination or disruption within the armed forces or using the mail to communicate any information promoting treason or insurrection.

In August 1917, the Socialist Party began distributing 15,000 anti-conscription leaflets in the United States. On one side, the pamphlet read, "Long Live The Constitution Of The United States; Wake Up America! Your Liberties Are in Danger," and included the Thirteenth Amendment, which had abolished slavery and involuntary servitude, printed along with messages encouraging resisting the draft through "peaceful measures." It argued that under the draft, "a conscripted citizen is forced to surrender his right as a citizen and become a subject." On the other side, the pamphlet contained more "assertive" calls for obstruction of the draft.

Schenck oversaw the production and distribution of the leaflets, and upon his subsequent prosecution, argued that his conduct was protected under the First Amendment and that the Espionage Act of 1917 was unconstitutional. The Supreme Court disagreed. In a unanimous opinion issued in 1919, not long after the end of the First World War, the Court asserted that though Schenck's communications may have been protected by the First Amendment during peacetime, the analysis was different during war. Justice Oliver Wendell Holmes, Jr., opined that not all speech is protected and famously analogized that Schenck's conduct was like shouting fire in a theater, creating panic. The Court said that the success, or lack thereof, of an individual's efforts to hinder the war effort did not determine whether speech was protected by the First Amendment. Rather, if the speech merely posed a clear and present danger, it was unprotected, regardless of whether the "danger" materialized. The Supreme Court found that the Constitution granted the Congress broad powers to promote the war effort, including the ability to restrict speech that hampered it. The Court held that the Espionage Act of 1917 was constitutional and upheld Schenck's and Baer's convictions, thus approving a "speech crime" against the state.

Schenck and *Debs v. United States* (1919), which was decided a week later, are widely considered the low point in protection of political speech under the First Amendment. As discussed more fully in the separate entry on the topic, the Clear and Present Danger Test outlived the First and Second World Wars, generally surviving until the Supreme Court abandoned that standard and its derivative—the "bad tendency test"—in its 1969 landmark decision in *Brandenburg v. Ohio*. Sections of the Espionage Act of 1917 challenged by Schenck survive to this day and have been used to prosecute modern crimes against the state, including those committed by Chelsea Manning and Edward Snowden.

See Also: *Abrams v. United States* (1919); *Brandenburg v. Ohio* (1969); Clear and Present Danger Test; *Debs v. United States* (1919); Espionage Act of 1917 and Sedition Act of 1918; Insurrection; Leaks of National Defense Information; Speech as Crime against the State; Treason

Resources

Schenck v. United States, 249 U.S. 47 (1919).

Smith, Stephen A. 2003. "Schenck v. United States and Abrams v. United States." In *Free Speech on Trial: Communication Perspectives on Landmark Supreme Court Decisions*, edited by Richard Parker, 20–35. Tuscaloosa: University of Alabama Press.

Waimberg, Joshua. 2015. "*Schenck v. United States*: Defining the Limits of Free Speech." *Constitution Daily, National Constitution Center*, November 2, 2015. Accessed June 16, 2023. https://constitutioncenter.org/blog/schenck-v-united-states-defining-the-limits-of-free-speech/.

Second Red Scare (McCarthyism)

McCarthyism refers to two separate but related concepts. First, McCarthyism connotes the extreme and irresponsible fear-mongering tactics of Senator Joseph McCarthy, a Republican Senator from Wisconsin, in the 1950s, in making baseless allegations that individuals were members of the Communist Party or were Soviet spies. Second, McCarthyism today references "a classic tactic … [in] the use of an unproven association with any individual, organization, or policy, which the accuser perceives as liberal or left, and, as a result, either un-American or even treasonous" (Shafritz 1988, 334–5).

Senator McCarthy abused his position on a subcommittee of the Senate Foreign Relations Committee to make unsubstantiated allegations that targeted individuals were guilty of treason and were disloyal to the United States. McCarthy oversaw several security investigations into the backgrounds and private lives of academics, scientists, entertainers, and government employees. McCarthy's mudslinging created an atmosphere of fear, and his tactics and the period in which he operated became known as McCarthyism and the McCarthy era. In time, McCarthy and his methods were discredited, and his claims regarding most of those he attacked were later determined to be spurious and without merit.

McCarthy burst onto the scene in February 1950 when he gave a speech claiming that "I have here in my hand a list of 205 that were known to the Secretary of State of being members of the Communist Party and who nevertheless are still working and shaping policy of the State Department" ("This Day in History" 2023). McCarthy never released the names, and the number of communist spies allegedly working in the State Department constantly changed. For the next four years, McCarthy made ad hominem attacks and harassed countless public servants and private individuals for his political gain and self-promotion. According to author Douglass Carter, "McCarthyism's greatest threat was not to individual liberty or even to the orderly conduct of government. It corrupted the power to communicate, which is indispensable to men living in a civilized society" (Safire 2008, 419). As President Dwight Eisenhower described it, "McCarthyism took its toll on many individuals and on the nation. No one was safe from charges recklessly made from inside the walls of Congressional immunity. Teachers, government employees, and even ministers became vulnerable … the cost was often tragic" (Safire 2008, 419).

McCarthy's career came to a careening halt when he claimed (without evidence) that the Department of the Army was harboring communists. His disastrous attack on the Army (and President Eisenhower) in 1954 brought an end to his political career. Because of his reckless behavior, McCarthy became one of the few US senators in history to be formally condemned and censured by the Senate, and he died shortly afterwards in 1957. "Today, any actions by public officials that flout individual rights and imply guilt by association would be considered by anyone sensitive to the concept of due process of law—as examples of McCarthyism" (Shafritz 1988, 335).

The "Second Red Scare" of the early Cold War, which coincided with McCarthyism, involved a period of renewed apprehension of communists, anarchy, and disloyalty. As had been the case during the "First Red Scare," these fears led to a variety of government actions to purportedly protect itself. During the Second Red Scare, these government responses included enacting the Internal Security Act of 1950, prosecuting alleged communists and "subversives" under the Smith Act, and several United States Supreme Court opinions upholding the government's authority to prohibit communist ideology, including *Dennis v. United States* (1951) and *Adler v. Board of Education* (1952).

See Also: Anarchy, Criminal; *Dennis v. United States* (1951); First Red Scare and the Palmer Raids (1919–20); Internal Security Act of 1950; Smith Act; Treason

Resources

Safire, William. 2008. *Safire's Political Dictionary*. Oxford: Oxford University Press, 418–19.

Shafritz, Jay. 1988. *The Dorsey Dictionary of American Government and Politics*. Chicago: The Dorsey Press, 334–5.

"This Day in History: Feb. 9, 1950: Sen. Joseph McCarthy Announces 'Enemies within.'" *Zinn Education Project: Teaching People History*. Accessed November 1, 2023. https://www.zinnedproject.org/news/tdih/mccarthy-red-scare.

Sedition

The term "sedition" and the modern meaning of it as a crime against the state was not used until the seventeenth century. According to the original meaning as defined by the *Oxford English Dictionary* (OED), the word "sedition" connoted "violent party strife" and especially "a factious contest attended with rioting and disorder" (OED 2023). Some of the earliest known examples of the use of the word "sedition" were in the context of describing strife or disagreement between individuals. According to the OED, a religious text from 1529 speaks of a rift between disciples, saying "as though these men were Apostles now specially sent by god to preche heresyses and sow sedicion among christen men." In another text from 1602, the author wrote: "When the Romanes were diuided, one faction labouring to oppresse another … such enimitie was called Sedition."

The meaning of the term began to change through libel/slander cases handled by the English Star Chamber Court. Today, the OED defines "sedition" as "conduct or language inciting to rebellion against the constituted authority in a state." Thus, "it was only towards the end of the sixteenth century that the secondary or more modern meaning of the word sedition began to emerge—the notion of inciting by words or writings disaffection towards the state or constituted authority. Thus, sedition came to be interpreted as words that fell short of treason and did not directly involve—although they might lead to—acts of violence" (Manning 1980, 101). Initially, the offense of "sedition" was meant to cover cases wherein an individual slandered or libeled the government, just like an individual might defame another through words or speech. However, over time, the concept of "sedition" was expanded to cover not only words that could incite rebellion against the government, but also conduct.

As the crime of sedition initially involved only spoken or written words critical of the government, or words that would bring the government or its leaders into disrepute, the offense was often referred to as "seditious libel." While the crime or civil action of seditious libel flourished in England for centuries, it fell into disfavor in the twentieth century in England, with the last reported prosecution occurring in 1972. In the United States, however, the concept of seditious libel was rejected by colonists long before the Revolutionary War in the 1735 colonial New York case entitled *Crown v. John Peter Zenger* (see Zenger, John Peter). With the acquittal of Zenger by a jury, the concept of a civil charge of seditious libel in America died. That is, as a civil cause of action, seditious libel ceased to be a viable option in American courts.

However, from time to time in American history, typically in moments of national crisis, the Congress has passed laws making it a crime to speak or write defamatory words about the government or to utter words which negatively impact the country's war effort. As part of the Alien and Sedition Acts (1798), the Congress enacted the Sedition Act of 1798, which made it a crime to write or publish any "false, scandalous, and malicious writings" about the president or Congress. This law lapsed when Thomas Jefferson took office, and its constitutionality was never challenged in court, although the Supreme Court in dicta (in comments without legal bearing) in *New York Times v. Sullivan* (1964), suggested it would be unconstitutional if heard by a modern Supreme Court. During the First World War, with the Sedition Act of 1918, the Congress again criminalized speech that criticized the war effort of the United States or the recruitment of soldiers. This legislation was quickly challenged but upheld by the Supreme Court in cases such as *Schenck v. United States* (1919) and *Abrams v. United States* (1919). The speech provisions of the Sedition Act of 1918 were largely repealed in 1921, but provisions regarding espionage and speech (found in the Espionage Act of 1917) are still in effect today. In 1940, the Congress again attempted to criminalize and abridge speech through the passage of the Smith Act, which criminalized the advocacy of or teaching of ideas relating to overthrowing the US government. Although parts of the Smith Act remain in effect today, major Supreme Court challenges to the constitutionality of the legislation occurred in cases like *Dennis v. United States* (1951) and *Yates v. United States* (1957).

Often today, people confuse sedition (words critical of the government or words advocating overthrowing the government) with seditious conspiracy. As defined by US federal law (18 United States Code 2384), seditious conspiracy is "if two or more persons … conspire to overthrow, put down or to destroy by force the Government of the United States, or to levy war against them, or to oppose by force the authority thereof, or by force to prevent, hinder or delay the execution of any law of the United States, or by force to seize, take, or possess any property of the United States." Thus, the crime of sedition alone entails words which typically are not criminal because of the First Amendment (see Speech as Crime against the State), unless the words amount to incitement of imminent lawless action against the government (see *Brandenburg v. Ohio* [1969]). Seditious conspiracy criminalizes the action (either the action to engage in conspiracy or the action of opposing the US government by force).

Finally, the concepts of seditious conspiracy and treason are often confused and people tend to use the terms interchangeably, but each connotes different things and has different requirements. In short, treason consists of "levying war" against the government or giving "aid and comfort" to its enemies and requires two witnesses to testify to the same treasonous conduct in open court. Seditious conspiracy does not require any of those items, merely conspiring or committing acts of rebellion or violence against the government.

See Also: *Abrams v. United States* (1919); Aid and Comfort (Aid to Enemies of the State); Alien and Sedition Acts (1798); *Brandenburg v. Ohio* (1969); Conspiracy, Criminal; *Dennis v. United States* (1951); Espionage Act of 1917 and Sedition Act of 1918; Jefferson, Thomas; Levying War; *Schenck v. United States* (1919); Sedition Act of 1798; Seditious Conspiracy; Smith Act; Speech and Crimes against the State; Treason; *Yates v. United States* (1957); Zenger, John Peter

Resources

Lewis, Anthony. 2007. *Freedom for the Thought That We Hate: A Biography of the First Amendment*. New York: Basic Books.

Manning, Roger. 1980. "The Origins of the Doctrine of Sedition." *Albion: A Quarterly Journal Concerned with British Studies* 12, no. 2 (September): 99–121.

Oxford English Dictionary. 2023. "Sedition." Oxford: Oxford University Press.

Sedition Act of 1798

The Sedition Act of 1798 was the most onerous, draconian, and potentially unconstitutional of the four laws collectively known as the Alien and Sedition Acts. The legislation came at a time of heightened hysteria over a potential war with France. The Federalist Party, who controlled the Congress, and President John Adams, believed the laws were necessary to keep public order and ensure domestic homeland security. The opposition party, known as Democratic-Republicans and led by Vice President Thomas Jefferson, viewed the laws as primarily an attempt by the Federalists to quell dissent and eliminate any subversive activities antithetic to the Federalist agenda. The Sedition Act of 1798, which went into effect on July 14, 1798, contained sweeping criminal prohibitions on writing, speaking, or uttering any words that might have the effect of bringing either the Congress or the President "into contempt or disrepute." Section 1 of the law even criminalized two or more people in combining or conspiring "together, with the intent to oppose any measure or measures of the government of the United States." Violations of this provision carried a punishment of a fine not exceeding five thousand dollars and imprisonment for a term of not less than six months but not more than five years.

Section 2 of the Act was the most infamous aspect of the legislation given its clear restrictions on freedom of speech. It criminalized writing, uttering, or publishing

> any false, scandalous and malicious writing or writings against the government of the United States, or either house of the Congress ... or the President ... with intent to defame ... or to bring them or either of them, into contempt or disrepute; or to excite against them either or any of them, the hatred of the good people of the United States, or to stir up sedition within the United States.

Punishments for conviction of an offense delineated in Section 2 of the Act were the same as those specified in Section 1.

Astonishingly, the Congress passed this law abridging speech less than eight years after ratification (in 1791) of the First Amendment to the Constitution, which declared that "Congress shall make no law ... abridging freedom of speech, or of the press." The United States Senate passed the legislation on July 4, 1798 (the date intentionally chosen to elicit emotions of patriotism); the United States House of Representatives then passed the bill on July 10, 1798; and President Adams signed it into law on July 14, 1798. As legal scholar Anthony Lewis noted, "ten days from start to finish: a swift course for a fateful statute" (Maxwell 2004, 11).

Opponents could not challenge the law in courts because the power of judicial review had not yet been created by Chief Justice Marshall in *Marbury v. Madison* (1803). Instead, members of the opposition party encouraged state governments to pass laws or ordinances calling on the Congress to rescind the law and/or stating that the state government would simply not adhere to the law. For instance, the Kentucky Resolution of 1798 declared that the Alien and Sedition Acts are "not laws," are "altogether void," "utterly void," and "of no force." The two most famous state-level reactions to the Alien and Sedition Acts came from Virginia and Kentucky and were authored by James Madison and Thomas Jefferson, respectively. These resolutions served as precedent for other actions by local governments against the federal government in the ensuing years. For instance, South Carolina used the Virginia and Kentucky Resolutions as legal authority to declare federal tariffs null and void in the state in the 1830s, and southern states utilized them in seceding from the United States at the onset of the American Civil War. In the early 2000s, over 330 state legislatures and local governments passed similar resolutions in opposition to the USA PATRIOT Act.

Unlike the lack of enforcement of the Alien Act and the Alien Enemies Act (also part of the Alien and Sedition Acts), President Adams sought to enforce the Sedition Act aggressively against the opposition party. Multiple people opposed to Federalist policies were prosecuted and convicted under the law. According to Anthony Lewis, "modern research has found that judges and federal marshals packed juries with Federalists in Sedition Act trials" (Lewis 2007, 14). Professor Peter Irons described the aggressive prosecutions as "a witch-hunt that rivaled those of colonial Salem and the more recent McCarthy era" (Irons 1999, 99). Historian Saul Cornell wrote that "the Sedition Acts precipitated the most serious constitutional crisis in the period after ratification [of the Constitution]" (Maxwell 2004, 3). Editors of major anti-Federalist newspapers were indicted, and the prosecutions successfully shut down multiple papers. A small number of prominent Democratic-Republican anti-Federalist politicians were also indicted and prosecuted under the law. The prosecutions resulted in high-profile trials involving freedom of speech and seditious libel in the early years of the United States, with most of the trials occurring during the Adams-Jefferson campaign election season. Indeed, Timothy Pickering, John Adams's Secretary of State was said to encourage "prosecutions that would silence pro-Jefferson papers during the election year" (Lewis 2007, 13).

The blatantly partisan and politicized nature of the law and its implementation was illustrated by the first person the Adams administration opted to prosecute, Congressman Matthew Lyon. Lyon's "egregious" political offense was to write a letter to the editor of a Vermont newspaper indicating that he thought Adams was involved in "a continual grasp for power, in an unbounded thirst for ridiculous pomp, foolish adulation and selfish avarice" (Lewis 2007, 13). Hardly words that would tend to incite a population to riot or lead to insurrection. The judge's charge to the jury was that they only had to determine whether Lyon wrote the letter, and if so, whether the language was intended to bring Adams into "disrepute." Lyon was sentenced to four months in prison and a thousand dollar fine. Ironically, while serving his prison sentence, Lyon was reelected to another term in the United States Congress, thoroughly routing his Federalist opponent.

A second political prosecution involved the case of Thomas Cooper. Cooper was a former British citizen, living in the United States, who had politically aligned himself with Thomas Jefferson. Cooper published an article alleging Adams borrowed money at too high an interest rate, needlessly maintained an Army and Navy, and interfered with the independence of the judiciary in a case involving a British defendant charged with murder. Hardly incendiary, the words published by Cooper were the type of political discourse and disagreement that the First Amendment was intended to protect. Nevertheless, like Matthew Lyon, Thomas Cooper was found guilty by a jury, ordered to pay a fine of four hundred dollars, and sentenced to be incarcerated for six months. Unlike other defendants who were pardoned by President Jefferson when he took office in March 1801, Cooper insisted on serving out his sentence on principle.

Perhaps the most notorious of the Sedition Act prosecutions involved the case of James Thompson Callender. Callender was a muckraker and scandalmonger whose targets over the course of his career included some of America's most famous early leaders, including George Washington, John Adams, Thomas Jefferson, and Alexander Hamilton. At the time of his prosecution Callender was under the employ of Thomas Jefferson and authored a book about Adams filled with unflattering commentary, such as referring to Adams as a "hoardy headed incendiary" and indicating that the choice in the election of 1800 was "between Adams, war and beggary, and Jefferson, peace and competency" (Lewis 2007, 14). Callender was convicted, fined two hundred dollars, and given a nine-month prison sentence.

Ironically, the relatives and descendants of America's most esteemed founding fathers were not immune from the adverse effects of this law. Benjamin Franklin spent many years of his life as a printer, and upon his death, bequeathed his printing press to his grandson, Benjamin Bache. When Bache published articles critical of President Adams in his newspaper, he was thrown in jail, where he sat for two years. Jefferson pardoned all those convicted under the Sedition Act when he took office. "Sadly, this did not free Bache from prison … [as] he had died behind bars just a few months before" (Coate 2006, 20).

The Sedition Act of 1798 is a cautionary tale of the willingness of Americans to give up sacred rights such as freedom of speech when faced with the specter of foreign fears. As James Madison wrote in a letter two months before passage of the Sedition Act of 1798, "[p]erhaps it is a universal truth that the loss of liberty at home is to be charged to provisions against danger, real or pretend, from abroad" (Lewis 2007, 21). More recently, in 1964, United States Supreme Court Justice William Brennan commented on the 1798 Sedition Act in the famous *New York Times Co. v. Sullivan* case. While Brennan never stated that the act violated the First Amendment's guaranty of freedom of speech, he indicated that it "first crystalized a national awareness of the central meaning of the First Amendment" and that "the attack upon its validity has carried the day in the court of history" (Maxwell 2004, 3). While Brennan may have been correct that it caused a heightened appreciation of the First Amendment, this heightened appreciation has not precluded a bevy of other questionable laws passed over the ensuing years when the country feared its national security was at peril.

See Also: Alien and Sedition Acts (1798); Alien Act (1798); Alien Enemies Act (1798); American Civil War and Treason; American Revolution and Treason; Espionage Act of 1917 and Sedition Act of 1918; Insurrection; Jefferson, Thomas; Second Red Scare (McCarthyism); Riot and Incitement to Riot; Sedition; Speech as Crime against the State; USA PATRIOT Act

Resources

An Act in Addition to the Act, Entitled "An Act for the Punishment of Certain Crimes against the United States," United States Statutes at Large 1 (1798): 596–7. Accessed May 21, 2022. https://www.archives.gov/milestone-documents/alien-and-sedition-acts#sedition.

Coate, Bill. 2006. *Shocking Secrets of American History: 115 Surprising Tales*. New York: MJF Books.

Hall, Kermit. 1992. *The Oxford Companion to the Supreme Court of the United States*. Oxford: Oxford University Press.

Irons, Peter. 1999. *A People's History of the Supreme Court*. New York: Viking.

Lewis, Anthony. 2007. *Freedom for the Thought That We Hate: A Biography of the First Amendment*. New York: Basic Books.

Maxwell, Bruce. 2004. *Homeland Security: A Documentary History*. Washington, DC: CQ Press.

Miller, John C. 1957. *Crisis in Freedom: The Alien and Sedition Acts*. Boston: Little, Brown and Company.

Sedition Act of 1918

See Espionage Act of 1917 and Sedition Act of 1918

Seditious Conspiracy

The crime of seditious conspiracy was promulgated by the United States Congress in partial response to John Brown's Raid against the Armory and Arsenal at Harpers Ferry, Virginia, in 1859, and the perceived inadequacies in dealing with cases like John Brown's under federal treason laws. The federal crime of treason is limited to "levying war" or "in adhering to their Enemies, giving them Aid and Comfort." Furthermore, Article III of the Constitution mandates that "no person shall be convicted of Treason unless on the Testimony of two Witnesses to the same overt Act, or on Confession in open Court." Much more broadly, the seditious conspiracy statute at 18 United States Code Section 2384 provides:

> [I]f two or more persons ... conspire to overthrow, put down or to destroy by force the Government of the United States, or to levy war against them, or to oppose by force the authority thereof, or by force to prevent, hinder or delay the execution of any law of the United States, or by force to seize, take, or possess any property of the United States ... they shall be fined under this title or imprisoned not more than twenty years, or both.

The seditious conspiracy statute criminalizes a wide array of conduct not expressly covered under US treason law and does away with the necessity of two witnesses testifying to the same overt act in open court. A review of Brown's 1859 case reveals that he would have been clearly and easily convicted under this federal statute. Indeed, the legislative history of the statute illustrates that the impetus for the law "arose out of the turmoil created in the nation by John Brown's dramatic 1859 raid on Harpers Ferry" (Tarrant 1971, 112). The chief sponsor of this law, Senator Stephen Douglas of Illinois (a contender for the US presidency in 1860), believed that the Congress clearly exercised its authority, granted by the Constitution, to "protect states and preserve the Union [and] Congress had exercised this power in repelling foreign invasion but had ... failed, up to this time, to make any law ... to deal with the type of invasion John Brown's thrust into Virginia" (Tarrant 1971, 114). Importantly, the seditious conspiracy statute gave prosecutors broad powers by making a simple conspiracy to engage in any of the listed items of force against the government a major felony under the federal law with potential incarceration of up to twenty years. The legislation was signed by President Lincoln and became law on July 31, 1861, and it remains a viable tool for federal prosecutors over 160 years later. It is occasionally described as the younger sibling of the offense of treason. In a March 1863 charge to a grand jury, United States District Judge Pelege Spargue stated, "Until the year 1861, [treason constituted] the only provisions of the criminal law for the suppression of acts directly tending to the destruction of the government" and the only possible charge against those intending to harm the government by force (Tarrant 1971, 107). The crime of seditious conspiracy was meant to fill this gap in federal law.

Prosecutions under the seditious conspiracy statute have been rare. Prior to 2022, the last time the federal government won a seditious conspiracy prosecution that went to trial was in the 1995 terrorism case of *United States v. Rahman* (1999). In *Rahman*, ten defendants were convicted of seditious conspiracy involving a widespread plot to engage in urban terrorism. The defendants were charged with various degrees of involvement in the 1993 bombing of the World Trade Center (see World Trade Center Bombing of 1993), as well as plotting other attacks: bombing bridges and tunnels and murdering a rabbi in New York City and assassinating the President of Egypt. The ringleader was Abdel Rahman, the so-called Blind Sheikh, as he was a blind Islamic scholar and cleric. Rahman called on his followers to commit "jihad" and instructed that they were to "do jihad with the sword, with the cannon, with grenades, with the missile … against God's enemies." According to the United States Court of Appeals for the Second Circuit in its reported decision upholding the conviction of Rahman and nine other defendants for seditious conspiracy, there was abundant evidence that the defendants viewed the United States and Egypt as the primary oppressors of Muslims and that the defendants believed the Qur'an mandated jihad against the United States and Egypt.

In unsuccessfully appealing their sentences, the defendants claimed that the seditious conspiracy statute bypassed the procedural protections of the offense of treason, that the statute ran afoul of the First Amendment, and that the over 160-year-old statute was vague and overbroad. While a treason prosecution does require compliance with the two-witness rule, the court ruled:

> [T]he plain answer is that the Treason Clause does not apply to the prosecution. The provisions of Article III, Section 3 apply to prosecutions for treason … [but the defendants] were not charged with treason. Their offense of conviction, seditious conspiracy under Section 2384, differs from treason not only in name and associated stigma, but also in its essential elements and punishment.

In rejecting the defendants' First Amendment claims, the court held that certain speech may be criminalized if coupled with action, citing Supreme Court cases such as *Dennis v. United States* (1951) and *Yates v. United States* (1957). In *Dennis v. United States*, the Supreme Court upheld the constitutionality of the Smith Act, which made it a crime to advocate, or to conspire to advocate, the overthrow of the US government by force or violence. In *Yates v. United States*, the Court interpreted the Smith Act to prohibit only the advocacy of concrete violent action, but not "advocacy and teaching of forcible overthrow as an abstract principle, divorced from any effort to instigate action to that end." Finally, in *Rahman* the Second Circuit Court of Appeals referred to the Supreme Court's ruling in *Brandenburg v. Ohio* (1969), which held a state may proscribe subversive activity when the advocacy is directed at and is likely to result in "imminent lawless action." The Second Circuit ruled that to be lawfully convicted for seditious conspiracy under Section 2384, "one must conspire to use force, not just to advocate the use of force [and] we have no doubt that this passes the test of constitutionality." Finally, while the court recognized that seditious conspiracy cases should be scrutinized to ensure that individuals are not being prosecuted for unpopular political views alone, the court nevertheless found that "Section 2384 is drawn sufficiently narrowly that we perceive no unacceptable risk of such abuse." Furthermore, the court indicated that the terms of Section 2384 are not vague or overbroad, but that "the terms of the statute are far more precise … and do not involve terms of such vague meaning."

The prosecution of the defendants in *United States v. Rahman,* and the resulting precedent of the case, establishes the continued viability of seditious conspiracy as a crime against the state. The charge of seditious conspiracy is a rarity. Indeed, the Justice Department has levied charges of seditious conspiracy in only a small number of cases going back decades. Nevertheless, the statute still represents good law and a viable offense at the disposal of federal prosecutors. About a decade and a half after the *Rahman* case, in 2010, the federal government unsuccessfully attempted to prosecute nine members of a Michigan militia (called the Hutaree) for seditious conspiracy. The judge acquitted the defendants in that case, holding that their anti-government speech did not amount to imminent lawless action and that the evidence was insufficient to establish that the defendants planned to act on their words and opinion. This was the last time the federal government would charge a defendant with seditious conspiracy until 2022.

Six members of the far-right Oath Keepers militia were indicted in June 2022 for seditious conspiracy in their roles in the Capitol Insurrection on January 6, 2021, and their alleged use of force to oppose the transfer of presidential power from Donald Trump to President Joseph Biden. According to prosecutors, the defendants trained for the event and stockpiled weapons at a hotel just outside Washington, DC, and were accused of conspiring to use violent force to stop the lawful transfer of power. To be successful in the prosecution, the government had to prove to a jury not only that the defendants engaged in a conspiracy and spoke about using force against the government, but also that they took concrete steps in furtherance of their alleged conspiracy. The defendants were tried in federal court for seditious conspiracy in November 2022 and found guilty. In a related victory for the federal government, in October 2022, a leader in another far-right militia group called the Proud Boys pleaded guilty to the charge of seditious conspiracy for his efforts at attempting to stop the transfer of presidential power on January 6, 2021. As of May 24, 2023, of the over one thousand individuals indicted for activities related to the January 6 events, over five hundred individuals have been sentenced with prison terms up to that point in time ranging from a few months to fourteen years. On May 25, 2023, the leader of the Oath Keepers, Stewart Rhodes, was sentenced to eighteen years in prison, making it the highest sentence relating to January 6 handed down to that point in time. At his sentencing hearing, Rhodes claimed that the Proud Boys were far more dangerous than his Oath Keepers. In early May 2023, an additional four members of the Proud Boys, including its leader, Henry "Enrique" Tarrio, were convicted of seditious conspiracy, and a fifth member on lesser charges. Sentences for these Proud Boy members, including its leader, were handed down at various points between June and September 2023. On September 5, 2023, Enrique Tarrio was sentenced to twenty-two years in prison, followed by thirty-six months of supervised release. This made Tarrio's sentence the longest prison sentence imposed on an individual involved in the events of January 6, 2021. Tarrio's group "conspired to prevent, hinder and delay the certification of the Electoral College vote and to oppose by force the authority of the government of the United States" (Office of Public Affairs, Department of Justice 2023). According to the DOJ, Tarrio received the longest sentence based upon his role and actions; however, his small group of compatriots also received similarly lengthy prison sentences, handed down in the summer of 2023. Of Tarrio's co-defendants, Ethan Nordean, was sentenced to eighteen years in prison, Joseph Biggs seventeen years, Zachary Rehl fifteen years, and Dominic Pezzola ten years. As of 2024, the DOJ continues to investigate and prosecute individuals who committed crimes on January 6, 2021.

See Also: Aid and Comfort (Aid to Enemies of the State); Assassination; *Brandenburg v. United States*; Brown, John; Capitol Insurrection on January 6, 2021; Conspiracy, Criminal; *Dennis v. United States* (1951); Insurrection; John Brown's Raid (1859); Levying War; Sedition; Smith Act; Terrorism; Treason; World Trade Center Bombing of 1993; *Yates v. United States* (1957)

Resources

Cohan, John Alan. 2003. "Seditious Conspiracy, the Smith Act, and Prosecution for Religious Speech Advocating the Violent Overthrow of Government." *St. John's Journal of Legal Commentary* 17: 199–245.

Lynch, Sarah N. 2022. "Oath Keepers Militia Trial Tests Prosecutors in U.S. Capitol Riot Case." *Reuters*, September 20, 2022. Accessed November 24, 2022. https://news.yahoo.com/oath-keepers-militia-trial-tests-101633568.html.

Office of Public Affairs, Department of Justice. 2023. "Proud Boys Leader Sentenced to 22 Years in Prison for Seditious Conspiracy and Other Charges Related to U.S. Capitol Breach." September 5, 2023. Accessed November 4, 2023. https://www.justice.gov/opa/pr/proud-boys-leader-sentenced-22-years-prison-seditious-conspiracy-and-other-charges-related.

Seditious Conspiracy, 18 U.S.C. Section 2384.

Shutz, Jacob. 2021. "The Last Time the Justice Department Prosecuted a Seditious Conspiracy Case." *Lawfare*, February 24, 2021. Accessed November 24, 2022. https://www.lawfareblog.com/last-time-justice-department-prosecuted-seditious-conspiracy-case.

Tarrant, Catherine M. 1971. "To 'Insure Domestic Tranquility': Congress and the Law of Seditious Conspiracy, 1859–1861." *The American Journal of Legal History* 15, no. 2 (April): 107–23.

United States Department of Justice. 2022. "News Release: Former Leader of Proud Boys Pleads Guilty to Seditious Conspiracy for Efforts to Stop Transfer of Power Following 2020 Presidential Election." October 6, 2022. Accessed November 24, 2022. https://www.justice.gov/opa/pr/former-leader-proud-boys-pleads-guilty-seditious-conspiracy-efforts-stop-transfer-power.

United States v. Rahman, 189 F.3d 88 (U.S. Second Circuit, 1999).

September 11, 2001

Commonly referred to as 9/11, the terrorist attacks that occurred on September 11, 2001, in New York City and Washington, DC, were the deadliest in US history, with approximately three thousand people killed. Up to that point, the next closest attack in terms of carnage and destruction was the 1995 Oklahoma City Bombing, which resulted in 168 deaths. While the Oklahoma City Bombing was an act of domestic terrorism committed by several of US citizens, 9/11 was an attack perpetrated by foreigners affiliated with the international terrorist network Al-Qaeda. Despite Al-Qaeda not being a sovereign nation, many have compared the 9/11 attack to the Japanese bombing of Pearl Harbor in 1941, which ushered the United States into the Second World War. The 9/11 attack led the United States into the War on Terror, which involved over a decade of military operations in Afghanistan and Iraq. Despite its foreign origin, the attack had profound influence on the protection of the homeland against future domestic threats and changed countless aspects of day-to-day life in America.

September 11, 2001, was a beautiful, crisp, sunny day in New York City, the tranquility of which would be instantaneously shattered by American Airlines flight 11, when it was intentionally flown directly into the North Tower of the World Trade Center at 8:46 a.m. A group of Al-Qaeda terrorist operatives had seized control of the cockpit with the express purpose of using the hijacked passenger plane as a missile. Seventeen short minutes later, another hijacked airplane (United Airlines flight 175) crashed into the South Tower of the World Trade Center at 9:03 a.m. The World Trade Center complex contained a variety of offices, shops, and restaurants, and an estimated 50,000 individuals worked in and around the complex each day. Initial estimates were that the death toll would exceed 10,000, but miraculously, and through the countless acts of heroism that day by ordinary individuals and first responders, the death toll was limited to just under 3,000. When the South Tower collapsed at 9:59 a.m. and the North Tower at 10:28 a.m., 348 firefighters and twenty-three New York Police Officers perished.

As the horrific events of the day continued to unfold, two more planes (United Airlines flight 93 and American Airlines flight 77) were commandeered by Al-Qaeda hijackers, who redirected them toward landmark buildings in Washington, DC. Many experts believe the terrorists intended to crash the planes into the United States Capitol and the White House, respectively. At 9:37 a.m., fifty-one minutes after the attack on the North Tower and thirty-four minutes after the attack on the South Tower, American Airlines flight 77 was flown into the Pentagon, killing 189 more individuals. Aboard the fourth hijacked plane (United Airlines flight 93), passengers learned about the previous plane hijackings and crashes through frenzied phone calls to loved ones and courageously attempted to overwhelm the hijackers and take back control of the plane. At 10:03 a.m., the plane crashed in Shanksville, Pennsylvania. While all forty passengers and crew perished in the crash, their heroic actions may have saved thousands of lives in Washington, DC.

The events of 9/11 shook the collective consciousness of the country like no other event since the bombing of Pearl Harbor in 1941. The sense of normalcy and safety in America had disappeared. Approximately forty-five days later, the USA PATRIOT Act was adopted. Many Americans were now willing to give the federal government more investigative and policing powers and to accept a reduction in civil liberties in the name of national security. Within a year, the Congress had drastically transformed the federal government with the passage of the Homeland Security Act of 2002, the first major sweeping reform of the federal government since the end of the Second World War. These laws are now part of the powerful legal arsenal of the United States in dealing with domestic crimes against the state.

In the aftermath of 9/11, there was wide public demand for information about the terrorist attack and how another event like it might be avoided in the future. President George W. Bush was initially reluctant to authorize or support the creation of an investigative committee or commission. However, he relented, and the 9/11 Commission, composed of five Democrats and five Republicans, was created by Congress on November 27, 2002, through Public Law 107-306. The official name was "The National Commission on Terrorist Attacks Upon the United States." The 9/11 Commission was tasked with determining what factors led to the September 11 attacks, investigating whether any nations were complicit with Al-Qaeda in the attacks, reviewing how the US intelligence communities acted (or failed to act) in handling intelligence warnings of an impending attack, and providing recommendations for restructuring how intelligence agencies should handle such threats in the future.

While the focus of the 9/11 Commission was international in scope, its bipartisan nature and investigative powers nevertheless serve as a blueprint for how the government can analyze momentous domestic events such as the Capitol Insurrection on January 6, 2021. Like the United States House Committee on the January 6 attacks (hereinafter the "J6 Committee"), the 9/11 Commission sifted through thousands of pages of documents and interviewed over 1,200 individuals. However, unlike the J6 Committee, which received only partial and tepid support from many Republican supporters, and with several witnesses even refusing to obey subpoenas to provide evidence, the 9/11 Commission conversely received strong bipartisan support from witnesses from multiple presidential administrations. While not testifying under oath, President Bush and Vice President Richard Cheney were interviewed in private by the ten-member Commission. Similarly, former President William Jefferson Clinton and Vice President Al Gore were interviewed. There were also nineteen full days of public hearings with many high-ranking current or former government officials testifying, including Colin Powell (Secretary of State), Donald Rumsfeld (Secretary of Defense), George Tenet (Central Intelligence Director), and Condoleezza Rice (National Security Advisor).

After two years of work, in July 2004, the 9/11 Commission released its final report, "The 9/11 Commission Report: The Final Report of the National Commission on Terrorist Attacks Upon the United States." The 567-page report is required reading for any individual wishing to make sense of the events leading up to September 11, 2001. The report delineates the development of the Al-Qaeda network, its fixation on attacking the United States, the 1998 attacks on United States embassies in Kenya and Tanzania, the foiled plot to attack Los Angeles in 1999, the 2000 attack on the United States Navy vessel the USS Cole, and, of course, the horrific attacks which occurred on September 11, 2001. The Report also analyzes to what degree other foreign states were complicit in support of Al-Qaeda and to what degree US intelligence communities failed to effectively identify the threats and thwart them. Finally, the Report made a series of recommendations to better protect the United States from similar attacks in the future. Notable recommended changes that were subsequently adopted included the creation of the Office of the Director of National Intelligence with oversight authority over all the separate intelligence agencies operating in the United States. The rationale for this recommendation was the same that led to the creation of the Department of Homeland Security through the Homeland Security Act of 2002, namely, the integration, uniformity, and intelligence sharing among various agencies. The Report also recommended the creation of a National Counterterrorism Center (which was subsequently established) as well as better crossflow of information and better training for the Central Intelligence Agency and the Federal Bureau of Investigation.

The legacy of the events of 9/11 cannot be overstated. Numerous planned attacks and crimes against the state have been prevented because of increased powers of federal law enforcement and the post-9/11 creation and operation of the Department of Homeland Security (DHS), which has itself become the lead force in preventing and responding to attacks against the United States, foreign or domestic.

See Also: Capitol Insurrection on January 6, 2021; Homeland Security Act of 2002; Insurrection; Oklahoma City Bombing (1995); Terrorism; USA PATRIOT Act

Resources

Dudziak, Mary L., ed. 2003. *September 11 in History: A Watershed Moment?* Durham, NC: Duke University Press.

National Commission on Terrorist Attacks upon the United States. 2004. *The 9/11 Commission Report: Final Report of the National Commission on Terrorist Attacks upon the United States*. New York: W.W. Norton.

Wright, Lawrence. 2006. *The Looming Towers: Al Qaeda and the Road to 9/11*. New York: Knopf.

Shay's Rebellion (1786–7)

Shay's Rebellion (1786–7) is often loosely associated with two other significant anti-taxation rebellions that occurred in the years following the American Revolution, namely, the Whiskey Rebellion (1794) and Fries's Rebellion (1798–9). However, each of the three "rebellions" was unique, originated from different economic and political factors, and should be distinguished. Fries's Rebellion was instigated by people in Pennsylvania who were upset at increased property taxes levied to pay for new military expenditures and to build up US defenses in the wake of a potential war with France. Fries's Rebellion also involved no deaths and little to no serious bodily harm. The people protesting the tax numbered only in the hundreds. On the other end of the spectrum, the Whiskey Rebellion was a massive popular uprising of up to 15,000 people in the western counties of Pennsylvania. These individuals were upset at having to pay taxes on whiskey to help pay for expenses and debts incurred by the state and federal governments during the American Revolution. President Washington called up 13,000 soldiers from the state militia to quell this rebellion. Both the Whiskey Rebellion and Fries's Rebellion occurred after the United States Constitution was ratified and went into effect in 1789. The insurgents of both these incidents sought relief from what they viewed as onerous taxes, not rebellion or revolution from the existing government.

In contrast, Shay's Rebellion was not about taxes per se, but about the abject poverty many people faced in western Massachusetts following the Revolutionary War and the lack of assistance from the state legislature and state court system to help these individuals. After the war, people faced massive debt and inflation. Farmers were unable to sell their produce, and creditors seized land and assets as payment. Thousands of dissatisfied individuals began blocking courts and skirmishing with state officials to preclude the courts from continuing to enforce these unpaid debts and to prevent the foreclosures of property. The goal was a regime change in Massachusetts as it related to both the court system and the legislature. As one writer aptly commented, "never, in all its history, has the government of that Commonwealth been in such imminent danger of overthrow" (Lyman 1894, 462).

Daniel Shay, a destitute farmer and former officer in the American Revolution, became the leader of the movement. Shay had served as a captain during the war and fought at Bunker Hill, Stony Point, Lexington, Concord, and in the campaign to capture British General John Burgoyne. Other men, like Luke Day (who fought with Benedict Arnold in the Quebec campaign) and Eli Parsons, also led contingencies of armed men and planned operations against state authorities. The "rebellion" was not a singular event, but a series of events stretching from August 1786 through January 1787. On August 28, 1786, a mob of about 1,500 armed individuals blocked the state courthouse located in Northampton, Massachusetts, preventing it from conducting business. Throngs of armed protesters also stopped the courts from operating in five separate counties. At the height of the movement, the rebellion forces had over four thousand followers. These actions prompted Massachusetts's Governor James Bowdoin to call out the state militia.

After a successful first round of stopping the courts from acting on debtor lawsuits and foreclosures, Shay's forces reorganized for another group of operations against the courts at various points across the state. Shay's plan was to attack the federal arsenal at Springfield, Massachusetts, on January 25, 1787. Then, once Shay's forces had seized additional arms and ammunition, the plan was to go on to attack elsewhere in the state. While sources vary, most agree that Shay had between 1,100 and 2,000 men at his disposal for the arsenal attack, with many of his other men spread out throughout other locations in the state. However, to Shay's dismay, the Springfield Armory and Arsenal were well supplied with artillery and small arms and were guarded by a large force of state militia commanded by well-experienced Major General William Shepherd. Shay's forces were easily and quickly repulsed by General Shepherd, who ordered a battery of artillery to fire when Shay's forces got close to the arsenal fortifications. After several warning shots over their heads, the cannon fired straight into the center of Shay's line, immediately causing "the utmost confusion," killing four men, and causing Shay's troops to flee in terror. Several days later, the rebel forces capitulated.

The state demanded an immediate surrender, with the stipulation that Shay's men put down their arms, take an oath of allegiance to the state, and go home. If this were done, pardons would be issued. The state issued approximately four thousand pardons for people with some part in Shay's Rebellion but excluded several hundred of the main instigators and planners. The more serious offenders were prosecuted for various crimes relating to rebellion against the state (including treason and sedition); however, except for a few key actors, these individuals were also pardoned shortly after their convictions. Of the remaining insurgency leadership (including Daniel Shay), each was found guilty of rebellion and treason and sentenced to death. Fortuitously for these "rebels," John Hancock would defeat James Bowdoin for the governorship and would assume office in May 1787 (immediately before some of the scheduled executions). Hancock had a much more favorable and lenient view of the insurgents than Bowdoin, and he pardoned all the remaining defendants, including Daniel Shay, in June 1788. Two individuals were executed in December 1787 for multiple criminal offenses (including theft and looting) unrelated to crimes against the state.

Shay's Rebellion is significant for several reasons. First, this was the first instance wherein *hundreds* of Americans were charged and convicted of treason for a single series of events. Second, the convictions stemming from Shay's Rebellion were the first to occur after the conclusion of the American Revolution but before the ratification of the United States Constitution. Third, the rebellion imperiled the governmental stability of Massachusetts and consequently threatened the stability (or lack thereof) of all states under the Articles of Confederation. Finally, with Shay's Rebellion fresh in the minds of the delegates of the 1787 Constitutional Convention, they were acutely aware of the need for a more powerful federal government to deal with future attacks on the state. Under the Articles of Confederation (1781–8), the federal government had little authority to stop such rebellions. The crime of treason was also not expressly covered in the Articles of Confederation, an omission that would be rectified when the new Constitution went into effect in 1789.

See Also: American Revolution and Treason; Arnold, Benedict; Fries's Rebellion (1799); Insurrection; Rebellion; Sedition; Treason; Whiskey Rebellion

Resources

Lyman, Payson R. 1894. "The Shays Rebellion in Massachusetts." *The American Historical Register and Monthly Gazette of the History, Military and Patriotic-Hereditary Societies of the United States of America* 19 (September/October): 462–75.

Richard, Leonard L. 2002. *Shay's Rebellion: The American Revolution's Final Battle*. Philadelphia: University of Pennsylvania Press.

Szatmary, David P. 1980. *Shay's Rebellion: The Making of an Agrarian Insurrection*. Amherst: The University of Massachusetts Press.

Smith Act

The Alien Registration Act of 1940 is commonly known as the Smith Act, named after the chief proponent of the legislation, Congressman Howard W. Smith. Coming on the eve of the Second World War and hostilities in Europe, the Smith Act aimed to curb subversive activities and speech against the United States as well as activities intended to demoralize the military and its servicemembers.

In the first section of the Smith Act, the Congress made it a felony offense "for any person, with intent to interfere with, impair, or influence the loyalty, morale, or discipline of the military or naval forces of the United States to advise, counsel, urge, or in any manner cause insubordination, disloyalty, mutiny, or refusal of duty by any member of the United States armed forces." The first section also prohibited any "written or printed matter which advises, counsels, or urges insubordination, disloyalty, mutiny, or refusal of duty."

Section Two criminalized any efforts to "advocate, abet, advise, or teach" the "desirability, or propriety of overthrowing or destroying" the US government, or "advocate, abet, advise, or teach ... the assassination of any officer" of the US government. The second section also prohibited the publication, circulation, distribution, or display of any written materials with the intention of "advocating, advising, or teaching" either the overthrow or destruction of the US government. Finally, the Smith Act criminalized any attempt "to organize or help to organize any society, group, or assembly of persons who teach, advocate, or encourage" the overthrow or destruction of the government, or "to be or become a member" of such an organization.

During and after the Second World War, dozens of individuals were prosecuted and convicted for violating the Smith Act. The first successful prosecutions were aimed at members of the Socialist Workers Party of Minneapolis and local labor organizations who went on strike or engaged in work stoppages during the War as a means of improving employment conditions. After the end of the Second World War and the start of the Cold War, the federal government began utilizing the Smith Act against the leadership of the American Communist Party. The government's position during this period was that communism was an ideology that sought the ultimate destruction or demise of the United States and, therefore, that membership and activities in the Communist Party were a violation of the Smith Act.

Multiple leaders of the American Communist Party were prosecuted and convicted in the late 1940s and early 1950s. In 1951, the Supreme Court in *Dennis v. United States* affirmed the convictions of eleven Party leaders and upheld the overall constitutionality of the Smith Act. In 1957, the Supreme Court again reviewed the constitutionality of the Smith Act in *Yates v. United States*, this time overturning the convictions of fourteen lower echelon members of the American Communist Party and sending the case back to the trial court for a determination as to whether the defendants were advocating an abstract political ideology or advocating actions that would entail the immediate destruction or overthrow of the government. In *Yates*, the Court indicated that the mere advocacy of abstract political doctrines, without the intention of immediate action, would not be actionable under the Smith Act based upon First Amendment considerations.

In 1961, the Supreme Court reviewed two cases (*Scales v. United States* and *Noto v. United States*) involving the portion of the Smith Act that made it a crime to be a member of an organization that advocated the overthrow of the United States. In *Scales v. United States*, the Supreme Court upheld the defendant's conviction because it was based not only on the defendant's membership in a political party, but also predicated on specific actions taken by the defendant in furtherance of the organization's goals. However, in *Noto v. United States*, the Supreme Court unanimously overturned the conviction of the defendant, holding that there was insufficient evidence to establish that the organization to which the defendant belonged was specifically engaged in advocating the overthrow or destruction of the government.

A significant portion of the Smith Act (Section Two of the original legislation) remains federal law, located at 18 United States Code Section 2385. The offense is entitled "Advocating overthrow of Government." However, the applicability and relevance of this provision of federal law are constrained by the Supreme Court's 1969 ruling in *Brandenburg v. Ohio*. In *Brandenburg*, the Court held that speech advocating illegal action or conduct is protected speech under the First Amendment unless that "advocacy is directed to inciting or producing imminent lawless action and is likely to incite or produce such action."

See Also: *Brandenburg v. Ohio* (1969); *Dennis v. United States* (1951); Speech as Crime against the State; *Yates v. United States* (1957)

Resources

18 United States Code Section 2385.

Cohan, John Alan. 2003. "Seditious Conspiracy, the Smith Act, and Prosecution for Religious Speech Advocating the Violent Overthrow of Government." *Journal of Civil Rights and Economic Development* 17 (Winter/Spring): 199–245.

Hunt, Alan Reeve. 1957. "State Control of Sedition: The Smith Act as the Supreme Law of the Land." *Minnesota Law Review* 41: 287–332.

"The Supreme Court, the Smith Act, and the 'Clear and Present Danger' Test." *St. John's Law Review* 32 (December 1957): 91–9.

Snowden, Edward

See Leaks of National Defense Information

Sovereign Citizens Movement

The Sovereign Citizens Movement is composed of a very loose and highly heterogeneous group of individuals. It is a movement that is hard to define in concrete terms given the divergent and bizarre beliefs of its members, with its only commonality the belief that the federal government is illegitimate and that individuals are sovereign entities. Members of the Sovereign Citizens Movement are typically anti-government extremists, often influenced by racist and antisemitic beliefs, who deny the validity of laws they believe are enacted by a corrupt and illegitimate federal government. Adherents believe that "even though they physically reside in this country, they are separate or 'sovereign' from the United States. As a result, they believe they don't have to answer to any government authority, including courts, taxing authorities, motor vehicle departments, or law enforcement" (FBI 2010). According to the FBI, members of the movement cause countless problems for the state: "For example, many sovereign citizens don't pay their taxes. They hold illegal courts that issue warrants for judges and police officers. They clog up the court system with frivolous lawsuits and liens against public officials to harass them. And they use fake money orders, personal checks, and the like at government agencies, banks, and businesses" (FBI 2010). The FBI has said that this Sovereign Citizen belief system lacks any organizational structure, adheres to no centralized monolithic set of principles, but should nevertheless be classified as "domestic terrorism" (Matza 2020).

Despite its loose organization, the Southern Poverty Law Center estimated that about 300,000 Americans identified with the Sovereign Citizen Movement in 2022. Hundreds of websites can be found on the internet espousing Sovereign Citizen Movement ideals and containing advice and fake pseudo-legal documents that people can use to avoid being held responsible by the actual state and/or federal government. These websites also encourage their members to post their confrontations with law enforcement on YouTube and other online streaming sites. Adherents to this belief system go by many names, including common-law citizens, preamble citizens, freemen, constitutionalists, and nonresident aliens.

The Sovereign Citizen Movement has its origins in the 1970s and, like the modern Militia Movement, traces its ancestry to a group called Posse Comitatus (roughly meaning "power to the country"). Posse Comitatus was founded by William Potter Gale, a racist and antisemitic activist, who believed his organization was needed to combat what he perceived as a federal government that undermined the rights of white people. Gale and his disciples "believed that the 'common law' (based upon interpretations of the Bible), as opposed to federal law, provided the only true legislative code for U.S. citizens" (Institute for Strategic Dialogue 2022, 2). And while considered a fringe movement in the 1970s–1980s, several high-profile incidents kept Gale and his beliefs in the public eye. For example, a North Dakota adherent (Gordon Kohl) violently resisted when United States Marshals attempted to arrest him for violating his parole. Denying the federal government's authority over him, Kohl shot and killed two law enforcement officers and wounded others. After four months on the run, Kohl was found in Arkansas, where a second firefight occurred, killing not only Kohl but also the local Sheriff.

Membership in the Sovereign Citizen Movement grew substantially in the aftermath of the standoffs between law enforcement and citizens at Ruby Ridge, Idaho, in 1992, and Waco, Texas, in 1993. While some adherents keep to themselves in large plots of land in western states, incidents of violence increased in the decade after Ruby Ridge and Waco. For instance, in 2000, Jerry Thompson used a samurai sword to behead his roommate during a dispute over owed rent. When police attempted to investigate, "Thompson refused to cooperate while claiming his status as a sovereign citizen made him immune to U.S. laws" (Strike Force 2020).

One of the most infamous adherents to the Sovereign Citizen Movement was a disgruntled resident of Michigan, who notified his state that he was no longer "a citizen of the corrupt political corporate State of Michigan and the United States of America" (ADL 2012, 3). This person engaged in several other bizarre actions, such as habitually writing "TDC" (meaning "threat, duress, coercion") next to the zip code on envelopes. He did this because he thought that using a federal zip code otherwise constituted a contract between himself and the federal government and that without somehow indicating his disagreement, he would be tacitly agreeing with the supremacy of federal law. This man was Terry Nichols, whose anti-government views very much aligned with Timothy McVeigh. Three years later, in 1995, Nichols conspired with McVeigh to design a bomb powerful enough to kill 168 people and destroy a building in the Oklahoma City Bombing.

The legal justifications and rationale for the Sovereign Citizen Movement are dubious and involve a tortured interpretation of US history and law. The simplest explanation adopted by many is that the United States started out as a "common law" country, but over time, the federal government slowly usurped the people's rightful sovereignty, making them pawns of an illegitimate federal government. Therefore, adherents feel they can divorce themselves from the federal system by rejecting contracts (such as driver's licenses, wedding licenses, hunting licenses, and social security identification cards) that they believe are forced upon citizens by the government in an attempt to get people to solidify federal authority.

Other beliefs within the Sovereignty Citizen Movement stem from a misinterpretation of the Fourteenth Amendment, ratified in 1868, which granted citizenship to all persons born or naturalized in the United States. Virtually all historians and scholars agree that one of the central purposes of the Fourteenth Amendment was to guarantee citizenship to millions of newly freed (formerly enslaved) individuals following the American Civil War and reverse the conclusion to the contrary stated by Chief Justice Taney in *Dred Scott v. Sanford* (1857). Yet, some in the Sovereign Citizens Movement believe that the Fourteenth Amendment created a second, optional type of federal citizenship, different from the original state citizenship rights they believed they had under a God-given "common law." These adherents believe that, before the 1868 ratification of the Fourteenth Amendment, no-one was a citizen of the United States and that, after 1868, individuals can opt out of the "new" federal citizenship. Many believe that the government misleads people into agreeing to federal citizenship by requiring things like government-issued documentation and the use of zip codes as part of the mail system. Some think that the federal government has gone so far as to set up "a corporate entity in a person's name when they are born, creating two separate identities. The corporate identities—so-called 'strawmen'—allegedly coexist alongside people's 'flesh and blood' personas. Sovereigns assume it is only this corporate identity which is subject to government legislation" (ADL 2012, 3–4). And "according to this theory, the government uses people's strawmen identities to set up secret trusts in their names that hold hundreds and thousands of dollars" (ADL 2012, 4). The Southern Poverty Law Center, which tracks extremist groups in the United States, has indicated that some adherents believe that "by filing a series of complex, legal sounding documents, the sovereign can tap into that secret Treasury account for his own purposes" (Matza 2020).

The damage to the state by this movement is significant. Members have resisted obeying laws (no matter how minor), set up "common law courts" and issued fake arrest warrants for various US officials (even had "trials" and called for executions in these courts), and issued fake documentation ranging from property deeds to car registrations to tax documents. One of the more common and universal practices of "sovereigns" involves something dubbed "paper terrorism." Paper terrorism entails saturating legitimate government offices with false and pseudo-legal paperwork so that the offices cease to operate effectively. In court cases, it is not uncommon for a "sovereign" litigant to flood the court with hundreds of nonsensical motions and requests for nonexistent legal remedies. Local county land offices are inundated with fake deeds and liens, simply overwhelming the ability of the legitimate government office to do its lawfully charged duties. The use of paper terrorism has been deemed effective by adherents to "damage the function of government institutions, to intimidate public officials, [and] flood opponents with pseudo-legal paperwork" (Institute for Strategic Dialogue 2022, 5). Responding to the onslaught of bogus paperwork "results in damage" to the state, "and disrupt[s] the functioning of government institutions, given the time consuming and costly procedures it takes to process and respond to these large amounts of paperwork" (Institute for Strategic Dialogue 2022, 5).

The Sovereign Citizens Movement also poses a real risk to life through their disregard of law enforcement. As noted, in 1983, Gordon Kohl killed three police officers who were trying to apprehend him for probation violations. In 1993, "sovereign" fugitives murdered a police officer in a shootout in Alabama. In 1994, adherents to the movement brutally attacked a county recorder outside her home. In 1995, Terry Nichols conspired with Timothy McVeigh to kill 168 people in the Oklahoma City Bombing. In 1996, a group of "Montana Freemen" held off federal authorities (who were attempting to arrest them for multiple offenses) in an eighty-one-day standoff. In 1997, members of the "Republic of Texas" engaged in a seven-day stand-off with federal authorities, with participants vowing "to wage an Alamo-style fight to the death." In 1998, two sovereign citizens shot two firefighters in Ohio because a firetruck blocked their vehicle. In 2010, two police officers were killed during a routine traffic stop by a father and son, both sovereign citizen adherents, who were traveling to give seminars on how to circumvent state and federal laws.

The illegal scheming of individuals in this movement continues to the present. In 2013, law enforcement arrested two Sovereign Citizen adherents in Nevada after a lengthy undercover investigation. The two "allegedly conspired to abduct police officers, hold them in custody and put them on trial in a common-law court. According to the police, they were plotting to torture and execute them" (Institute for Strategic Dialogue 2022, 6). In 2020, a group of Michigan men were arrested after a plot to kidnap Michigan Governor Gretchen Whitmer was uncovered. Participants in this conspiracy allegedly contemplated executing her for crimes against the citizens of Michigan. As reported by the BBC, "a growing movement of people who believe that laws do not apply to them threatens police and law enforcement around the world" (Matza 2020) and destabilizes the state.

See Also: American Civil War and Treason; Conspiracy, Criminal; Militia Movement (Modern); Oklahoma City Bombing (1995); Ruby Ridge (1992); Terrorism; Waco (1993)

Resources

Anti-Defense League (ADL). 2012. "ADL 100: Special Report: The Lawless Ones: The Resurgence of the Sovereign Citizen Movement." Second edition. Accessed May 10, 2023. https://www.adl.org/sites/default/files/documents/assets/pdf/combating-hate/Lawless-Ones-2012-Edition-WEB-final.pdf.

Anti-Defense League (ADL). 2017. "Backgrounder: Sovereign Citizen Movement." February 6, 2017. Accessed May 10, 2023. https://www.adl.org/resources/backgrounder/sovereign-citizen-movement.
Federal Bureau of Investigation. 2010. "FBI Bulletin: Stories: Domestic Terrorism: The Sovereign Citizen Movement." April 13, 2010. Accessed May 10, 2023. https://archives.fbi.gov/archives/news/stories/2010/april/sovereigncitizens_041310/domestic-terrorism-the-sovereign-citizen-movement.
Institute for Strategic Dialogue. 2022. "Sovereign Citizen: Anti-government Movement That Believes the US Government Illegitimately Rules over Them." Accessed May 10, 2023. https://www.isdglobal.org/wp-content/uploads/2023/01/Sovereign-Citizens-Explainer.pdf.
Matza, Max. 2020. "What Is the 'Sovereign Citizen' Movement?" *BBC News*, August 5, 2020. Accessed May 10, 2023. https://www.bbc.com/news/world-us-canada-53654318.
Strike Force. 2020. "The Dangers of the Sovereign Citizen Movement: Domestic Terrorism with Little Understanding: People Who Believe They Are Immune to U.S. Laws." September 10, 2020. Accessed May 11, 2023. https://strikesource.com/2020/09/04/the-dangers-of-the-sovereign-citizen-movement/.

Speech as Crime against the State

Through a modern lens, the notion that speech against the government could be criminalized seems counter to the principles of liberty embodied in the Constitution, especially the First Amendment's protections against infringements of speech and the press. And yet, through much of US history, government has criminalized speech it claimed was harmful to government or society.

Though there is little evidence regarding what members of Congress participating in the ratification process thought the Free Speech and Free Press Clauses of the First Amendment meant, it is reasonable to assume many followed the views of eminent English jurist William Blackstone, who over a century earlier had opined:

> The liberty of the press is indeed essential to the nature of a free state; but this consists in laying no previous restraints upon publications, and not in freedom from censure for criminal matter when published. Every freeman has an undoubted right to lay what sentiments he pleases before the public; to forbid this, is to destroy the freedom of the press: but if he publishes what is improper, mischievous, or illegal, he must take the consequences of his own temerity.

Blackstone observed the ill effects of allowing government to control speech in advance ("prior restraint") in England, and warned "[t]o subject the press to the restrictive power of a licenser, as was formerly done, both before and since the Revolution, is to subject all freedom of sentiment to the prejudices of one man, and make him the arbitrary and infallible judge of all controverted points in learning, religion and government." And yet, Blackstone also accepted the need for government and society to punish "dangerous or offensive writings" after they were published as also necessary for "solid foundations of civil liberty" (Blackstone 1872).

The Framers of the Constitution were thus attempting to reach a balance that allowed government and society to protect themselves from falsehood while preventing the same government from engaging in the tyranny Blackstone had observed in England. This was observed much later by Justice Felix Frankfurter when he opined in a concurrence in *Dennis v. United States* (1951):

> The historic antecedents of the First Amendment preclude the notion that its purpose was to give unqualified immunity to every expression that touched on matters within the range of political interest .... "The law is perfectly well settled," this Court said over fifty years ago, "that the first ten amendments to the Constitution, commonly known as the Bill of Rights, were not intended to lay down any novel principles of government, but simply to embody certain guaranties and immunities which we had inherited from our English ancestors, and which had from time immemorial been subject to certain well-recognized exceptions arising from the necessities of the case." [Citation omitted]. That this represents the authentic view of the Bill of Rights and the spirit in which it must be construed has been recognized again and again in cases that have come here within the last fifty years.

The evolution of the understanding of the meaning of the First Amendment has had a significant impact on the extent to which speech "against the state" can be criminalized. Though the Speech and Press Clauses of the First Amendment provoked apparently little debate at the time of their ratification, they became central to the debate over the Sedition Act of 1798 and subsequent attempts by the government to criminalize speech. President Thomas Jefferson's argument against the Sedition Act of 1798 included articulation of a more libertarian view of individual speech rights, planting a seed that would eventually bloom into the Supreme Court's modern free speech jurisprudence, but not before a century and a half of a generally allowing government to criminalize speech. During the American Civil War, the Supreme Court declined to decide the significant free speech question posed by the arrest and conviction by military commission of a politician who made anti-war statements (*Ex Parte Vallandigham* [1864]). In a host of cases, including *Abrams v. United States* (1919), *Schenck v. United States* (1919), *Debs v. United States* (1919), *Gitlow v. New York* (1925), *Whitney v. California* (1927), *Dennis v. United States* (1951), and *United States v. O'Brien* (1968), the Supreme Court created and employed standards like the Clear and Present Danger Test to uphold various laws criminalizing speech against the government, including sedition laws, criminal anarchy laws, and criminal syndicalism laws. Indeed, under the precedent of the time, speech itself could constitute not only a crime against the state, but the ultimate crime against the state, namely treason (see, for example, Radio Traitors and Anti-State Propaganda during the Second World War).

However, after decades of attempting to preserve the balance alluded to by Blackstone and Frankfurter, in the 1960s, the Supreme Court ultimately embraced a more libertarian view of free speech rights that has endured to this day. In *New York Times v. Sullivan* (1964), the Supreme Court unanimously proclaimed "we consider this case against the background of a profound national commitment to the principle that debate on public issues should be uninhibited, robust, and wide-open, and that it may well include vehement, caustic, and sometimes unpleasantly sharp attacks on government and public officials." And in *Brandenburg v. Ohio* (1969), the Supreme Court summarized its own jurisprudence as having "fashioned the principle that the constitutional guarantees of free speech and free press do not permit a State to forbid or proscribe advocacy of the use of force or of law violation except where such advocacy is directed to inciting or producing imminent lawless action and is likely to incite or produce such action." Thus, criminal *action*, rather than mere speech or controversial and even dangerous *ideas*, became the lynchpin of crimes against the state.

To be sure, some laws criminalizing speech as a crime against the state still exist and have been repeatedly upheld by the Supreme Court. These include laws against sharing government secrets, such as the Espionage Act of 1917 (though see the important exception for prior restraint of the press, as articulated in *New York Times v. United States* [1971]), laws against providing material support to terrorist organizations, and laws prohibiting false statements, such as libel, defamation, and perjury. But the balance between individual and press liberty on the one hand and the government's proclaimed need for self-preservation on the other weighs decidedly in favor of curtailing speech as a crime against the state.

See Also: *Abrams v. United States* (1919); American Civil War and Treason; Anarchy, Criminal; *Brandenburg v. Ohio* (1969); Clear and Present Danger Test; Criminal Syndicalism; *Debs v. United States* (1919); *Dennis v. United States* (1951); Espionage Act of 1917 and Sedition Act of 1918; *Ex Parte Vallandigham* (1864); *Gitlow v. New York* (1925); Jefferson, Thomas; Material Support Crimes; *New York Times v. United States* (1971); *O'Brien, United States v.* (1968); Perjury, False Statements, and the Obstruction of Justice; Radio Traitors and Anti-State Propaganda during World War Two; *Schenck v. United States* (1919); Sedition; Sedition Act of 1798; Treason; *Whitney v. California* (1927)

Resources

Blackstone, William. 1872. *Commentaries on the Laws of England.* Edited by Thomas M. Cooley. Second, revised edition. Chicago: Callaghan and Company, 151–2.
Bracken, Harry M. 1994. *Freedom of Speech: Words Are Not Deeds*. Westport, CT: Praeger.
Kersch, Ken I. 2003. *Freedom of Speech, Rights, and Liberties under the Law*. Santa Barbara, CA: ABC-CLIO.
Levy, Leonard. 1960. *Legacy of Suppression: Freedom of Speech and Press in Early American History*. Cambridge, MA: Harvard University Press.
Levy, Leonard. 1985. *Emergence of a Free Press*. Oxford: Oxford University Press.

Stevens, Aaron (1831–60)

Aaron Stevens was executed by the Commonwealth of Virginia for acts of treason, murder, and attempted insurrection in March 1860. Stevens was one of John Brown's provisional army of twenty-one men and one of Brown's trusted lieutenants who was involved in John Brown's Raid, the attack upon, and seizure of, the United States Armory and Arsenal at Harpers Ferry, Virginia (now West Virginia) in October 1859. Alongside Brown in court, Stevens was indicted by the Commonwealth of Virginia on October 26, 1859. The treason charge was premised upon three separately defined acts of treason under Virginia law. As specified in the indictment, Stevens was charged with committing treason as follows: "feloniously and traitorously make rebellion, and levy war against the said Commonwealth of Virginia"; attempting to form "a government, separate from and hostile to the existing government of said commonwealth"; giving his "allegiance and fidelity to said usurped government"; and engaging "in open battle and deadly warfare with the civil officers and soldiers in the law service of said Commonwealth of Virginia." Stevens's trial was delayed due to the possibility that he might be transferred into custody of the federal government for trial for treason. While this was being negotiated, Stevens sat in a Virginia jail from late October 1859 through February 1860. Stevens was not transferred to federal custody, and he was put on trial by Virginia in February 1860, convicted of all counts, and executed on March 16, 1860. Stevens was the seventh and final person executed by the Commonwealth of Virginia for crimes stemming from the attack on the federal Armory and Arsenal.

Stevens was a former United States Army soldier who enlisted at age sixteen in a Massachusetts Volunteer regiment to fight in the Mexican American War. He was honorably discharged after the war and entered civilian life. He enlisted again in the mid-1850s and served as a bugler in a United States Army dragoon regiment. At Taos, New Mexico, he was court-martialed and convicted of committing battery against a superior officer and sentenced to death. President Franklin Pierce commuted Stevens's sentence to three years of hard labor at Fort Leavenworth, Kansas. Stevens was imprisoned for a brief time before making his escape in 1856 and joining Brown and his men in "Bleeding Kansas" (a period of violent clashes between citizens in the fight to determine whether Kansas would be a free or slave state). Stevens provided military training to the men in Brown's provisional army. During John Brown's invasion of Harpers Ferry on October 16–17, 1859, Stevens led a group of Brown's men and captured several local townspeople as hostages, including Lewis Washington, the great grandnephew of George Washington and a prominent citizen who served on the staff of the governor of Virginia. On October 17, Stevens was shot and captured by townspeople as he attempted to negotiate with them on behalf of Brown under a flag of truce. During the prosecution of Brown, Lewis Washington was called as a witness and testified that he heard Aaron Stevens asking a hostage if the hostage was in favor of the institution of slavery. When the hostage responded in the affirmative, Stevens retorted, "then you are the first man I would hang" (McGinty 2009, 154).

See Also: Brown, John; Insurrection; John Brown's Raid (1859); Levying War; Rebellion; Treason; *Virginia v. Brown* (1859)

Resources

McGinty, Brian. 2009. *John Brown's Trial*. Cambridge, MA: Harvard University Press.
Oates, Stephen. 1970. *To Purge This Land with Blood*. Amherst: The University of Massachusetts Press.

Surratt, Mary E. (1820–65)

Mary Surratt was the first woman in US history executed by the federal government. Surratt was executed in July 1865 for her role in the conspiracy to assassinate President Abraham Lincoln. Along with seven other accomplices, Surratt was charged with conspiring to murder the president of the United States and was unanimously convicted of the charges by an eleven-member military commission on June 30, 1865. The conviction and recommended death sentence were transmitted to President Andrew Johnson on July 5, 1865, and Surratt was executed by hanging on July 7. President Johnson referred to Surratt's boarding house in Washington, DC, where several conspirators who were involved in the Lincoln assassination stayed and held clandestine meetings, as the "nest that hatched the eggs" of vipers who would murder the president. When Surratt was executed, it was described as "the biggest hanging America ever had" (Lewis 1994, 205).

Few historians debate that Surratt was an ardent secessionist and felt no strong love or loyalty for the Union. During the Civil War, her son, John Surratt, Jr., served as a Confederate spy and a liaison between Confederate President Jefferson Davis and Secretary of War Judah Benjamin and Confederate spies in Canada. Union spies in Canada testified during the prosecution of the conspirators that John Surratt, Jr., and John Wilkes Booth were heard discussing the possible assassination of Lincoln during meetings with Southern sympathizers in Canada. By many accounts, Mary Surratt was captivated by the actor John Wilkes Booth, who visited Surratt's Washington, DC, boarding house often with Mary's son, John. Mary Surratt was said to be so taken by Booth that she displayed a picture of him alongside photos of Confederate General Robert E. Lee and Confederate President Jefferson Davis. An abundance of evidence suggests that Booth and Surratt's son, John Surratt, Jr., conspired together to kidnap the president before hatching the assassination plot. Booth would frequently bring other individuals later proven to be involved in the plot to murder Lincoln to Mary Surratt's boarding house, including David Herold, Lewis Powell, and George Atzerodt.

Mary Surratt lived a hardscrabble existence and was bitter by the onset of the Civil War. Her husband, John Surratt, Sr., owned a tavern thirteen miles outside of Washington, DC, in a little hamlet aptly named Surrattsville. By 1863, John Surratt, Sr., had died and Mary Surratt was forced to lease the tavern and move to a boarding house she owned on H Street in Washington, DC. While living in DC, Mary Surratt made several trips to Surrattsville, and one of those trips on the eve of the Lincoln assassination would constitute strong circumstantial evidence of her guilt. During her trial, she was frequently referred to as the "widow-woman."

Lincoln succumbed to the gunshot wound to his head in the early hours of April 15, 1865. Two days later, on April 17, Mary Surratt and her whole household, including co-conspirator Lewis Powell, were arrested, and taken into custody. Beginning May 10, Surratt and seven other co-conspirators were charged before a military tribunal of eleven military judges/commissioners. Over the course of the trial, an immense amount of evidence was submitted for the military commission's consideration and between 300 and 400 witnesses testified. Because Surratt was charged with "conspiracy" to murder President Lincoln, and not attempting to murder Lincoln herself, the government only needed to prove that Surratt had knowledge of the plan, did not renounce the conspiracy, and committed at least one overt act in furtherance of the conspiracy. The overt act in furtherance of the conspiracy also provides additional evidence to a judge or jury that the accused was indeed aware of the criminal enterprise, took the plans seriously, and wished to support the planned endeavor.

There were two witnesses who were instrumental in proving Surratt's guilt and sealing her fate. The first person was 26-year-old Louis Weichmann, originally a friend of John Surratt, Jr., who was invited to live at Mary Surratt's boarding house in DC. The second witness was John M. Lloyd, a tenant at the Surrattsville tavern. After the aborted kidnapping attempt of Lincoln by John Surratt, Jr., Weichmann became suspicious of the occupants of Surratt's boarding house and witnessed a few hushed conversations, furtive looks, and what looked like clandestine meetings. Thinking that there might be connection between this activity and the recent kidnapping attempt, Weichmann reported his concerns to the War Department. An official at the War Department instructed Weichmann to keep his eyes on the group and report any other suspicious behavior or illegal activity.

On the eve of the Lincoln's assassination, Mary Surratt requested that Weichmann drive her coach and accompany her to Surrattsville. Weichmann testified that Surratt brought with her two packages and, upon arrival, carried them into the Surrattsville tavern and gave them to John Lloyd. Surratt described the items as "things of Booth's" and instructed Lloyd to have the items ready for when Booth called to retrieve them the next day. According to testimony, the bundle contained a spyglass and a revolver for Booth. Additionally, Surratt told John Llyod to keep the "shooting irons" handy and have them ready to give to Booth when he arrived at the Surrattsville tavern. The "shooting irons" were two rifles hidden in the tavern that Booth attempted to retrieve after the assassination and as he tried to escape. Weichmann's testimony was corroborated by John Lloyd.

Weichmann was a very believable witness and never wavered in his belief as to Mary Surratt's guilt. For decades after, Weichmann was harassed by secessionist sympathizers, and there were several attempts on his life. Weichmann spent almost twenty years under federal protection. Later in life, he swore to his sisters that "he never doubted her [Surratt's] guilt after it [Lincoln's assassination] happened" (Lewis 1994, 227). Perhaps more persuasively, Weichmann made a deathbed statement reiterating his belief in Surratt's guilt. Many people are convinced that "deathbed statements are better than sworn testimony … [because] no man will send his soul climbing through the stars to God weighted down with a lie" told moments before death (Lewis 1994, 231). As his life ebbed away, Weichmann's mind was on the Surratt trial and execution thirty-seven years before. He called his sisters for a pen and paper and penned his last words: "June 2, 1902; This is to certify that every word I gave in evidence at the assassination trial was absolutely true; and now I am about to die and with love. I recommend myself to all truth-loving people" (Lewis 1994, 232). Very soon after he signed his name to this statement, Weichmann died.

The verdict in Surratt's trial was unanimous for conviction, although five of the eleven members signed a statement appealing to President Andrew Johnson to show leniency and commute the imposed death sentence, primary due to Surratt's age (mid-40s) and gender. Never in its history had a woman been executed by the United States. President Johnson ignored the clemency recommendation from the five commissioners, and Surratt was executed by hanging on July 7, 1865.

In retrospect, the strongest argument made by Surratt's lawyers during trial was not in attempting to discount John Lloyd or Louis Weichmann's testimony. Rather, Surratt's counsel argued that a trial by a military commission was illegal and improper. First, the crime alleged against Surratt was that she engaged in a conspiracy in the execution of "traitorous acts." Her counsel argued that considering this, the charge should have been treason—which is a civilian charge, not a military one. In fact, in one of the federal government's first treason cases, President Thomas Jefferson did not attempt to try Aaron Burr in a military court but relied on civilian authorities and the civilian court system. More perplexing to Surratt's lawyers, the leader of the confederacy, Jefferson Davis, had just been indicted by a federal grand jury, and his prosecution was headed to a civilian court as well, yet Surratt's fate was being decided by a military tribunal.

Surratt's lawyers conceded that military commissions and tribunals are proper over military members of the Army and the Navy and in instances where martial law is in place and the civilian courts are not operating. However, Surratt was a civilian and not acting in a theater of military conflict. Surratt's defense argued that she, as an American citizen, had a constitutional right to be indicted by federal grand jury, a right to due process, and a right to a public trial and an impartial civilian jury. In response, United States Attorney General James Speed weakly argued that since the target of the crime was the Commander-in-Chief of the Army and Navy and the offense took place in an area (Washington, DC) still under military control, Surratt was committing an offense against the military and thus military commissions, not civilian courts, were proper. Attorney General Speed's rationale has been characterized as "woefully inadequate" (Downey 2010, 266). Indeed, the jurisdictional arguments of Surratt's lawyers were so sound that they were adopted by the United States Supreme Court in a unanimous opinion a mere ten months later. In *Ex Parte Milligan* (1866), the Supreme Court held that private citizens not connected with the military, involved in a crime not committed in war, should have their cases heard in civilian courts (with civilian judges and juries) if the civilian courts are open and hearing cases. This ruling came ten months too late for Mary Surratt.

See Also: American Civil War and Treason; Assassination; Burr, Aaron; *Burr, United States v.* (1807); Conspiracy, Criminal; Davis, Jefferson; *Ex Parte Milligan* (1866); Martial Law; Treason

Resources

Downey, Arthur T. 2010. *Civil War Lawyers: Constitutional Questions, Courtroom Dramas, and the Men behind Them.* Chicago: The American Bar Association.

Leonard, Elizabeth D. 2004. *Lincoln's Avengers: Justice, Revenge, and Reunion after the Civil War.* New York: W.W. Norton & Company.

Lewis, Lloyd. 1994. *The Assassination of Lincoln: History and Myth.* Lincoln: University of Nebraska Press.

T

Terrorism

Terrorism is often defined as an act of mass violence committed upon a civilian population to achieve political goals or to further a political agenda. The goal of a terrorist is to undermine the public's sense of security and through these means achieve concessions from the government. Domestic terrorism, as a crime against the state, was not included as a specific offense under the United States Code until after the horrific events of 9/11 and the passage of the USA PATRIOT Act a brief time later. Since 2001, several states have also criminalized acts of terrorism as distinct offenses as well.

The concept of terrorism stretches back over several thousand years. Many scholars trace the origins of the word to the Latin verb *tersere*, which means to fear or dread or to be afraid. The Latin phrase *terror cimbricus*, employed by the Romans in 113 BC, referred to the hysteria and fear of the Roman population as the armies of one of Rome's neighboring tribes, the Cimbri, approached. In the mid-1790s, the word "terrorism" was coined to describe the horror exhibited by the French population in response to the actions of Maximilien Robespierre. Robespierre oversaw the Jacobian forces (i.e., French revolutionaries) during the waning years of the French Revolution. Thousands of civilians were apprehended and executed by guillotine during Robespierre's Reign of Terror. The word quickly entered the common vernacular and was added to the *Oxford English Dictionary* by the end of the 1790s. While Robespierre used mass executions as a power of the state to intimidate and frighten the populace (i.e., the application of force by a government directed at a civilian population), in the twentieth century, the term "terrorism" commonly connotes mass violence aimed at a government to effectuate political goals or change policies of that government.

The United States has experienced many terrorist events over its history. Three notable examples from the nineteenth century and early twentieth centuries are the Pottawatomie Massacre in 1856, the activities of the Ku Klux Klan (KKK) during and after Reconstruction, and anarchist activities in the early 1900s. The main perpetrator of the Pottawatomie Massacre was radical abolitionist John Brown. He led an attack and directed the mass murder of multiple civilians to put terror in the hearts of pro-slavery settlers in Kansas. Brown had the additional goal of effectuating change in the policies of Kansas toward the issue of slavery in the territories. After the American Civil War, defiant Southerners created the KKK to intimidate the newly enfranchised Black population in the South and to obstruct reconstruction efforts by the North. The KKK committed hundreds of murders and other acts of violence directed at Black citizens and white Northerners residing in the South. In the early 1900s, anarchists sent dozens of bombs and explosive devices to prominent politicians and business leaders, leading to the First Red Scare and Palmer Raids of the early 1920s.

Post Second World War, the deadliest period for terrorism within the United States was an eight-year period from 1993 through 2001. In 1993, Islamic terrorists planned to destroy the World Trade Center in New York City by parking a vehicle packed with explosive devices in the underground parking facility beneath the World Trade Center (see World Trade Center Bombing of 1993). On

April 19, 1995, Timothy McVeigh and accomplice Terry Nichols targeted the Alfred P. Murrah Federal Building in Oklahoma City (see Oklahoma City Bombing). McVeigh detonated a rental truck packed with explosives that destroyed a substantial portion of one side of the building and killed 168 individuals, including multiple government employees and more than a dozen children. It was the largest terrorist attack on US soil prior to the September 11, 2001, attack. During this same eight-year period, the United States also suffered multiple terrorism attacks abroad, including an attack on a residential US military building (Khobar Towers) in Saudi Arabia in 1996, resulting in the death of nineteen services members and injuring over 400; attacks on US embassies in Tanzania and Kenya in 1998, resulting in the death of 223; and an attack on the USS Cole as it was anchored off the coast of Yemen, resulting in the death of seventeen service members on board. Though disaster had been largely averted in the first World Trade Center Bombing in 1993, a second more massive attack on the civilian population working in the World Trade Center complex occurred eight years later. This attack, committed by Al-Qaeda terrorists on September 11, 2001, involved hijacking and crashing four commercial airplanes (two planes into the World Trade Center buildings, one plane into the Pentagon, and one plane which would crash outside of Somerset, Pennsylvania). This was the bloodiest terrorist attack on the United States in its history and resulted in the deaths of approximately three thousand individuals. The attacks ushered in President George W. Bush's decade-long War on Terror, one of the most significant aspects of US foreign policy at the dawn of the twenty-first century.

During the latter half of the twentieth century, dozens of international treaties pertaining to international terrorism and multiple United Nations Security Council Resolutions about international terrorism were put into place in the attempt by the international community to prevent terrorist attacks. Historically, however, the crime of terrorism was not defined in the domestic legal systems of most countries, including the United States. Many countries (responding to their own domestic problems with terrorism) eventually enacted domestic laws criminalizing the act of terrorism. For example, in 1989, the UK passed its Prevention of Terrorism Act which defined terrorism as "the use of violence for political ends and includes any use of violence for the purpose of putting the public or any section of the public in fear" (Beckman 2007, 9). Article 571 of the Spanish Criminal Code defined terrorism as "belonging, acting in the service of, or collaborating with armed groups whose objective is to subvert the constitutional order or seriously alter public peace" (Beckman 2007, 118–19). As evidenced by the difference between the British and Spanish definitions of the crime of terrorism, there exist variations as to what constitutes the crime of terrorism on the domestic level. While the UK's definition of terrorism tracks the accepted usage of the term (i.e., "the use of violence for political ends"), Spain defines terrorism more broadly to include belonging in, acting in the service of, or collaborating with armed groups whose objective is to subvert the constitutional order or alter the public peace.

Prior to 9/11, while the United States Code contained several definitions of "terrorism," those provisions were related to immigration and to international terrorism and the designation of international terrorist organizations. For example, 22 United States Code Section 2656f(d) provided the following definition: "The term terrorism means premediated, politically motivated violence perpetrated against non-combatant targets by sub-national groups or clandestine agents, usually intended to influence an audience." However, this definition pertained to how the term "terrorism" is utilized in Congress's mandated "Annual Country Reports on Terrorism" and did not define or criminalize the act of terrorism within the United States. Indeed, prior to October 2001, US federal criminal law statutes only defined the term "international terrorism" and did not address acts of domestic terrorism occurring within the territory jurisdiction of the United States.

After the events of September 11, 2001, and the subsequent signing of the USA PATRIOT Act into law on October 26, 2001, 18 United States Code Section 2331 was amended to incorporate an assortment of actions as constituting terrorism under a new federal designation of "domestic terrorism." The law defined domestic terrorism as follows:

> (A) involves acts dangerous to human life that are a violation of the criminal laws of the United States or of any State; (B) appears to be intended—(i) to intimidate or coerce a civilian population, (ii) to influence the policy of a government by intimidation or coercion, (iii) to affect the conduct of a government by mass destruction, assassination, or kidnapping; and … ; (C) occur primarily within the territorial jurisdiction of the United States.

Yet, in passing this statute, Congress did not specify any criminal penalties or punishments to accompany the designation of "domestic terrorism." This means that under federal law a person cannot be charged with a separate offense for domestic terrorism as a stand-alone charge.

However, the lack of criminal punishments for domestic terrorism does not allow the perpetrator to avoid adverse consequences. First, being found to have committed an act of domestic terrorism is an extenuating circumstance that may allow a judge to provide a more stringent sentence for an underlying criminal offense that the person may have committed (e.g., homicide, battery, arson, etc.). Second, the designation of a person's actions as "terrorism" allows for a heightened number of law enforcement tools in conducting a criminal investigation under the terms of the USA PATRIOT Act before the person's case reaches federal court. Third, if there is probable cause to believe a person's assets and property were involved in an act of domestic terrorism, the federal government can immediately seize and/or freeze those assets based on the probable cause determination alone. These assets can be temporarily seized without warning or a hearing. If the government wishes to permanently seize the assets, a civil hearing is required. However, the standard of proof is much lower in these asset forfeiture cases ("preponderance of the evidence") as opposed to a criminal prosecution ("beyond a reasonable doubt"). Furthermore, because the seizure of assets entails only a civil (and not criminal) hearing, the accused is not entitled to an attorney if they cannot afford one, unlike in a criminal case.

Because Section 802 of the Patriot Act (Pub. L. No. 107–52; Section 802 now codified at 18 United States Code Section 2331) did not create a new criminal offense for "domestic terrorism" by providing appropriate criminal punishments, defendants are still charged with the underlying criminal acts (i.e., the acts which are dangerous to human life and that are a violation of the criminal laws of the United States or of any State). Additionally, it is a federal criminal offense to provide support to terrorists or terrorist organizations, and numerous individuals are prosecuted and convicted for this related offense on a yearly basis. For example, in February 2022, three defendants pleaded guilty in federal court (United States District Court for the Southern District of Ohio) for conspiring to provide material support to terrorists after they participated in a plan to disable and/or destroy parts of the power grid throughout the United States to promote a white supremacist scheme. In 2002, John Walker Lindh, the "American Taliban," was charged with numerous offenses, including providing material support and resources to terrorist organizations. To date, this is the most common way cases of terrorism are handled in the domestic legal system; that is, the defendant may be charged with providing support or assistance to a terrorist organization (see Material Support Crimes), along with charges for underlying offenses the person may have committed, ranging from murder to mayhem to arson.

Because it is addressed in federal law, many state governments have declined to pass separate criminal laws pertaining to terrorism, but a handful of state governments have done so. For example, the State of New Jersey defines the crime of terrorism as the attempt, threat, or conspiracy to do any of the following: "(1) to promote an act of terror; or (2) to terrorize five or more persons; or (3) to influence the policy or affect the conduct of government by terror; or (4) to cause by an act of terror the impairment or interruption of public communications, public transportation, public or private buildings, common carriers, public utilities, or other public services." Similarly, the State of West Virginia defines and criminalizes a "terrorist act" that is

> likely to result in serious bodily injury or damage to property or the environment; and intended to: (i) intimidate or coerce the civilian population; (ii) influence the policy of a branch or level of government by intimidation or coercion; (iii) affect the conduct of a branch or level of government by intimidation or coercion; or (iv) retaliate against a branch or level of government for a policy or conduct of the government.

And while several states have domestic terrorism as a separate criminal offense, prosecutions are rare. Most often, perpetrators are charged with the "underlying illegal actions of violence, and not the offense of terrorism" itself (Beckman 2007, 10). Many argue that the sub-elements of the offense are "amorphous and ambiguous at best and the definition remains subjective in terms of its sub-elements" (Beckman 2007, 10). It is for this reason that state governments, and indeed many countries, "chose to try terrorists under the applicable [underlying] criminal code violations (e.g., homicide, battery, kidnapping, et cetera), and not based upon the charge of 'terrorism'" (Beckman 2007, 10). Framed this way, the cases are easier for the government to prosecute and convict under the rigorous "beyond a reasonable doubt" standard of proof.

See Also: American Civil War and Treason; Brown, John; First Red Scare and Palmer Raids (1919–20); John Brown's Raid (1859); Lindh, John Walker; Material Support Crimes; Pottawatomie Massacre (1856); September 11, 2001; Treason; USA PATRIOT Act; World Trade Center Bombing of 1993

Resources

Beckman, James. 2007. *Comparative Legal Approaches to Homeland Security and Anti-Terrorism*. Hampshire: Ashgate Publishing Limited.

Fine, Jonathan. 2010. "Political and Philological Origins of the Term 'Terrorism.'" *Middle Eastern Studies* 46: 271–88.

Lansford, Thomas, and Robert P. Watson. 2003. *Debating the War on Terrorism*. Dubuque, IA: Kendall/Hunt Publishing Company.

United States Attorney's Office (Southern District of Ohio), Department of Justice. 2022. "3 Men Plead Guilty to Domestic Terrorism Crime Related to Plans to Attack Power Grids." February 23, 2022. Accessed June 24, 2022. https://www.justice.gov/usao-sdoh/pr/3-men-plead-guilty-domestic-terrorism-crime-related-plans-attack-power-grids.

Wilkinson, Paul. 1974. "Concepts of Terror and Terrorism." In *Political Terrorism: Studies in Comparative Politics*, edited by Paul Wilkinson, 9–31. London: Palgrave.

Texas v. White (1869)

Texas v. White involved something like a crime against the state, not committed by an individual or organization, but rather by a state itself. It involved what may be the ultimate crime against the state—the attempted violent overthrow of the federal government through secession and armed rebellion—and was committed by Texas and the ten other states who were members of the Confederate States of America and fought against the United States in the American Civil War. In *Texas v. White*, the Supreme Court addressed some of the consequences of Texas's participation in the rebellion. The Court's opinion was significant in resolving the legal question as to whether states could unilaterally secede from the United States, and whether secession of a state was valid even if approved by state leaders and a majority of citizens of the state.

The case itself dealt with a lawsuit by the state of Texas against a company called White & Chiles. During the waning days of the Civil War, the rebel Texas government had endorsed bonds to White & Chiles as a form of payment for various supplies to support the rebellion. The bonds Texas transferred were federal US bonds, which had originally been provided by the federal government to Texas before the Civil War to settle a border issue. White & Chiles later sold off most of the bonds. When, after the Civil War, the newly reconstituted State of Texas demanded the return of the bonds for White & Chiles's non-performance on the contract, White & Chiles refused. Texas then sought an injunction directing that the federal government not pay the bondholders and to compel the bondholders to surrender the bonds back to the state of Texas.

The United States Supreme Court exercises original jurisdiction in lawsuits brought by states against citizens of other states. Nevertheless, the Court's jurisdiction was a central question in this case. The defendants argued the Supreme Court's original jurisdiction included only suits brought by states, and that Texas was not a state because of its armed rebellion. The Court agreed that if Texas was not a state, it did not have jurisdiction. Ultimately, the question was whether Texas's secession and armed rebellion meant it had ceased to be a state. The Court held that when Texas became part of the United States in 1845, "she entered into an indissoluble relation" and there was "not place for reconsideration, except through revolution or through consent of the States." The Court further held that Texas's secession and all acts undertaken by the secessionist legislature of Texas were "absolutely null … [and] were without operation in law." The Court distinguished between a state in the sense of a people or political community and state *government*. Ultimately, the Court held "the state did not cease to be a State."

The Court then turned to the question of whether contracts entered by the temporary government of Texas during its period of attempted secession were valid. Despite finding that Texas had never ceased to be a state, and thus the Court had jurisdiction to hear the case, the Court determined that the temporary "insurgent government" could not divest the state of Texas of its title to the bonds. Moreover, contracts to support levying war against the United States were of themselves unenforceable. The Supreme Court declared the contract with White & Chiles was invalid and the bonds had to be returned to the state of Texas.

See Also: American Civil War and Treason; Levying War; Rebellion

Resources

Texas v. White, 74 US 700 (1869).

Threats against Government Officials

While freedom of speech is one of the most sacrosanct of American rights, in some circumstances, it is possible for one's words to constitute a crime against the state (see Speech as Crime against the State). Over the years, the Supreme Court has interpreted the First Amendment as not protecting certain narrow categories of speech. For instance, individuals may be prosecuted for speech that incites violence (referred to as the "advocacy of illegal action") if the standards of *Brandenburg v. Ohio* (1969) are satisfied. Similarly, speech solely intended to terrorize or to communicate a threat is not protected speech under the First Amendment and is referred to as a "true threat."

Political criticism and satire, insults directed politicians, and threats made in jest to prove a point are protected speech, but truly threatening speech is not protected and may be criminalized. While courts and scholars differ as to the exact meaning of what constitutes a "true threat," it is commonly held that, in determining whether a true threat is made, one asks whether a reasonable person hearing the words would perceive such "statements to be threatening" in nature and not made in jest (Gilbert 2004, 870). According to the United States Court of Appeals for the Second Circuit, for example, "to qualify as a true threat, a statement must be so 'unequivocal, unconditional, immediate and specific as to the person threatened as to convey a gravity of purpose and imminent prospect of execution'" (Gilbert 2004, 870). In *Virginia v. Black* (2003), the United States Supreme Court decided that it was not necessary for a speaker to intend to carry out a threat for the language to nevertheless constitute a true threat.

Under 18 United States Code Section 871, it is a felony (subject to five years imprisonment) to utter words "containing any threat to take the life of, to kidnap, or to inflict bodily harm upon the President of the United States, the President-elect, the Vice President or other officer next in the order of succession to the office of President, or Vice President-elect." Similarly, 18 United States Code Section 879 makes it a crime to threaten to

> kill, kidnap, or inflict bodily harm upon a former President or a member of the immediate family of a former President, a member of the immediate family of the President, the President-elect, the Vice President, or the Vice President-elect, or a major candidate for the office of President or Vice President, or a member of the immediate family of such a candidate.

In *Watts v. United States* (1969), the United States Supreme Court considered how serious the threat must be against the president for it to be categorized as a true threat. Eighteen-year-old Robert Watts, who opposed the Vietnam War, stated that "if they ever made me carry a rifle the first man I want to get in my sights is L.B.J." For these words, Watts was prosecuted and convicted for threatening the life of the president of the United States. However, the Supreme Court overturned Watts's conviction, ruling that the words were too tenuous in nature and, considering the laughter from the surrounding crowd after the words were uttered, the Court classified Watts's comments as "a kind of very crude offensive method of stating a political opposition to the President" and not a true threat. The Court also noted that the statement was made during a political debate and that the alleged threats were contingent on the speaker being inducted into the military, something the speaker stated would never occur.

In the same year (1969) of the Watts decision, the United States Court of Appeals for the Ninth Circuit upheld the conviction of a person who threatened the life of the president in *Roy v. United*

States. The defendant, Richard Roy, was a United States Marine stationed at a military base in the United States that the president was to visit the next day. Roy joked with other Marines about how they were going to "get him with cannons and how everybody was going to shoot them off" when the president arrived. Then, a brief time later, Roy picked up a telephone, asked for the operator, and stated "Tell the President that he should not come aboard the base or he would be killed … I hear the President is coming to base. I am going to get him." Roy was prosecuted and convicted for threatening the president and his conviction was upheld, with the court considering the defendant's speech to be sufficiently serious and not made in jest.

Beyond the president and vice president, other government officials are protected from being subjected to threatening speech as well. Any threat against any government official in the furtherance of their government business is a federal felony under 18 United States Code Section 115. Specifically, under Section 115, any individual who "threatens to assault, kidnap or murder a member of the immediate family of a United States official, a United States judge, a Federal law enforcement officer, or an official whose killing … with intent to impede, intimidate, or interfere with such official, judge, or law enforcement officer while engaged in the performance of official duties, or with intent to retaliate against such official, judge, or law enforcement officer on account of the performance of official duties" is subject to potential incarceration of up to thirty years.

A typical example of a successful prosecution under 18 United States Code Section 115 can be seen in the federal case *United States v. Gray* (1987). In this case, a disgruntled litigant in a court case wrote a letter to the judge threatening to kill him and his family. Specifically, the letter stated in part that "I am going to kill you, but before I kill you, I am going to kill your family one by one in front of you." The trial court concluded that this letter was sent with the "intent to intimidate or retaliate against [a judge] on account of the performance of his official duties." This person was then convicted under Section 115 and the conviction was upheld by the United States Court of Appeal for the Ninth Circuit.

Unfortunately, it is common for disgruntled taxpayers to threaten employees of the Internal Revenue Service (IRS). Threatening taxation officials can be traced back to early events in American history like the Whiskey Rebellion, Fries's Rebellion, and the Boston Tea Party. Consequently, Congress has enacted a special statute protecting its taxation employees, 26 United States Code Section 7212, which provides that "whoever corruptly or by force or threats of force (including any threatening letter or communication) endeavors to intimidate or impede any officer or employee of the United States acting in an official capacity under this title, or in any other way corruptly or by force or threats of force (including any threatening letter or communication) obstructs or impedes, or endeavors to obstruct or impede, the due administration of this title, shall, upon conviction" be subject to a prison sentence of up to three years.

An example of a prosecution under this statute can be seen in *United States v. Darby* (1994). Defendant James Peter Darby became irate over a tax notice and called the local IRS multiple times, asking one person if she knew "how long it takes to bury a person?" and "do you know how long it takes to kill a person?" He continued, "I am tired of the IRS with their G** d*mn bullsh**. If I don't hear from you today, it's going to be a massacre." He ended the conversation saying that he normally did not threaten people, but that he was in Vietnam, and he could "kill again." In another phone call on the same day, Darby informed the IRS employee that Darby had gone to the local hardware store and bought pipes and supplies. He then asked "how would you like to have a pipe bomb delivered to your place of employment? This is not a bomb threat." On a previous occasion, Darby had verbally assaulted and threatened another IRS employee, stating in part that "he does not eat his victims, he just kills them and blows them up; the Internal Revenue Service people in Durham would be dead; and if the Internal Revenue Service had a flower fund, they would need one for the funerals in Durham." Darby was convicted, and his conviction affirmed by the United States Court of Appeal for the Fourth Circuit.

In recent years, threats to elected officials have increased. According to the Department of Justice (DOJ), "from 2012–2018, federal threat charges were filed in about 160 cases per year" (Jackman 2023). The number of recorded threats against members of Congress "rose from 4,000 in 2017 to more than 9,600 in 2021, then declined last year [2022] to 7,501" (Jackman 2023). After investigating the 7,501 cases in 2022, federal law enforcement "determined only 313 qualified as true threats, or about 4 percent." Of those 313 cases forwarded to DOJ for prosecution, only "22 of the 313, or about 7 percent" were prosecuted (Jackman 2023). Despite the increased number of threats against members of Congress, the number of successful prosecutions has dropped. According to the United States Capitol police, "there were 51 threats to members of Congress charged federally in 2019, about 13 percent of the cases referred. Ten percent were prosecuted in 2020, and 9 percent in 2021" (Jackman 2023). While the number of referrals remains statistically low compared to the overall number of threats, many of the referred cases involve language that clearly is not political satire or humor and in no way adds to political discourse or contributes to a robust marketplace of ideas. For instance, one person prosecuted left four hundred voice mail messages for a single congressperson, saying in one of the messages "well, so I'm gonna murder you. It is justified" (Jackman 2023). Another prosecuted individual posted messages on a website announcing an upcoming political event, saying "Thank you for the address!!! I'm coming to murder all of you" (Jackman 2023).

Even threats communicated against non-federal officials can constitute a federal criminal offense, such as threatening a state court judge through social media. Federal criminal law also covers any threat made against any individual wherein interstate commerce is impacted or utilized. Congress has the constitutional authority to regulate conduct that involves or impacts interstate commerce (i.e., commerce or activities that cross state lines). Interstate communications are included under the definition of "interstate commerce," so any communications that utilize the United States Postal Service, telephone lines, internet postings or phone texts or chats, etc., are subject to federal criminal law. The statute 18 U.S. Code Section 875 indicates that "whoever transmits in interstate or foreign commerce any communication containing any threat to kidnap *any person* or any threat to injure the person of another, shall be fined under this title or imprisoned not more than five years, or both." Threatening a government official (state or federal) through interstate communications (mail, telephone, e-mail, internet postings, et cetera) is a separate felony offense under Section 875. Threats against government officials can often constitute a crime against the state as such threats attempt to impede the elected official's fulfillment of his or her governmental duties. While not all threats against public officials will constitute a crime against the state (e.g., threats made because of some pre-existing personal grudge or some other wholly personal reason), many threats are made based upon dissatisfaction of the government's official execution of his or her job duties in furtherance of governmental interests, or to impede the official in execution of his or her duties.

See Also: *Brandenburg v. Ohio* (1969); Fries's Rebellion (1799); Speech as Crime against the State; Whiskey Rebellion

Resources

18 U.S. Code Section 115. 2023. "Influencing, Impeding, or Retaliating against a Federal Official by Threatening or Injuring a Family Member."
18 U.S. Code Section 871. 2023. "Threats against President and Successors to the Presidency."
18 U.S. Code Section 875. 2023. "Interstate Communications."
18 U.S. Code Section 879. 2023. "Threats against Former Presidents and Certain Other Persons."
26 U.S. Code Section 7212. 2023. "Attempts to Interfere with Administration of Internal Revenue Laws."
Gilbert, Lauren. 2004. "Mocking George: Political Satire as 'True Threat' in the Age of Global Terrorism." *University of Miami Law Review* 58 (April): 843–89.
Jackman, Tom. 2023. "Reported Threats on Congress Remain High, but Prosecutions Decline: Federal Prosecutors Charged Fewer than Two Dozen People out of More than 7,500 Threats Capitol Police Reviewed Last Year." *The Washington Post*, February 18, 2023.

Tokyo Rose (Iva Toguri D'Aquino) (1916–2006)

Tokyo Rose was a mythicized name dreamed up by American service members in the Second World War that came to be applied to one woman by the end of the War, Iva Toguri D'Aquino. At the beginning of the war, there were at least thirteen separate female voices being broadcast to American servicemembers throughout the Pacific. Servicemembers began using the name "Tokyo Rose" to refer to any of those broadcasters. Iva Toguri D'Aquino was one such broadcaster who, while in Japan, began broadcasting a show called "Zero Hour" and originally went by the name Orphan Ann. "Ann" was short for "announcer" and "orphans" shorthand for "Orphans of the Pacific," a popular phrase to describe American GIs in the Pacific. Americans were also familiar with the name from the comic strip "Little Orphan Annie." By the Summer or Fall of 1943, Orphan Ann and Tokyo Rose became synonymous in the minds of many service members. There were certainly other "radio traitors" during the Second World War, but Tokyo Rose ruled the Pacific Theatre airwaves, just as Axis Sally (Mildred Gillars) ruled the airwaves over Germany.

D'Aquino's life was laced with ironies and tragedies. It started in the most American way possible, with her birth on the fourth of July in 1916. She lived in California for her first twenty-five years, attending the University of California at Los Angeles (UCLA) as a pre-med student. In July 1941, D'Aquino traveled to Tokyo to visit a sick relative, but became stranded in Japan after Pearl Harbor when the United States would not permit her to return home. During her absence from the United States, and unbeknownst to D'Aquino, her parents were relocated to a Japanese American Internment Camp where they were confined for three years during the war. In Japan, D'Aquino tried to find gainful employment as a typist but found that her English-speaking abilities were primarily suited for working with Japanese radio stations.

D'Aquino, who was considered an enemy alien by the Japanese, worked alongside several allied prisoners of war (POWs) on a radio show called "Zero Hour" for Radio Tokyo. Some of the POWs worked subtly to subvert the anti-American message in the broadcasting booth and in the scripts being read by the broadcasters. It was an hour-long program, and D'Aquino typically talked for twenty minutes, with the rest of the time filled with musical broadcasting. D'Aquino viewed herself as a sweetheart to American GIs, and the Department of Justice (DOJ) viewed her broadcasting as "innocuous." In one post-war study, the vast majority of servicemembers surveyed said that they enjoyed listening to Tokyo Rose because it had "good entertainment," and less than 10 percent of the servicemembers surveyed felt demoralized by the broadcast.

The Army investigated and released D'Aquino in 1946 as it did not find sufficient evidence of criminality, and she returned to the United States in 1947. Upon her return stateside, prominent American journalist Walter Winchell clamored for D'Aquino's prosecution, causing a public outcry and prompting the DOJ to prosecute. In 1949, in United States Federal District Court in San Francisco, she was charged with eight counts of treason (ultimately found guilty of one of the eight counts) and was also charged with perjury, false statements, and obstruction of justice. The treason charges were based on the claim that D'Aquino provided aid and comfort to an enemy of the United States through her radio transmissions. While D'Aguino was targeted for prosecution, none of the POWs involved with broadcasting in Japan were charged, nor were over two hundred Japanese Americans who were forced to work in propaganda roles in Japan during the war.

The trial started on July 5, 1949, and lasted twelve weeks. Even though the government had 340 hours of "Zero Hour" tapes that were hauled into court each day, and though there was sufficient time in a such a long trial, none were played to the jury and no evidence was heard from the tapes that could be considered "overt propaganda" or "deliberately designed materials to demoralize soldiers," charges made in the indictment. The jury instead heard evidence from two men who testified to what they claimed they heard on the tapes—claims that both men recanted in the 1970s. Kenkichi Oki and George Mitsushio testified to the same act of treason (a requirement under the Treason Clause), claiming that they witnessed D'Aquino speak these words into a microphone: "Now you fellows have lost all your ships. You really are orphans of the Pacific. Now how do you think you will ever get home?" (National Registry of Exoneration 2023). The tapes were never checked to verify these words were spoken as alleged. The jury was divided and deliberated for seventy-eight hours. Finally, on September 29, 1949, D'Aquino was convicted of one count of treason and sentenced to a ten-year prison sentence, a fine of $10,000, and revocation of her US citizenship. The trial cost $750,000 (the equivalent of $9,511,639 in 2023), making it the most expensive government prosecution in history at that time. D'Aquino's lawyer simply muttered walking out of the courtroom: "Guilty without evidence."

After serving six years and two months, D'Aquino was released for good behavior in 1956 and took up residence in Chicago. In the 1970s, investigators reinterviewed people involved in D'Aquino's case and found that it was replete with fraud and governmental misconduct. In 1976, the two key government witnesses who were essential to ensuring that D'Aquino was found guilty of treason were discovered to have been lying. Specifically, during the recorded interview, both men admitted that they had been forced to provide false testimony and withhold vital information during D'Aquino's trial. They indicated that the Federal Bureau of Investigation had harassed and threatened them and that other government witnesses were bribed by US officials to provide damaging testimony. "Oki and Mitsushio admitted that they had never heard D'Aquino make any treasonous broadcasts or statements, a complete turnaround from their testimony during the trial" (The National Registry of Exoneration 2023). This investigation and the interviews were published in full by the *Chicago Tribune* in 1976. On January 19, 1977, President Gerald Ford pardoned D'Aquino and restored her American citizenship in the process. She died at the age of ninety on September 26, 2006, in Chicago, Illinois.

See Also: Aid and Comfort (Aid to Enemies of the State); Axis Sally (Mildred Gillars); Perjury, False Statements, and Obstruction of Justice; Radio Traitors and Anti-State Propagandists during World War Two; Treason

Resources

Federal Bureau of Investigation. 2023. "Iva Toguri D'Aquino and 'Tokyo Rose.'" Accessed May 15, 2023. https://www.fbi.gov/history/famous-cases/iva-toguri-daquino-and-tokyo-rose.

Howe, Russell Warren. 1990. *The Hunt for "Tokyo Rose."* New York: Madison Books.

Leggett, John. 1976. "Tokyo Rose: Traitor or Scapegoat." *The New York Times*, December 5, 1976. Accessed May 15, 2023. https://www.nytimes.com/1976/12/05/archives/tokyo-rose-traitor-or-scapegoat-after-world-war-ii-an-american-girl.html.

McCurry, Justin. 2006. "'Tokyo Rose' Dies at 90." September 27, 2006. Accessed May 15, 2023. https://www.theguardian.com/world/2006/sep/27/secondworldwar.usa.

The National Registry of Exonerations. 2023. "Iva Toguri D'Aquino." Accessed May 15, 2023. https://www.law.umich.edu/special/exoneration/Pages/casedetailpre1989.aspx?caseid=332.

Treason

In common vernacular, treason generally refers to disloyalty to one's government. As a legal offense, treason typically involves activity relating to the attempted overthrow of one's government or in providing aid and comfort to an enemy of one's country. An early example of treason was the assassination of Julius Caesar by a cabal of Roman senators in 42 BC, with the intention of overthrowing the ruling governmental regime. Marcus Junius Brutus, one of the Roman senators involved in the assassination and a close friend (and perhaps a relative) of Julius Caesar, was instrumental in Caesar's assassination and reputedly one of the last senators to stab Caesar to death. In commenting on the traitorous act, Caesar is said to have turned to Brutus and uttered his last words: "Et Tu, Brute" (Latin for "you as well, Brutus?"). Brutus was later hunted down and killed for his attempted seizure of power and his involvement in the assassination of Caesar. One of the more notorious examples of treason from England involved the Gunpowder Plot of 1605. Guy Fawkes and a group of Catholic rebels attempted to blow up the Houses of Parliament to overthrow the Protestant King James I. The rebels packed thirty-six barrels of explosives in a subterrain chamber underneath the House of Lords. The plot was discovered and foiled on November 5, 1605, the evening before the day the King and all the government officials were scheduled to meet in the House of Lords. November 5 has become known as Guy Fawkes Day, and his capture is memorialized and celebrated throughout England every year on that day with bonfires and fireworks.

The legal accusation of treason carries a particular connotation and constitutionally defined meaning. American treason law is based in part on the English Treason Statute of 1351. While the 1351 statute contained six distinct types of treason that one could commit against the Crown, the United States adopted only two of these, namely "levying war" against one's government or providing its enemies "aid and comfort." Many state governments contain the same verbiage defining treason in their constitutions. As of 2023, forty-three of the fifty state governments define treason as a criminal offense either under a state constitutional provision, a state statute, or both.

Treason is the only criminal offense enshrined in the United States Constitution, defined in Article III as "levying war against [the United States], or in adhering to their Enemies, giving them Aid and Comfort." Some suggest that the Framers of the Constitution envisioned treason as the most serious offense that could be committed against the state and wanted it enshrined in the Constitution for that reason. Others suggest that its inclusion in the Constitution was intended to limit the use of treason charges and prosecutions by the government. All the signers of the Declaration of Independence were characterized as being guilty of treason against Great Britain (see American Revolution and Treason) and were, perhaps, especially sensitive of the charge and afraid of its potential misuse. Treason charges could potentially be used to curtail and suppress peaceful political opposition and persecute those in the political minority. As James Madison wrote in Federalist Paper 43:

> As treason may be committed against the United States, the authority of the United States ought to be enabled to punish it. But as new-fangled and artificial treasons have been the great engines by which violent factions, the natural offspring of free government, have usually wreaked their alternate malignity on each other, the convention, have, with great judgment, opposed a barrier to this peculiar danger, by inserting a constitutional definition of the crime, fixing the proof necessary for conviction of it, and restraining the Congress, even in punishing it, from extending the consequences of guilt beyond the person of its author.

Thus, the Treason Clause in the Constitution also requires that to be convicted of treason, the accused must have committed an overt act that demonstrates the traitorous behavior and that the overt act must be attested to in open court by at least two independent witnesses. The Crimes Act of 1790 carried forward this definition of treason into the very first federal criminal law.

Almost immediately after the ratification of the United States Constitution in 1789, the country faced large-scale opposition and resistance of federal authority (specifically taxation laws) in the Whiskey Rebellion in 1794 and Fries's Rebellion in 1799. The leaders of both resistance groups were the first defendants tried and convicted of treason against the nascent US government. Three notorious examples of treason against the United States occurred prior to the American Civil War and were perpetrated by Benedict Arnold, Aaron Burr, and John Brown. During the Revolutionary War, Benedict Arnold conspired to deliver the military fortifications at West Point, New York, to the British, thereby committing treason against the American colonies. Shortly after the Revolutionary War, Aaron Burr, the third vice president of the United States, was indicted and accused of plotting to take control of the Louisiana Territory in 1807. While Burr escaped legal liability for the offense of treason, it remains one of the most high-profile treason cases in the early years of the Republic. Finally, radical abolitionist John Brown was convicted of treason in 1859 by Virginia for leading a raid on the United States Armory and Arsenal at Harpers Ferry, Virginia, in the hopes of sparking a slave revolt. Brown was the first American, and remains one of the few, to be executed for the offense of treason in the United States.

Acts of treason have likely occurred during every American war, though convictions for treason have not. In the United States' first war after the signing of the Constitution, the specter of treason charges loomed large. Unlike the American Revolutionary War, which itself constituted treason against Great Britain, the War of 1812 occurred between sovereign nations, and for the first time, the country needed to weigh the right of dissension against the crime of treason. The war was deeply unpopular, with much regional dissension, especially in the Northeast. For the first time in the country's history, fears that the charge of treason could be misused to curtail and suppress peaceful political opposition were real and no longer an abstract constitutional principle to be debated (see War of 1812 and Treason). During the American Civil War, hundreds of thousands of acts of treason were committed, but none of the individuals were held responsible after the war (see American Civil War and Treason). During the Second World War, the federal government successfully prosecuted numerous individuals for treason against the United States, including multiple well-known cases involving Americans engaged in propaganda against the United States, such as Axis Sally, Tokyo Rose, and Martin James Monti. The last treason conviction upheld by the United States Supreme Court took place in 1952 in *Kawakita v. United States* and involved an American and Japanese dual-citizen who worked at a factory in Japan that became a POW camp during the Second World War. In another Second World War prosecution, Sergeant John Provoo, who had allegedly offered his services to the Japanese while he was held as an American prisoner of war, was indicted for treason in 1954. Provoo was convicted, but his conviction was overturned on appeal. Provoo's treason indictment would be the last in a United States court until 2006, when Adam Gadahn was indicted for treason for producing anti-American propaganda for Al-Qaeda. He was killed in a drone strike, so the case never went to trial. Thus, except for the Gadahn indictment in 2006, treason has not been pursued as a viable criminal charge against suspected defendants since the early 1950s.

There have been numerous federal and state court cases discussing and defining the perimeters and requirements for the offense of treason. Some of the prominent lower federal court decisions include cases such as *United States v. Burr* (1807), *United States v. Hoxie* (1808), and *United States v. Hanway* (1851). Multiple Supreme Court cases have either upheld treason convictions or discussed discrete aspects of treason law as part of the Court's overall body of jurisprudence. Some of the more notable cases include *Ex Parte Bollman* (1807), *United States v. Greathouse* (1863), *Carlisle v. United States* (1872), *Haupt v. United States* (1947), and *Kawakita v. United States* (1952). Each of these cases added vital details to understanding the challenges of bringing a successful treason prosecution.

The first Supreme Court case dealing exclusively with issues pertaining to treason law as the central issue occurred in 1945 in *Cramer v. United States*. While other cases added bits and pieces to the overall understanding of the offense of treason, the Supreme Court's decision in *Cramer v. United States* was especially important as it was the Court's very first interpretation of the meaning of the "overt act" requirement contained in the Treason Clause in Article III, and it provided the first in-depth, comprehensive explanation of what the term providing "aid and comfort" to the enemy meant under the Treason Clause. The *Cramer* decision was also important in its determination that the government was not constitutionally limited to the charge of treason and the Treason Clause in prosecuting crimes against the state. The Supreme Court suggested in *Cramer* that Congress could also properly criminalize related offenses such as seditious conspiracy, espionage, and sabotage.

Treason was first codified in federal law in the Crimes Act of 1790. Currently, the United States Congress has codified the offense of treason at 18 United States Code Section 2381 as entailing the following:

> Whoever, owing allegiance to the United States, levies war against them or adheres to their enemies, giving them aid and comfort within the United States or elsewhere, is guilty of treason and shall suffer death, or shall be imprisoned not less than five years and fined under this title but not less than $10,000; and shall be incapable of holding any office under the United States.

However, Article III of the Constitution mandates that "no person shall be convicted of treason unless on the testimony of two witnesses to the same overt Act, or on Confession in open Court." Article III, Section 3, also empowers Congress "to declare the Punishment of treason," but prohibits punishment entailing the "Corruption of Blood, or Forfeiture except during the Life of the Person attainted."

See Also: Aid and Comfort (Aid to Enemies of the State); American Civil War and Treason; American Revolution and Treason; Arnold, Benedict; Assassination; Axis Sally (Mildred Gillars); Brown, John; Burr, Aaron; *Burr, United States v.* (1807); *Carlisle v. United States*; Corruption of Blood; *Cramer v. United States* (1945); Crimes Act of 1790; English Treason Statute of 1351; Espionage; *Ex Parte Bollman* (1807); Fries's Rebellion (1799); Gadahn, Adam Yahiye; *Greathouse, United States v.* (1863); *Hanway, United States v.* (1851); *Haupt v. United States* (1947); *Hoxie, United States v.* (1808); *Kawakita v. United States* (1952); Levying War; *Monti, United States v.* (1949); Radio Traitors and Anti-State Propaganda during World War Two; Sabotage; Seditious Conspiracy; Tokyo Rose; War of 1812 and Treason; Whiskey Rebellion

Resources

Beckman, James. 2022. "Abolitionist John Brown's Treason against the Commonwealth of Virginia: A Lesson for State Governments about the Culpability of Non-Residents for Treason against the State." *British Journal of American Legal Studies* 11: 61–79.

Hurst, James Willard. 1971. *The Law of Treason in the United States: Collected Essays*. Westport, CT: Greenwood Press.

Larson, Carlton F. W. 2006. "Forgotten Constitutional Law of Treason and the Enemy Combatant Problem." *University of Pennsylvania Law Journal* 154: 853–926.

Larson, Carlton F. W. 2020. *On Treason: A Citizen's Guide to the Law*. New York: Ecco, an imprint of HarperCollins.

Simon, Walter G. 1961. "The Evolution of Treason." *Tulane Law Review* 35, no. 4: 667–704.

Turner, Nat (1800–31)

Nat Turner was an enslaved individual in Southampton County, Virginia, who commanded one of the biggest slave rebellions and attempted insurrections in US history. The Nat Turner Slave Rebellion is notable for not only the violence and numerous murders of those attempting to liberate themselves from slavery, but also the brutal violence and extrajudicial murders committed by white mobs and Virginia militia units in the aftermath of the uprising. While some have classified Turner's rebellion as an example of terrorism, the white response involved far more murders and terror imposed on the local Black population. Nat Turner's insurrection was the bloodiest slave rebellion in US history.

Most of what is known about Nat Turner, his early life, and the planning of the rebellion, comes from a written confession that Turner wrote from his jail cell from November 1 to November 3, 1831. From his early childhood, Turner was told that he had unique powers from God and that he was fated for a momentous event. As he grew older, Turner became the spiritual leader among the local enslaved population. At some point in the 1820s, Turner claimed that he began to have visions from God, visions that prompted him to plan and then lead the rebellion. In May 1828, Turner believed he had been informed by spirits that he would soon be given a sign to commence a war of rebellion against the white population. He waited about three years for that sign; although he told seven of his most trusted friends that he had received the sign and that the uprising was to take place on Independence Day, July 4, 1831. Yet, Turner temporarily delayed the rebellion, until he claimed to have received another sign, telling him that his attack should commence on August 21, 1831.

On the morning of August 21, 1831, Turner and a group of his men went into the home of Turner's enslaver, Joseph Travis, and killed him first. In his confession, Turner described Travis as "a kind master, [who] placed the greatest confidence in me; in fact, I had no cause to complain of his treatment of me" (Greenberg 1996, 48). Turner and his men murdered the entire Travis family, five family members in all. The group moved from farm to farm with orders from Turner to murder all white inhabitants, regardless of gender or age. Multiple children were murdered. Turner admitted in his confession to murdering even infants. In describing the murder of the Travis family in his confessions, Turner stated: "The murder of this family, five in number, was the work of a moment, not one of them awoke; there was a little infant sleeping in a cradle, that was forgotten, until we had left the house and gone some distance, when Henry and Will returned and killed it" (Greenberg 1996, 49). Because Turner and his men lacked firearms, almost all the murders were committed using axes, knives, wooden fence posts, and other crude implements or tools, making the murders very gruesome. Multiple individuals had limbs cut off, skulls split, or heads decapitated.

As the group went from farm to farm killing the white inhabitants, they gathered recruits along the way. While the size of Turner's "army" has been debated by historians, most put it in the range of seventy to eighty men at the apex of its activities. The number of white inhabitants murdered during the rebellion is also unclear. Most scholars estimate that fifty-five to sixty individuals were murdered by Turner's group. When Turner believed his group was at its greatest size and strength, he decided to attack the county seat of government in Jerusalem. However, by this point, local militia units had responded and repulsed Turner's men in a series of skirmishes. The rebellion was over by August 23, although Turner himself evaded capture for two months, until October 30, 1831.

During the immediate aftermath of the rebellion, local militia units and mobs summarily murdered at least 125 people whom they believed might have some connection to Turner's group. Many historians believe that many of these individuals had no knowledge of Turner and/or had not participated in supporting Turner in any fashion. The true number of extrajudicial murders of Black people in the aftermath of Turner's rebellion will never be known, but many scholars believe the Black death toll was much higher than 125 individuals.

The indictment against Turner and his captured men indicated that they were "charged with making insurrection, and plotting to take away the lives of divers free white persons." Of the fifty-two charged individuals listed in the August 1831 indictment, thirty people were convicted and sentenced to death. Surprisingly given the hostile political climate, thirteen trials ended in "not guilty" verdicts. A few other defendants had charges dismissed due to jurisdictional or evidentiary issues. Of the thirty defendants who were found guilty and were scheduled to be executed, only nineteen would die on the gallows, as eleven had their punishment commuted or reduced by Virginia Governor John Floyd. Turner was tried on November 5 and executed on November 11, 1831.

After the Turner rebellion, inhabitants of southern communities became more fearful of slave rebellions and the possibility of being murdered in their beds. As such, Virginia and other southern states made their existing "slave codes" more onerous and increased the number of daily "slave patrols." These patrols would "police" the countryside, and enslaved individuals were often required to carry a "pass" to travel beyond the farm or plantation of their enslavement. In the name of protecting communities, these patrols committed countless acts of harassment, violence, and other crimes against vulnerable Black individuals. While Turner's goal was to strike a blow against the institution of slavery and free himself and others from inhuman and immoral bondage, the insurrection became a crime against the state when Turner turned his forces toward the county seat in Jerusalem and attacked the local government.

See Also: Insurrection; Rebellion; Terrorism

Resources

Greenberg, Kenneth S., ed. 1996. *The Confession of Nat Turner and Related Documents*. Boston: Bedford/St. Martin's.

Oates, Stephen B. 1990. *The Fires of Jubilee: Nat Turner's Fierce Rebellion.* New York: Perennial, an imprint of HarperCollins.

U

Unabomber

See Kaczynski, Theodore ("Unabomber")

United States v. U.S. District Court (1972)

The Fourth Amendment to the United States Constitution enshrined a key liberty of the American people: "the right of the people to be secure in their persons, houses, papers, and effects, against unreasonable searches and seizures." It further detailed the process by which the government could obtain a Warrant: "no Warrants shall issue, but upon probable cause, supported by Oath or affirmation, and particularly describing the place to be searched, and the persons or things to be seized." The United States Supreme Court has generally interpreted the Fourth Amendment to mean that for a non-consensual search or seizure to be "reasonable," the government must, with a few exceptions, first obtain a warrant. Why was this right so important to the Founders? Because the government of Britain had routinely trampled on individual privacy in the name of protecting the government. Observation of the abuses of such power led early American revolutionaries, Massachusetts lawyer James Otis foremost among them, to demand that government not be permitted to violate the privacy of individual citizens in this way. In 1761 during a long speech railing against British abuses of power, Otis famously asserted "A man's house is his castle." President John Adams, who attended Otis's speech and would later sign into law the notorious Alien and Sedition Acts that greatly enhanced government power against individual liberties, later credited Otis with birthing the American revolutionary movement in that moment.

Many view the Fourth Amendment as creating a fundamental tension between collective security and liberty. In the context of crimes against the state, the weighing of the Fourth Amendment's protection of individual liberty against the interests of national security is particularly acute. When thinking about national security in the context of the Fourth Amendment, the government is typically searching for evidence that will prevent crimes against the state—hostile acts or threats to the structure or existence of the United States government.

In the 1960s, the Judicial Branch began to contemplate the effect of the Fourth Amendment on national security investigations. Executive Branch intelligence and law enforcement agencies interpreted some courts' jurisprudence as allowing warrantless searches (surveillance) for national security purposes. This was the central question in *United States v. U.S. District Court*, also known as the *Keith* case after Judge Damon Keith, the district court judge who issued the contested ruling.

In 1968, the Central Intelligence Agency (CIA) office in Ann Arbor, Michigan, was bombed. Three defendants were charged with conspiring to bomb the office, and one of the defendants, Lawrence Plamondon, was charged with carrying out the bombing. The government obtained evidence against

Plamondon by wiretapping his telephone, but the government had not obtained a warrant from a judge before conducting the wiretap and refused to disclose the contents of much of the electronic surveillance it had obtained. The defendants argued that the government's wiretap and eavesdropping on Plamondon's conversations violated the Fourth Amendment. The government responded by arguing that there is, or should be, a national security exception to the Fourth Amendment's warrant requirement. The government asserted that if the Court required prior judicial review of national security-related searches, it would impede the president's authority and responsibility to protect the nation's security. The government further argued that national security-related investigations are extremely complex and secretive, and the court system is ill-equipped to understand and keep pre-surveillance warrant requests secret. Moreover, national security-related searches are often an attempt to collect intelligence rather than evidence of criminal activity for the purposes of arresting a suspect, and the government contended the Fourth Amendment was not intended to apply to these sorts of searches. Finally, the government suggested that if a court must review a national security-related search, the review should happen after the search has occurred and courts should only find a search unlawful if the government unreasonably relied on the national security exception without any justification.

The Supreme Court unanimously held that the Fourth Amendment's warrant requirement applies equally to criminal investigations and intelligence gathering, as both risk infringing constitutionally protected liberties. Responding to the government's suggestion that requiring a warrant unduly impedes national security-related searches, the Court opined that the Fourth Amendment's reasonableness requirement must be read in conjunction with the warrant requirement. The Fourth Amendment's requirement that law enforcement obtain a warrant before conducting a search serves an important function in a free society, ensuring a judge, a neutral person not involved in the Executive Branch's law enforcement goals, plays a role in determining when the government is justified in invading its citizens' privacy. Otherwise, the Executive Branch's law enforcement efforts might become overzealous and unrestrained. The Court found the Fourth Amendment specifically requires the Judicial Branch to play a role *before* the government sets out to search for evidence of criminal activity, because if the Judicial Branch only played a role in approving a search after it happened, searches that did not uncover evidence of criminal activity would never be reviewed.

The group charged with conspiring to bomb the CIA office in *Keith* was a domestic organization, the White Panther Party, made up of US citizens. As a result, the government was conducting electronic surveillance of internal threats to national security. The Supreme Court in *Keith* specifically noted that its decision only analyzed whether a warrant was required in domestic national security cases. The Court recognized that some national security-related searches are focused on foreign security threats, and it did not address whether a warrant would be required if the subject of a search or surveillance was a foreign power or its agents. This is an interesting distinction when considering the possibility that domestic security threats may be as damaging to the state as foreign threats.

See Also: Alien and Sedition Acts (1798)

Resources

Merriam, Eric, and Douglas B. McKechnie. 2021. *National Security Law*. St. Paul, MN: West Academic, 133–42.

United States v. U.S. District Court, 407 U.S. 297 (1972).

USA PATRIOT Act

Just over a month after the September 11, 2001, and 2001 anthrax attacks, Congress enacted the "Uniting and Strengthening America by Providing Appropriate Tools Required to Intercept and Obstruct Terrorism Act of 2001" (USA PATRIOT Act or Patriot Act). The Patriot Act provided the government with several new significant avenues to fight terrorism, including increased surveillance powers, increased sharing of intelligence across federal agencies, and increased immigration authority.

Within a week after September 11, 2001, Attorney General John Ashcroft submitted draft legislation giving sweeping powers to the law enforcement and intelligence branches of the government. President George W. Bush asked Congress to pass the massive legislation—about 342 pages long—"in days." While the legislation was not passed within a week as suggested by Ashcroft and Bush, it was rapidly passed by Congress, within roughly forty-five days following September 11. Given the sheer volume and the fact that the legislation spanned hundreds of provisions and amended dozens of existing statutes, many Congressmembers admitted to not even reading the legislation before it came up for a vote. In the final vote, only sixty-six Representatives (of 435) and one Senator (of 100) voted against the legislation. It was signed into law by President Bush on October 26, 2001.

One of the very important aspects of the Patriot Act is that it effectively removed a wall of separation between domestic law enforcement and foreign intelligence operations. Since the 1970s, Congress had placed strict barriers preventing the crossflow of information between the Federal Bureau of Investigation (FBI) and the Central Intelligence Agency (CIA). After enactment of the Patriot Act, US foreign intelligence services could pass along to domestic law enforcement information in their possession about the activities of US citizens who may be violating domestic laws. For instance, providing material support to terrorist organizations had been a crime since the 1990s, but there had been few prosecutions. After the Patriot Act, the floodgates opened when the CIA could share with the FBI information like American names found on terrorist laptops and bank accounts wherein those individuals were listed as providing financial or material support to terrorists or terrorist organizations.

The Patriot Act defined several new crimes as well. For example, before 2001, only "international terrorism" was defined in the United States Code. The Patriot Act amended 18 United States Code 2332 to now include acts of "domestic terrorism." Now, a person who commits an act dangerous to human life that is a violation of criminal law and appears to intimidate or coerce a civilian population or appears to influence a government policy by intimidation or coercion can be prosecuted and convicted of terrorism under federal law. The Patriot Act also amended the Racketeer Influenced and Corrupt Organization (RICO) statute to include terrorist conspiracies as prohibited under RICO.

Regarding surveillance authority, the Patriot Act significantly revised the Foreign Intelligence Surveillance Act (FISA), boosting the government's ability to gather intelligence and counterintelligence efforts by other nations. These new authorities were controversial for many reasons, including the fact that they ostensibly broadened the government's ability to also surveil Americans. For example, the Patriot Act expanded the use of FISA surveillance authorization from situations where the "primary" purpose was obtaining foreign intelligence to situations where a "significant" purpose of the authorization was to obtain foreign intelligence, greatly broadening the scope of authorized investigatory activities. For instance, law enforcement could listen to phone conversations without a warrant if the federal agent averred that a "significant purpose" of the investigation was to gather foreign intelligence. Additionally, the Patriot Act expanded FISA's initial authorization of electronic surveillance to allow administrative subpoenas, without prior judicial oversight, to search "tangible things" like books and paper documents. "National security letters" constitute another data collection practice allowed by the Patriot Act and utilized frequently by law enforcement. With a national security letter, a federal agent may direct a person to provide the law enforcement agency with certain records, again without a warrant. National security letters were typically utilized to obtain things like financial records, university records, internet activity, purchasing invoices, etc. According to the *New York Times* in 2005, "the letters have proven a favorite tool, with *tens of thousands* issued since the 2001 attacks" (Lichtblau 2005, A1). In a report to the House of Representatives and the Senate, the FBI disclosed that it sent out 9,254 national security letters within a one-year period (2005) to financial institutions, telephone and internet providers, and other companies, and involving over 3,500 US citizens.

In addition to these new surveillance and investigatory powers, to combat terrorism, the Patriot Act enacted new criminal laws and increased penalties for others. The Patriot Act notably increased the use of the material support law criminalizing aiding organizations the US government designated as foreign terrorist organizations. The increased surveillance authority and enhanced material support laws were instrumental in over three hundred prosecutions, including *United States v. Al-Arian* (2005).

The Patriot Act stirred significant controversy from the beginning. Some believe it was enacted too hastily, under the cover of the fear of terrorism gripping the nation at the time. Numerous claims that no one had read the entire bill received significant popular attention. Furthermore, the American public was for years unaware of the extent to which the broad surveillance activities authorized by the Patriot Act were used by the government until Edward Snowden's leak of national defense information revealed a massive electronic surveillance program of Americans conducted by the National Security Agency and the Federal Bureau of Investigation. Snowden's leaks caused such a public uproar that these surveillance activities were significantly curtailed by Congress in 2015. The Patriot Act's authorization of indefinite detention of terror suspects also raised civil liberties concerns.

After several re-authorizations, Congress allowed most provisions of the Patriot Act to expire in 2020. Additionally, the "Uniting and Strengthening America by Fulfilling Rights and Ensuring Effective Discipline Over Monitoring Act of 2015" (USA FREEDOM Act or Freedom Act) rolled back some key Patriot Act provisions. For instance, the Freedom Act significantly curtailed some of the authorities the government had used to conduct bulk collection and surveillance, required greater transparency of Foreign Intelligence Surveillance Court (FISC) decisions and authorized appointment of amicus curiae ("friends of the court") to make legal arguments before the FISC to "advance the protection of individual privacy and civil liberties," and allowed individuals and companies greater freedom to report or disclose their participation or non-participation in bulk data collection by the government.

During its existence, the Patriot Act ostensibly enhanced the government's ability to protect against terrorist attacks and other crimes against the state, but clearly came at the expense of individual liberty and freedom from government intrusion. The Patriot Act and the Homeland Security Act of 2002 came after the terrorist attacks of September 11, 2001, and both pieces of legislation revolutionized how the government protected itself based upon what occurred in the days and weeks leading up to the attacks. As threats change and transform, governments must be sufficiently nimble to respond to these new threats, and indeed major new laws adding to government authority often come after crimes against the state have occurred. For instance, after the Oklahoma City Bombing in 1995, Congress responded with the Anti-Terrorism and Effective Death Penalty Act of 1996. After the terroristic racist threats of the KKK in the late 1860s, Congress responded with the Enforcement Acts of 1870. However, overregulation comes at a price. As Benjamin Franklin once noted, those who "can give up essential liberty to obtain a little temporary safety deserve neither liberty nor safety." Or as Supreme Court Justice Sandra Day O'Connor admonished the country more recently, it "would indeed be ironic if, in the name of national defense, we would sanction the subversion of one of those liberties … which makes the defense of the Nation worthwhile" (Chrishti 2004).

See Also: *Al-Arian, United States v.* (2005); Anti-Terrorism and Effective Death Penalty Act of 1996; Anthrax Attacks (2001); Enforcement Acts of 1870; Homeland Security Act of 2002; Leaks of National Defense Information; Material Support Crimes; Oklahoma City Bombing (1995); September 11, 2001; Terrorism

Resources

Beckman, James. 2006. *Comparative Legal Approaches to Homeland Security and Anti-Terrorism.* Hampshire: Ashgate Publishing, 1–50.

Chrishti, Muzaffar. 2004. "U.S. Supreme Court Affirms Rights of Non-Citizen Detainees." *Migration Policy Institute*, August 1, 2004. Accessed November 1, 2023. https://www.migrationpolicy.org/article/us-supreme-court-affirms-rights-non-citizen-detainees.

Lichtblau, Eric. 2005. "Congress Nears Deal to Renew Antiterror Law: Sweeping U.S. Powers Are Mostly Preserved." *The New York Times*, November 17, 2005, A1.

Merriam, Eric, and Douglas B. McKechnie. 2021. *National Security Law.* St. Paul, MN: West Academic, Chapters 7 and 8.

USA FREEDOM Act of 2015.

USA PATRIOT Act.

V

Vesey's Rebellion (1822)

Named after its leader Denmark Vesey, the Vesey Rebellion (1822) was potentially one of the two most massive slave rebellion plots in North America prior to the American Civil War. The other was Nat Turner's Rebellion in 1831. These slave rebellions (along with Gabriel's Rebellion in 1800 and John Brown's attack on the United States Armory and Arsenal in 1859) kept the South in a collective and perpetual state of paranoia and fear. It also motivated white-dominated states to enact draconian laws on Black communities in the hope of protecting their villages and hamlets from rebellion and violence.

Denmark Vesey (1767–1822) spent the first twenty years of his life in bondage before purchasing his freedom in December 1799. While he briefly contemplated emigrating to Sierra Leone, his wife and many children were still being held in bondage. Thus, Vesey decided to stay and plan a rebellion, which would culminate with victorious rebels casting off their chains of captivity, leaving Charleston, and emigrating to Haiti to provide support to the beleaguered Haitian government; the plan was to kill as many slave owners in Charleston and liberate as many enslaved individuals as possible. Vesey planned his rebellion in meticulous detail for four years.

The Vesey Rebellion was to take place in Charleston, South Carolina, in July 1822, on Bastille Day (July 14), which was selected to reference the French Revolution of 1789–99. However, close collaborators of Denmark Vesey revealed the rebellion plans to their respective owners, who in turn notified James Hamilton, the mayor of Charlestown, who called out the city's militia. The militia arrested close to one hundred accomplices in June 1822, a month before the rebellion was planned to occur. After the initial arrest of the chief conspirators, one of the participants stated that the insurgents were expecting upward of 6,600 recruits. Others testified to up to 9,000 supporters. Not counting the surrounding regions, the enslaved population in Charleston alone was 12,621. Of the 131 individuals arrested, Hamilton convened a special court to prosecute ninety-one individuals (with many defendants tried separately over several separate extended court sessions). Many scholars analyzing the trials have explained that African American witnesses were coerced and, in some instances, tortured, that there were major discrepancies and omissions to the transcript of the proceedings, and that there was rampant collusion between government witnesses. Enslaved defendants could not challenge certain evidence or testify in court and were denied adequate legal representation. Even the rapidity of the hearing of the chief planner of the rebellion suggests that the trials were suspect; Denmark Vesey, who was represented by counsel and offered evidence, was captured on June 21, 1822, and executed less than two weeks later, on July 2, 1822.

Ninety-one individuals were charged with "attempting to raise an insurrection." Of the ninety-one charged, sixty-seven were convicted and twenty-three acquitted. Thirty-five convicted individuals (including Denmark Vesey) were executed by hanging and thirty-two were deported and sold into bondage abroad. Some scholars have alleged that the forty individuals (of the 131 initially arrested) who were not prosecuted were pressured into providing evidence or face charges themselves. Similarly, it has been suggested that some of the twenty-three acquittals were due to the acquitted defendant's willingness to cooperate with the state in the prosecutions and offer useful information.

Finally, there were four white defendants tried separately in October 1822. Charged with "a misdemeanor to inciting slaves to insurrection," all four were found guilty. However, unlike the severe punishments faced by the Black defendants, the harshest punishment of the lead white defendant (accused of conspiring to provide transportation to Haiti for the Denmark Vesey's men after the insurrection was accomplished) was twelve months in prison and a $1,000 fine. Two of the other white defendants were each sentenced to three months in prison and a $100 fine, and the fourth received a punishment of six months incarceration and a $500 finc. All four of these white defendants had knowledge of Vesey's intentions and could therefore be found to be a part of the conspiracy just like the sixty-seven Black defendants who were either executed or exiled.

After the punishments, state and city officials enacted several restrictive laws meant to prevent such a rebellion from occurring in the future. The South Carolina General Assembly prohibited the entry of any free Blacks into the state, and ordinances against teaching African Americans to read were enforced with renewed vigor. Cities began organizing slavery patrols and daily militia activities to deal with any insurrection that might occur in the future. These local southern militias and slave patrols would eventually form a key component of the confederate Army several decades later.

See Also: American Civil War and Treason; Brown, John; Gabriel's Rebellion (1800); Insurrection; John Brown's Raid (1859); Rebellion; Turner, Nat

Resources

Egerton, Douglas R., and Robert L. Paquette. 2017. *The Denmark Vesey Affair: A Documentary History*. Gainesville: University of Florida Press.

Johnson, Michael P. 2001. "Denmark Vesey and Co-Conspirators." *The William and Mary Quarterly* 58 (October): 915–76.

Pearson, Edward A., ed. 1999. *Designs against Charleston: The Trial Record of the Denmark Vesey Slave Conspiracy of 1822*. Chapel Hill: University of North Carolina Press.

Virginia v. Brown (1859)

The prosecution of John Brown for treason, homicide, and attempting a slave insurrection has been described as one of the most consequential cases in American legal history. As a result of his actions and trial, Brown was the first person ever executed in the United States for treason. The United States has never executed an American for treason during peacetime. The only Americans ever executed for treason in its history by either the federal or state governments were John Brown and three of his co-conspirators, Edwin Coppoc, Albert Hazlett, and Aaron Stevens, for their roles in John Brown's Raid on Harpers Ferry. For this reason, *Virginia v. Brown* ranks as one of the most important treason cases in US history. Numerous eminent legal scholars have echoed this sentiment, calling it "the most important criminal trial in the history of the United States" (McGinty 2009, 18), "the most significant, or perhaps ... consequential, trial in United States history" (Lubet 2001, 426), and a "national media sensation, the first genuine 'trial of the century'" (Larson 2020, Chapter 5). Indeed, "the trial [of] John Brown, in some ways more than the Harpers Ferry raid itself, did much to hasten, and perhaps even make inevitable, the onset of the Civil War" (Lubet 2002, 50). Paraphrasing author David Reynolds, in the end, Brown had his greatest effect not with his weapons or his attack on the Armory and Arsenal at Harpers Ferry, but with words spoken in court during his trial. As Henry David Thoreau observed, Brown's words in court were his rifles, more powerful than any gun he carried at Harpers Ferry (Reynolds 2005, 334).

Only one day following Brown's capture by United States Marines at Harpers Ferry, with ten of his men killed in the process, Brown and his surviving conspirators were transferred for trial to the county seat at Charles Town, Virginia, approximately eight miles from Harpers Ferry. The main prosecutor, Andrew Hunter, who was specifically appointed by Virginia Governor Henry M. Wise to handle the Brown case, received negative publicity in the Northern press almost immediately when he promised that Brown would be "arraigned, tried, found guilty, sentenced and hung, all within ten days" (National Park Service 1974, 53). To the outsider and the non-Virginian lawyer, the process appeared rushed.

Along with four of his accomplices then in custody (Edwin Coppoc, John Copeland, Aaron Stephens, and Shields Green), John Brown was indicted for treason against the Commonwealth of Virginia, the murder of four townspeople and one United States Marine killed during the attempt to capture Brown, and attempting to cause a slave insurrection. Each defendant pleaded "not guilty" and requested a separate trial. The Commonwealth elected to prosecute Brown first.

While the time for execution after sentencing was not mandated under Virginia law, Hunter's statement of an arraignment, trial, and sentence all being accomplished in ten days was in accordance with prevailing Virginia criminal procedure laws. Virginia law required that a trial had to occur in the same session as when the defendant was indicted. The Circuit Court of Jefferson County, Virginia, only held court twice a year in Jefferson County, and the court had just convened (by pre-arrangement before Brown's raid) on October 20, 1859. The court was mandated to meet in Jefferson County from October 20 to November 10, 1859, at which time the term ended, and the court moved to Winchester. This meant that any indictment must be tried and handled and concluded in a twenty-day period, unless for good cause shown. Brown was captured on October 18, transferred to Charles Town on October 20, arraigned on October 25, and indicted by the Grand Jury on October 26. Brown's three-and-half-day trial started on October 27, and the jury retired to deliberate on October 31 and returned a conviction of guilty on all charges approximately forty-five minutes later. Brown was sentenced on November 2 and scheduled to be executed on December 2, 1859. Since the court's session ended on November 10, Andrew Hunter had only eight days to spare under the applicable Virginia due process statute. Thus, Hunter really had just over ten days to do as he had promised (minus the execution stage—Brown's execution would take place exactly thirty days after his sentencing on November 2 on December 2, 1859). In the landmark and classic book on John Brown by Oswald Garrison Villard (William Llyod Garrison's grandson) written fifty years after Brown's execution, Villard pointedly addressed the criticisms of some of his fellow Northerners about the trial's rapidity, by writing that these Northern lawyers and critics were "probably ignorant of the Virginia Statute governing the case. After this lapse of time, it is plain that the authorities had ample justification in this statute, and in the popular excitement, in expediting the trial; that the outcome of a deferred trial would have been the same is also obvious. It certainly cannot be successfully maintained that substantial injustice was done to John Brown by the celerity of his conviction" (Villard 1910, 482).

Brown did not hide behind legal technicalities during his trial. The law governing Brown's trial came from the 1849 Virginia Code. The 1849 Code of Virginia, chapter 208, section 16, specified that "no person shall be tried for a criminal offense while insane." Furthermore, the next section (section 17) specified that "if the jury finds persons insane at the time of the offense, court may dismiss prosecution and either discharge the prisoner or order him removed to a lunatic asylum." Moments after one of his lawyers (Lawson Botts) stood up in court on Thursday, October 28, and indicated that he had affidavits from Ohio attesting to insanity in the Brown family, Brown, still weak from wounds and lying on a cot, immediately rose to condemn efforts to exonerate him on what he insisted were spurious grounds. Speaking about the insanity defense, Brown said "I look upon it as a miserable artifice and pretext; I view it with contempt more than otherwise." Brown went on to say that "if I am insane, of course I should think I know more than all of the rest of the world. But I do not think so. I am perfectly unconscious of insanity, and reject, so far as I am capable, any attempt to interfere in my behalf on that score." Brown did not want the world to think that only the insane opposed slavery.

There was ample evidence and testimony that Brown had committed the charges listed in the indictment. One of the charges was the murder of five individuals during his attack on the armory, namely George Turner, Thomas Boerly, Hayward Shepherd (a free African American living in town and the first person killed during the raid), Fontaine Beckham (the mayor of Harpers Ferry), and United States Marine Luke Quinn. Since the conclusion of the case, there has been some scholarly debate as to whether Virginia had authority to prosecute the homicide charges relating to Luke Quinn and Fontaine Beckham, as they were killed within the grounds of the United States Armory and subject to the exclusive federal jurisdiction of the United States. Yet, it was indisputable that all five of these men were killed by Brown's men during the attack on the Armory.

On appeal, Brown's lawyers would argue that there was insufficient evidence that Brown himself had shot and killed any of the five individuals. However, this level of detail was not required by the court under the common law doctrine of accomplice liability. The doctrine of accomplice liability provides that if one has knowledge of a criminal enterprise and takes any steps in furtherance or in assistance to that crime, it is as if the person was principal perpetrator of the crime. In instructing the jury in the charges against John Cook, one of Brown's co-conspirators, the trial judge (Richard Parker) explained if Cook assisted in some fashion and "if the prisoner at the bar was present at the murders charged … then he is alike guilty with the parties who directly committed the murders." Judge Parker also explained that "presence did not require … actually standing by during the murders, but only that [one] was within sight and close enough to aid and assist the actual perpetrators." And the prosecutor, Andrew Hunter, explained to the jury that Brown had not only participated in the murder of Virginia citizens, but "that he was the chief director of the whole movement." If one has knowledge of the criminal enterprise and commit acts in furtherance of that enterprise, Hunter said, "no matter whether he was present on the spot or a mile off, he is equally guilty."

Another of the three charges in the indictment was attempting to cause a slave insurrection. By Brown's own words and actions, this was the reason for his attack at Harpers Ferry: to liberate the enslaved, arm them, and overthrow the institution of slavery by force. Brown told one of his financial supporters that if he were successful in his plans, "the whole country from the Potomac to the Savannah would be ablaze." During the raid, Brown temporarily liberated several enslaved people on farms on the outskirts of Harpers Ferry, and some joined Brown's army of liberation.

Finally, Brown was indicted for treason against the Commonwealth of Virginia. There was little doubt about the legitimacy and exercise of a state's treason power. The record of the 1787 Constitutional Convention makes clear that the Framers intended that the crime could be equally applied to treason against the federal or a state government. Furthermore, the text of the United States Constitution itself expressly references state treason charges. The Extradition Clause, located in Article IV, section 2, clause 2, provides that "a person charged in any state with treason, felony, or other crime who shall free from justice ... shall ... be returned to the state from which he fled." Finally, the major state treason trial of *Dorr v. Rhode Island* (1844), a case which stemmed from a popular sovereignty uprising called Dorr's Rebellion, occurred just fifteen years before the Brown prosecution, and the legitimacy of state treason charges was firmly upheld in that case.

Thus, Brown's lawyers did not contest the authority of Virginia to prosecute Brown for treason (both at trial and on appeal), but instead argued that "no man is guilty of treason, unless he be a citizen of the State or Government against which the treason so alleged has been committed." And alternatively, if a non citizen could be held liable under a state's treason statute, Brown's lawyers argued that he did not violate Virginia's treason statute.

The trial court (and jury) concluded that even a brief temporary presence in the state would be sufficient to be covered by treason law. While treason is a breach of allegiance against a sovereign, the court determined that allegiance can be permanent or temporary and even owed to a state by an alien or foreigner. This determination was in accordance with the writings of common law jurists going back centuries and most recently, as it related to Brown's case, the 1820 holding of the United States Supreme Court in *United States v. Wiltberger*. In this ruling, Chief Justice John Marshall writing for the majority stipulated the pre-requisites for a proper treason prosecution as follows: "treason is a breach of allegiance, and can be committed by him only who owes allegiance either perpetual or temporary."

After the Civil War, the Supreme Court expressly ratified the correctness of the court's ruling in Brown's case in the treason-related cases of *Carlisle v. United States* (1872) and *Radich v. Hutchins* (1877). In *Radich*, the Supreme Court ruled that a subject of the Russian Emperor owed allegiance to the United States while domiciled in Texas during the Civil War. In *Carlisle*, the Supreme Court held that British citizens were accountable under US treason laws, even during a temporary stay within the charging jurisdiction.

Since treason charges were proper against Brown as a non citizen, Brown was left contesting that he did not violate Virginia's treason statute. The Virginia Code of 1849 (the statute in effect at the time of Brown's trial in 1859) defined treason as including any of the following acts:

> (1) Levying war against the Commonwealth; (2) Adhering to its enemies, giving them aid and comfort; (3) Establishing, without authority of the legislature, any government within its limits separate from the existing government; (4) Holding or executing, in such usurped government,

> any office, or professing allegiance or fidelity to it; or (5) Resisting the execution of the laws under color of its authority.

The easiest elements of treason for the prosecutors to prove in Brown's case were establishing a government separate from the existing government and holding an office or professing allegiance to that alternate government. The most convincing evidence of Brown's guilt lay not in any act of violence that he committed between October 16 and 18, 1859, but in a document that he authored eighteen months earlier. Brown's "Provisional Constitution and Ordinances for the People of the United States" (drafted partially in the home of Frederick Douglass in February 1858) was roughly modeled on the United States Constitution. It sought to reform by excising—indeed criminalizing and rendering subject to extreme penalties—the institution of slavery. Brown's Provisional Constitution, a blueprint for the organization and governance of his followers if their abolitionist enterprise should last, was read to all his men on Sunday morning, October 16, 1859, immediately preceding the raid. All of Brown's men took oaths of allegiance and fidelity to Brown immediately before the raid and several of Brown's men were found with commissions for offices in Brown's provisional government in their possession after their capture.

Brown's Provisional Constitution was submitted as evidence in his trial and the Preamble, along with Articles 7, 45, and 48, were read into the record. Article 48 directed that all persons associated with Brown's Provisional Constitution should take an oath of allegiance to the newly constituted government. While Article 46 of Brown's Constitution specified that it was not designed to overthrow the United States Government or State governments, the document nonetheless established a competing government designed by Brown, with offices and officers (including Brown as Commander in Chief). When Brown was asked by Governor Wise on October 18, 1859, where he intended to set up his "provisional government," Brown responded "here, in Virginia, where I commenced operations." This statement not only lent strength to the argument that Brown intended to stay in Virginia for some time and was not merely a transitory character, but also that he violated a particular aspect of Virginia's treason statute. Prosecutor Andrew Hunter summarized Brown's guilt quite persuasively:

> The prisoner had attempted to break down the existing Government of the Commonwealth, and establish on its ruins a new Government: he had usurped the office of Commander-in Chief of this new government, and, together with his whole band, professed allegiance and fidelity to it; he represented not only the civil authorities of the state, but his own military; he is doubly, trebly and quadruply [sic] guilty of treason.

At the end of the trial, it is interesting to note that Brown himself admitted that the crimes against him were proven. In Virginia and many other states during this era, defendants were precluded from testifying under oath and offering evidence under the so-called self-interested party rule. It was believed that the testimony would not be truthful and would be self-serving in many instances. Instead, many courts, like those in Virginia, allow the defendant to make what was called an allocution—an unsworn statement made before sentencing. When Brown spoke, he admitted that the charges against him had been adequately proven. Brown stated in part that he would not or should not have been punished if he acted on "behalf of the so-called rich, powerful, the intelligent, the so-called great," that such actions should have been "deemed an act worthy of reward rather than punishment." But in making this point, Brown also clearly admitted his own guilt for the crimes. Brown stated "it was unjust that I should suffer such a penalty. *Had I interfered in a manner which I admit* and which I admit has been fairly proved—for I admire the truthfulness and candor of the greater portion of the witnesses who have testified in this case" (emphasis in original).

Thus, despite the composition of the jury (two-thirds were slave owners collectively enslaving fifty-five individuals), a slave-holding judge, and the rapidity of the trial, Brown ultimately admitted to his crimes, instead arguing that God's law (Nature Law) should negate his criminality (rather than denying that he had in fact violated Virginia's laws). Brown stated on November 2 in open court in his allocution "that he was entirely satisfied with the treatment [he] received on [his] trial," and "it has been more generous than I expected."

Brown's lawyers filed a lengthy appellate document with the Virginia Supreme Court of Appeals on November 18, 1859. Typically, after the filing of a Writ of Error (asking the court for a review of legal issues and/or trial court errors), it was common for the Virginia Supreme Court of Appeals to hold oral arguments on the issue. Furthermore, in all appellate actions, and regardless of the Virginia Supreme Court's ultimate ruling in the case, the court normally issued a judgment explaining why it resolved the case the way it did and clarifying any confusing issues of law. Yet, in Brown's case, his lawyers filed the Writ of Error on November 18, 1859, and it was summarily rejected by the court very next day (November 19). No oral arguments were scheduled or requested, and no legal opinion was issued. Instead, the Virginia Supreme Court of Appeals simply declared that everything that occurred at the trial court level was correct, stating in an extreme economy of words, that "the judgment of the circuit court was plainly right." "Plainly right" is not helpful language for legal scholars and practitioners trying to ascertain the correct legal rules and practices within the courts of the state—then or now.

See Also: Brown, John; *Carlisle v. United States*; Coppoc, Edwin; Cook, John E.; Dorr's Rebellion (1841–42); Hazlett, Albert; Insurrection; John Brown's Raid (1859); Stevens, Aaron; Treason

Resources

Beckman, James. 2009. "John Brown Trial of 1859 and Virginia Insanity Defense Laws Explored." *Magazine of the Jefferson County Historical Society* 75: 45–60.

Beckman, James. 2022. "Abolitionist John Brown's Treason against the Commonwealth of Virginia: A Lesson for State Governments about the Culpability of Non-Residents for Treason against the State." *British Journal of American Legal Studies* 11: 63–79.

Larson, Carlton F. W. 2020. *On Treason: A Citizen's Guide to the Law*. New York: HarperCollins Publishers, Inc. (Kindle Edition).

Lubet, Steven. 2001. "John Brown's Trial." *Alabama Law Review* 52: 425–66.

Lubet, Stephen. 2002. *Nothing but the Truth: Why Trial Lawyers Don't, Can't, and Shouldn't Have to Tell the Whole Truth*. New York: New York University Press.

McGinty, Brian. 2009. *John Brown's Trial*. Boston: Harvard University Press.

National Park Service. 1974. *John Brown's Raid*. Washington, DC: United States National Park Service.

Reynolds, David. 2005. *John Brown, Abolitionist*. New York: Vintage Books.

Villard, Oswald Garrison. 1910. *John Brown's Raid: Fifty Years After*. Boston: Houghton Mifflin Company.

W

Waco (1993)

The name/term Waco refers to a series of events that took place at a religious compound located outside of Waco, Texas, from February to April 1993. The incident involved several law enforcement branches of the federal government and a fringe religious movement called the Branch Davidians that many have characterized as a religious cult. The Branch Davidian compound was located at Mount Carmel, Texas, a short distance outside Waco. The confrontation between federal law enforcement and the Branch Davidians resulted in four federal agents being killed on February 28, 1993, followed by a fifty-one-day standoff between the federal government and the Branch Davidians before federal agents assaulted and subdued the compound on April 19, 1993. As federal law enforcement tried to gain control of the compound, the complex burned to the ground in a conflagration, with almost all the remaining Branch Davidians dying inside. In the end, four federal agents, and approximately eighty civilian Branch Davidians, including two dozen children, were dead.

The incident at Waco in 1993 represents one of the largest confrontations in US history between a civilian group and federal law enforcement and compares to the Colfax Massacre almost a century earlier in terms of the number of participants and resulting fatalities. Former United States Attorney General Ramsey Clark, who represented some of the surviving Branch Davidians, stated that "[h]istory will clearly record, I believe, that these assaults on the Mt. Carmel church center remain the greatest domestic law enforcement tragedy in the history of the United States" (Lichtblau 2000). In the aftermath, the few surviving members of the Branch Davidian compound who were able to escape the conflagration were subsequently indicted and prosecuted in federal court for various federal crimes ranging from conspiracy to murder federal agents to the possession of illegal firearms and explosives. Nine of the twelve indicted were convicted of some of the charges and faced and served lengthy prison sentences. There were also many lawsuits against the federal government by survivors or next of kin of those in the compound under both Federal Tort Claims Act and so-called *Bivens* lawsuits (lawsuits against federal agents in their individual and personal capacity) and several federal investigations as to the correctness of the actions of federal law enforcement in the handling of the incident.

The confrontation between the Branch Davidians at the Mount Carmel Complex and the federal government had its genesis when investigations were commenced by the United States Bureau of Alcohol, Tobacco, and Firearms (ATF) for suspected widespread violations of various federal firearms laws. The charismatic leader of the Branch Davidians was a man named David Koresh, a name he adopted and used instead of his actual name, Vernon Howell. Koresh claimed to be the Messiah called for in the Bible's book of Revelations. Among other things, Koresh claimed to be able to raise bodies from the dead and that God personally spoke to him in his interpretation of Scripture. The ATF alleged that the Branch Davidians at the compound were stockpiling and selling massive quantities of explosive devices and automatic weapons in violation of the National Firearms Act of

1934 (NFA) and the Gun Control Act of 1968 (GCA). Koresh also stated on a television interview that the possession of machine guns and other illegal weapons was the modern-day equivalent of possessing swords that were sanctioned in Biblical times and needed for the defense of his "flock" in the final days of the world and in defense of the Armageddon battle of good versus evil.

The case first came to the attention of the ATF in May 1992 when a representative of the United Parcel Service (UPS) contacted authorities because he noticed that a package destined to be delivered at the Mount Carmel Compound contained what looked like illegal gun parts, explosive devices, and black powder. With this information, the ATF opened an investigation and began its undercover activities, including placing an undercover agent (Robert Rodriguez) within the Branch Davidian compound itself and maintaining an observation post in an adjacent house about a mile away from the compound. Additional information justifying the eventual search warrant was the fact that another mail carrier told authorities he had been delivering packages to the compound that he believed contained grenades and materials needed to convert AR-15 semi-automatic weapons into fully automatic weapons that would operate much like a military M-16. Finally, at least one neighbor recalled hearing machine gun fire coming from the Mount Carmel complex.

The ATF's investigation resulted in a search and arrest warrant dated February 25, 1993, and culminated in the ATF's attempted execution of warrants to search the compound on February 28, 1993. While the date of the execution of the warrants was meant to be a secret to maintain the element of surprise, a local reporter was tipped off in advance by the ATF in hopes of positive publicity (the name of the ATF operation was dubbed "Showtime"). However, in an unforeseen twist of fate, the news reporter stopped and asked directions of a postal worker for how to get to the Mount Carmel complex. This postal worker happened to be a relative of David Koresh and tipped off Koresh. Shortly after this interaction between the news reporter and the postal worker, Koresh received a phone call, and then immediately turned to the undercover ATF agent inside the compound and said, "They are coming Robert." Thus, the Branch Davidians were heavily armed, and lying in wait for the ATF's arrival.

Over sixty ATF agents were tasked with assisting with the execution of the warrants. Expecting violence and non-compliance, ATF agents attested afterward that they wrote their blood type on their arms in the event they were injured and needed an immediate blood transfusion and medical care. Upon attempting to enter the compound on February 28, 1993, a firefight including heavy weapons fire quickly ensued. Several ATF agents present, who were military veterans and had seen combat action in Vietnam, stated that the resulting firefight was worse than anything they had previously witnessed. After a tense exchange of gunfire lasting approximately two hours, and with ATF agents running out of ammunition, the ATF retreated. Four ATF agents had been killed and sixteen wounded. Six Branch Davidians were also killed.

The FBI was brought in to attempt a resolution, but a fifty-one-day standoff ensued. Early on, some progress was made when Koresh agreed to let nineteen children leave the compound without their parents. However, over ninety people, including dozens of children, remained in the compound. Koresh was given several deadlines to leave the compound, but he refused each time. Koresh claimed he would leave the compound if a lengthy statement of his perceived "wrongs" were read verbatim on local radio stations, but, after this was done, Koresh and his followers still refused to leave. According to multiple witnesses, the occupants inside the Branch Davidian compound were preparing for an Armageddon-style confrontation with law enforcement.

Finally, on April 19, 1993, United States Attorney General Janet Reno authorized an assault of the compound. This decision was reportedly made based upon several factors, including a fatigued and frustrated FBI Hostage Negotiation unit, allegations of abuse and mistreatment of children inside the compound, and concern that other militia units might be in route to reinforce and bolster the Branch Davidian defense of the compound. In attempting the breach of compound, the FBI played warnings over a speaker explaining that they would not be shooting into the compound, that a military vehicle was being utilized to insert tear gas into the compound, and that occupants of the compound should come out unarmed. Because of the magnitude of the operation (both on February 28 and April 19), a variety of military equipment was utilized, including Bradley fighting vehicles and Black Hawk helicopters, and multiple military advisors were consulted—many from the Texas National Guard. The use of this equipment (and coordination with the Texas National Guard) would subsequently give rise to claims of violation of the century-and-a-half old Posse Comitatus Act (PCA)—claims that were rejected in subsequent governmental reviews by both the United States Treasury Department and the United States Department of Justice (DOJ), as well as in federal court during the resolution of multiple wrongful death cases against the government. The use of the military equipment and advisors was determined to not be a violation of the PCA because these resources were provided by the National Guard (and not active-duty Armed Forces) and the PCA does not preclude the National Guard from acting in pursuant to state functions and in protection of the state. The three DELTA force members and two senior United States Army officers present at the time of the April 19 raid on the compound acted only in an advisory capacity and as observers and did not take part in an active role in the events.

Unfortunately, after six hours of injecting tear gas into various locations within the compound, only nine Branch Davidians fled the building. A later investigation revealed that a vast majority of the occupants were wearing gas masks and barricaded in the complex bunker. Then, fires were seen erupting at several spots in the compound. After a yearlong investigation by the DOJ Office of Special Counsel, and interviewing multiple witnesses, it was determined that the Branch Davidians had stockpiled drums and cans of gasoline throughout the hallways of the compound and intended to set the building aflame if it looked like the building was breached by federal authorities.

In the aftermath, investigators found seventy-six deceased Branch Davidians within the charred remains of the compound. Many individuals appeared to have been crushed by rubble from the building or died from suffocation and smoke inhalation. More troubling, government reports speculated that some Branch Davidians were refused exit by their fellow Branch Davidians. Additionally, at least twenty of the seventy-six, including five children under the age of fourteen, died from gunshot wounds from within the compound. An expert employed as part of the DOJ Danforth Inquiry opined that the gunshot wounds to several victims "support self-destruction either by overt suicide, consensual execution (suicide by proxy), or less likely, forced execution" (Danforth 2000, 21–2).

Of the few surviving Branch Davidians and several who had left the compound before the assault, twelve were indicted for various federal offenses ranging from the conspiracy to murder federal law enforcement officers to criminally possessing and using various firearms, including illegal machine guns and assault weapons. Charges against one of the defendants were dropped when this person turned state-witness and provided testimony against the other defendants. At the end of an almost two-month federal jury trial, all the charged defendants were acquitted of the most serious charge, conspiring to, or aiding and abetting in, the murder of federal law enforcement agents. However, five of the charged defendants were convicted of committing voluntary manslaughter of the federal agents, as well as utilizing a firearm during the commission of a crime. Additionally, of the eleven remaining defendants, eight were convicted of possessing or utilizing a firearm, including one convicted of conspiracy to possess a machine gun and another convicted of possessing a grenade. One of the additional defendants pleaded guilty to forcibly resisting entry by law enforcement personnel acting under a lawful warrant. Four of the twelve originally indicated defendants were acquitted and/or cleared of all indicted charges. Imposed sentences ranged from three to forty years, with those defendants convicted of voluntary manslaughter receiving the highest sentences. After several appeals wherein the defendants challenged the length of the sentences imposed (including appellate review of the case by the United States Supreme Court), the original federal district court trial judge reduced the sentences of those defendants who had received forty-year sentences by twenty years each, meaning the most serious offenders would be released after serving fifteen years. By July 2007, all the defendants in this case had been released from federal incarceration.

The incident at Waco was subject to multiple independent reviews, ranging from an investigation by the United States Department of the Treasury (see Resources), the DOJ (the so-called Danforth Inquiry; see Resources), as well as numerous federal lawsuits against the federal government and individual federal agents. The Danforth Inquiry was the last and most definitive analysis of what transpired at Waco. After spending $12 million in the investigation, reviewing over two million documents, thousands of pounds of physical evidence, and interviewing close to a thousand witnesses, the Danforth inquiry exonerated the actions of federal law enforcement (both the ATF and the FBI). Some of the key findings of the Danforth Inquiry included the following: federal agents did not start the fire; federal agents did not shoot at the Branch Davidians on April 19; there was no improper or illegal use of the US military or Texas National Guard; there was no massive conspiracy or cover-up by the government; and the responsibility for what occurred at Waco was attributable to David Koresh and his followers, who shot and killed four ATF agents, wounded sixteen others, shot at FBI agents trying to insert tear gas into the compound, burned down the compound themselves when faced with impeding arrest, and shot and killed twenty of their own people, including children.

Unfortunately, the Waco saga did not end on April 19, 1993. On April 19, 1995, on the two-year anniversary of Waco, Timothy McVeigh committed the worst act of domestic terrorism on US soil when he parked a truck packed with explosive devices next to a federal building in Oklahoma City, Oklahoma, and detonated the truck, killing 168 people, including nineteen children under the age of six (see Oklahoma City Bombing). McVeigh's primary motivation for the attack was to seek revenge for what had occurred at Waco, Texas. The events that transpired at Ruby Ridge in 1992 and in Waco in 1993 infuriated McVeigh. He targeted the Alfred P. Murray federal building to seek revenge because it housed several federal agencies, including ATF and FBI offices. In law enforcement's extensive investigation after the Oklahoma City attack, McVeigh was identified in an FBI photograph of anti-government protestors gathered outside of the Mount Carmel complex at Waco, Texas, in March 1993, before the conflagration that occurred on April 19, 1993. He had travelled to Waco to observe the standoff between the Branch Davidians and federal law enforcement. McVeigh also gave a brief television interview at that time. Finally, a reporter indicated that he saw McVeigh loitering outside the Waco federal courthouse during the trials, selling bumper stickers and other paraphernalia. Thus, the tragedy at Waco was the impetus for the 1995 Oklahoma City bombing, the largest domestic terrorist attack on US soil.

See Also: Colfax Massacre (1873); Conspiracy, Criminal; Oklahoma City Bombing (1995); Ruby Ridge (1992); September 11, 2001; Terrorism

Resources

Danforth, John C. 2000. Interim Report to the Deputy Attorney General Concerning the 1993 Confrontation at the Mt. Carmel Complex WACO, TEXAS (July 21) (by order of 2256–99 of the Attorney General). Washington, DC: Office of Special Counsel. Accessed May 29, 2022. https://www.hsdl.org/?abstract&did=731749.

Lichtblau, Eric. 2000. "Report Clears Feds in Deaths of Davidians." *The Los Angeles Times*, July 22, 2000.
Report of the Department of the Treasury on the Bureau of Alcohol, Tobacco, and Firearms investigation Vernon Wayne Howell also known as David Koresh. September 1993. Washington, DC: U.S. Government Printing Office. Accessed May 29, 2022. https://www.policinginstitute.org/wp-content/uploads/2018/02/DOT-Report-ATF-Investigation-of-David-Koresh_Sept-1993.pdf.

Walker, John Anthony, Jr. (1937–2014)

John Anthony Walker Jr. was one of the most damaging spies in US naval history. *The New York Times* reported in 1990 that "it's been estimated by some intelligence experts that Mr. Walker provided enough code-data information to alter significantly the balance of power between Russia and the United States" (O'Connor 1990, A35). Walker was also the ringleader of an espionage cabal, described as the "most damaging case of espionage in United States history" (Lease 2023).

According to the Department of Justice (DOJ), this was "the most damaging espionage ring uncovered in the United States in three decades" (Skelton 1985, A1). During sentencing for one of Walker's co-conspirators (Jerry Whitworth), the DOJ released declassified documents quoting a high-ranking Soviet intelligence officer as saying that the Soviets believed the Walker spy operation was the most important "in the KGB's history" ("Spy Given Two Life Terms" 1986).

Walker joined the Navy in 1955 and began spying for the Soviet Union in 1967. By that time, he had attained the rank of Warrant Officer. In 1969, he befriended Navy radioman Jerry Whitworth at the Naval Training Center in San Diego. Whitworth became Walker's first co-conspirator. When Walker was transferred to a position aboard a supply trip and his intelligence information dried up, Walker recruited Whitworth to send classified secret material to Walker, who in turn forwarded the information to his Soviet handlers. Whitworth continued to provide classified material to Walker until Whitworth's retirement in 1983. Walker himself retired from the Navy in 1976. Unwilling to give up his espionage career with the Soviets, or the hundreds of thousands of dollars he was receiving from the Soviets, Walker recruited his older brother Arthur James Walker, a retired Navy commander and military contractor, who provided Walker with additional materials to pass along to the Soviets. Walker also recruited his son, Michael Lance Walker, an active-duty sailor in the Navy, to begin providing classified information in 1983. Walker tried recruiting his daughter when she was serving in the Army, although she refused her father's recruitment efforts when she decided to leave the Army to become a full-time mother.

Over the course of a seventeen-year career in espionage, Walker assisted the Soviet Union with deciphering over one million encrypted Navy communications, providing Navy radio cipher cards, and showing the Soviets how to defeat Navy cipher machines, and provided a bevy of other top-secret information. Caspar Weinberger, Secretary of Defense during the Reagan administration, stated that Walker gave the Soviets "access to weapons and sensor data and naval tactics, terrorist threats, and surface, submarine, and airborne training, readiness and tactics" (Gordon 1987). John Lehman, Secretary of the Navy in the Reagan administration, stated that Walker's espionage enabled the Soviets to know precisely where all US submarines were positioned at any given moment. Lehman stated that had a conflict erupted in that time period, the United States would have been immediately defeated because of Walker's espionage.

Walker's espionage unraveled along with his marriage. His ex-wife notified the Federal Bureau of Investigation (FBI) that he had been spying for the Soviet Union for years. The FBI interviewed Walker's daughter, Laura, who corroborated that her father was a Soviet spy and that he had tried to recruit her to commit espionage on his behalf. After both wife and daughter passed their polygraph tests, the FBI began surveillance that led to Walker's arrest. He was observed attempting to make an intelligence dead-drop of a package containing 124 pages of classified information in May 1985. He was taken into custody on May 20, 1985, by law enforcement agents claiming they needed Walker's assistance after an alleged automobile accident. John Walker was arrested in what has become known as the Year of the Spy, during which Aldrich Ames, Robert Hanssen, and Larry Wu-Tai Chin were also active and/or arrested. It is unclear how much Walker was compensated over the course of his seventeen years of spying, but it is believed he was paid more than $1 million (an approximation confirmed in a government report), making him one of the highest paid spies in American history.

In late 1985, John Anthony Walker walked into federal court to plead guilty to the offense of espionage in providing naval operations intelligence to the Soviet Union, as well as conspiracy to commit espionage. John Walker's son, Michael Lance, was arrested aboard the USS *Nimitz*. His footlocker was filled with classified government documents. John Walker's brother, Arthur, and his co-conspirator Jerry Whitworth were arrested as well. Arthur Walker was prosecuted for espionage first. Before the charges could even be read in court, Arthur Walker began blurting out his guilt during his arraignment. He was convicted and sentenced to three life sentences. All of the conspirators were convicted of violating the Espionage Act of 1917.

John Walker agreed to cooperate with prosecutors and testify against his co-conspirator Jerry Whitworth. As part of the cooperation agreement, John Walker would plead guilty and provide testimony against Whitworth at trial. Whitworth's espionage was considered by the trial court to be just as damaging to US intelligence and national defense, if not greater. Whitworth did not cooperate with authorities and faced an array of charges, including the following: one count of conspiracy to deliver national defense information to a foreign government, 18 United States Code § 794(c); six counts of delivery of national defense information to a foreign government, 18 United States Code § 794(a); one count of unlawfully obtaining national defense information, 18 United States Code § 793(b); four counts of making false tax returns, 26 United States Code § 7206(1); and one count of conspiracy to defraud the United States, 18 United States Code § 371. He was found guilty on every charge except the one count of unlawfully obtaining national defense information. The federal judge at Whitworth's trial called Whitworth "one of the most spectacular spies of this century." While prosecutors requested a 150-year prison sentence for Whitworth, the judge ignored this recommendation and sentenced him to a 365-year prison sentence, the harshest prison sentence for an espionage case since Julius and Ethel Rosenberg were put to death in 1953, and a punishment he is still serving at a federal high security prison in California.

In exchange for John Walker's cooperation, the government agreed that the prosecutors would only request a twenty-five-year sentence for John Walker's son, Michael Lance, a sentence he subsequently received. Therefore, except for Michael Lance Walker, all the other members of the spy ring received at least a life sentence. John Walker's older brother, Arthur, received three life sentences plus forty years and died in prison in 2014. John Walker received a life sentence and also died in prison in 2014, six weeks after the death of his brother.

See Also: Ames, Aldrich Hazen "Rich"; Chin, Larry Wu-Tai; Conspiracy, Criminal; Espionage; Espionage Act of 1917 and Sedition Act of 1918; Hanssen, Robert Philip; Rosenberg, Julius and Ethel; Year of the Spy (1985)

Resources

Blum, Howard. 1987. *I Pledge Allegiance: The True Story of the Walkers: An American Spy Family*. New York: Simon & Schuster Books.

Earley, Pete. 1989. *Family of Spies: Inside the John Walker Spy Ring*. New York: Bantam Books.

Gordon, Michael. 1987. "Weinberger Says the Walkers Gave Soviet Much Key Data." *The New York Times*, April 17, 1987.

Hunter, Robert W. 1999. *Spy Hunter: Inside the FBI Investigation of the Walker Espionage Case*. Annapolis, MD: Naval Institute Press.

Lease, Lawrence. 2023. "Walker Spy Ring: The Worst Case of Espionage in U.S. History." *Hubpages*, October 20, 2023. Accessed November 4, 2023. https://discover.hubpages.com/politics/The-Jonathan-Walker-Spy-Ring.

Morain, Dan. 1986. "Whitworth Given 365-Year Sentence: Castigated by Judge, Spy Also Is Fined $410,000; Penalty Harshest since '53." *The Los Angeles Times*, August 29, 1986.

O'Connor, John. 1990. "American Spies in Pursuit of the American Dream." *New York Times*, February 4, 1990, A35.

Skelton, Nancy. 1985. "Jerry Whitworth, Accused in Espionage Ring: No One Really Knew the Fourth Spy Suspect." *Los Angeles Times*, June 9, 1985, A1.

"Spy Given Two Life Terms: Final Edition." 1986. *Patriot-news* (Harrisburg, PA), November 6, 1986.

War of 1812 and Treason

In the United States' first war after the ratification of the Constitution, treason was an ever-present concern. Unlike the American Revolutionary War, which itself constituted treason against Great Britain, the War of 1812 occurred between sovereign nations, as the United States declared war on Great Britain. Though many reasons for the war have been suggested, a core underlying concern was the young country's fears for its national security. In light of these fears, the fact that the war was immediately and deeply unpopular, especially in New England, led to further fears of treason.

President James Madison's war against Britain was unpopular among Federalists and New Englanders from the start. Viewed by some opponents as merely a political ploy ("a war of party and not of country"), viewed by many New England religious leaders as deeply immoral, and viewed by businessmen as economically ruinous, Federalists vehemently opposed the Declaration of War and continued voicing opposition after the war commenced. Massachusetts Governor Caleb Strong refused President Madison's request that the Massachusetts militia serve in the war. And "when Acting Secretary of War James Monroe bluntly informed Strong that his state would have to bear unilaterally all subsequent military defense costs," Strong claimed that the federal government had "virtually abandoned the five New England states," and these states would have no choice but to convene a regional convention to discuss ongoing problems "within the federal union" (Richards 1989, 496). Many Federalist leaders believed a departure from the Union would be best for New England. Newspapers began promoting secession as an option. Governor Strong, who had been a delegate to the Constitutional Convention in 1787, opened direct negotiations with representatives of Great Britain about whether Massachusetts and New England might have their own truce or peace with Great Britain. Such actions have led some to characterize New England's Federalists as a "borderline treasonous cabal." Strong "was also willing to consider that Massachusetts, as a sovereign state, negotiate a separate peace agreement with the British" (Richards 1989, 496).

By Winter 1814, Federalists were fed up with a war that, as they had feared from the beginning, had devastated the maritime economy of New England, the party's primary locus of power. They called a meeting in December 1814 in Hartford, Connecticut. Now known as the Hartford Convention, the Federalists discussed how to increase their power within the United States, including proposing several constitutional amendments. But several delegates also suggested New England secede, earning the Hartford Convention a reputation as treasonous. In fact, some have pointed to the Hartford Convention and events leading up to it to demonstrate that secession was not a concept invented by the American South in the years leading up to the American Civil War. When Madison's government signed a peace treaty in late December 1814, the contrast between the Federalists' contemplated sedition and Madison's Democratic-Republican wartime victory ruined the Federalist party that John Adams and Alexander Hamilton had birthed. The Federalists would nominate only one more presidential candidate before collapsing. Indeed, "the very term 'Hartford Convention' became a synonym for disloyalty and treason, and the Federalist Party, which rapidly declined after the war, never lived down its notoriety" (Hickey 1989, 234).

Talk of treason during the War of 1812 was not limited to state secession. At least one person engaged in overt treason in New England and another was tried in federal court in Maryland for alleged treason. In New York, a state court ruled against military authorities who attempted to deal with treason cases through prosecuting the civilian via a military court-martial. Specifically, in *Smith v. Shaw* (N.Y. Sup. Ct. 1815), the court awarded a $799.25 damages verdict against a federal military officer for illegal detention of a civilian. The military claimed that the person was detained for treasonous behavior in advance of a court-martial. The court held that the military lacked this authority, stating "None of the offenses charged against [the detainee] were cognizable by a court-martial, except that which related to being a spy; and if he was an American citizen, he could not be charged with such an offense. He might be amenable to the civil authority for treason; but could not be punished under martial law, as a spy." The court went on to explain that "[i]f the defendant was justifiable in doing what he did, every citizen of the United States would, in time of war, be equally exposed to the like exercise of military power and authority."

Even before the war began, some Federalists in New England worked to preserve relations with Great Britain, and some went much further than that. At least one American provided meaningful intelligence to the British he had collected from various well-placed Federalists, including the Chief Justice of the Vermont Supreme Court. Francis Duclos, an American Revolutionary War veteran, relayed to Britain significant information regarding US war preparations, including where Canada would be attacked in the event of a war, how the United States was manning and supplying its armies, and where in Vermont the British should strike. This likely did not constitute treason at the time (for failing to meet the "Aid and Comfort" to the enemy requirement of the Treason Clause), as war had not yet been declared and Britain was not yet "the enemy." That is, under the Treason Clause, it would have been legally impossible for Duclos to commit treason by providing aid and comfort to the British because the United States was not an open armed conflict or a declared war. At a minimum, however, Duclos's actions did meet the definition of espionage. Duclos's efforts during the war certainly did constitute providing "aid and comfort" to the enemy: throughout the war he smuggled cattle to British forces in Canada and warned people in Canada of an impending attack by American forces. Though not tried for treason, Duclos was imprisoned and heavily fined for smuggling.

In 1814, after sacking Washington, DC, burning the Capitol and President's House, the British Army marched toward Baltimore, Maryland. Along the way, some townspeople in Upper Marlboro, Maryland, captured four British stragglers and an apparent deserter. In turn, the British took hostage several prominent town leaders and threatened to "lay the town in ashes" if the British prisoners were not returned immediately. John Hodges, a town official, convinced the American general holding the British prisoners, General Robert Bowie, to let him return the prisoners to the British Army. The town was saved; Hodges was indicted for high treason.

Hodges was charged with "adhering to the enemy, giving him aid and comfort." Apparently, the grand jury found Hodges's actions met the constitutional definition of treason but expressed its desire that he not be prosecuted, given that his motive was to save the town. Nevertheless, in May 1815, three months after the Treaty of Ghent had officially ended the war, Hodges was tried for treason in federal court in Maryland. As was common at the time, the case was heard by a jury and two judges, one of whom, Gabriel Duval, was a United States Supreme Court Justice sitting as a Circuit Justice, and the other a District Judge.

After several witnesses for the prosecution and defense, much of which focused on whether Hodges knew one of the men he returned to the British was a deserter, the prosecutor "prayed the court to direct the jury that the mere act of delivering up prisoners or deserters is an overt act of high treason." In the prosecutor's mind, there were only two questions: did Hodges deliver the prisoners and did he intend to do so? If their answer was yes to both questions, treason was established. Hodges's defense counsel argued that Hodges's actions were justified by his motive to save the town and secure release of the hostages, to which the prosecution rebutted that motive was not an excuse for treason. In his instructions to the jury, Justice Duvall stated that in his opinion the act of delivering the prisoners constituted "adhering to the enemy" and that when an act constitutes treason, only a threat to one's life—not to property—can serve as a justification or excuse. The District Judge countered that "he did not entirely agree with the chief justice." According to the trial report, after instructions and final argument, "The jury, without hesitating a moment, rendered a verdict of not guilty." Thus, though acts of treason occurred during the War of 1812, and secession was overtly discussed, no one was convicted of treason.

See Also: Aid and Comfort (Aid to Enemies of the State); American Civil War and Treason; American Revolutionary War and Treason; Espionage; Treason

Resources

American State Trials: A Collection of the Important and Interesting Criminal Trials Which Have Taken Place in the United States, from the Beginning of Our Government to the Present Day. ed. John D. Lawson. 1918. St. Louis: F. H. Thomas Law Book Company, 164.

Chapman, Jennifer Elisa. 2019. "*United States v. Hodges*: Developments of Treason and the Role of the Jury." *Denver Law Review* 97: 117.

Henderson, Robert. 2011. "Patriots or Traitors? The Leaking of Secret U.S. War Plans to the British in 1812." *Access Heritage: The War of 1812*. Accessed June 6, 2023. https://www.warof1812.ca/patriotstraitors.htm.

Hickey, Donald R. 1989. "Hartford Convention." In *The Encyclopedia of the War of 1812*, edited by David Heidler and Jeanne Heidler, 233–4. Annapolis, MD: Naval Institute Press.

Mahnken, Kevin. 2012. "Fractures of 1812." *Humanities* 33, no. 6 (November/December). Accessed February 15, 2024. https://www.neh.gov/article/fractures-1812.

Richards, Miles S. 1989. "Strong, Caleb." In *The Encyclopedia of the War of 1812*, edited by David Heidler and Jeanne Heidler, 495–6. Annapolis, MD: Naval Institute Press.

United States v. Hodges, 2 Wheeler's Criminal Cases 477 (1815).

Weapons of Mass Destruction

Shortly after the World Trade Center bombing of 1993, as part of the Violent Crime Control and Law Enforcement Act, Congress first criminalized the possession or use of weapons of mass destruction (WMDs). Codified at 18 United States Code Section 2332a, this law made it a federal offense to use or attempt to use, or conspire to use, a WMD in the United States or against United States interests abroad. As originally drafted, Section 2332a applied only to the use, conspiracy to use, or attempted use of WMDs, and did not apply to the threatened use of WMDs or mere transportation, receipt, or possession of WMDs. As part of the Anti-Terrorism and Effective Death Penalty Act (1996), following the Oklahoma City Bombing in 1995, Section 2332a was amended and broadened to allow for the prosecution of individuals who threaten to use WMDs against a person in the United States, even if the device is not ultimately used. Further amendments to Section 2332a now make it a crime, subject to up to life imprisonment, to transport or receive a WMD with the intent to use it against another person at some future point, or knowingly possess a WMD in furtherance of a federal crime of violence. Consequences for violating any of the above variations (i.e., use, threatened use, conspiracy to use, possessing in furtherance of a federal crime of violence, transporting or receiving with the intent to use it) carry a punishment of any number of years up to a possible life sentence, and in cases "where death results," the statute provides for imposition of the death penalty as a possible punishment as well.

Some mistakenly think of WMDs as including only things like a nuclear weapon or a so-called dirty bomb (a bomb containing explosives and radioactive material) or envision the United States Army's unsuccessful search for Saddam Hussein's alleged missing large-scale WMDs in the early 2000s in Iraq. Under US law, WMDs are defined much more broadly (under 18 United States Code § 2332c) as "any destructive device," "any weapon that is designed or intended to cause death or serious bodily injury through the release, dissemination, or impact of toxic or poisonous chemicals, or their precursors," "any weapon involving a biological agent, toxin, or vector," or "any weapon that is designed to release radiation or radioactivity at a level dangerous to human life." A WMD does not need to be a nuclear device, it could be as small as a grenade or a vial containing Anthrax or Ebola.

Under 18 United States Code Section 921, a destructive device is defined as including any of the following: "any explosive, incendiary, or poison gas; bomb; grenade; rocket having a propellant charge of more than four ounces; missile having an explosive or incendiary charge of more than one-quarter ounce; mine, or device similar to any of the devices described." Some critics have argued that the ambiguity at the end of this definitional section (i.e., "or device similar to any of the devices described") leaves the statute open for potential abuse. Critics also argue that this broad definition can potentially lead to the criminalization of non-dangerous substances or objects that do not pose a significant threat as true weapons of mass destruction.

Finally, under 18 United States Code Section 178, the term "biological agent" means "any microorganism (including, but not limited to, bacteria, viruses, fungi, rickettsiae or protozoa), or infectious substance, or any naturally occurring, bioengineered or synthesized component of any such microorganism or infectious substance, capable of causing death, disease, or other biological malfunction in a human, an animal, a plant, or another living organism; or causing the deterioration of food, water, equipment, supplies, or material of any kind; or causes a deleterious alteration of the environment." Under 18 United States Code Section 178, the term "toxin" means the "toxic material or product of plants, animals, microorganisms (including, but not limited to, bacteria, viruses, fungi, rickettsiae, or protozoa), or infectious substances, or a recombinant or synthesized molecule, whatever their origin and method of production, and includes any poisonous substance or biological product that may be engineered as a result of biotechnology produced by a living organism; or any poisonous isomer or biological product, homolog, or derivative of such a substance." Finally, the term "vector" means a "living organism, or molecule, including a recombinant or synthesized molecule, capable of carrying a biological agent or toxin to a host."

WMD-related charges and convictions are rare compared to other federal criminal law offenses. However, there are several high-profile cases where individuals have been indicted and convicted for the use or threatened use of WMDs. One of the most widely known examples is the 1997 criminal prosecutions of Timothy McVeigh and Terry Nichols for the Oklahoma City Bombing in 1995. They were both charged and convicted under the original 1994 version of the statute. McVeigh was convicted and executed by the federal government in 2001. Nichols is serving a life sentence. Another example can be seen in the 2013 Boston Marathon Bombing. Dzhokhar Tsarnaev was indicted and convicted on several counts, including using a WMD resulting in death. Tsarnaev was sentenced to death, but the sentence was later reduced to life imprisonment without parole following an appeal. Similarly, in 2005, Eric Rudolph was charged with a series of bombings that occurred between 1996 and 1998, including at several abortion clinics and the Centennial Olympic Park in Atlanta during the 1996 Summer Olympics. He used powerful explosives in his attacks and explosives packed with nails to increase the resulting damage and potential human carnage, leading to charges under the federal WMD statute (18 United States Code § 2332a). Finally, in *United States v. Padilla*, Jose Padilla, also known as Abdullah al-Muhajir, was arrested in 2002 and accused of planning to build and explode a radiological "dirty bomb" in the United States in Chicago. After his capture, he was charged with multiple offenses, including conspiracy to use a WMD. However, shortly thereafter, he was transferred to military detention as an enemy combatant and, as discussed more completely elsewhere in this book (see *Padilla, United States v.*), a legal battle ensued between Padilla and the government that spanned years and several federal appellate court rulings. Years later, he was finally brought to stand trial in civilian court, the case came full circle, and he was tried in the same civilian jurisdiction where he was first arrested and detained in 2002. Ironically, however, he was not charged for the alleged possession of a WMD plot that had served as the government's justification for several years of military custody. Instead, Padilla was charged in federal court with conspiracy to commit murder, kidnapping, providing material support to terrorists and terrorist organizations, and maiming of persons *overseas*. He was convicted and received a twenty-one-year sentence.

See Also: Anti-Terrorism and Effective Death Penalty Act 1996; Boston Marathon Bombing (2013); Conspiracy, Criminal; Material Support Crimes; Oklahoma City Bombing (1995); *Padilla, United States v.* (2004–2014); Rudolph, Eric Roberts; World Trade Center Bombing of 1993

Resources

18 U.S.C. Section 2332a, Use of Weapons of Mass Destruction.

Weather Underground

The Weather Underground (also known as the Weathermen, Weatherman, Weatherman Underground, and Weather Underground) was an extremist militant organization pledged to the violent overthrow of the government of the United States and the overthrow of the capitalist system. The Weather Underground was in operation from the late 1960s through the early 1980s and was responsible for dozens of bombings across the country. The group was responsible for multiple high-profile bombings of various government offices, banks, and businesses. Group members also blew up cars, committed armed robberies, engaged in domestic terrorism, and participated in countercultural figure Timothy Leary's escape from a California prison and his escape to Algeria. A majority of members of the Weather Underground left the group in the late 1970s or early 1980s, and it was completely disbanded by the early 1980s.

The Weather Underground was the violent offspring of the Students for Democratic Society (SDS). The SDS, founded in the early 1960s, was founded principally to protest the Vietnam War, although it was also engaged in combating racism and poverty in America. Non-violence was the chief tool of the SDS, and at its height, it boasted over a hundred thousand members at college campuses across the United States. The SDS was taken over by members of the Weather Underground at the SDS convention at the Coliseum in Chicago in June 1969. While the Weather Underground took over the name and SDS structure, group members disavowed non-violence as a tactic and embraced violence as its chief strategy. One of the claimed goals of the Weather Underground was to commit acts of violence to "bring the war home" to the average American citizen. The group named itself the Weatherman after lyrics from a Bob Dylan song. The group believed insurrection and then revolution in America was imminent. The group also claimed inspiration from radical abolitionist John Brown, dedicating a 1973 self-published book to Brown and naming its short-lived newsletter "Osawatomie" (a reference to both the Pottawatomie Massacre and Brown, who was sometimes referred to as Osawatomie Brown).

The group established communes and collective houses in Cleveland, Chicago, Detroit, San Francisco, Seattle, Cincinnati, and Milwaukee, with the idea of connecting the disaffected students at college campuses with non-college working-class youth in blue collar neighborhoods, although the communes were known for the hedonistic activities of its members. The group's first big, planned event after its takeover of the SDS was called "The Days of Rage," scheduled to take place in October 1969 in Chicago. The goal was to violently confront the police and vandalize properties. Organizers of the event anticipated tens of thousands of protestors to show up (based upon earlier SDS membership numbers); instead, only several hundred individuals attended. Those who did show up vandalized banks and stores in downtown Chicago, fought with the police, and engaged in a riot. Police arrested 287 rioters for the massive property damage inflicted during the event, disorderly conduct, and resisting arrest, among other things. Several days prior to the event, the Weather Underground planted dynamite and destroyed the Haymarket Affair police statue in Chicago. The explosion was so violent that it shattered the windows of nearly one hundred adjacent structures. The City of Chicago would rebuild the statue, only to have it bombed and destroyed again by Weather Underground operatives in October 1970.

As the size of the former SDS dwindled down to a hundred or so members of the Weather Underground, the group became more radical and militant. Many of its members believed that all Americans were complicit in the country's activities in Vietnam and the rampant racism and police violence that existed in the United States, and therefore, were legitimate targets. The leadership intended to engage in random bombings intended to kill people, as well as damage property, with the mindset of the "bigger the damage and destruction, the better." At the end of 1969, leaders approved a plan to change the group into an underground organization that would commit acts of sabotage and violence and changed its name to "Weather Underground Organization."

The group was planning an act of blatant terrorism and mass murder for the spring of 1970. They had targeted a Non-Commissioned Officers Army Ball that was scheduled to take place at Fort Dix, New Jersey. However, on March 6, 1970, as members of the group were putting the final charges on an explosive device that was to be used for the bombing, the device prematurely exploded at the Weather Underground's West 11th Street townhouse in New York City (Greenwich Village). The explosion killed three Weather Underground members in the townhouse at that time and destroyed the building.

After the March 1970 explosion, the Federal Bureau of Investigation (FBI) stepped up its investigations and surveillance of the Weather Underground. The FBI had a specific unit assigned to the group that was known as FBI Squad 47 or the FBI Weatherman Squad. This unit went undercover in hopes of infiltrating the group, although almost all members evaded the FBI. At this time, the group decided to go into hiding. Many members of the group would spend most of the next decade hidden from public view and in hiding from family and friends. Years later, some leaders of the group (e.g., Bernardine Dohrn, Bill Ayers, Mark Rudd) would claim that after the West 11th townhouse incident, they would not target innocent Americans as targets in their bombings. These leaders claimed that they picked targets to avoid hurting bystanders and typically gave anonymous warnings to clear the buildings or areas shortly before planted bombs were scheduled to detonate. While warnings were given in many instances for bombings, other acts of Weather Underground violence involved the loss of life. For example, multiple members of the Weather Underground were involved in acts of armed robberies in which police officers were killed. In May 1970, the Weather Underground issued a "Declaration of a State of War" that pronounced war on the US government. In October 1970, the FBI placed three members of the group on the FBI's Ten Most Wanted List, namely Dohrn, Power, and Saxe.

While too numerous to detail, some of the more high-profile bombings were as follows: National Guard Association (May 1970); New York City Police Headquarters (June 1970); Presidio Army base (July 1970); Bank of America Headquarters (July 1970); New York Queens Courthouse (October 1970); Harvard Center for International Affairs (October 1970); California Marion County Courthouse (October 1970); United States Capitol (February 1971); multiple California Department of Corrections Offices (August 1971); New York Department of Corrections (September 1971); Pentagon (May 1972); New York 103rd Police Precinct (May 1973); ITT Headquarters (September 1973); United States Health, Education, and Welfare Offices in California (March 1974); California Attorney General's Office (May 1974); Gulf Oil Headquarters (June 1974); Banco de Ponce office in New York (June 1975); and United States State Department (June 1975). At various times between 1970 and 1975, members of the group firebombed police cars, threw Molotov cocktails into a sitting judge's house (1970), and conspired to bomb a California Senator's home (1977), among other things. Weather Underground members were paid \$20,000–\$25,000 to help Timothy Leary escape from a California prison (he was serving a ten-year prison sentence), and the group was successful in helping Leary escape in September 1970 and flee to Algeria.

Multiple members of the Weather Underground were on the FBI's Ten Most Wanted List at various points between 1970 through 1980. From 1976 through 1981, many Weather Underground members slowly begin to quit the organization and turn themselves in to authorities, some after decades of hiding as fugitives. While a few notable members of the group had federal charges dropped against them or received minor punishment or probation after the disclosure of misconduct by FBI agents, numerous members of the Weather Underground were prosecuted and convicted for other various offenses and received lengthy prison sentences (ranging from three to seventy years). The names and individual crimes of these ex-Weather Underground members are too numerous to delineate here.

See Also: Brown, John; Haymarket Affair (1886); Insurrection; Pottawatomie Massacre (1856); Riot and Incitement to Riot; Sabotage; Terrorism

Resources

Eckstein, Arthur M. 2016. *Bad Moon Rising: How the Weatherman Underground Beat the FBI and Lost the Revolution*. New Haven, CT: Yale University Press.

FBI Records on the Weather Underground. 2022. Accessed July 17, 2022. https://vault.fbi.gov/Weather%20Underground%20(Weathermen).

Grathwohl, Larry, and Frank Reagan. 1976. *Bringing Down America: An FBI Informer with the Weathermen*. New Rochelle, NY: Arlington House Publishers.

Weaver, Randy

See Ruby Ridge

West Virginia Coal Wars

The West Virginia Coal Wars were a series of labor disputes between miners and mining companies from 1912 to 1921. When union workers demanded better pay and conditions, mining companies hired private security guards to act as strikebreakers, and on multiple occasions during the decade violence ensued. Multiple West Virginia governors declared martial law to address the breakdowns of local government during the hostilities. Ultimately, the fighting culminated with the Battle of Blair Mountain, which required the mobilization of 2,500 troops from two infantry divisions of the United States Army to quell and was the largest (by number of participants) insurrection in US history other than the American Civil War.

In 1912, thousands of miners from mines in the Paint Creek and Cabin Creek areas went on strike. Mining company security guards evicted striking miners and their families from company housing, then prohibited them from using company-owned infrastructure such as local roads and running water. The strikebreakers killed several striking miners, and miners retaliated with force. After several thousand miners declared their intent to destroy the mines, and in light of the warring parties' complete disregard for local law enforcement efforts, Governor William Glasscock declared a *state of war* existed, and declared martial law. In addition to sending state troops to confiscate the miners' weapons and attempt to keep peace, Governor Glasscock appointed a military commission to hear criminal cases in the area.

In 1920, when several hundred miners in Matewan, West Virginia, joined a union, their employer fired them and evicted them from their company-owned homes. Local law enforcement arrested one mining company agent, alleging the evictions were illegal. Subsequently, agents of the mining company's security contractor returned to evict more miners from a mine company's housing area. Local law enforcement, including Police Chief Sid Hatfield, unsuccessfully attempted to stop the evictions. Though accounts differ as to who began shooting first, the eventual "shootout" left ten people dead: the town mayor, two miners, and seven mine company security agents. Chief Hatfield was subsequently charged with murdering the mining company agents and for allegedly destroying another mining camp. On August 1, 1921, as Chief Hatfield voluntarily appeared at the courthouse to stand trial, he and another co-defendant were assassinated by mining company security agents.

The unrest resulting from the Battle of Matewan and assassination of Chief Hatfield led to increased miner organization across the state. In late August, many thousands of miners, many of whom were armed, assembled in and then marched en masse to the mountains outside Logan, West Virginia. In the ensuing "Battle of Blair Mountain," the Logan County Sheriff attempted to resist the miners with a force that was significantly outnumbered (roughly 2,000 police, state militia, and mine company security agents against the miners with thousands more) but better equipped. After a week of fighting, President Warren G. Harding ordered 2,500 federal troops to the area to secure peace. The miners yielded to the federal forces. Over 500 miners were subsequently convicted of a range of faced trial for murder and insurrection. Though dozens were indicted, only one miner, Walter Allen, was convicted of treason *against the state* for his activities in leading the miners' march that led to the Battle of Blair Mountain. By historical coincidence, Allen was tried for treason against West

Virginia in the same courthouse in Charles Town where John Brown had been tried and convicted for treason against the state of Virginia in 1859 and condemned to hang. Allen's fate was less severe: he was sentenced to ten years in prison and, while released on bail pending appeal of his conviction, disappeared. Bill Blizzard, the other labor ringleader, was found not guilty of treason in the same courthouse by the Jefferson County, West Virginia, jurors.

The West Virginia Coal Wars were important not only for the participants and the principles for which they fought, but because of they are the most recent significant examples of a governor's use of military tools like declarations of war, martial law, and military commissions to respond to crimes against the state like violent unrest. This also was the last time a state government charged a defendant with treason. The West Virginia Supreme Court of Appeals repeatedly approved the governor's military actions, though some dissenting Justices questioned whether the mine uprisings constituted war or insurrection sufficient to justify martial law.

While the West Virginia Coal Wars may have been the most significant example of labor unrest considered to rise to the level of insurrection, it was but one of many instances of such unrest leading to the use of military forces to address the purported insurrection. Other instances of violent labor unrest include the Colorado Coalfield Wars, the Ludlow Massacre, and the violence associated with a strike at the Albert Lea meatpacking plant in Minnesota in 1959, which led to the most recent declaration of martial law in the United States. Though these and other instances of widespread violence or disregard for civil authorities in the midst of a private dispute were significant, when considering crimes against the state, it is important to distinguish between such actions and true insurrection or rebellion where the usurpation or replacement of government is the object of the violence rather than accomplishing one's preferred outcome in a dispute with another private entity or individual. Violent conflict between labor unions, corporations, and strike breakers may overwhelm local government's ability to enforce the peace, and thus may trigger government military responses similar to those one might expect in the context of an actual insurrection or rebellion, such as calling out the militia pursuant to the Insurrection Act or martial law, but such situations likely do not constitute crimes against the state absent the intent to injure the state itself.

See Also: American Civil War and Treason; Insurrection; Insurrection Act; John Brown's Raid (1859); Martial Law; Rebellion; Treason; *Virginia v. Brown* (1859)

Resources

Corbin, David Alan, ed. 1990. *The West Virginia Mine Wars: An Anthology*. Charleston, WV: Appalachian Editions.

Laurie, Clayton D. 1991. "The United States Army and the Return to Normalcy in Labor Dispute Interventions: The Case of the West Virginia Coal Mine Wars, 1920–1921." *West Virginia History* 50: 1–24.

Lee, Howard B. 1969. *Bloodletting in Appalachia: The Story of West Virginia's Four Major Mine Wars and Other Thrilling Incidents of Its Coal Fields*. Morgantown: West Virginia University Library.

Merriam, Eric. 2022. "Necessary Necessity: Courts' Historical Assessment of the Condition Precedent for Martial Law." *Oklahoma Law Review* 75: 203–12.

Savage, Lon. 1990. *Thunder in the Mountains*. Pittsburgh: University of Pittsburgh Press.

Shogan, Robert. 2004. *The Battle of Blair Mountain: The Story of America's Largest Labor Uprising*. Boulder, CO: Westview Press.

Sullivan, Ken, ed. 1991. *The Goldenseal Book of the West Virginia Mine Wars*. Charleston, WV: Quarrier Press.

Wheeler, Hoyt N. 1976. "Mountaineer Mine Wars: An Analysis of the West Virginia Mine Wars of 1912–1913 and 1920–1921." *The Business History Review* 50, no. 1: 69–91.

Whiskey Rebellion

The Whiskey Rebellion is significant for multiple reasons. This early insurgency against the United States occurred within a brief time following the ratification of the United States Constitution and tested whether the new country could enforce its own laws and successfully negate forces of secession caused by disagreement with unpopular federal laws. The Whiskey Rebellion exemplified the largest opposition by a distinct group against the federal government from the American Revolution until the American Civil War. The Whiskey Rebellion also represented the largest peacetime standoff between federal forces and a civilian population, vastly outnumbering the nineteenth- and twentieth-century confrontations at the Colfax Massacre and Waco, Texas, in 1873 and 1993, respectively. One of the key differences between the Whiskey Rebellion and these two events is the lack of significant bloodshed and fatalities during the Whiskey Rebellion as compared with what transpired at the Colfax Massacre and at Waco. Additionally, the Whiskey Rebellion holds a unique place in American law, as the events during the Whiskey Rebellion gave rise to the first treason trials in the history of the United States after the ratification of the United States Constitution in 1789. Over twenty people were escorted to Philadelphia, Pennsylvania, to stand trial for treason, although only two would ultimately be found guilty. The Whiskey Rebellion resulted in the highest number overall indictments for treason for any single event in US history (the second highest number of indictments came from the Christiana Revolt in 1851).

The origins of the Whiskey Rebellion stem from Alexander Hamilton's taxation scheme to raise federal funds to pay off state debts incurred during the Revolutionary War. With few avenues for raising federal funds, excises and custom duties were one of the few tools at the disposal of the federal government to raise money, and the taxation of alcohol and spirits was a prime target. The excise tax on whiskey enacted in 1791 covered not only the sale, but also its manufacture in private stills, and even the personal consumption of the distilled spirituous liquors. In the western regions of Pennsylvania (and indeed at other remote frontier establishments), whiskey, and especially Monongahela rye, was considered an all-purpose commodity. Many poorer farmers and frontiersman used the distilled whiskey for a range of purposes from cooking to medicine, to a source of currency and a medium of exchange to barter for other commodities needed on the frontier. It was common for town ministers and teachers to be compensated for their services with jugs of whiskey instead of money. The frustration over the taxation of distilled whiskey was exacerbated by the fact that indigent farmers were taxed even for the whiskey distilled for their personal consumption. Many of these frontiersmen were intensely private and disliked federal tax collectors peering around their properties. Finally, the fact that the federal tax collectors were compensated with a portion of the taxes collected did not sit well with many of the farmers and frontiersman.

Almost immediately after the tax was enacted in 1791, acts of violence began to occur. In October 1791, a group of disenchanted frontiersmen kidnapped a federal tax collector from his bed in Pittsburgh, Pennsylvania, and forced the federal revenue official to walk five miles, where he was stripped naked and branded with a red-hot iron. Over the next couple of years as the insurrection developed, numerous federal tax collectors were assaulted, terrorized, tarred and feathered, and harassed in numerous other ways. Occupants of Pittsburgh were under constant fear that the burgeoning village of several hundred homes would be burned to the ground. The whiskey stills of people who paid the taxes were often destroyed. Mail bags were seized by the insurgents and citizens were targeted for harassment based upon the contents of confiscated mail. John Neville, the head federal revenue officer in western Pennsylvania had his home and outbuildings burned to the ground by the mob. More troubling, insurgents began communicating with other frontiersman in neighboring territories west of the Alleghany mountains and "there was talk of establishing a separate trans-Alleghenian nation, or of marching on Philadelphia to force on the federal government measures dictated by the frontier" (Flexner 1974, 316). Rebel forces resisting federal authority ballooned to between five thousand and seven thousand individuals. At one point, estimates placed the rebel forces as large as 15,000 men.

By 1794, the federal government had enough. Before assembling troops to put down the festering rebellion, the Militia Act of 1792 (a precursor to the Insurrection Act) demanded a justice of the United States Supreme Court to certify that law enforcement had lost control of the situation and that the situation was beyond the control of local authorities to remediate. Thus, on August 8, 1794, Supreme Court Justice James Wilson delivered an opinion which stated that western Pennsylvania was in a state of rebellion that necessitated calling up the army. President George Washington made one last attempt at peacefully resolving the dispute, issuing a proclamation ordering that the mob "disperse and retire peaceably to their homes" by September 1, 1794 (Flexner 1974, 316). When this did not happen, Washington called up militia units from New Jersey, Maryland, and Virginia, a combined force of 12,950 soldiers. While Washington led the troops as far as Reading, Pennsylvania, he then turned the command of the forces over to Revolutionary War General "Light Horse" Harry Lee and Secretary of the Treasury Alexander Hamilton (one of Washington's trusted aides during the Revolutionary War).

In the face of this formidable federal force, the mob disintegrated, dispersed, and fled into the surrounding wilderness. The alleged leader of the rebellion, David Bradford, was never captured or charged. George Washington was said to remark to John Jay that the rebels had been shown "a perfect sense of their misconduct without spilling a drop of blood" (Flexner 1974, 319). In total, approximately 150 individuals were arrested under suspicion of aiding in the rebellion. Of those 150 people, in May 1795, thirty-five defendants were indicted in the Circuit Court for the Federal District of Pennsylvania for a wide variety of crimes associated with the Whiskey Rebellion. The indictments of two individuals were dropped (one died prior to his trial and the other was released because of mistaken identity). Nine other indicted defendants were charged with minor federal offenses and received modest punishments. The remaining twenty-four defendants were each charged with serious federal crimes, including treason against the United States. Nineteen of the twenty-four were convicted of lesser federal crimes. When President Washington learned that none of these individuals were principal actors or instigators in the rebellion, he pardoned them. Only two of the original thirty-five indicted defendants, John Mitchell and Philip Vogel, were found guilty of treason and sentenced to death by hanging. However, President Washington also pardoned both Mitchell and Vogel on November 5, 1795, believing one to be a mere "simpleton" and the other to be "insane."

As mentioned, the Whiskey Rebellion served as the precipitating event to the very first federal treason trials in the United States following the ratification of the Constitution in 1789. In overseeing the treason trials of Mitchell and Vogel, presiding federal Circuit Court Judge William Patterson set forth an early understanding of what the term "levying war" meant for treason prosecutions under Article III of the Constitution in *Mitchell, United States v.* (1795). Article III, section 3, of the United States Constitution (the Treason Clause), defines treason, in part, as "levying war" against the United States. In instructing the jury at the close of the prosecution of Mitchell and Vogel, Judge Patterson instructed the jury that any armed opposition to the enforcement of federal law should be considered "levying war" against the government. This would be the definition of "levying war" and treason in the subsequent trial of John Fries (for Fries's Rebellion) in 1799. However, the broad concept of "levying war" as including any act in armed defiance of federal laws or the violent violation of federal laws was eventually disavowed by federal courts by the mid-1850s. Most notably, this interpretation of "levying war" for treason purposes was rejected in *United States v. Hanway* (1851), a case resulting from the Christiana Revolt and the refusal of people to follow or assist a deputized federal marshal (and in some cases, violently resist the federal marshal) in the enforcement of the Fugitive Slave Act of 1850.

Beyond the narrow confines of the operation and application of treason law, the federal response to the Whiskey Rebellion illustrated that the new federal government had the political will and ability to suppress violent resistance to federal laws and to quell incipient secessionist movements. While the Whiskey Rebellion is often mentioned along with Shay's Rebellion in 1786 and Fries's Rebellion in 1799 as examples of early anti-taxation protests, the Whiskey Rebellion stands alone in its magnitude and its real and palpable threat to the stability of the nascent United States. While all three events were motivated by a desire to not follow unpopular tax laws, neither Shay's Rebellion nor Fries's Rebellion ever garnered more than a few hundred followers. This is easily contrasted with the thousands of rebels arrayed against the federal government during the Whiskey Rebellion.

See Also: American Revolution and Treason; Christiana Revolt (1851); Colfax Massacre (1873); Fries's Rebellion (1799); *Hanway, United States v.* (1851); Insurrection; Insurrection Act; Levying War; *Mitchell, United States v.* (1795); Rebellion; Shay's Rebellion (1786–7); Treason; Waco (1993)

Resources

Boyd, Steven R. 1985. *The Whiskey Rebellion: Past and Present Perspective*. Westport, CT: Greenwood Press.
Flexner, James Thomas. 1974. *Washington: The Indispensable Man*. Boston: Little, Brown and Company.
Slaughter, Thomas P. 1988. *The Whiskey Rebellion: Frontier Epilogue to the American Revolution*. Oxford: Oxford University Press.

Whitney v. California (1927)

Charlotte Anita Whitney was a member of the national Communist Labor Party of America (CLPA) and helped found the Communist Labor Party of California. Among other things, the CLPA's platform included a declaration that "it was in full harmony with 'the revolutionary working class parties of all countries,' and that its purpose was 'to create a unified revolutionary working class movement in America,' organizing the workers as a class in a revolutionary class struggle to conquer the capitalist state for the overthrow of capitalist rule, the conquest of political power and the establishment of a working class government, the Dictatorship of the Proletariat, in place of the state machinery of the capitalists, which should make and enforce the laws, reorganize society on the basis of Communism, and bring about the Communist Commonwealth."

The California Criminal Syndicalism Act (Syndicalism Act) prohibited criminal syndicalism, which the Syndicalism Act defined as "any doctrine or precept advocating, teaching or aiding and abetting the commission of crime, sabotage [defined as meaning willful and malicious physical damage or injury to physical property], or unlawful acts of force and violence or unlawful methods of terrorism as a means of accomplishing a change in industrial ownership or control, or effecting any political change." Thus, like most criminal syndicalism laws, the Syndicalism Act was concerned with attempts to disrupt industry or government. Ms. Whitney was convicted of syndicalism for her membership in the Communist Party and her support of the party's platform advocating a revolutionary class struggle to conquer the capitalist state and institute communism.

In *Whitney v. California* (1927), the Supreme Court rejected Ms. Whitney's argument that the Syndicalism Act violated her rights to free speech, expression, and association. With little analysis of the free speech ramifications, the majority observed that "the offense denounced by the [Syndicalism] Act is the combining with others in an association for the accomplishment of the desired ends through the advocacy and use of criminal and unlawful methods" and that "such united and joint action involves even greater danger to the public peace and security than the isolated utterances and acts of individuals." Accordingly, the majority held that the Syndicalism Act was not an unreasonable or arbitrary exercise of the police power of the State, and therefore constitutional.

In one of the most well-known opinions regarding free speech ever issued by a Supreme Court Justice, Louis Brandeis, joined by Justice Oliver Wendell Holmes, Jr., authored an impassioned concurrence in defense of free speech rights. Justice Brandeis observed that the Syndicalism Act prohibited not only the practice of criminal syndicalism, but also the mere association with those who proposed to advocate criminal syndicalism. He also noted that the Court had not settled on a fixed understanding of the clear and present danger test for determining when abridging the rights of free speech and assembly would be justified.

But Brandeis's most well-known contribution to First Amendment jurisprudence was his full-throated argument in favor of broad rights to free speech. Brandeis's strong defense of free speech merits directly quoting some of his more powerful passages. Brandeis noted:

> Those who won our independence believed that the final end of the State was to make men free to develop their faculties, and that, in its government, the deliberative forces should prevail over the arbitrary. They valued liberty both as an end, and as a means. They believed liberty to be the secret of happiness, and courage to be the secret of liberty. They believed that freedom to think as you will and to speak

> as you think are means indispensable to the discovery and spread of political truth; that, without free speech and assembly, discussion would be futile; that, with them, discussion affords ordinarily adequate protection against the dissemination of noxious doctrine; that the greatest menace to freedom is an inert people; that public discussion is a political duty, and that this should be a fundamental principle of the American government.

Brandeis continued, arguing that:

> Fear of serious injury cannot alone justify suppression of free speech and assembly. Men feared witches and burnt women. It is the function of speech to free men from the bondage of irrational fears. To justify suppression of free speech, there must be reasonable ground to fear that serious evil will result if free speech is practiced. There must be reasonable ground to believe that the danger apprehended is imminent. There must be reasonable ground to believe that the evil to be prevented is a serious one.
>
> . . .
>
> In order to support a finding of clear and present danger, it must be shown either that immediate serious violence was to be expected or was advocated, or that the past conduct furnished reason to believe that such advocacy was then contemplated.
>
> Those who won our independence by revolution were not cowards. They did not fear political change. They did not exalt order at the cost of liberty. To courageous, self-reliant men, with confidence in the power of free and fearless reasoning applied through the processes of popular government, no danger flowing from speech can be deemed clear and present unless the incidence of the evil apprehended is so imminent that it may befall before there is opportunity for full discussion. If there be time to expose through discussion the falsehood and fallacies, to avert the evil by the processes of education, the remedy to be applied is more speech, not enforced silence.
>
> . . .
>
> The fact that speech is likely to result in some violence or in destruction of property is not enough to justify its suppression. There must be the probability of serious injury to the State. Among free men, the deterrents ordinarily to be applied to prevent crime are education and punishment for violations of the law, not abridgment of the rights of free speech and assembly.

Justice Brandeis believed that most speech and association should *not* be considered a "crime against the state" but rather that broad speech rights were essential to a healthy state. Justice Brandeis's more libertarian view of free speech rights would be vindicated four decades later when, in *Brandenburg v. Ohio* (1969), the Supreme Court struck down a similar criminal syndicalism law, abandoned the clear and present danger test in favor of the imminent incitement test, and overruled *Whitney v. California*.

See Also: *Brandenburg v. Ohio* (1969); Clear and Present Danger Test; Criminal Syndicalism; Speech as Crime against the State

Resources

Whitney v. California, 274 U.S. 357 (1927).

Wilmington Insurrection of 1898

The Wilmington Insurrection of 1898 was a violent—and successful—overthrow of elected government. Described by some as the only successful coup d'état to occur in US history, it is perhaps the most significant example of election-related violence committed by white supremacists in the American South. As with the Colfax Massacre (1873), The Battle of Liberty Place (1874), and the Eufaula Election Massacre and Spring Hill Insurrection (1874), the purpose of the Wilmington Insurrection was to retake control of governments that had been lost by white Democrats through enfranchisement of Black voters and the federal government's Reconstruction policies.

By the late 1890s, Wilmington, North Carolina, was a shining example of a mixed-race community. The largest city in North Carolina at the time, the important port city was governed by a multi-racial "Fusionist" government comprised of Republicans and Populists, supported in large part by Black voters, poor white farmers, and a few pro-Reconstruction white members of the middle and upper class. The government included Black men in elected and appointed roles, such as city aldermen, police officers, and magistrates. Wilmington's Black professional class included sixty-five doctors, lawyers, and teachers. Numerous Black-owned businesses proliferated, including in the city's central business district. Black residents were buying property, owning their own homes. And the Black male literacy rate exceeded that of whites. In fact, Wilmington was home to the only Black-owned daily newspaper in the United States at the time, the *Wilmington Daily Record*, owned and edited by Alexander Manly.

In 1896, Fusionists won every state-wide election in North Carolina, including the governorship. Residents of Wilmington were represented in Congress by a Black representative. This political success served as the final catalyst for the backlash from a white supremacy-based Democratic Party that determined to retake control in 1898. Furnifold Simmons, who had briefly served as a member of Congress in the late 1880s before he was unseated by a Black Republican, was the architect of the Democratic Party's 1898 statewide campaign. A Democratic Party handbook, published in the summer of 1898, made clear its intention: "This is a white man's country and white men must control and govern it" (State Democratic Executive Committee of North Carolina 1898, 38). Throughout the state, Simmons established "White Government Unions" of local white supremacists who met regularly to strategize a return to power.

By the 1890s, the Democratic Party's tactics had been well-rehearsed throughout the South. Democratic leader and editor of the *Raleigh News and Observer* Josephus Daniels observed that the Party relied on a three-pronged attack to win the 1898 election: men who could write, men who could speak, and men who could "ride." The Democratic Party employed newspaper propaganda, inflammatory speakers, and physical intimidation to fan the flames of white supremacy, whipping up a furor against Black participation in government and society that boiled over in the election of 1898.

Newspapers glorified Democrats and vilified Fusionists and Black citizens, often using editorials and vitriolic cartoons depicting Blacks as monkeys, vampires, and the Devil. Daniels even admitted later in life his paper's bias toward Democrats and that its stories were not fully researched and probably could not be "sustained in a court of justice." Newspapers in the state routinely spread claims that Black men were incompetent and that they wanted political power so they could have sex with—or rape—white women, a claim repeated by acclaimed suffragist Rebecca Felton. In a speech in August 1898, Felton promoted lynching to protect white women from being raped by Black men, saying "if it needs lynching to protect woman's dearest possession from the ravening human beasts—then I say lynch, a thousand times a week if necessary." Daniels bragged of the newspaper campaign's success, claiming "people on every side were at such a key of fighting and hate that the Democrats would believe almost any piece of rascality." When Alexander Manly responded to Felton's speech in an editorial opinion in the *Wilmington Daily Record* that white rape of Black women was much more frequent and that intimate contact between white women and Black men was often consensual, the white supremacists of Wilmington would have their rallying cause. Speechmakers such as prominent Democrat and former United States Attorney Charles Aycock and Wilmington Democrat Alfred Moore Waddell used their orations to instigate fear of "Negro domination." Orators sometimes cited Nat Turner's slave revolt to stoke fears of a violent Black uprising and as justification for suppressing Black power. White militias, including the Red Shirts (similar to the White League in other states), acted at the behest of Democratic Party leaders. Often riding on horseback, they intimidated Black voters and anyone who supported them.

The white supremacist plan throughout the state made no attempt at secrecy. On the eve of the state-wide election of 1898, Waddell gave a speech demanding that white men "do your duty" by looking for Black voters. Waddell commanded that if white men found a Black voter they should "tell him to leave the polls and if he refuses kill, shoot him down in his tracks. We shall win tomorrow if we have to do it with guns" (Luckhurst 2021). And win they did. In the 1898 election, the Democrats swept state and local elections.

In Wilmington, several groups of white supremacists planned to retake the city from the Fusionists. In addition to the overt election campaign activities of the Democratic Party, secret groups such as "Group Six" and the "Secret Nine"—a group of influential businessmen led by Hugh MacRae—conspired to regain control. Democratic businessmen used economic tactics to successfully pressure several Wilmington Republican businessmen to align with white supremacy and the Democrats. And employing the state party's three-pronged approach, local leaders relied on speakers, writers, and "riders." In a series of speeches in Wilmington and around the state, Waddell urged whites to "choke the current of the Cape Fear [River] with [Black] carcasses" to win the election and escape "the intolerable conditions under which we live" (Waddell 1898). The city's white-owned newspapers printed not only Democratic campaign rhetoric, but inflammatory articles concerning threats of Black violence, excerpts of speeches by Waddell and other white supremacists, and glorification of Red Shirt and White Government Union activity. These groups regularly held rallies and paraded through African American neighborhoods brandishing weapons.

November 8, 1898—Election Day—was a tense, but largely peaceful day in Wilmington. As was the case throughout the state, Wilmington area Democrats secured victory in state local elections due to the successful intimidation tactics that kept many Black voters from the polls, some outright election fraud in counting ballots, and some prior Fusionist capitulation in not putting forward Black candidates in some elections to preserve peace. Despite the victory, the Democrats were unsatisfied, especially because the Fusionist city government would remain in power until the following year's city elections. The white supremacist frenzy created before the election was not quelled by the election victory.

The day after the election, Waddell gave a speech at a large assembly of white voters. Led by Waddell and MacRae, a group of white leaders created and articulated a White Man's Declaration of Independence. The group then communicated its demands to the leaders of the African American community, demands that included the removal of Alexander Manly from the city. When the group of Black leaders did not reply by the time specified on the morning of November 10, Waddell led a crowd to a local armory. Using Manly's earlier editorial comments about white rape of Black women and consensual romance between the races as pretext, Waddell and many hundreds of armed white men rode into Wilmington and torched the *Daily Record* building, destroying the printing press.

Manly had been alerted to the impending violence and escaped the city, pretending at one Red Shirt checkpoint to be white. Armed with rifles, pistols, and even a Gatling gun, the mob then spread throughout the town, killing as many as sixty Black residents and destroying Black-owned businesses and homes. Though several white men were wounded in the conflict, none were killed. Waddell and his men ultimately turned their sights on local government, transforming the riotous massacre into an insurrection. They marched to city hall and, at gunpoint, demanded the resignation of the Republican mayor, the Board of Aldermen, and chief of police. The officials all promptly resigned, and Waddell declared himself to be mayor.

After the insurrection, thousands of Black residents fled Wilmington, decimating the Republican political base and returning the balance of political power to the Democrats. The Black middle class declined, many Black businesses shuttered, and the Black residents who remained moved their businesses and homes from the central business district to traditionally Black neighborhoods. Schools attended by Black students received significantly less funding than white schools, and Black literacy rates quickly dropped. The formerly Black-majority city became a white-majority city. After the insurrection, no Black citizen served in public office in Wilmington until 1972.

The events in Wilmington on November 10, 1898, were not isolated, but rather part of a well-documented and overt statewide conspiracy by upper-class white businessmen to regain control of government in North Carolina using any means necessary. The massacre of Black citizens and violent takeover of a duly elected government in Wilmington were not covered up, but rather celebrated and used to promote white supremacy throughout the state and the South. As the 1898 Wilmington Race Riot Commission concluded, "Because Wilmington rioters were able to murder blacks in daylight and overthrow a legitimately elected Republican government without penalty or federal intervention everyone in the state, regardless of race, knew that the white supremacy campaign was victorious on all fronts."

As it did throughout the South, the successful return to power by white supremacist Democrats in North Carolina led to active continuing efforts to disenfranchise Black citizens. In 1899, the legislature passed a law requiring new voters to pay a poll tax and a state constitutional amendment requiring voters to demonstrate they could read and write any section of the Constitution. Because the latter requirement discriminated against not only many Black residents of the state, but also many illiterate whites, the amendment included a "grandfather clause" that allowed a voter to bypass the literacy requirement if they or one of their lineal ancestors were eligible to vote prior to January 1, 1867. These efforts were profoundly successful. In 1896, 126,000 Black men had registered to vote in North Carolina. In 1902, the number was 6,100. With the ensuing white supremacist-based Democratic Party control, racial hierarchy laws known as "Jim Crow" would predominate for decades to come.

In the years after the Wilmington insurrection, men seeking stature in the Democratic Party and with voters would proudly claim to have participated in the attack. And the leaders of the insurrection were indeed rewarded. After usurping the office, Afred Waddell was elected mayor of Wilmington in 1899, an office he held until 1905. Hugh MacRae was elected to be a Wilmington city alderman and donated land for a "whites only" park near Wilmington that bore his name until 2020. Charles Aycock was elected governor of North Carolina in 1900. In a 1903 speech in Baltimore, Maryland, titled "The Negro Problem," Aycock proclaimed "I am proud of my State … because there we have solved the negro problem … We have taken him out of politics and have thereby secured good government under any party and laid foundations for the future development of both races. We have secured peace, and rendered prosperity a certainty" (Connor and Poe 1912, 161–2). Josephus Daniels was appointed Secretary of the Navy by President Woodrow Wilson, and Ambassador to Mexico by President Franklin D. Roosevelt. Rebecca Felton was appointed by the Governor of Georgia to serve temporarily in the United States Senate, becoming the first female Senator in United States history. Furniford Simmons served as a United States Senator from North Carolina for thirty years.

For many years, the insurrection was cast by politicians, journalists, and even some historians, as a race riot started by Black residents and put down by heroic white citizens who were preserving peace and defending white honor. These narratives usually blamed Alexander Manly for pushing whites too far in attempting to revolutionize the social order. Today some still attempt to characterize the insurrection as noble and necessary. In 2005, a group purporting to be the "1898 Wilmington Institute for Education & Research" produced a website claiming "to clearly show the various reasons for the change in government and violence in Wilmington in November, 1898" (1898 Wilmington Institute 2005). The "Institute" then blamed Black citizens for the violence and argued the insurrection was not a coup, but rather a rightful replacement of a local government illegally controlled by the Republican governor. Charles Aycock is quoted extensively, including his white supremacist views.

In 2000, over 100 years after the insurrection, the North Carolina General Assembly enacted legislation creating a commission to examine the events of November 10, 1898, and its effects. Even this commission was called the 1898 Wilmington *Race Riot* Commission, though it produced an exhaustive account that concluded that the insurrection was "part of a statewide effort to put white supremacist Democrats in office and stem the political advances of black citizens." The Commission recommended ten pieces of legislation aimed to address the long-standing damage to the Black community caused by the Wilmington Insurrection; the North Carolina Legislature enacted none of them.

Actions in the modern era demonstrate that the racial hostilities underlying the Wilmington Insurrection have not been completely resolved. In June 2020, three Wilmington police officers were fired after a recording emerged in which they used racial slurs. Echoing the sentiments of Simmons, Waddell, Felton, MacRae, and Aycock from a century before, one officer vowed to "go out and start slaughtering them f[ing] [Black people]" and "wipe 'em off the f[ing] map" to "put 'em back four or five generations." Another officer referred to an African American judge in Wilmington as a "f[ing] negro magistrate" (Castagno 2020).

After the failed Capitol Insurrection on January 6, 2021, historians and journalists drew parallels to the successful Wilmington insurrection, noting the similarities in attempts by politicians to undermine election results. The lack of accountability for the perpetrators of the Wilmington insurrection, which opened the door to the decades of trampling African Americans' civil rights that followed, was highlighted as a reason why accountability for the Capitol Insurrection was essential. Interestingly, many of the insurrectionists who stormed the Capitol on January 6 streamed—perhaps unknowingly—past a statue of Charles Aycock displayed in the United States Capitol's Statuary Hall over 100 years after the successful insurrection he helped foment.

See Also: Battle of Liberty Place (1874); Capitol Insurrection on January 6, 2021; Colfax Massacre (1873); Conspiracy, Criminal; Eufaula Election Massacre and Spring Hill Insurrection (1874); Insurrection; Turner, Nat

Resources

1898 Wilmington Institute for Education & Research. 2005. "1898 Wilmington Race Riot." Accessed November 3, 2023. http://www.1898wilmington.org/.

"1898 Wilmington Race Riot Report." *1898 Wilmington Race Riot Commission*, May 31, 2006.

Castagno, Peter. 2020. "Wilmington NC Police Officers Fired after Genocidal Comments: 'We Are Just Going to Go Out and Start Slaughtering Them F—— Ni——.'" June 28, 2020. Accessed November 3, 2023. https://citizentruth.org/wilmington-nc-police-fired-90-cases-dropped-after-audio-revealed-cops-wanted-to-slaughter-them-fing-ns/.

Connor, Robert D. W., and Clarence Poe. 1912. *The Life and Speeches of Charles Brantley Aycock*. New York: Doubleday, Page and Company.

Luckhurst, Toby. 2021. "Wilmington 1898: When White Supremacists Overthrew a US Government." *BBC*, January 17, 2021. Accessed June 19, 2023. https://www.bbc.com/news/world-us-canada-55648011.

Prather, Leon. 2006. *We Have Taken a City: The Wilmington Racial Massacre and Coup of 1898*. Wilmington, NC: Dram Tree Books.

State Democratic Executive Committee of North Carolina. 1898. The Democratic Hand Book.

Umfleet, LeRae Sikes. 2020. *A Day of Blood: The 1898 Wilmington Race Riot*. Durham: North Carolina Office of Archives and History.

Waddell, Alfred Moore. 1898. "Waddell Speech, Thalian Hall, Wilmington, NC, October 24, 1898." Accessed November 4, 2023. https://core.ecu.edu/umc/wilmington/scans/ticketTwo/waddellSpeech.pdf.

Zucchino, David. 2020a. "The 1898 Wilmington Massacre Is an Essential Lesson in How State Violence Has Targeted Black Americans." *Time*, July 1, 2020.

Zucchino, David. 2020b. *Wilmington's Lie (Winner of the 2021 Pulitzer Prize): The Murderous Coup of 1898 and the Rise of White Supremacy*. New York: Atlantic Monthly Press.

Wolverine Watchmen

The Wolverine Watchmen (Watchmen) was a relatively small and unknown group among a subset of groups in the Militia Movement who refer to themselves as "boogaloo boys" or the "boogaloo movement." The boogaloo movement is a loosely related collection of groups united by a desire for a second American Civil War or American Revolution. Among several grievances, the Watchmen objected to various restrictions imposed by Michigan Governor Gretchen Whitmer and the Michigan government during the Covid-19 pandemic in 2020. The Watchmen gained notoriety when the Federal Bureau of Investigation (FBI) exposed their plot to kidnap Governor Whitmer, attack the state capitol, attack law enforcement personnel, and overthrow the government.

Though the Watchmen discussed numerous plans for attacking government personnel, and participated in protests at the Michigan State Capitol that some alleged were opportunities to surveil the building for a later attack, the group ultimately settled on kidnapping Governor Whitmer and either abandoning her on a boat in the middle of Lake Michigan or taking her to Wisconsin and subjecting her to trial for being a tyrant. The Watchmen trained in a variety of ways, including weapons training, making improvised explosive devices, and assaulting a faux building some members had constructed from PVC pipes and plywood they called the "kill house." The group conducted physical surveillance of Governor Whitmer's vacation lake home, though some members had difficulty locating the house. After conducting surveillance, the Watchmen determined that in order to slow law enforcement response and aid in their escape, they would blow up a bridge. When several Watchmen arrived at a warehouse to purchase explosives for the bridge destruction, they were arrested by FBI agents. As other members would soon discover, several "members" of the group were FBI informants.

During its investigation of the group, the FBI discovered the Watchmen had purportedly discussed kidnapping Virginia Governor Ralph Northam and South Carolina Governor Henry McMaster. The FBI also found one Watchmen member's hit list of politicians he wanted to hang as "anti-Americans."

After the foiled kidnapping plot, several members of the Watchmen were charged with a variety of federal and state crimes, including conspiracy to commit kidnapping, conspiracy to use a weapon of mass destruction, and providing material support for terrorist acts. Several men were convicted in federal and state court trials, though some were also acquitted.

The Watchmen's almost comically inept plans and efforts led many to believe they never posed a serious threat of kidnapping the governor or launching a meaningful attack against state government. Furthermore, at trial, it was argued they were simply "big talkers" whose talk amounted to no criminal actions and was even protected by the First Amendment. And the significant role of several FBI informants in leading the training and planning for the purported kidnapping led some members to claim they had been entrapped by the FBI.

Michigan Attorney General Dana Nessel asserted the Watchmen were engaged in far more than inappropriate comments and were, in fact, domestic terrorists. Attorney General Nessel also contended that some protests in which the Watchmen had participated at the Michigan State Capitol were practice for the Capitol Insurrection on January 6, 2021. Governor Whitmer, the target of the plot, stated the Watchmen were more appropriately characterized as domestic terrorists than militia members. She blamed President Donald Trump in part, saying he had given "comfort to those who spread fear and hatred and division" (Egan 2020). After leaving office, President Trump characterized the kidnapping plot as a "fake deal," implying there had never been a legitimate plan or intent to kidnap the governor (C-Span 2020).

See Also: American Civil War and Treason; American Revolution and Treason; Capitol Insurrection on January 6, 2021; Conspiracy, Criminal; Insurrection; Material Support Crimes; Militia Movement (Modern); Seditious Conspiracy; Weapons of Mass Destruction

Resources

"Barry Croft Jr. Sentenced to More than 19 Years for Role in Plot to Kidnap Michigan Governor Gretchen Whitmer." 2022. *CBS News*, December 28, 2022.

Bensinger, Ken, and Jessica Garrison. 2021. "Watching the Watchmen." *BuzzFeed News*, July 20, 2021.

C-Span. 2020. "President Trump on Gov. Whitmer Kidnapping Plot." October 17, 2020. Accessed November 3, 2023. https://www.c-span.org/video/?c4916262/president-trump-gov-whitmer-kidnapping-plot.

Egan, Paul. 2020. "Gov. Whitmer Denounces Hate Groups, Says President Donald Trump Is 'Complicit.'" *Detroit Free Press*, October 8, 2020.

Fawcett, Eliza. 2022. "Three Michigan Men Sentenced to Prison Terms for Aiding Plot against Whitmer." *New York Times*, December 15, 2022.

King, Jon. 2022. "Wolverine Watchmen Defendants Sentenced to Prison over Plot to Kidnap and Murder Whitmer." *Michigan Advance*, December 15, 2022.

World Trade Center Bombing of 1993

After the events of September 11, 2001, many have described the 1993 World Trade Center Bombing as "forgotten," or worse "unknown" to the average American today. Yet, the attack killed six, injured over 1,000, and was, up to that point in time, the deadliest act of international terrorism that had occurred on US soil. It was the warning shot across the bow of the United States and tragically foreshadowed a much deadlier attack on the World Trade Center eight and half years later. Additionally, the planned scale of the 1993 attack was immense in scope and, had it been successful, could have even surpassed the carnage of 9/11. The 1993 plot leader, Ramzi Yousef, admitted to the Federal Bureau of Investigation (FBI) that the plan contemplated a sufficiently powerful explosion in the subterrain parking garage below the North Tower to destroy the building and cause the North Tower to topple over into the South Tower. Yousef admitted that he hoped his plan would kill 250,000 Americans in and around the World Trade Center complex. Ironically, according to experts, Yousef's plan might have succeeded had he parked his explosive packed van closer to the World Trade Center's poured concrete foundation. The vehicle was parked away from the foundation, not adversely impacting the structural integrity of the building. Even so, the detonation caused a blast crater approximately six stories deep and 200 feet wide.

The 1993 attack took place on February 26, 1993, at about 12:17 pm. The plot was schemed up by a small group of anti-American Islamic terrorists who wished to punish America for its foreign policy and support of Israel. One of the conspirators to the plot was Mohammed Salameh, who rented a van that accomplices packed with highly explosive chemicals and parked under the World Trade Center Complex. Unwisely, Salameh returned to the rental car company on March 4, 1993, trying to get his $400 security deposit back, claiming the vehicle had been stolen. Unbeknownst to Salameh, through incredible crime scene work, FBI analysts were able to retrieve the vehicle identification number from the vehicle and trace it back to Salameh's rental. In a subsequent search of Salameh's apartment, other suspects were identified and arrested. The police also found bomb-making material tied to the men in a New York storage facility.

After a trial involving 1,000 exhibits, 200 witnesses, and over four months of court proceedings, the four primary culprits of the 1993 bombing were tried, convicted, and sentenced to life in prison on March 4, 1994. Yet, the man considered the mastermind behind the plot, Ramzi Yousef, was not captured until 1995, and only after he participated in other terrorist plots around the globe. Yousef was finally convicted in 1997 and sentenced in a United States District Court in January 1998, receiving a sentence of life imprisonment plus 240 additional years. Yousef proclaimed to the judge and the courtroom observers "Yes, I am a terrorist and proud of it."

In the investigation of the 1993 bombing, investigators were led to a radical extremist Islamic cleric named Omar Abdel Rahman, known to many as the "Blind Sheikh." Rahman preached violence against the United States for its support of Israel and Egypt, and several of the 1993 bombing defendants attended his mosque. Rahman had been twice tried and acquitted for attempting to incite the assassination of Egyptian President Anwar Sadat. However, because of the excellent investigative work tying the 1993 bombers to Rahman and conducting additional surveillance, on June 24, 1994, FBI agents caught a group of men associated with Rahman constructing bombs in a warehouse to be used for future attacks. Rahman and his accomplices were charged with planning to simultaneously blow up the Holland and Lincoln Tunnels (under the Hudson River), the George Washington Bridge, and the United Nations headquarters. Rahman and his fellow accomplices were all found guilty in 1995 and sentenced to life in prison. Rahman was also charged and convicted of seditious conspiracy, a serious federal offense used sparingly and only a handful to times since its original passage as a law during the American Civil War. After the Capitol Insurrection on January 6, 2021, approximately a dozen defendants (members of either the Proud Boys or Oath Keepers) have pled guilty or been found guilty by a jury of seditious conspiracy, the first time the federal government has utilized seditious conspiracy since the Rahman prosecution. Journalist Peter Bergen has stated that, while in prison and until his death in 2017, Rahman continued to exert a powerful influence over radical Muslims. Bergen described Rahman as the "spiritual guide of 9/11" (Schudel 2017).

Just as the Blind Sheik had radicalized and incited many to plan various terrorist attacks and execute the 1993 World Trade Center bombing, the chief architect of the bombing was encouraged and supported by his uncle, Khalid Sheikh Mohammed (KSM). KSM had sent his nephew money and resources for various terrorism plans, including wiring funds before the 1993 World Trade Center Bombing. After Ramzi Yousef's arrest in 1995, KSM continued to rise in the ranks of the Al-Qaeda terrorist network, eventually becoming a top aide to Osama Bin Laden and considered to be the "principal architect" of September 11, 2001. Thus, the actors behind these terrorists' attacks and the events themselves should not be viewed in isolation as there were many connections. Tragically, the 1993 World Trade Center bombing would be surpassed in its lethality by the 1995 Oklahoma City Bombing and the 9/11 terrorist attacks.

See Also: American Civil War and Treason; Assassination; Capitol Insurrection on January 6, 2021; Oklahoma City Bombing (1995); Seditious Conspiracy; September 11, 2001; Terrorism

Resources

"1993: World Trade Center Bomb Terrorizes New York." *BBC News: On This Day*. Accessed February 18, 2023. http://news.bbc.co.uk/onthisday/hi/dates/stories/february/26/newsid_2516000/2516469.stm.

Agrawal, Nina. 2018. "First World Trade Center Bombing, Long since Overshadowed by 9/11, Is Remembered on 25th Anniversary." *The Los Angeles Times*, February 26, 2018. Accessed February 18, 2023. https://www.latimes.com/nation/la-na-world-trade-center-1993-htmlstory.html.

Bashinsky, Ruth. 2017. "At World Trade Center Memorial, a Bombing Is Forgotten." *The New York Times*, February 20, 2017. Accessed February 18, 2023. https://www.nytimes.com/2017/02/19/nyregion/world-trade-center-memorial-1993-bombing-forgotten.html.

CNN Editorial Research. 2023. "1993 World Trade Center Bombing Fast Facts." Accessed February 18, 2023. https://www.cnn.com/2013/11/05/us/1993-world-trade-center-bombing-fast-facts/.

Peltz, Jennifer. 2018. "Precursor to 9/11; Trade Center Bomb Echoes after 25 Years." *AP News*, April 21, 2018. Accessed February 18, 2023. https://apnews.com/article/north-america-bombings-new-york-ap-top-news-us-news-ef2094670c454917831ae081c5a516a0.

Schudel, Matt. 2017. "Omar Abdel Rahman, Imprisoned 'Blind Sheikh' Linked to Terrorist Efforts, Dies at 78." *The Washington Post*, February 18, 2017. Accessed November 3, 2023. https://www.washingtonpost.com/world/omar-abdel-rahman-blind-sheik-convicted-in-1993-world-trade-center-attack-dies-at-78/2017/02/18/807c4f2c-f603-11e6-8d72-263470bf0401_story.html.

Wright, Lawrence. 2006. *The Looming Towers: Al Qaeda and the Road to 9/11*. New York: Knopf.

Y

Yates v. United States (1957)

In 1951, fourteen leaders of the Communist Party of California were convicted in federal district court of violating the Smith Act for "conspiring (1) to advocate and teach the duty and necessity of overthrowing the Government of the United States by force and violence, and (2) to organize, as the Communist Party of the United States, a society of persons who so advocate and teach, all with the intent of causing the overthrow of the Government by force and violence as speedily as circumstances would permit."

The Supreme Court overturned the convictions on the basis that the trial court had misunderstood the Supreme Court's prior guidance in *Dennis v. United States* (1951). Specifically, the Supreme Court believed the trial court had incorrectly interpreted *Dennis* to mean that mere doctrinal advocacy of forcible overthrow of the government was punishable if the defendant(s) were engaged in such advocacy with the intent to accomplish the overthrow of the government. In *Yates*, the Supreme Court clarified that such advocacy was "too remote from concrete action" to be regarded as the kind of indoctrination preparatory to *action* the Court had condemned in *Dennis*. The *Yates* Court explained that "[t]he essence of the *Dennis* holding was that indoctrination of a group in preparation for future violent action, as well as exhortation to immediate action," by advocacy found to be directed to *action* and employing "language of incitement," is not constitutionally protected "when the group is of sufficient size and cohesiveness, is sufficiently oriented towards action, and other circumstances are such as reasonably to justify apprehension that action will occur." To the *Yates* Court, the essential distinction is that, for the Smith Act to apply, those to whom the advocacy of government overthrow is addressed "must be urged to *do* something, now or in the future, rather than merely to *believe in* something."

The Supreme Court determined that the prosecution's theory of the case in *Yates* was that the fourteen charged defendants had all been members of the Communist Party of California, that the Party constituted a conspiratorial group, and that membership in the conspiracy could therefore be proved by showing that the individual petitioners were actively identified with the Party's affairs, and thus they were parties to the Party's tenets. The Court acknowledged that if advocacy of the abstract doctrine of forcible overthrow was sufficient under the Smith Act, the evidence would have been sufficient to show that the Communist Party engaged in such advocacy. But the Supreme Court found that the evidence of actual advocacy to *action* by the individual defendants or the Communist Party of California was lacking in the case. Thus, the flaw in the prosecution's case was not the idea that membership in a group alone could make one guilty of conspiracy to overthrow the government, but rather that the evidence was insufficient to demonstrate that the group had actually advocated action to overthrow the government.

Importantly, the Supreme Court's decision in *Yates* was not premised on a newly articulated understanding of the First Amendment, or on a constitutional basis at all. Rather, the Court held that the trial court had incorrectly misinformed the jury as to what the Smith Act actually prohibited. A little over one decade later, in *Brandenburg v. Ohio* (1969), the Supreme Court would articulate a new understanding of what speech the First Amendment does and does not protect in this area.

See Also: *Brandenburg v. Ohio* (1969); Conspiracy, Criminal; *Dennis v. United States* (1951); Smith Act

Resources

Yates v. United States, 354 U.S. 298 (1957).

Year of the Spy (1985)

In the United States, espionage and spying can be traced back to the American Revolution and the actions of Benedict Arnold. Since the end of the Second World War, there have been numerous high-profile cases of espionage and spying, usually involving the Soviet Union, and after 1993, Russia. Examples of notorious early post-Second World War cases involved Alger Hiss, Julius and Ethel Rosenberg, and Rudolph Abel, among others. High-profile cases involving alleged violations of the Espionage Act of 1917 continued in the first and second decades of the twenty-first century, involving individuals such as Edward Snowden, Bradley/Chelsea Manning, and Jack Teixeira (see Leaks of National Defense Information). Yet, throughout American history, one year in particular stands out as being particularly damaging to the United States as relating to espionage: 1985. Consequently, 1985 has been dubbed "The Year of the Spy."

The year 1985 was especially damaging to the United States for two main reasons: first, there were an unusual high number of American governmental officials caught engaged in espionage in 1985; and second, virtually all the US foreign intelligence operatives were lost (i.e., killed/executed) in the Soviet Union over an eighteen-month period. A career Central Intelligence Agency (CIA) officer stated that "the inventory of lost agents and operations over the last fifteen months was devasting" (Bearden and Risen 2003, 191). At its climax, news of American sources being identified and executed by the Soviet Union was received almost on a weekly basis. In subsequent years, within the hallways of CIA headquarters at Langley, CIA officials referred to "the losses of 1985" in describing the carnage of that particular year. The losses of foreign espionage assets assisting the United States were so high primarily because of the actions of two American traitors, Federal Bureau of Investigation (FBI) agent Robert Hanssen and CIA analyst Aldrich Ames, who both began providing the Soviet Union the identities/names of American foreign assets as well as other sensitive materials in great volume in 1985. In fact, the high loss of foreign agents is what convinced the CIA of the presence of a "mole" within the agency. The CIA initiated a "mole hunt" in 1985 that would eventually lead in 1993 to Aldrich Ames being identified as one of the two spies responsible for the losses, and Ames was arrested in 1994. Hanssen was not arrested until 2001, in part because the United States attributed its many asset losses in 1985 (and to lesser extent in other years) chiefly to Ames, which delayed the investigation and apprehension of Hanssen for seven more years.

If 1985 were not sufficiently unusual, the Year of the Spy also saw the double defection of one of highest Soviet defectors to ever switch over (temporarily) to the United States, Vitaly Yurchenko, a high-ranking KGB intelligence officer. Yurchenko defected to the United States in August 1985, provided tantalizing intelligence on an array of Soviet intelligence practices (and information damning Ronald William Pelton and Edward Lee Howard, two American spies captured in 1985). However, by November 1985, Yurchenko had escaped his US detail team and re-defected back to the Soviet Union, bizarrely claiming at a press conference that he had been drugged by CIA agents in Rome, brought to the United States, and interrogated over the course of three months. When the CIA presented various signed "confessions" written in Yurchenko's own handwriting, and tape recordings of Yurchenko in his own voice freely giving up Soviet state secrets, Yurchenko and the Soviets claimed that all the damning evidence was provided "always when he was under the influence of the CIA's drugs" (Bearden and Risen 2003, 142). Perhaps one of the strangest aspects of the Yurchenko story was the fact that when he first arrived in the United States to be debriefed, he was first met by Aldrich Ames, who individually debriefed Yurchenko. America's biggest yet-to-be-discovered traitor and spy, Aldrich Ames, interviewed one of the highest-ranking defections from KGB intelligence. A high-ranking CIA officer suggested that Ames insisted on being the first interviewer of Yurchenko to establish for himself that Yurchenko did not know that Ames was a Soviet spy and the highest-ranking "mole" within the CIA. If Yurchenko had such knowledge, Ames would be exposed as a spy. Thus,

> Ames decided he had to test Yurchenko as soon as possible. So in the back of the car as they drove away from Andrews [Andrews Air Force Base], he broke off their conversation long enough to hand him a note that he had prepared earlier. 'If you have any particularly important information which you wish to provide only to the Director [of the CIA] or another senior U.S. official, tell me, and I will take you to him.' Yurchenko grinned at Ames and said he had no message that required such special care. The confirmation came as a relief [to Ames] (Bearden and Risen 2003, 79).

Beyond the extraordinarily high number of American spies executed by the Soviet Union in 1985 due to the treachery of Ames and Hanssen, the other reason that 1985 was dubbed the Year of the Spy was because of the high number of arrests that year of Americans spying for foreign countries. There were at least fourteen arrests for espionage associated with 1985—nine of which were considered prominent cases: John Anthony Walker, Edward Lee Howard, Jonathan Jay Pollard, Clayton Lonetree, Larry Wu-Tai Chin, Ronald William Pelton, Richard Kelly Smyth, Sharon W. Scranage, and Randy Miles Jeffries. Walker, Pollard, Chin, and Pelton are covered separately in this book. Some additional information involving those *not* covered elsewhere is briefly summarized here.

Clayton Lonetree was a United States Marine Sergeant stationed in Moscow to provide security at the American Embassy. He was targeted and "had fallen into the oldest KGB trap in the business … the classic 'honey trap'" (Bearden and Risen 2003, 195). Lonetree, lonely and single, was targeted by a 25-year-old KGB agent named Violetta Seina. An intimate secret "relationship" developed between the two, despite the clear American policy prohibiting the fraternization between Marine Guards and Soviet women. Then, once Lonetree was compromised, Seina introduced Lonetree to her "Uncle Sasha," who was a more senior KGB handler who began to blackmail intelligence from Lonetree (Bearden and Risen 2003, 195). When Lonetree was reassigned to security at the American embassy in Vienna, "Uncle Sasha" followed him there. Wracked with guilt of spying for the Soviets throughout 1985, Lonetree pulled aside the CIA head officer in Vienna at a Christmas party and openly confessed. Lonetree was so distressed that he was described by a CIA agent as "terrified," and "barely under control, almost psychotic" (Bearden and Risen 2003, 193). He turned himself in of his own volition in 1986, was court-martialed, and served nine years for his espionage. Much of the damage from leaked intelligence initially attributed to Lonetree was later determined to have come from Ames.

In another "honey trap" scheme, Sharon Scranage, a young CIA secretary working in Ghana, was seduced by Michael Agboutui Soussoudis, a Ghanese agent, to solicit US intelligence. Scranage discussed the names of CIA informants operating in Ghana. Some information from Scranage was passed on to the intelligence services in Cuba, Libya, and East Germany. Scranage received a five-year sentence for violating the Espionage Act and the Intelligence Identities Protection Act.

Edward Lee Howard was a former CIA agent, who was hired by the CIA in 1980, but fired in 1983 when it was revealed that he lied about his past and had substance abuse issues. It was believed that Howard began revealing classified information in 1984. In 1985, Yurchenko named Howard and Pelton as spies. Knowing he was under surveillance and investigation, Howard defected to the Soviet Union in late 1985 and lived in Russia until his death in 2002.

Unlike most of the captured spies, Richard Kelly Smyth was not a full-time government employee, but a private businessperson who consulted for the government on aerospace issues. Smyth owned his own company, Milco International Incorporated, and provided some services for NASA. In the early 1980s, Smyth illegally exported fifteen shipments containing 810 items known as "krytrons" to a foreign country. A "krytron" is an electrical switch used in triggering the denotation in nuclear devices. He was arrested in May 1985, but jumped bail and fled to Spain, at which point he and his wife lived as fugitives undiscovered until 2001. In July 2001, he was arrested and extradited back to the United States and pleaded guilty in December 2001 for violating provisions of the Arms Export Control Act, which, among other things, prohibited the smuggling of weapon technology to foreign countries.

Lastly, Randy Miles Jeffries was a low-level clerical worker for a company called Acme Reporting, which provided reporting and stenography services to federal agencies. While Jeffries was a clerk for the FBI from 1978 to 1980, he was suspended for heroin possession. His subsequent job with Acme Reporting was to photocopy and bundle classified documents for delivery to various agencies and to dispose of those documents when no longer needed. On December 14, 1985, Jeffries conspired with a coworker to disclose to Soviet intelligence several classified reports, including one called "US House of Representatives, Department of Defense Command Control Communication and Intelligence Programs, C31, Closed Session, Subcommittee on Armed Services, Washington, DC." He distributed these documents successfully on December 14 and again on December 17, when KGB agents paid Jeffries an astonishingly low $60. Jeffries attempted to meet with Soviet intelligence again on December 20 to pass along a few more documents—but this time for a lot more money, namely $50,000. Unfortunately for Jeffries, the December 20 meeting was with FBI undercover agents, and Jeffries was apprehended and arrested. Jeffries pleaded guilty under the Espionage Act and received a three-to-nine-year sentence. Jeffries apologized at his sentencing, claiming he was motivated not by treason or to hurt his country, but rather because of an ongoing drug addiction and utter desperation on his part. As was reported by *UPI*, "Jeffries' December arrest capped off what came to be known as the 'year of the spy' because an unprecedented number of Americans—14—were arrested and charged with espionage" (Neal 1986). However, the Year of the Spy cases did not conclude until Richard Kelly Smyth was finally convicted and sentenced to prison in December 2001.

See Also: Abel, Rudolf Ivanovich; American Revolution and Treason; Ames, Aldrich Hazen "Rich"; Arnold, Benedict; Espionage; Espionage Act of 1917 and Sedition Act of 1918; Chin, Larry Wu-Tai; Conspiracy, Criminal; Hanssen, Robert Philip; Hiss, Alger; Intelligence Identities Protection Act; Leaks of National Defense Information; Pelton, Ronald William; Pollard, Jonathan Jay; Rosenberg, Julius and Ethel; Treason; Walker, John Anthony, Jr.

Resources

Bearden, Mitt, and James Risen. 2003. *The Main Enemy: The Inside Story of the CIA's Final Showdown with the KGB.* Part One: The Year of the Spy, 1–197. Ballantine Books: New York.

Lamar, Jacob V., Jr. 2005. "Spies, Spies, Everywhere." *Time Magazine*, June 21, 2005. Accessed May 19, 2023. https://web.archive.org/web/20080604015023/http://www.time.com/time/magazine/article/0,9171,1074834,00.html.

Neal, Andrea. 1986. "Randy Miles Jeffries Apologized Thursday for Trying to Sell Secrets to the Soviet Union." *UNITED PRESS INTERNATATIONAL (UPI)*, March 13, 1986. Accessed May 19, 2023. https://www.upi.com/Archives/1986/03/13/Randy-Miles-Jeffries-apologized-Thursday-for-trying-to-sell/8784511074000/.

Z

Zenger, John Peter (1697–1746)

The 1735 Trial of John Peter Zenger for seditious libel stands as a seminal case. The trial was a milestone historical moment in formulating early American thought about what freedom of speech should entail prior to the ratification of the First Amendment in 1791, and indeed for years after ratification of the Amendment as well. The resulting acquittal of John Peter Zenger for charges of seditious libel illustrated early American intolerance of seditious libel being a legitimate crime against the state or an act punishable by the state, and the case foreshadowed the eventual death knell of the doctrine in America.

John Peter Zenger was a German immigrant who came to the United States at an early age and began apprenticing for William Bradford, New York's only printer at that time. After the apprenticeship, Zenger began publishing *The New York Weekly Journal.* During this time, the New York Governor (William Cosby) became embroiled in a series of disputes and a lawsuit with the former Royal Governor Rip Van Dam. Cosby also attacked certain members of the sitting judiciary. When Cosby won a lawsuit involving back pay in a two to one verdict by the New York Supreme Court, the dissenting judge (Chief Justice Lewis Morris) in the case wrote a caustic dissenting opinion detailing why he felt the verdict was wrong and that Cosby had attempted to manipulate the New York jury system. Cosby was so infuriated with Morris's dissent that he had him removed from the bench.

At this point, publisher John Peter Zenger entered the fray by reporting favorably on Lewis Morris's candidacy for an assembly seat for Westchester County and publishing articles criticizing Cosby's reign as governor. After several months of strident and critical articles, Cosby set his sights on shutting down Zenger's paper. However, on two separate occasions (in January 1734 and October 1734), the sitting grand jury refused to hand down indictments against Zenger. Cosby was so outraged that the grand jury would not indict Zenger that he ordered New York's public executioner to publicly burn all copies of Zenger's paper. Furthermore, in a clear effort to bypass New York's grand jury system (which had twice refused to indict), Cosby had his attorney general (Richard Bradley) file an "indictment by information" with the court. This led to a bench warrant being issued for Zenger's arrest, wherein Zenger was arrested by the sheriff and spent the next eight months (pending trial) behind bars at New York's Old City Jail. For the period, an outrageously high bail amount of 800 pounds was set to ensure that Zenger would remain behind bars, and pre-trial confinement of eight months was also considered harsh.

At the time, the offense of seditious libel was a crime against the state meant to protect government officials from being scandalized, criticized, or vilified through written or spoken word. And unlike today, the truth of the words spoken or written was not a defense to a conviction for seditious libel. If the speakers' words tended to scandalize or hold the government official in contempt, the crime of seditious libel had been committed, even if the speaker's words were true. Put more simply, nobody had a right to criticize the government, even if the criticism was true.

The next step of the legal proceedings had the effect of revolutionizing free speech cases in the United States for centuries to come and served as a death knell to the English crime of seditious libel being adopted in America. Zenger's lawyer stated that the defense would not contest that Zenger had published the papers and waived the right to examine any of the state witnesses. He argued for the release of the 38-year-old printer, because what Zenger had printed was true and should not be considered a crime in colonial America. Zenger's lawyer argued that "it is the cause of liberty, the liberty both of exposing and opposing arbitrary power by speaking and writing—Truth!" Because the defense lawyer waived the right to examine any witnesses, the presiding judge sent the prosecution witnesses home and instructed the jury that they must find in favor of the prosecution. In addition to explaining to the jury the law of seditious libel and that truth is not a defense, the judge also added: "As [the defense attorney] has confessed the printing and publishing of these libels, I think the jury must find a verdict for the king." In summation in the case, the defense lawyer had offered no laws or facts that would exonerate his client from the English offense of seditious libel, but simply argued that the law of England in this area should not automatically extend to New York or other colonies.

The judge again reiterated to the jury that the facts and evidence were clear and there were therefore no issues to adjudicate. The judge ordered the jury to find Zenger guilty of the charged offense. Yet, a brief time later, the jury returned to the court and announced its verdict of not guilty. Reported yells of "huzzahs" and "shouts of joy" were heard from the gallery.

To be clear, the Zenger verdict set forth no new rules or laws regarding seditious libel in America. Rather, by a grand jury failing to indict twice, and the jury's ultimate return of a not-guilty verdict in the face of a contrary order from the bench, citizens of New York were signaling their distaste and opposition to charges of seditious libel in America. It was the first time in America the press had in essence won the right to criticize the government, using truth as a defense against government attempts at legally stifling speech.

Approximately fifty years later, during the very first session of the United States Congress, members of Congress debated a new proposed Bill of Rights, which included the First Amendment. One of the Congressional members present that day was Gouvenor Morris (the great-grandson of Lewis Morris—removed from the bench by Cosby and the catalyst for the start of the Zenger saga). Morris characterized "The trial of Zenger in 1735 as the gem of American freedom, the morning star of that liberty which subsequently revolutionized America" (*Dennis v. United States* 1950, n173). Influenced by the Zenger trial, the members of the first session of the United States Congress approved of language in the First Amendment that provided Congress shall make no law regarding the abridgement of speech. However, controversially, this constitutional prohibition did not preclude Congress from nevertheless subsequently passing the Sedition Act of 1798 or the Sedition Act of 1918.

See Also: Alien and Sedition Acts (1798); Espionage Act of 1917 and Sedition Act of 1918; Sedition; Sedition Act of 1798; Speech as Crime against the State

Resources

Dennis V. United States. 1950. Brief for Petitioner, 1950 WL 78749, footnote 173.

Finkleman, Paul, ed. 1997. *A Brief Narrative of the Case and Trial of John Peter Zenger*. New York: Brandywine Press.

Lewis, Walker. 1960. "The Right to Complain: The Trial of John Peter Zenger." *American Bar Association Journal* 46 (January): 27–30, 108–11.

Moglen, Eblen. 1994. "Considering Zenger: Partisan Politics and the Legal Profession in Provincial New York." *Columbia Law Review* 94: 1495–524.

Sutherland, Arthur, ed. 1964. "A Brief Narrative of the Case and Trial of John Peter Zenger." *Harvard Law Review* 77: 787–90.

Index

9/11, *see* September 11, 2001

A Plea for Captain John Brown 92, 230
A Theory of Justice 93
Abel, Rudolph 17–18, 437
abortion clinic bombings 328, 413
Abrams v. United States 19–20, 102–3, 152, 182, 186, 342
academic freedom 25, 240
accomplice liability 255, 396
Adams, John
    Alien & Sedition Acts, support of 28–30, 225–6, 344–5
    birthplace of 334–5
    Committee on Spies, member of 35
    criticism of 345
    Direct Tax Act, signed into law 170
    Federalist Party, creation of 409
    Fries's Rebellion, actions in response to 172, 217
    in general 72
    Otis, James, support of 387
Adarand Constructors, Inc. v. Pena 242
Adler v. Board of Education 340
advocacy of illegal action 22, 205, 374
ADX Florence Supermax Prison 292, 329
Afghanistan, US actions in 62, 191, 197, 257, 291, 351
Aid and Comfort
    Burr, U.S. v., as discussed in 77
    Capitol Insurrection, relating to 141
    Carlisle v. U.S., as discussed in 32, 85
    Committee of Spies Resolution, discussed in 35–6
    Confederacy, support of as providing 129, 139
    Cramer v. U.S., as discussed in 118–19, 382
    definition, meaning, and evolution of 21–4, 33–4
    Disqualification Clause, as discussed in 132, 139
    English Treason Statute of 1351, element of 148
    Gadahn, Adam, charges against 180
    in general 347
    Greathouse v. U.S., as discussed in 183–4
    Haupt v. U.S., as discussed in 199
    Propaganda against US type of of 51, 311, 378
    Rhode Island treason law, covered in 142
    Treason Clause, part of 343, 380–2
    Virginia treason law, covered in 397–8
    War of 1812, actions in 283, 409–10
Al-Arian, v. United States 25–6, 265, 390
Al-Awlaki, Anwar 62, 197
Al-Marri v. Hanft 30
Al-Muhajir, Abdullah 413
Al-Qaeda
    capture of operative 221
    in general 43, 197
    Hasan, Nidal, relationship to 198
    intelligence leaked to 194
    Lindh, John Walker, relationship to 257
    military attack against 44
    Padilla, Jose, relationship to 291–2
    propaganda of 62, 180, 381
    September 11, 2001 351–2, 370
    terrorist organization 23, 236, 264, 433
Alcatraz 183, 239
Alfred P. Murrah Building 44, 287, 370, 404
Alien Act 27–8, 225–6, 345
Alien Enemies Act 27–30, 345
Alien Registration Act of 1940, *see* Smith Act
Alien and Sedition Acts
    Adams, John, signed by 28, 170
    in general 44, 211
    Homeland Security Act, relation to 211
    Jefferson, Thomas, opposition to 225–6
    Kentucky and Virginia Resolutions, relation to 344
    main provisions of 28–9, 342
    Sedition Act of 1918, relation to 342–3
    subparts to 27–8, 30, 344
Allen, Walter 417–18
American Airlines Flight 11 351
American Airlines Flight 93 351
American Airlines Flight 77 351
American Airlines Flight 444 233–4
American Civil War—Amnesty and Pardons 31–2, 85, 129–32, 139–40
American Civil War and Treason
    Amnesty and Pardon for 31–2
    analysis of 33–7
    Carlisle v. U.S., discussed in 85
    Davis, Jefferson, relation to 129–33
    Disqualification Clause, relation to 139–40
    Ex Parte Milligan, discussed in 158–9
    Ex Parte Vallandigham, discussed in 162
    in general 129
    Greathouse v. U.S., discussed in 183–4
    largest act of treason 112, 318, 381
    prosecutions, lack thereof 381
    rebellion, example of 316
    Texas v. White, discussed in 373

American Communist Party 356
American flag, *see* Flag Disrespect as Crime against the State
American Revolution and Treason
 analysis of 35–7
 Arnold, Benedict, role in 47–8
 Bacon's Rebellion, influence upon 53
 English Treason Statute, violation of 380
 Espionage, practiced in 150
 Jefferson, Thomas, role in 225
 rebellion, distinguished from 316
 War of 1812, distinguished from 381, 409
Ames, Aldrich
 actions of 38–9
 Chin, Larry, relation to 87
 espionage, leading example of 150
 Espionage Act, violation of 153, 220–1
 Hanssen, Robert, relation to 194
 leaks of intelligence information, leading example of 245
 Walker, John, relation to 406
 Year of the Spy, start of Ames's espionage 439
amnesty, *see* American Civil War—Amnesty and Pardons
Anarchy, Criminal
 analysis of 40–1
 Clear and Present Danger, factor in analysis 103–4
 Gitlow v. New York, discussed in 181
 Haymarket Affair, major factor in 201
 McKinley assassination, factor in 267–8
 Pennsylvania v. Nelson, discussed in 294
 Sacco-Vanzetti Case, major factor in 334–5
 Supreme Court cases, as covered in 363
 syndicalism, relation to 123
Anderson, Osbourne 203
Anderson, Jane 311, 314
Andre, John 47–8
Anthrax attacks 42–3, 389
Anti-Terrorism and Effective Death Penalty Act 44–6, 211, 264, 288, 390, 412
Army-Air Corps 55, 273
Army Court of Criminal Appeals 246, 277
Army of Northern Virginia 34, 254
Arnold, Benedict
 actions of 47–8
 Burr, Aaron, commander of during Revolution 72
 Davis, Jefferson, and Arnold, held in infamy 129
 espionage, early American example 437
 "Founding Traitor," labeled as 150
 highest ranking traitor 129, 273
 Quebec, revolutionary wartime service at 354
Arnold, Samuel 255
Articles of Confederation 257
Aryan Nation 324
Ashcroft, John 25, 257, 389
Assange, Julian 150, 153, 245–7
assassination
 analysis, history, and elements of 49–50
 anarchy statutes, criminalized under 41
 Brown, John, characterized as 230
 Caesar, Julius 380
 Diem, Ngo Dinh, assassination of 295
 federal statute (18 USC 2333), covering 328, 371
 Hatfield, Sid, assassination of 417
 January 6, 2021, threatened assassination 82
 King, Martin Luther, Jr., assassination of 218
 Lincoln, Abraham, assassination of 31, 60, 67, 253–6, 288, 366–7
 McKinley, William, assassination of 40, 267–8
 McVeigh, Timothy assassination plans 287
 New York Anarchy Statute, criminalized under 181
 Sadat, Anwar, assassination of 432
 Smith Act, criminalized under 356
 Teixeira, Jack, planned 248
association, freedom of 123, 223–4, 240, 265, 270, 422–4
Atzerodt, George 254–5, 366
Authorization for the Use of Military Force (AUMF) 191, 291
Aycock, Charles 426–8
Axis Sally 51–2, 273, 311, 314, 378, 381
Azzam the American, *see* Gadahn, Adam

Bache, Benjamin 29, 346
Bacon, Nathanial 53–4
Bacon's Rebellion 53–4, 225, 316
Baer, Elizabeth 338
Barr, Bill 80
Barrett, Richard 82
Barry, Joseph 203–4
Bas v. Tingy 23
Battle of Athens, Tennessee 55–6
Battle of Blair Mountain 252, 417
Battle of Canal Street, see Battle of Liberty Place
Battle Hymn of the Republic 130, 228, 230
Battle of Liberty Place 57–9, 106, 124, 156, 217, 425
Berger, Victor 139
Berkeley, William 53–4
Best, Robert H.313–14, 316
Betts, U.S. v. 319
Biden, Joseph 79–80, 218, 220, 248, 262, 349
Bill of Attainder 140
Bill of Rights 181, 223, 362, 442
Bin Laden, Osama 180, 194, 257, 433
Bitch of Berlin, *see* Axis Sally
Black Muslims/Black Power 100
Black Panther Party 100

Black, Hugo 137, 223
Blackstone, William 23, 131, 259, 337, 362–3
Blair House 50, 308
Blair, Francis 336
Bleeding Kansas 66, 111, 203, 228, 304, 365
Blennerhessett Island 73, 75
Blind Sheikh 348, 432
Blizzard, Bill 252–3
Blockade 22, 305–6
Blue Ridge Mountains 66, 228
Bollman, Erick 77, 157
Bolshevik Revolution 17, 41, 122, 165, 268
Boogalo Movement 430
Booth, John Wilkes
  Brown, John, witness to execution 60, 67
  Christiania Revolt, schoolmate of participant 89
  life, Lincoln plots, and assassination aftermath 60–1
  Lincoln Assassination, perpetrator of 49, 253–6, 288, 366
Border Ruffians 203, 304
Boston Marathon bombing 62–3, 413
Boston Tea Party 35, 375
Boumediene v. Bush 166
Bowden, James 354–5
Bradley, Joseph 106
Branch Davidians 287, 401–4
Brandeis, Louis 19, 64–5, 103–4, 182, 422–3
Brandenburg v. Ohio
  Abrams v. U.S., relation to *20*
  in analysis of anarchy laws 41
  Clear and Present Danger, relation to 104
  Dennis v. U.S., relation to 137
  discussion of case 64–5
  Hess v. Indiana, relied on as precedent 205
  Pennsylvania v. Nelson, relation to 294
  riot and incitement to riot, application of case 318
  Schenck v. United States, relation to 338
  Sedition Act of 1918, relation to 152
  seditious and *Brandenburg* test 342–3
  Seditious Conspiracy and Brandenburg test 348
  Smith Act and Brandenburg test 357
  Speech as Crime, relation to 363
  Syndicalism and Brandenburg test 123
  threats of violence and Brandenburg test 374
  Whitney v. California, relation to 423–4
  Yates v. U.S., relation to 436
Brandenburg, Clarence 64, 104
Brandford, David 420
Brennen, William 346
British Army 35–6, 47–8, 410
Brown, John
  actions in attacking US Armory and Arsenal 228–31
  actions and life of 66–7
  Booth, John Wilkes, guarding execution site 60
  Cook, John, involvement with 111–2
  Copeland, John, involvement with 113–14
  Coppoc, Edwin, involvement with 115–16
  definition of treason in his case 34
  Dorr's Rebellion, in relation to Brown 142
  financial supporter of 130
  in general 131, 178, 393
  Green, Shields, involvement with 187–8
  Hazlett, Albert, involvement with 203–4
  Kaczynski, Theodore, views on 235–6
  Milligan, Lambdin and Brown compared 159
  Pottawattamie Massacre, role in 304, 369, 414
  prosecution by Virginia 239, 283, 395–9
  Seditious Conspiracy statute, reason for 347
  song about 67, 130, 230
  Stevens, Aaron, involvement with 367
  Thoreau, Henry David, views on 92
  treason, leading American example 383
  Vallandigham, Clement, interrogation of 162
  Weather Underground, inspired by 416
  West Virginia Coal War defendants tried in same courthouse as Brown 417–18
Brutus, Marcus Junius 61, 288, 380
Buchanan, James 229, 304
Bundy, Ammon 69–70, 215
Bundy, Cliven 69, 215
Bundy, Ryan 69
Bundy Standoff 69–70, 215, 270, 288
Bureau of Alcohol, Tobacco, and Firearms (ATF) 287, 324, 401–2
Bureau of Land Management (BLM) 69
Burger, Ernest 160
Burgoyne, John 47, 354
Burr, Aaron
  actions against US 75
  actions with co-conspirators 157
  Levying War, arguable application of Treason Clause 251–2
  life of 72–4
  Jefferson, Thomas, and threatened invocation of Insurrection Act against 217, 226–7
  prosecution of, generally 23, 75–8, 367
Burr, v. U.S. 73–8, 149, 157, 251–2, 367, 381
Bush, George H.W. 175, 218, 220
Bush, George W.
  commutation of sentence for I. Lewis "Scooter" Libby 300
  cooperation with 9/11 Commission 352
  creation of 9/11 Commission 352
  Hamdi v. Rumsfeld, role in 191
  Hurricane Katrine, contemplated use of military 218
  "Plame Affair" scandal during term 221

U.S. v. Padilla, role in 292
USA Patriot Act, role in passage 389
War on Terror, role in 272
Butler, Benjamin 275

Caesar, Julius 49, 288, 380
Caliber, *see* Rosenberg, Julius and Ethel
Callender, James Thompson 345
Campos, Pedro Albizu 308
Cantrell, Paul 55
Capitol Insurrection on January 6
background and events of day 79–84
Black Panther activities, contrasted with 100
conspiracy against rights 146
criminal conspiracies on day 109
Disqualification Clause, for participation in 139–41
House Select Committee on Investigation 352
Insurrection Act, whether threshold was met for insurrection 217
militia groups, participation in 269, 287–8, 430
mutiny, potential charge for participating service members 278
Seditious Conspiracy, prosecutions for from day 349, 430
Trump, Donald, role in alleged incitement questioned 319
Wilmington Insurrection of 1898, compared with 428
Capitol Square, Richmond, Virginia 177–8
Capitol, US *see* Capitol Insurrection on January 6
Cardozo, Benjamin 40
Carlisle v. U.S. 32–3, 85–6
Carter, Jimmy 49, 175
Centennial Olympic Park, Atlanta, Georgia 328, 413
Chambers, Whittaker 208–10
Chandler, Douglas 311, 313–14
Charles II, King 54, 259
Chase, Salmon 131–2
Chase, Samuel 171, 251
Cheney, Liz 79, 82
Cheney, Richard 221, 300, 352
Chin, Larry 87–8, 293, 406–7, 438
Christiana Revolt 89–91, 130, 195, 251–2, 419, 421
Civil Disobedience and Crimes against the State
analysis, definition, and application of 92–9
in *Hirabayashi, U.S. v.*, claims of 206
Kaczynski, Theodore, rejection of 233
in *O'Brien v. U.S.*, claims of 285
Snowden, Edward, claims of 247
in *Street v. New York*, claims of 168–9
in *U.S. v. Walli*, claims of 333
Civil Rights Movement and Crimes against the State 99–101, 168
Clark, John H.19
Clear and Present Danger
Abrams v. U.S., discussed in 19–20
analysis and definition of doctrine 102–5, 363
Brandenburg v. Ohio, discussed in 64–5
Dennis v. U.S., discussed in 137
Gitlow v. New York, discussed in 182
Schenck v. U.S., discussed in 338
Whitney v. California, discussed in 422–3
Clinton, Bill 44, 175–6, 242, 352
Coke, Edward 148, 239
Cold War 17, 23, 41, 210, 220, 340, 356
Colfax Massacre
analysis of event 106–7
Battle of Liberty Place, relation to 57
Cruikshank, U.S. v., role in 124–5
Eufaula Election Massacre, relation to 156
Insurrection Act, use to suppress 217
WACO, compared with 401, 419
Whiskey Rebellion, compared with 419
Wilmington Insurrection, compared to 425
Committee on Spies 35, 225
Communism and McCarthyism 340
Communist Control Act 108
Communist Labor Party of the United States 64, 422
Communist Party, discussed in *Whitney* 422
Communist Party, generally 166, 173, 208–9, 240, 322, 340
Communist Party of California 435
Communist Party of Pennsylvania 294
Communist Party of the United States 104, 108, 136–7
Confederate Secret Service 61, 254
Confederate States of America
Aid & Comfort to 85
in Civil War 33, 61
Davis, Jefferson, role in 58, 129–31, 367
defeat of 254, 316
Disqualification Clause 31, 139
in *Ex Parte Milligan* 158
in *Ex Parte Vallandigham* 162
former members of 145
oath, not to join 57
in *Prize Cases* 305–6
State membership 373
United Daughters of 155
Conspiracy, Criminal
in Abel, Ruldolph, prosecution 18–19
in *Al-Arian, U.S. v.* 25–6
in Aldrich, Ames case 39
in Bundy Standoff 70
in *Burr, U.S. v.* 72, 77–8, 157, 217, 227
Capitol Insurrection on January 6, charges in 83
in Chin, Larry, prosecution 87
in Colfax Massacre 124
Communist Control Act, provision of 103

in Copeland, John, prosecution 113
definition and elements of 109–10
DeJonge v. Oregon, discussed in 136–7
Enforcement Acts, provision in 145–6
Espionage Act, provision of 245
in *Ex Parte Milligan* 158–9
First World War, prosecutions in 122
in Gabriel's Rebellion 177–8
in Green, Shields, prosecution 187
in Hanssen, Robert, case 193
in Hazlett, Albert, case 204
in *Hoxie, U.S. v.*, discussed in 214
Insurrection Act, provision of 219
in Lincoln assassination 49, 253, 255, 366–7
Lindh, John Walker, charge in 257
Material Support crimes, element of 264–5
McKinley, William, assassination, lack thereof 267
in McVeigh, Timothy, prosecution 288
in Padilla, Jose, prosecution 292
in Pollard, Jonathan, prosecution 301
in Rosenberg, Julius and Ethel case 23, 320–2
scheme to kidnap Gretchen Whitmer 360, 430
Sedition Conspiracy, distinguished from 343
terrorism, conspiracy to (in New Jersey) 274
Trump, Donald, indictment for 300
in Vesey's Rebellion 393
WACO, charges of 401, 403–4
Weaver, Randy, charges of 325
Walker, John, charges of 407
Weapons of Mass Destruction, to use 412–13
Yates v. U.S., discussed in 435
Constitutional Convention of 1787 77, 142, 148, 355, 397, 409
Constructive Treason 148, 213–14, 227, 251
Continental Congress 35, 195, 225
Cook, John 111–16, 187–8, 203, 396
Cooper, Thomas 345
Copeland, John 112–15, 187–8, 203, 230, 395
Coppoc, Barclay 115–16
Coppoc, Edwin 66, 112–16, 187–8, 203–4, 230, 395
Corruption of Blood 117, 121, 148, 382
Cosby, William 441
counterfeiting 120, 148
covert agent 220–1
Cramer, Anthony 118–19
Cramer v. U.S. 118–19, 149, 199–200, 272, 382
Crimes Act of 1790 31, 117, 120–1, 298, 381–2
Criminal Syndicalism
anarchy statutes, relation to 41
in *Brandenburg v. Ohio* 64, 104
Clear and Present Danger Test, analyzed under 363
definition and elements of 122–3
in *DeJonge v. Oregon* 136
in general 334
passage of state statutes covering 186, 268
Pennsylvania v. Nelson, analyzed under 294
sabotage, relation to 331
Whitney v. California, discussed in 422–4
Cruikshank, U.S. v. 106, 124–5, 146
curfews 95–7, 206
Customs and Border Patrol Protection 211, 269
cybercrimes 126
cybersecurity 126–8
Czolgosz, Leon 267

Dahlgren, Ulric 253
Danforth Inquiry 403–4
Daniels, Josephus 425, 427
D'Aquino, Iva, *see* Tokyo Rose
Darby, James 375–6
Darby, U.S. v. 375–6
Dasche, George 160–1
Daschele, Thomas 42
Davis, Jefferson 33–4, 58, 129–33, 183, 253–4, 366–7
death penalty
assassination, punishment for 50
Crimes Act of 1790, punishment under 120
Hanssen, Robert, avoidance of 193
Hasan, Nidal, sentence of 198
Kaczynski, Theodore, avoidance of 236
McVeigh, Timothy, sentence of 287
Rosenberg, Julius and Ethel, sentence of 322
Rudolph, Eric, avoidance of 328
Tsarnaev, Dzhokhan, sentence of 62
Weapons of Mass Destruction, possible punishment for use 413
Debs, Eugene 102, 122, 134
Debs v. U.S. 102, 134–5, 152, 186, 338, 363
Declaration of Independence 35–6, 195, 225, 380
defamation 209, 363
Degan, William 324–5
DeJonge, Dirk 136
DeJonge v. Oregon 136
Delaney, Edward 311, 313–14
Democratic Party
during Civil War 158
in Louisiana 57, 106
in Presidential Election, 1916 185
in South in 1890s 425–7
in South during Reconstruction 124, 155
Democratic-Republican Party 27–9, 226, 344–5, 409
Dennis v. U.S.
case description and facts 137–8
Clear and Present Danger test, application of 64, 104, 363
communist ideology, prohibition of 341
Smith Act, constitutionality of 340–3, 348, 356
speech, freedom of, generally 362–3

Yates v. U.S., interpretation of *Dennis* 435
Zenger, Peter, trial, commentary on 441
Department of Defense 82, 241, 245, 261, 281, 295
Department of Homeland Security 127, 211, 352–3
Department of Justice
Capitol Insurrection on January 6, prosecution of 79, 82–3, 348–9
criminal conspiracy, practice in charging 109
Debs, U.S. v., role in 134
Green Corn Rebellion, role in 185–6
Hanssen, Robert, case, role in 193
Hirabayashi, U.S. v., role in 207
Internal Security Act, registration with 223–4
IWW, prosecution of 122
Korematsu, U.S. v., role in 241
Palmer Raids, role in 167
Plame, Valerie, case, role in 221
Riot Act, prosecutions under 319
Ruby Ridge, review of 326
Rudolph, Eric, case, role in 328
Second World War, Radio Propagandists, role in 311–15
Teixeira, Jack, prosecution 248
Threats against Officials, data from 376
Tokyo Rose, case, role in 378–9
WACO, review of 403
Walker, John, case, role in 406
Department of State 193, 208–9, 245, 314, 340, 415
deportation 27–8, 30, 45, 165–6, 223
detention
Anti-Terrorism and Effective Death Penalty Act, under 45
Bollman, Erick, detention of 157
Fries's Rebellion, detention during 171
Hamdi v. Rumsfeld, discussed in 191
Haupt, Hans Max and Herbert Hans, detention of 332
illegal detention of civilians 409–410
illegal detention by militia groups 270
Internal Security Act, under 223–4
Milligan, Lambdin, detention of 158, 162
Padilla, Jose, detention of 291–2, 415
Palmer Raids, detention during 166
USA Patriot Act, authorized 390
Dewitt, John 206, 241
Direct Tax Act 170
dirty bomb 291–2, 412–13
Disqualification Clause 120, 131, 139–41, 215, 316
Dohrn, Bernardine 415
Dorr, Thomas 142–3
Dorr v. Rhode Island 397
Dorr's Rebellion 142–3, 259, 262, 283, 316, 397
Douglass, Frederick 90, 111, 187, 228–9, 398
Douglass, William O. 65, 200
draft, military
card 95, 97, 275, 285
in general 96, 122, 134, 185–6, 338
Dred Scott v. Sandford 113, 124, 187, 359
Drexel, Constance 311, 313–14
Duclos, Francis 410
due process
in general 123–4, 145, 166, 192, 267, 340, 368
Due Process Clause 124, 136, 181
Duncan v. Kahanamoku 261

Egypt, use of spies in antiquity 150
Ehrichman, John 297
Eichman, U.S. v. 169
Eisenhower, Dwight D. 108, 200, 209, 218, 239, 320–2, 340
Electoral College 79, 349
Ellsberg, Daniel 153, 245, 247, 249, 281, 295–7
Embargo Act 213–14, 217, 227
Emerson, Ralph Waldo 67, 230
enemy combatant 161, 191–2, 291–2, 413
Enforcement Acts 106, 124, 140, 145–7, 218–19, 390
English Star Chamber Court, influence on sedition law 342
English Treason Statute of 1351
aid and comfort to enemy, element of 21, 23
analysis and definition of 148–9
application in American Revolution 35–6
counterfeiting, element of 120
influence on American treason law 380
levying war, element of 251
Equal Protection 123–4, 145, 218
espionage
Abels, Rudolph, conduct of 17
Abrams v. U.S., discussed in 19–20
Ames, Adrich, conduct of 38–9, 220
analysis, definition, and elements of 150–1
Chin, Larry, conduct of 87
Clear and Present Danger, relation to 102–4
Cook, John, conduct of 111
Cramer v. U.S., discussed in 382
crimes against state, example of 97, 109
cyber activities, commission by 127
Debs v. U.S., discussed in 134
Espionage Act of 1917 150–3, 320, 338, 342, 363
Ex Parte Quirin, discussed in 160
Fuchs, Klaus, conduct of 173–4
in general 197, 211
Green Corn Rebellion 185–6
Hanssen, Robert, conduct of 193–4, 220
Haupt v. U.S., discussed in 199
Hiss, Alger, conduct of 208–10, 298

Internal Security Act, power to prevent 223
Japanese-American internment camps, to prevent 241
leaks of defense information as 245–9
Manning, Chelsea/Bradley, conduct of 94
Pelton, Ronald William, conduct of 293
Pentagon Papers, publication of as 281, 295–7
Pollard, Jonathan, conduct of 301–3
radio propaganda during Second World War as 311–15
Rosenbergs, Julius and Ethel, conduct of 320–2
Snowden, Edward, conduct of 94
Walker, John, conduct of 406–7
War of 1812 and espionage 409–10
Year of the Spy and espionage 437–9
Espionage Act of 1917
Abels, Rudolph, violation of 17
Abrams v. U.S., violation of 19–20
Ames, Adrich, violation of 38–9, 220, 245
analysis, definition, and elements of 150, 152–3, 245–9
Assange, Julian, violation of 245–6
Chin, Larry, violation of 87
Clear and Present Danger, relation to 102–4
Cramer v. U.S., violation of 382
Debs v. U.S., violation of 134
Ellsberg, Daniel, violation of 245, 297
Ex Parte Quirin, violation in 160
in general 211
Green Corn Rebellion, violation in 185–6
Hanssen, Robert, violation of 193–4, 220, 245
Haupt v. U.S., violation of 199
leaks of defense information, violation of 245–9
Manning, Chelsea/Bradley, violation of 94, 150, 246–7
Pelton, Ronald William, violation of 293
Pentagon Papers, violation of 281, 297
Pollard, Jonathan, violation of 301–3
Rosenbergs, Julius and Ethel, violation of 320–2
Russo, violation of 245, 249
Schenck v. United States, violation of 338–9
Snowden, Edward, violation of 94, 150, 247
Teixeira, Jack, violation of 245, 248–9
Trump, Donald, alleged violation of 110, 150, 299–300
Walker, John, violation of 406–7
Winner, Reality, violation of 245, 248
Year of the Spy, violations during 437–9
Eufaula Election Massacre 106, 155–6, 425
evacuation order 96
Ex Parte Bollman 73, 77, 157, 214, 382
Ex Parte Milligan 33, 130, 158–60, 162, 191, 368
Ex Parte Quirin 118, 159, 160–1, 191, 199, 332
Ex Parte Vallandigham 162–3, 363
Exclusion Zone 96, 206, 241
Executive Order 9066 206, 241
Executive Order 12333 50
Extradition Clause, US Constitution 397

Federal Bureau of Investigation
Abels, Rudolph, case, role in 17
Al-Arian case, role in 25
Ames, Adrich, case, role in 38, 437–8
CCA, opposition to 108
Cramer v. U.S., role in 118
Ellsberg and Russo, case, role in 297
enhanced training after 9/11 352
FALN, investigation of 175
Flynn, Michael, case, role in 299
Hanssen, Robert, case, role in 193, 437
Hasan, Nidal, case, role in 197
Haupt v. U.S., role in 160
Hirabayashi, Gordon, case, role in 96, 206
Hiss, Alger, case, role in 209
Kaczynski, Theodore, case, role in 233
Kawakita, Tomoya, case, role in 238
Lindh, John Walker, case, role in 257
McVeigh, Timothy, case, role in 287–8
Monti, James, case, role in 273
Padilla, Jose, case, role in 291
Palmer Raids, role in 166
Patriot Act, new powers 389–90
Pollard, Jonathan, case, role in 302
Puerto Rican National Party, case, role in 308
Ruby Ridge, review of 326
Rudolph, Eric, case, role in 328
Scranage, case, role in 221
Second World War propaganda cases, investigation of 311
Tokyo Rose, case, role in 379
Trump, Donald, investigation of 153
Tsarnaev brothers, case, role in 62
Walker, John, case, role in 406–7
Weather Underground, investigation of 415
website, defacement of 126
Winner, Reality, case, role in 248
Wolverine Watchmen, investigation of 430
World Trade Center Bombing of 1993, investigation of 43
federal preemption 41, 123, 294
Federalist Papers 117, 380
Federalist Party 28, 211, 226, 344–5, 409
Feklisov, Alexander 321
Felton, Rebecca 425–8
Field, Stephen J. 23, 183, 306
Fifteenth Amendment 124–5, 145, 155
Fifth Amendment 223–4
First Amendment
Abrams v. U.S., discussed in 19–20

aid and comfort of enemies through speech 22–3
Alien and Sedition Acts, relation to 226, 344–6
Brandenburg v. Ohio, discussed in 64, 205, 357
Clear and Present Danger Doctrine, relation to 102–3
Cruikshank, U.S. v., discussed in 124
Debs, U.S. v., discussed in 134
Dennis, U.S. v., discussed in 137
Espionage Act and First Amendment 152, 246, 249, 338
Flag Disrespect and First Amendment 168–9
IIPA, potential violation of 220
ISA, constitutionality of under First Amendment 223
in general 245–6, 294, 313, 430
Gitlow v. New York, discussed in 41, 181–2
Keyishian v. Board of Regents, discussed in 240
material support crimes, constitutionality of under 265
national security concerns and First Amendment 279, 282
prohibition of pre-publication censorship 279–80
riot laws and First Amendment 318
sedition and seditious conspiracy, relation to 343, 348
seditious libel, relation to 441–2
speech and First Amendment protection 362–3
syndicalism, relation to 123
threats (verbal) and First Amendment 374
Yates v. U.S., discussed in 356, 435–6
First Red Scare and Palmer Raids
analysis of period 165–7
bombings during 369
Haymarket Affair, relation to 201
in general 334
laws enacted as result of 240, 268, 340
Flag Disrespect as Crime against the State 152, 168–9, 275, 285
Flag Protection Act 169
FLAME 127
Flynn, Michael 299
Ford, Gerald 49, 180, 253, 277, 379
Ford's Theatre 254–5
Foreign Intelligence Surveillance Act 389–90
Foreign Intelligence Surveillance Court 390
Foreign Terrorist Organization 25, 264–5, 390
Fort Hood, Texas 197
Fort Leavenworth, Kansas 198, 273, 365
Fort Monroe, Virginia 130–1
Fourteenth Amendment
Clear and Present Danger, relation to 104
Cruikshank, U.S. v., discussed in 124–5
Dejonge v. Oregon, discussed in 136
Disqualification Clause and Jefferson Davis 34, 131–2
Disqualification Clause, generally 139, 259
Enforcement Act, relation to 145, 218
Gitlow v. New York, discussed in 181
insurrection & rebellion, specified in 215, 316
Sovereign Citizens Movement, view of 359
Fourth Amendment 387–8
Framers, Constitutional
Aid and Comfort Clause, views on 21, 23
Levying War Clause, views on 251
martial law, views on 262
Treason Clause, views on 75, 275, 363, 381–2, 410
France, pseudo-war with 23, 27–30, 44, 170, 225–6, 344, 354
Frankfurter, Felix 223, 241, 264, 362–3
Franklin, Benjamin 29, 36, 72, 346, 390
Freedom of Assembly
Cruikshank, U.S. v., discussed in 124
Debs, U.S. v., discussed in 134
Dejonge v. Oregon, discussed in 136
Dennis, U.S. v., discussed in 137
Gitlow v. New York, discussed in 181
ISA, potential violation of 223
riot laws, constitutionality under 318
Smith Act, constitutional under 356–7
Whitney v. California, discussed in 422–4
Freedom of Press
Brandenburg v. Ohio, discussed in 64, 104, 318, 363
Dejonge v. Oregon, discussed in 136
in general 249, 362
U.S. v. New York Times, discussed in 281
Freedom of Speech, *see* Speech as Crime against State
French Revolution 28, 37, 364
Fries, John 170–1
Fries's Rebellion
analysis of event 170–2
Hoxie, U.S. v., influenced by 213–14
in general 129, 215
Insurrection Act, to quell 217, 270
rebellion, early example of 316
Shay's Rebellion, compared with 354
treason law, early influence on 251–2
Whiskey Rebellion, compared with 251, 375, 381
Frohwerk v. U.S. 102–3, 152, 186
Fromme, Lynette "Squeaky" 49, 253
Fuchs, Klaus 173–4, 320
Fuerza's Armadas de Liberacion Nacional (FALN) 175–6
Fugitive Slave Act of 1793 89
Fugitive Slave Act of 1850 89–91, 195–6, 252, 421
Fugitive Slave Clause, US Constitution 89
Fusionist 425–6

Gabriel's Rebellion 177–9, 228, 316, 393
Gadahn, Adam 119, 180, 198, 381

Gale, William Potter 358
Galleanists 165
Galvan v. Press 223
Gandhi, Mahatma 93–4
Garfield, James 49, 60, 253
General Order Number 38 162
George the Third, King 35
German State Radio 314–15
German Waffen-S.S. 273
Gesell, Gerhard 281
Getman, George 170–1
Gillars, Mildred, *see* Axis Sally
Gitlow, Benjamin 181
Gitlow v. New York
  analysis and main case description 181–2
  anarchy statute upheld as constitutional 40–1, 201, 268
  Clear and Present Danger doctrine, relation to 102–3, 363
  Due Process Clause binding on State governments 136
  Holmes, Oliver Wendall, dissent in 65
Glasscock, William 417
Goebbels, Joseph 51, 312–13
Gold, Harry 173, 320–1
Goldfus, Emil Robert, *see Abel v. U.S.*
Goldman, Emma 166, 201, 267
Gorsuch, Edward 89–91
Grant, Ulysses S. 49, 57–8, 146, 217, 253–4
Gravel, Michael 296
Gravel v. U.S. 296
Gray, U.S. v. 375
Greathouse, Ridgely 183
Greathouse, U.S. v. 22–3, 118, 183–4, 306, 382
Green Corn Rebellion 185–6, 316
Green, Israel 229
Green, Shields 112–15, 187–8, 203, 230, 395
Greenglass, David 173–4, 320–1
Greenglass, Ruth 321–2
Greenwood, New York 189
Grier, Robert 91, 195
Gritz, James Bo 325
GRU (Soviet Intelligence Agency) 38, 248
Gulf of Tonkin 295
gun control 269, 287, 402
Gunpowder Plot of 1605 380
Gurfein, Murray 281
Guy Fawkes Day 380

Habeas Corpus 45, 145–6, 157–8, 160, 191, 291, 305–6, 316
Hale, Edward 23
Halter v. Nebraska 168
Hamdi, Yasser 191–2
Hamdi v. Rumsfeld 159, 161, 191–2, 292
Hamilton, Alexander 72, 345, 409, 419–20
Hamilton, James 393
Hammond, Dwight and Steven 69–70
Hanauer v. Doane 32
Hancock, John 355
Hand, Learned 104, 137
Hanssen, Robert
  Ames, Adrich, compared with 38
  analysis, life, and action 193–4
  Espionage Act, prominent offender 153, 220, 245
  highest paid spy 87
  motivation for 150
  Year of the Spy, active during 406–7, 437–8
Hanway, Caster 90–1, 130, 195–6
Hanway, U.S. v. 90–1, 195–6, 251–2, 271, 381–2, 421
Harpers Ferry Raid, *see* John Brown's Raid
Harris, Kevin 325–6
Harris, William 203–4
Hartford Convention 409
Hasan, Nidal 197–8
Hatfield, Sid 417
Haupt, Hans Max and Herbert 160, 199–200, 332
Haupt v. U.S. 24, 160, 199–200, 332, 382
Hawthorne, Nathaniel 67, 230
Hayanen, Reino 17–18
Haymarket Affair 40, 201, 414
Hazlett, Albert 66, 112, 115, 203, 230, 395
Herney, Frederick 170–2
Herold, David 255, 366
Hess v. Indiana 205
Hinckley, John, Jr. 49
Hirabayashi, Gordon 95–7
Hirabayashi, U.S. v. 95–7, 206–7
Hiss, Alger 150, 208–10, 298–9, 437
Hiss, Gregory 205
Hitler, Adolf 51, 273, 311, 313–14
Hodges, John 410
Hoffman, Ogden 183
Holder v. Humanitarian Law Project 265
Holmes, Oliver Wendell, Jr.
  Abrams v. U.S., views in 19–20
  anarchist bombing target 165
  Clear and Present Danger, views in evolution of doctrine 102–4
  Gitlow v. New York, dissenting view in 65, 182
  Hiss, Alger, relationship to 208
  Schenck, U.S. v., views in case 338
  Whitney v. California, views in 422
Homeland Security Act 46, 211, 351–2, 390
Hoover, J. Edgar 108, 166, 311, 320
House of Representatives Select Committee on Investigation of January 6 79–81, 83, 352

House of Representatives Un-American Activities Committee (HUAC) 208–9
Howard, Edward Lee 437
Hoxie, Frederick 213–14
Hoxie, U.S. v. 213–14, 227, 251, 271, 381
Hughes, Charles Evan 279
Hugo, Victor 230
Hunter, Andrew 111–13, 395–8
Horiuchi, Lon 325–7

Idaho v. Horiuchi 325–7
Imminent Incitement Test 64–5, 102, 423–4
Imminent Lawless Action 41, 104, 137, 205, 343, 348–9, 357, 363
Independence Hall 89, 195
Industrial Workers of the World (IWW) 122–3, 185–6
insanity defense 235–6, 313, 396
insurrection
- analysis, definition, and elements 215–16
- anarchy compared with 40
- Bacon's Rebellion, first insurrection in New World 53–4
- Brown, John, convicted of 395–9
- Bundy Standoff as insurrection 70
- Burr, Aaron, attempted insurrection 75
- Capitol Insurrection on January 6 79–84, 319, 349
- Colfax Massacre as insurrection 106–7, 125
- conspiracy to commit on January 6 109, 146
- Cook, John, convicted of 111
- Copeland, John, convicted of 113
- Coppoc, Edwin, convicted of 115
- crime against state 97
- Disqualification Clause, relation to 132, 139–41
- Enforcement Act, power to suppress 145
- Espionage Act, criminalized mail to incite 338
- Eufaula Election Massacre and Spring Hill Riot as 155–6
- Fries's Rebellion, prosecutions for 170, 251
- Gabriel's Rebellion, convicted of 178
- Green, Shields, convicted of 187
- Greenwood, New York, Insurrection 189
- Hazlett, Albert, convicted of 203–4
- Insurrection Act 217–19
- Internal Security Act, power to detain to prevent 223
- John Brown's Raid as insurrection 228–30
- Levying War compared with Insurrection 183, 196, 251–2, 271
- martial law, in response to 262–3
- militias (government) to suppress 270
- power of president to quell 226–7, 259, 261–2, 305–6
- rebellion compared with 316
- Stevens, Aaron, convicted of 365
- Turner, Nat, insurrection 384–5
- Vesey insurrection 393–4
- Weather Underground, goal of 414
- Whiskey Rebellion, as 419–21
- Wilmington Insurrection of 1798 425–8

Insurrection Act
- analysis of main provisions and history 216, 217–19, 316–17
- Enforcement Act amendment to 145
- fear of misuse after 2020 Presidential election 82
- Jefferson, Thomas, expansion to 226–7
- martial law, relation to 261–2
- precursor to act used to quell Whiskey Rebellion 420
- violent labor disputes and possible invocation of act 418

Intelligence Identities Protection Act 220–2, 300
Internal Security Act 108, 152–3, 223–4, 340
International Working People's Association 40
internment
- camps 52, 206, 312, 378
- order 97, 206, 241
- generally 96, 224, 241

interstate commerce 305, 318, 376
Iraq, invasion of 62, 197, 221, 246, 351, 412
Iredell, James 171
Ivins, Bruce Edwards 43

Jackson, Robert 118–19, 137, 168, 241–2, 262
January 6, *see* Capitol Insurrection on January 6, 2021
Jefferson, Thomas
- actions and position as President 225–7
- Alien and Sedition Acts, opposition to 28–9, 342, 344–6
- Bacon's Rebellion, influence on 53
- Burr, Aaron, dispute with 72–3
- Burr, Aaron, role in prosecution of 75–7, 367
- Committee on Spies, member of 35
- constructive treason, proponent of 213, 271
- Embargo Act of 1808, proponent of 213
- Insurrection Act, request for passage of 217
- Revolutionary War, almost captured by Benedict Arnold 48
- right to revolution, proponent of 316

Jeffries, Randy Miles 438
Jim Crow 99, 106, 156, 427
John Brown's Body 67, 130, 230
John Brown's Fort 67, 83, 115, 203, 229
John Brown's Raid
- analysis of action and events of attack 228–30
- comparison of other state treason cases 283
- Cook, John, involvement in attack 111
- Copeland, John, involvement in attack 113
- Coppoc, Edwin, involvement in attack 115
- goal of attack 304

Green, Shields, involvement in attack 187
Hazlett, Albert, involvement in attack 203
leading treason case in US 381
overview of event 66
Seditious Conspiracy statute, raid impetus for legislation 347
Stevens, Aaron, involvement in attack 365
trial of John Brown for treason and insurrection 395–9
Johnson, Andrew
1865 amnesty order pardoning confederates 31, 33, 129
1867 amnesty order pardoning Jefferson Davis 132
1868 amnesty order pardoning confederates 85
commutation of Lambdin Milligan sentence 158
issued proclamation blaming Confederacy for Lincoln assassination plot 254
refusal to commute or pardon Mary Surratt 366–7
target in Lincoln assassination plot 49, 253
Jones Family 185–6
Judiciary Act of 1789 120, 283

Kaczynski, David 235
Kaczynski, Theodore (Unabomber) 95, 233–6, 288
Kagi, John 113
Kaltenbach, Fred W. 311–13
Kane, John J. 91, 195
Kawakita, Tomoya 238–9
Kawakita v. U.S. 238–9, 381–2
Keils, Elias 155
Keith Case 387
Kellogg, William Pitt 57–8, 106
Kennedy Farmhouse 203, 229
Kennedy, John F. 49, 60, 218, 239, 253, 313
Kentucky and Virginia Resolutions of 1798 226, 344
Kenya, US embassy attack on 352, 370
Keyishian v. Board 240
KGB 17–18, 38, 194, 321–2, 406, 437
Khruschev, Nikita 321
King, Martin Luther, Jr. 49, 93–4, 99, 218
King, Samuel 142
Kiriakou, John 221
Kline, Henry 90, 195
Kohl, Gordon 358, 360
Koischwitz, Max Otto 51
Korematsu, Fred 95–7, 241–2
Korematsu v. U.S. 95–7, 206, 241–2
Koresh, David 401–2, 404
Ku Klux Klan Act, *see* Enforcement Acts

labor disputes 217, 262, 417
Lackawanna defendants 265
Larson, Carlton F.W. 33, 36, 129, 132, 336–7
Leaks of National Defense Information 94, 150, 153, 245–9, 390, 437
Leary, Lewis Sheridan 113–14
Leary, Timothy 414–15
Leavitt, Humphrey H. 22
Lee, Robert E.
assassination, view on propriety of 254
capture of John Brown 60, 66, 229
in general 368
pardon, lack thereof 129
statue of 58
treason, failure to prosecute for 33, 132
Levying War
acts of assembly and preparation, failure to constitute 78, 157
American Civil War, acts of as constituting 33–4
American Revolution, acts of as constituting 35–7
analysis, definition, and evolution of term 251–2
Burr, Aaron, actions of 72, 77–8
Christiana Revolt, acts of as failure to constitute 89, 91, 196
conspiracy to engage in, failure to constitute 78, 157
contract to, unenforceability of 373
definition, basic 77–8, 343
in Dorr's Rebellion 142, 259
elements of 21–3
English Treason Statute of 1351, element of 148–9, 380
in Fries's Rebellion 170–2
Greathouse, U.S. v., discussed in 183–4
intent to engage in 213–14
meaning, modern interpretation of 89, 91, 196
obsolete view of 271, 420–1
State government, act of against a 283, 397
threats of violence, failure to constitute 271
Treason Clause, US Constitution 48, 119, 347, 380
Lewis, Anthony 279, 344–5
Libby, I. Lewis "Scooter" 221, 300
Libertarian 40, 63, 226, 363, 423–4
Liberty City Six 265
Lincoln Assassination
analysis of event 253–6
Booth, John Wilkes, involvement in 60–1, 67, 288
in general 21, 129
plot to 49
Surratt, Mary, involvement in 366–8
Lindh, John Walker 191, 257–8, 264, 371
Livingston, Henry Brockholst 213–14, 251
Lloyd, John 367
Lonetree, Clayton 438
Longstreet, James 57–8, 129
Lopez, Oscar 175–6
Los Alamos 173, 320
Ludlow Massacre 418

Luther, Martin 259
Luther v. Borden 143, 259–62
Lynch, Mark 283
Lyon, Matthew 345

MacRae, Hugh 426–8
Madison, James 117, 344, 346, 380, 409
Malheur National Wildlife Refuge 70
malware 126–7
Manhattan Project 173, 320
Manly, Alexander 425–8
Manning, Bradley/Chelsea 94, 150, 153, 245–7, 338, 437
Mansfield, Pat 55
Manson, Charles 49, 253
Mar-a-Lago Club 150, 299–300
Marbury v. Madison 73, 76, 344
Marshall, John
  in *Burr, U.S. v.*, 23, 73, 75–6, 251
  Ex Parte Bollman, opinion in 157
  United States v. Wiltberger, opinion in 131, 239, 337, 397
martial law
  analysis, definition, and elements of 261–3
  criminal syndicalism, to quell 122
  deference to military, when invoked 241
  Dorr's Rebellion, to quell 142, 259
  Enforcement Act, to quell KKK activities 146
  Ex Parte Milligan, discussed in 159
  Ex Parte Vallandigham, discussed in 162
  Insurrection Act, contrasted with 218
  Mumford, William Bruce, incident 275, 336
  Surratt, Mary, case, factor in 367–8
  War of 1812, not invoked 410
  West Virginia Coal Wars, declared in 252, 417–18
Martin, Luther 77
Martin v. Mott 217
Marxist ideology 122, 137, 175, 309
material support crimes
  Aid and Comfort to Enemies, by providing 22–3
  Al-Arian, Sami, charged with 25
  analysis, definition, and elements of 264–5
  Anti-Terrorism and Effective Death Penalty Act, first criminalized in 44, 288
  Lindh, John Walker, charged with 257, 373
  Padilla, Jose, charged with 291–2, 415
  popular charge in terrorism cases 371
  speech, as possible material support crime 363
  Wolverine Watchmen, charged with 430
McCarran, Pat 223
McCarran Act, *see* Internal Security Act
McCarthy, Joseph 209, 340
McEnergy, John 57–8, 106
McKinley assassination 40, 49, 60, 253, 267–8
McKinley, William, *see* McKinley assassination
McNamara, Robert 295
McVeigh, Timothy
  bombing in Oklahoma City 287–8, 259, 370
  incarceration of before execution 39, 236
  militia affiliation of 269
  motivation for bombing 63, 404
  Ruby Ridge, influence on 287, 324
  Waco, influence on 287, 404
  Weapons of Mass Destruction, charged with using 413
Mexican American War 92, 129, 275, 365
Michigan militia 269, 349, 430
military commissions 158–62, 363, 366–8, 417–18
military detentions 162, 191, 291–2, 413
military tribunals 130, 158–61, 199, 334, 368–9
Militia Act of 1792 217, 420
Militia Act of 1903 270
militia movement (modern) 269–70, 288, 358, 430
Milligan, Lambdin 158
Minersville School District v. Gobitis 168
Miselis, U.S. v. 314
misprision 85, 120
Mitchell, John 271–2, 420
Mitchell, John (US Attorney General) 281, 296
Mitchell, U.S. v. 118, 251, 271–2, 420
Mitsushio, George 281, 379
Mohammed, Khalid Sheikh 433
mole (spying) 38–9, 194, 437
Monroe, James 177–8, 409
Montana Freeman 360
Monti, Martin James 52, 273, 381
Monti, U.S. v. 52, 273, 381
Morris, Lewis 442
Mosser, Thomas 235
Mount Carmel Complex 401–2, 404
Mudd, Samuel 254–5
Mulligan, Hercules 150
Mumford, William Bruce 275, 336
Munley, Kimberley D. 197
Murphy, Frank 200, 241
mutiny
  analysis, definition, and elements of 276–8
  crime against the state, example of 109
  Debs, Eugune, encouragement to 102, 134
  Espionage Act, incitement of as crime under 152, 185
  Smith Act, incitement of as crime under 356

National Association for the Advancement of Colored People (NAACP) 99, 277
National Firearms Act of 1934 324, 401–2
National Guard
  deployment on January 6 82
  in Green Corn Rebellion 185
  in Militia Act of 1903 270

Posse Comitatus Act, relation to 403
Teixeira, Jack, member of 248
National Security Act of 1947 220
National Security Advisor 44, 299, 352
National Security Agency 95, 247, 293
National Security Letters 389–90
Native Americans, treatment of 53–4, 92
Naturalization Act 28–9, 226
Nauta, Waltine 110
Nazi 41, 51, 118–19, 173, 273, 312–14
Near v. Minnesota 22, 279–82
Nelson, Steve 294
Nessel, Dana 430
New England 48, 73, 287, 409–11
New York Times
Pentagon Papers publication 153, 279, 281–2, 295–7
Unabomber Manifesto, publication of 235
Wikileaks, publication of 246
New York Times v. Sullivan 226, 342, 346, 362
New York Times v. U.S. 279, 281–2, 295–7, 363
New York v. Lynch 283
Newby, Dangerfield 230
Nichols, Terry 269, 287–8, 359–60, 370, 413
Nixon, Richard 87, 205, 208–9, 224, 295, 297
Nobel Peace Prize 99, 320
Non-Detention Act 224, 291
Northern Alliance 191, 257
Northwestern University, bombing of 234
Noto v. U.S. 356–7
Novak, Robert 221

O'Brien, David 285
O'Brien v. U.S. 95, 275, 285–6, 363
O'Connor, Sandra D. 191, 242, 390–1
O'Laughlin, Michael 255
O'Neil, Eric 194
Oath Keepers 69–70, 81, 83, 269, 349, 433
Obama, Barack 175, 207, 246–7, 269, 299
Oberlin College 113–14, 188, 228
Office of Director of National Intelligence 50, 126, 352
Oki, Kenkichi 379
Oklahoma City Bombing
analysis of incident 287
Anti-Terrorism and Effective Death Penalty Act, influenced by 44, 211, 264, 390
in general 178
McVeigh, Timothy, perpetrator of 236, 269, 287, 359
Nichols, Terry, conspiracy with McVeigh 269, 287–8, 359–60, 370
Ruby Ridge, influence of on bombing 324
September 11, 2001, compared with 351
timing of 63
Waco, influence of on bombing 404
Weapons of Mass Destruction, use of 412–13
World Trade Center bombing (1993), compared with 433
Olympic Park Bombing, *see* Rudolph, Eric
Operation Ivy Bells 293
Operation Pastorius 160, 199–200, 332
Osawatomie, *see* Brown, John
Otis, James 387

Padilla, Jose 291–2, 413
Padilla, U.S. v. 192, 291–2, 413
Padilla v. Hanft 192, 292
Palmer, A. Mitchell 165–6
Palmer Raids, *see* First Red Scare and Palmer Raids
paper terrorism 360
pardons, *see* American Civil War—Amesty and Pardons
Parker, William 90–1
Patriot Act, *see* USA Patriot Act
Patriot Movement 70
Patterson, William 171, 251, 420
Pearl Harbor 96, 206, 238, 241, 351, 378
Peierls, Robert 173
Pelosi, Nancy 82
Pelton, Ronald 293, 437
Pence, Mike 80–2
Pennsylvania Sedition Act 294
Pennsylvania v. Nelson 41, 123, 294
Pentagon Papers 153, 245, 279, 281–2, 295–7
People v. Upshaw 318
Perjury, False Statements, and Obstruction of Justice
Al-Arian, Sami, charged with 25
analysis, definition, and elements of crimes 298–300
Cramer, Anthony, false statements made 118
Crimes Act of 1790, type of 120
Espionage Act, obstruction as crime 152
Hiss, Alger, charged with perjury 208–9
Libby, I. Lewis, charged with 221
speech, limitation upon 363
Tokyo Rose, charged with 378–9
Trump, Donald, alleged obstruction of justice under Espionage Act 153
Pierce, Franklin 129, 365
piracy 120
Plame (Wilson), Valerie 221, 300
Plamondon, Lawrence 387–8
Polk, James K. 336
Pollard, Anne 302
Pollard, Jonathan 293, 301–3, 438
polygraph test 221, 301, 406
Port Chicago Mutiny 276–7
Portland jihad cell 265
Posse Comitatus (militia group) 358
Posse Comitatus Act of 1878 218, 403

Pottawatomie Massacre 66, 111, 229, 304, 369, 414
Pound, Ezra 311
Powell (Paine), Lewis 49, 254–5, 366
Praetorian Guard (militia group) 69
Presidential Assassination Statute 50
Presidential Medal of Freedom 207, 210, 242
Presidio Mutiny 277
Prior Restraint, doctrine against 137, 279–82, 362–3
prisoners of war 31, 161, 238, 253–4, 378
Prize Cases 305–6
Proclamation 179 85
Proud Boys 81, 83, 269, 349, 433
Provisional Constitution 66–7, 228, 398
Provoo, John 119, 180, 381
Provoo, U.S. v. 180
Puerto Rican Nationalist Party Revolt 50, 175, 308–9

Qua Warranto, Writ of 140
Quinn, Luke 229, 396

Radich v. Hutchins 33, 397
Radio Traitors and Anti-State Propaganda during Second World War 51, 273, 311–15, 363, 378–9
Rahman, Omar Abdel, *see* Blind Sheik
Rawls, John 93–5
Reagan, Ronald 49, 175, 209–10, 267, 406
rebellion
  Bacon's Rebellion 53–4
  definition of 316–17
  Disqualification Clause, grounds for 139–41
  Dorr's Rebellion 142–3
  Fries's Rebellion 170–2
  Gabriel's Rebellion 177–8
  Green Corn Rebellion 185–6
  Vesey Rebellion 393–4
  Whiskey Rebellion 419–21
Reconstruction Act of 1867 57
Red Scare, *see* First Red Scare and Palmer Raids & Second Red Scare (McCarthyism)
Red Shirts 428
Reffitt, Guy Wesley 83
Republic of Texas (militia group) 360
Revolutionary War, *see* American Revolution and Treason
Rex v. Casement 21
Rhodes, Stewart 81, 83, 349
Richmond Grays 60
riot and incitement to riot 318–19, 414
Rise Above Movement (hate group) 319
Robel, U.S. v. 224
Roberts, Anthony 195
Robertson, Thomas 83
Robespierre, Maximilien 369
Roosevelt, Franklin D. 51, 160–1, 206, 217, 241, 311–14, 427–8
Roosevelt, Theodore 49, 267
Rosenberg, Julius and Ethel
  Abel, Rudolph, relation to 17
  analysis of events and legal case 320–2
  Espionage Act, prosecution under 153
  espionage charges instead of treason 23
  Fuchs, Klaus, relation to 173–4
  Hiss, Alger, relation to 208
  motivation to spy 150
  notorious Cold War espionage case, example of 437
Roy, Richard 375
Roy v. U.S. 374–5
Ruby Ridge 178, 248, 269–70, 287, 324–7, 359, 404
Rudd, Mark 415
Rudolph, Eric 288, 328–9, 413

sabotage
  analysis, definition, and elements of 331–3
  civil disobedience, impermissibility of 95
  Ex Parte Quirin, discussed in 160–1
  Haupt v. U.S., discussed in 198–200
  Internal Security Act, power to prevent 223
  IWW, campaign of 122
  Weather Underground, campaign of 415
Sabotage Act 331–3
Sacco, Nicola 334–5
Sacco-Vanzetti Case 334
Sagebrush Rebellion 69
Salameh, Mohammed 432
Salazar, Hipolito 131, 336–7
Salt March 93
Scales v. U.S. 356
Schenck, Charles 338
Schenck v. U.S.
  Abrams v. U.S., relation to 19–20
  analysis of case and ruling 338
  Brandenburg v. Ohio, relation to 64
  Clear and Present Danger test, role in development of 102–4, 182, 363
  Debs, U.S. v., relation to 134
  Espionage Act, prosecution under 186
  Sedition Act of 1918, constitutionality under 152, 342
Scranage, Sharon W. 221, 438
Seattle General Strike 165
secession, legality of, *see Texas v. White*
Second Amendment 124–5, 270
Second Red Scare (McCarthyism) 108, 152, 165, 208, 240, 294, 340–1
Secret Service, US 50, 81–2, 211, 287, 308
Secret Six 112, 130, 228–9

Sedition Act of 1798
- Adams, John, signed into law by 170, 387
- analysis, definition, and main provisions 28–9, 255, 344–6
- constitutionality of 226, 342
- Jefferson, Thomas, views on 29, 226
- Sedition Act of 1918, compared with 152

Sedition Act of 1918 134, 152–3, 168, 342, 442
sedition, concept and meaning 342–3
sedition, contrasted with seditious conspiracy and treason 343
Seditious Conspiracy
- analysis, definition, and elements 347–9
- Capitol Insurrection on January 6, prosecutions of 83, 269–70, 349
- criminal conspiracy, contrasted with 109
- FALN and prosecutions of 175
- treason, contrasted with 345
- World Trade Center bombing (1993), prosecutions of 348–9

Seditious Libel 342, 345, 441
Seina, Violetta 438
Selective Service Act of 1917 185, 285, 338
Self-Interested Party Rule 398
Sella, Aviem 303
Senate Select Committee on Intelligence 38, 193
September 11, 2001
- analysis of attack 351–3
- Anthrax Attacks, shortly after 42
- *Ex Parte Quirin*, renewed relevancy after 161
- Fort Hood shooting (2009), compared with 197
- in general 180, 257
- Homeland Security Act, impetus for 211
- Oklahoma City bombing, compared with 287, 370
- riot in New York City, shortly after 318
- USA Patriot Act, impetus for 25, 44, 264, 371, 381
- World Trade Center bombing (1993), compared with 370, 432

Seward, William 49, 253–5
Shakespeare, William 49
Shay, Daniel 171, 354–5
Shay's Rebellion 129, 171, 316, 354–5, 421
Shepherd, Hayward 229, 396
Shepherd, William 355
Sheridan, Philip 57–8
Shippen, Peggy 47–8
Simmons, Furnifold 425, 428
slave patrols 385, 394
slave rebellions 177–8, 215, 228, 384, 393–4
Smith Act
- acts made criminal under 343, 356–7
- analysis of statute and elements 356–7
- *Dennis v. U.S.*, discussed and upheld in 104, 137, 348
- federal preemption of state law by 294
- registration requirement of 224
- Second Red Scare, example of legislation passed during 340
- *Yates v. U.S.*, discussed in 435–6

Smith, Gerrit 130, 228
Smith v. Shaw 409–10
Smyth, Richard Kelly 438
Snowden, Edward
- civil disobedience, claims of 94–5
- electronic surveillance program, leaked by 387–8
- Espionage Act, prosecution under 150, 153, 338, 437
- leaks of defense information, modern 245, 247–8
- Pelton, Ronald, relation to 293

Sobell, Martin 320–2
Socialist Party 103, 181, 185–6, 338
Sons of Liberty 158
Southern Poverty Law Center 269, 358–9
Sovereign Citizens Movement 69, 269, 358–9
Soviet embassy 38, 194, 293
Spangler, Edman 255–6
Spann, Johnny Michael "Mike" 257
Speech as Crime against State
- advocacy of illegal action 40, 294, 343
- aid and comfort to enemies, speech providing 22
- analysis and overview 362–3
- flag burning 169
- Intelligence Identities Protection Act, publication of names 220
- Sedition Act of 1798, potential violation of free speech 226
- threats against government officials, prohibition on 374–6

Speed, James 131, 368
Spence, Gerry 325–6
Spence v. Washington 169
Spies v. Illinois 201
Spies, August 201
Springfield, US Armory and Arsenal 171, 354
Sprott, U.S. v. 22
Stanton, Edwin 253, 255
Sterling, E.R. 134
Sterling v. Constantin 262
Stevens, Aaron
- actions and life of 365
- captured during attack on US Armory and Arsenal 187, 230
- pre-trial incarceration of 203
- treason, execution for 66, 112, 204, 395

Stevens, Bob 42
Stevens, Thaddeus 130, 195
Story, Joseph 143, 148
Stowe, Harriett Beecher 66

Street, Sidney 168–9
Street v. New York 168–9
Strong, Caleb 409
Stuart, J.E.B. 66, 229
Students for a Democratic Society (SDS) 100, 414
Stuxnet 126–7
Subversive Activities Act 223
Subversive Activities Control Board 108, 223–4
Subversive Activities, generally 223, 225, 344, 356
Supermax Prison 194, 236, 288, 292, 329
Surratt, Mary 49, 61, 254–5, 366–8
syndicalism, *see* criminal syndicalism

Taliban 191, 257, 291–2, 371
Taney, Roger B. 124, 359
Tanzania, US embassy attack on 352, 370
Tarrio, Henry "Enrique" 349
Taylor, Zachary 129
Taylor v. Mississippi 168
Teixeira, Jack 150, 153, 245, 248–9, 437
Ten-Point Plan, Black Panthers 100
Tennessee v. Garner 326
terrorism
  analysis, definition, and elements of 369–72
  Anti-Terrorism and Effective Death Penalty Act, to combat 44–6
  biological 42
  domestic 62–3, 326, 414, 430
  Fuerza's Armadas de Liberacion Nacional, actions of 175–6
  Hasan, Nidal, actions of 198
  Homeland Security Act, to combat 211
  Kaczynski, Theodore, actions of 233–6
  material support of 25–6, 264–5
  Oklahoma City bombing 287
  Pottawatomie Massacre 304
  USA Patriot Act, to combat 389
  Weather Underground, actions of 414–16
  World Trade Center Bombing of 1993 432
Texas v. Johnson 169, 275, 285–6
Texas v. White 32–3, 131, 373
The Civil Rights Cases 124–5
Thiel, Walter 118–19
Thirteenth Amendment 145, 338
Thompson, Bennie 80, 82
Thompson, Jerry 359
Thoreau, Henry David 67, 92–3, 230, 395
Threats against Government Officials 374–5
Three-Percenters 81, 269
Todd, Mark 197
Tokyo Rose (Iva Toguri D'Aquino) 52, 180, 239, 311, 378–9, 381
Townsville Mutiny 276–7
Travis, Joseph 384
treason
  aid and comfort to enemies, component of 21–4
  American Civil War, during 33–4
  American Revolution, during 35–7
  Burr, U.S. v. 75–8
  constructive treason, definition of and obsolete view of 148, 251, 213–14, 271
  definition and elements of 380–2
  English Treason Statute 148–9
  Levying War, component of 251–2
  Radio Traitors and Anti-State Propaganda during Second World War 51, 273, 311–15, 363, 378
  restrictive (and modern view) of "levying war" and treason 252
  Treason Clause, US Constitution, requirements therein 21, 380–2
  Virginia v. Brown 395–9
  in West Virginia Coal Wars 417–18
Treaty of Paris 37
trespass, crime of 81–3, 97, 333
Truman, Harry S. 49–50, 208, 211, 223, 291, 308
Trump, Donald J.
  actions on January 6, 2021 79–83
  conspiracy, indictment for 109–10
  Disqualification Clause 140–1
  Enforcement Act 146
  Espionage Act, potential violation of 150, 153
  false statements, allegedly made by 299–300
  in general 248, 430
  Insurrection Act, contemplation on January 6 218
  martial law, contemplated by 262–3
  pardons, issued by or contemplated 221, 247, 299–300, 303
Trump v. Hawaii 242
Tsarnaev, Dzhokhar and Tamerlan 62–3, 413
Turner, Nat 95, 177–8, 384–5
Turpin, U.S. v. 332
Tyson, Dave 257

Unabomber, *see* Kaczynski, Theodore
Unabomber Manifesto 234–5
Underground Railroad 66, 89–90, 195
Underwood, John C. 130, 132
Uniform Code of Military Justice 161, 246, 276
Unite the Right 319
United Airlines Flight 175 351
United States ex rel Turner v. Williams 267
United States v. U.S. District Court 387–8
Uranium 126, 221, 332
USA Patriot Act
  analysis of major details of law 389–91

domestic terrorism added to US Code 328, 372
extended powers under 25, 45–6
information sharing between federal agencies 264
opposition to 345
passage after September 11, 2001 44, 211, 351
USS Cole 352, 370

Vallandingham, Clement 162
Vanzetti, Bartolomeo 334–5
Venona Cables 173, 210, 321–2
Vesey, Denmark 95, 177–8, 393–4
Vesey's Rebellion 177–8, 228, 316, 393–4
Vicksburg Massacre 217
Virginia jihad network 265
Virginia Plot of 1800, *see* Gabriel's Rebellion
Virginia v. Black 374
Virginia v. Brown
analysis of case and proceedings 395–9
Brown, John, conviction and execution 67
Brown, John, prosecution in 66
treason against a State, leading example of 34, 142, 283
treason by a non-citizen/non-resident 239
Vogel, Philip 271–2

Waco
analysis of incident 401–4
Anti-Terrorism and Effective Death Penalty, factor in passage of 211
McVeigh, Timothy, factor in radicalization of 287
militia groups, rise in membership as a result of 269–70, 359
Oklahoma City bombing, factor influencing terror attack 287
Waddell, Alfred 426–8
Walker, Arthur 407
Walker, John 87, 295, 406–7, 438
Walker, Michael Lance 406–7
Walli, U.S. v. 333
War of 1812 283, 409–11
War on Terror 30, 159, 257, 351, 370
Warmoth, Henry 57
Washington, George
Arnold, Benedict, relationship with 47–8
espionage of 150
in general 72, 172, 229, 345
subordinates of 47
Whiskey Rebellion, actions in 170–1, 217, 420
Washington, Lewis 66, 187, 365
Watts, Robert 374
Weapons of Mass Destruction 221, 412–13
Weather Underground 95, 100, 175, 414–16
Weaver, Randy 324–7
Weaver, Sammy 325–6
Weaver, Vicki 324–6
Weichmann, Louis 366–7
Weinberger, Caspar 302, 406
West Point military garrison 48, 381
West Virginia Coal Wars 252, 262, 417–18
West Virginia State Board of Education v. Barnette 168
Whiskey Rebellion
analysis of event 419–21
Colfax Massacre, compared to 419
Fries's Rebellion, compared to 170–1
intention of protestors 213–15, 251–2
Militia Act, utilized to suppress by Washington 217
rebellion, act of 316
Shay's Rebellion, compared to 354
Treason trials of John Mitchell and Philip Vogel 271–2, 420
Waco, compared to 419
White Government Union 425–6
White League 57–8, 106, 155, 426
White Mountain Militia 69
White Panther Party 388
Whitmer, Gretchen 270, 360, 430
Whitney, Charlotte Anita 422
Whitney v. California 64, 102–3, 123, 142, 363, 422–4
Whitworth, Jerry 406–7
Wikileaks 245–7
Wilkinson, James 72–3, 75–6
Willard, Ashbel 111–2
Wilmington Insurrection 106, 156, 217, 425–8
Wilson, James 148, 420
Wilson, Joseph 221
Wilson, Valerie Plame, *see* Plame (Wilson), Valerie 221, 300
Wilson, Woodrow 185, 427
Wiltberger, U.S. v. 131, 239, 337, 397
Winchester Medical College 114, 188
Winner, Reality 153, 245, 248
Wise, Henry 111, 115
Wolverine Watchmen 270, 430–1
Working Class Union (WCU) 185–6
World and Islam Studies Enterprise 25
World Trade Center 351, 369–70, 432–3
World Trade Center Bombing
analysis of bombing 432–3
Anti-Terrorism and Effective Death Penalty Act, factor in passage 44
domestic terrorism, example of 369–70
incarceration of Ramzi Yousef 236, 288
material support crimes, factor in passage of law 264
sedition conspiracy, conviction for 347–9
weapons of mass destruction, usage in 412–13

Yalta Conference 208, 210
Yasui v. U.S. 95–7, 206–7
Yasui, Minoru 95–7, 206–7
Yates v. U.S. 137, 343, 348, 356, 435–7
Year of the Spy
  analysis and overview of period 437–9
  Chin, Larry, arrest during 87
  Espionage Act, violations during 153, 245
  Pelton, Ronald, arrest during 293
  Pollard, Jonathan, arrest during 301–3
  Scranage, Sharon, arrest during 221
  Walker, John, arrest during 406
Young, John 139
Young, U.S. v. 22, 118
Youngstown Sheet & Tube Co. v. Sawyer 262, 291
Yousef, Ramzi 236, 288, 432–3
Yurchenko, Vitaly 437–8

Zedong, Mao 87
Zenger, John Peter 342, 441–2

About the Authors

James A. Beckman, JD, LLM, is Professor of Legal Studies at the University of Central Florida, USA.

Eric Merriam, JD, LLM, is Associate Professor at the University of Central Florida, USA, where he is appointed jointly to the Legal Studies Department and the School of Politics, Security, and International Affairs.